# ¡Qué chévere! 1

**Author**

Alejandro Vargas Bonilla

**Contributing Writers**

Margarita María Cárdenas
Inés Greenberger
Sandra Mercado

EMC Publishing®

ST. PAUL

**Development Editor:**
Kristin Hoffman

**Associate Editor:**
Tanya Brown

**Director of Production:**
Deanna Quinn

**Production Editor:**
Bob Dreas

**Cover and Text Designer:**
Leslie Anderson

**Senior Digital
Production Specialist:**
Julie Johnston

**Digital Production Specialist:**
Grant Ertl

**National Consultants:**
Mary Lindquist, Liz Sacco

*Cover photo: Casa Batlló,
Barcelona, Spain*

AP® is a registered trademark of the College Board, which was not involved in the production of, and does not endorse, this product.

Care has been taken to verify the accuracy of information presented in this book. However, the authors, editors, and publisher cannot accept responsibility for Web, e-mail, newsgroup, or chat room subject matter or content, or for consequences from application of the information in this book, and make no warranty, expressed or implied, with respect to its content.

**Trademarks:** Some of the product names and company names included in this book have been used for identification purposes only and may be trademarks or registered trade names of their respective manufacturers and sellers. The authors, editors, and publisher disclaim any affiliation, association, or connection with, or sponsorship or endorsement by, such owners.

**Credits:** Acknowledgements, Literary Credits, and Photo Credits follow the Index.

We have made every effort to trace the ownership of all copyrighted material and to secure permission from copyright holders. In the event of any question arising as to the use of any material, we will be pleased to make the necessary corrections in future printings. Thanks are due to the aforementioned authors, publishers, and agents for permission to use the materials indicated.

ISBN 978-0-82196-922-9 (print)
ISBN 978-0-82197-892-4 (eBook Version 2.0)

© 2016 by EMC Publishing, LLC
875 Montreal Way
St. Paul, MN 55102
Email: educate@emcp.com
Website: www.emcp.com

24 23 22 21 20 19 18 17 16          4 5 6 7 8 9 10

# Welcome to ¡Qué chévere!

Learning a new language is **¡chévere!** (cool), and Spanish is a logical choice. By the end of the year you will be able to use Spanish in some basic, real-life situations. Plus, knowing another language will open up lots of doors for you.

## Spanish by the numbers

- Over 6.5 million American students choose to study Spanish.
- 350 million people speak Spanish as their first language.
- Soon 50 million people living in the United States will be Spanish speakers.
- Spanish is the 4th most commonly spoken language in the world.
- In 21 countries Spanish is the official language.

It is clear that Spanish is an important world language. Tell a classmate which fact above is the most surprising to you and why, and explain why you signed up to learn Spanish this year.

## You already know some Spanish!

Spanish will be easy for you to learn. It is easy to pronounce and spell, plus you already speak some Spanish. With a classmate, take turns saying, or guessing, what the words below mean.

| hola | zorro | hombre | enchilada | pueblo | amigo |
| --- | --- | --- | --- | --- | --- |
| bodega | fiesta | guacamole | don Quijote | niño | patio |
| chipotle | sombrero | piñata | chica | adiós | hacienda |

Can you organize the words into categories (for example, people, places, celebrations)? Can you add any more words to these categories? Work with your classmate to prepare a graphic organizer.

## What you will learn

In your first year of Spanish, you will learn how to meet and greet other people, go shopping, describe people, say where you are going, and what you'll do when you get there. You will be able to discuss a range of topics such as your favorite pastimes, your family and friends, celebrations, and vacation plans. You will be able to participate in conversations, present information, and understand essential written and audio texts. It is also important to learn Spanish in terms of the cultures where it is spoken, so you will learn the practices, products, and perspectives of the Spanish-speaking world as you learn the Spanish language.

## Opening windows

You will find that Spanish allows you to speak with more people in the United States; travel successfully to places like Mexico, Costa Rica, Puerto Rico, and Spain; become a better student by knowing another language; build your vocabulary in English; and understand the English language better. In the future, you might choose to study abroad, work in a field in which Spanish is needed, or vacation in Spanish-speaking countries. *¡Abre la ventana al mundo!* (Open the window to the world!)

**"Cuando los hombres buscan la diversidad, viajan."** —Wenceslao Fernández Florez (1879–1964)

"When people look for diversity, they travel." (Spanish author)

—Alejandro Vargas Bonilla
    Author of **¡Qué chévere!**

# Table of Contents

## Contexto cultural: Estados Unidos

**Contexto cultural: México**

Contexto cultural: Puerto Rico y República Dominicana

Contexto cultural: Costa Rica y Nicaragua

**Contexto cultural: Venezuela y Colombia**

Contexto cultural: Argentina y Chile

Contexto cultural: Panamá y Ecuador

## Contexto cultural: Perú y Guatemala

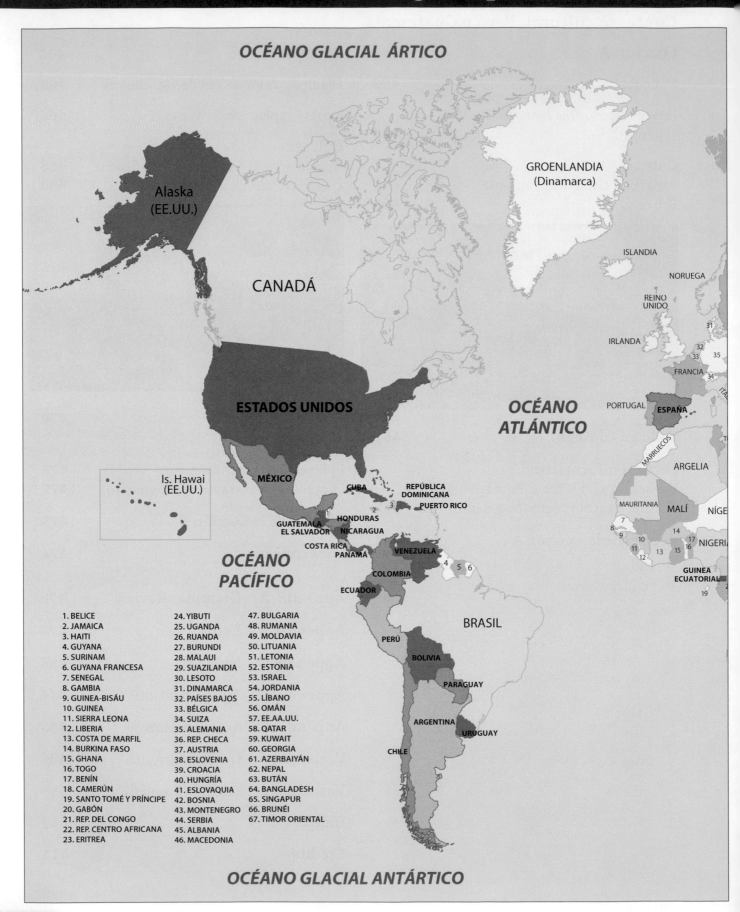

OCÉANO GLACIAL ÁRTICO

GROENLANDIA
(Dinamarca)

ISLANDIA

NORUEGA

REINO
UNIDO

IRLANDA

Alaska
(EE.UU.)

CANADÁ

31

32
33    35

FRANCIA
34

OCÉANO
ATLÁNTICO

PORTUGAL    ESPAÑA

ESTADOS UNIDOS

MARRUECOS

ARGELIA

Is. Hawai
(EE.UU.)

MÉXICO

MAURITANIA    MALÍ    NÍGE

CUBA    REPÚBLICA
DOMINICANA

7

PUERTO RICO

14

HONDURAS

2

3

8

GUATEMALA
EL SALVADOR

NICARAGUA

9    10

17
16

NIGERIA

COSTA RICA

1

11    13    15

PANAMÁ    VENEZUELA

12

OCÉANO
PACÍFICO

COLOMBIA

4    5    6

GUINEA
ECUATORIAL

ECUADOR

19

BRASIL

PERÚ

BOLIVIA

PARAGUAY

ARGENTINA

URUGUAY

CHILE

OCÉANO GLACIAL ANTÁRTICO

1. BELICE
2. JAMAICA
3. HAITI
4. GUYANA
5. SURINAM
6. GUYANA FRANCESA
7. SENEGAL
8. GAMBIA
9. GUINEA-BISÁU
10. GUINEA
11. SIERRA LEONA
12. LIBERIA
13. COSTA DE MARFIL
14. BURKINA FASO
15. GHANA
16. TOGO
17. BENÍN
18. CAMERÚN
19. SANTO TOMÉ Y PRÍNCIPE
20. GABÓN
21. REP. DEL CONGO
22. REP. CENTRO AFRICANA
23. ERITREA

24. YIBUTI
25. UGANDA
26. RUANDA
27. BURUNDI
28. MALAUI
29. SUAZILANDIA
30. LESOTO
31. DINAMARCA
32. PAÍSES BAJOS
33. BÉLGICA
34. SUIZA
35. ALEMANIA
36. REP. CHECA
37. AUSTRIA
38. ESLOVENIA
39. CROACIA
40. HUNGRÍA
41. ESLOVAQUIA
42. BOSNIA
43. MONTENEGRO
44. SERBIA
45. ALBANIA
46. MACEDONIA

47. BULGARIA
48. RUMANIA
49. MOLDAVIA
50. LITUANIA
51. LETONIA
52. ESTONIA
53. ISRAEL
54. JORDANIA
55. LÍBANO
56. OMÁN
57. EE.AA.UU.
58. QATAR
59. KUWAIT
60. GEORGIA
61. AZERBAIYÁN
62. NEPAL
63. BUTÁN
64. BANGLADESH
65. SINGAPUR
66. BRUNÉI
67. TIMOR ORIENTAL

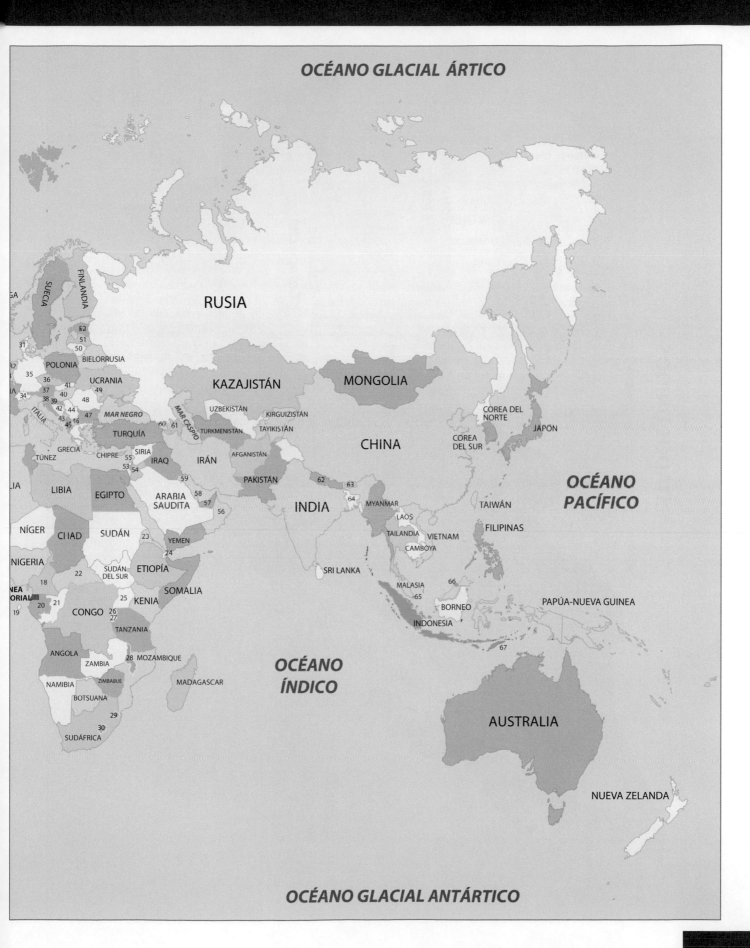

OCÉANO GLACIAL ÁRTICO

RUSIA

SUECIA
FINLANDIA

52
51
31
50
BIELORRUSIA
POLONIA
35 36
UCRANIA
32
41
37
40
49
KAZAJISTÁN
MONGOLIA
34
39
48
38
42 44
47
MAR NEGRO
MAR CASPIO
ITALIA
43 45 16
UZBEKISTÁN
KIRGUIZISTÁN
60
61
COREA DEL
TURQUÍA
TURKMENISTÁN
TAYIKISTÁN
NORTE
CHINA
JAPÓN
GRECIA
CHIPRE
SIRIA
COREA
DEL SUR
TÚNEZ
55
IRAQ
IRÁN
AFGANISTÁN
53 54
59
OCÉANO
LIBIA
EGIPTO
PAKISTÁN
62
63
PACÍFICO
58
ARABIA
57
64
SAUDITA
INDIA
TAIWÁN
56
MYANMAR
NÍGER
CHAD
SUDÁN
23
LAOS
FILIPINAS
YEMEN
TAILANDIA
VIETNAM
24
NIGERIA
CAMBOYA
SUDÁN
ETIOPÍA
22
DEL SUR
SRI LANKA
NEA
SOMALIA
66
TORIAL
MALASIA
PAPÚA-NUEVA GUINEA
18
25
KENIA
65
19
20
21
CONGO
26
BORNEO
27
INDONESIA
TANZANIA
ANGOLA
67
ZAMBIA
28
MOZAMBIQUE
OCÉANO
ZIMBABUE
NAMIBIA
MADAGASCAR
ÍNDICO
BOTSUANA
29
AUSTRALIA
30
SUDÁFRICA

OCÉANO
ÍNDICO

NUEVA ZELANDA

OCÉANO GLACIAL ANTÁRTICO

# MÉXICO

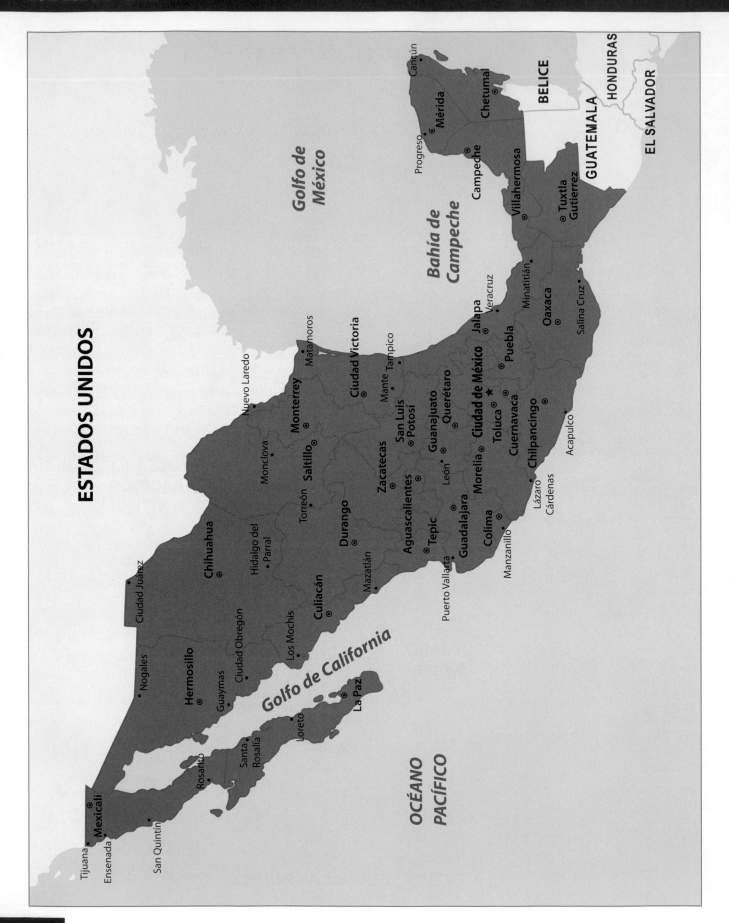

# AMÉRICA CENTRAL Y EL CARIBE

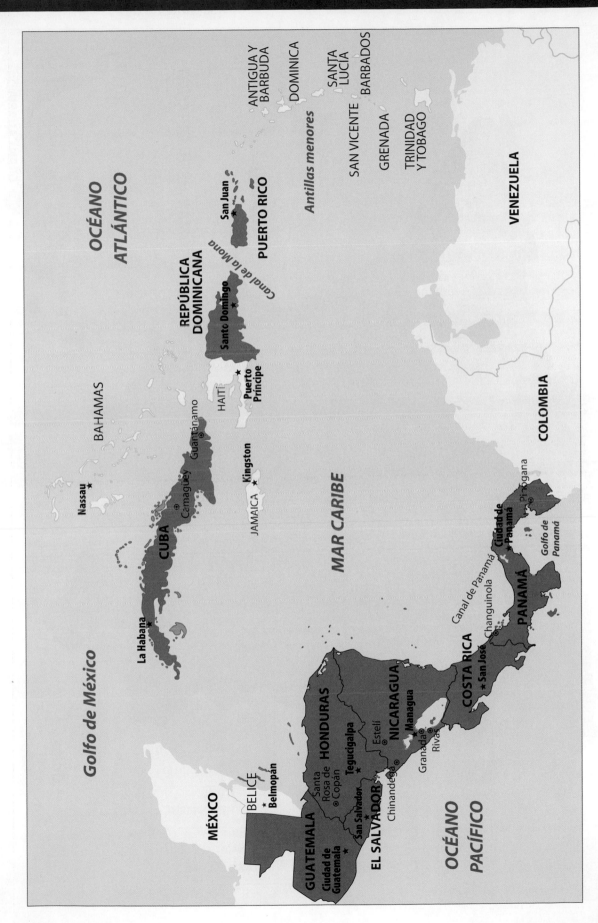

# ESPAÑA

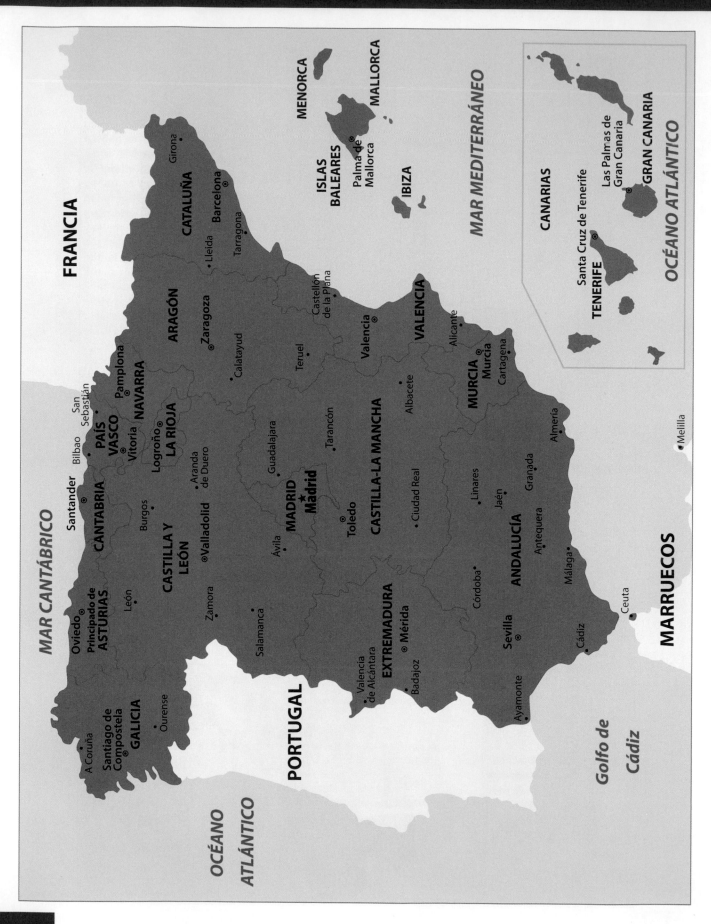

# AMÉRICA DEL SUR

NICARAGUA
COSTA RICA
San José
PANAMÁ
Ciudad de Panamá
Cúcuta
Maracaibo
Valencia
Mérida
Caracas
Barcelona
Puerto España
TRINIDAD Y TOBAGO

VENEZUELA
Medellín
Bucaramanga
Bogotá, D.C.
Puerto Ayacucho
Cali
COLOMBIA
Mitú

Georgetown
Linden
Paramaribo
Cayenne
GUYANA
SURINAME
GUYANA FRANCESA

OCÉANO ATLÁNTICO

Quito
ECUADOR

Cuenca
Piura
Chiclayo
Trujillo
Chimbote
Huaraz
PERÚ
Iquitos
Pucallpa
Huancayo
Ayacucho
Lima
Ica
Cusco
Juliaca
Arequipa
Tacna
Arica
Iquique

Manaus
Belém

BRASIL

BOLIVIA
La Paz
Santa Cruz
Cochabamba
Sucre
Tarija
PARAGUAY

Brasília

OCÉANO PACÍFICO

Antofagasta

Pedro Juan Caballero
Asunción
Ciudad del Este

Salta
San Miguel de Tucumán
La Rioja
Resistencia

Río de Janeiro
São Paulo

Pôrto Alegre

La Serena

Córdoba
Santa Fe
Tacuarembó

Valparaíso
San Juan
Mendoza
Rosario
URUGUAY

Santiago
Buenos Aires
Montevideo

CHILE
Concepción
ARGENTINA
Mar del Plata

OCÉANO ATLÁNTICO

Neuquén
Bahía Blanca

Puerto Montt

Rawson
Comodoro Rivadavia

Coyhaique

Río Gallegos

Islas Malvinas
(territorio británico de ultramar)

Georgias del sur (R.U.)

Punta Arenas
Río Grande

xix

Cartagena, Colombia

El Salto Ángel, Venezuela

Orquídea, Ecuador

Puerto Madero, Buenos Aires

*kal, Guatemala*

*ogotá, Colombia*

*Guacamaya, selva venezolana*

*Isla Saona, República Dominicana*

xxi

Moáis, Isla de Pascua, Chile

Santiago, Chile

Machu Picchu , Perú

Islas Galápagos, Ecuador

celote, Costa Rica

Cavernas de Mármol, Chile

astillo de San Felipe del Morro, Puerto Rico

Plaza Mayor, Madrid

Carnaval Internacional de la Amistad, Honduras

Parque eólico, España

Andalucía, España

Park Güell, Barcelona

Pirámides de Sal, Bolivia

Volcán de Izalco, El Salvador

San Blas, Panamá

Punta del Este, Uruguay

Oso perezoso, Costa Rica

México, D.F.

Ciudad de Panamá, Panamá

esierto de Atacama, Chile

uesto de frutas, Bolivia

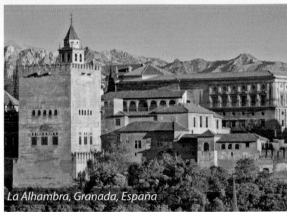
La Alhambra, Granada, España

Glaciar Perito Moreno, Argentina

xxvii

### ¿Sabías que...?

You already speak some Spanish! If you have ever talked about enjoying a barbecue, going out to the patio, dancing salsa, wearing a poncho, or visiting Florida or the Grand Canyon, then you have used Spanish words. Spanish is all around you. *¡Qué chévere!*

# 1

# ¡Mucho gusto!

Scan the QR code to watch this episode of *El cuarto misterioso*.

**José meets up with his friend Francisco in Coyoacán Park. Who are Ana and Conchita?**

**A. José's friends**
**B. Francisco's friends**
**C. two girls they both just met**

*Essential Question*

**?**

**How do people reach out to communicate with others?**

## Mis metas

**Lección A  I will be able to:**

▸ spell words in Spanish
▸ ask for and give names
▸ greet and say good-bye
▸ use Spanish punctuation appropriately
▸ talk about birthdays in Spanish-speaking countries
▸ greet people with appropriate gestures
▸ identify where Spanish is spoken in the world
▸ say where I am from
▸ state my age
▸ count to twenty
▸ use definite articles with some country names
▸ explain cognates and false cognates
▸ talk about ten wonders of the Spanish-speaking world

**Lección B  I will be able to:**

▸ ask and tell how someone is feeling
▸ recognize the difference between informal and formal Spanish
▸ express courtesy
▸ ask for and state the time
▸ count up to 100
▸ read a simple narrative in Spanish

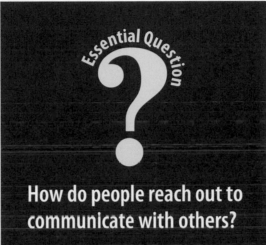

Why is this teenager dancing with her father at a formal party?

El mundo hispanohablante

# ¡Hola! ¿Cómo te llamas?

Yo me llamo Esteban, ¿y tú?

¡Hola! ¿Cómo te llamas?

¡Mucho gusto!

¡Adiós!

¡Hasta luego!

## Para decir más

| | |
|---|---|
| ¿Qué hay de nuevo? | *What's new?* |
| ¡Chao! | *Bye!* |
| ¡Nos vemos! | *See you!* |

## Un poco más

Some letters with similar sounds are often given different names in order to distinguish them:

| **b** | be larga | **v** | ve corta |
|---|---|---|---|
| **i** | i latina | **y** | i griega, ye |
| **r** | ere (single r) | **rr** | erre (rolled double rr) |

Some letter combinations are often given their own names:

**ll**  elle (instead of *ele, ele*)

**ch**  che (instead of *ce, hache*)

**rr**  erre (instead of *ere, ere*)

**a b c d e f g h**

a   be   ce   de   e   efe   ge   hache

**i j k l m n ñ**

i   jota   ka   ele   eme   ene   eñe

**o p q r r r s t**

o   pe   cu   ere   erre   ese   te

**u v w x y z**

u   ve   doble ve   equis   ye   zeta

el alfabeto

**B**
mayúscula

**b**
minúscula

## Para conversar

*T*o ask and answer how to spell something:

**¿Cómo se escribe** Raúl? **¿Con** ere?
*How do you spell Raúl? With an r?*

**Sí**, con ere mayúscula, a, u con **acento**, ele.
*Yes, with a capital r, a, u with an accent, l.*

## Los nombres 🎧

### 1 ¿Cómo se escribe? 🎧

Escribe los nombres que oyes.

**MODELO** Carlos

Me llamo Daniel.

Me llamo Jimena.

### Un poco más

#### Los apodos

Nicknames (*apodos*) are common in Spanish. Examples include *Isa* (for *Isabel*), *Fina* or *Pepa* (for *Josefina*), *Lola* (for *Dolores*), *Lupe* (for *Guadalupe*), *Paco* or *Pancho* (for *Francisco*), *Pepe* (for *José*) and *Quique* (for *Enrique*). Personal characteristics are also used for nicknames in Spanish: *Flaco* (Slim).

| muchachos | | |
|---|---|---|
| Alejandro | Guillermo | Mario |
| Andrés | Héctor | Mateo |
| Antonio | Hernán | Miguel |
| Benjamín | Hugo | Nicolás |
| Carlos | Jaime | Pablo |
| Daniel | Jesús | Pedro |
| David | Jorge | Rafael |
| Diego | José | Raúl |
| Eduardo | Juan | Ricardo |
| Enrique | Julián | Roberto |
| Esteban | Julio | Rodrigo |
| Felipe | Luis | Santiago |
| Fernando | Manuel | Tomás |
| Francisco | Marcos | Víctor |

| muchachas | | |
|---|---|---|
| Adriana | Gabriela | Patricia |
| Ana | Gloria | Paula |
| Andrea | Inés | Paz |
| Ángela | Isabel | Pilar |
| Carmen | Jimena | Raquel |
| Carolina | Julia | Rosa |
| Catalina | Laura | Sandra |
| Claudia | Liliana | Sara |
| Cristina | Luz | Sofía |
| Diana | María | Teresa |
| Elena | Marta | Valeria |
| Elisa | Mercedes | Verónica |
| Esperanza | Mónica | Victoria |
| Eva | Natalia | Yolanda |

### 2 Muchachos y muchachas

Read the names below. Next to each Spanish name, write the name that you think is the English equivalent.

| Muchachos | | Muchachas | |
|---|---|---|---|
| José | | Elena | |
| Alejandro | | Marta | |
| Antonio | | María | |
| Felipe | | Catalina | |

### 3 Nombres de personas

Imagine that someone asks you how to spell these names. Select the letter in parentheses that would best complete your answers.

1. Guillermo se escribe con ___ (*ele / elle*).
2. Victoria se escribe con ___ (*ve / u*).
3. Carmen se escribe con ___ (*ere / erre*).
4. Héctor se escribe con ___ (*jota / hache*).
5. Yolanda se escribe con ___ (*ye / elle*).

## 4 Mini-diálogos

Escoge la respuesta correcta. *(Choose the correct answer.)*

1. Hola, me llamo Raquel.
   A. Mucho gusto.
   B. Hasta luego.

2. Hola, ¿cómo te llamas?
   A. Mucho gusto. ¿Y tú?
   B. Me llamo Gloria.

3. ¿Cómo se escribe José?
   A. Con jota minúscula.
   B. Con jota mayúscula.

4. ¡Hasta luego!
   A. ¡Adiós!
   B. ¡Mucho gusto!

# ¡Comunicación!

## 5 Nombres en español        Interpersonal Communication

Write a list of three names of *muchachos* and three names of *muchachas* from the boxes on the previous page. Take turns with a classmate reading out the names on your lists. Ask each other how they are spelled and write them according to each other's dictation.

MODELO
A: María
B: ¿Cómo se escribe?
A: Se escribe con eme, a, ere, i con acento, a.
B: ¿Con eme minúscula?
A: No, con eme mayúscula.

*¿Cómo se escribe?*

## 6 ¡Mucho gusto!

Escribe una frase apropiada para cada situación. *(Write an appropriate phrase for each situation.)*

1. You meet up with a friend on the street.
2. You want to know a person's name.
3. You are meeting someone for the first time.
4. Somebody has just told you her name, and then she asks your name.
5. You have to leave for a little while.
6. You don't know how to spell a word.
7. You want to know if the letter B in a word is capitalized.
8. You are leaving a party.

# Diálogo

## ¡Hola!

**Carmen:** ¡Hola! ¿Cómo te llamas?

**Hugo:** Yo me llamo Hugo. ¿Y tú?

**Carmen:** Me llamo Carmen.

**Hugo:** ¡Mucho gusto, Carmen!

**Carmen:** ¿Cómo se escribe Hugo?

**Hugo:** Se escribe con hache mayúscula, u, ge, o. Hasta luego.

**Carmen:** Adiós.

### 7  ¿Qué recuerdas?

Answer the following questions according to the dialogue *¡Hola!*

1. What is the boy's name?
2. What is the girl's name?
3. Did they know each other before today? How do you know?
4. What does the boy want to know?
5. What does the girl ask the boy?

### 8  Algo personal

1. ¿Cómo te llamas?
2. ¿Cómo se escribe tu nombre?

### 9  ¿Cuál es la respuesta correcta? 🎧

Escoge una respuesta correcta a lo que oyes. *(Choose a correct response to what you hear.)*

Adiós     Sí, con hache.

Me llamo Carmen

¡Mucho gusto, Carmen!

## 💬 ¡Comunicación!

### 10  ¿Cómo te llamas? 👥   Interpersonal Communication

With a classmate, act out the roles of two students who are meeting for the first time.

• Introduce yourselves.

• Ask the spelling of the other's name.

• Say good-bye.

# Gramática

## Punctuation

*¿Cómo te llamas? ¿Y tú? ¡Hola! ¡Mucho gusto!*

Have you noticed any upside-down punctuation marks in Spanish? It is not a mistake. Written Spanish requires two question marks and two exclamation points.

- The first question mark is inverted (¿) and marks the beginning of a question. The second is placed at the end of the question, just as in English.

- The first exclamation point is likewise inverted (¡) and marks the beginning of an exclamation. The second is used just as in English.

- No other punctuation (e.g., period, comma) follows this pattern.

- Opening punctuation marks do not necessarily come at the very beginning of a sentence: *Inés, ¿cómo se escribe tu nombre?*

### 11 La puntuación correcta

Corrige la puntuación en el diálogo. (*Correct the punctuation in the dialogue.*)

**A:** Hola!

**B:** ¡Hola Cómo te llamas?

**A:** Me llamo Inés Y tú?

**B:** Yo me llamo Andrés

**A:** ¡Mucho gusto, Andrés

**B:** Mucho gusto. Cómo se escribe Inés? Con i?

**A:** Sí, con i mayúscula, ene, e con acento, ese

**B:** Adiós, Inés!

*¡Mucho gusto!*

### 12 ¿Cuál es el orden?

Escribe oraciones lógicas usando las siguientes pistas. (*Write complete sentences using the following cues.*)

**MODELO**    llamo / Me / Alejandro / .
**Me llamo Alejandro.**

1. ¡ / ! / Hola

2. llamas / ? / te / ¿ / Cómo

3. Carlota / . / llamo / Me / ¿ / tú? / Y

4. Yo / Carlota / Jaime / . / me / gusto, / ! / llamo / ¡Mucho

5. se / ¡Mucho / ¿ / Cómo / Jaime? / gusto / ! / escribe

6. escribe / Se / jota / i, / con / eme, / mayúscula, / a, / e / .

## Estrategia

### Recognizing classroom expressions

The following expressions are commonly heard in a classroom. Recognizing them will help you understand instructions. Look for examples of these expressions in your textbook. Do they help you understand what to do in the activities?

| | | | |
|---|---|---|---|
| **Abre/Abran (el libro).** | *Open (your book).* | **Haz/Hagan....** | *Make (or do)....* |
| **Busca/Busquen... en la página....** | *Look for... on page....* | **Lee/Lean....** | *Read....* |
| **Cierra/Cierren (el libro).** | *Close (your book).* | **Levanta/Levanten (la mano).** | *Raise (your hand).* |
| **Contesta/Contesten....** | *Answer....* | **Mira/Miren.** | *Look.* |
| **Da/Den....** | *Give....* | **Pasa/Pasen a (la pizarra).** | *Go to (the board).* |
| **Di/Digan....** | *Say (or tell)....* | **Responde/Respondan....** | *Respond....* |
| **Escoge/Escojan....** | *Choose....* | **Saca/Saquen (una hoja de papel).** | *Take out (a sheet of paper).* |
| **Escribe/Escriban....** | *Write....* | **Señala/Señalen (el mapa).** | *Point at (the map).* |
| **Escucha/Escuchen.** | *Listen.* | **Siéntate/Siéntense.** | *Sit down.* |
| **Habla/Hablen en español.** | *Speak in Spanish.* | | |

## ¡Comunicación!

### 13 ¡Acción! — Interpersonal/Presentational Communication

You are a scriptwriter for a video in Spanish. Write a scene in which two Spanish-speaking teenagers meet on the street. Use the graphic organizer below to prepare your script. Then, write out the script. Have two classmates act it out. Be sure to include:

• speakers greeting one another

• asking each other's name and how to spell it

• saying good-bye

Add stage directions where appropriate so that readers and actors can visualize the scene.

| Speaker | Lines | Stage directions |
|---|---|---|
| **Luis** | **¡Hola!** | *Holds out his hand* |
| | | |
| | | |
| | | |

# Cultura

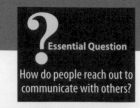

## Una gran celebración

Let's party! Family celebrations are a popular reason for Spanish speakers to reach out and stay connected. Birthdays (*los cumpleaños*) are important social events that bring families and friends together. They are often celebrated with music, eating, and dancing and may last until the early morning hours.

In several Spanish-speaking countries, a girl's fifteenth birthday (*la quinceañera* or *la fiesta de quince*) is a very special occasion, as it marks the fact that the girl is now a young woman. Traditions for this coming-of-age celebration include a religious ceremony in the morning, followed by a reception or a formal dance at home or in a banquet hall. The girl makes a grand entrance with her father, who might make a formal speech to mark the occasion. Then father and daughter share a waltz. The guest of honor may have a court composed of maids of honor and their escorts, potentially dressed in formal attire. Today, many girls prefer a special gift rather than a formal dance. Boys celebrate their fifteenth birthday like any other *cumpleaños*, with an informal party, an outing, or a special dinner with their family. And everybody loves a birthday cake with candles accompanied, of course, by the "Happy Birthday" song.

*Mi papá y yo en mi quinceañera*

**🔍 Búsqueda:** quinceañera

### Comparaciones

Compare how teenagers in the Spanish-speaking world celebrate birthdays to how teens celebrate in other countries.

### Productos

While some Spanish-speaking cultures have their own birthday songs, sung in varying rhythms, others have developed Spanish lyrics set to the tune of "Happy Birthday."

¡**Cumpleaños** *feliz!*

(Melodía de "Happy Birthday")

Cumpleaños feliz,

Cumpleaños feliz,

Que los sigas cumpliendo

¡hasta el año tres mil!

(Happy birthday, happy birthday.
May you continue having birthdays
until the year 3000!)

### 14 Comprensión

1. How do Spanish speakers reach out and stay connected?
2. Describe a *quinceañera*.
3. How does a boy's fifteenth birthday compare to a girl's?

### 15 Analiza

1. What do you think of coming-of-age milestones like the *quinceañera*? Do we have something similar in the United States?
2. If you lived in a Spanish-speaking culture, how would you choose to celebrate your fifteenth birthday? Why?

Hola. ¿Qué tal?

# Abrazos, besos y más

Do you kiss and hug family members and friends when you greet them? How do Spanish speakers start the communication process? You now know the right words—but what about the gestures? Greeting others in an informal situation can be quite expressive in Spanish-speaking cultures. When greeting friends and relatives, men commonly exchange a handshake (*un apretón de manos*) accompanied by a hug (*un abrazo*) as they pat each other on the back. Women and girls give each other a light kiss (*un beso*) on the cheek (or on both cheeks in Spain), even if they have just been introduced for the first time. Men and women who know each other may also exchange a kiss on the cheek. Meanwhile, the verbal exchange may include inquiries as to the person's well-being as well as that of family members. The same gestures are often repeated when saying good-bye, accompanied by greetings to pass on to family members or mutual friends. The next time you see people greeting in Spanish, listen—and watch—to see how they communicate.

🔍 **Búsqueda:** nonverbal communication in the latino world

## Perspectivas

Although they look like gestures of familiarity, *el abrazo* and *el beso* are considered common forms of greeting among Spanish speakers, even for an initial introduction. What value(s) can you infer from this practice?

Mucho gusto.

## 16 Comprensión

Say *sí* or *no* for each statement about greetings and good-byes in Spanish-speaking countries.

1. Words are very important in a greeting, but so are gestures.
2. Men exchange hugs when they greet and/or are introduced to someone.
3. Girls greet each other with a kiss on the cheek, but women use a handshake instead.
4. Gestures used in good-byes are very different from those used in greetings.
5. Good-byes often include references to family members or friends.

## 17 Analiza

What one word or phrase might best describe the main characteristic of greetings in a Spanish-speaking culture?

## Comparaciones

Compare and contrast how you greet family members and friends with the way Spanish speakers generally greet theirs.

# Vocabulario 2

## Soy de las Américas 🎧

### Los países hispanohablantes

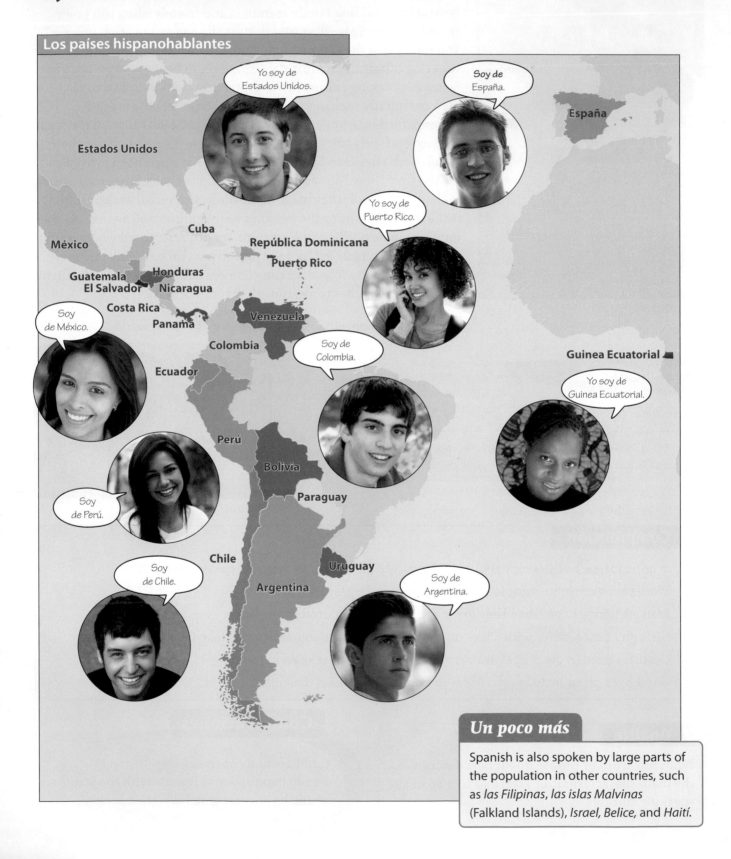

**Un poco más**

Spanish is also spoken by large parts of the population in other countries, such as *las Filipinas*, *las islas Malvinas* (Falkland Islands), *Israel*, *Belice*, and *Haití*.

## Para conversar

*T*o ask and tell where you are from:

¿De **dónde eres**?
*Where are you from?*

Soy de Buenos Aires, **la capital** de Argentina.
*I am from Buenos Aires, the capital of Argentina.*

¿Y tú? ¿**Eres** de **aquí**?
*And you? Are you from here?*

**No**. Yo soy de (los) Estados Unidos.
*No. I am from the United States.*

*T*o ask and tell your age:

¿**Cuántos años tienes**?
*How old are you?*

**Tengo** quince **años**.
*I am fifteen years old.*

### Los números del 0 al 20

| | | | |
|---|---|---|---|
| 0 | cero | | |
| 1 | uno | 11 | once |
| 2 | dos | 12 | doce |
| 3 | tres | 13 | trece |
| 4 | cuatro | 14 | catorce |
| 5 | cinco | 15 | quince |
| 6 | seis | 16 | dieciséis |
| 7 | siete | 17 | diecisiete |
| 8 | ocho | 18 | dieciocho |
| 9 | nueve | 19 | diecinueve |
| 10 | diez | 20 | veinte |

### Para decir más

| | |
|---|---|
| ¿Dónde queda Asunción? | *Where is Asunción (located)?* |
| ¿También eres de Paraguay? | *Are you from Paraguay, too?* |
| ¿Qué edad tienes? | *What is your age?* |
| Tengo catorce. | *I'm fourteen.* |

### 18 Los números

In pairs, begin counting from *cero* and count by twos to *veinte*. Start over, beginning with *once*, and count by twos to *diecinueve*.

### 19 Los países

Practice saying the names of the Spanish-speaking countries you hear. Write the name of each country after it is repeated.

### Un poco más

When asked where you are from, be sure not to answer, "*Soy de América*" or "*Soy americano*" (I am American). Remember that America covers two continents and includes all of North, Central, and South America. Instead, say "*Soy estadounidense.*" You may need to practice that a few times for it to come out easily!

*Soy de Honduras. ¿Y tú?*

## 20  Países y capitales

Using the maps in the front of your textbook, match the countries with their corresponding capitals.

1. Argentina
2. República Dominicana
3. Costa Rica
4. España
5. Perú
6. Venezuela

A. Caracas
B. Madrid
C. Lima
D. San José
E. Santo Domingo
F. Buenos Aires

## 21  ¿Cuál es el intruso?

Busca al intruso y explica por qué. *(Look for the intruder and explain why.)*

**MODELO**  Cuba / Tegucigalpa / Nicaragua
**Tegucigalpa is a capital, not a country.**

1. Uruguay / Paraguay / España
2. Bogotá / La Paz / Chile
3. Lima / Asunción / Madrid
4. Honduras / Guatemala / Bolivia
5. México / Colombia / Ecuador
6. Puerto Rico / Costa Rica / La Habana

## 22  Sumas en español    Conéctate: las matemáticas

In groups of four, create two teams of two. A student from Team A says a number from *uno* to *veinte*. A student from Team B writes the number, and then says another number, which when added to the first gives a sum of 20. A correct answer scores one point. Then Team B starts the next round.

**MODELO**  Team A: seis
Team B: catorce

Soy de aquí. ¿Y tú?

## 23  Una conversación

Completa la siguiente conversación.

A: ¡Hola! ¿De **(1)** eres?

B: Yo **(2)** de Lima, la **(3)** de Perú. ¿Y tú? ¿Eres **(4)** aquí?

A: No, yo **(5)** de Panamá. ¿**(6)** años tienes?

B: **(7)** catorce años.

# Diálogo 🎧

## ¿De dónde eres, Hugo?

**Carmen:** ¿De dónde eres, Hugo?

**Hugo:** Soy de Bogotá, la capital de Colombia. ¿Y tú? ¿Eres de aquí?

**Carmen:** No. Yo soy de México. ¿Cuántos años tienes, Hugo?

**Hugo:** Tengo dieciséis años. ¿Y tú?

**Carmen:** Yo tengo quince años.

## 24 ¿Qué recuerdas?

Say *si* or *no* for each statement according to what you heard in the dialogue.
Correct the false statements.

1. Carmen wants to know where Hugo is from.
2. The capital of Colombia is La Paz.
3. Hugo already knows where Carmen is from.
4. Carmen is not from Mexico.
5. Carmen is sixteen years old.
6. Hugo is one year older than Carmen.

## 25 Algo personal 🎧

1. ¿De dónde eres?
2. ¿Cuántos años tienes?

## 26 Las capitales 👥 Conéctate: la geografía

Working in pairs use the maps at the front of the textbook to say the name of a Spanish-speaking country to your partner. He/She will give the capital.

## 27 ¿Cuántos años tienes? 🎧

Escribe los números que oyes.

**MODELO**  16

1

2

3

4

# Gramática

## Definite Articles and Countries

Some Spanish speakers use the definite articles (*artículos definidos*) **el**, **la**, and **los** with these country names, whereas others prefer to omit the articles. Their use is optional, but the tendency is to omit them.

| | | |
|---|---|---|
| **la** Argentina | → | Argentina |
| **el** Ecuador | → | Ecuador |
| **los** Estados Unidos | → | Estados Unidos |
| **el** Paraguay | → | Paraguay |
| **el** Perú | → | Perú |
| **la** República Dominicana | → | República Dominicana |
| **el** Uruguay | → | Uruguay |

### Un poco más

**Definite articles and nouns**

Every singular noun in Spanish—not just countries—uses either the article *el* or *la* for the word "the."

### Estrategia

**Linking articles to nouns**

Try to learn each new noun with its appropriate article, *el* or *la*. That way, you'll choose the right article automatically, the way native speakers do.

### 28  ¿Qué países son?

Look at the map and list the names of the 22 Spanish-speaking countries. If the country name can take a definite article, include it. See how many you can name without looking at the map in the vocabulary presentation or in the front of your book. Include as many capitals as you can, also.

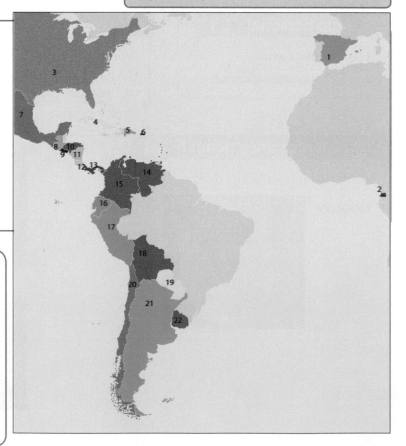

### 29  Los artículos definidos

Look back at the definite articles in front of each country name in the *Gramática* box. Answer these questions.

1. Why do you think that some countries use *la* while other countries use *el*?

2. Can you tell why *los Estados Unidos* is the only country that has a different article?

## 30 ¿Eres de…?

Selecciona la respuesta más apropiada. *(Select the most appropriate response.)*

1. ¿Eres de Venezuela?
2. ¿Eres de la Argentina?
3. ¿Eres de España?
4. ¿Eres de Ecuador?
5. ¿Eres de Honduras?

A. Sí, soy de la capital, Tegucigalpa.
B. Sí, soy de la capital, Quito.
C. Sí, soy de la capital, Madrid.
D. Sí, soy de la capital, Caracas.
E. Sí, soy de la capital, Buenos Aires.

## 31 Visita un país

What countries or cities in the Spanish-speaking world would you like to visit?
Explain what you find interesting or attractive about your choice(s).

# ¡Comunicación!

## 32 ¡Mucho gusto!    Interpersonal Communication

With a classmate, take turns greeting each other, asking one another's name, age, and where each of you is from. In your answer, choose a city and country from one of the Spanish-speaking countries. You may use the cities depicted in the photos below as some possible options.

*Ciudad de Panamá, Panamá*

*Santiago, Chile*

*Bogotá, Colombia*

*Quito, Ecuador*

# Gramática

## Cognates

- Words in Spanish often resemble English words you already know. For example, *acento* is similar to the English word **accent**. Words that resemble one another and that have the same meaning in two languages are called **cognates** (*cognados*). Do you recognize these cognates?

  *computadora*   *celular*   *fabuloso*

  *vocabulario*   *persona*   *capital*

*Buenos Aires, la capital de Argentina*

- When words look similar but have entirely different meanings in Spanish and English, they are known as **false cognates** or false friends (*falsos amigos*). Here are a few examples:

  | *colegio* | school  | *sin*     | without   |
  |-----------|---------|-----------|-----------|
  | *éxito*   | success | *carpeta* | folder    |
  | *lectura* | reading | *librería* | bookstore |

## 33  Cognados y profesiones

Indica la letra de la foto que corresponde con la profesión de las siguientes personas.

A

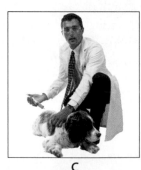

C

D

B

1. Es veterinario.
2. Es actor de televisión.

3. Es dentista.
4. Es policía.

## 34 Los cognados 🎧

Practice pronouncing these cognates. Try to guess the meaning of the words as you say them.

1. favorito
2. estudiar
3. el chocolate
4. formal

5. México
6. el actor
7. la persona
8. la capital

9. el animal
10. la televisión
11. el restaurante
12. el teléfono

13. la posibilidad
14. el diálogo
15. el vocabulario

# ¡Comunicación!

## 35 Un artículo en español 👥 Interpretive Communication

Read this article without using a dictionary. Prepare a list of the cognates and other words you think you can guess or connect to English. Then, write a short summary in English. With a classmate, read your summaries to each other and compare.

Página web +

◀ ▶ www.famosos.com

★★★★★

Hay muchas páginas web donde tú puedes encontrar biografías, fotos recientes, y más datos sobre personas importantes y famosas. ¿Te interesa algún actor o actriz? ¿Un músico popular? ¿O quizá un científico o un astronauta? Búscalo en nuestra página web. Usa palabras de búsqueda como el nombre de la persona, un libro que escribió o una película en que actuó. Vas a obtener mucha información.

*Penélope Cruz*

# ¡Comunicación!

## 36 ¿De dónde eres? 👥 Interpersonal/Presentational Communication

Working with a partner, create a dialogue in which you greet each other, ask for one another's names and ages, and where each of you is from. Each person should prepare at least four lines. Practice the dialogue and then present it in class. Remember to use appropriate gestures.

*¿De dónde eres tú?*

## Comunidades

Many Spanish virtual communities can provide opportunities for you to:
• connect with Spanish speakers in your area and around the world;
• practice Spanish with native speakers via text, audio chat, or video;
• get to know other cultures and customs;
• make new friends.
Best of all: By taking part in a virtual community, you will improve your Spanish-speaking skills and by doing so you will learn more about your own language.

# Todo en contexto

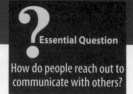
## ¡Comunicación!

### 37 Yo soy... Presentational Communication

You are a new student in Spanish class, and you want to reach out to your classmates and communicate with them. Create a short presentation about yourself in Spanish. Use a graphic organizer like the one below to prepare your information. Practice and then present it to the class.

| | |
|---|---|
| Greeting | |
| My name (in Spanish) | |
| Spelling of my name | |
| My age | |
| Where I am from (city/state/country) | |

## ¡Comunicación!

### 38 ¡Es tu turno! Interpersonal Communication

Now get to know five of your new classmates by asking them for the same information you presented about yourself in the previous activity. As you interview them, fill in a chart like the one below with the appropriate information. Be sure to have your classmates spell their names.

| Nombre | Edad | Origen |
|---|---|---|
| | | |
| | | |
| | | |
| | | |
| | | |

## ¡Comunicación!

### 39 Una quinceañera Interpersonal Communication

In groups of three or four, prepare a skit about a *cumpleaños* or *quinceañera*. You are getting to know some of the other guests. Ask and answer questions about names, ages, and places of origin. (You are all from Spanish-speaking countries.) Remember to use appropriate gestures.

MODELO
> A: Hola, me llamo Luisa.
>
> B: ¡Mucho gusto, Luisa! ¿De dónde eres?
>
> A: Soy de...

*Me llamo Luisa.*

# Lectura informativa

## Antes de leer

1. What countries in the Spanish-speaking world would you like to visit? Why?

2. What important historical or geographical facts do you know about any of these countries?

3. What famous Spanish-language writer, athlete, or historical figure do you admire? What is that person's country of origin?

### Estrategia

**Know the culture**

One way to reach out to, and communicate with, people from a different country is to get to know something about their culture. If you have the opportunity to meet or interact with Spanish speakers, do some research on a well-known individual or site from that country. This will show your new friends that you value their culture and its contributions.

## Visita las maravillas del mundo hispanohablante

¿Sabías que el mundo hispanohablante tiene[1] el desierto más árido del planeta (el desierto de Atacama en Chile)? También tiene la catarata[2] más alta[3] (el Salto Ángel en Venezuela), la pirámide más grande[4] (la Pirámide de Quetzalcóatl en México) y la capital más alta del mundo (La Paz). Y tiene además la universidad más antigua de las Américas (la Universidad Autónoma de Santo Domingo, fundada en 1538).

[1] has    [2] waterfall    [3] highest    [4] largest

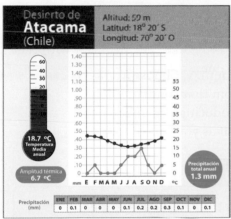

Datos del desierto de Atacama, Chile          La Paz, Bolivia          El Salto Ángel, Venezuela

**Búsqueda:** desierto de atacama, salto ángel, pirámide de quetzalcóatl, universidad autónoma de santo domingo

### 40 Comprensión   Interpretive Communication

Corrige las siguientes oraciones. *(Correct the following sentences.)*

1. The driest jungle in the world is in Chile.

2. *La Paz* is the oldest capital city in the world.

3. The oldest university in the world is in the Dominican Republic.

4. *El Salto Ángel* is a volcano in Venezuela.

5. The biggest pyramid in the world, outside of Egypt, is in Mexico.

### 41 Analiza

1. What is the most surprising fact that you learned in the reading "*Visita las maravillas del mundo hispanohablante*"? Which world records, if any, did you already know?

2. Which of the places would you like to visit the most? Explain why, using information from the reading and other knowledge you might have for that country.

## Extensión

Let's look at five additional wonders of the Spanish-speaking world:

1. The cathedral in Sevilla, España is the largest Gothic building in Europe.

2. Guinea Ecuatorial is one of the most humid countries on the planet.

3. *Ojos del Salado*, Argentina is the highest active volcano on the planet.

4. Cusco, Perú is the oldest continuously inhabited city in South America.

5. Granada, Nicaragua is the oldest colonial (Spanish) city in Central America.

*Cusco, Perú*

# Escritura

### 42 Un nuevo amigo | Presentational Communication

You are starting an exchange with an e-pal from a Spanish-speaking country. Choose a country and research one place, person, or thing of special interest from that country. After you have done your research, compose an e-mail in Spanish introducing yourself to your new acquaintance. Provide as much information about yourself as you can. Ask your e-pal about himself or herself also. Then mention one fact about that country from your research that interests you in particular. The words in *Para escribir más* may be helpful as you compose your message.

### Para escribir más

| | |
|---|---|
| me gusta | *I like* |
| me interesa | *I am interested in* |
| yo quiero | *I want* |
| conocer | *to get to know* |
| tu país | *your country* |
| fantástico | *fantastic* |

### Estrategia

**Organize your thoughts before writing**

Before you begin a writing assignment, you should always jot down your ideas. A visual map of your thoughts could be in the form of an outline, a graphic organizer like a mind map, a table or chart, or whatever fits your particular style. Once you have your thoughts down (on paper or in digital format), you can decide how you are going to organize them and then move on to composing your paragraph, e-mail, essay, etc.

emcpassport.com
WB 16
LA 6
GV 9

## A Escuchar: ¿Cuántos años tienen? 🎧 (p. 11)

Listen to the names and ages. Then match each person with his or her age.

1. Cristina
2. Daniel
3. Gabriela
4. Miguel
5. Camila
6. Eduardo

A. 19
B. 11
C. 10
D. 5
E. 14
F. 13

## B Vocabulario/Gramática: Diálogos (pp. 2, 10–11)

Completa los diálogos con las palabras apropiadas.

**I**  **A:** Hola. ¿Cómo te **(1)**?

**B:** Me **(2)** Valeria.

**A:** ¿Se escribe con **(3)** minúscula?

**B:** No. Se escribe con ve **(4)**.

**II**  **A:** ¿Y **(5)**? ¿Cómo te llamas?

**B:** **(6)** me llamo Natalia.

**A:** ¿De dónde **(7)**, Natalia?

**B:** Yo **(8)** de Madrid, la capital de España.

## C Vocabulario/Gramática: Signos de puntuación (pp. 2, 6, 10–11)

Usa la puntuación correcta en el diálogo. Usa los signos de interrogación, exclamación, los puntos (*periods*) y las letras mayúsculas y minúsculas.

**A:** yo me llamo elisa cómo te llamas tú

**B:** me llamo esteban mucho gusto!

**A:** ¿eres de la argentina

**B:** sí soy de buenos aires, la capital y tú

**A:** yo soy de aquí soy estadounidense

**B:** eres de Estados Unidos!

## D Gramática: Los países hispanohablantes (p. 10)

Write the name of each country next to its capital. Use the articles whenever appropriate.

| | | | |
|---|---|---|---|
| 1. San Juan | | 5. Quito | |
| 2. Lima | | 6. Santo Domingo | |
| 3. La Habana | | 7. La Paz | |
| 4. Washington, D.C. | | 8. Montevideo | |

## E Gramática: ¿Qué palabra es? (p. 16)

Di qué quiere decir cada palabra en inglés. (*Tell what each word means in English.*) ¡Ojo! Cuidado con los falsos amigos. (*Watch out! Careful with false friends.*)

1. fabuloso
2. carpeta

3. teléfono celular
4. lectura

Sort the words from the list in three groups: *saludos* (greetings), *fiestas* (parties), and *despedidas* (good-byes), and write them where they belong. Use a table like the one below.

| quinceañera | dos besos |
|---|---|
| abrazo | cumpleaños |
| hola | adiós |
| hasta luego | apretón de manos |

| Saludos | Fiestas | Despedidas |
|---|---|---|
|  |  |  |
|  |  |  |
|  |  |  |

## Vocabulario

### Despedidas

Adiós.
Hasta luego.

### Números

cero
uno
dos
tres
cuatro
cinco
seis
siete
ocho
nueve
diez
once
doce
trece
catorce
quince
dieciséis
diecisiete
dieciocho
diecinueve
veinte

### Países

la Argentina
Bolivia
Chile
Colombia
Costa Rica
Cuba
el Ecuador
El Salvador
España
los Estados Unidos
Guatemala
Guinea Ecuatorial
Honduras
México
Nicaragua
Panamá
el Paraguay
el Perú
Puerto Rico
la República Dominicana
el Uruguay
Venezuela

### Palabras interrogativas

¿cómo?
¿(de) dónde?

### Personas

tú
yo

### Saludos

Hola.
Mucho gusto.

### Verbos

eres
me llamo
se escribe
soy
te llamas
tengo
tienes

### Otras expresiones

el acento
aquí
la capital
¿Cómo te llamas?
con
¿Cuántos años tienes?
de
¿Eres (tú) de...?
hispanohablante
la mayúscula
la minúscula
el muchacho, la muchacha
no
el país
sí
Tengo (*number*) años.
y

### El alfabeto

| a | b | c | d | e | f | g | h |
|---|---|---|---|---|---|---|---|
| i | j | k | l | m | n | ñ | |
| o | p | q | r | rr | s | t | |
| u | v | w | x | y | z | | |

## Gramática

### Punctuation

Written Spanish requires two question marks and two exclamation points, one at the beginning (written upside down) and the other at the end of interrogative and exclamative sentences.

### Definite articles and countries

Some Spanish speakers use the definite articles e*l*, *la*, *los*, and *las* with country names.

| la Argentina | los Estados Unidos |
|---|---|
| el Ecuador | el Perú |

### Cognates

Words in Spanish and English that resemble one another and that have the same meaning are cognates. For instance, *acento* in Spanish looks similar to the English word **accent**. When a word in Spanish looks similar to a word in English but they do not have the same meaning, they are false cognates. For example, *colegio* means school, not **college**.

## Lección B

# Vocabulario 1

El mundo hispanohablante

WB 1–4
LA 1–2
GV 1–2

emcpassport.com

## Saludos y despedidas 🎧

Buenos días. ¿Cómo está usted, señora Torres?

Estoy bien, Raúl, gracias.

¿Cómo estás, Natalia?

¿Qué tal?

Bien. ¿Y ustedes?

Muy bien.

Hasta mañana, Isa...

Hasta pronto, Isa...

AM 8:00 **Buenos días.**

PM 2:00 **Buenas tardes.**

PM 9:00 **Buenas noches.**

Buenas tardes. ¿Cómo está usted, Sra. López?

Estoy regular, gracias.

### Un poco más

#### Las abreviaturas

Just as Mr. is a shortened form of the word mister in English, *Sr.* is an abbreviation (*abreviatura*) for *señor* in Spanish.

Other abbreviations: *Srta.* (*señorita*), *Sra.* (*señora*), *Ud.* (*usted*), *Uds.* (*ustedes*), *Dr.* (*doctor*), and *Dra.* (*doctora*).

## Para conversar

**T**o greet people formally:

Buenas tardes, **señor** y señora
Martínez. ¿Cómo **están** ustedes?
*Good afternoon, Mr. and Mrs. Martínez.*
*How are you?*

**T**o ask and say how other people are:

| | |
|---|---|
| ¿Cómo **está él**? | ¿Y **ella**? ¿Cómo está? |
| *How is he?* | *And she? How is she?* |
| Él está muy bien. | Ella está **mal**. |
| *He is very well.* | *She is (doing) badly.* |

**T**o say goodbye:

**Buenas noches**, señor Pérez.
*Good night, Mr. Pérez.*

Hasta mañana, **señorita** Rodríguez.
*See you tomorrow, Miss Rodríguez.*

### Para decir más

| | |
|---|---|
| Así así. / Más o menos. | *So-so.* |
| ¿Cómo te va? | *How are things?* |
| Nada nuevo. | *Nothing new.* |
| ¿Qué cuentas? | *What's up? What's new?* |

### 1  ¿Saludo o despedida?

Di si lo que oyes es: **un saludo**; **una despedida**; **un saludo y una despedida**. *(Say if what you hear is: a greeting, a farewell, or a greeting and a farewell.)*

### 2  Dos diálogos

Completa los dos diálogos con las palabras del recuadro. *(Complete the two dialogues with the words from the box.)*

| hasta pronto | él | estás | yo | qué | hasta luego | tú | usted | buenos |
|---|---|---|---|---|---|---|---|---|

**Diálogo I**

**A:** **(1)** días, Sra. Torres. ¿Cómo está **(2)**?

**B:** **(3)** estoy bien, gracias.

**A:** ¿Y el señor Torres?

**B:** **(4)** también (*also*) está bien.

**Diálogo II**

**A:** Hola, Tony, ¿**(5)** tal?

**B:** Regular, ¿y **(6)**?

**A:** Así, así. ¡**(7)**!

**B:** ¡**(8)**!

### 3  Cuatro mini-diálogos

Completa los siguientes cuatro diálogos de una manera lógica. *(Complete the following four dialogues in a logical way.)*

**A:** ¡Hola! ¿Qué **(1)**?

**B:** Bien, **(2)**, ¿y tú?

**A:** Buenos días, Sra. Fernández.
¿Cómo **(3)** Ud.?

**B:** **(4)** bien, gracias.

**A:** ¿Cómo **(5)** Pedro?

**B:** **(6)** está regular.

**A:** ¿**(7)** está Julia?

**B:** Ella **(8)** muy mal.

# Diálogo 🎧

## Buenos días

**Alicia:**   Buenos días, Quique. ¿Cómo estás?

**Quique:**   Estoy muy bien. ¿Y tú? ¿Qué tal?

**Alicia:**   Bien, gracias. Adiós, Quique.

**Quique:**   Adiós, no. Hasta pronto.

## 4  ¿Qué recuerdas?

Escribe **sí** o **no**.

1. Alicia and Quique meet up one afternoon.
2. Quique is feeling really well.
3. Alicia is not feeling well.

4. Alicia thanks Quique for doing her a favor.
5. Quique plans to see Alicia again soon.
6. It is in the evening when they say good-bye.

## ¡Comunicación!

### 5  Algo personal  👥  Interpersonal Communication

Greet four or five students in class and ask how each one is. Your classmates then answer and ask how you are. You may incorporate the expressions from the *Para decir más* box to extend your conversations.

**MODELO**

A:  Buenos días/Buenas tardes, (*name of student B*). ¿Qué tal?

B:  Mal. ¿Y tú?

A:  Muy bien, gracias. ¿Por qué mal?

B:  Me duele la cabeza.

### Para decir más

| | |
|---|---|
| ¿Por qué? | *Why?* |
| Me duele la cabeza. | *I have a headache. / My head hurts.* |
| Me duele el estómago. | *I have a stomachache. / My stomach hurts.* |
| Estoy mucho mejor. | *I am much better.* |

### 6  ¿Cuál es una respuesta correcta? 🎧

Escoge una respuesta correcta a lo que oyes.

*Bien, gracias*

**Buenos días**

Adiós, no. Hasta pronto.

# Gramática

## The Spanish "You": Formal and Informal

- Spanish has several words for **you**. Use the informal **tú** when talking to someone with whom you use a first name. Use the more formal **usted** (abbreviated **Ud.**) when talking to someone you would address using a title (*señor Torres, señorita Jiménez*).

- The plural **you** is **ustedes** (abbreviated **Uds.**) in all the Spanish-speaking world, but in Spain you have two choices:

    1) use the polite and formal **ustedes** (or **Uds.**) when talking to two or more people you address using a title;

    2) use the informal **vosotros** (for males or a combination of males and females) or **vosotras** (for females) when talking to two or more friends, family members, or younger people.

|  | singular | plural |
|---|---|---|
| informal | tú | **ustedes (Uds.)**<br>**vosotros** (*masculine/mixed*)<br>**vosotras** (*feminine*) |
| formal | usted (Ud.) | **ustedes (Uds.)** |

### Un poco más

When using the informal *vosotros* or *vosotras* in Spain, the greeting *¿Cómo están?* or *¿Cómo están ustedes?* becomes *¿Cómo estáis?, ¿Cómo estáis vosotros?, ¿Cómo estáis vosotras?*

---

## 7 Saludando correctamente

How would you address (talk to) these people? Choose either *tú, Ud., Uds., vosotros,* or *vosotras*.

1. a friend at school
2. your sister
3. your teacher
4. an elderly couple you have just met
5. the principal at your school
6. two friends (Latin America)
7. two female friends (Spain)
8. two male friends (Spain)

---

## 8 El saludo correcto

Would you use *tú, Ud., Uds., vosotros,* or *vosotras* when talking to these people? Some may have more than one possible answer.

**1.** Sr. y Sra. Uribe   **2.** Jaime   **3.** Juan y Marta   **4.** Srta. Vázquez   **5.** Teresa y Raquel

## 9 Saludos

Greet these people in Spanish according to the time and ask how they are feeling.

MODELO    Carmen
          **Buenos días, Carmen. ¿Cómo estás?/¿Qué tal?**

**1.** Ana y Marisa
(México)

**2.** Juana y Julito
(España)

**3.** la Sra. Gómez
(República Dominicana)

**4.** Elena, Mónica y Marta
(España)

**5.** Paco (Ecuador)

**6.** el Sr. Fernández y
el Sr. García (España)

## ¡Comunicación!

### 10 ¿Cómo están Uds.?   Interpersonal Communication

You have just walked up to some friends in a Latin American country. In groups of three, talk about how you are feeling. Be sure everyone in the group practices each of the roles shown (A, B, and C).

MODELO    A: *(Greet two classmates and ask how they feel.)*
          B: *(Say how you feel.)*
          C: *(Say how you feel and ask how student A feels.)*
          A: *(Say how you feel.)*

### 11 ¿Cómo estáis?

Pretend you are on an exchange program in Spain. Greet the following members of your host family and ask how they feel.

**1.** your sisters

**2.** your parents

**3.** your male cousins

**4.** your little brother

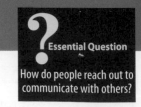

# La cortesía en el mundo hispanohablante

Connecting to and communicating with others means showing proper respect. If you want to approach people in Spanish speaking cultures, it is important to learn a few basic terms that show courtesy. The expressions *Perdón* and *Con permiso* are equivalent to "Excuse me." However, these expressions are used in different situations.

Use *Perdón* if you need to interrupt a conversation, want to indicate you do not understand what someone said, or if you accidentally bump into someone. *Perdón* is also very important if you need to get someone's attention, for example to ask for directions on the street or call out to a server in a restaurant.

*Con permiso,* on the other hand, is used more specifically to ask someone to let you pass by or to politely let someone know you are about to leave.

And remember to preface requests with *Por favor* (Please) and finish with *Gracias* or *Muchas gracias* for any small courtesy or kindness. Being polite to others will get you a long way among Spanish speakers!

*Muchas gracias*

**Búsqueda:** perdón vs con permiso

## Prácticas

Among many Spanish speakers, it is customary to stand relatively close to each other while conversing. Because English speakers tend to keep more of a distance between themselves and another person, this proximity may be misinterpreted as an invasion of one's personal space, which it is not. *No es falta de cortesía* (lack of manners); it is simply the way many Hispanics interact with one another.

## 12 Comprensión

1. Explain the difference between *perdón* and *con permiso*.
2. What would you say to someone if you accidentally spilled your beverage on that person's lap?
3. What would you say if you needed to leave before a conversation is over?

## 13 Analiza

1. Why do you think is it important to learn and use the correct register (level of formality) when addressing people in other cultures?
2. How do you react when you feel someone is standing too close to you and is invading your personal space? Would you react differently if you knew it were due to a cultural norm?

# Más sobre los saludos

Relating to others is a vital part of Spanish-speaking cultures, and the way people connect is almost as varied as the relationships themselves. Allow yourself to experience this the next time you are among Spanish speakers or the next time you watch a program or movie in Spanish (great media for observing cultural norms!). There are differences between formal and informal language and when each of these is used. For example, formal greetings like *Buenas tardes* and *¿Cómo está Ud.?* are used differently from the very informal *Hola* or *¿Qué hay?* (What's new?).

There are other notable cultural differences in when and with whom greetings are exchanged. Spanish speakers are careful to greet everyone in the room in a social setting. Greetings are exchanged upon entering a store or stepping into an elevator.

*Buenas tardes.*

When exiting, good-byes are equally as common.

Residents of large cities and residents of small towns will also interact among themselves differently. A small town naturally lends itself to greater familiarity and more informal interactions which are reflected in different types of greetings and good-byes.

As a student of the Spanish language, you are also a student of the culture. Observe and learn so you will be able to connect and communicate with Spanish speakers all over the world.

**Búsqueda:** normas de cortesía imágenes

*Hola, ¿qué tal?*

## Comparaciones

Spanish speakers are expected to greet each person individually when they enter a room. Before leaving, they also go around the room saying individual goodbyes. Is this a custom where you live?

## Perspectivas

Spanish speakers have a proverb that says, *"A la tierra que fueres, haz lo que vieres."* ("When in Rome, do as the Romans do.") What inference can you make about the advice this cultural perspective is giving? How would you apply it in your study of a new culture?

## 14 Comprensión

1. Name three things to observe regarding *los saludos* when you are in a group of Spanish-speakers or observing them.
2. Give one formal greeting and one informal greeting.

## 15 Analiza

1. Why is it important to learn the formal and informal ways to greet and say good-bye in Spanish?
2. Why is it important to learn about the culture while learning a language?

## La hora

Con permiso, por favor.

¡Con mucho gusto!

¿Qué hora es?

Es la una y media.

¡Estoy mal!

¡Lo siento!

¡Muchas gracias!

¡De nada!

### La hora

Es la una menos cinco.

Es la una y cuarto.

Es la una.

Es la una y media.

Es la una y cinco.

Son las dos menos cuarto.

Es mediodía.

Es medianoche.

## Para conversar

**T**o ask for the time:
   **Perdón**. ¿Qué hora es?
   *Excuse me. What time is it?*

Son las once **de la mañana**.
*It is eleven o'clock in the morning.*

Es la una **de la tarde**.
*It is one o'clock in the afternoon.*

Son las siete **de la noche**.
*It is seven o'clock in the evening.*

### Para decir más

| | |
|---|---|
| **Disculpe Ud., ...** | *Excuse me, ...* |
| **No hay de qué.** | *It's nothing.* |
| **¿Qué hora tiene?** | *What time do you have?* |

## Los números del 20 al 100

| 20 | veinte | 25 | veinticinco | 30 | treinta | 60 | sesenta |
| 21 | veintiuno | 26 | veintiséis | 31 | treinta y uno | 70 | setenta |
| 22 | veintidós | 27 | veintisiete | 32 | treinta y dos | 80 | ochenta |
| 23 | veintitrés | 28 | veintiocho | 40 | cuarenta | 90 | noventa |
| 24 | veinticuatro | 29 | veintinueve | 50 | cincuenta | 100 | cien |

## 16 Los números hasta cien

Escribe los números que oyes.

MODELO   30

## 17 Números en serie   Conéctate: las matemáticas

Completa de forma lógica las siguientes series de números hasta 100.

1. cero, cinco, diez…
2. cero, siete, catorce…
3. cero, once, veintidós…
4. cero, trece, veintiséis, treinta y nueve…

*Tres por cuatro son doce.*

## 18 La hora

Choose the correct time.

1. 1:15
   A. Es la una.
   B. Es la una y cuarto.
   C. Es la una y media.

2. 3:30
   A. Son las tres.
   B. Son las tres y cuarto.
   C. Son las tres y media.

3. 7:45
   A. Son las siete y cuarto.
   B. Son las siete menos cuarto.
   C. Son las ocho menos cuarto.

4. 10:50
   A. Son las diez y diez.
   B. Son las once menos diez.
   C. Son las diez menos diez.

## 19 Situaciones

Escoge la mejor frase para cada situación. *(Choose the best sentence for each situation.)*

1. You need to know the time.
   A. ¿Qué hora es?
   B. Lo siento.
   C. Es la una.

2. You need to use an empty chair at somebody's table.
   A. Con permiso.
   B. Con mucho gusto.
   C. ¿Qué tal?

3. Someone offers you a seat in a crowded train.
   A. ¡Estoy mal!
   B. Muchas gracias.
   C. De nada.

4. You want to apologize to your friend for being rude.
   A. Lo siento.
   B. De nada.
   C. Con permiso.

## ¡Comunicación!

### 20 ¿Cuánto es tres por tres? 👥 Interpersonal Communication    Conéctate: las matemáticas

Work with a partner to play the "multiplication question" game. Take turns asking a question and responding. Use the model as a guide.

> **MODELO**    A: ¿Cuánto es siete por siete? *(How much is seven times seven?)*
> B: Es cuarenta y nueve.

## ¡Comunicación!

### 21 Con permiso 👥 Interpersonal/Presentational Communication

Role play a conversation between two strangers on the street. Use the outline below to prepare. Switch roles. Present your dialogue to the class.

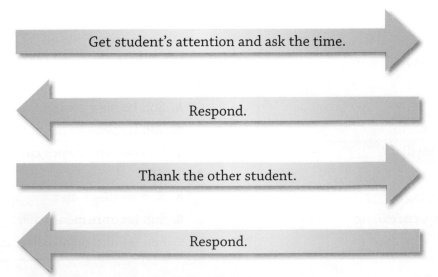

Get student's attention and ask the time.

Respond.

Thank the other student.

Respond.

# Diálogo

## ¿Cómo te llamas?

**Quique:** Por favor, ¿qué hora es?

**Paloma:** Son las tres y diez.

**Quique:** Muchas gracias. Perdón, ¿cómo te llamas?

**Paloma:** Me llamo Paloma.

**Quique:** Mucho gusto. Me llamo Quique.

**Paloma:** Con permiso.

**Quique:** Sí, lo siento.

---

## 22 ¿Qué recuerdas?

1. ¿Qué hora es en el diálogo?
2. ¿Qué dice el muchacho antes de preguntar el nombre a la muchacha? *(What does the boy say before asking the girl's name?)*
3. ¿Cómo se llama la muchacha?
4. ¿Cómo se llama el muchacho?
5. ¿Qué dice la muchacha antes de bajar del autobús? *(What does the girl say before getting off the bus?)*

---

## 23 Algo personal

1. ¿Qué hora es?
2. ¿Cómo te llamas?

---

## 24 ¿Qué hora es?

Escribe la hora que oyes. *(Write the time you hear.)*

**MODELO** 9:25

3:10    1:30    6:00    4:20

9:25    12:40    5:15

---

## 25 Si aquí es... ¿qué hora es en... ? | Conéctate: la tecnología

Find a world clock online and use it to determine the time at the locations indicated, assuming that in New York it is 1:30 AM.

1. En Madrid, España, es/son __.
2. En Los Ángeles, California, es/son __.
3. En Sidney, Australia, es/son __.
4. En La Paz, Bolivia, es/son __.

# Gramática

## Telling Time

- You can find out what time it is by asking *¿Qué hora es?*
- When giving the time in Spanish, use **Es la una** to refer to one o'clock and **Son las** (+ number) to indicate any other hour.

    1:00 **Es la** una.                2:00 **Son las** dos.

- To add minutes **after** the hour, use **y** (+ number of minutes through *veintinueve*). To indicate time **before** the hour, use **menos** (+ number of minutes through *veintinueve*).

    2:29 **Son las** dos **y** veintinueve.          2:31 **Son las** tres **menos** veintinueve.

- Add **y cuarto** for a quarter past the hour, **y media** for half past the hour, and **menos cuarto** for a quarter to the hour.

    4:15 **Son las** cuatro **y cuarto**.          4:30 **Son las** cuatro **y media**.

    4:45 **Son las** cinco **menos cuarto**.

- When using a digital timepiece, people usually add as many minutes as shown, through 59.

    7:45 **Son las** siete **y** cuarenta y cinco.          7:57 **Son las** siete **y** cincuenta y siete.

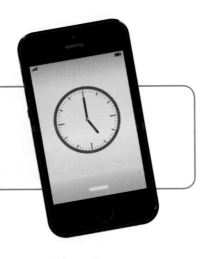

### 26 La hora

Escribe la hora.

**MODELO** Son las cinco.

**¡Ojo!** 👁

To tell the time before the hour, be sure to look at the hour that is coming and subtract the minutes remaining:

6:50 = 10 minutes to 7 = 7 minus 10 = *las siete menos diez.*

# Gramática

## Expressions for AM and PM

| | | |
|---|---|---|
| AM | **de la mañana** | in the morning |
| PM | **de la tarde** | in the afternoon |
| | **de la noche** | at night |

Two additional useful expressions:

| | |
|---|---|
| *Es mediodía.* | It is noon. |
| *Es medianoche.* | It is midnight. |

### Un poco más

Some Spanish-speaking countries use the 24-hour clock, counting the hours from 1:00 through 24:00. In this system 1:00 is AM and 24:00 is midnight. 1:00 PM would be *las trece,* and 10:00 PM is *las veintidós.*

---

### 27 La profesora y el estudiante

Completa el siguiente diálogo de una manera lógica.

**Lorenzo:** Buenos **(1)**, Sra. Vargas.

**Sra. Vargas:** ¡Hola, Lorenzo! ¿Cómo **(2)**?

**Lorenzo:** Estoy bien, **(3)**. ¿Y **(4)**?

**Sra. Vargas:** **(5)** muy bien.

**Lorenzo:** **(6)**, ¿**(7)** hora es?

**Sra. Vargas:** **(8)** las diez y media de la **(9)**.

**Lorenzo:** ¿No son **(10)** nueve y media?

**Sra. Vargas:** No.

**Lorenzo:** ¡Uy! Tengo clase de español. Hasta **(11)**.

**Sra. Vargas:** Adiós, hasta **(12)**.

---

### ¡Ojo! 👁

Remember the difference between telling time on an analog and a digital timepiece. With a digital timepiece, you tell the exact number of minutes after the hour.

## 🗨 ¡Comunicación!

### 28 Perdón, ¿qué hora es? 👥 Interpersonal Communication

With another student, imagine you have stopped someone on the street to politely ask what time it is. Take turns asking for and stating the indicated time.

MODELO
A: Perdón, ¿qué hora es?
B: Son las siete y cuarto (y quince) de la mañana.
A: Muchas gracias.

7:15 AM

# Todo en contexto

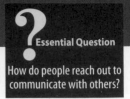

## ¡Comunicación!

### 29 Hola, amigo 👥 Interpersonal/Presentational Communication

Role play a conversation between two friends who run into each other on the street. Be prepared to present it to the class.

⟷ Greet and ask how each other is.

⟶ Ask the time.

⟵ Say the time.

⟶ Say you have Spanish class. Excuse yourself and say see you soon.

⟵ Say good-bye.

## ¡Comunicación!

### 30 Un diálogo 👥 Presentational Communication

In a small group, brainstorm a dialogue in which you use some or all of the expressions from the word bank. Add as many additional expressions as you wish. Be creative! Write your dialogue, then present it to the class using appropriate gestures and other non-verbals.

perdón  con permiso  vosotros

Ud.

mal  muy mal  lo siento

de nada

*De nada.*

# Lectura

## Antes de leer

### 31 Los cognados

1. Give five examples of cognates you know.
2. Find at least five cognates in the reading that follows.

### Estrategia

**Using cognates for understanding**

Spanish will be more enjoyable to read if you learn some techniques that will help you recognize cognates. For example, many words that end in *-ión* have English counterparts that end in -tion, such as *información* (information).

## El mundo hispanohablante 🎧

**República Bolivariana de Venezuela**
Capital: Caracas

**República de Colombia**
Capital: Bogotá

**Salto Ángel**
(catarata más alta del mundo[1])

**Gabriel García Márquez**
(ganador[2], Premio Nobel de literatura)

**Carolina Herrera**
(diseñadora de modas[3])

**Shakira**
(cantante[4])

**República de Chile**
Capital: Santiago

**Jorge Luis Borges**
(escritor[5])

**Coté de Pablo**
(actriz: *NCIS*)

**República Argentina**
Capital: Buenos Aires

**Viggo Mortensen**
(actor - Él vivió[6] en Argentina.)

**Isabel Allende**
(escritora famosa)

[1] world's highest waterfall   [2] winner   [3] fashion designer   [4] singer   [5] writer   [6] he lived

🔍 **Búsqueda: personas, sitios famosos en sudamérica**

El rey[1] don Felipe VI de Borbón y la reina doña Letizia
(Madrid, España)

Reino de España
Capital: Madrid

Frida Kahlo
(pintora[2] famosa)

Alicia Alonso
(bailarina famosa)

Estados Unidos Mexicanos
Capital: México, D.F.

República de Cuba
Capital: La Habana

Estado Libre Asociado de Puerto Rico
Capital: San Juan

República de El Salvador
Capital: San Salvador

República de Costa Rica
Capital: San José

Sonia Sotomayor
(Juez Asociada[3], Corte Suprema de Justicia - Sus papás son de Puerto Rico.)

Harry Shum, Jr.
(actor: *Glee*)

J.D. Pardo
(actor: *Revolution*)

[1] king   [2] painter   [3] Associate Justice

**Búsqueda:** personas, sitios famosos del mundo hispanohablante

---

## 32 Comprensión    Interpretive Communication

Match the person/s in the column on the left with the country of origin in the column on the right.

1. Frida Kahlo
2. Jorge Luis Borges
3. Isabel Allende
4. el rey don Felipe VI y la reina doña Letizia
5. Gabriel García Márquez y Shakira

A. Colombia
B. República de Chile
C. España
D. República Argentina
E. Estados Unidos Mexicanos

---

## 33 Analiza

1. If you could have a conversation with one of the famous people mentioned in the reading "*El mundo hispanohablante*" on these two pages, who would it be and why?
2. What would you ask this person? Why?

# Repaso de la Lección B

## A Escuchar: La hora 🎧 (pp. 30, 34–35)

Escribe las horas que escuchas.

**MODELO**   2:10 PM

## B Vocabulario/Gramática: ¿Cómo están? (pp. 23–24)

Greet these people in Spanish and ask how they are feeling. How might they respond?

**MODELO**   Paula

A: **Hola, Paula. ¿Cómo estás?/¿Qué tal?**

B: **Estoy muy bien, gracias.**

Paula

**1.** Sr. y Sra. Gómez   **2.** Antonio   **3.** Jaime y María

**4.** Srta. Sosa   **5.** Tere y Julia

## C Vocabulario: Los números (p. 31)

Escribe el número que falta en la serie. *(Write the missing number in the series.)*

**1.** diez, veinte, treinta, __, cincuenta, sesenta

**2.** quince, treinta, cuarenta y cinco, __, setenta y cinco, __

**3.** ochenta, ochenta y cinco, noventa, noventa y cinco, __

**4.** veintiuno, veintitrés, __ , veintisiete

## D Vocabulario/Gramática: América y España (pp. 23, 26)

Completa las oraciones (*sentences*) con una palabra apropiada.

**1.** ¿Cómo estáis __?

**2.** Buenos días, señores. ¿Cómo están __?

**3.** Hola, Pancho, ¿cómo __?

**4.** ¿Cómo está __, Srta. Baez?

Indicate which of these expressions you would use in the following situations.

*Con permiso.*    **De nada.**    *Con mucho gusto.*

*¿Perdón?*    *Dos, por favor.*    *No, muchas gracias.*

1. You want to politely refuse an offer to do something.

2. A friend asks you for help.

3. Someone thanks you for doing something.

4. You are on an elevator standing behind other people, and you want to exit.

5. You politely ask for two movie tickets.

6. Someone speaks to you so quickly in Spanish that you cannot understand.

## Vocabulario

| Cortesía | La hora | Números | Otras expresiones | Saludos y despedidas |
|---|---|---|---|---|
| con mucho gusto | de la mañana | veintiuno | bien | Buenas noches. |
| con permiso | de la noche | veintidós | mal | Buenas tardes. |
| de nada | de la tarde | veintitrés | muy | Buenos días. |
| (muchas) gracias | Es la… / Son las… | veinticuatro | pronto | Hasta mañana. |
| lo siento | Es medianoche. | veinticinco | ¿Qué tal? | Hasta pronto. |
| perdón | Es mediodía. | veintiséis | regular | |
| por favor | la hora | veintisiete | | |
| | la mañana | veintiocho | | **Verbos** |
| | menos | veintinueve | | es |
| **Gente** | la noche | treinta (y uno, y dos, etc.) | | está (él, ella) |
| él | ¿Qué hora es? | cuarenta | | está (Ud.) |
| ella | la tarde | cincuenta | | están (Uds.) |
| el señor (Sr.) | y cuarto | sesenta | | estás (tú) |
| la señora (Sra.) | y media | setenta | | estoy (yo) |
| la señorita (Srta.) | | ochenta | | son |
| usted (Ud.) | | noventa | | |
| ustedes (Uds.) | | cien | | |
| vosotros/as | | | | |

## Gramática

| Formal/Informal you | | |
|---|---|---|
| | **singular** | **plural** |
| **informal** | tú | ustedes (Uds.) vosotros/vosotras (Spain) |
| **formal** | usted (Ud.) | ustedes (Uds.) |

| Time | |
|---|---|
| ¿Qué hora es? | *What time is it?* |

Es mediodía. (*It's noon.*)
Es medianoche. (*It's midnight.*)

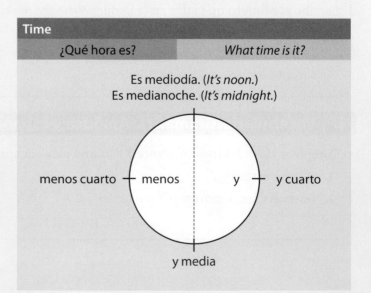

# *Para concluir*

## Proyectos

### A ¡Manos a la obra!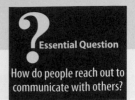

You have been asked by a person in the Spanish-speaking world to create a social networking page communicating the person's information and achievements out to other countries. Working in groups of three or four, choose a country where Spanish is the official language. Then choose a person from that country to research. How is this person special? In what way does he or she reflect the country's culture? Use online resources and, if possible, ask someone from that country for information. Then, create a visual to share with the class publicizing the person's major achievements.

*Gabriel García Márquez (1927–2014)*

### B En resumen

Use the graphic organizer below to classify what you learned about communicating with others in Spanish-speaking culture. In the first column list all the expressions you know for approaching or greeting a Spanish speaker. In the next column, write when or with whom you would use each expression. In the third column indicate any special gestures that might accompany the expression. Finally, imagine a situation somewhere in the Spanish-speaking world where you would apply some of these words and gestures. Fill in the fourth column of the chart and describe your imaginary scenario to another student.

| Expresiones | Cuándo/ Con quién | Gestos | Situación |
| --- | --- | --- | --- |
|  |  |  |  |
|  |  |  |  |
|  |  |  |  |
|  |  |  |  |
|  |  |  |  |

### Extensión

As you learn Spanish this year, you will also learn about the cultures of the people who speak Spanish. Who are they? What is their history? What contributions have they made to the world? Read newspapers, watch television, and search the Internet to develop a greater appreciation for the influence Spanish has had, and continues to have, on the world.

*¿Hablas español?*

## C ¡A escribir!

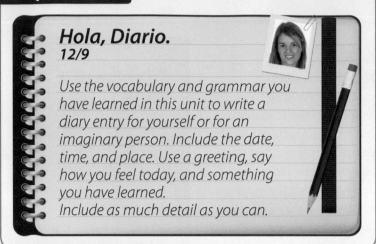

**Hola, Diario.**
12/9

*Use the vocabulary and grammar you have learned in this unit to write a diary entry for yourself or for an imaginary person. Include the date, time, and place. Use a greeting, say how you feel today, and something you have learned.*
*Include as much detail as you can.*

### Estrategia

**Writing the date in Spanish**

Dates in Spanish are written differently from English. The day is given first, followed by the month and then the year. For example, January 16, 2018 would be *16/1/2018*, and October 4 would be *4/10*.

## D Un viaje ideal   Conéctate: la geografía

Draw your own map of the Spanish-speaking world. Include the names of the Spanish-speaking countries and their capital cities. Do online research to find major bodies of water, large mountain chains, and other features, and include those in your illustration. Indicate on the map the three places you would most like to visit. Present the map to the class, stating briefly where you would like to go and why.

## E Una lista de cognados   Conéctate: las ciencias

Many words in the sciences are similar in English and Spanish. Use what you know about word endings to think of scientific words that might have cognates in Spanish. Then check your guesses in the dictionary. Find at least five new cognates. If any of your guesses turns out to be a false cognate, write the meaning of the Spanish word.

MODELO   astronomy   *astronomía*

### Estrategia

**Using the dictionary**

When you come across a word that looks like a cognate, check the context to make sure it is not a *falso amigo*. If the context does not dispel your doubt, use a dictionary to get a clear and accurate understanding of what the word means and whether it is really equivalent to the similar-looking English word.

## F Artistas famosos   Conéctate: el arte

You have already seen references to several famous writers, including Nobel Prize winners, whose native language is Spanish. Now do an online search for famous painters, sculptors, or musicians who come from Spanish-speaking cultures. Do you recognize any of their works? List ten people from ten different countries. Include his or her country of origin and the title of one famous work. Keep an eye out for mention of these artists in upcoming units.

**Búsqueda:** pintores, escultores, músicos famosos del mundo hispanohablante

# Vocabulario de la Unidad 1

el **acento** accent 1A
**Adiós** Good-bye 1A
el **alfabeto** alphabet 1A
**aquí** here 1A
la **Argentina** Argentina 1A
**bien** well 1B
**Bolivia** Bolivia 1A
**Buenas noches** Good night 1B
**Buenas tardes** Good afternoon 1B
**Buenos días** Good morning 1B
la **capital** capital 1A
**catorce** fourteen 1A
**cero** zero 1A
**Chile** Chile 1A
**cien** one hundred 1B
**cinco** five 1A
**cincuenta** fifty 1B
**Colombia** Colombia 1A
**¿cómo?** how?, what? 1A; *¿Cómo te llamas?* What is your name? 1A
**con** with 1A; *con mucho gusto* I would be very glad to 1B; *con permiso* excuse me, may I 1B
**Costa Rica** Costa Rica 1A
**¿Cuántos años tienes?** How old are you? 1A
**cuarenta** forty 1B
**cuatro** four 1A
**Cuba** Cuba 1A
**de** from 1A; *¿de dónde?* (from) where? 1A; *de la mañana* in the morning, AM 1B; *de la noche* at night, PM 1B; *de la tarde* in the afternoon, PM 1B; *de nada* you are welcome 1B
**diecinueve** nineteen 1A
**dieciocho** eighteen 1A
**dieciséis** sixteen 1A
**diecisiete** seventeen 1A
**diez** ten 1A
**doce** twelve 1A
**dos** two 1A
el **Ecuador** Ecuador 1A
**él** he 1B
**El Salvador** El Salvador 1A
**ella** she 1B
**eres** you (informal) are 1A; *¿Eres (tú) de...?* Are you from...? 1A
**es** you (formal) are, he/she/it is 1B; *Es la una.* It is one o'clock. 1B; *Es medianoche.* It is midnight. 1B; *Es mediodía.* It is noon. 1B

**España** Spain 1A
**está (él, ella)** (he/she) is/ 1B; *está (Ud.)* you (formal) are 1B
los **Estados Unidos** United States 1A
**están (Uds.)** you (pl.) are 1B
**estás (tú)** you (informal) are 1B
**estoy** I am 1B
**Guatemala** Guatemala 1A
**Guinea Ecuatorial** Equatorial Guinea 1A
**Hasta luego** See you later 1A; *Hasta mañana.* See you tomorrow. 1B; *Hasta pronto.* See you soon. 1B
**hispanohablante** Spanish-speaking 1A
**Hola** Hello 1A
**Honduras** Honduras 1A
**hora** hour, time 1B
**lo siento** I am sorry 1B
**mal** badly 1B
**mañana** tomorrow 1B
la **mañana** morning 1B
la **mayúscula** capital letter 1A
**me llamo** my name is 1A
**menos (cinco, cuarto, etc.)** minus, to, until, before (to express time) 1B
**México** Mexico 1A
la **minúscula** lowercase letter 1A
la **muchacha** girl, young woman 1A
el **muchacho** boy, young man 1A
**(muchas) gracias** thank you (very much) 1B
**Mucho gusto.** Glad (Nice) to meet you. 1A
**muy** very 1B
**Nicaragua** Nicaragua 1A
**no** no 1A
la **noche** night 1B
**noventa** ninety 1B
**nueve** nine 1A
**ochenta** eighty 1B
**ocho** eight 1A
**once** eleven 1A
el **país** country 1A
**Panamá** Panama 1A
el **Paraguay** Paraguay 1A
**perdón** excuse me, pardon me 1B
el **Perú** Peru 1A
**por favor** please 1B

**pronto** soon, quickly 1B
**Puerto Rico** Puerto Rico 1A
**¿Qué hora es?** What time is it? 1B
**¿Qué tal?** How are you? 1B
**quince** fifteen 1A
**regular** average, so-so, regular 1B
la **República Dominicana** Dominican Republic 1A
**se escribe** it is written 1A
**seis** six 1A
el **señor (Sr.)** gentleman, sir, Mr. 1B
la **señora (Sra.)** lady, madame, Mrs. 1B
la **señorita (Srta.)** young lady, Miss 1B
**sesenta** sixty 1B
**setenta** seventy 1B
**sí** yes 1A
**siete** seven 1A
**son** *Son las* (+ number). It is (+ number) o'clock. 1B
**soy** I am 1A
la **tarde** afternoon 1B
**te llamas** your name is 1A
**tengo** I have 1A; *Tengo (number) años.* I am (number) years old. 1A
**tienes** you have 1A
**trece** thirteen 1A
**treinta (y uno, etc.)** thirty (one, etc.) 1B
**tres** three 1A
**tú** you (informal) 1A
**uno** one 1A
el **Uruguay** Uruguay 1A
**usted (Ud.)** you (s.) 1B
**ustedes (Uds.)** you (pl.) 1B
**veinte** twenty 1A
**Venezuela** Venezuela 1A
**vosotros/as** you (Spain, pl.) 1B
**y** and 1A; *y cuarto* quarter past, quarter after 1B; *y media* half past 1B
**yo** I 1A

## ¿Sabías que...?

Almost 40 percent of all Hispanics in the United States are bilingual, but many others don't even speak Spanish! This is due to the fact that they were born in the United States, and English is their native language. About one-third of all Hispanics in the United States speak only English at home.

# 2

# ¡Al colegio!

Scan the QR code to watch this episode of *El cuarto misterioso*.

**What do José and Conchita have in common?**

A. They both like music.
B. They both like math.
C. They both like soccer.

**Essential Question**

**?**

**How does education promote understanding of different cultures?**

## Mis metas

**Lección A** **I will be able to:**

▶ ask and tell who someone is
▶ ask and tell where someone is from using subject pronouns and the verb **ser**
▶ give examples of Spanish in everyday life
▶ identify Hispanic influence in the United States
▶ ask and tell how to say a word in Spanish
▶ talk about one or several people, places, or classroom objects
▶ talk about grades in Spanish-speaking countries

**Lección B** **I will be able to:**

▶ discuss school schedules
▶ describe classroom objects and clothing
▶ talk on the phone in Spanish
▶ talk about what people do and need using **-ar** verbs
▶ talk about student exchange programs and schools in the Spanish-speaking world
▶ identify technology items
▶ ask for and provide contact information
▶ talk about where things are and how people are using the verb **estar**
▶ read and discuss a poem by Gina Valdés

Estados Unidos

What is the oldest city in the United States? Who founded it?

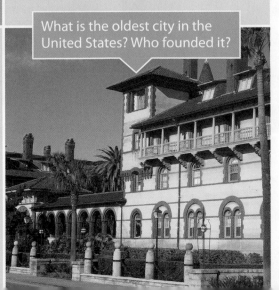

## ¿Cómo se llama?

## Para conversar 🎧

*T*o ask and answer about people you don't know:

¿**Quiénes** son **ellos**?
*Who are they?*

Ellos son Felipe y Rafael.
*They are Felipe and Rafael.*

¿De dónde son ellos?
*Where are they from?*

¡**Ay**! ¡Lo siento! No **sé**.
*Oh! I'm sorry! I don't know.*

### Para decir más

| | |
|---|---|
| ¡Claro! | Of course! |
| No estoy seguro/a. | I am not sure. |
| ¿Sabes... ? | Do you know...? |
| ¡Seguro! | Sure! |

### 1 ¿Quién? 🎧

Selecciona la foto de la persona o personas apropiadas.

A    B    C    D

### 2 ¿Cuál es la respuesta?

Match the questions in the column on the left with the answers in the column on the right.

1. ¿Cómo te llamas?
2. ¿De dónde eres?
3. ¿Cómo se llama ella?
4. ¿Quién es él?
5. ¿De dónde es ella?
6. ¿Quiénes son ellos?
7. ¿De dónde son ellos?
8. ¿Cuántos años tienes?

A. Soy de Perú.
B. Son de España.
C. Es Alejandro.
D. Tengo quince años.
E. Es de Panamá.
F. Me llamo Mateo.
G. Se llama Adriana.
H. Son Diego y Mario.

*Ellas son Vanessa y Victoria.*

## 3 Es de...

Completa el diálogo con las palabras apropiadas. *(Complete the dialogue with the appropriate words.)*

**Laura:** Miguel, ¿cómo **(1)** llama ella?

**Miguel:** ¿Ella? Se **(2)** Carolina.

**Laura:** ¿Y de **(3)** es ella?

**Miguel:** **(4)** es de Nicaragua.

**Laura:** ¿Y **(5)**? ¿De dónde son?

**Miguel:** Ellos **(6)** de Uruguay.

**Laura:** Y él, ¿quién **(7)**?

**Miguel:** ¿**(8)**? Es Felipe.

**Laura:** ¿Es él **(9)** Uruguay?

**Miguel:** No. **(10)** es de los Estados Unidos.

*¿De dónde son ellos?*

## 4 Forma preguntas

Choose one item from each column to create questions. Mix and match to make as many question combinations as possible. Be sure to use proper punctuation on the questions.

**MODELO** ¿Quién es él?

| Quién(es) | son | ella |
| Cómo | es | ellos |
| De dónde | se llama | él |

## 5 Ahora, forma respuestas

For each question you created in Activity 4, write an appropriate answer.

**MODELO** Él es Pablo.

# ¡Comunicación!

## 6 Diálogo    Interpersonal Communication

With a classmate, take turns asking and answering questions about the students in your Spanish class.

**MODELO** A: ¿Cómo se llama ella?

B: Se llama Mercedes.

# Diálogo

## ¿Cómo se llama ella?

**Raúl:** Laura, ¿quién es?

**Laura:** ¿Él?

**Raúl:** No, ella. ¿Cómo se llama ella?

**Laura:** Se llama Diana.

**Raúl:** ¿Es de aquí?

**Laura:** No, ella es de Los Ángeles.

*(Later)*

**Diana:** ¿Quién eres tú?

**Raúl:** Perdón. Me llamo Raúl.

**Diana:** Mucho gusto, Raúl.

**Raúl:** Mucho gusto, Diana.

### 7  ¿Qué recuerdas?

1. ¿Quién es el muchacho?
2. ¿Es Laura un muchacho?
3. ¿Cómo se llama la muchacha de Los Ángeles?

### 8  Algo personal

1. ¿Eres tú de California? ¿De dónde eres?
2. ¿Cómo se llama la capital de los Estados Unidos?

### 9  ¡No es lógico!

Escucha la información y corrige lo que no es lógico. *(Listen to the information and correct what is not logical.)*

**1.** Raúl

**2.** Laura y Diana

**3.** María

# Gramática

## Subject Pronouns

- You already have used subject pronouns in Spanish to talk about one person (*yo, tú, Ud., él, ella*). Now, you will use subject pronouns to talk about more than one person. Note that Spanish does not have a pronoun equivalent to the English pronoun "it."

| Subject Pronouns | | | |
|---|---|---|---|
| **yo** | *I* | **nosotros** <br> **nosotras** | *we (masc., mixed)* <br> *we (fem.)* |
| **tú** | *you (informal)* | *(Spain only)* <br> **vosotros** <br> **vosotras** | *you (pl., informal) (masc., mixed)* <br> *you (pl., informal) (fem.)* |
| **usted (Ud.)** <br> **él** <br> **ella** | *you (formal)* <br> *he* <br> *she* <br> *it* | **ustedes (Uds.)** <br> **ellos** <br> **ellas** | *you (pl.)* <br> *they (masc., mixed)* <br> *they (fem.)* |

- You will often use subject pronouns (*pronombres personales*) to replace the names of people in a sentence in Spanish.

| | |
|---|---|
| *¿De dónde es **Inés**?* | Where is **Inés** from? |
| ***Ella** es de Ecuador.* | **She** is from Ecuador. |
| *¿De dónde son **Jaime y Marta**?* | Where are **Jaime and Marta** from? |
| ***Ellos** son de Uruguay.* | **They** are from Uruguay. |

- The plural forms *nosotras, vosotras,* and *ellas* refer only to females, while the subject pronouns *nosotros, vosotros,* and *ellos* are used to refer either to males only or to a mixed group of both males and females.

| | |
|---|---|
| *¿Anita y Rosa?* ***Ellas** son de Guatemala.* | Anita and Rosa? **They** (feminine) are from Guatemala. |
| *¿Carlos y Jaime?* ***Ellos** son de Miami.* | Carlos and Jaime? **They** (masculine) are from Miami. |
| *¿Enrique y Elena?* ***Ellos** son de Colombia.* | Enrique and Elena? **They** (mixed) are from Colombia. |

## 10  Los pronombres

Replace the subject with the corresponding pronoun.

*Ud., Sr. Vargas*

| MODELOS | Ana | **Ella** |
|---|---|---|
| | *(you)*, Sra. Vega | **Ud.** |

1. Martín
2. *(you)*, Sr. Pérez
3. *(you)*, Susi
4. José y Juan
5. Eva y yo *(fem.)*

6. tú y Pablo
7. Estefanía
8. Miguel y yo
9. Ud. y la Sra. Gómez
10. Gabriela y Marina

# Gramática

## Subject Pronouns and the Verb *ser*

- You have already used most of the subject pronouns with the following forms of the verb **ser** (to be) to identify people and to say where they are from.

| ser | | | | | |
|---|---|---|---|---|---|
| yo | **soy** | *I am* | nosotros/as | **somos** | *we are* |
| tú | **eres** | *you are* | vosotros/as | **sois** | *you are* |
| Ud.<br>él<br>ella | **es** | *you are*<br>*he is*<br>*she is*<br>*it is* | Uds.<br>ellos<br>ellas | **son** | *you are*<br>*they are*<br>*they are* |

- To make a sentence negative in Spanish, place *no* before the verb.

| | |
|---|---|
| *Alicia es de California.* | Alicia is from California. |
| *Alicia **no** es de Arizona.* | Alicia is **not** from Arizona. |
| *Me llamo Esteban.* | My name is Esteban. |
| *No me llamo Miguel.* | My name is **not** Miguel. |

### Un poco más

**The word no**

The word *no* means the same as the English word **no**, but it can also mean **not**.

*No, ella no se llama Susi.*

**No**, her name is **not** Susi.

---

## 11  ¿De dónde son los estudiantes?

Completa las oraciones con la forma correcta del verbo **ser**. (*Complete the sentences with the correct form of the verb* ser.)

1. ¿ __ tú de St. Paul, Minnesota?
2. Él __ de Portland, Washington.
3. Ellas __ de Houston, Texas.
4. Ud. __ de Macon, Georgia.
5. Nosotros __ de San Francisco, California.
6. Yo __ de (*name of your city and state*).
7. Ana y yo __ de (los)....
8. Tú y yo __ de Sarasota, Florida.
9. Marta __ de Denver, Colorado.
10. Thalía y Gloria __ de Boston, Massachusetts.

---

## 12  ¡No! 🎧

Show that you disagree with these statements by making them negative.

**MODELO**  Teresa y Daniel son de España.
**Teresa y Daniel no son de España.**

1. Soy de París.
2. Diana es de Nueva York.
3. Ella es de aquí.
4. Me llamo Hernán.
5. Se llama Luz.
6. Nosotros somos de la Argentina.

*¿De dónde son Uds.?*

## 13 Personas famosas en los Estados Unidos 👥

With a classmate, take turns asking and answering where some well-known people are from.

Shakira es de Colombia.

> **MODELO**  Shakira / Colombia
>
> A: ¿De dónde es Shakira?
>
> B: Ella es de Colombia.

1. Penélope Cruz y Enrique Iglesias / España
2. Jennifer López y Christina Aguilera / Estados Unidos
3. Horatio Sanz / Chile
4. Carlos Vives y Juanes / Colombia
5. Mariano Rivera / Panamá
6. Sofía Vergara / Colombia

# ¡Comunicación!

## 14 Somos de muchos países 👥   Interpersonal Communication

With a partner, discuss where the following people are from, according to the illustration.

> **MODELO**  Roberto
>
> A: ¿De dónde es Roberto?
>
> B: Es de (los) Estados Unidos.

1. Camilo
2. Diego
3. tú
4. Rodrigo y Diana
5. Clara, tú y yo
6. la Srta. Jaramillo
7. yo
8. el Sr. y la Sra. Díaz
9. Juan
10. Elena

## 15 Famosos del mundo hispano

Research the following famous Spanish-speaking people, and use the words in *Para decir más* to say what field of expertise they have in common.

**MODELO**  Jorge Luis Borges, Isabel Allende, José Martí
**Ellos son escritores.**

1. Joaquín Phoenix, Penélope Cruz, Sofía Vergara
2. Isaac Albéniz, Alberto Ginastera, Plácido Domingo
3. Rafael Nadal, Juan Pablo Montoya, Lionel Messi
4. Fernando Botero, Pablo Picasso, Diego Rivera
5. Antonio Machado, Gina Valdés, Rafael Pombo
6. Pablo Casals, Andrés Segovia, Carlos Santana
7. Rafael Correa, Cristina Fernández de Kirchner, Enrique Peña Nieto

### Para decir más

| | |
|---|---|
| actor(es) | *actors* |
| atleta(s) | *athletes* |
| cantante(s) | *singers* |
| escritor(es) | *writers* |
| músico(s) | *musicians* |
| pintor(es) | *painters* |
| poeta(s) | *poets* |
| político(s) | *politicians* |
| presidente(s) | *presidents* |

## ¡Comunicación!

## 16 Una persona famosa de... 👥 Interpersonal Communication

Find information about these famous people on the Internet and complete a chart like the one below. Then, exchange information with a classmate, taking turns asking and answering the questions. Finally, add three additional names and see if your partner recognizes them.

**MODELO**  A: **¿De dónde es Isabel Allende?**
B: **Ella es de Chile.**
A: **¿Cuántos años tiene?**
B: **Tiene 72 años.**
A: **¿Qué es?**
B: **Es escritora.**

*Lionel Messi es de la Argentina.*

| Persona famosa | ¿De dónde es? | ¿Cuántos años tiene? | ¿Qué es? |
|---|---|---|---|
| Isabel Allende | Chile | 72 | escritora |
| Lionel Messi | | | |
| Juanes | | | |
| Verónica Charlyn Corral Ang | | | |
| Fernando Botero | | | |
| Penélope Cruz | | | |
| Mariano Rajoy | | | |

**?** Essential Question

How does education promote understanding of different cultures?

## El español en tu vida

Is there Spanish in your life beyond what you are learning in class? You might be surrounded by Spanish language and culture and not even realize it! Take your school, for example. Is there a *patio* or a *cafetería* (Spanish for "coffee shop")? Have you seen *tacos, burritos,* or *bananas* on the lunch menu? You may have studied *mesas* or *tornados, cóndores* or *coyotes* in science class. All these words are of Spanish origin.

Many teens in the U.S. dance to rhythms like *salsa, merengue,* or *cumbia.* Perhaps you have taken a *siesta* or gone to a Zumba class. If you have done any of these things, you have enjoyed some of the many Hispanic influences in the United States. You have come closer to understanding other cultures by experiencing their food, music, and activities.

*En el patio del colegio*

Now, by taking Spanish in school, you are learning how people from Hispanic cultures speak, think, live, and interact. You will find it easier to communicate with people from Spanish-speaking countries by understanding the language and, in turn, some of their culture. And you will start to see not just your differences, but also the many things you have in common.

🔍 **Búsqueda:** spanish in everyday english

*Una mesa en el estado de Arizona*

### Prácticas

In areas with a large Hispanic population, school bands often play Hispanic or Latin music. In Florida or Louisiana there might be a Latin jazz band with *congas* (tall, narrow drums tapped with the hands), *bongós* (small twin drums), *maracas,* or a *güiro* (a hollow gourd with ridges that are scraped with a stick). *Las claves* are a pair of smooth sticks tapped rhythmically together. Many schools in California and Texas have *mariachi* bands with trumpets, *guitarras,* and a large bass *guitarrón.*

*Esta banda toca música latina.*

### 17 Comprensión

1. Name five Spanish words that have been incorporated into the English language.
2. What aspects of Hispanic culture is a young person likely to come across in everyday life?
3. What are some things you can learn by studying Spanish, in addition to the language itself?

### 18 Analiza

1. Why do you think the type of rock formation shown above is called a *mesa*?
2. What aspect of Hispanic culture in the United States have you encountered most? What can you learn from it?
3. Why is it important to be educated about all cultural influences in the United States?

# La influencia hispana en los Estados Unidos

El rodeo americano

Do you associate United States history with Spain? How about United States geography with Mexico? Making connections like these will help you better understand the factors that shaped, and continue to influence, this country's identity. Fifty-five years before the Pilgrims arrived on the Mayflower, the Spanish city of *San Agustín* was flourishing in what is now Florida. The iconic cowboy tradition in the American Southwest traces its roots to the Mexican *ranchos* and—even further back—to Spain. Spanish language influence is also evident in many geographical names like Los Angeles, Monterey, and the Grand Canyon, while Mexico and other Latin American countries continue to have an impact on the culture and economy of the United States.

San Agustín, Florida

Currently in the United States, almost one in every four public school students is Hispanic, and over thirty million people speak Spanish every day. Opportunities to connect to the language and culture are all around. Major cities offer Spanish-language newspapers, television, and radio stations, due to the demand from the growing Hispanic population. Bilingual signs are seen on public transportation, at doctor's offices, and in grocery stores. Even voting ballots are now available in both English and Spanish. Start your language education in school and expand it out to the community and beyond by taking advantage of the history and influence of Spanish and Hispanic culture in the United States.

**Búsqueda:** hispanic influences in the united states

## Comparaciones

Are there any places near where you live that have geographical names of Spanish origin? What are they? Do you know what the names mean?

## Perspectivas

"When it comes to describing their identity, most Hispanics in the United States prefer their family's country of origin over pan-ethnic terms." What does this conclusion from a Pew Survey tell you about Spanish-speakers' views of terms like *hispano* or *latino*?

### 19 Comprensión

1. Who established the first city in the United States?
2. In what aspects of American culture can you find Hispanic influence?

### 20 Analiza

1. What status do you think the Spanish language will have in the U.S. in another twenty years?
2. How do Latin American countries continue to have an impact on the culture and economy of the United States?

# Vocabulario 2

## El blog de Juana: ¿Qué hay en la clase? 🎧

INICIO | CLASE DE ESPAÑOL | MI ESCUELA | MIS AMIGOS | MI FAMILIA

Me llamo Juana. Yo soy de Puerto Rico. Ricardo es **mi nuevo amigo** de la República Dominicana. Somos **estudiantes en la clase** de español. Nuestro **profesor** es el señor Jaime Hernández.

el mapa

la estudiante

el estudiante

**¿Qué hay** en la clase?

la puerta

la ventana

la pared

la pizarra

el profesor

la chica

el pupitre

el chico

la silla

el reloj

el libro

la página

la tiza

el marcador

la mochila

el lápiz

el cuaderno

el bolígrafo

el borrador

la regla

el papel

la revista

el periódico

el sacapuntas

## Para conversar

**T**o say that you don't understand something:

Perdón, no **comprendo**.
*Pardon me, I don't understand.*

**T**o ask for the meaning of a word:

**¿Qué quiere decir la palabra escritorio?**
*What does the word* escritorio *mean?*

Quiere decir *desk.*
*It means desk.*

**¿Cómo se dice** *wastebasket*?
*How do you say wastebasket?*

Se dice **cesto de papeles**.
*You say cesto de papeles.*

### Para decir más

| | |
|---|---|
| la calculadora | *calculator* |
| el calendario | *calendar* |
| el cartel | *poster* |
| la computadora | *computer* |
| el resaltador | *highlighter* |

### En otros países

| | |
|---|---|
| el bolígrafo | *el esfero (Colombia)* |
| | *el boli (España) la pluma (México)* |
| el borrador | *la goma (España)* |
| | *la goma de borrar (Argentina)* |
| el cesto de papeles | *la caneca (Colombia)* |
| | *el basurero, el papelero (Argentina)* |
| | *el bote (Mexico)* |

## 21 ¿Cuál es el intruso?

Busca al intruso y explica por qué.

**MODELO**  la chica / el profesor / el mapa
**el mapa: The other two are people.**

1. el lápiz / el reloj / el bolígrafo
2. el cesto de papeles / el libro / la revista
3. el pupitre / el borrador / la silla
4. mi amiga / mi profesora / mi regla
5. la pared / la mochila / la ventana
6. el amigo / el escritorio / el estudiante

## 22 ¿Qué es? 🎧

Identifica los objetos que oyes. (*Identify the objects you hear.*)

| A | B | C | D | E | F |

## 23 ¿Qué necesitas?

What object(s) would you use if you needed to do the following?

El reloj

**MODELO**   sharpen a pencil

**el sacapuntas**

1. throw away a piece of paper
2. find the location of *Guinea Ecuatorial*
3. carry books and notebooks
4. check the time
5. sit down
6. read thirty pages
7. write on a white board
8. write a first draft

## 24 Categorías

Use a chart like the one below to sort the words from the box in the categories listed.
The first row is shown as an example.

amigo   lápiz   papel   pizarra   tiza

estudiante   chica   periódico   escritorio

bolígrafo   cuaderno   revista

pupitre   silla   profesor

libro

| People | Furniture | For reading | For writing |
|---|---|---|---|
| **profesor** | **pupitre** | **libro** | **lápiz** |
| | | | |
| | | | |
| | | | |

# Diálogo

## La nueva estudiante de Los Ángeles

**Carlos:** ¿Quién es la chica con la mochila?

**Raúl:** ¿Qué quiere decir la palabra *mochila*?

**Carlos:** Quiere decir *backpack*.

**Raúl:** Ella es la estudiante nueva de Los Ángeles.

**Carlos:** ¿Cómo se llama?

**Raúl:** Se llama Diana y es mi amiga.

**Diana:** Perdón, chicos. ¿Cómo se dice *clock* en español?

**Carlos:** Se dice *reloj*.

**Diana:** Muchas gracias.

## 25 ¿Qué recuerdas?

1. ¿Qué quiere decir la palabra mochila?
2. ¿De dónde es la chica con la mochila?
3. ¿Quién es la estudiante nueva?
4. ¿Es la estudiante nueva amiga de Carlos?
5. ¿Cómo se dice *clock* en español?
6. ¿Hay un reloj en la clase?

## 26 Algo personal

1. ¿Tienes una mochila?
2. ¿Tienes un reloj? ¿Qué hora es?

## 27 ¿Sí o no?

¿Son lógicos los diálogos? Corrige lo que no es lógico.

# ¡Comunicación!

## 28 ¿Cómo se dice? — Interpersonal Communication

Work with your partner. Take turns asking and answering questions about the things in your classroom and how to say them in Spanish. Use the model as a guide.

**MODELO**  A: ¿Cómo se dice *desk*?
  B: Se dice pupitre.

*¿Qué quiere decir?*

# Gramática

## Using Definite Articles with Nouns

Nouns refer to people, places, things, or concepts. All nouns in Spanish have a gender; they are either masculine or feminine.

- Nouns that end in **-o** or consonants like **-r** or **-l** are generally masculine and are often used with the definite article **el** (the), whereas nouns that end in **-a**, **-ción**, or **-dad** are usually feminine and are often used with the definite article **la** (the).

| masculino | **el** chico | **el** borrado**r** | **el** pape**l** |
|---|---|---|---|
| femenino | **la** chic**a** | **la** pronuncia**ción** | **la** posibili**dad** |

- Some nouns are irregular; they do not follow these patterns.

| masculino | **el** día | **el** problem**a** |
|---|---|---|
| femenino | **la** man**o** | **la** radi**o** |

- Some nouns that refer to people may have only one form. The gender of the person is indicated by the definite article.

| masculino | **el** estudiante | **el** artista |
|---|---|---|
| femenino | **la** estudiante | **la** artista |

- Nouns also have a number: singular (one) or plural (more than one). If a noun ends in a vowel, add **-s** to make it plural. If a noun ends in a consonant, add **-es** to make it plural. The accompanying plural of the definite articles are **los** (masculine) and **las** (feminine). In Spanish, articles and nouns have to agree in gender and number.

| singular | **el** amigo | **el** papel | **la** amiga | **la** pared |
|---|---|---|---|---|
| plural | **los** amigos | **los** papel**es** | **las** amigas | **las** pared**es** |

- For nouns that end in **-z**, change the **-z** to **-c** in the plural.

| singular | el lápi**z** | la lu**z** (*light*) |
|---|---|---|
| plural | los lápi**c**es | las lu**c**es |

- It may be necessary to add or remove an accent mark when making a noun plural.

| singular | el ex**a**men (*test*) | la lec**ción** |
|---|---|---|
| plural | los ex**á**menes | las lec**cio**nes |

*La mano*

*El artista*

*El chico y la chica*

*Las luces*

## 29 Objetos en la clase 🎧

Da cada sustantivo con su artículo definido. Sigue el modelo. (*Give each noun with its definite article. Follow the model.*)

**MODELO**    pupitre    **el pupitre**

1. puerta
2. cuaderno
3. ventana
4. borrador
5. escritorio
6. lápiz
7. lección
8. página
9. mapa
10. actividad

## 30 ¡Más de uno!

**¡Ojo!**

Remember to make the definite article and the noun plural.

Forma el plural de las palabras. (*Form the plural of the words.*)

1. la regla
2. el día
3. el marcador
4. la noche
5. el periódico
6. la actividad
7. el profesor
8. el lápiz

## 31 Periódicos y revistas

Identify the nouns in these magazine and newspaper headlines and ads and tell which ones are masculine (*masculino*) and which are feminine (*femenino*).

1. **CULTURA** Exposición **Por la puerta grande**

2. ¡Es la hora de **comer bien!**

3. **OPINIÓN** *Contra la* **Pared** por Felipe Lopéz

4. BENTO El reloj que marca la hora

5. Los lápices PRISMACOLOR *Dan color a tu clase*

6.  El papel **reciclado** está de moda

7. Todo está en las Páginas Amarillas

## 32 Más objetos

Say the definite article that corresponds to each item.

1. silla
2. pupitres
3. sacapuntas
4. estudiantes (*a boy and a girl*)
5. mochilas
6. borrador

# Gramática

## ¡Comunicación!

**33 ¿Quién es...?** 👥 **Interpersonal Communication**

You and a classmate are looking at pictures of friends. Working in pairs, take turns asking and answering questions about the people shown. For each question, mention what the person is holding, using the word *con*. Answer by giving the person's name and then say who he or she is.

MODELO    A:  ¿Quién es el chico con la mochila?
            B:  Se llama Martín y es mi amigo.

*Se llama Martín.*

**1.** Sr. Cardona

**2.** Pilar

**3.** Srta. Jiménez

**4.** Juan Pablo

**5.** Esteban

**6.** Natalia

## Using Indefinite Articles with Nouns

You know how to use the definite articles **el**, **la**, **los**, and **las** to designate *specific* persons or things. Indefinite articles refer to *nonspecific* people or things.

- The singular forms of the indefinite articles are **un** and **una**.

| masculino | | femenino | |
|---|---|---|---|
| **el** lápiz | **un** lápiz | **la** página | **una** página |
| **the** pencil | **a** pencil | **the** page | **a** page |

- The plural forms of the indefinite articles are **unos** and **unas**.

| masculino | | femenino | |
|---|---|---|---|
| **los** lápices | **unos** lápices | **las** páginas | **unas** páginas |
| **the** pencils | **some/a few** pencils | **the** pages | **some/a few** pages |

### Un poco más

Las palabras **un**, **una** y **uno**

The words **un** and **una** before a noun can also mean the number one. **Uno** (the number one) is never used before a noun.

*dos cuadernos y **un** libro*
*tres chicos y **una** chica*

## 34 ¿Qué hay en la clase?

Completa el párrafo con **un**, **una**, **unos** o **unas** para indicar qué hay en la clase. (*Complete the paragraph with **a**, **an**, or **some/a few** to indicate what is in the classroom.*)

La clase tiene cuatro paredes y dos ventanas. La profesora es la Sra. Martínez. En la clase hay **(1)** escritorio, **(2)** cesto de papeles, **(3)** sillas y **(4)** pupitres con **(5)** libros, **(6)** lápices y **(7)** bolígrafos. En las paredes hay **(8)** reloj, **(9)** sacapuntas y **(10)** pizarra. En la mochila hay **(11)** marcadores, **(12)** regla y **(13)** libro de español.

*La profesora es la Sra. Martínez.*

## 35 ¿Es o son?

Di lo que ves en cada foto. (*Say what you see in each photo.*)

MODELO   Es una chica.
Son unos pupitres.

1

2

3

4

5

6

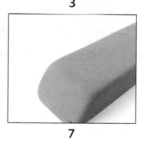
7

8

## ¡Comunicación!

## 36 Personas nuevas   Presentational Communication

Some new people have come to your school. You will introduce one of them to the class. Prepare by writing all the information you can about that person. Use the table as a guide. Then, introduce the person to the class, giving all the information you collected.

MODELO   Es el nuevo profesor.
Se llama Sr. Madero y es de Palo Alto, California.

| ¿Quién es? | ¿Cómo se llama? | ¿De dónde es? |
|---|---|---|
| el nuevo profesor | Sr. Madero | Palo Alto, California |
| | | |

# Lectura informativa

## Antes de leer

1. Is your course load in school very demanding?

2. What grades do you generally get in science? In language arts? In technology courses? In math?

3. Do your teachers include comments with your grades?

### Estrategia

**Look for a topic sentence**

Often the topic sentence will provide a very concise idea of what the entire paragraph is about. Keep this topic sentence in mind as you read. It will serve as a guide in figuring out unfamiliar words or difficult sentences. Although topic sentences may appear anywhere in a paragraph, they often appear at the beginning.

## Las notas en el colegio

**Libreta de calificaciones**

Nombre del alumno: Clara Ruiz

Grado: 9

Semestre: 1

| Materia | Nota | Comentario del profesor |
|---|---|---|
| Literatura española | 9,5 | Excelente |
| Historia de América | 7 | Regular |
| Matemáticas | 6,5 | Debe mejorar[1] |
| Ecología | 4,5 | Muy deficiente |
| Inglés | 5 | Deficiente |
| Tecnología | 8,5 | Bien |
| Ciencias sociales | 9 | Muy bien, buena participación en clase |
| Álgebra | 5,5 | Deficiente |
| Física | 4 | Muy deficiente |
| Educación artística | 10 | Excelente |
| Educación física | Aprobado | Buena participación en clase |

[1]Needs improvement

*Clara tiene una mala nota*

Las notas en muchos países hispanohablantes no son las letras A–F. Los estudiantes reciben[1] un número en una escala de 1–10. El número 10 es la nota más alta[2]. Cero es la nota más baja. Generalmente, el estudiante aprueba[3] con una nota de 6 o más[4]. Una nota de seis es equivalente a una C en los Estados Unidos. Los profesores también[5] usan frases descriptivas, por ejemplo "excelente" para una nota de diez, "bien" para una nota de ocho y "deficiente" para una nota de cinco.

[1]get  [2]highest  [3]passes  [4]more  [5]also

**Búsqueda:** grading systems in latino countries

## 42 Comprensión — Interpretive Communication

1. How is the grading system described in *"Las notas del colegio"* different from the one generally used in schools in the United States?

2. What is a passing grade in the system described?

3. What do you think is the equivalent grade in a school in the United States to the *"Aprobado"* Clara received in *educación física*?

## 43 Analiza

1. What is the topic sentence of the reading *"Las notas en el colegio"*?

2. From Clara Ruiz's grades, what areas might she like to study in college?

3. Would you prefer the grading system described for Spanish-speaking countries to the one you have in your school? Explain why or why not, using information from the reading and your own experience.

# ✎ Escritura

## 44 ¡Tienes suerte! — Presentational Communication

You are in luck! Today you get a chance to fill out your own report card. Draw or print out a report card form in Spanish. Provide your own information. List your subjects in Spanish. If you do not know the name of a subject in Spanish, be sure to ask your teacher *"¿Cómo se dice?"* Then, using the Hispanic grading method, write the grades you think you will actually get in this grading period. Add a brief comment after each grade. The words on Clara's report card and in *Para escribir más* may be helpful.

**Libreta de calificaciones**

Nombre del alumno:

Grado:

Semestre:

| Materias | Nota | Comentario del profesor |
| --- | --- | --- |
|  |  |  |
|  |  |  |
|  |  |  |
|  |  |  |
|  |  |  |
|  |  |  |
|  |  |  |
|  |  |  |

### Para escribir más

| | |
| --- | --- |
| álgebra | Algebra |
| biología | Biology |
| educación física | Physical Education |
| estudios sociales | Social Studies |
| geometría | Geometry |
| historia | History |
| Bien | Good |
| Debe mejorar | Needs improvement |
| Debe participar más | Should participate more |
| Deficiente | Unsatisfactory |
| Muy bien | Very good |
| Sobresaliente | Oustanding |

# Repaso de la Lección A

## A  Escuchar: ¿Qué hay en las fotografías? 🎧 (pp. 56–57)

Selecciona la foto que corresponde con lo que oyes.

**A**

**B**

**C**

**D**

**E**

**F**

## B  Vocabulario: Ellos son... (pp. 46–47)

En pareja (*match*) las preguntas con las respuestas.

1. ¿Cómo te llamas?
2. ¿Quién es él?
3. ¿Cómo se llama ella?
4. ¿De dónde son Uds.?
5. ¿Quiénes son ellos?
6. ¿De dónde son Ernesto y Luis?
7. ¿De dónde es Adriana?

A. Somos de Perú.
B. Son de Costa Rica.
C. Es el nuevo profesor.
D. Es de Uruguay.
E. Me llamo Julito.
F. Se llama Jimena.
G. Son mis amigos.

## C  Gramática: Están en... 👥 (p. 60)

Completa las oraciones con los artículos definidos (*definite articles*) apropiados.

1. __ reloj está en __ pared.
2. __ profesor está en __ clase.
3. __ tiza está en __ pizarra.
4. __ libros están en __ escritorio.
5. ¿Cómo se dice __ palabra *eraser* en español?
6. __ estudiante nuevo se llama Guillermo.

## D  Gramática: En mi clase hay... (p. 62)

Completa las oraciones con los artículos indefinidos (*indefinite articles*) apropiados.

1. En mi clase hay __ pupitres, __ escritorio y __ silla para el profesor.
2. También (*also*) hay __ mapa y __ ventana en la pared.
3. Yo tengo __ lápiz, __ papeles, __ marcadores y __ libro en mi pupitre.

## E  Cultura: Fiesta hispana en los Estados Unidos  *(pp. 54–55)*

You have been asked to help plan an Hispanic-themed *fiesta* for your community. Research some ideas for food (*la comida*), music (*la música*), and dancing (*los bailes*), and summarize your findings in a graphic organizer, as seen here. Then, create an attractive invitation that will make everybody want to come.

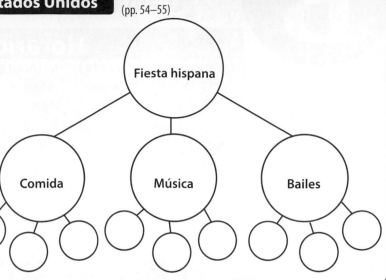

## Vocabulario

| Objetos en la clase | |
|---|---|
| el bolígrafo | la pared |
| el borrador | el periódico |
| el cesto de papeles | la pizarra |
| el cuaderno | la puerta |
| el escritorio | el pupitre |
| el lápiz | la regla |
| el libro | el reloj |
| el mapa | la revista |
| el marcador | el sacapuntas |
| la mochila | la silla |
| la página | la tiza |
| el papel | la ventana |

**Personas**

el amigo/la amiga
el chico/la chica
ellas
ellos
el estudiante/la estudiante
nosotras
nosotros
el profesor/la profesora

**Palabras interrogativas**

¿qué?
¿quién
¿quiénes?

**Verbos**

comprendo
 (comprender)
hay
(no) sé
son (ser)

**Otras expresiones**

¡Ay!
¿Cómo se dice...?
 Se dice...
¿Cómo se llama (Ud./él/ella)?
(Ud./Él/Ella) se llama...
el, la, los, las
en la clase
la palabra
mi
nuevo/a
¿Qué quiere decir...?
 Quiere decir...
un, una, unos, unas

## Gramática

| Subject pronouns | |
|---|---|
| yo | nosotros/as |
| tú | vosotros/as |
| Ud./él/ella | Uds./ellos/ellas |

| The verb *ser* | |
|---|---|
| soy | somos |
| eres | sois |
| es | son |

### Definite and indefinite articles with nouns

In Spanish definite and indefinite articles match nouns in number and gender.

| | | Definite article | Noun | Indefinite article | Noun |
|---|---|---|---|---|---|
| masculine | singular | el | chico | un | chico |
| | plural | los | chicos | unos | chicos |
| femenine | singular | la | chica | una | chica |
| | plural | las | chicas | unas | chicas |

# Vocabulario 1

## ¿Cuántas clases tienes? 🎧

### Horario de clases

| HORA | LUNES | MARTES | MIÉRCOLES | JUEVES | VIERNES | SÁBADO | DOMINGO |
|------|-------|--------|-----------|--------|---------|--------|---------|
| 7:55 | biología | biología | biología | biología | biología | | |
| 8:50 | inglés | inglés | inglés | inglés | inglés | | |
| 9:45 | computación | computación | computación | computación | computación | | |
| 10:40 | historia | historia | historia | historia | historia | En **mi colegio** NO HAY CLASES. ¡No **estudiamos**! | |
| 11:35 | español | español | español | español | español | | |
| 12:30 | ALMUERZO | | | | | | |
| 1:00 | música | arte | música | música | arte | | |
| 1:55 | matemáticas | matemáticas | matemáticas | matemáticas | matemáticas | | |

Yo **hablo** en español, ¿y tú?

la clase de español

la clase de historia

la clase de biología

la clase de inglés

la clase de matemáticas

la clase de computación

la clase de música

la clase de arte

¿A qué hora terminas la clase?

A las tres y media.

negro verde amarillo blanco gris azul rojo

los colores

**la ropa**

**la camiseta**

**la falda**

**el pantalón**

**los jeans**

**los calcetines**

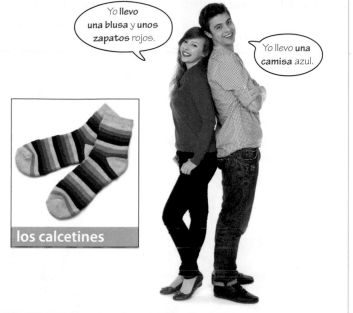

*Yo llevo una blusa y unos zapatos rojos.*

*Yo llevo una camisa azul.*

## Para conversar

***T**o talk on the phone:*

¡**Aló**! ¿Ernesto?
*Hi! Ernesto?*

Soy yo, Rosa.
*It's me, Rosa.*

¿**Cómo**?
*What?*

***T**o talk about what you need:*

¿Qué **necesitas** para...?
*What do you need for...?*

Necesito...
*I need...*

***T**o talk about classes and schedules:*

¿**Cuántas** clases tienes?
*How many classes do you have?*

¿Qué **día** tienes clase de...?
*What day do you have... class?*

### Para decir más

| | |
|---|---|
| ¿Bueno?/¿Hola?/¿Mande? | Hello? (When talking on the phone) |
| ¿Con quién hablo? | Who is speaking? |
| ¿Puedo hablar con…? | May I speak with…? |
| No está. | He/she is not here. |

### 1 ¿Qué ropa llevan?

Name five people in class and say what each is wearing.

**MODELO** **Carlos lleva unos jeans y una camiseta.**

### En otros países

| | |
|---|---|
| los jeans | *los mahones (Puerto Rico)* |
| | *los bluejeans (Colombia)* |
| | *el bluyín (Venezuela)* |
| | *los vaqueros (España)* |
| | *los pantalones de mezclilla (México)* |

# Gramática

## ¡Comunicación!

### 18 ¿Qué estudian?   Interpersonal/Presentational Communication

Survey your classmates to find out what they are studying in school. Choose three classes (*arte, biología, computación, historia, matemáticas,* or *música*). Find out how many boys and how many girls in class study those three subjects. Record the results under the headings *Chicos* and *Chicas.* Summarize your findings for the rest of the class.

| Matemáticas | |
| --- | --- |
| **Chicos** | **Chicas** |
| 卌 | 卌 |
| 卌 | 卌 |
| ‖ | ‖ |

**MODELO**

A: Pedro, ¿estudias matemáticas?

B: Sí, estudio matemáticas.

**En resumen:** Doce chicos y doce chicas estudian matemáticas.

*Sí, estudio matemáticas.*

## Talking About Schedules: *¿A qué hora?*

- To ask when something is going to occur, ask: *¿A qué hora* **(+ verb + event)***?*
- To answer, say: **Verb +** *a la/las* **(+ time)** or simply *A la/las* **(+ time)**.

| | |
| --- | --- |
| *¿A qué hora es* la clase de español? | **When (At what time) is** Spanish class? |
| *Es a la* una. | **It is at** one o'clock. |
| *A la* una. | **At** one o'clock. |

**Note:** The twenty-four hour clock (also known as military time) often appears in railroad, airline, and bus schedules or in movie and theater advertising. When expressing time this way, the day begins at one minute after midnight. The numbers one to twelve refer to the time of day between one o'clock in the morning and twelve noon. After noon, each hour is added to twelve; 13:00 hours (*las trece horas*) would be the equivalent of 1:00 PM. (*Es la una de la tarde.*)

### 19 Mi horario en el colegio 🎧

Contesta las siguientes preguntas.

1. ¿A qué hora es tu clase de español? ¿A qué hora termina?
2. ¿A qué hora es tu clase de inglés? ¿A qué hora termina?
3. ¿A qué hora es tu clase de historia? ¿A qué hora termina?
4. ¿A qué hora es tu clase de matemáticas? ¿A qué hora termina?

*¿Qué hora es?*

# ¡Comunicación!

## 20 Las clases de Juan José | Interpretive Communication

Mira el horario de Juan José. Luego, responde las preguntas sobre su día escolar.
(*Look at Juan José's schedule. Then answer the questions about his school day.*)

**EL COLEGIO MONTES HORARIO DE CLASES**

| HORA | LUNES | MARTES | MIÉRCOLES | JUEVES | VIERNES | SÁB/DOM |
|---|---|---|---|---|---|---|
| 7:55 - 8:45 | matemáticas | biología | matemáticas | biología | matemáticas | |
| 8:50 - 9:40 | español | español | español | español | español | |
| 9:45 - 10:35 | inglés | inglés | historia | inglés | historia | NO HAY CLASES |
| 10:40 - 11:30 | educación física | arte | educación física | arte | educación física | |
| 11:35 - 12:05 | A L M U E R Z O | | | | | |
| 12:10 - 1:00 | música | computación | música | computación | música | |

1. La clase de inglés es los lunes, martes y __.
2. ¿A qué hora es la clase de matemáticas?
3. ¿Qué días y a qué horas es la clase de computación?
4. ¿A qué hora termina el almuerzo?
5. ¿Cuándo es la clase de biología?
6. ¿Qué clase es los martes y jueves a las diez y cuarenta?
7. ¿A qué hora terminan las clases?
8. ¿Qué días no hay clases?

# ¡Comunicación!

## 21 La ropa y los horarios | Interpersonal/Presentational Communication

Ask several classmates what they are wearing, what classes they are taking, when the classes are and when they end. Take notes and then report back to the class what you have learned about one of your classmates.

| Nombre | Ropa | Clases y hora | Terminan |
|---|---|---|---|
| Bob | jeans negros, camiseta gris | música a las 8:45, biología a las 10:15, inglés a la 1:30 | 3:10 |
| | | | |

**MODELO** Bob lleva unos jeans negros y una camiseta gris. Estudia música a las nueve menos cuarto, biología a las diez y cuarto e inglés a la una y media. Las clases terminan a las tres y diez.

# Vocabulario 2

¿Cuál es tu número de teléfono?

Es el 7-25-67-47.

Perdón. ¿Es el 6-14-74-36?

Tienes el número **equivocado**. Es el 6-14-74-63.

Tengo **un examen** de computación mañana.

¿Dónde está Uruguay?

¡Mira! Allí está.

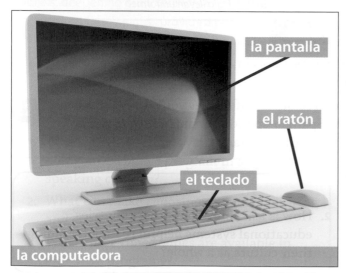

la pantalla

el ratón

el teclado

la computadora

la impresora láser

el disco compacto (CD)

| | |
|---|---|
| **punto (.)** | dot (for Internet and e-mail addresses) |
| **arroba (@)** | at (for e-mail address) |

## Para conversar 🎧

*T*o talk about the location of something:

¿Dónde está mi libro de español?     *Where is my Spanish book?*

¿Está en el escritorio **o** en la mochila?     *Is it on the desk or in the backpack?*

No está en el escritorio. **Tampoco** está en la mochila.     *It isn't on the desk. It isn't in the backpack, either.*

¡Mira! Allí está, **sobre** la computadora.     *Look! There it is, on top of the computer.*

*T*o ask for contact information:

¿Cuál es tu...     *What is your...*

número de **fax**?     *fax number?*

número de teléfono **celular**?     *cell phone number?*

**dirección de internet**?     *Web address?*

dirección de **correo electrónico**?     *e-mail address?*

### Para decir más

| el archivo | *file* |
|---|---|
| la internet/la Red | *Internet* |
| la página web | *website* |
| el portátil | *laptop* |
| navegar por la Red | *to surf the Web* |

### 26 ¿Qué necesitan? 🎧

Write the names Pilar and Julio. Next, listen and list under each name what Pilar and Julio need before they leave for college. Then circle any items on the lists that they both need.

### 27 El ratón

Choose the appropriate words to complete the dialogue.

| allí | dónde | tampoco | está | sé |
|---|---|---|---|---|

Susi:     ¿**(1)** está mi ratón?

Chucho:     ¿Tu ratón? No **(2)**.

Alicia:     ¿**(3)** en la computadora?

Susi:     No, y **(4)** está en el escritorio.

Chucho:     **(5)** está, ¡en la silla!

*¿Dónde está el ratón?*

# Gramática

## Present Tense of *-ar* Verbs

- You have already learned how to conjugate regular *-ar* verbs, as well as the verb **ser**. Notice that the *-ar* verbs you have seen all indicate what the subject is doing. They are action verbs.

    La clase **termina**.          Tú **estudias** español.

- The verb **ser** does not indicate an action, but rather a state of being. It gives information about the subject.

    *Él* **es** *mi amigo*.          *Ellas* **son** *de Honduras*.

- Now you will learn another *-ar* verb that indicates a state of being: ***estar***.

## Talking About Location or How Someone Feels: *estar*

The verb ***estar*** (to be) is an *-ar* infinitive, but it is irregular in the present tense. You have already seen several forms of this verb.

| estar | | | | | |
|---|---|---|---|---|---|
| yo | **estoy** | *I **am*** | nosotros nosotras | **estamos** | *we **are*** |
| tú | **estás** | *you **are*** | vosotros vosotras | **estáis** | *you **are*** |
| Ud. él ella | **está** | *you **are*** *he **is*** *she **is*** *it **is*** | Uds. ellos ellas | **están** | *you **are*** *they **are*** *they **are*** |

***Estar*** indicates location or a state of being (a condition) at a given moment.

- **location:**

    *¿Dónde* **está** *el profesor?*          Where **is** the teacher?
    ***Está*** *en clase.*          **He is** in class.

- **state of being or condition:**

    *¿Cómo* **estás***?*          How **are you**?
    ***Estoy*** *bien, gracias.*          **I am** well, thanks.

### Un poco más

**States of being**

Other states of being at a given moment are: *cansado/a* (tired), *contento /a* (happy), *triste* (sad), and *solo /a* (alone).

*Marcos está cansado.*

*Amalia está contenta.*

*Ramiro está triste.*

## 33 ¿Dónde están?

Marcela is sending e-mail messages to family and friends across the United States. With a classmate, talk about where these people are located according to the illustration.

MODELO
A: ¿Dónde está Nacho?
B: Nacho está en Chicago.

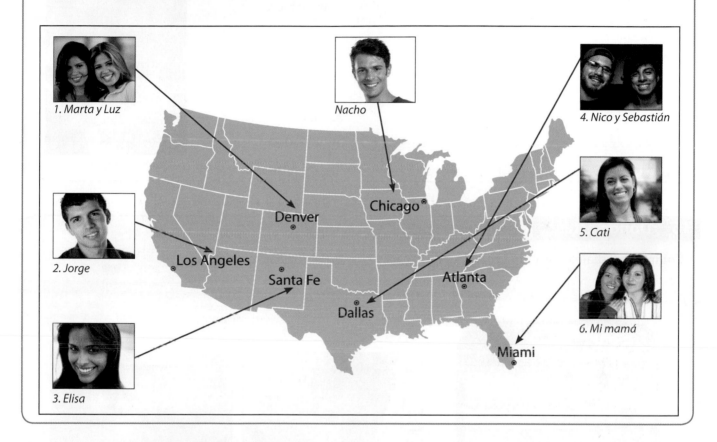

## 34 ¿Dónde están las ciudades? Conéctate: la geografía

Amalia is studying for a geography quiz. Can you tell her where each of the following Spanish-speaking cities is located?

MODELO
Malabo
**Malabo está en Guinea Ecuatorial.**

1. Concepción
2. Potosí
3. Maracaibo
4. San Antonio y Santa Fe
5. La Plata
6. Santiago
7. Cali
8. Montevideo
9. Managua
10. Sevilla y Madrid

*Malabo está en Guinea Ecuatorial.*

## 35 ¿Cómo estás?

Usa la forma correcta de una palabra del recuadro y el verbo **estar** para decir cómo están estas personas. *(Use the correct form of a word from the box and the verb* estar *to tell how these people are.)*

| cansado/a | contento/a | solo/a | mal |
|-----------|------------|--------|-----|
| bien | triste | regular | muy bien |

**MODELO**   Pedro
**Pedro está cansado.**

1. Uds.
2. yo
3. tú

4. ella
5. nosotros
6. mis amigos

*¿Cómo estás?*

## 36 ¿Dónde estás?

Completa el diálogo usando los verbos de la caja y sus *(their)* formas apropiadas.

| estar | estudiar | terminar | necesitar |
|-------|----------|----------|-----------|

Hola, Samuel. ¿Dónde (1)?

(2) en el colegio.

¿(3)?

Sí, pero (4) cansado. (5) en cinco minutos.

Rita y yo (6) en el parque.

¿No hay un examen mañana a las ocho?

Sí.

¿No (7) estudiar Uds.?

Sí. ☺

*Samuel está en el colegio.*

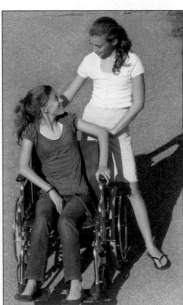

*Ellas están en el parque.*

## 37 Busca las cosas en la clase

Mira la ilustración de la clase de geografía y contesta las preguntas en español.

> **MODELO**  ¿Dónde está el profesor?
> **Está en clase.**

1. ¿Dónde está el reloj?
2. ¿Dónde está la estudiante?
3. ¿Dónde están los libros verdes?
4. ¿Dónde está el mapa de México?
5. ¿Dónde está la revista *Shock*?
6. ¿Dónde están las sillas?
7. ¿Dónde está el periódico?
8. ¿Dónde están los libros de biología?
9. ¿Dónde está el colegio Highland High?
10. ¿Dónde está Mazatlán?
11. ¿Qué hora es?

## ¡Comunicación!

### 38 ¿Dónde están?   Interpersonal Communication

Pretend you are looking for someone or something in your classroom. Working with
a classmate, take turns asking about where several people and objects are. Be sure
to be polite and say "please" and thank the other person for information about each
person or object you are trying to find. Use the words in *Para decir más* to give more
specific locations.

> **MODELO**  A: Por favor, ¿dónde está Ramiro?
> B: Está al lado de Celia.
> A: Gracias.

### Para decir más

| | |
|---|---|
| al lado de | *next to* |
| cerca de | *near* |
| debajo de | *under* |
| delante de | *in front of* |
| detrás de | *behind* |

## ¡Comunicación!

### 39 Un nuevo horario   Interpersonal/Presentational Communication

Create your ideal schedule for next year. Include six classes and a lunch period. Then,
in pairs, create a telephone conversation in which you compare your two schedules.
For example, find out if you have the same classes and when you have your lunch
period. Role play your conversation for the class.

# Todo en contexto

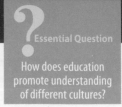
## ¡Comunicación!

### 40 Compara colegios 👥 Interpersonal Communication

You and a friend are completing a one-year exchange program in a Spanish-speaking country. Working with a classmate, act out a dialogue where you compare experiences in your host schools. Talk about the topics below and use the model as a guide.

| los horarios | las actividades | las notas | la ropa que llevan | las clases |
|---|---|---|---|---|

MODELO
A: ¿Qué clases tienes?
B: Tengo historia, matemáticas, geografía, biología y educación física. ¿Y tú?
A: Yo tengo computación, música, inglés, matemáticas y español.

## ¡Comunicación!

### 41 ¿Qué necesitamos? 👥 Interpersonal Communication

The school year is about to start, and you call a friend from an office supply store to find out what items he or she needs.

Call your friend and ask what items he or she needs.

Say what school supplies you need for different classes, as well as clothing and tech items.

Tell your friend what items are in the store.

Say thank you and good-bye.

*Mis amigas y yo estamos contentas.*

# Lectura

## Puentes y fronteras/*Bridges and Borders* (selecciones)
### de *Gina Valdés*

### Sobre la autora

Gina Valdés is a Chicana (Mexican-American) poet. Born in Los Angeles, California, she grew up on both sides of the Mexican border. She is now a professor of Chicano literature and culture and bilingual creative writing. She has taught at universities throughout the United States. In her bilingual book of Chicano poetry, *Puentes y fronteras* (*Bridges and Borders*), Valdés reflects on the difficulties faced by Hispanics who dream of moving to the United States.

### Antes de leer:

#### 42 Preparación para la lectura

1. Where do a lot of Hispanic immigrants enter the United States? Why?
2. What difficulties might Hispanic immigrants face when they move to the United States?

### Estrategia

**Using the title to make predictions**

You can use a title of a selection to predict what its content will be. What does the title *Puentes y fronteras/Bridges and Borders* suggest to you? Why does the author choose a bilingual title? Brainstorm with a partner what you think some of the most important themes of this work might be. Write your ideas down. After you read the poem on the next page, go back to your list of ideas and find out if your predictions were right.

### Extensión

The poem on the next page is in the tradition of one of the oldest styles of Spanish poetry, called a *copla*. The *coplas* were popular in medieval Spain because they were short and easily memorized. Minstrels sang *coplas* to villagers they encountered in their travels. This established an oral tradition that passed stories and information from one person to another for centuries. Today, many Spanish-speaking countries maintain the *copla* tradition. Usually a *copla* is a short poem, often improvised and set to music, that tells about people and their daily lives. If you were to use the words of this poem as the lyrics of a song, what type of music would you choose?

*Cruzando la frontera* (Crossing the border)

# Puentes y fronteras/*Bridges and Borders* (selecciones) 🎧
## de *Gina Valdés*

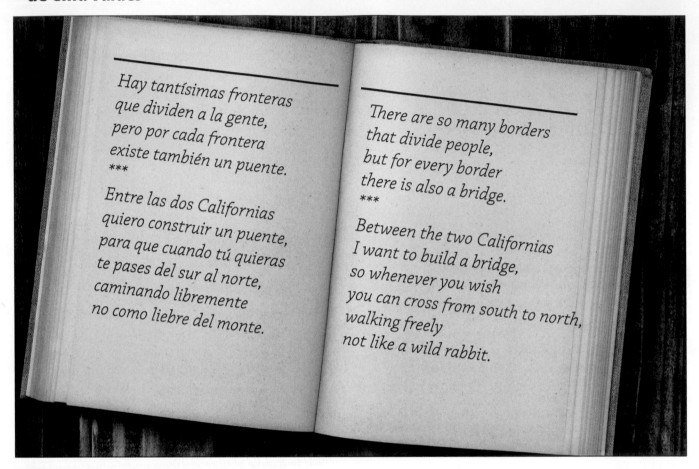

Hay tantísimas fronteras
que dividen a la gente,
pero por cada frontera
existe también un puente.
***

Entre las dos Californias
quiero construir un puente,
para que cuando tú quieras
te pases del sur al norte,
caminando libremente
no como liebre del monte.

There are so many borders
that divide people,
but for every border
there is also a bridge.
***

Between the two Californias
I want to build a bridge,
so whenever you wish
you can cross from south to north,
walking freely
not like a wild rabbit.

🔍 **Búsqueda:** gina valdés, chicano

## 43 Comprensión

1. What are the "two Californias" the poet talks about?
2. Who would cross the border "like a wild rabbit" (*como liebre del monte*)?
3. Which words rhyme in the Spanish poem? Do any words rhyme in the English version?

## 44 Analiza

1. Why do you think the author uses the old style of *coplas* to express her modern poetry?
2. Besides the physical border, in what other ways are the Mexican and American cultures divided? What is the significance of the *puente*?
3. Knowing what you've learned about Gina Valdés, find elements in this poem that reflect her life experience.

# Repaso de la Lección B

## A Escuchar: ¿Qué clase es? 🎧 (pp. 70–71)

Di **sí** o **no** si lo que oyes en las seis oraciones se refiere a las clases del colegio. (*Say* **yes** *or* **no** *if what you hear in the six sentences refers to classes at school.*)

## B Vocabulario: La ropa (pp. 70–71)

Describe la ropa en cada foto. (*Describe the clothing in each picture.*)

MODELO **Son unos jeans azules.**

1

2

3

4

5

## C Gramática: Estudiamos mucho (p. 78)

You are in a school in a Spanish-speaking country. Use the correct form of *estudiar* to talk about what subjects you and your friends are studying now.

1. Yo __ matemáticas.
2. ¿ __ (tú) física y biología también?
3. Laura __ música y arte.
4. ¿ __ tú y tus amigos historia hoy?
5. Marco y Pepe __ inglés y computación.
6. ¡Sofía y yo __ mucho!

## D Gramática: Unas conversaciones (pp. 78, 88)

Fill in the conversations with the appropriate form of the verbs according to the context.

| llevar | hablar | necesitar | terminar | estudiar | estar |
|--------|--------|-----------|----------|----------|-------|

1. A: ¿ __Uds. español?
   B: Sí, __ español y e inglés.
2. A: ¿Cómo __ Ud., Sra. Vázquez?
   B: __ bien, gracias.
3. A: ¿ __ (tú) jeans a la escuela?
   B: No __ jeans, pero mis amigos sí __ jeans.
4. A: ¿ __ Ana un cuaderno para la clase?
   B: No, pero Alberto sí __ un cuaderno.
5. A: ¿A qué hora __ las clases?
   B: La clase de español __ a las dos.
6. A: ¿ __ (tú) mucho para los exámenes?
   B: No, no __ mucho.

You're attending classes in a Spanish-speaking country. What differences do you notice between your school in the United States and your host school? Include information from the culture reading "*El colegio*" and use a Venn diagram to compare and contrast your findings. Try to write as much in Spanish as possible. Here are some topics to get you started:

- uniforms
- electives
- popular sports
- extracurricular activities
- learning a second language

## Vocabulario

### Clases

el arte
la biología
el colegio
la computación
el español
la historia
el horario
el inglés
las matemáticas
la música

### Por teléfono

aló
¿cuál?
la dirección
  de correo
  electrónico/de
  internet
el número de
  teléfono/de
  fax/de teléfono
  celular/
  equivocado
el teléfono

### Ropa

la blusa
el calcetín
la camisa
la camiseta
la falda
los jeans
el pantalón
la ropa
el zapato

### Colores

amarillo/a
azul
blanco/a
gris
negro/a
rojo/a
verde

### Tecnología

la arroba
la computadora
el disco
  compacto (CD)
la impresora
  láser
la pantalla
el punto
el ratón
  (pl. los ratones)
el teclado

### Días

el domingo
el jueves
el lunes
el martes
el miércoles
el sábado
el viernes

### Otras expresiones

a
allí
el almuerzo
¿a qué hora?
el color
¿cómo?
¿cuántos/as?
el día
el examen
el horario
¡mira!
o
sobre
tampoco
tu

### Verbos

estar
estudiar
hablar
llevar
necesitar
terminar

## Gramática

### Noun-adjective agreement

In Spanish, adjectives must match the gender and number of the nouns they describe.

|  | Masculine | Feminine |
|---|---|---|
| **Singular** | un zapato negro. | una blusa amarilla. |
| **Plural** | unos zapatos negros. | unas blusas amarillas. |

### Talking about schedules: ¿A qué hora?

To ask and answer when something is going to occur:
  Question: **¿A qué hora es** la clase de español?
  Answer:  **Es a las** dos.

### Present tense of -ar verbs

| hablar | |
|---|---|
| hablo | hablamos |
| hablas | habláis |
| habla | hablan |

### The verb estar

| estoy | estamos |
|---|---|
| estás | estáis |
| está | están |

# *Para concluir*

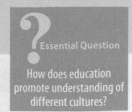

## Proyectos

### A  ¡Manos a la obra!

Choose a Spanish-speaking country and research online about its educational system and culture. You may want to include what classes students typically take, how many classes they have in a day, what time classes end, what their grading system is, what they wear to school, and so on. Prepare a class presentation combining your knowledge from *Unidad 2* and what you've discovered in your research. Try to present as much in Spanish as possible. Compare your findings with school life in the United States. Illustrate your presentation with a Venn diagram to list differences and similarities.

### B  En resumen

For each culture reading in *Unidad 2,* answer the Essential Question "How does education promote understanding of different cultures?" Be sure to include information from the *Perspectivas* and *Prácticas* features as well. Use the chart to organize your ideas.

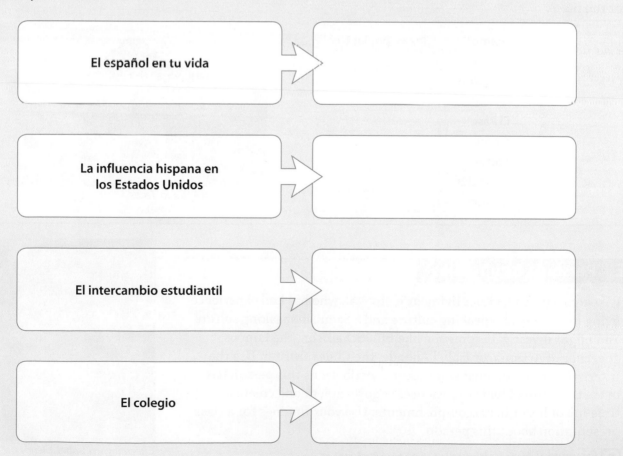

El español en tu vida →

La influencia hispana en los Estados Unidos →

El intercambio estudiantil →

El colegio →

## C ¡A escribir!

Choosing an outfit to wear to school takes too much time! So you've decided to plan ahead and make a list of the clothes you are going to wear. Copy the table below and fill in an outfit for each day. As you plan for the weekend, do your choices change? Include at least three items and colors. Then compare your list with those of your classmates.

| lunes | martes | miércoles | jueves | viernes | sábado | domingo |
|---|---|---|---|---|---|---|
| un pantalón gris, una camisa azul y unos zapatos negros | | | | | | |

## D El español en los Estados Unidos    Conéctate: la geografía

The Spanish were amongst the first Europeans to explore what is now the United States. As a result, many places in the United States bear Spanish names. Copy the table below and in the right-hand column write the location and English meaning of the place.

| Alamo | Texas; poplar tree |
|---|---|
| Alcatraz | |
| Boca Raton | |
| Colorado | |
| El Paso | |
| Florida | |
| Fresno | |
| Los Angeles | |
| Nevada | |

El Álamo, San Antonio, Texas

## E Personas biculturales

Research a person, either living or historical, who has had experience living in an English-speaking culture and a Spanish-speaking culture. You might investigate someone like Bill Richardson, the famous governor of Arizona, or Isabel Allende, the Chilean writer. Use the Internet to find out what significant contributions this person has made to culture, literature, science, or government and create a timeline of his or her accomplishments. Use your findings for a class presentation about this person.

**Búsqueda:** famous hispanics in the united states

Chilean writer Isabel Allende

# Vocabulario de la Unidad 2

**a** to, at, in *2B*

**¿a qué hora?** at what time? *2B*

**allí** there *2B*

el **almuerzo** lunch *2B*

**aló** hello (telephone greeting) *2B*

**amarillo/a** yellow *2B*

el **amigo,** la **amiga** friend *2A*

la **arroba** at (the symbol @ used for e-mail addresses) *2B*

el **arte** art *2B*

**¡ay!** oh! *2A*

**azul** blue *2B*

la **biología** biology *2B*

**blanco/a** white *2B*

la **blusa** blouse *2B*

el **bolígrafo** pen *2A*

el **borrador** eraser *2A*

el **calcetín** sock *2B*

la **camisa** shirt *2B*

la **camiseta** jersey, polo, t-shirt *2B*

el **cesto de papeles** wastebasket *2A*

el **chico,** la **chica** boy, girl *2A*

la **clase** class *2A*

el **colegio** school *2B*

el **color** color *2B*

**¿Cómo?** How? *2B*

**¿Cómo se dice...?** How do you say...? *2A*

**¿Cómo se llama (Ud./él/ella)?** What is (your/his/her) name? *2A*

**comprendo (comprender)** I understand (to understand) *2A*

la **computación** computer class *2B*

la **computadora** computer *2B*

el **cuaderno** notebook *2A*

**¿cuál(es)?** which one(s)? *2B*

**¿cuántos/as?** how many? *2B*

el **día** day *2B*

la **dirección** (de correo electrónico /de internet) address (e-mail / Internet) *2B*

el **disco compacto** (CD) compact disc *2B*

el **domingo** Sunday *2B*

**el, la** the *2A*

**ellas** they (f.) *2A*

**ellos** they (m.) *2A*

**en** in, on, at *2A*

el **escritorio** desk *2A*

el **español** Spanish *2B*

**estar** to be *2B*

el **estudiante,** la **estudiante** student *2A*

**estudiar** to study *2B*

el **examen** exam, test *2B*

la **falda** skirt *2B*

**gris** grey *2B*

**hablar** to speak *2B*

**hay** there is, there are *2A*

la **historia** history *2B*

el **horario** schedule *2B*

la **impresora láser** laser printer *2B*

el **inglés** English *2B*

los **jeans** jeans, blue jeans *2B*

el **jueves** Thursday *2B*

el **lápiz** pencil *2A*

el **libro** book *2A*

**llevar** to wear *2B*

**los, las** the (m.pl.), the (f.pl.) *2A*

el **lunes** Monday *2B*

el **mapa** map *2A*

el **marcador** marker *2A*

el **martes** Tuesday *2B*

las **matemáticas** mathematics *2B*

**mi** my *2A*

el **miércoles** Wednesday *2B*

**¡mira!** look! *2B*

la **mochila** backpack *2A*

la **música** music *2B*

**necesitar** to need *2B*

**negro/a** black *2B*

**nosotros/as** we *2A*

**nuevo/a** new *2A*

el **número de teléfono/de fax/ de teléfono celular** phone number/fax number/cell phone number *2B*

la **página** page *2A*

la **palabra** word *2A*

el **pantalón** pants *2B*

la **pantalla** screen *2B*

el **papel** paper *2A*

la **pared** wall *2A*

el **periódico** newspaper *2A*

la **pizarra** blackboard *2A*

el **profesor,** la **profesora** teacher *2A*

la **puerta** door *2A*

el **punto** dot (term used in Internet address) *2B*

el **pupitre** desk *2A*

**¿qué?** what? *2A*

**¿Qué quiere decir...?** What does ... mean? *2A*

**¿quién?** who? *2A*

**¿quiénes?** who (pl) *2A*

**quiere decir** it means *2A*

el **ratón** (computer) mouse *2B*

la **regla** ruler *2A*

el **reloj** clock, watch *2A*

la **revista** magazine *2A*

**rojo/a** red *2B*

la **ropa** clothing *2B*

el **sábado** Saturday *2B*

el **sacapuntas** pencil sharpener *2A*

**sé** I know *2A*

**se dice** you say *2A*

**ser** to be *2A*

la **silla** chair *2A*

**sobre** on, over, on top of *2B*

**tampoco** neither *2B*

el **teclado** keyboard *2B*

el **teléfono** telephone *2B*

**terminar** to finish *2B*

la **tiza** chalk *2A*

**tu** your *2B*

**(Ud./Él/Ella) se llama...** (your/ his/her) name is ... *2A*

**un, una** a, an, one *2A*

**unos, unas** some, any, a few *2A*

la **ventana** window *2A*

**verde** green *2B*

el **viernes** Friday *2B*

el **zapato** shoe *2B*

### ¿Sabías que...?

*La Ciudad de México*, officially known as *México, D.F.*, was built by the Aztecs on an island in Lake Texcoco in 1325. Its original name was *Tenochtitlán*, derived from the Aztec words for rock and prickly pear (a type of cactus native to the region).

# 3

# ¡En la ciudad!

Scan the QR code to watch this episode of *El cuarto misterioso*.

Ana and her mother view the photos that she took of Mexico City. What did Ana photograph?

A. city celebrations
B. city landmarks
C. city landscapes

*Essential Question*

## ?

## How do major cities tell their stories?

## Mis metas

**Lección A  I will be able to:**

▶ talk about places in the city
▶ invite using **¿Quieres?** and **¿Por qué no?**
▶ introduce a friend and express courtesy
▶ ask and answer questions
▶ talk about interesting places to visit in Mexico City
▶ talk about Diego Rivera's murals
▶ talk about modes of transportation and proximity
▶ express a problem
▶ ask and say where someone is going using the verb **ir**
▶ talk about Mexico City's subway

**Lección B  I will be able to:**

▶ talk about more places in the city
▶ ask and say what people are going to do using **ir a** + infinitive
▶ talk about Mexico's three cultures
▶ talk about Mexico City's landmarks and cuisine
▶ have a conversation in a restaurant
▶ talk about what people do using **-er** verbs
▶ talk about Frida Kahlo and her art

México

Why is this large park in *México, D.F.* called *Chapultepec*?

## ¿Adónde vamos en la ciudad? 🎧

¡El Zócalo de **la Ciudad** de México es **fantástico**!

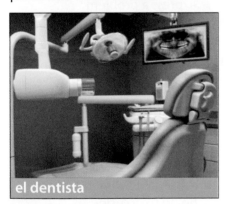

el dentista

el hotel

el restaurante

el banco

la oficina

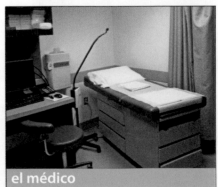

el médico

el parque

la escuela

el cine

la biblioteca

## Para decir más

| un lugar | a place |
|---|---|
| ¡Por supuesto! | Of course! |
| ¡Me encantaría! | I'd love it! |
| Hoy no, gracias. | Not today, thanks. |
| ¿Otro día? | Some other day? |

## Para conversar 🎧

**T**o introduce a friend and express courtesy:

Gabriel, **te presento** a mi amiga Laura.
*Gabriel, let me introduce you to my friend Laura.*

**¡Tanto gusto**!
*So glad (to meet you)!*

**¡Encantado/a**!
*Delighted (to meet you)!*

**¡El gusto es mío**!
*The pleasure is mine!*

**T**o ask and say where someone is going:

Ana, **¿adónde vas**?
*Ana, where are you going?*

**Voy** a la escuela. Voy a **tomar el autobús**.
*I am going to (the) school. I am going to take the bus.*

¡Yo **también**!
*Me too!*

**T**o make a suggestion and express agreement:

**¿Por qué** no **caminamos**?
*Why don't we walk?*

¡Buena idea! **¡Vamos**!
*Good idea! Let's go!*

**T**o invite and accept an invitation:

**¿Quieres ir a la fiesta** de Natalia?
*Do you want to go to Natalia's party?*

**¡Claro**! **¡Quiero ir**! Natalia es muy **simpática**.
*Of course! I want to go! Natalia is very nice.*

**T**o find out more information:

**¿Cuándo** es la fiesta?
*When is the party?*

**¿Sabes** quiénes **van**?
*Do you know who is going?*

## 1 La ciudad 🎧

Selecciona la foto que corresponde con lo que oyes. *(Select the photo that matches what you hear.)*

A

B

C

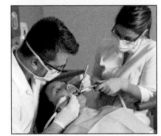

D

E

F

## 2 ¿Cuál es el intruso?

Busca al intruso y explica por qué. *(Look for the intruder and explain why.)*

**MODELO**    la escuela / el dentista / la biblioteca
**el dentista: A school and a library have books.**

1. el autobús / la fiesta / el cine
2. la oficina / el parque / el banco
3. el restaurante / el hotel / el médico

4. tomar el autobús / caminar / encantado
5. fantástico / simpático / también
6. adónde / cuándo / claro

## 3 ¿Qué dices?

Empareja cada oración de la columna I con la respuesta adecuada de la columna II.
*(Match each sentence from Column I with the appropriate response from Column II.)*

**I**

1. Fernando, te presento a mi amiga Ana.
2. ¿Por qué no vamos al cine?
3. ¿Sabes cuándo es la fiesta de la escuela?
4. Voy a tomar el autobús, ¿y tú?
5. ¿Adónde vas?

**II**

A. Sí. Es el sábado.
B. Yo también. ¿Vamos?
C. ¡Encantado!
D. Voy al dentista, ¿y tú?
E. ¡Claro! ¿Cuándo quieres ir?

## Diálogo 🎧

### En la Ciudad de México

**Marisol:** ¡Hay una fiesta fantástica en la ciudad!

**Tomás:** ¿Cuándo es la fiesta?

**Pilar:** Es mañana en el Zócalo. ¿Por qué no vamos?

**Tomás:** ¡Claro! ¡Vamos! Y... Olga va también, ¿no? Es muy simpática.

**Pilar:** Sí, ella va.

**Tomás:** ¡Ah, muy bien!

**Pilar:** Allí está mi amiga. ¡Hola, Ana! Te presento a Tomás.

**Tomás:** Tanto gusto.

**Ana:** Encantada. ¿Por qué no caminamos al parque?

**Tomás:** Sí, quiero caminar.

### 4 ¿Qué recuerdas? 🎧

1. ¿Dónde están los muchachos?
2. ¿Dónde hay una fiesta?
3. ¿Cómo es Olga?
4. ¿Va Tomás al Zócalo?
5. ¿Adónde quiere ir Ana?

### 5 Algo personal 🎧

1. ¿Eres tú simpático/a? ¿Y tus amigos/as?
2. ¿Hay un parque en tu ciudad? ¿Cómo se llama?
3. ¿Caminas a la escuela?

## ¡Comunicación!

### 6 Te presento a mi amigo 👥 Interpersonal Communication

Enrique introduces Cristina to his friend Felipe. With two classmates play the roles of Enrique, Cristina, and Felipe. Switch roles to play all the parts. Use a variety of expressions in your responses.

MODELO    A: Hola Felipe. Te presento a mi amiga, Cristina.

B: Encantado, Cristina.

C: Mucho gusto.

# Gramática

## Making Introductions: *te, le, les*

Follow these guidelines when you wish to introduce people:

**te** (to one person, informal)    *Laura, **te presento** a Gabriel.*

**le** (to one person, formal)    *Sra. Durán, **le presento** a María.*

**les** (to two or more people,    *Luis y José, **les presento** a Margarita.*
informal and formal)

**Note:** When speaking **about** someone with a title, use the definite article *el*, *la*, *los*, *las*

*Emilia, **te** presento a **la** Sra. Ayala.*

Remember that you have several responses to choose from when meeting someone, among them: ***Encantado/a, Mucho gusto, Tanto gusto,*** *or* ***El gusto es mío***.

### Un poco más

Two titles of respect in addition to *Sr., Sra.,* and *Srta.* are ***don*** (masculine) and ***doña*** (feminine). They do not require a definite article and are used with a person's first name when talking to or about adults you know very well: ***Don** Diego, **le** presento a **doña** Teresa.*

---

### 7 ¿Quiénes son?

Completa las presentaciones con **te**, **le** o **les**, según corresponda (*as needed*).

1. Jorge, __ presento al Sr. Francisco Ortiz.
2. Profesor Vallejo, __ presento a doña Marina.
3. Rodolfo y Ana, __ presento al Sr. Rodríguez.
4. Doña Ana, __ presento a la Srta. Medina.
5. Sr. y Sra. Gaviria, __ presento a don Carlos.
6. Paco y Antonio, __ presento al Sr. Pedraza.
7. Rodrigo y Pablo, __ presento a Diana y a Catalina.
8. Rosario, __ presento a don Carlos y a Ernesto.
9. Don Miguel, __ presento a mi amiga Pilar.
10. Papá, __ presento a los Villegas.

### 8 Presentaciones 🎧

Indica la letra de la foto que corresponde con lo que oyes.

A

B      C

D

# *Gramática*

## Using Contractions: *al, del*

- When the prepositions **a** and **de** precede the masculine singular definite article **el**, a contraction is required to create **al** and **del**.

$$a + el = al$$   $$de + el = del$$

*Tomás y Pilar, les presento **al** director **del** banco, el señor Rojas.*

- However, **a** and **de** do not contract with the feminine **la** or the plurals **los** and **las**.

| **a** | | | | **de** | | |
|---|---|---|---|---|---|---|
| | singular | plural | | | singular | plural |
| masculine | a + el **al** | a + los **a los** | masculine | de + el **del** | de + los **de los** |
| feminine | a + la **a la** | a + las **a las** | feminine | de + la **de la** | de + las **de las** |

*Sr. Gómez, le presento **a la** directora **de la** escuela, la Sra. Ayala.*

### 9 ¿Adónde vas?

Completa el diálogo con las palabras del recuadro según corresponda.

| a la | al | de la | del |
|---|---|---|---|

*El Parque de Chapultepec, México, D.F.*

**Roberto:** Hola Marcos, ¿adónde vas?

**Marcos:** Voy **(1)** clase **(2)** Srta. Rodríguez, ¿y tú?

**Roberto:** Voy **(3)** oficina **(4)** Sr. Martínez. Oye, ¿por qué no vamos **(5)** cine por la tarde?

**Marcos:** ¡Claro! Y luego vamos **(6)** Parque de Chapultepec. Es fantástico.

**Roberto:** ¡Buena idea! ¡Adiós!

### 10 De visita en la ciudad

You and two classmates are greeting some friends and family who have decided to visit Mexico City. Introduce everyone using the words shown.

**MODELO**   Hernando / presento a / el profesor de música, el Sr. Villamil
**Hernando, te presento al profesor de música, el Sr. Villamil.**

1. Carmen y Gabriel / presento a / Edgar
2. Sra. Giraldo / presento a / la Sra. Suárez
3. Sr. y Sra. Ruiz / presento a / el profesor de historia de / el colegio, el Sr. Botero
4. Isabel / presento a / el amigo de / el Sr. Rueda, don Carlos
5. Enrique y Sonia / presento a / el amigo de / el profesor Osorio
6. don Martín y doña María / presento a / la amiga de Silvia, Juliana
7. Ana / presento a / Jorge

# ¡Comunicación!

In groups of three, act out the following situations, taking turns to play the part of each person.

• Introduce your friend Rosario to your next door neighbor *Sr.* Villegas, and his mother, *doña* Ana.

• A friend introduces you to one of the exchange students at her school. Respond to the introduction with courtesy.

*Clara, te presento a Ana.*

# ¡Comunicación!

In groups of three or four, pretend you are guests at a *quinceañera* party at the home of the study abroad program director. Practice introducing one another in Spanish and then start conversations with the other guests. Ask where they are from, how they are, if they speak Spanish and English, and so on. Exchange phone numbers with at least one other person. Remember to use appropriate greetings, gestures, and responses in your conversations.

## Repaso rápido

## Question Words *(Palabras interrogativas)*

You are already familiar with several words used for asking information questions.

| | | | |
|---|---|---|---|
| *¿**Cómo** estás?* | **How** are you? | *¿**Dónde** están ellos?* | **Where** are they? |
| *¿**Cuál** es tu cuaderno?* | **Which (one)** is your notebook? | *¿**Por qué** está ella allí?* | **Why** is she there? |
| *¿**Cuáles** son?* | **Which (ones)** are they? | *¿**Qué** es?* | **What** is it? |
| *¿**Cuándo** es la clase de español?* | **When** is the Spanish class? | *¿**Quién** es de Cancún?* | **Who** is from Cancún? |
| *¿**Cuánto** es?* | **How much** is it? | *¿**Quiénes** son ellos?* | **Who** are they? |
| *¿**Cuántos** hay?* | **How many** are there? | | |

**Note:** ***Qué**** can be used before a noun: *¿**Qué** autobús tomas?* (What bus are you taking?)

*Cuál* or *cuáles* cannot be used before a noun; *cuál* (or *cuáles*) is usually followed by a verb: *¿**Cuál** es tu número de teléfono?* (What is your telephone number?)

### 13 ¿Qué palabra es?

Selecciona la palabra interrogativa adecuada.

1. *¿Cómo/Dónde* hay una fiesta fantástica?

2. *¿Quién/Qué* va a la fiesta?

3. *¿A qué/Cuándo* hora es la fiesta?

4. *¿Por qué/Dónde* vamos al parque?

5. *¿De dónde/quién* es ella?

6. *¿De cuál/qué* ciudad son ellos?

7. *¿Cuál/Qué* es tu número de teléfono?

8. *¿Cómo/Dónde* está ella?

# Gramática

## Asking Questions: Ways to Form Questions

- One way to ask a question is by making your voice rise at the end of the sentence.

    *Hay una biblioteca en la ciudad.* → *¿Hay una biblioteca en la ciudad?*

- You can also create a question by adding a tag word such as *¿no?* or *¿verdad?* to the end of a sentence, much as you might add **isn't he/she?** or **right?** in English.

    *Eva va al restaurante, ¿no?*　　Eva is going to the restaurant, **isn't she?**
    *Uds. van al Zócalo, ¿verdad?*　　All of you are going to the Zócalo, **right?**

- Another way to ask a question in Spanish is to place the subject after the verb.

    **Tomás está** en el parque.　　→　　*¿Está Tomás en el parque?*
    　　1　　2　　　　　　　　　　　　　　2　　1

- When forming information questions with interrogative words (*¿cómo?, ¿cuál?, ¿cuándo?,* and so forth), the verb precedes the subject, just as in English:

    ¿Question word + verb + subject + ... ?
    *¿Cuándo van ellos a la fiesta?*　　**When are they going** to the party?

- Some interrogative words may be used in combination with various prepositions:

    ¿Preposition + question word + verb + subject + ... ?
    *¿De dónde eres tú?*　　**Where** are you **from**?

---

### 14 En forma de pregunta 🎧

Cambia las siguientes oraciones a preguntas.

> **MODELO**　　La amiga de Pilar es simpática.
>
> **¿Es la amiga de Pilar simpática?**

1. Ana es la amiga de Pilar.
2. Ana y Tomás estudian música en la Ciudad de México con la Sra. Alvarado.
3. La Sra. y el Sr. Alvarado son de Puebla.
4. Los dos chicos caminan en el Parque de Chapultepec.
5. Ellos hablan con la Sra. Alvarado en el Museo de Antropología.
6. La Sra. Alvarado toma el camión a Puebla.

### 15 ¿Sí o no? 👥

Con un(a) compañero/a de clase, contesta las preguntas creadas en la Actividad 14. Contesta con **sí** o **no** y una oración completa.

> **MODELO**　　A: ¿Es la amiga de Pilar simpática?
> 　　　　　　　B: Sí, la amiga de Pilar es simpática./No, la amiga de Pilar no es simpática

*La amiga de Pilar no es simpática.*

## 16 Necesito información

Completa las preguntas con la palabra interrogativa correcta.

1. ¿ ___ va al restaurante, Sergio o Marcos?
2. ¿ ___ años tienes?
3. ¿ ___ está Elena, bien o mal?
4. ¿ ___ está el libro, en la clase o en la biblioteca?
5. ¿ ___ es Jorge? ¿Simpático?
6. ¿ ___ estudiantes hay, veinte o treinta?
7. ¿ ___ es la profesora de español, la Sra. Jiménez o el Sr. Vallejo?
8. ¿ ___ vas al médico, mañana o el martes?

¿Quién?

¿Cómo?

¿Cuántos?

¿Cuándo?

¿Dónde?

## 17 Muchas preguntas

Make as many different questions as you can for each of the following statements.

**MODELO**  Mañana hay una fiesta fantástica en el Zócalo.
**¿Qué hay mañana en el Zócalo?/¿Dónde hay una fiesta mañana?/**
**¿Cuándo es la fiesta?**

1. Doña Cecilia necesita el horario de autobuses.
2. El Sr. Galindo camina en el Parque de Chapultepec.
3. El Zócalo está en el D.F.
4. César, Ignacio y Pedro estudian en una escuela en Mazatlán.

## ¡Comunicación!

## 18 Preguntas personales   Interpersonal Communication

Con un(a) compañero/a de clase, contesta las preguntas.

1. ¿Eres simpático/a?
2. ¿Vas mucho a la biblioteca pública?
3. ¿Adónde vas con tus amigos?
4. ¿Hay un parque en tu ciudad?
5. ¿Vas a muchas fiestas? ¿Con quién(es) vas?
6. ¿ . . . ?

*¿Están en el Parque de Chapultepec?*

# ¡Comunicación!

## 19 Una entrevista · Interpersonal/Presentational Communication

Usa la gráfica para entrevistar (*interview*) a cinco compañeros de clase y tomar apuntes (*notes*). Usa los apuntes para presentar la información a la clase. Sigue (*follow*) el modelo.

| ¿Cómo te llamas? | ¿Cómo estás? | ¿Cuántos años tienes? | ¿De dónde eres? | ¿Adónde vas el sábado con los amigos? |
|---|---|---|---|---|
| Juan | bien | 16 | España | al cine |
| | | | | |
| | | | | |
| | | | | |
| | | | | |

MODELO    Juan está bien. Tiene 16 años. Es de España. El sábado va al cine con los amigos.

# ¡Comunicación!

## 20 Planes por teléfono · Interpersonal Communication

Create a telephone conversation with a classmate. Make plans and be sure to include where to go, when, who is going, and at what time.

MODELO
A: ¡Aló!
B: Hola, Pedro. Soy Juan. ¿Quieres ir al cine?
A: ¿Cuándo?
B: El viernes.
A: ¿Quiénes van?
B: Marcos, tú y yo.
A: ¿A qué hora?
B: A las siete.
A: Sí, ¡vamos!

*¡Vamos al cine!*

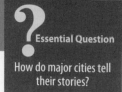

# *Cultura*

*El Zócalo*

## De visita en la Ciudad de México

Mexico City is sinking at the rate of 8 inches per year! Why? The Aztecs built their capital city *Tenochtitlán* on an island in the middle of a lake. Current day *México, D. F.* has grown into the largest city in the western hemisphere (21 million people), and its battle with water issues continues. The *Zócalo*, Mexico City's main square, is home to the centuries-old *Catedral Metropolitana*, which used to sit at a noticeable angle due to the sinking of the city but has since been restored. The other famous building in the *Zócalo* is the *Palacio Nacional*, the seat of government of Mexico. The *Zócalo* (official name *Plaza de la Constitución*) is also home to an enormous Mexican flag (*bandera*) which is raised and lowered each day. It is stored in the *Palacio Nacional* overnight. The *Zócalo* attracts Mexicans and visitors for cultural and social events as well as political protests.

**Q Búsqueda:** el zócalo, la ciudad de méxico, la bandera de méxico, diego rivera

**Productos**   Conéctate: el arte

Diego Rivera was a famous Mexican artist. His large *murales* in the *Palacio Nacional* are a celebration of Mexico's national identity; they include scenes from pre-Hispanic civilizations up through the Mexican Revolution of 1910 and the struggles of modern day Mexico. Diego painted many of his murals between 1929 and 1951 as an alternate history for Mexicans who cannot read and write.

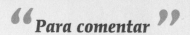
**"*Para comentar*"**

What aspects of daily life are represented in the mural of *la Gran Tenochtitlán*?

*Murales de Diego Rivera, Palacio Nacional: la Gran Tenochtitlán*

## 21 Comprensión

1. What was the original factor that caused Mexico City to start sinking?
2. What is *el Zócalo*? Name three main attractions there.
3. Who was Diego Rivera and where can you find examples of his work?

## 22 Analiza

1. Similar to *el Zócalo*, what public spaces in the United States play host to major celebrations and protests? And in other parts of the world?
2. Why do you think Rivera's works are a source of Mexican pride?

# El Parque de Chapultepec 🎧

El Parque de Chapultepec es un parque enorme en el centro de la Ciudad de México. Es un espacio verde, un oasis en medio de la contaminación de la capital. El Parque de Chapultepec es llamado "el pulmón[1] de la ciudad". *Chapultepec* quiere decir "en el cerro del chapulín[2]" en náhuatl, la lengua de los aztecas. En el parque hay muchas atracciones que visitar: un zoológico, un parque de atracciones, un castillo[3], el Museo Nacional de Antropología y unos monumentos a los niños[4] héroes. Muchos mexicanos y turistas visitan el parque todos los días.

[1]lung    [2]at the grasshopper hill    [3]castle    [4]boys

*Un chapulín en el Parque de Chapultepec*

🔍 **Búsqueda:** el parque de chapultepec, los niños héroes

*Las estatuas de los niños héroes*

## Comparaciones

Is there a park in your city or region that has special features?

## Perspectivas

How much do residents of Mexico City value *El Parque de Chapultepec*? Look online to find out how many visitors there are to the park annually. Find out who visits the park and why it's an important attraction in the city.

## 23 Comprensión    Interpretive Communication

Indica si la frase es correcta. Si no, corrígela.

1. *El Parque de Chapultepec* is a small green space in *México, D.F.*
2. Among the attractions in the park are a zoo, an amusement park, and a museum.
3. The name of the park has its origin in Nahuatl, the language of the Mayan people.
4. Only residents of the city visit the park.
5. The main idea of the reading is that *El Parque de Chapultepec* is called the "lung" of Mexico City.

*El parque de atracciones en el Parque de Chapultepec*

# Vocabulario 2

## ¿Cómo vamos? 🎧

¡Vamos a la ciudad!

en bicicleta

a caballo

a pie

en tren

en moto(cicleta)

en autobús

en carro

en camión

en taxi

en barco

en metro

en avión

## En otros países

| el autobús | la buseta (Colombia) |
| | el camión (México) |
| | el camello (Cuba) |
| | el colectivo (Chile, Paraguay, Uruguay) |
| | la guagua (República Dominicana, Cuba) |
| | el micro (Bolivia, Chile, Perú) |
| el carro | el coche (España) |
| el metro | el subte(rráneo) (Argentina) |

## Para decir más

| en bote | by (small) boat |
| en patines | on roller/ice skates |
| en patines en línea | on inline skates |
| en monopatín | by skateboard |

## Para conversar

***T***o express proximity:

El Parque de Chapultepec está **lejos del** Zócalo. Necesitas tomar el metro.
*Chapultepec Park is far from the Zócalo. You need to take the subway.*

La escuela está **cerca de** la biblioteca. Vamos a pie.
*The school is near the library. Let's go on foot.*

***T***o express a problem:

Don Manuel tiene **un problema porque** no tiene **transporte para** ir a la oficina.
*Manuel has a problem because he doesn't have transportation to get (go) to the office.*

### 24  ¿Qué medio de transporte es?

Selecciona la foto que corresponde con lo que oyes.

A

B

C

D

E

F

G

H

### 25  Medios de transporte

Say which means of transportation you would use to go to the following places.

**MODELO**  la oficina de tu papá
**en autobús**

1. la escuela
2. Puerto Rico
3. el parque
4. México, D.F.
5. el dentista
6. el cine

### 26  ¿Cómo vas?

Find photos in magazines or on the Internet to make flashcards of various means of transportation. On the back of each, identify what it is in Spanish. With a partner, take turns having short conversations using the illustrations as prompts.

**MODELO**  A: *(hold up a picture of a taxi)* **¿Cómo vas?**

B: **Voy en taxi.**

# Diálogo

## ¿Qué?

**Tomás:** Hola, Olga, tú vas mañana a la fiesta, ¿verdad?

**Olga:** ¿Cómo? Estás muy lejos.

**Tomás:** Lo siento. ¿Vas tú mañana a la fiesta en el Zócalo?

**Olga:** Estás muy cerca, Tomás.

**Tomás:** Perdón.

**Olga:** No, no voy porque no tengo transporte.

**Tomás:** Bueno, no hay problema.

**Olga:** ¿Por qué no hay problema?

**Tomás:** Porque yo tengo carro para ir a la fiesta.

---

### 27 ¿Qué recuerdas?

1. ¿Quién está lejos?
2. ¿Con quién habla Tomás?
3. ¿Por qué no va Olga a la fiesta?
4. ¿Por qué no hay problema?

---

### 28 Algo personal

1. ¿Qué transporte tomas para ir a la escuela?
2. ¿Qué tomas para ir al parque? ¿Está lejos o cerca?
3. ¿Vas a fiestas con amigos? Explica.

---

## ¡Comunicación!

### 29 ¿Qué transporte tomas?    Interpersonal Communication

Invita a tu compañero/a a un lugar (*place*) en la ciudad. Tu compañero/a va a responder.

**MODELO**    A: ¿Por qué no vamos al cine?

B: ¡Sí, vamos! Está lejos de aquí. Vamos en autobús.

# Gramática

## Saying Where Someone Is Going: *ir*

- The verb **ir** (to go) is irregular in the present tense.

| ir | | | |
|---|---|---|---|
| yo | **voy** | nosotros nosotras | **vamos** |
| tú | **vas** | vosotros vosotras | **vais** |
| Ud. él ella | **va** | Uds. ellos ellas | **van** |

- The verb **ir** is usually followed by the preposition *a* (or the contraction *al*) and a destination.

*¿Por qué no **vamos** a la biblioteca?* — Why don't **we go to** the library?
**Voy** *al cine.* — **I am going to the** movies.

**Note:** When you want to suggest going somewhere or doing something ("Let's go somewhere/do something!"), use **vamos** *a* (+ place or infinitive).

*¡**Vamos** a la ciudad hoy!* — **Let's go** into town today!
*¡**Vamos** a tomar el autobús!* — **Let's** take the bus!

### 30 ¡Vamos!

Completa las siguientes oraciones con la forma apropiada de **ir**.

**MODELO**     Nuria y Rosario **van** al Museo Nacional de Antropología.

1. Tomás __ a la fiesta en el Zócalo, ¿no?
2. Nosotros __ a la fiesta con él, ¿verdad?
3. El Sr. y la Sra. Morales __ en avión a Veracruz.
4. Andrea y tú __ en metro a un restaurante en el D.F., ¿verdad?
5. ¡Claro! Andrea y yo __ con Mauricio al Castillo de Chapultepec.
6. Tú __ a la Ciudad de México con ellos.
7. Ud. __ al hotel en el centro.
8. Elena __ a la escuela a pie.
9. Ud. y su amigo __ a Panamá en barco.
10. Yo __ a (*give a location*).

*El Castillo de Chapultepec*

## 31 ¿Adónde van en la ciudad?

Indica adónde van las siguientes personas.

**MODELO** Héctor

**Héctor va a la oficina.**

**1.** yo

**2.** tú

**3.** Pablo

**4.** las muchachas

**5.** Nicolás

**6.** Ud.

## 32 ¿Adónde van?

Con un(a) compañero/a, pregunta y responde con las palabras indicadas.

**MODELO** Gloria / al banco / en carro

**A: ¿Adónde va Gloria? Al banco, ¿verdad?**

**B: Sí, va al banco. Va en carro.**

**1.** don Francisco / el médico / en taxi

**2.** los muchachos / el restaurante / en autobús

**3.** Emilia y yo / el dentista / a pie

**4.** la Sra. López / la oficina / en metro

**5.** tú / el cine / en bicicleta

**6.** Pablo y tú / la escuela / en autobús

**7.** Ud. / la ciudad / en tren

**8.** tu familia / Puerto Rico / en barco

**9.** el Sr. Pantoja / la biblioteca / en camión

**10.** las muchachas / el parque / a caballo

**!Ojo!** 👁

Do you remember how to answer when *tú*, *Ud.*, and *Uds.* are the subjects in the question?

## 33 ¿Cómo van? 🎧

Say how these people are going to arrive at the places indicated.

**MODELO**  Ángela y Carlota / cine
**Ángela y Carlota van al cine en autobús.**

**1.** Uds. / parque

**2.** nosotros / oficina

**3.** Uds. / restaurante

**4.** Jaime / banco

**5.** tú / Zócalo

**6.** yo / Isla Mujeres

## 💬 ¡Comunicación!

### 34 ¿Cómo vamos? 👥 Interpersonal Communication

Working in pairs, alternate suggesting places to go in the city and how you might go
to each one. You may disagree with your partner on the transportation suggestion
and offer an alternative.

**MODELO**  A: ¿Vamos al banco?
B: ¡Claro! Vamos en bicicleta.
A: No. Está lejos. Vamos en carro.

*¡Vamos al banco en bicicleta!*

# ¡Comunicación!

## 35 El Hotel San Gabriel 👥    Interpretive/Interpersonal Communication

Con un(a) compañero/a de clase, contesta las preguntas sobre el folleto (*brochure*) del Hotel San Gabriel en la Ciudad de México. Al final, haz (*make*) dos preguntas originales para tu compañero/a.

1. ¿Dónde está el Hotel San Gabriel?
2. Necesitas transporte. ¿Cuál es el número de teléfono?
3. ¿Cómo se llama el cine? ¿Y el banco?
4. ¿Dónde está la Oficina de Turismo?
5. ¿Cuántos restaurantes hay cerca del hotel?
6. ¿Está la Cafetería Don Chang cerca o lejos del hotel? ¿Cómo sabes?
7. La Azteca es un restaurante fantástico. ¿Vas tú allí?
8. ¿Adónde van Uds. mañana?
9. ¿. . . ?
10. ¿. . . ?

**DIRECCIONES Y TELÉFONOS DE URGENCIA Y DE INTERÉS**

| Urgencia | Teléfono |
|---|---|
| Policía | 091 |
| Médico | 297 33 33 |
| **Interés** | |
| Recepcionista | 97 |
| Autobús | 256 29 39 |
| Taxi | 299 43 01 |
| Restaurante La Azteca<br>  Calle Ponce, 75 | 357 55 02 |
| Cafetería Don Chang<br>  Avenida de la Defensa, 99 | 291 77 86 |
| Banco Nacional<br>  Calle Once, 50 | 356 19 61 |
| Oficina de Turismo<br>  Avenida de la Defensa, 98 | 354 00 01 |
| Cine Máximo<br>  Calle 23 y Calle Ponce | 459 78 03 |
| Metro—Información y horario | 290 10 16 |

PARA MÁS INFORMACIÓN, FAVOR LLAMAR • AL/A LA RECEPCIONISTA AL 97.

Avenida de la Defensa 23 • México, D.F. • 294 87 86/297 87 42

# ¡Comunicación!

## 36 ¡Viajamos por México! 👥    Presentational Communication

Work with a partner to plan trips to five different cities in Mexico. Do online research to find means of transportation to get from one place to another; use a variety throughout your trip (bus, plane, boat, car, etc.). Start and end your trip in the same city, and make sure your destination for one leg is your origin for the next leg. Be prepared to share your findings with the class. Use the *modelo* as a guide for your presentation.

| Origen | Destino | Fecha | Día | Hora de salida (*departure*) | Hora de llegada (*arrival*) | Medio de transporte | Costo |
|---|---|---|---|---|---|---|---|
| | | | | | | | |
| | | | | | | | |
| | | | | | | | |
| | | | | | | | |
| | | | | | | | |

**MODELO**    Mi compañero/a y yo vamos a __ de __ . Vamos el __ de __ .
Salimos a las __ y llegamos a las __ . Vamos en __ . El costo es __ dólares/pesos.

# Todo en contexto

## 🗨 ¡Comunicación!

### 37 ¿Por qué no vamos?  👥  Interpersonal Communication    Conéctate: las matemáticas

Tú y tu amigo/a están en el Gran Hotel de la Ciudad de México y hablan de adónde van a ir.

**Nota:** 1km = 0.6 miles

**MODELO**   el restaurante (19.2 km)

A: ¿Por qué no vamos al restaurante?
B: ¡Sí, vamos! ¿Está cerca?
A: No, está lejos. Vamos en metro (taxi, carro, autobús).

1. el Zócalo (1 km)
2. el Parque de Chapultepec (12 km)
3. el Palacio de Bellas Artes (1.5 km)
4. el Restaurante Sanborns (800 metros)
5. el Cinemex (17 km)
6. el Museo de Antropología (6.3 km)
7. Puerto Vallarta (651 km)

*El Palacio de Bellas Artes está cerca del Zócalo.*

## 🗨 ¡Comunicación!

### 38 ¡Conoce la Ciudad de México!  👥  Interpersonal/Presentational Communication

Imagine you and your friends are planning to spend the day in Mexico City. Create a list of at least five questions you might ask your friends to help plan the schedule for the day. Use a variety of the *palabras interrogativas* from this lesson, and include as many Mexico City landmarks as you can. Then, in groups of three or four, review the questions each person has created and choose the ones you want to include in your discussion. Role play your discussion for the class.

# Lectura informativa

## Antes de leer

1. Have you ever ridden a subway?

2. Is there one where you live or in a city nearby?

3. Do you use public transportation? If so, what do you use? If not, why not?

### Estrategia

**Cognates**

Remember that cognates are words that look alike and have the same meaning in two or more languages. Scan the reading for all cognates and other words you recognize, and you'll see how much you already understand!

*El metro de la Ciudad de México*

## El metro de la Ciudad de México 🎧

### Red[1] del Sistema de Transporte Colectivo

Todos los días, cinco millones de personas en la Ciudad de México toman el metro para ir a todas partes. Es el medio de transporte más popular en la ciudad y el más barato[2] del planeta. Solo cuesta US $0.20. El metro es un transporte moderno, limpio[3], seguro y eficiente. ¡Úsalo!

[1] network   [2] cheapest   [3] clean

## Mapa de la red

El metro de la Ciudad de México es el primer sistema que usa símbolos y colores para identificar las estaciones.

🔍 **Búsqueda:** el metro de la ciudad de méxico

*El mapa del metro*

## 39 Comprensión    Interpretive Communication

1. Describe Mexico City's subway.

2. What system is used to identify the subway stations?

3. How do you know the metro is a popular mode of transportation in Mexico City?

## 40 Analiza

1. What is the main idea of the *Lectura informativa*?

2. In your opinion, why do so many people take the metro in Mexico City every day? Can you find evidence in the reading? Can you infer other reasons from what you know about Mexico City?

## Extensión

The logo that corresponds to the name of each metro station is a representative symbol for that station's name. When the metro first opened in 1972, there was a high illiteracy rate in Mexico City, so this system of symbols rather than words made it easier for people to find their way around the city. In the examples, the photos on the right show the inspiration for the symbols on the left.

**Q Búsqueda:** los símbolos del metro de la ciudad de méxico

*Los símbolos de unas estaciones del metro*

# ✏ Escritura

## 41 ¿Qué significan los símbolos?   Presentational Communication

Your class is going to create an informational brochure about the symbols used for the metro stations in Mexico City, and you have been assigned to write captions for four of the symbols shown above. Go online and find more information about these symbols, what they represent and why, and summarize your information in a chart like the one below.

### Para escribir más

| | | | |
|---|---|---|---|
| **el acueducto** | *aqueduct* | **el mercado** | *market* |
| **la campana** | *bell* | **el pato** | *duck* |
| **la fuente** | *fountain* | **las plumas** | *headdress* |
| **la pirámide** | *pyramid* | **significa** | *means* |
| **las manzanas** | *apples* | **viene de** | *comes from* |

| Símbolo | Nombre de la estación | ¿Qué representa? | ¿Por qué? |
|---|---|---|---|
|  | Chapultepec | un chapulín | La estación está cerca del Parque de Chapultepec. *Chapultepec* significa "cerro del chapulín". Viene del náhuatl *chapulli (grasshopper)* y *tepec (hill)*. |
| | | | |
| | | | |
| | | | |

When the brochure is complete, display it in your classroom or in the school media center.

# 🗨 ¡Comunicación!

## 42 ¡Te toca a ti!   Presentational Communication

If you had to design a symbol for a subway station in your city or region, what would it be and why would you choose that logo? Use the same chart as in *Actividad 41* to organize your ideas, and be prepared to present a visual of your symbol plus your explanation to the class.

# Repaso de la Lección A

## A  Escuchar: ¿Qué transporte toman? 🎧 (p. 114)

Selecciona la foto que corresponde con lo que oyes.

A          B          C          D          E

## B  Vocabulario/Gramática: ¿Adónde y cómo van? (pp. 114, 117)

Completa las frases con la forma correcta del verbo **ir** y un medio de transporte lógico.

> **MODELO**    Ud. **va** a Puerto Rico. Está lejos. **Va en barco**.

1. Julia __ al parque. Está cerca. __ ___.

2. Mis amigos y yo __ al cine. Está lejos. __ ___.

3. El Sr. Vargas __ a la oficina. Está lejos. __ ___.

4. (Tú) __ a la escuela. Está lejos. __ ___.

5. Pepe y Paco __ a la biblioteca. Está cerca. __ ___.

6. (Yo) __ al/a la ___. Está ___. __ ___.

## C  Gramática: En la fiesta (pp. 106–107)

Completa las tres conversaciones.

**Roberto:**        Sr. y Sra. Ortega, **(1)** presento **(2)** amigo **(3)** Sr. Gómez, don Fernando.
**Sr. Ortega:**     Tanto **(4)**, don Fernando.
**Don Fernando:**   **(5)**.

**Sra. Tovar:**     Sra. Santos, **(6)** presento **(7)** profesora de español, Alejandra Pinel.
**Sra. Santos:**    **(8)**, Sra. Pinel.
**Sra. Pinel:**     **(9)**.

**Marcos:**         Hola. Me llamo Marcos. **(10)**.
**Estefanía:**      **(11)**.

## D  Gramática: ¿Cuál es la pregunta? (p. 108)

Completa la pregunta con una palabra interrogativa apropiada.

1. **A:** ¿ __ estudiantes hay en la clase?
   **B:** Hay treinta y cinco.

2. **A:** ¿ __ es?
   **B:** Es un bolígrafo.

3. **A:** ¿ __ está Marta?
   **B:** Bien.

4. **A:** ¿ __ van al restaurante?
   **B:** Pedro y Elena.

5. **A:** ¿ __ está Marcos en la biblioteca?
   **B:** Necesita estudiar.

6. **A:** ¿ __ es la fiesta de los Carallo?
   **B:** El sábado.

## E   Cultura: De visita en la Ciudad de México (pp. 112–113)

¿Qué recuerdas de la Ciudad de México? Completa la gráfica con información.

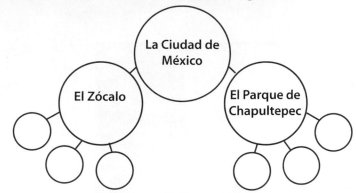

## Vocabulario

| La ciudad | Palabras interrogativas | Transporte | Verbos | Otras expresiones |
|---|---|---|---|---|
| el banco | | a caballo | caminar | |
| la biblioteca | ¿adónde? | a pie | ir | al |
| el cine | ¿cómo? | el autobús | presento | cerca (de) |
| la ciudad | ¿cuál? | el avión | quieres | ¡claro! |
| el/la dentista | ¿cuáles? | el barco | quiero | del |
| la escuela | ¿cuándo? | la bicicleta | sabes | El gusto es mío. |
| el hotel | ¿cuánto? | el caballo | tomar | encantado/a |
| el/la médico/a | ¿cuántos? | el camión | ¡vamos! | fantástico/a |
| la oficina | ¿dónde? | el carro | | la fiesta |
| el parque | ¿por qué? | en (means of | | lejos (de) |
| el restaurante | ¿qué? | transportation) | | le/les/te |
| | ¿quién? | el metro | | presento a |
| | ¿quiénes? | la moto(cicleta) | | para |
| | | el taxi | | porque |
| | | el transporte | | el problema |
| | | el tren | | simpático/a |
| | | | | también |
| | | | | Tanto gusto. |
| | | | | ¿verdad? |

## Gramática

### Making introductions: *te, le, les*

| | to one person | to two or more people |
|---|---|---|
| informal | te | les |
| formal | le | les |

### Irregular verb: *ir*

The verb **ir** is usually followed by the preposition *a* and a destination.

| ir | |
|---|---|
| voy | vamos |
| vas | vais |
| va | van |

### Asking questions

- raise voice at the end of a sentence
- add a tag word, ¿no? or ¿verdad?
- place the subject after the verb
- use a question word (*¿cómo?, ¿cuál?, ¿qué?*) that precedes the verb

## Vocabulario 1

### En el centro 🎧

En **el centro** hay **muchos** edificios **grandes**.

el museo

el edificio

la tienda

el teatro

el concierto

el/la cantante

la plaza

la avenida / la calle

## Para conversar 🎧

*T*o talk about what someone is going to do:

¿Qué vas a **hacer hoy**?

*What are you going to do today?*

Voy a ir al concierto de mi cantante **favorito**.

*I'm going to go to the concert of my favorite singer.*

### Para decir más

| | |
|---|---|
| el café | *café, cafeteria* |
| (la oficina de) correos | *post office* |
| el hospital | *hospital* |
| la iglesia | *church* |
| la mezquita | *mosque* |
| la sinagoga | *synagogue* |

### 1  En el centro 🎧

Selecciona la foto del lugar apropiado, según lo que oyes.

A

B

C

D

E

F

G

H

### 2  La ciudad

Completa las oraciones con expresiones del Vocabulario 1.

1. El autobús va por las ___ del centro.
2. Gabriela y Ana van al ___ de arte moderno.
3. Mañana hay un ___ de una banda popular en un ___ grande en el centro.
4. Hay muchos bancos en la ___ Wall en Nueva York.
5. El Zócalo es una ___ grande en el ___ de la Ciudad de México.
6. La oficina de mi mamá está en un ___ grande.
7. Frank Sinatra es un ___ favorito de mi papá.
8. Una ___ es una calle grande.

### 3  El cine vs. el teatro

¿Cuál es la diferencia entre (*between*) un cine y un teatro? ¿Qué tienen en común (*common*)? Usa el diagrama de Venn.

el cine          el teatro

movie          play

## Diálogo 🎧

### Vamos al museo

**Tomás:** Olga, ¿qué vas a hacer el sábado?

**Olga:** Voy a ir al centro con Pilar.

**Tomás:** ¿Van a las tiendas?

**Olga:** No. Vamos al museo de arte.

**Tomás:** El museo está en un edificio grande.

**Olga:** Sí, luego, vamos al restaurante El Charro. ¿Vas?

**Tomás:** ¡Claro! ¿Está el restaurante en la calle Versalles?

**Olga:** No, está en la Avenida de la Independencia.

---

### 4  ¿Qué recuerdas? 🎧

1. ¿Qué va a hacer Olga el sábado?
2. ¿Va ella a las tiendas?
3. ¿Cómo es el edificio del museo?
4. ¿Dónde está el restaurante?

---

### 5  Algo personal 🎧

1. ¿Qué vas a hacer el sábado?
2. ¿Hay muchos edificios grandes en el centro de tu ciudad?
3. ¿En qué calle está tu colegio?

---

### 6  ¿Qué vas a hacer hoy? 🎧

Indica la letra de la foto que corresponde con lo que oyes.

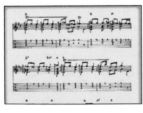

A

B

Avenida de la Independencia

C

D

# *Gramática*

## Talking About the Future: *ir a* + Infinitive

- Say what you are going to do or what is going to happen by using the present tense of **ir** followed by **a** and an infinitive (*infinitivo*).

$$\boxed{\textbf{ir } + \textbf{ a } + \textit{infinitive}}$$

*Laura **va a ser** médica.*  Laura **is going to be** a doctor.

*Uds. **van a caminar** en la ciudad, ¿verdad?*  You **are going to walk** in the city, right?

- The expression **Vamos a** + infinitive can be used to make a suggestion.

**Vamos a** *caminar en el parque.*  **Let's** walk in the park.

---

### 7  Van a ir a diferentes lugares

Ask where these people are going tomorrow in downtown Guadalajara, using tag questions.

**MODELO**  Juan / restaurante El Amanecer

**Juan va a ir al restaurante El Amanecer, ¿verdad?**

1. Uds. / museo de arte
2. Manolo / fiesta en la plaza
3. Fabiola y Gerardo / teatro
4. nosotros / tiendas

5. Doris / oficina
6. Ud. / banco
7. tú / biblioteca
8. doña Ester / médico

---

### 8  ¿Adónde van a ir?

Haz oraciones lógicas usando palabras y expresiones de cada columna.

**MODELO**  **Los Martínez van a ir al cine a las seis.**

| I | II | III |
|---|---|---|
| los Martínez | ir al cine | el lunes |
| la Sra. Sandoval | caminar al concierto | en la tarde |
| nosotros | estar en el restaurante | a las seis |
| yo | llevar ropa nueva | a las diez y media |
| doña Angelina | caminar al edificio nuevo | el domingo |
| Ariel Tovar | visitar el museo | al mediodía |
| tú | hablar en la plaza | en la noche |
| Mónica y José Ruiz | tomar el autobús | a las tres y media |

# ¡Comunicación!

## 9  En el D.F.  👥  Interpretive Communication

As part of a summer study program, you have the opportunity to take classes at *la UNAM* (*la Universidad Autónoma de México*), and a classmate has prepared a list to help you find your way around the city. Answer the questions about the places to go.

1. ¿Cómo vas a ir a los museos de Chapultepec?
2. ¿Qué museo de arte está en Chapultepec?
3. ¿A qué museos vas a ir?
4. Tomas un taxi a la Calle 16 de Septiembre. ¿De qué plaza vas a estar cerca?
5. ¿Dónde está el restaurante con "mole fantástico"?
6. ¿Dónde está el Palacio de Bellas Artes? ¿Cómo vas a ir allí?
7. Quiero ir al Museo de Arte Moderno. ¿Sabes el número de teléfono del museo?

**Adónde ir en el D.F.**

Parque de Chapultepec (ir en metro):
- Museo Nacional de Antropología
- Museo Nacional de Historia (en el Castillo)
- Casa del Lago (parque de atracciones)
- Museo Tecnológico
- Museo de Arte Moderno (en Av. Reforma): 776-83-41
- Museo de Historia Natural

Otros lugares interesantes:
- Palacio de Bellas Artes (museo y teatro en el Centro Histórico)
  - Está en la Alameda Central y la Avenida Juárez. (camiones Nº 16 ó 52) Información: 683-48-05
- El Zócalo (plaza central)
  - Calle 16 de Septiembre (cerca de la Calle Seminario)

- La Plaza de las Tres Culturas
  - Almacenes S/N, Tlatelolco

Restaurantes:
- La Bodega (¡Mole fantástico!)
  Popocatépetl 25, Colonia Hipódromo Condesa, Zona Centro
  Teléfono: 525-84-73

- SpaceNet Café
  Calz. del Hueso 160 local 3-B Fuentes Plaza Ex Hacienda Coapa, Zona Sur
  Teléfono: 567-35-52

# ¡Comunicación!

## 10  Sus propios planes  👥  Interpersonal Communication

Working in pairs, use the list from the previous activity to make your own plans for what you are going to do while in Mexico City.

**MODELO**
A:  ¿Vamos a ir al Museo de Antropología?
B:  Sí. Vamos a tomar el autobús. Está lejos.

## Comunidades

Knowing Spanish helps you connect with your community in a whole new way! You might be able to practice your Spanish *en un restaurante*, *en un museo*, *en una tienda*, or simply strolling along a city street.

# ¡Comunicación!

## 11  ¿Qué van a hacer mañana?  👥👥  Interpersonal/Presentational Communication

Usa la gráfica para hablar con dos compañeros de clase y tomar apuntes (*notes*). Usa los apuntes para presentar la información a la clase.

| Nombre | ¿Adónde vas a ir? | ¿Está cerca o lejos? | ¿Cómo vas? | ¿Cuándo vas? |
|--------|-------------------|----------------------|------------|--------------|
| Miguel | a la tienda de ropa | lejos | en metro | al mediodía |
|  |  |  |  |  |

**MODELO**  Miguel va a ir a la tienda de ropa. Está lejos. Va en metro al mediodía.

**?** Essential Question

How do major cities tell their stories?

# La Plaza de las Tres Culturas 🎧

México tiene una historia de muchas culturas. En la Plaza de las Tres Culturas en el centro de la Ciudad de México hay tres períodos históricos representados. Las ruinas de unos templos y unas pirámides aztecas representan la cultura pre-hispánica (antes del año 1521); la iglesia[1] católica de Santiago de Tlatelolco representa el período colonial (1521–1821), y un edificio moderno representan al México de hoy. En la plaza hay un monumento dedicado a los aztecas que murieron[2] en una masacre en 1521 cuando Hernán Cortés y los españoles conquistaron México. También hay un monumento dedicado a los estudiantes que murieron en la plaza en 1968 durante una protesta contra la injusticia y la violencia. En el Museo Nacional de las Culturas (cerca del Zócalo) hay más información de las diversas culturas de México.

[1]church [2]died

La Plaza de las Tres Culturas

🔍 **Búsqueda:** la plaza de las tres culturas, el museo nacional de las culturas

## Productos

Mexico City tells its story with landmarks and monuments commemorating its rich cultural history. The Aztec ruins in the *Templo Mayor* near the *Zócalo* and the *Monumento a la Raza* in *el centro* both speak to the indigenous culture that forms an integral part of Mexico's history. *El Ángel de la Independencia* and the *Monumento a la Revolución* commemorate the Mexicans' struggle for freedom and a better life. The *Monumento a los Niños Héroes* and the *Hemiciclo* (semicircle) *a Benito Juárez* depict the reverence with which the Mexicans treat their national heroes. Their national pride can be heard in the popular *dicho* by *los chilangos* (residents of Mexico City), *"Sí, se puede"*. ("Yes, it's possible.")

El Ángel de la Independencia

## 12 Comprensión — Interpretive Communication

1. What three cultures are represented in *La Plaza de las Tres Culturas*?
2. How is each represented?
3. To whom are the two monuments in the *Plaza de las Tres Culturas* dedicated?

## 13 Analiza

1. Explain the connection between the famous monuments in Mexico City and the popular saying by its residents, *"Sí, se puede"*.
2. Explain how Mexico City tells its story through *La Plaza de las Tres Culturas* and the monuments placed around the metropolis.

## Antes de leer

Which foods from the box do you think had their origin in Spain and which in Mexico? Make two lists.

| | | | |
|---|---|---|---|
| tomatoes | olive oil | beef | corn |
| meat | peppers | cheese | beans |

### Comparaciones

Are there dishes unique to your region that contain what some people might deem "exotic" ingredients? What is the history behind those regional dishes?

# La comida de las tres culturas

"Excuse me waiter, there's a fly in my soup." Well, in some Mexican dishes, it might be part of the recipe! In pre-Hispanic times, Mexican food included corn, beans, and chilis (still staples today) but also insects like *chapulines* (grasshoppers) as a protein source. During the colonial period, Mexican cuisine incorporated the influence of Spanish tastes and ingredients: meat, olive oil, and dairy, especially cheese. The Mexico City of today has quite a varied cuisine due to the influx of people from all over the country and the world. There are restaurants reviving the indigenous style of cooking, some even incorporating sustainable protein from the 300 to 550 species of edible insects native to Mexico. There are restaurants that serve the more traditional fare of *enchiladas*, *tamales*, and the very popular *mole*, a thick, spicy, dark brown sauce made from chilis, chocolate, and spices and often served with *pollo* (chicken). In the capital *los chilangos* (residents of Mexico City) enjoy street cuisine, with *tacos* and *tortas* (Mexican sandwiches) being two popular choices sold by vendors.

*¿Quieres un plato de chapulines?*

*Quiero una torta.*

**Búsqueda:** la comida mexicana, el mole, la torta

## 14 Comprensión

1. Explain the evolution of Mexican cuisine from pre-Hispanic times to present day.
2. What are popular foods sold by street vendors in Mexico City?

## 15 Analiza

1. What can you infer about Mexicans' attitude toward food after reading the selection? Give details to support your answer.
2. How does Mexico City tell its story through its food?

### Perspectivas

In 2010, UNESCO (United Nations Educational, Scientific and Cultural Organization) proclaimed Mexican cuisine to be "intangible cultural heritage." Why do you think Mexicans value their cuisine?

## En el restaurante

En el restaurante ellos comen comida mexicana.

el mesero

el menú

### Las comidas

la ensalada

los frijoles

el pescado

el pollo

### Los verbos

comer

tomar

ver

leer

### Las bebidas

el agua

el jugo
de naranja

el refresco

### *Para decir más*

| Para tomar | | Para comer | |
|---|---|---|---|
| el café | coffee | la carne | meat |
| el chocolate | hot chocolate | la hamburguesa | hamburger |
| la gaseosa | soft drink | el pan | bread |
| la leche | milk | el postre | dessert |
| el té | tea | las papas fritas | french fries |

### *En otro país (España)*

| | |
|---|---|
| los frijoles | las alubias |
| el jugo | el zumo |
| el menú | la carta |
| el mesero | el camarero |

## Para conversar 🎧

**T**o have a conversation in a restaurant:

**Oye**, Natalia, ¿qué vas a comer?
*Hey, Natalia, what are you going to eat?*

**Bueno** (**Pues**), **siempre** como pollo, **pero** hoy voy a comer pescado.
*Well, I always eat chicken, but today I am going to eat fish.*

¿Por qué no le **preguntas** al mesero qué hay de tomar?
*Why don't you ask the server what there is to drink?*

**De acuerdo**. Le voy a preguntar **ahora**.
*Okay. I am going to ask him now.*

**T**o have a conversation with the server:

Cecilia **hace una pregunta**: Mesero, ¿tiene pollo en mole hoy?
*Cecilia asks a question: Waiter, do you have chicken in mole (sauce) today?*

**¡Cómo no**! **Un momento**, por favor.
*Of course! One minute (moment), please.*

*¿Hay pollo en mole en el menú?*

---

### 16  ¿Dónde está? 🎧

Di si lo que oyes está en **un restaurante** o en **un colegio**.

---

### 17  ¿Cuál es el intruso?

Busca al intruso, la palabra que no pertenece al grupo, y explica por qué.

> **MODELO**  el agua / la ensalada / el refresco
> **la ensalada: Water and soft drinks are beverages.**

1. el pescado / el pollo / los frijoles
2. toma / quiero / como
3. cómo / bueno / pues
4. preguntar / comer / hacer una pregunta
5. leer / ver / mesero
6. los frijoles / la ensalada / el pescado

---

### 18  En el restaurante

Completa las siguientes oraciones con una palabra del Vocabulario 2.

1. Las chicas leen las comidas y las bebidas en el ___.
2. El ___ pregunta a las chicas, "¿Qué van a comer?"
3. Las chicas toman ___ mineral.
4. La ___ que toma el señor de camisa azul es un jugo de naranja.
5. Hoy Natalia va a ___ pollo porque es su favorito.
6. Pablo no va a comer luego; quiere comer ___.

# Diálogo

## ¿Qué van a comer?

**Tomás:** Perdón, ¿sabe dónde está el restaurante El Charro?

**Señora:** ¡Sí! Está allí, cerca de la biblioteca, en la Avenida de la Independencia.

**Tomás:** Muchas gracias.

*(Más tarde)*

Hola, Olga. Hola, Pilar.

**Olga:** ¡Hola, Tomás! Oye, ¿qué vas a comer?

**Tomás:** Yo siempre como pollo en mole.

**Mesera:** ¿Qué van a comer, señoritas?

**Olga:** Este... quiero el pescado y un refresco.

**Pilar:** Yo voy a comer unos frijoles y a tomar un jugo de naranja.

**Mesera:** De acuerdo.

---

## 19 ¿Qué recuerdas?

1. ¿Dónde está el restaurante El Charro?
2. ¿Qué come Tomás siempre?
3. ¿Qué va a comer Olga?
4. ¿Va Pilar a comer una ensalada?

---

## 20 Algo personal

1. ¿Dónde está tu restaurante favorito?
2. ¿Qué comida vas a comer allí?
3. ¿Tomas agua mineral, jugo de naranja o refresco?

---

## 21 ¿Cuál es la respuesta?

Escoge la letra de la respuesta correcta.

A. Sí, pero hoy no quiero pollo en mole.

B. Está allí, cerca de la biblioteca.

C. Pues, un momento, por favor...
Voy a comer pescado hoy.

D. Quiero tomar agua mineral, por favor.

### Para decir más

**Um . . . , Huh? Well . . .** Do you ever use these words when speaking to buy yourself time to think? These "filler words" also exist in Spanish. Try adding them to pauses in your conversation, and you will sound more natural

| a ver | let's see |
|-------|-----------|
| bueno | okay, well |
| este | well, so |
| mira | look, hey |
| oye | hey, listen |

# Gramática

## Conjugating Regular -*ar* Verbs

In Unit 2 you learned how to conjugate regular -*ar* verbs: remove the -*ar* and add the endings -*o*, -*as*, -*a*, -*amos*, -*áis*, -*an*.

| | |
|---|---|
| *¿Tomas el autobús a la escuela?* | Do you take the bus to school? |
| *No, camino porque la escuela está cerca.* | No, I walk because the school is close. |

## Saying What Someone Does: Present Tense of -*er* Verbs

- Form the present tense of regular -*er* verbs such as *comer* (to eat), *comprender* (to understand), and *leer* (to read) by first removing the -*er* ending and then attaching endings that correspond to each of the subject pronouns shown in this chart.

| comer | | | |
|---|---|---|---|
| yo | com**o** | nosotros<br>nosotras | com**emos** |
| tú | com**es** | vosotros<br>vosotras | com**éis** |
| Ud.<br>él<br>ella | com**e** | Uds.<br>ellos<br>ellas | com**en** |

- Three additional verbs that end in -*er*, *hacer* (to do, to make), *saber* (to know information), and *ver* (to see), are regular **except** for the yo forms.

  *hacer*  yo **hago**      *saber*  yo **sé**      *ver*  yo **veo**

- In addition, the *vosotros* form of *ver* does not require an accent mark: *vosotros* **veis**.

  **Veo** *la calle Versalles.*                    **I see** Versalles Street.

  *¿***Veis** *vosotros la Avenida Suárez en el mapa?*   **Do you see** Suárez Avenue on the map?

---

### 22  ¿Qué comes?

Working in pairs, take turns asking questions about whether each of you does or does not eat the items listed.

**MODELO**   tacos

A: **¿Comes tacos?**
B: **Sí, (No, no) como tacos.**

1. ensalada          2. frijoles          3. pescado          4. pollo

## 23 ¿Qué tienen en común?

Read the following statements and say who else does the same thing, according to the cue in parentheses. Add an expression such as *pues* or *bueno* before each sentence.

Leo periódicos en español.

> **MODELO** Leo periódicos en español y comprendo muy bien. (*Elena*)
>
> **Pues, Elena lee periódicos en español y comprende muy bien también.**

1. Josefina lee una revista y toma jugo de naranja. (*yo*)
2. El Sr. y la Sra. Correa leen libros en español. (*nosotros*)
3. El profesor comprende inglés y español. (*José y Ana*)
4. Comemos pescado y ensalada en el centro hoy. (*los Peña*)
5. Roberto come tacos en el restaurante Los Rancheros. (*tú*)

## 24 ¿Comprenden y hablan inglés y español?

Say that the following people all understand and speak English and Spanish.

> **MODELO** Alejandro
>
> **Alejandro comprende y habla inglés y español.**

1. yo
2. tú
3. mi amiga y yo
4. el profesor
5. los estudiantes en la clase de español
6. la chica nueva

## 25 Un viernes en El Charro

Completa el párrafo con la forma correcta de los verbos entre paréntesis.

Los viernes, mi amiga Pilar y yo siempre (**1.** *comer*) en el restaurante El Charro. Hoy muchos chicos del colegio (**2.** *comer*) aquí. En la mesa número uno, Paco y María (**3.** *leer*) el menú. Paco no (**4.** *saber*) qué comer. María siempre (**5.** *comer*) pescado. En la mesa dos, el mesero pregunta a Jorge, Daniel y Patricia qué van a comer. Ellos (**6.** *hacer*) una pregunta al mesero: "Nosotros no (**7.** *ver*) tacos en el menú. ¿Hay tacos aquí?" "Sí, ¡cómo no!" responde el mesero. En la mesa tres estamos Graciela y yo. Graciela (**8.** *leer*) el menú. Yo siempre (**9.** *comer*) ensalada, pero no (**10.** *saber*) qué tomar hoy. Graciela dice "Un momento, por favor". Yo (**11.** *ver*) que ella no (**12.** *comprender*) una palabra del menú. Luego, ella dice "¡Ahora (**13.** *comprender*)! Yo quiero el pollo en mole y un refresco por favor". "De acuerdo".

## 26 Todos hacen algo

Using the verbs *comer*, *comprender*, and *leer*, tell what these people are doing.

**MODELO** el chico
**El chico come pollo.**

**1.** Graciela

**2.** Camilo

**3.** las muchachas

**4.** ellos

**5.** Edgar y Vivian

**6.** Mónica

## 27 ¿Qué hacen?

Working with a partner, read the following statements about Alfredo and his friends. Tell your partner that you do the same things as Alfredo, and then ask what your partner does.

**MODELO**
A: **Alfredo va a un colegio grande en el centro.**
B: **Pues, yo también voy a un colegio grande en el centro. ¿Y tú?**
A: **Yo (no) voy a un colegio grande en el centro.**

**1.** Alfredo sabe historia.

**2.** Alfredo siempre lee muchas revistas y periódicos.

**3.** Los sábados Alfredo y Rebeca hacen pollo en mole.

**4.** Alfredo y Tomás hacen muchas preguntas en la clase de biología.

**5.** Alfredo comprende español.

**6.** Alfredo, Rebeca y Tomás comen pescado y pollo.

## 28 Describe lo que ves

Say what these people do, see, or know according to what you see in each illustration.

**1.** Gabriel y María

**2.** ellos

**3.** Mónica

**4.** Diego

**5.** los Montoya

**6.** la Sra. Ruiz

# ¡Comunicación!

## 29 ¡Vamos al Charro! | Interpersonal Communication

In groups of four, two students play the role of friends who are considering going to a popular restaurant in town, El Charro. The other two students should pretend they often go to eat at El Charro. Then, four of you meet on the street and discuss the restaurant (the restaurant's name, if it is new, where it is, etc.). Be sure to ask your friends what they eat when they go to El Charro. Then say what you are going to eat when you go there. Switch roles.

### Estrategia

**Review and recycle** ♻

When doing an activity that requires consolidating previously learned material and adding a touch of creativity, you should always look back at appropriate sections earlier in the unit and/or lesson: *vocabulario, diálogo, para conversar, gramática, cultura*. Borrow set phrases and create your own combinations. Don't be afraid to experiment!

# ¡Comunicación!

## 30 ¿Qué leen tus compañeros de clase? | Interpersonal/Presentational Communication

Survey your classmates to find out their reading habits. Fill in the chart. Be prepared to summarize your findings in a short paragraph. Use the modelo as a guide.

| ¿Cómo te llamas? | ¿Lees mucho o poco? | ¿Qué lees ahora? |
|---|---|---|
| **Kristin** | **mucho** | **The Hunger Games** |
| | | |
| | | |

MODELO    **Seis estudiantes leen mucho y nueve leen poco. Dos leen *Ender's Game*. Tres no leen nada. Kristin y yo leemos. . .**

# Todo en contexto

## ¡Comunicación!

### 31 Visita el museo    Interpretive Communication

Use the advertisement to answer the questions.

1. What time span does the permanent collection cover?
2. How can you find out about temporary exhibits?
3. Give three other facts you learn about the museum from this advertisement.
4. Why do you think 1521 is an important year?

MUSEO NACIONAL DE ANTROPOLOGIA

**¡Ven a visitar el Museo de Antropología en el Parque de Chapultepec!**

Visita nuestra colección permanente de piezas pre-hispánicas, objetos que tienen 3.2 milliones de años hasta objetos del año 1521

Visita nuestro sitio web para ver una lista de exposiciones temporales

Horario: 9,00-19,00 todo el año
Entradas: $57.00 pesos MX
Entrada gratis: Gente mayor de
60 años y menores de 13 años de edad

Estaciona el carro por sólo $16 pesos MX por hora
Ofrecemos visitas guiadas y escolares
Ofrecemos audioguías

## ¡Comunicación!

### 32 En un restaurante    Interpersonal Communication

Role play a conversation between two friends in a restaurant.

⟷ Greet and ask how each other is.

➝ Ask what he/she is going to eat.

⟵ Say what you always eat. Ask what he/she is going to eat.

➝ Say what you are going to eat and drink.

⟵ Say what you want to drink but you don't see it on the menu.

➝ Tell him/her to ask the server.

⟵ Agree.

# Lectura

## Antes de leer

### 33 Vocabulario — Conéctate: el arte

Selecciona las palabras de la columna I que van con las palabras en inglés de la columna II.

| I | II |
|---|---|
| **1.** un estilo | **A.** a painting |
| **2.** un autorretrato | **B.** a husband |
| **3.** una pintora | **C.** a painter, artist |
| **4.** un tema | **D.** a self–portrait |
| **5.** un cuadro/una pintura | **E.** a theme |
| **6.** un esposo | **F.** a style |

### Estrategia

**Anticipating special vocabulary**

It will be easier for you to read and understand specialized subject matter if you try anticipating some of the words and expressions you may encounter. Identifying specialized vocabulary beforehand will help you zero in on what a writer is saying since your mind will already be thinking about the topic.

### 34 Compara y contrasta

Visuals are an important tool to use in preparation for reading. Look at the photo of Frida Kahlo below and her self-portrait. Before reading about her on the next page, work with a partner to compare and contrast the two images. Decide which you prefer and why.

*La pintora Frida Kahlo en 1931*

*Autorretrato con mono (Self-Portrait with Monkey), Frida Kahlo, 1938. Albright–Knox Art Gallery, Buffalo, N.Y.*

# Frida Kahlo, una artista universal, famosa e importante (1907–1954)

Me llamo Frida Kahlo. Soy una pintora mexicana. Vivo[1] en la Ciudad de México, en la zona de Coyoacán, en una casa azul. Vivo con mi esposo, Diego Rivera, quien también es un artista mexicano.

Diego y yo pintamos cuadros que tienen un impacto social; son una combinación del arte y la política. Los murales de Diego representan la historia de México. Mis pinturas representan temas universales: los aspectos negativos de la industrialización (la contaminación del aire) y la naturaleza. También pinto representaciones de mis problemas físicos. De muchacha tuve[2] polio, y a los dieciocho años tuve un accidente de tráfico. Sufro de dolor[3] crónico y lo expreso en mis cuadros.

Mi esposo y yo estamos muy orgullosos[4] de la cultura indígena. (Los indígenas son las personas nativas de México.) Llevo ropa de estilo indio, y en mis autorretratos represento la cultura indígena con el uso de plantas, animales y colores de la naturaleza.

[1] I live   [2] I had   [3] pain   [4] proud

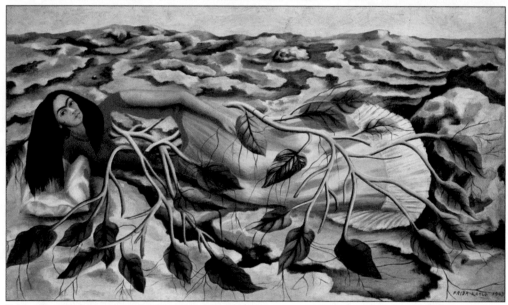

Raíces (Roots), Frida Kahlo, 1943. Private collection.

🔍 Búsqueda: frida kahlo, diego rivera

## 35 Comprensión   Interpretive Communication

1. Give three facts you learn about Frida Kahlo in the first paragraph.
2. Compare and contrast Diego's works with Frida's.
3. What autobiographical elements does Frida include in her works?

## 36 Analiza

1. Comment on the title of the selection. Why do you think her works are important and have stood the test of time?
2. Knowing what you do about Frida and her works, comment on the painting entitled *Raíces*.

# Repaso de la Lección B

## A  Escuchar: ¿En el restaurante o en el centro? 🎧 (pp. 126–127, 133–134)

Escucha las seis oraciones. Di si lo que oyes está en **el restaurante** o en **el centro**.

## B  Vocabulario: La palabra lógica (pp. 126–127, 133–134)

Completa las oraciones con una palabra lógica del vocabulario.

1. Un __ es una lista de comidas y bebidas.
2. En la __ en el centro de la ciudad hay un monumento a la independencia.
3. El __ pregunta, "¿Qué van a comer?"
4. Hay mucho tráfico en las __ de la ciudad.
5. Don Armando va a tomar un __ de naranja.
6. Una comida típica en México es __ con mole.
7. La oficina de mi papá está en un __ grande en el centro.
8. Los estudiantes hacen muchas __ en la clase de matemáticas cuando no comprenden.
9. En el __ de Arte Moderno hay muchas pinturas famosas.
10. Siempre tomo refrescos, pero hoy voy a tomar __ mineral.

## C  Gramática: ¿Qué hacen? (p. 136)

Completa las frases con la forma correcta del verbo entre paréntesis.

1. Yo no (*saber*) qué comer hoy. Voy a (*leer*) el menú.
2. Los estudiantes (*comprender*) al profesor.
3. **A:** Marta, ¿qué (*ver*) en el menú?
   **B:** (*ver*) muchas comidas fantásticas.
4. **A:** Javier, ¿qué (*hacer*) el sábado?
   **B:** (*ir*) a un concierto en el Palacio de Bellas Artes.
5. Pilar y yo siempre (*hacer*) planes para el viernes.
6. **A:** Elena, ¿qué (*ir*) a hacer tú y Jorge hoy?
   **B:** (*ir*) a ir al teatro.
7. Yo siempre (*hacer*) la comida para mi familia.
8. Los estudiantes (*leer*) muchos libros en la clase de inglés.

## D  Gramática: Planes (p. 129)

Según (*according to*) el calendario de Josefina, ¿qué van a hacer ella, sus amigos y su familia? Escribe seis oraciones.

**MODELO**  yo / ver televisión

**El lunes voy a ver televisión.**

| lunes | martes | miércoles | jueves | viernes | sábado | domingo |
|---|---|---|---|---|---|---|
| yo / ver televisión | papá y yo / ir al concierto | Ana y yo / leer libros en la biblioteca | yo / hacer planes con Marcos | Marcos y yo / comer en un restaurante mexicano | mamá y yo / ir a la tienda de ropa | mi familia y yo / estar en el centro |

## E    Cultura: La comida  (p. 132)

How are your eating habits similar to and different from the Mexicans'? Include information from the culture reading "La comida de las tres culturas" to compare and contrast. Use the Venn Diagram. Try to write as much in Spanish as possible.

Yo como          Los mexicanos comen

## Vocabulario

| En la ciudad | En un restaurante | Verbos | Otras expresiones |
|---|---|---|---|
| la avenida | el agua (mineral) | comer | ahora |
| la calle | la bebida | hacer | bueno |
| el centro | la comida | ir a (+ *infinitive*) | el/la cantante |
| el edificio | la ensalada | leer | ¡cómo no! |
| el museo | los frijoles | preguntar | el concierto |
| la plaza | el jugo (de naranja) | saber | de acuerdo |
| el teatro | el menú | tomar | favorito/a |
| la tienda | el/la mesero/a | ¡vamos a (+ *infinitive*)! | grande |
|  | el pescado | ver | hacer una pregunta |
|  | el pollo |  | hoy |
|  | el refresco |  | el momento |
|  |  |  | mucho/a |
|  |  |  | oye |
|  |  |  | pero |
|  |  |  | pues |
|  |  |  | siempre |

## Gramática

### Present tense of -er verbs

Some regular **-er** verbs include *comer, comprender,* and *leer*.

| comer | |
|---|---|
| com**o** | com**emos** |
| com**es** | com**éis** |
| com**e** | com**en** |

### Talking about the future: *ir a* + infinitive

**Ir a** + infinitive is the equivalent to what someone is "going" to do in the near future.

*Voy a ir a la fiesta.*     **I am going to go** to the party.

# *Para concluir*

## Proyectos

### A ¡Manos a la obra! 👥

Mexico City tells its "story" through its three cultures (pre-Hispanic, colonial, modern day). These cultures can be seen in many places around the capital: monuments, museums, green spaces, restaurants, etc. In small groups decide which "culture" you find most interesting and create a tour for the rest of the class. Use online resources and maps to plot your itinerary. Be sure to include visuals for your in-class presentation.

### B En resumen

Copy the diagram below and fill in the boxes in the right-hand column to indicate how each aspect of Mexico City contributes to its story.

| | |
|---|---|
| **el Zócalo** | site of festivals and protests |
| **el Palacio Nacional** | |
| **el Parque de Chapultepec** | |
| **el Museo de Antropología** | |
| **el metro** | |
| **la Plaza de las Tres Culturas** | |
| **la comida** | |
| **el arte de Frida Kahlo** | |

## Extensión

Research another major city in the Spanish-speaking world, and tell its story. Include landmarks and monuments, art, food, and any other items that make it unique.

## C ¡A escribir!

Write a paragraph in Spanish about what you and your friends and family are going to do this week. Use *Actividad D* on p. 143 as a guide to help you get started. Incorporate vocabulary from *Unidad 3* as well as previously learned vocabulary. Include sequencing words to connect your thoughts.

## D   Fechas históricas   Conéctate: la historia

The following years stand out in the history of Mexico City. Research their historical significance and fill in the left side of the chart. Find dates of historical significance for your city or region and fill in the right side of the chart.

| México, D.F. | | Mi ciudad | |
|---|---|---|---|
| Year | Historical significance | Year | Historical significance |
| 1521 | | | |
| 1821 | | | |
| 1910 | | | |
| 1968 | | | |

## E   En el Restaurante Danubio   👥   Conéctate: las matemáticas

You are going out to dine at the *Restaurante Danubio* in Mexico City. Choose what you would like to order. Include a soup or salad, a main course, a beverage, and a dessert. Calculate the total price and include 15% for tax and 15% for tip. Take the total in pesos and convert to U.S. dollars using an online currency converter. Is this similar to the cost of a meal in a restaurant in your area? Provide data to justify your answer. Using your menu selections, role play a restaurant scene with a partner.

## F   Frida Kahlo y Diego Rivera   Conéctate: el arte

Go online and research additional works by Frida Kahlo and Diego Rivera. Choose one piece by each artist and compare and contrast their themes and styles.

### Restaurante Danubio
#### Menú

**Ensaladas**

| | |
|---|---|
| Ensalada mixta | 85 pesos |
| Ensalada especial Danubio | 120 pesos |

**Sopas**

| | |
|---|---|
| Consomé de pollo | 75 pesos |
| Sopa de tomate | 88 pesos |

**Para comer (platos fuertes)**

| | |
|---|---|
| Mojarra (pescado) | 165 pesos |
| Calamares | 190 pesos |
| Filete con champiñones | 180 pesos |
| Filete a la parrilla | 180 pesos |
| Pollo frito | 80 pesos |
| Pollo a la cacerola | 95 pesos |
| Medio pollo | 110 pesos |

**Bebidas**

| | |
|---|---|
| Refrescos | 35 pesos |
| Limonada o Naranjada | 40 pesos |
| Agua mineral | 30 pesos |

**Postre**

| | |
|---|---|
| Helado | 55 pesos |
| Fruta | 50 pesos |

# Vocabulario de la Unidad 3

**a caballo** on horseback *3A*
**a pie** on foot *3A*
**¿adónde?** (to) where? *3A*
el **agua (mineral)** (mineral) water *3B*
**ahora** now *3B*
**al** to the *3A*
el **autobús** bus *3A*
la **avenida** avenue *3B*
el **avión** airplane *3A*
el **banco** bank *3A*
el **barco** boat, ship *3A*
la **bebida** drink *3B*
la **biblioteca** library *3A*
la **bicicleta** bicycle *3A*
**bueno** well, okay *3B*
el **caballo** horse *3A*
la **calle** street *3B*
**caminar** to walk *3A*
el **camión** truck *3A*
el **cantante, la cantante** singer *3B*
el **carro** car *3A*
el **centro** downtown, center *3B*
**cerca (de)** near *3A*
el **cine** movie theater *3A*
la **ciudad** city *3A*
**¡claro!** of course! *3A*
**comer** to eat *3B*
la **comida** food *3B*
**¡cómo no!** of course! *3B*
el **concierto** concert *3B*
**¿cuándo?** when? *3A*
**de acuerdo** agreed, okay *3B*
**del** of the, from the *3A*
el **dentista, la dentista** dentist *3A*
el **edificio** building *3B*
**El gusto es mío.** The pleasure is mine. *3A*
**en** (means of transportation) by *3A*
**en carro** by car *3A*
**encantado/a** delighted *3A*
la **ensalada** salad *3B*
la **escuela** school *3A*
**fantástico/a** fantastic, great *3A*
**favorito/a** favorite *3B*
la **fiesta** party *3A*
los **frijoles** beans *3B*
**grande** big *3B*
**hacer** to do, to make *3B*

**hacer una pregunta** to ask a question *3B*
el **hotel** hotel *3A*
**hoy** today *3B*
**ir** to go *3A*
**ir a** *(+ infinitive)* to be going (to do something) *3B*
el **jugo (de naranja)** (orange) juice *3B*
**le/les/te presento a** let me introduce you to *3A*
**leer** to read *3B*
**lejos (de)** far (from) *3A*
el **médico, la médica** doctor *3A*
el **menú** menu *3B*
el **mesero, la mesera** food server *3B*

el **metro** subway *3A*
el **momento** moment *3B*
la **moto(cicleta)** motorcycle *3A*
**mucho/a** much, a lot of *3B*
el **museo** museum *3B*
la **naranja** orange *3B*
la **oficina** office *3A*
**oye** hey, listen *3B*
el **parque** park *3A*
**para** for, to, in order *3A*
**pero** but *3B*
el **pescado** fish *3B*
la **plaza** plaza, public square *3B*
el **pollo** chicken *3B*
**¿por qué?** why? *3A*
**porque** because *3A*
**preguntar** to ask *3B*
el **problema** problem *3A*
**pues** thus, well, so, then (pause in speech) *3B*

**¿quiénes?** who? (pl.) *3A*
**quieres** (do) you want *3A*
**quiero** I want *3A*
el **refresco** soft drink, refreshment *3B*
el **restaurante** restaurant *3A*
**saber** to know *3B*
**sabes** you know *3A*
**siempre** always *3B*
**simpático/a** nice, pleasant *3A*
**también** also, too *3A*
**Tanto gusto.** So glad (to meet you). *3A*
el **taxi** taxi *3A*
el **teatro** theater *3B*
la **tienda** store *3B*
**tomar** to take; to drink *3B*
el **transporte** transportation *3A*
el **tren** train *3A*
**¡vamos a** *(+ infinitive)*! let's (do something/go somewhere)! *3B*
**¡vamos!** let's go! *3A*
**ver** to see; to watch *3B*
**¿verdad?** right? *3A*

## ¿Sabías que...?

Hispanics highly value group relationships, particularly among family members. Families expand to include extended family and close friends. Emotional support from relatives is an essential part of the culture.

# Unidad

# 4

# La familia y los amigos

Scan the QR code to watch this episode of *El cuarto misterioso*.

**Why do Ana and Conchita go to José's house?**

A. to pick him up for school
B. to take him out to eat
C. to eat lunch at his house

*Essential Question*

**?**

How do cultural values shape relationships in Hispanic countries?

## Mis metas

**Lección A  I will be able to:**

▸ talk about family and relationships

▸ use possessive adjectives to describe relationships among people

▸ talk about what people do using **-ir** verbs

▸ talk about Puerto Rico, its languages, and its people

▸ use **estar** to describe people and things

▸ explain the Hispanic naming tradition

**Lección B  I will be able to:**

▸ talk about activities people like and don't like to do

▸ discuss the role of the family in the Dominican Republic

▸ describe typical Dominican music

▸ describe friends and family

▸ use the verbs **ser** and **estar** correctly

▸ talk about the importance of baseball in the Dominican Republic

Puerto Rico

República Dominicana

What is the name of this fort in San Juan, and why was it built?

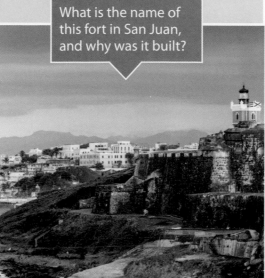

## La familia

**Familia González López**

esposo

Pedro
mi abuelo

Ana María
mi abuela

esposa

**Familia García Paz**

Guillermo
mi abuelo

Patricia
mi abuela

los abuelos

hijos

hijos

Álvaro
mi tío

Cristina
mi tía

Rodrigo
mi padre

Isabel
mi madre

Alejandro
mi tío

Clara
mi tía

hija única

hijos

hijos

Soy José. Esta es mi **familia**.

Sarita
mi prima

José
yo

Mónica
mi hermana

Natalia
mi prima

Enrique
mi primo

los nietos

Sarita, Natalia y Enrique son **los sobrinos** de mis padres.

Esta es **la casa** donde **vivimos**.

| MI FAMILIA | MI ESCUELA | MIS AMIGOS | MIS VACACIONES | MIS VIAJES |

Esta **foto** es de **mis** abuelos; ellos son muy **cariñosos**.

Mi prima Diana es muy **bonita** y **popular**. Siempre **sale** con **sus** amigos.

En esta foto están mis primos, mis tíos favoritos y mis **otros** abuelos.

Me llamo Elisa. Nosotros vivimos en Puerto Rico. Yo **quiero mucho** a **toda** mi familia.

Mi papá y mi hermano van a **la playa** en **el verano**.

## Para conversar

*T*o talk about your relatives:

¿Tienes muchos **parientes**?
*Do you have a lot of relatives?*

José es muy **amable** y **guapo**, pero mi primo Enrique es el **más divertido**.
*José is very nice and handsome, but my cousin Enrique is the most fun.*

Mis abuelos **nunca** están mucho **tiempo** en casa porque salen mucho con sus amigos. ¡**Qué** bueno!
*My grandparents never spend much time at home because they go out a lot with their friends. How great!*

*Tengo muchos parientes.*

### Para decir más

| | |
|---|---|
| el hermanastro | *stepbrother* |
| la hermanastra | *stepsister* |
| el padrastro | *stepfather* |
| la madrastra | *stepmother* |
| el medio hermano | *half brother* |
| la media hermana | *half sister* |
| materno/a | *maternal* |
| paterno/a | *paternal* |

### Un poco más

**Los papás o los padres**

Some people prefer to use the terms *mamá* and *papá* instead of *madre* and *padre*. Regardless of which term you use, when referring to both parents simultaneously, use the masculine plural form: *padres* or *papás* (parents).

*el padre + la madre = los padres*

*el papá + la mamá = los papás*

## 1 ¿Quiénes son?

Completa las oraciones con las palabras del recuadro según la información en el Vocabulario 1.

| | | |
|---|---|---|
| la tía | la hermana | el abuelo |
| el primo | el esposo | la hija |

1. Enrique es __ de José.
2. Isabel es __ de Alejandro.
3. Sarita es __ de Álvaro y Cristina.
4. Pedro es __ de José y Mónica.
5. Clara es __ de Mónica.
6. Guillermo es __ de Patricia.

*¿Qué es José de Enrique?*

## 2 ¿Cierto o falso? 🎧

Di si lo que oyes es **cierto** o **falso**, según la información en el Vocabulario 1. Si es falso, di la respuesta correcta.

## 3 José y su familia

Completa el párrafo sobre José y su familia. Usa expresiones del Vocabulario 1.

Soy José González García. Mi **(1)** se llama Mónica. Ella es muy popular. Mi **(2)**, Sarita, es la hija **(3)** de mi **(4)** Álvaro y mi **(5)** Cristina. Ellos son divertidos. El **(6)** Alejandro es el **(7)** de mi **(8)**, Isabel. Mi **(9)** es Rodrigo. Quiero mucho a mi padre. También quiero mucho a mi **(10)** Pedro. ¡Soy el **(11)** favorito de él!

## 4 ¿Quién es quién?

Empareja cada pregunta de la columna I con la respuesta adecuada de la columna II. Usa el árbol genealógico que aparece en el Vocabulario 1.

*¿Quién es el sobrino de Alejandro?*

**I**

1. ¿Quién es el padre de Enrique?
2. ¿Quiénes son los padres de Sarita?
3. ¿Quiénes son los abuelos maternos (*maternal*) de José?
4. ¿Cómo se llama la mamá del padre de José?
5. ¿Quiénes son las tías de Mónica?
6. ¿Quiénes son los primos de Natalia?
7. ¿Quiénes son los padres de Rodrigo y Cristina?

**II**

A. Álvaro y Cristina
B. Mónica y José
C. Alejandro
D. Pedro y Ana María
E. Ana María
F. Guillermo y Patricia
G. Cristina y Clara

# Diálogo 🎧

## En la fiesta del abuelo

**José:** Hola, Javier. Te presento a mi prima, Julia.

**Julia:** Mucho gusto.

**Javier:** Encantado, Julia.

**José:** Ella es la nieta favorita de mi abuelo Pedro.

**Javier:** Tu abuelo es muy amable.

**Julia:** Sí, y muy cariñoso. Vivimos con él en Puerto Rico todo el verano.

**José:** ¡Mira, allí está el abuelo!

**Javier:** ¡Ay, sí! ¡Allí está! ¿Quiénes están con él?

**Julia:** La señora de rojo es la esposa de mi tío Juan, y la chica de azul es su hija.

**Javier:** ¡Es muy guapa!

## 5 ¿Qué recuerdas? 🎧

1. ¿Cómo se llama la nieta favorita de Pedro?
2. ¿Quién es amable y cariñoso?
3. ¿Quién es la señora de rojo?
4. ¿Quién es la chica de azul?

## 6 Algo personal 🎧

1. ¿Dónde está tu casa? ¿Estás en casa mucho?
2. En tu familia, ¿quién es amable? ¿Divertido/a? ¿Popular?
3. ¿Tienes muchos parientes? ¿Quiénes son?
4. ¿Cómo se llaman tus abuelos? ¿Y tus tíos?
5. ¿Tienes sobrinos? ¿Cómo se llama(n)?
6. ¿Cuántos primos tienes?
7. ¿Quién es tu pariente favorito? ¿Por qué?

# 💬¡Comunicación!

## 7 Parientes favoritos 👥   Interpersonal Communication

Con dos compañeros/as de clase, hablen de un pariente favorito.

**MODELO**
A: Daniel, te presento a Julia, mi prima favorita.
B: Mucho gusto. Y tú, ¿tienes un pariente favorito?
C: Sí, es mi tío Eduardo y es muy divertido.

## 8 ¿Quién es? 🎧

Escucha la información y, luego, escoge la letra de la respuesta correcta.

**A.** Guillermo    **B.** Cristina    **C.** Natalia    **D.** Rodrigo

## Adjectives

You will recall that adjectives (e.g., colors) may be masculine or feminine and singular or plural since they must match the gender and number of the noun they are describing. To make a singular adjective plural, add **-s** if the adjective ends in a vowel or **-es** if the adjective ends in a consonant. Although most adjectives usually follow the nouns they modify, adjectives of quantity such as *cinco, mucho (mucha), otro (otra), todo (toda)*, and words that ask a question precede their nouns but still must agree in number and gender with the nouns they are modifying.

| | |
|---|---|
| *Tod**os** mis prim**os** son divertid**os**.* | All my cousins are fun. |
| *¿Cuánt**as** herman**as** tienes?* | How many sisters do you have? |

### 9 Mi familia en San Juan

Completa las oraciones con la forma apropiada de las palabras en paréntesis.

**MODELO**  Tengo __ parientes en San Juan. (*mucho*)
Tengo **muchos** parientes en San Juan.

1. Mi tía __, Juana, es de San Juan. (*favorito*)
2. ¡Qué __ es mi tía Juana! (*amable*)
3. También tengo dos primas __ en San Juan, Susi y Marina. (*divertido*)
4. Pero no __ mi familia está en San Juan. (*todo*)
5. Mi __ prima, María, está con mi tía, Paula, en Ponce. (*otro*)
6. ¡Qué __ son María y la tía Paula! (*simpático*)
7. La tía María es __. (*cariñoso*)
8. Ella es muy __ también. (*bonito*)
9. Susi, Marina y María son __ populares. (*todo*)
10. Mis primos son unos cantantes __. (*fantástico*)
11. ¡Tengo unos parientes __! (*increíble*)

*Tengo muchos parientes en Puerto Rico.*

*Un poco más*

### Exclamaciones

The word *qué* may be followed by an adjective (or other descriptive phrase) to express strong feelings, much as you might use **How...!** in English: *¡Qué amable!* (How nice!)

# Gramática

## Expressing Possession: Possessive Adjectives

- Possessive adjectives (*adjetivos posesivos*) express possession or describe relationships between or among people. In Spanish, possessive adjectives precede the noun they modify and agree in number with that noun.

| mi(s) | hermano(s) hermana(s) | my | brother(s) sister(s) |
|---|---|---|---|
| tu(s) | tío(s) tía(s) | your (informal) | uncle(s) aunt(s) |
| su(s) | sobrino(s) sobrina(s) | your (formal) | nephew(s) niece(s) |
| su(s) | sobrino(s) sobrina(s) | his | nephew(s) niece(s) |
| su(s) | sobrino(s) sobrina(s) | her | nephew(s) niece(s) |
| nuestro(s) nuestra(s) | hermano(s) hermana(s) | our | brother(s) sister(s) |
| vuestro(s) vuestra(s) | tío(s) tía(s) | your (informal) | uncle(s) aunt(s) |
| su(s) | sobrino(s) sobrina(s) | your (formal) | nephew(s) niece(s) |
| su(s) | sobrino(s) sobrina(s) | their | nephew(s) niece(s) |

**Note:** The forms *nuestro/nuestra* and *vuestro/vuestra* must also agree in gender with the nouns they modify.

| | |
|---|---|
| *Alejandro es **nuestro** tío.* | Alejandro is **our** uncle. |
| *Clara es **nuestra** tía.* | Clara is **our** aunt. |

- To clarify the meaning of *su* and *sus*, or to add emphasis to what you are saying, replace the possessive adjective with *de* plus a pronoun or a person's name.

  *Es **su** tía.* → *Es la tía **de ella**. (Es la tía **de Natalia**.)*

*¿Son ellos tus tíos?*

## 10 ¿Quiénes son? 👥🎧

En parejas, alternen en preguntar y confirmar quiénes son las siguientes personas. (*In pairs, take turns asking and confirming who the following people are.*)

**MODELO** Verónica / hermana

A: ¿**Es Verónica tu hermana?**

B: **Sí, es mi hermana.**

1. Pablo / hermano
2. Rodrigo y José / primos
3. doña Amalia y don Rogelio / abuelos
4. ellas / tías
5. María / sobrina
6. él / tío

## 11 Fotos de mis parientes

Diana and her cousins, Isabel and Rafael, are discussing the photos Diana took with her new smartphone. Complete their conversation with the possessive adjectives indicated by the cues in parentheses.

**MODELO** Isabel: Aquí hay una foto de **nuestros** abuelos en la playa. (*nosotros*)

**Rafael:** Están con **(1)** madre. (*nosotros*)

**Diana:** ¿Hay dos fotos de **(2)** tía? (*yo*)

**Isabel:** Sí. Una con doña Evelina y don Enrique, y otra es con **(3)** padres. (*tú*)

**Rafael:** Aquí están doña Evelina y don Enrique en **(4)** casa nueva. (*ellos*)

**Isabel:** ¿Están todos **(5)** nietos en la foto con ellos? (*ellos*)

**Diana:** No, yo no estoy en la foto y soy **(6)** prima favorita. (*Uds.*)

**Rafael:** Pues, mi foto favorita está aquí con **(7)** hermano, Jenny la *au pair* y yo en el parque. ¡Qué día tan divertido! (*tú*)

## 12 ¿Quiénes son los invitados?

Use the appropriate possessive adjective to complete this guest list for a cookout at your home.

1. Julia y __ amigas, Amy y Paula
2. la Sra. y el Sr. García y __ tres hijos
3. los González y __ sobrino, Enrique
4. Juana Ruiz y __ dos hermanas
5. Amalia y Rogelio de la Torre y __ madre
6. el doctor Diego Fernández y __ familia

*Aquí están nuestros invitados.*

# Gramática

emcpassport.com

WB 6–7
LA 4
GV 7–8

**Repaso rápido**

## Conjugating Regular -er Verbs

In Unit 3 you learned how to conjugate regular **-er** verbs: remove the **-er** and add endings **-o**, **-es**, **-e**, **-emos**, **-éis**, **-en**.

*¿Com**es** en la cafetería de la escuela?*  Do you eat in the school cafeteria?
*Sí com**o** allí. La comida es muy buena.*  Yes, I eat there. The food is really good.

## Saying What Someone Does: Present Tense of -ir Verbs

- To form the present tense of a regular **-ir** verb, such as *vivir* (to live), remove the **-ir** ending and then attach endings that correspond to each of the subject pronouns shown in the chart.

**Note:** The endings are the same as those of *-er* verbs except for *-imos* and *-ís*.

| vivir | | | |
|---|---|---|---|
| yo | **vivo** | nosotros nosotras | **vivimos** |
| tú | **vives** | vosotros vosotras | **vivís** |
| Ud. él ella | **vive** | Uds. ellos ellas | **viven** |

- Another verb that ends in **-ir**, *salir* (to go out, to leave), is regular in all forms except the first-person singular: *yo* **salgo**.

***Salgo** a las dos.*  **I leave** at two.
***Salimos** a las cuatro.*  **We leave** at four.

### 13  ¿Adónde enviar las invitaciones?

Juan's cousin, Sara, is contacting family and friends to invite them to her mother's birthday party. Complete this paragraph with the appropriate forms of the verb *vivir*.

Nosotros **(1)** aquí en San Juan. Los tíos **(2)** cerca de nosotros aquí en la capital, pero los abuelos **(3)** lejos de nosotros en Ponce. La hermana de mi madre, la tía Juana, también **(4)** en San Juan. Mis primos, Clara y Rafael, **(5)** en Mayagüez, pero van a estar en Miami. Noli, mi hermana, **(6)** en Orlando pero va a estar en casa de sus primos, Carmen y Jorge. Ellos **(7)** en Rincón. Y tú, ¿dónde **(8)**? ¿Vienes tú a nuestra fiesta?

*Vivimos en una casa. ¿Dónde vives tú?*

## 14 ¿Dónde viven? 👥 🎧

With a classmate, take turns asking and answering questions about where various people live. Answer using the words in parentheses.

**MODELO** tu hermano (*San Juan*)

A: ¿Dónde vive tu hermano?

B: Vive en San Juan.

1. el hijo único de tu tío Alfonso (*Ponce*)
2. ellos (*una casa grande y nueva*)
3. Hernán (*la casa de su tío*)
4. mi tía (*París*)
5. tu madre y tu padre (*San Juan*)
6. tú (?)

## 15 ¿A qué hora salen? 👥 🎧

Working in pairs, take turns asking and telling when the following people are leaving their houses to arrive on time for the birthday party.

**MODELO**  ¿Los tíos?

A: ¿A qué hora salen los tíos?

B: Ellos salen a las cinco de la tarde.

1. ¿Los abuelos?
2. ¿Nosotros?
3. ¿La madre de una amiga?
4. ¿La tía Rosa y Julia?
5. ¿Tú?

## 🗨 ¡Comunicación!

## 16 ¿Cómo es tu familia? 👥  Interpersonal Communication

With a classmate, talk about your relatives (where they live, what they are like, what they do, and so on). You may wish to include in your questions and answers some of the adjectives you have learned thus far: *amable, bonito, cariñoso, divertido, fantástico, favorito, guapo, popular,* and *simpático*. You can also use expressions from the *Para decir más* box to indicate their professions.

**MODELO** A: ¿Cómo se llama tu tía?

B: Se llama Andrea. Es profesora y vive en Nueva York. Es muy simpática.

### Para decir más

| | |
|---|---|
| el abogado/la abogada | *lawyer* |
| el dentista/la dentista | *dentist* |
| el ingeniero/la ingeniera | *engineer* |
| el médico/la médica | *doctor* |
| el profesor/la profesora | *teacher* |

# ¡Comunicación!

## 17 Tu familia y mi familia  Interpersonal Communication

Imagine you attend school in Puerto Rico. With a classmate, talk about where different members of your family live. Use words from each column to create your sentences. Be sure to use the correct form of the verb *vivir*.

MODELO  A: ¿Dónde viven tus abuelos?
B: Mis abuelos viven cerca de la Playa de Luquillo.

| I | II | III | IV |
|---|---|---|---|
| | | | Bayamón |
| tu primo | | | Mayagüez |
| tus abuelos | | aquí en | Arecibo |
| Uds. | vivir | en | San Juan |
| tus hermanas | | lejos de | el Yunque |
| tú | | cerca de | el Morro |
| tus tíos | | | Ponce |
| | | | la Playa de Luquillo |

# ¡Comunicación!

## 18 ¿Dónde viven?  Presentational Communication

Create a family tree, of your real family or an imaginary one. Use real photos or images from magazines or the Internet. Label each person with a name and a relationship. Be sure to include yourself! Present your "family" to the class and be prepared to answer your classmates' questions like the ones below. Use the expressions in the *Para decir más* box on p. 158 to help with professions.

- ¿Quién es tu prima favorita?
- ¿Cómo se llama tu padre?
- ¿Dónde viven tus abuelos?
- ¿Qué es tu madre? (profesión)
- ¿Cómo es tu abuela?

*Él es mi abuelo.*

## Descubre los dos idiomas de Puerto Rico

*El español de Puerto Rico representa tres culturas.*

Puerto Ricans value preserving the past as well as anticipating the future. Nowhere is this more evident than in their relationship to the two official languages spoken on the island, Spanish and English. The Spanish spoken in Puerto Rico was shaped by a blending of three races: Taíno, Spanish, and African. The English influence is a result of Puerto Rico's status as Commonwealth of the United States and its future relationship with the mainland.

Taíno Indians occupied Puerto Rico when Christopher Columbus arrived to the New World and claimed the island for Spain. Many Taíno words form part of the Puerto Rican vocabulary of today, such as *canoa*, *hamaca*, *maraca*, *güiro*, *iguana*, *manatí*, *barbacoa*, *yuca*, and *huracán*.

The biggest historical influence on the language of Puerto Rico comes from Spain, evidenced in the fact that Spanish was the only official language of the island until the beginning of the 20th century.

The African influence on Puerto Rican Spanish comes from the languages spoken by the slaves brought to the island by the Spaniards in the 16th century. Examples can be seen in terms such as *bomba* (a dance), *congo* (a type of drum), and *mondongo* (tripe soup).

The Puerto Ricans' relationship with English grows stronger every day and will surely continue to grow in the future. As a Commonwealth of the United States, Puerto Rico has adopted English as the other official language of the island, and up to 51 per cent of its residents polled would like to see it as the only one. The English influence can be seen in expressions incorporated literally, like "home run," to words that have been borrowed but given a Spanish "twist" like *lonchar* (to eat lunch) used instead of *almorzar*.

**Q Búsqueda:** languages of puerto rico, santos of puerto rico

### 19 Comprensión

1. What are the two official languages of Puerto Rico?
2. What three cultures in Puerto Rico's history shaped the Spanish spoken there today? Give examples of borrowed words.
3. Describe Puerto Rico's connection to the English language.

### 20 Analiza

1. It is said the essence of a culture is its language. Do you agree? Explain.
2. Why do you think the Three Kings are some of the figures most often represented in the *santos*?

### Productos   Conéctate: el arte

Continuing a Catholic tradition brought over by the Spaniards, the Puerto Ricans in each town established a long-standing relationship with a patron saint who acts on the townspeople's behalf before God. In addition, individual homes have their own patron saint in the form of a *santo* to protect the family. The *santos* are carved religious figures that have been produced since the colonial era by craftsmen called *santeros*. The most popular figures represent male Catholic saints, the Virgin Mary, and the Three Kings.

*Los tres Reyes Magos*

# La isla del encanto y su gente encantadora 🎧

¿Por qué llaman a Puerto Rico "la isla del encanto[1]" y a su gente "encantadora[2]"? Puerto Rico es una isla perfecta para vivir y visitar. El clima, las playas, la fauna, la flora, la música, el arte, la comida, la gente, ¡todo es un encanto!

Los puertorriqueños son personas abiertas y muy amables que valoran sobre todo las relaciones familiares y las relaciones con los amigos. En Puerto Rico y en muchos países hispanos la familia no solamente incluye a los padres y a los hijos sino también a los abuelos, tíos, primos y a miembros de la familia extendida. La familia ofrece un sólido sistema de apoyo[3]. La casa está considerada como el centro principal de la vida social y un lugar de confort, calor y solidaridad familiar. Ocasiones especiales como cumpleaños, bodas[4] y aniversarios se celebran normalmente en la casa y no en lugares públicos.

El Castillo de San Felipe del Morro

Para los puertorriqueños, un típico fin de semana consiste en salir con la familia al cine o a comer. Si son de la capital, San Juan, van a visitar galerías de arte o fortalezas[5] históricas como el Castillo de San Felipe del Morro, construido en 1591 para proteger la isla. También van a comer en familia en los cafés del Viejo San Juan y escuchar conciertos de alegre música caribeña. A muchas familias les gusta pasar el día en playas como la de Luquillo o caminar por parques tropicales como El Yunque.

Deliciosa comida puertorriqueña

[1]enchantment  [2]charming  [3]support  [4]weddings  [5]forts

🔍 **Búsqueda:** el morro, el yunque, viejo san juan, las playas de puerto rico

## Comparaciones

In Latin culture, families celebrate special occasions at home. Where and with whom do you celebrate special occasions?

## Perspectivas

How do Puerto Ricans feel about being a Commonwealth of the United States? Find a recent poll online depicting the percentage of Puerto Ricans who would prefer to be independent versus the percentage of those who are content with the current situation.

## 21 Comprensión   Interpretive Communication

1. What makes Puerto Rico a great place to live and to visit?
2. What do Puerto Ricans value?
3. Give three examples of how Puerto Ricans spend their free time.

## 22 Analiza

1. What is the main idea of the reading?
2. Would you like to live in Puerto Rico? Explain why or why not using information from the readings.

Luquillo, Puerto Rico

# Vocabulario 2

## ¿Cómo están? 🎧

Está abierta.

Está cerrada.

Está cansado.

Está nerviosa.

Están contentos.

Está triste.

Está frío.

Está caliente.

Está enferma.

## Para conversar 🎧

*T*o describe people and things:

Mi padre es médico. Siempre está **ocupado**. Nunca está **libre**.
*My father is a doctor. He is always busy. He is never free.*

Mi madre toma el tren todos los días. Ella siempre está **apurada**.
*My mother takes the train every day. She is always in a hurry.*

Mi hermano está **loco**; nunca estudia para los exámenes.
*My brother is crazy; he never studies for exams.*

La casa de mi tía Sofía siempre está **limpia**, pero su carro siempre está **sucio**.
*My aunt Sofía's house is always clean, but her car is always dirty.*

### Para decir más

| | |
|---|---|
| alegre | *happy* |
| desilusionado/a | *disappointed* |
| enojado/a | *upset* |
| entusiasmado/a | *excited* |
| feliz | *happy* |
| preocupado/a | *worried* |

### 23 ¿Cómo están? 🎧

Selecciona la letra de la ilustración que corresponde con lo que oyes.

A

B

C

D

## ¡Comunicación!

### 24 ¿Cómo está tu familia? 👥 Interpersonal Communication

Find photos in magazines or on the Internet to make flash cards of different moods or conditions from Vocabulario 1. On the back of each card identify what it is in Spanish. With a partner, take turns having short conversations using the illustrations as prompts.

MODELO   A: *(holds up a picture of a woman running after a taxi)*
              ¿Cómo está?
          B: Está apurada.

*Ella está apurada.*

# Diálogo

## ¿Por qué estás triste?

**Javier:**  Julia, ¿por qué estás triste?

**Julia:**  Mi abuelo está enfermo.

**Javier:**  ¿Don Pedro García Montoya?

**Julia:**  Sí, y estoy muy nerviosa.

**Javier:**  Él va a estar bien.

**Julia:**  Gracias. Eres muy amable.

**Javier:**  Bueno, adiós. Estoy apurado.

**Julia:**  ¿Adónde vas?

**Javier:**  Voy a casa, estoy muy cansado.

## 25  ¿Qué recuerdas?

1. ¿Quién está triste?
2. ¿Por qué está triste?
3. ¿Cómo se llama el abuelo?
4. ¿Quién está nervioso?
5. ¿Adónde va Javier?

## 26  Algo personal

1. ¿Estás triste o contento/a? Explica.
2. ¿Estás enfermo/a?

## 27  ¿Cómo están todos?

Listen as several people talk about how they are feeling. Then match the names with the description that fits each person.

1. Ángel
2. Esperanza
3. Benjamín
4. Natalia
5. Josefina
6. Verónica

A. Está contenta.
B. Está muy ocupado.
C. Está nerviosa.
D. Está apurado.
E. Está triste.
F. Está enferma.

*Está nerviosa.*

# Gramática

## Using *estar* to Express Location

In Unit 3 you learned how to use the verb *estar* to express location.

| | |
|---|---|
| ¿Dónde **están** ellos? | Where **are** they? |
| Ellos **están** en el parque. | They **are** at the park. |
| La escuela **está** lejos del parque. | The school **is** far from the park. |
| Mi casa **está** cerca de la biblioteca. | My house is **near** the library. |

## Describing People and Things with *estar*

**Estar** can also be used with adjectives to describe conditions that are likely to change (*caliente, cansado, frío*) or to express how someone or something is at a given moment (*bonito, nervioso, sucio*).

| | |
|---|---|
| El agua **está** caliente. | The water **is** hot. |
| ¿**Está** él triste? | **Is** he sad? |
| Ellos **están** apurados. | They **are** in a hurry. |
| ¡**Estás** muy bonita hoy! | **You are** (look) very pretty today! |
| El carro **está** limpio. | The car **is** clean. |

**Note:** Some adjectives that describe appearance or personality can be used with either **ser** or **estar**, but with a difference in meaning.

| | |
|---|---|
| Elena **está** guapa hoy. | Elena **is** (looks) pretty today. |
| Armando **es** un muchacho guapo. | Armando **is** a good-looking boy. |

## 28 Descripciones

Describe what you see in these photos. Complete the following sentences with the correct form of *estar* and an appropriate adjective.

**1.** Antonio y Carlos __.

**2.** La playa __.

**3.** La comida __.

**4.** Los refrescos __.

**5.** Susana __.

**6.** El profesor Ríos __.

## 29 Un picnic en familia 👥

Your family is having a party at your house, and you have invited one of your friends. Take turns asking a classmate questions about some of the things you see, using the words provided. Answer each question using the cues in parentheses.

**MODELO** estar cansado / tus hermanos (*mi hermana*)

A: ¿Están cansados tus hermanos?

B: No, no están cansados, pero mi hermana está cansada.

1. estar muy enfermo / tu abuelo (*mi abuela*)
2. estar sucio / el carro de tu padre (*el carro de mi tía*)
3. estar apurado por ir al parque / tus primos (*mis tíos*)
4. estar abierta / la puerta del garaje (*ventanas*)
5. estar libre para ir al cine mañana / tú (*mis amigas*)
6. estar triste / tus tíos (*la nueva esposa de mi primo*)
7. estar ocupado / tus hermanas (*tú y yo*)
8. estar nervioso / tus sobrinos (*mi prima*)

## 30 ¿Cómo está tu familia?

Make a list of your family members, including yourself, and tell how each person is feeling today. Then give a reason why the person is feeling that way. You may include some of the following words in your descriptions: *apurado, contento, enfermo, loco, nervioso, triste, ocupado.*

**MODELO** Mi hermana está contenta hoy porque está con sus amigos.

*Mi hermana está contenta porque está con sus amigos.*

## ¡Comunicación!

## 31 ¿Cómo está? 👥 Interpersonal Communication

With a classmate, discuss what you see in the illustration on p. 167. Talk about who the people are and describe how they feel or what condition they are in. You also may ask and answer questions about anything else you see.

**MODELO** A: ¿Cómo está Andrea?

B: Está ocupada.

A: ¿Cuántas personas hay en la casa hoy?

B: Hay cinco personas.

## ¡Comunicación!

### 32 Un juego con estar 👥 Interpersonal Communication

Working in groups, form two concentric circles with three to four students in each circle. Students in the inside circle face students in the outside circle and begin a conversation about their families' health or emotional condition. Next, students in the outer circle move one step to the right and begin a similar conversation with a new partner. Be sure to have a conversation with everyone in the opposing circle.

MODELO
A: Hola, Ana. ¿Qué tal?
B: Estoy bien, pero ocupada. Y tú, ¿cómo estás?
A: Yo estoy bien, gracias. ¿Cómo están tus primos?
B: Están nerviosos porque mañana tienen un examen.

# Repaso de la Lección A

## A Escuchar: ¿Quién es? 🎧 (p. 150)

Escucha las seis oraciones y di si lo que oyes es **cierto** o **falso**.
Corrige las oraciones falsas.

## B Vocabulario: ¿Cómo está? (pp. 162–163)

Completa las oraciones escogiendo un adjetivo correcto de la lista.

| | | |
|---|---|---|
| ocupado/a | enfermo/a | cerrado/a |
| contento/a | cansado/a | nervioso/a |

**MODELO**    Son las ocho, y la clase es a las ocho y cinco. Pedro está **apurado**.

1. Estoy triste porque mi abuela está muy __.

2. Mi papá tiene mucho que hacer; está muy __.

3. Mi hermano está __ porque tiene un examen mañana.

4. Él está __ porque estudia mucho.

5. La puerta está __.

6. Estoy muy __ porque mañana voy a una fiesta.

## C Gramática: ¿Una familia grande? (p. 155)

Completa el párrafo con el adjetivo posesivo apropiado.

Yo tengo dos hermanas muy simpáticas. (**1.** *Sus / Mis*) hermanas se llaman Julia y Marisa. (**2.** *Nuestras / Nuestra*) tía Rita, (**3.** *su / sus*) esposo, Julián, y (**4.** *sus / su*) dos hijos viven con nosotros. Rita es la hermana de (**5.** *su / mi*) padre. (**6.** *Nuestros / Tu*) primos se llaman Ernesto y José y son muy divertidos. Mi amiga Clara siempre me pregunta: "¿Cuántas personas viven en (**7.** *tu / su*) casa?". Y yo siempre contesto: "¡Muchas!, pero me gusta mucho tener una familia grande".

## D Gramática: ¿Estar, vivir o salir? (pp. 157, 165)

Completa las oraciones con la forma correcta de **estar**, **vivir** o **salir**, según el contexto.

1. Mi padre __ muy contento hoy.

2. Yo __ a las 8:30 para el colegio.

3. **A:** Hola chicos, ¿ __ Uds. libres para salir?

   **B:** No, __ muy ocupados.

4. ¿ __ tú en una casa grande?

5. **A:** ¿Por qué __ tú triste hoy?

   **B:** No __ triste; estoy cansada.

6. Las ventanas __ abiertas.

7. **A:** ¿ __ Uds. cerca de Ponce?

   **B:** No, __ lejos de allí.

8. Hoy yo __ muy cansado.

9. ¿ __ Uds. mucho los fines de semana?

10. **A:** ¿Dónde __ tus primos? ¿Lejos?

    **B:** No, ellos __ aquí en Ponce, cerca de mi casa.

## E  Cultura: Descubriendo Puerto Rico

(pp. 160–161)

Completa la gráfica con la información que has leído (*you have read*) sobre Puerto Rico.

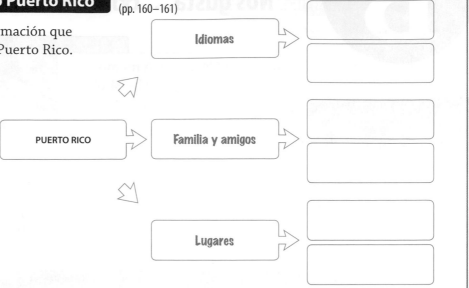

Idiomas

PUERTO RICO

Familia y amigos

Lugares

*El Viejo San Juan en San Juan, Puerto Rico*

## Vocabulario

| Para describir | | Familia | Otras expresiones | Verbos |
|---|---|---|---|---|
| abierto/a | loco/a | el abuelo, la abuela | la casa | salir |
| amable | más | el esposo, la esposa | la foto(grafía) | vivir |
| apurado/a | mi, mis | la familia | mucho | |
| bonito/a | nervioso/a | el hermano, la hermana | nunca | |
| caliente | nuestro(s), nuestra(s) | el hijo, la hija | la playa | |
| cansado/a | ocupado/a | la madre | ¡qué (+ *description*)! | |
| cariñoso/a | otro/a | el nieto, la nieta | el tiempo | |
| cerrado/a | popular | el padre | el verano | |
| contento/a | su, sus | los padres | | |
| divertido/a | sucio/a | el pariente, la pariente | | |
| enfermo/a | todo/a | el primo, la prima | | |
| frío/a | triste | el sobrino, la sobrina | | |
| guapo/a | tu, tus | el tío, la tía | | |
| libre | único/a | | | |
| limpio/a | | | | |

## Gramática

### Expressing possession: possessive adjectives

Possessive adjectives describe relationships among people and must agree in number and gender with the noun.

| Singular possessive adjectives | | Plural possessive adjectives | |
|---|---|---|---|
| mi | nuestro, nuestra | mis | nuestros, nuestras |
| tu | vuestro, vuestra | tus | vuestros, vuestras |
| su | su | sus | sus |

### Describing people and things with *estar*

*Estar* can be used with adjectives to describe conditions that are likely to change or to express how someone or something is at a given moment.

| Regular *-ir* verbs: *vivir* | |
|---|---|
| viv**o** | viv**imos** |
| viv**es** | viv**ís** |
| viv**e** | viv**en** |

*Salir* has an irregular *yo* form ➞ **salgo**.

## Diálogo

### Me gusta mucho

**Andrés:** Felipe, ¡vamos a la playa!

**Felipe:** ¿A la playa? ¿Te gusta la playa?

**Andrés:** Sí, me gusta mucho.

Natalia y otros amigos van a ir allí.

**Felipe:** Bueno, yo quiero ir al partido de fútbol.

**Andrés:** Ah, sí... pero me gusta más nadar.

**Felipe:** A ti no te gusta nadar. A ti te gusta Natalia.

**Andrés:** ¿Por qué no vamos al partido y, luego, a la playa?

**Felipe:** Está bien, chico. ¡Vamos!

### 4  ¿Qué recuerdas?

1. ¿A quién le gusta mucho la playa?
2. ¿Quiénes van a ir a la playa?
3. ¿De qué hay un partido?
4. ¿Qué le gusta a Andrés hacer en la playa?
5. ¿Adónde van los muchachos hoy?

### 5  Algo personal

1. ¿Te gusta ir a la playa?
2. ¿Te gusta ir a los partidos de fútbol?
3. ¿Qué te gusta hacer?

## Estrategia

### Using contextual cues

The context in which a word is used often determines its meaning. One example of this is *chico*, which can mean **boy** or **small**. In the dialogue, however, Felipe uses *chico* as a term of friendship that Andrés does not take literally, much as you might use the word **buddy** or **pal**. Additional terms that are used include *hombre*, *compa* (from *compadre*), *chica*, *niña*, and *guapa* (used among female friends). Other contextual cues include facial expressions and gestures. Looking at the context often indicates the intended meaning of words.

### 6  ¿Qué les gusta?

Write the names Natalia and Andrés. Next, listen and list under each person's name what he or she likes to do. Then circle any item on the lists that they both like to do.

*¿Qué les gusta?*

# Gramática

## Using *gustar* to State Likes and Dislikes

- To talk about what you like or dislike, use the verb *gustar*. Use the words *me, te, le, nos, os,* or *les* before the singular *gusta* to say what someone likes when referring to an infinitive or a singular noun. Use the same *me, te, le, nos, os,* or *les* before *gustan* when referring to a plural noun.

| me | nos | + | gusta *(followed by an infinitive or singular noun)* |
|---|---|---|---|
| te | os | | |
| le | les | | gustan *(followed by a plural noun)* |

| | | |
|---|---|---|
| Singular noun: | *¿Te gusta el libro?* | **Do you like** the book? |
| Plural noun: | *Me gustan todos los libros.* | **I like** all books. |
| Infinitive: | *Me gusta mucho leer.* | **I like** to read a lot. |

**Note:** The verb *gustar* really means "to please" or "to be pleasing." *Me gusta* really means "(Something) is pleasing to me." *Te, nos,* and *os* refer to you, us, and you (pl.) respectively. In the case of *le* and *les*, it is not clear to whom something is pleasing, only that it is one person or more than one. Use context clues to infer.

*Ana va mucho a la playa.* **Le gusta** *nadar.*    Ana goes to the beach a lot. **She likes** to swim.

- Make a sentence negative by placing *no* before *me, te, le, nos, os,* or *les gusta/gustan.*

| | |
|---|---|
| *No me gusta estudiar.* | **I do not like** to study. |
| *¿No te gustan las fotos de Ana?* | **Don't you like** Ana's pictures? |
| *No nos gusta ver televisión.* | **We do not like** to watch t.v. |

---

### 7  ¿Te gusta(n)…? 🎧

Contesta las siguientes preguntas.

1. ¿Te gusta el colegio?
2. ¿Te gusta la clase de español?
3. ¿Te gusta hacer la tarea?
4. ¿Te gustan los sábados?
5. ¿Te gustan los partidos de fútbol en la televisión?

*¿Te gusta ir de compras?*

# ¡Comunicación!

## 8 Gustos 👥 Interpersonal Communication

En parejas, alternen en preguntar y contestar si lo que (*what*) ven en la foto les gusta(n) o no.

**MODELO**    A: ¿Te gusta jugar al tenis?

B: Sí, (No, no) me gusta jugar al tenis.

1

2

3

4

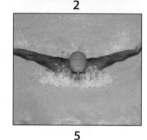

5

6

# ¡Comunicación!

## 9 ¿Qué les gusta hacer? 👥 Presentational Communication

Working in small groups, create a list to conduct a survey of what activities your classmates enjoy. (The list should consist of the same number of activities as there are members in your group.) Each person in your group selects one activity from the list and asks other students in class if they like that activity. Finally, one person from each group should give a summary (*resumen*) of the results of the survey to the class.

**MODELO**    A: ¿Te gusta bailar?

B: Sí, me gusta./No, no me gusta.

Resumen:  A tres estudiantes les gusta bailar y a un estudiante no le gusta escuchar música.

**ENCUESTA**

| ¿Te gusta...? | Sí | No |
|---|---|---|
| 1. bailar | ✓ | |
| 2. escuchar música | | ✓ |
| 3. hacer la tarea | ✓ | |
| 4. jugar al fútbol | ✓ | |
| 5. ir de compras | | |

# Gramática

## Using *a* to Clarify or Emphasize What You Are Saying

You can add **a** plus someone's name, a noun, or a pronoun to clarify an otherwise confusing sentence or to emphasize what you are saying. Look at the following:

| | | |
|---|---|---|
| | **A mí** | **me** *gusta bailar con amigos.* |
| | **A ti** | **te** *gusta bailar con amigos.* |
| singular | **A Ud.** | |
| | **A él** (**A Paco / A tu primo**) | **le** *gusta bailar con amigos.* |
| | **A ella** (**A Tere / A tu amiga**) | |

| | | |
|---|---|---|
| | **A nosotros/as** | **nos** *gusta bailar con amigos.* |
| | **A vosotros/as** | **os** *gusta bailar con amigos.* |
| plural | **A Uds.** | |
| | **A ellos** (**A Paco y a Jorge**) | **les** *gusta bailar con amigos.* |
| | **A ellas** (**A Tere y a Elena**) | |

*A ellos les gusta cantar en inglés.*

### 10  Las preferencias de mis parientes

Completa el siguiente párrafo con la palabra apropiada de cada columna.

| me | |
|---|---|
| te | |
| le | gusta |
| | gustan |
| nos | |
| les | |

En mi casa a todos nosotros **(1)** mucho escuchar música y ver la televisión. A mi papá **(2)** todos los deportes en la televisión, como el fútbol, el béisbol y el básquetbol. A mi mamá **(3)** un programa de música clásica en la radio. A mis hermanos **(4)** los conciertos de rock y de música latina en la televisión pero también **(5)** escuchar música en su MP3. A mamá y a mis hermanas siempre **(6)** un programa de televisión donde hablan de la construcción, de la remodelación y de la decoración de las casas. ¡Es su programa favorito! Personalmente, a mí **(7)** los programas que le permiten a uno comprar por internet productos fantásticos. Y a ti, ¿qué **(8)** escuchar en la radio o ver en la televisión?

## 11 ¿Es claro?

Working in pairs, take turns reading these unclear sentences and clarify them by adding the given cues and making any other changes necessary. Follow the model.

**MODELO**  A: Le gusta escuchar la radio y bailar. (*Diana*)
B: ¿A quién?
A: A Diana le gusta escuchar la radio y bailar.
B: Les gusta bailar merengue. (*mis hermanas*)
A: ¿A quiénes?
B: A mis hermanas les gusta bailar merengue.

1. Les gustan mucho los conciertos de música dominicana. (*los Suárez*)
2. Les gusta ir de compras. (*mis primas*)
3. Le gustan los partidos de béisbol. (*Eduardo*)
4. Le gusta patinar sobre ruedas. (*ella*)
5. Les gusta jugar al tenis. (*Sara y Alberto*)
6. Les gustan mucho las ciudades de Santo Domingo y Puerto Plata en la República Dominicana. (*la Sra. y el Sr. García*)

## 12 ¿Qué les gusta?

The following people all have strong opinions about what they like and what they do not like. In pairs, take turns asking and answering questions using the cues below, clarifying each person's preference.

**MODELO**  ella / nadar / jugar al tenis
A: ¿A ella le gusta nadar?
B: ¡No! ¡A ella no le gusta nadar! Le gusta jugar al tenis.

1. tú / ver televisión / ir al cine
2. Uds. / jugar al fútbol / jugar al béisbol
3. él / tocar el piano / bailar
4. ellas / ir de compras / escuchar música en la radio y cantar
5. los Fernández / las playas de Puerto Rico / las playas de la República Dominicana
6. los estudiantes / contestar en inglés / contestar en español

*Me gustan las playas de la República Dominicana.*

## 13 ¿Les gusta a todos en tu familia?

Working with a classmate, take turns asking and answering questions about what everyone in your family likes to do. If there is someone who does not like an activity that follows, say who that person is.

**MODELO** bailar

A: ¿Les gusta bailar a todos en tu familia?

B: Sí, nos gusta bailar a todos. / No, no nos gusta bailar a todos porque a mi padre no le gusta bailar.

1. ir a restaurantes
2. leer libros
3. pasear en el parque
4. vivir en los Estados Unidos
5. visitar a la familia
6. salir de casa los sábados
7. ir a conciertos de rock

*Nos gusta bailar.*

## 14 Los conozco bien

Name at least six people who are important in your life, and say how you know each person. (They are either family or friends.) Then say something each person likes and at least one thing the person does not like.

**MODELO** A mi amigo Josué le gustan los partidos de béisbol.

No le gusta jugar al tenis.

## ¡Comunicación!

## 15 ¿Qué nos gusta hacer?     Interpersonal Communication

With a classmate, find out four things that both of you like.
Write down your findings using *Nos gusta(n)*.

**MODELO** A: ¿Te gusta cantar?

B: No, no me gusta. ¿A ti te gusta tocar el piano?

A: ¡Sí, claro! Me gusta mucho.

A y B: *Write:* Nos gusta tocar el piano.

*¿Te gusta tocar el piano?*

# ¡Comunicación!

## 16 Me gusta... pero no me gusta...   👥   Interpersonal/Presentational Communication

In small groups, talk about the activities you like most and least. Assign one member of the group to take notes of the group's preferences and dislikes and present the information to the class.

**MODELO**
A: A mí me gusta bailar pero no me gusta cantar. ¿Y a Uds.?

B: A mí me gusta ver la televisión pero no me gusta escuchar la radio.

C: A mí me gusta nadar pero no me gusta patinar sobre ruedas.

B: *Writes and then says:* **A** (*name of student A*) **le gusta bailar pero no le gusta cantar, a** (*name of student C*) **le gusta nadar pero no le gusta patinar sobre ruedas y a mí me gusta ver la televisión pero no me gusta escuchar la radio.**

# ¡Comunicación!

## 17 ¿Qué te gusta?   👥   Presentational Communication

Make a list of seven activities or items that are common in your daily life. Then ask your classmates if they like the activity or item. When you find someone who likes what you named, write his or her name next to the corresponding activity or item. You have ten minutes to locate one person for each activity or item on your list. Next, summarize your findings in several short sentences. Finally, report the results to the class.

*A ellas les gusta ver videos en la tableta.*

**MODELO**   los partidos de tenis

A: **María, ¿te gustan los partidos de tenis?**

B: **Sí, me gustan.**

A: *Writes* **María** *next to* **los partidos de tenis** *and says:* **A María le gustan los partidos de tenis.**

**ENCUESTA**

| ¿Le gusta/Le gustan? | Sí | No | Nombre |
|---|---|---|---|
| 1. los partidos de tenis | ✓ | ◡ | María A. |
| 2. jugar al béisbol | ◡ | ◡ | |
| 3. ... | ◡ | ◡ | |

# La evolución de la familia dominicana

Cultural values include the ideas, customs, and traditions that people have passed down for generations. In the 21st century, modernization, urbanization, and a higher cost of living have affected the lifestyle and customs of cultures around the world. How have these changes affected the family structure and cultural values in the Spanish-speaking world?

One result of societal changes has been that the Hispanic family, traditionally composed of parents, children, grandparents, aunts and uncles, has given way to a smaller, nuclear structure. In the Dominican Republic, households with extended families of seven or more people used to be common. Today the average household consists of 3.5 people. Why is that? Many families have moved from rural areas to urban settings, where jobs are more plentiful but living spaces are smaller, thus unable to accommodate large extended families. Family members might immigrate to other countries seeking better employment opportunities. (The ties to family remain strong, however, as these immigrants send remittances to their relatives back home.) Parents

*Una familia dominicana*

are opting to have fewer children as a result of a higher cost of living. And finally, there is an increasing number of single-parent households, a trend that can be seen in many parts of the world.

Despite this rapid evolution of their society, the *dominicanos* have managed to retain many of their traditional values. Families, although smaller, continue to be centers of supportive relationships among their members. A relaxed and informal lifestyle still promotes close relationships among friends and neighbors. And of course the love of music is as alive as ever, so social gatherings with traditional food and dance are frequent pastimes, both in the home as a center of social life, as well as in clubs and places outside the home.

**Búsqueda:** dominican family lifestyles

### Perspectivas

Read this translation of one blogger's comment during *el Mes de la Familia* in the Dominican Republic: "This is a time to reflect upon and review the values we are instilling in our children and how we are raising our families in a society that each day has become more corrupt, silent and complicit in all that is bad." What does this reveal about the attitude toward family in the Dominican Republic today?

*Una familia dominicana en la playa*

## 18 Comprensión

1. What do cultural values include?
2. How have societal changes affected the Dominican lifestyle and family structure?
3. What traditional Dominican values have not been affected by societal changes?

## 19 Analiza

1. What positive and negative changes do you see in the evolution of the Dominican family?
2. How does the love of music and dance promote positive relationships in the Dominican Republic?

# Dos dominicanos famosos: El merengue y la bachata

¿Cuál es una buena manera de relacionarse con la gente[1]? ¡Cantar y bailar! Y los dominicanos son expertos. Aman la música y el baile. Un artista musical favorito de los dominicanos es Juan Luis Guerra, el cantante de merengue más famoso de la República Dominicana. El merengue es un ritmo antiguo que representa, en sus instrumentos, la mezcla de culturas que forman la identidad dominicana. El acordeón representa la cultura europea; la güira[2], la cultura taína (la cultura indígena); y la tambora[3], la africana. Los dominicanos escuchan y cantan merengue en las tiendas, en los carros, en los restaurantes, en la calle y hasta en el

autobús. Este ritmo divertido invita a bailar en fiestas familiares y en discotecas. Muchos padres y abuelos dominicanos se enamoraron[4] bailando merengue. Hoy el merengue es popular en todo el mundo.

La bachata es un ritmo más moderno que se originó[5] en la República Dominicana en los años 60. La palabra "bachata" tiene su origen en África y se refiere a las fiestas en las calles. A diferencia del merengue, es una música romántica y nostálgica que habla del amor. Los instrumentos de la bachata son la guitarra, la güira, el tambor bongó y las maracas. Al igual que el merengue, sus instrumentos reflejan la influencia europea, taína y africana, una mezcla que forma la identidad dominicana. Hoy en día, la bachata es tan popular como el merengue. ¡En la República Dominicana no hay fiesta sin merengue y bachata!

[1] people   [2] percussion instrument   [3] two-headed drum   [4] fell in love   [5] originated

*Nos gusta bailar el merengue.*

🔍 **Búsqueda:** juan luis guerra, el merengue, la bachata

## Productos 🎧

*Bachata rosa* recibió el Premio Grammy para el Mejor Álbum Latino Tropical Tradicional. Su autor es Juan Luis Guerra. El álbum combina este ritmo antiguo dominicano con el sonido del sintetizador moderno. Vendió (*it sold*) más de cinco millones de copias y popularizó la bachata en todo el mundo.

## Comparaciones

What type of music is currently popular where you live? What do you like about it? Does it promote positive or negative relationships?

## 20 Comprensión   Interpretive Communication

1. Who is Juan Luis Guerra?
2. What cultures influenced the development of *merengue* and *bachata*?
3. What is one difference between *merengue* and *bachata*?

*¿De dónde es Juan Luis Guerra?*

## 21 Analiza

1. Why do you think music and dance are important in the Dominican culture? Do you think music and dance can make a difference in how people relate to each other?
2. Do you think music and dance can promote negative relationships? Explain.

# Vocabulario 2

## ¿Cómo somos? 🎧

| INICIO | MIS ACTIVIDADES | DEPORTES | MIS AMIGOS | MI FAMILIA |
|---|---|---|---|---|

pelirroja

canosa

calvo

rubia

moreno

alto y bajo

cómica

inteligente

tonto

gorda

delgado

importante

buena

malo

rápido

lento

egoísta

generosas

horrible

feo

ideal

## Para conversar 🎧

*T*o talk about likes and dislikes:

Me gusta leer. Es **interesante**.
*I like to read. It is interesting.*

A mí me gusta estudiar español. Es **fácil**.
*I like to study Spanish. It is easy.*

No me gusta ir a partidos de fútbol. Es **aburrido**.
*I don't like to go to soccer games. It is boring.*

A mí no me gusta tocar el piano. Es **difícil**.
*I don't like to play the piano. It is difficult.*

**Para decir más**

| | |
|---|---|
| **flaco/a** | *skinny* |
| **gracioso/a** | *witty* |
| **listo/a** | *clever* |
| **travieso/a** | *mischievous* |
| **veloz** | *fast* |
| **el gato** | *cat* |
| **la mascota** | *pet* |
| **el perro** | *dog* |

### 22  ¿Cómo es? 🎧

Mira las fotos y contesta las preguntas con sí o no, según lo que oyes.

1

2

3

4

5

6

7

8

## ¡Comunicación!

### 23  ¿Quién es y cómo es?   Presentational Communication

Create a chart of six friends or relatives and indicate their relationship to you.
Under each name, write words that describe the person in terms of physical traits
(*características físicas*) and personality traits (*características de personalidad*). Describe
one person from your chart to the class. Bring in a photo of the person you are
describing.

| Nombre | Relación | Características físicas | Características de personalidad |
|---|---|---|---|
| Lisa | Es mi amiga. | Es baja y delgada. | Es cómica y divertida. |

# Diálogo

## ¿Cómo es ella?

**Felipe:**   ¿Cómo es tu amiga Natalia?

**Andrés:**   Es morena y es muy inteligente.

**Felipe:**   ¡Qué bien!

**Andrés:**   Sí, y también es muy guapa.

**Felipe:**   ¿De dónde es ella?

**Andrés:**   Ella es de Santo Domingo.

**Felipe:**   ¡A las muchachas de Santo Domingo les gusta bailar!

**Andrés:**   Sí, ella baila muy bien el merengue. ¡Mira, allí está!

**Felipe:**   ¡Ah, sí!, con la chica pelirroja.

## 24 ¿Qué recuerdas?

1. ¿Cómo es Natalia?
2. ¿De dónde es Natalia?
3. ¿A quiénes les gusta bailar?
4. ¿Con quién está Natalia?

## 25 Algo personal

1. ¿Cómo eres tú?
2. ¿Cómo es tu amigo/a favorito/a?
3. ¿Dónde estás ahora?

## 26 ¿Cuál es el opuesto?

You will hear some descriptions of people and objects. Give the opposite (*el opuesto*) of each adjective you hear.

**MODELO**   gordos

*Ana es morena y Susi es rubia.*

## Ser y estar

You have already seen several forms of the verbs *ser* and *estar*. These verbs are both irregular in the present tense. Here is a review of their forms.

| ser | |
|---|---|
| soy | somos |
| eres | sois |
| es | son |

| estar | |
|---|---|
| estoy | estamos |
| estás | estáis |
| está | están |

### 27 ¿Cómo son?

Describe your relatives, your friends, and yourself, using the appropriate form of **ser** and one or two adjectives. You may make up any of the information you wish.

**¡Ojo!** 👁

Be sure to change the endings on the adjectives (number and gender) to match the person(s) being described.

**MODELO**  el profesor / la profesora de inglés

**El profesor de inglés es calvo y muy divertido.**

1. yo
2. mi madre
3. mis abuelos
4. mi dentista
5. mi amiga favorita
6. los otros estudiantes de la clase de español y yo

### 28 ¿Cómo están en la clase?

Completa las oraciones con la forma apropiada de **estar**.

1. Mi amiga favorita no __ en la clase.
2. Yo __ en mi clase de español ahora.
3. Tres estudiantes __ enfermos hoy.
4. ¿Cómo __ tú hoy?
5. Nosotros __ muy cansados pero también __ contentos porque mañana es sábado.
6. La profesora es simpática y hoy __ muy bonita.
7. La comida __ caliente, pero en diez minutos va a __ fría.
8. Las ciudades de Punta Cana y Puerto Plata __ en la República Dominicana.

*¿Cómo estás?*

# Gramática

## Uses of *ser* and *estar*

Both **ser** and **estar** are equivalent to the English verb **to be**. However, the two verbs are used in very different situations.

- **Ser** may be used to express origin.

  *Soy de Santo Domingo.*          **I am** from Santo Domingo.

- **Ser** is also used to indicate characteristics that distinguish people or objects from one another.

  *Lorenzo es bajo.*          Lorenzo **is** short.

- **Estar** is used to express a temporary condition.

  *¡Qué cansada está hoy!*          How tired **she is** today!

- **Estar** may also refer to where someone or something is located.

  *¿Dónde está la biblioteca?*          Where **is** the library?

**Note:** Although **estar** is generally used to express location, **ser** is used to refer to the location of an event, in which case it means "to take place."

  *¿Dónde es el concierto?*          Where **is** the concert (taking place)?

### 29 ¿Uso *ser* o *estar*?

Usa la forma correcta de **ser** o **estar** para completar las siguientes oraciones.

1. Juan Luis Guerra __ de la República Dominicana.
2. Nosotros __ contentos de estar en familia.
3. Germán __ el tío de Marta.
4. No __ cansado. ¡__ apurado!
5. El carro __ de Ernesto y Gisela.
6. ¿Dónde __ el concierto de merengue?
7. ¡Qué simpática __ tú!
8. Su casa __ en Santo Domingo.

*¿Cómo están Uds.?*

9. ¿ __ (tú) enfermo o __ bien?
10. La ciudad de Santo Domingo __ en la República Dominicana.

### 30 Descripciones

En parejas, describan a las personas de las fotos. Usen oraciones con **ser** y **estar**.

1

2

3

4

# ¡Comunicación!

## 31 Escribe una biografía 👥 Presentational Communication

Bring to class an image from a magazine, an online site, or another source, of a famous person from a Spanish-speaking country (e.g., singer, athlete, television/film star). Next, working in small groups, assign a "biographer" to write down what others say about, and how they describe, each person. (Everyone in the group should have a turn as the biographer.) One student holds up a picture and identifies the person. Each group member (except the biographer for that round) adds a sentence describing that person, and the biographer writes down the information. After the biographies are completed, each member of the group introduces his or her famous person to the class including all of the information the biographer recorded.

Gael García Bernal es un actor guapo y popular.

MODELO
> A: Es Gael García Bernal. Es un actor popular.
>
> B: Es guapo y muy inteligente.
>
> C: Es de México.
>
> D: Sus padres son actores también.

| Nombre | ¿Qué es? | ¿Cómo es? |
|---|---|---|
| Gael García Bernal | Es un actor popular. | Es guapo y muy inteligente. |
| | | |
| | | |
| | | |

# ¡Comunicación!

## 32 Di quién es 👥 Interpersonal Communication

Search the Internet or other source to find out about a celebrity. Find out where the person is from, what the person is like, why the person is famous, and so on. Take notes, and try to include as much information as possible. Do not name the celebrity. Your classmate must ask you a maximum of twenty *sí/no* questions to try to guess the identity of the person. The round ends when your classmate guesses the name of the celebrity. Then switch roles.

### Para decir más

| | |
|---|---|
| actor/actriz | *actor/actress* |
| atleta | *athlete* |
| bailarín/bailarina | *dancer* |
| cantante | *singer* |
| cómico/a | *comedian* |
| coreógrafo/a | *choreographer* |
| músico/a | *musician* |

MODELO
> A: ¿Es de Puerto Rico?　　A: ¿Es rubia?　　A: ¿Es Shakira?
>
> B: No.　　　　　　　　　　B: Sí.　　　　　B: ¡Sí! Es Shakira.
>
> A: ¿Es de Colombia?　　　A: ¿Es cantante?
>
> B: Sí.　　　　　　　　　　B: Sí

# ¡Comunicación!

**33  ¿Quién soy?**  👥  **Interpersonal Communication**

Now it's your turn to be a celebrity. Your classmates will ask you questions using **ser** and **estar** to determine your identity. They may ask where you are from, your basic personal characteristics, your profession, and so on. Here are some possible questions.

- ¿De dónde eres?
- ¿Eres guapo/a? ¿Rubio/a? ¿Moreno/a? ¿Alto/a? ¿Bajo/a?
- ¿Eres actor/actriz? ¿Cantante? ¿Comediante? ¿Atleta?
- ¿Eres muy popular? ¿Dónde?
- ¿Cómo estás hoy? ¿Contento/a? ¿Nervioso/a?
- ¿Estás siempre muy ocupado/a?
- ¿Estás en un programa de televisión? ¿En una película? ¿En un equipo (*team*)?

# ¡Comunicación!

**34  Entrevista**  👥  **Interpersonal/Presentational Communication**

Interview three classmates you do not know well and take notes in a chart like the one below. Ask them the questions in the chart. Then switch roles. Finally, write a summary describing how you are alike and different, making positive statements only. Present the results to the class.

| ¿Cómo te llamas? | ¿Cómo estás hoy? | ¿Cómo eres? | ¿Cómo es tu familia? | ¿Qué te gusta hacer? | ¿Qué no te gusta? |
|---|---|---|---|---|---|
| Mónica | apurada | inteligente | divertida | bailar | patinar sobre ruedas |
|  |  |  |  |  |  |

**MODELO**  Resumen: Mi compañera se llama Mónica. Hoy está apurada. Es inteligente. Su familia es divertida. A Mónica le gusta bailar. No le gusta patinar sobre ruedas.

*¿Cómo es tu familia?*

*¿Qué te gusta hacer?*

*Nos gusta bailar.*

# Todo en contexto

## ¡Comunicación!

### 35 La familia dominicana 👥 Interpersonal Communication

Here is a picture of a traditional Dominican family. With a classmate, take turns pointing to the people in the photo, asking your partner questions about them, and responding to your partner's questions. Keep in mind what you know about Dominican cultural values as you create your questions and descriptions.

Include the following information:

- name (must be in Spanish)
- where he/she is from
- where he/she lives now
- whether he/she lives with other members of the family
- physical description
- personality description
- what he/she likes to do and with whom

*¿Cuántas personas hay en esta familia?*

**MODELO**

A: ¿Cómo se llama?

B: Se llama José Luis Canó.

A: ¿De dónde es?

B: Es de Santo Domingo.

A: ¿Dónde vive?

B: Vive en Punta Cana.

A: ¿Con quiénes vive?

B: Vive con sus hijos y sus nietos.

**República Dominicana**

Puerto Plata
Santiago de los Caballeros
San Juan de la Maguana
★ Santo Domingo
Punta Cana

## ¡Comunicación!

### 36 El merengue en la vida de los dominicanos 👥 Presentational Communication

Merengue is the most popular musical form in the Dominican Republic. You've been asked to make a presentation about it and its influence on the life of Dominicans. In groups of three, use the culture reading *"Dos dominicanos famosos: El merengue y la bachata"* and the Internet to find out more about merengue's origins, instruments, famous songs, renowned interpreters, and places where you can hear it and dance to it. First organize your information and then prepare your presentation. Use visuals and recordings of merengue when you present to the class.

orígenes

canciones

instrumentos

Merengue

cantantes

dónde se escucha y se baila

# Lectura

## Antes de leer

### 37 Preparación 🎧

1. ¿Qué deporte (*sport*) te gusta jugar?
2. ¿Cuál es el deporte más popular donde vives?
3. ¿Te gusta jugar al béisbol?
4. ¿Te gusta ver los partidos de béisbol en vivo o en la televisión?

### Estrategia

**Skimming**

Before beginning to read an article, quickly look over the contents. Skimming through the reading will give you an idea what the article is about and will tell you whether the content interests you or not. To skim the article that follows, read the title and first line or two of each paragraph, note capitalized words, and look for clues in the supportive visuals such as photographs.

### 38 Las Grandes Ligas

Selecciona los equipos de la columna de la derecha que van con las ciudades de la columna de la izquierda.

| I | II |
|---|---|
| 1. Seattle | A. los Medias Blancas |
| 2. Pittsburgh | B. los Bravos |
| 3. Chicago | C. los Cardenales |
| 4. Cincinnati | D. los Indios |
| 5. San Luis | E. los Rojos |
| 6. Oakland | F. los Marineros |
| 7. Boston | G. los Padres |
| 8. San Diego | H. los Medias Rojas |
| 9. Atlanta | I. los Atléticos |
| 10. Cleveland | J. los Piratas |

*Adrián Beltré*

## El béisbol: Un deporte nacional 🎧

El béisbol, o pelota, no solo es un deporte muy popular en los Estados Unidos, también es muy popular en muchos países hispanos, sobre todo en la República Domincana. ¿Sabes cuántos beisbolistas de las Grandes Ligas son dominicanos? ¡Más de 130! Unos muy famosos son David Ortiz (los Medias Rojas de Boston), Alberto Pujols (los Ángeles de Los Ángeles), José Reyes (los Mets de Nueva York) y Adrián Beltré (los Rangers de Texas). En la República Dominicana también hay muchas academias y campamentos de béisbol, donde chicos de varios países aprenden[1] y practican el béisbol.

[1] learn

La familia Martínez tiene dos hijos que juegan al béisbol. Pedro Martínez entra a una academia de béisbol a los 14 años. Unos agentes de las Grandes Ligas de los Estados Unidos visitan la academia para buscar[1] nuevos talentos. Allí ven a Pedro y a su hermano Ramón y firman[2] contratos con los dos. Ramón Martínez se une a[3] los Dodgers de Los Ángeles. Pedro Martínez se une a los Mets de Nueva York y a los Medias Rojas de Boston.

Pedro y Ramón Martínez

Ahora, los hermanos no juegan profesionalmente, pero son administradores. Pedro y su familia tienen una fundación, la Fundación Pedro Martínez y Hermanos. Allí, niños y niñas se educan y se preparan para triunfar no solamente en el béisbol sino[4] en la vida[5]. De los 130 jugadores dominicanos que juegan actualmente[6] en las Grandes Ligas, muchos están allí gracias a fundaciones como la Fundación Pedro Martínez y Hermanos.

Una academia de béisbol en la República Dominicana

[1] to look for  [2] they sign  [3] joins  [4] but  [5] life  [6] now

David Ortiz

🔍 **Búsqueda:** academias de béisbol, beisbolistas dominicanos en las grandes ligas

---

## 39 Comprensión 🎧 Interpretive Communication

1. ¿Cuántos jugadores de béisbol dominicanos hay en las Grandes Ligas?
2. ¿Adónde van los agentes de las Grandes Ligas de Estados Unidos a buscar nuevos talentos?
3. ¿Qué hace la familia Martínez para ayudar (help) a su comunidad?

## 40 Analiza

1. Why do you think there are so many outstanding Dominican ball players in the U.S. leagues?
2. Would you like to attend a baseball camp in the Dominican Republic? Why?
3. In what other Spanish-speaking countries do you think there might be baseball academies? Why?
4. What might make the *Fundación Martínez y Hermanos* different from traditional baseball academies? Do you think this makes it more effective than traditional academies, or less? Why?

Alex Rodríguez, una leyenda del béisbol profesional, es hijo de dominicanos.

## A  Escuchar: ¿Cómo son? 🎧  (pp. 174–175, 185–186)

Selecciona la foto que corresponde con lo que oyes.

| A | B | C | D | E |

## B  Vocabulario: Los opuestos  (pp. 185–186)

Completa las oraciones con el opuesto.

**MODELO**   Esteban es alto, no es **bajo**.

1. El carro de mi papá es rápido, no es __.
2. La clase de matemáticas es difícil, no es __.
3. Mi papá es delgado, no es __.
4. La chica es guapa, no es __.

5. El chico es bueno, no es __.
6. Jugar al fútbol es divertido, no es __.
7. Mi hermana es generosa, no es __.
8. Los estudiantes no son tontos, son __.

## C  Gramática: ¿Qué les gusta?  (pp. 177, 179)

Write sentences using the correct forms of *gustar* and the appropriate indirect object pronouns (*me, te, le, nos, les*).

1. A nosotros / gustar / nadar
2. ¿A Uds. / gustar / el béisbol?
3. A mi hermana / gustar / ir de compras
4. A mí / gustar / los partidos de tenis

5. A Juan Carlos y a Sandra / gustar / cantar
6. A mis padres y a mí / gustar / el merengue
7. A él no / gustar / las tareas difíciles
8. ¿Y a ti / que / gustar / hacer?

## D  Gramática: ¿Ser o estar?  (p. 189)

Completa las oraciones con la forma correcta de **ser** o **estar**.

1. ¿Dónde __ la casa de tu tía?
2. Yo __ de Santo Domingo.
3. Ellos __ contentos de estar en la playa.
4. Yo no __ gordo, __ delgado.
5. ¡Nosotros __ divertidos!

6. Él __ enfermo.
7. ¿Dónde __ el concierto de Juan Luis Guerra?
8. ¿__ Uds. de aquí?
9. ¿Por qué __ Julio triste hoy?
10. __ las tres de la tarde.

## E  Cultura: Valores culturales en la República Dominicana (p. 183)

How have societal changes in the 21st century affected the Dominican family? Refer to the reading *La evolución de la familia domincana* in this unit and search online sources to answer this question. Copy the Venn diagram below and use it to organize your findings.

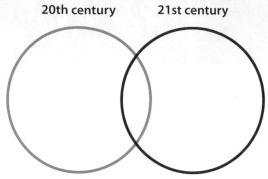

20th century          21st century

## Vocabulario

| Para describir | | Otras expresiones | Verbos |
|---|---|---|---|
| aburrido/a | gordo/a | el béisbol | bailar |
| alto/a | horrible | el fútbol | cantar |
| bajo/a | ideal | me | comprar |
| bueno/a | importante | mí | contestar |
| calvo/a | inteligente | nos | escuchar |
| canoso/a | interesante | el partido | gustar |
| cómico/a | lento/a | el piano | ir de compras |
| delgado/a | malo/a | la radio | jugar (ue) |
| difícil | moreno/a | la tarea | jugar a (+ *sport/game*) |
| egoísta | pelirrojo/a | la televisión | mirar |
| fácil | rápido/a | el tenis | nadar |
| feo/a | rubio/a | ti | patinar (sobre ruedas) |
| generoso/a | tonto/a | | tocar |
| | | | ver (la televisión) |

## Gramática

### Using *gustar* to state likes and dislikes

| **Singular** – followed by an infinitive verb or singular noun | | **Plural** – followed by a plural noun | |
|---|---|---|---|
| **Me gusta** el libro. | **Nos gusta** bailar. | **Me gustan** los libros. | **Nos gustan** las computadoras. |
| **Te gusta** comer. | **Os gusta** el español. | **Te gustan** los frijoles. | **Os gustan** los zapatos. |
| **Le gusta** el tenis. | **Les gusta** hablar. | **Le gustan** los discos compactos. | **Les gustan** las camisas. |

### *Ser* vs. *estar*

| When to use *ser* | When to use *estar* |
|---|---|
| Origin – **Soy** de Colombia. | Temporary condition – **Estoy** enfermo. |
| Characteristic – *Él* **es** bajo. | Location – **Estás** en Nueva York. |
| Location of an event – *La fiesta* **es** en la casa de Antonio. | |

# *Para concluir*

## Proyectos

### A ¡Manos a la obra! 👥

With a group of classmates, pretend you are members of an extended Spanish-speaking family from either Puerto Rico or the Dominican Republic. Each student should choose one member of the family and prepare a description of the person, stressing several physical and personality traits, and some likes and dislikes. Point out some things that make you similar or different from other members of the "family," as well as activities you do together, and where and when you do them. Then introduce yourselves to the class as a family, with each member in turn talking briefly about him or herself. Be sure to give yourselves Spanish names.

**MODELO**   Me llamo Julia Ogando. Soy de Santo Domingo pero ahora vivo en Puerto Plata. Estoy muy contenta porque vivo con mis hijos y nietos. A mí me gusta Puerto Plata porque tiene playas muy bonitas y a mí me gusta nadar y caminar por la playa. Soy una persona muy cariñosa y me gusta jugar con mis nietos.

*Una familia dominicana*

### B En resumen 👥

In *Unidad 4* you have learned how cultural values shape relationships in Puerto Rico and the Dominican Republic. Use the chart below to organize the information you have gathered. Work with a classmate to review the values mentioned in the readings on pp. 160–161 and 183–184, and show how they affect relationships in one or both of the countries studied in the unit. The first one has been done for you as an example. When you have completed the chart, share your ideas with another pair.

| Los valores | Las relaciones |
|---|---|
| the past | Puerto Ricans stay connected to their Taíno, African, and Spanish heritage by keeping those influences alive through language. |
| family | |
| traditions | |
| the present | |
| music | |
| the future | |

## ¿Sabías que...?

Everybody loves a celebration! Spanish-speaking countries seem to celebrate holidays almost every month. There are civic holidays, historic holidays, patron saint holidays. Nicaragua even has a holiday that involves dogs and one to celebrate its national poet, Rubén Darío.

# 5

# La rutina y la diversión

Scan the QR code to watch this episode of *El cuarto misterioso*.

**What is happening in this scene?**

A. Un mariachi toca en la boda de Conchita.

B. Un mariachi toca para la fiesta de cumpleaños de Conchita.

C. Un mariachi toca para la fiesta de Ana.

## *Pregunta clave*

**?**

How do key activities in a society reflect its values?

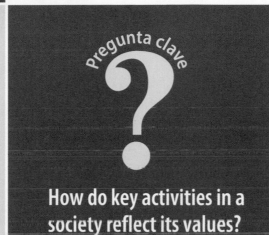

Why are these dogs dressed up, and where are they going?

Nicaragua    Costa Rica

## *Mis metas*

**Lección A   I will be able to:**

▶ identify objects in an electronics store

▶ talk about what people have using the verb **tener**

▶ express strong feelings using **¡Qué** + adjective/noun**!**

▶ discuss how nature conservation and political neutrality are present in Costa Rica

▶ describe activities for the coming week

▶ use the personal **a** when needed in front of direct objects

▶ use direct object pronouns

▶ discuss Monteverde Cloud Forest Reserve in Costa Rica

**Lección B   I will be able to:**

▶ talk about holidays and celebrations

▶ tell where someone comes from using the verb **venir**

▶ describe festivals in Nicaragua

▶ talk about the months of the year and birthdays

▶ count using numbers from 101 to 999,999

▶ ask for and give the date

▶ discuss Rubén Darío and the annual celebration in his honor

### Todo en electrónicos

Me llamo Esteban. Mis **compañeros** y yo **pasamos** mucho tiempo en la tienda de **artículos electrónicos.**

Nos gusta **entrar** a ver los artículos nuevos **que** tienen **cada semana.**

la tableta

el estéreo

los audífonos

la consola de juegos

el quemador de CDs

el reproductor de MP3

¿Va a comprar el DVD?

¡Caramba! No tengo mucho dinero.

el dinero

el reproductor de CDs

el reproductor de DVDs

el DVD

## Para conversar 🎧

$T$o ask for items in a store:

Perdón, **buscamos** el CD de **canciones** de **la película** *Estoy loco de **amor** por tí.* ¿Lo **tienen**?
*Excuse me, we are looking for the CD with songs from the movie I Am Crazy in Love with You. Do you have it?*

¡Claro que lo tenemos!
*Of course we have it!*

¡**Qué sorpresa**! A ver **si** también tienen el DVD de la película.
*What a surprise! Let's see if you also have the DVD of the movie.*

No, no lo tenemos en este momento.
*No, we don't have it at the moment.*

¡**Qué lástima**!
*What a shame!*

### Para decir más

| | |
|---|---|
| la aplicación/el app | *app* |
| el blog | *blog* |
| el grabador de video digital | *digital video recorder (DVR)* |
| los videojuegos | *videogames* |
| descargar música | *to download music* |
| Me lo llevo. | *I'll take (buy) it.* |

### 1 ¿Cuál es el intruso?

Busca al intruso y explica por qué.

**MODELO** estéreo / compañeros / audífonos

**compañeros: Estéreo y audífonos son artículos electrónicos.**

1. amor / pasar / entrar
2. CDs / DVDs / semana
3. CD / dinero / DVD
4. ¡Qué lástima! / ¿Qué tal? / ¡Qué sorpresa!
5. consola de juegos / reproductor de CDs / canciones
6. reproductor de MP3 / reproductor de DVDs / tableta

*¿Qué videojuegos te gustan?*

### 2 ¿Qué es? 👥

Find photos in magazines or online to make flash cards of different kinds of electronic equipment. On the back of each, write the name in Spanish. With a partner take turns having short conversations and using the photos as props.

**MODELO** A: *(hold up a picture of a CD burner)* ¿Qué es?

B: **Es un quemador de CDs.**

## 3 ¿Qué buscan? 🎧

Selecciona la foto que corresponde con lo que oyes.

**A**

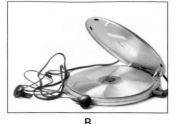

**B**

**C**

**D**

**E**

**F**

## 4 Completa las frases

Completa en forma lógica las frases de la izquierda con las frases de la derecha.

**1.** Buscamos el DVD...

**2.** Nosotros pasamos...

**3.** No sabemos si...

**4.** ¡Qué lástima! No tenemos...

**5.** El chico entra...

**6.** ¡Caramba! No tengo dinero...

**A.** ...para comprar la tableta.

**B.** ...a la tienda de artículos electrónicos.

**C.** ...el CD con la canción *Locos de amor*.

**D.** ...tiempo cada semana en la tienda de artículos electrónicos.

**E.** ...de la película *Locos de amor*.

**F.** ...tienen audífonos para reproductores de MP3.

*A mí me gusta escuchar música en mi reproductor de MP3.*

# Diálogo

## Me gustan las tiendas

**Marta:** Vamos a ver si tienen el CD de Alejandro Sanz en la tienda.

**Sofía:** ¿Otra tienda? No tenemos más dinero.

**Marta:** Solo quiero mirar si tienen el disco compacto.

Buenas. Buscamos el CD de Alejandro Sanz.

**Señor:** No, no tenemos CDs de Alejandro Sanz.

**Marta:** ¡Qué lástima! Bueno, gracias.

**Sofía:** ¡Ahora sí! ¡Vamos a casa!

**Marta:** No. ¿Por qué no vamos a otra tienda?

**Sofía:** ¡Caramba! ¡Qué sorpresa!

## 5 ¿Qué recuerdas?

1. ¿Qué van a ver Marta y Sofía si tienen en la tienda de artículos electrónicos?
2. ¿Tienen el CD de Alejandro Sanz en la tienda de artículos electrónicos?
3. ¿A quién le gustan las tiendas?
4. ¿Van a casa las chicas?

*¿Tienes un CD de Alejandro Sanz?*

## 6 Algo personal

1. ¿Cuál es tu disco compacto favorito?
2. ¿Qué canción te gusta? ¿Por qué?
3. ¿Te gustan las tiendas de artículos electrónicos? Explica.
4. ¿Qué artículos electrónicos tienes en casa?

## ¡Comunicación!

## 7 ¿Y tú? **Presentational Communication**

yo          mi compañero/a

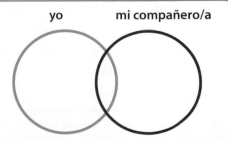

Pregúntale a tu compañero/a las mismas preguntas de la Actividad 6 y anota sus respuestas. Luego usa un diagrama de Venn para comparar tus respuestas y las respuestas de tu compañero/a. Haz una presentación a la clase con los resultados.

**MODELO** Nuestro CD favorito es. . .

# Gramática

## Saying What Someone Has: *tener*

- The verb **tener** (to have) is an irregular verb.

| tener | | | |
|---|---|---|---|
| yo | **tengo** | nosotros<br>nosotras | **tenemos** |
| tú | **tienes** | vosotros<br>vosotras | **tenéis** |
| Ud.<br>él<br>ella | **tiene** | Uds.<br>ellos<br>ellas | **tienen** |

| | |
|---|---|
| *Tengo una consola de juegos nueva.* | **I have** a new gaming console. |
| *Mi tío tiene mucho dinero.* | My uncle **has** a lot of money. |

- **Tener** is sometimes used in Spanish expressions where the verb **to be** is used in English. One such expression is *tener* (+ number) *años*, which you have already used to talk about someone's age.

| | |
|---|---|
| *¿Cuántos años **tienes**?* | How old **are you**? |
| *Tengo veinte años.* | **I am** twenty years old. |
| *¿Cuántos años **tienen** Uds.?* | How old **are you**? |
| *Tenemos quince años.* | **We are** fifteen years old. |

## 8 Un DVD para Sara

Completa el diálogo con las formas apropiadas de **tener**.

**Esteban:** Quiero ver si la tienda de artículos electrónicos **(1)** un DVD para Sara.

**Paula:** ¿Qué DVD buscas?

**Esteban:** Ella no **(2)** el nuevo DVD de la película de Leo DiCaprio.

**Paula:** Bueno, vamos a preguntar.

**Esteban:** Hola, señor. ¿**(3)** Uds. el nuevo DVD de la última película de Leo DiCaprio?

**Señor:** Nosotros **(4)** muchos DVDs, pero no **(5)** el DVD de la última película de Leo DiCaprio.

**Esteban:** ¡Caramba! ¡Qué lástima! Muchas gracias.

**Paula:** Son las siete, nosotros **(6)** una hora. ¿Vamos a otra tienda?

**Esteban:** Está bien, pero sabes, yo **(7)** un problema. No **(8)** dinero. ¿Cuánto **(9)** tú?

**Paula:** Pues, Esteban, yo tampoco **(10)** dinero.

*¿Qué DVDs tienes?*

## 9 ¿Qué tienen todos?

Working in pairs, take turns asking one another questions about what various people have. Answer according to the photos, adding any details you wish.

MODELO    don Manuel

        A: ¿Qué tiene don Manuel?

        B: Tiene un DVD de la película de Matt Damon.

**1.** tú

**2.** Sandra y su hermano

**3.** yo

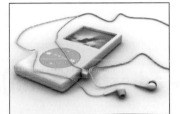

**4.** Ud.

**5.** Emilia y Anita

**6.** nosotros

## 10 ¿Cuántos años tienen?   Conéctate: las matemáticas

Di cuántos años tienen las siguientes personas de acuerdo al año en que nacieron (*were born*).

**1.** Kathy / 1961

**2.** Doña Marta / 1927

**3.** Daniel y Estefanía / 2002

**4.** Keeley / 1989

**5.** Rafael y Gustavo / 1976

**6.** el Sr. Cortés / 1956

**7.** yo / 1953

**8.** tú / ?

## ¡Comunicación!

## 11 Tengo mucha música   Interpersonal Communication

Working in pairs, talk about your interests in entertainment, such as what kind of music and films you like, how many CDs of different types of music you have, which CDs or DVDs you have, and what equipment you use to play them. Try to determine what interests you have in common (*en común*) and how your interests differ. Be creative!

MODELO    A: ¿Te gusta la música hip hop?

        B: Sí, me gusta mucho. Tengo muchas canciones en mi reproductor de MP3. ¿A ti te gusta?

# Gramática

## 12 Tenemos en casa... 👥  Interpersonal Communication

Working in small groups, take turns talking about your families' entertainment preferences. First, mention specific people in your families. Then tell family members' favorite music, television and radio programs (programas de televisión y radio), electronic games, and movies. Finally, be sure to include what kind of electronics your families have for their entertainment preferences.

**MODELO**

A: Tengo dos hermanos. Les gusta jugar con su consola de juegos y ver películas en la tableta. ¿Tienes hermanos?

B: Yo tengo un hermano. Le gusta escuchar música indie en su reproductor de MP3 y ver películas en DVD. ¿Y en tu familia?

C: Yo no tengo hermanos, pero tengo muchos tíos. A ellos les gustan los CDs de música clásica.

## Expressing Strong Feelings with ¡Qué (+ adjective/noun)!

There are times when you may wish to express strong feelings—both positive and negative—about something or someone. In Spanish, use **qué** followed by an adjective as the equivalent of **How...!** Similarly, when **qué** is followed by a person, place, or thing, it is equivalent to **What a...!**

| ¡**Qué** (+ adjective)! | ¡**Qué** (+ noun)! |
|---|---|
| ¡**Qué** fantástico!   **How** fantastic! | ¡**Qué** película!   **What a** movie! |
| ¡**Qué** aburrido!   **How** boring! | ¡**Qué** lástima!   **What a** shame! |

## 13 ¿Cómo reaccionas?

Using qué and an adjective or noun, react to the following circumstances.

**MODELO**   A good friend buys you a gift card to download music.
¡Qué amable!

1. You are watching a very funny movie.
2. It is very hot outside.
3. You just dropped a brand new MP3 player in a bathtub full of water.
4. Your parents tell you some really sad news.
5. You have just learned how to use your new smartphone.

## 14 ¿Qué opinas?

Write captions for the following photos, using *qué* plus a noun.

MODELO   ¡Qué reproductor de MP3!

1

2

3

4

5

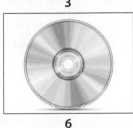

6

## 15 Me gusta

The following people have just purchased some new items. Say what they have and express how much you like each purchase.

MODELO   Beatriz / una tableta nueva
**Beatriz tiene una tableta nueva. ¡Qué tableta!**

1. mis primos / un estéreo nuevo
2. Carmen / una computadora rápida
3. Alicia / dos DVDs fantásticos
4. los Vargas / un carro BMW rápido
5. tú / un CD nuevo de Juanes
6. Ud. / una casa bonita

## ¡Comunicación!

## 16 ¡Qué tienda tan chévere!   Interpersonal/Presentational Communication

With a partner, create a dialogue about shopping in an electronics store that carries computers, DVD and CD players, gaming consoles, and other electronic equipment. Express how you feel about each item and add any other details you wish. Be creative! Then perform the dialogue in front of the class.

MODELO   A: Oye, Juan. ¡Mira! ¡Qué estéreo!
B: Sí, muy bonito, pero es mucho dinero. Roberto tiene uno.

Aguas termales de Arenal

# Costa Rica: País pequeño[1] pero de gran riqueza[2]

**?Pregunta clave**

How do key activities in a society reflect its values?

Are you adventurous? If you like activities such as zip-lining over a cloud forest, spotting tropical wildlife, visiting an active volcano, or kayaking in a mangrove, Costa Rica is your place! When Christopher Columbus disembarked in Cariari (now the city of Puerto Limón) in 1502, he named the land *Costa Rica* (rich coast) because he thought the area offered a wealth of gold and silver. Today, this small Central American country has wealth of other kinds: fertile soil, over half a million species of wildlife, and abundant rivers that provide 90 percent of the country's electricity. Costa Rica can also be proud of its thriving democracy and its well-educated and peace-loving population.

*Ticos* (Costa Ricans) are very appreciative of their natural resources. They have a system of incentives that has helped reduce deforestation to almost zero. They maintain the largest percentage of protected areas in the world (a full 25 percent of their total area is natural parks and wildlife refuges), and they have made ecotourism into a booming business. Locals and visitors admire jaguars, tapirs, giant green turtles, several unique monkey species, and stunning birds, such as the quetzal and the scarlet macaw. Whales are seen breaching off the coast, and frogs come in shades of green, blue, red, brown, yellow, and black. Locals and guests can also visit the Arenal Volcano and its nearby hot springs for some relaxation after a day of taking in the sights of Costa Rica.

In addition to tourism, other important industries add to the wealth of this small country: agriculture, particularly coffee and bananas; pharmaceuticals; and electronics. Costa Rica: a small country rich in human and natural resources.

[1] small    [2] wealth

**Búsqueda:** costa rica nature, ecotourism, arenal

## 17  Comprensión

1. What are two important characteristics of the Costa Rican people?
2. How is Costa Rica a "wealthy" country?
3. What industries does Costa Rica have in addition to tourism?

## 18  Analiza

1. What role does wildlife play in Costa Rica's environment and economy?
2. What values are reflected in the reading *"Costa Rica: País pequeño pero de gran riqueza"*? Does the United States share any of those same values? Explain.

## Prácticas

Costa Ricans use their own regional words and expressions. For example, they refer to themselves as *ticos* or *ticas*, which is a typical ending they add to everyday words (*chico* → *chiqui***tico**). You might also hear the phrase *pura vida* (pure life), which is a very popular positive reaction to almost any situation.

Other popular expressions:

| | |
|---|---|
| **¡Buena nota!** | *Okay!* |
| **el chunche** | *thing (whatchamacallit)* |
| **maje** | *buddy, pal* |

## Comparaciones

What special words and expressions do you and your friends use when talking to each other? Would people outside your region and/or age group understand them?

# Costa Rica: Un país pacífico y patriótico 🎧

Un día en 1948, el presidente de Costa Rica, José Figueres Ferrer, declaró el fin del ejército[1] en el país. Años después, en 1987, el presidente Óscar Arias Sánchez recibió el Premio Nobel de la Paz por su participación en los procesos de paz en América Central. Hoy en día Costa Rica tiene otro tipo de ejército: uno de profesores y estudiantes para "batallar" contra la ignorancia y la pobreza[2]. El dinero que ya no usan para armas ahora lo usan para la educación y la cultura. Costa Rica invierte[3] más dinero en educación que cualquier otro país de América Latina. Actualmente[4], aproximadamente el 95 por ciento de la población adulta sabe leer y escribir.

*Los niños celebran el Día de la Independencia en Costa Rica.*

Los costarricenses valoran la paz y la educación, y aman[5] su país. Todo esto se ve cuando Costa Rica celebra su Día de la Independencia el 15 de septiembre. Ese día en las calles hay desfiles[6] de estudiantes, bailes típicos y bandas de colegio. La noche del 14 de septiembre, los niños y niñas desfilan con faroles[7] de colores. Con estas y otras costumbres, los costarricenses expresan el amor por su nación.

[1]army   [2]poverty   [3]invests   [4]currently   [5]love   [6]parades   [7]lanterns

🔍 **Búsqueda:** josé figueres ferrer, óscar arias sánchez, faroles de color costa rica

## Perspectivas

*El Museo Nacional de Costa Rica en San José*

In 1950, a fortress in San José, which formerly housed the country's military headquarters, became the official site of the *Museo Nacional de Costa Rica*. What values of the Costa Rican people does this conversion reveal?

## Productos 🎧

En el delta del río (*river*) Diquis, en el oeste de Costa Rica, hay unas misteriosas esferas de piedra (*stone*). Son el producto de civilizaciones indígenas antiguas. Su forma es perfecta y su diámetro varía desde pocos centímetros hasta 2,5 metros. Unas pesan (*weigh*) 16 toneladas. Las esferas son un ejemplo del arte y la tecnología precolombina pero no sabemos qué representan ni por qué están allí.

*Esferas de piedra precolombinas*

## 19 Comprensión   Interpretive Communication

1. What did Costa Rican President Figueres Ferrer declare in December 1948?
2. What types of "battles" would be fought from then on?
3. How do Costa Ricans celebrate Independence Day?

## 20 Analiza

Try to imagine what the ancient stone spheres were used for in pre-Columbian times (prior to 1492).

# Vocabulario 2

## ¡Qué semana tan ocupada!

INICIO | **MIS ACTIVIDADES** | DEPORTES | MIS AMIGOS | MI FAMILIA

Me llamo Sarita. Siempre estoy **tan** ocupada. Me gusta mucho escuchar música, **hacer deporte**, leer y hablar por teléfono **todos los días**.

¿Qué **actividades** haces en la semana?

### UNA SEMANA TÍPICA

**LUNES**

ir a **la práctica** de fútbol

**MARTES**

ir a **la librería** a comprar libros

**MIÉRCOLES**

**montar** en bicicleta con unos compañeros

**JUEVES**

ir a la práctica de tenis

**VIERNES**

**llamar** a Julián por teléfono ¿**Lo** llamo el viernes o el sábado?

Los viernes estoy **un poco** cansada, pero necesito hacer las tareas para el lunes.

### EL FIN DE SEMANA

**SÁBADO**

pasar la tarde en el parque con mi **gata** y mi **perro**

**DOMINGO**

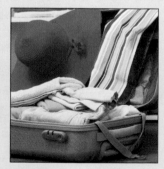

llamar a preguntar a qué hora **abren** la tienda "Su Música" el domingo

hacer **la maleta** para ir a visitar a los abuelos ¡Sé que **me** quieren ver!

## Para conversar

**T**o talk about what you are going to do:

¿Qué vas a hacer el fin de semana **que viene**?

*What are you going to do next weekend?*

Voy a **hacer un viaje** con mis padres, pero **primero** necesito una maleta nueva.

*I am going to take a trip with my parents, but first I need a new suitcase.*

¿Qué vas a hacer con tu perro? ¿Lo **llevas**?

*What are you going to do with your dog? Are you taking him?*

### Para decir más

| | |
|---|---|
| viajar | *to travel* |
| antes | *before* |
| durante | *during* |
| después | *afterwards* |
| el próximo fin de semana | *next weekend* |
| abierto/a | *open* |
| cerrado/a | *closed* |
| segundo | *second* |

---

### 21 Las actividades de Javier la semana que viene

Selecciona la letra de la foto que corresponde con lo que oyes.

**A**

**B**

**C**

**D**

**E**

**F**

---

### 22 El horario de Cristina

Unscramble the following sentences to find out about a typical week in Cristina's life.

**MODELO**   el lunes / de tenis / práctica / tiene
**El lunes tiene práctica de tenis.**

1. tiene / el martes / un partido de fútbol

2. en bicicleta / monta / el miércoles / con unas compañeras

3. el jueves / con una amiga / de compras / va / a la librería

4. un examen de inglés / el viernes / tiene

5. hace / el sábado / para / la maleta / ir de viaje / a Limón

6. de la película / compra / nuevo / el DVD / el domingo / de Cameron Diaz

# Diálogo

## La semana que viene

**Marta:** ¡Caramba, tico! Estoy tan ocupada la semana que viene.

**Tomás:** ¿Por qué? ¿Qué vas a hacer?

**Marta:** El lunes voy a estudiar para el examen de biología.

**Tomás:** Yo también, pero estoy un poco cansado.

**Marta:** El martes tengo práctica de tenis y, luego, de fútbol.

**Tomás:** ¡Pues, Marta, te gusta hacer muchos deportes!

**Marta:** El miércoles voy a la librería y el sábado voy a hacer un viaje.

**Tomás:** ¿Adónde vas?

**Marta:** A casa de mi tía en Puntarenas. ¡Ay! La voy a llamar. Adiós.

**Tomás:** ¡Adiós! ¡Qué semana!

## 23 ¿Qué recuerdas?

1. ¿Quién está muy ocupada la semana que viene?
2. ¿Qué va a hacer Marta primero?
3. ¿Quién está un poco cansado?
4. ¿Qué deportes le gusta hacer a Marta?
5. ¿Adónde tiene que ir de viaje Marta?

## 24 Algo personal

1. ¿Estás un poco cansado/a hoy? Explica.
2. ¿Te gustan los deportes? ¿Cuáles?
3. ¿Qué haces primero los fines de semana? ¿Y luego?

¿Te gusta jugar al fútbol?

## 25 ¿Cuándo?

Marta dice lo que tiene que hacer. Indica el día en que va a hacerlo, según el diálogo.

| lunes | martes | miércoles | jueves | viernes | sábado |
|-------|--------|-----------|--------|---------|--------|

## 26 Las actividades de Tomás

Escribe en una hoja de papel lo que vas a escuchar.

# Gramática

## Direct Objects and the Personal *a*

- A direct object (*complemento directo*) is the person or thing in a sentence that receives the action of the verb directly and answers the question **what?** or **whom?**

- Add the word **a** (called the *a personal*) before any direct object that refers to a person. Note, however, that you should not use the *a personal* with the verb *tener*.

| | | |
|---|---|---|
| *Veo la tableta.* | (I see **what?**) | I see the tablet. |
| *Veo **a** Miguel.* | (I see **whom?**) | I see Miguel. |
| *Tomás tiene dos hermanas.* | (He has **what?**) | Tomás has two sisters. |

**Note:** Some people place an **a** in front of a direct object that refers to a pet they consider part of the family.

*Veo **al** perro.*    I see the dog.

---

### 27 Busca el complemento directo

Indica el complemento directo en las siguientes oraciones.

**MODELO**    Hago **la tarea** en la biblioteca.

1. Mis padres hacen la maleta para su viaje.
2. Elisa ve películas en DVD los fines de semana.
3. Mis amigas y yo compramos ropa en la tienda de moda.
4. Miras fotos en tu tableta.
5. Tú y Juan escuchan canciones en el reproductor de MP3.
6. Mi hermano Pepe toca el piano.
7. Ud. y el profesor Gutiérrez abren sus clases a las ocho menos cuarto.
8. Llamamos a nuestros abuelos los fines de semana.
9. Voy a comprar los audífonos si no necesito mucho dinero.

### 28 ¿A quién veo?

Completa las siguientes oraciones con la **a** personal cuando sea necesario.

1. ¿Tienes __ tres hermanos?
2. Voy a llamar __ mi primo el lunes.
3. Sí, quiero __ mi mamá.
4. Llevo __ mi primo al colegio.
5. ¿Te gusta escuchar __ música en un reproductor de MP3?
6. El sábado voy a ver __ una película en mi nuevo reproductor de DVD.

*Veo a mi gato.*

7. Veo __ mis abuelos cada semana.
8. Llevo __ mi gato a casa de mis padres.
9. Busco __ un quemador de CDs.
10. Mi padre busca __ mi madre en la tienda.

# Gramática

## Direct Object Pronouns

- The following direct object pronouns (*pronombres de complemento directo*) can replace a direct object if the direct object has already been stated or if it is understood. The pronoun must agree in number and gender with the direct object it is replacing or to which it is referring.

| Los pronombres de complemento directo | | | |
|---|---|---|---|
| **me** | *me* | **nos** | *us* |
| **te** | *you* (tú) | **os** | *you* (vosotros/as) |
| **lo** | *him, it, you* (Ud.) | **los** | *them, you* (Uds.) |
| **la** | *her, it, you* (Ud.) | **las** | *them, you* (Uds.) |

- Notice in the following examples that direct object pronouns usually precede the conjugated form of the verb, and any negative expressions (such as *no* or *nunca*) are placed before the object pronouns. In addition, the direct object pronouns **lo**, **la**, **los**, and **las** can refer to either people or objects.

| | |
|---|---|
| *¿**Me** llamas?* | You'll call **me**? |
| *Sí, yo **te** llamo.* | Yes, I'll call **you**. |
| *¿Dónde está Eva? No **la** veo.* | Where is Eva? I don't see **her**. |
| *Busco el DVD y el CD. No **los** veo.* | I'm looking for the CD and the DVD. I don't see **them**. |

- Sometimes the direct object pronoun **lo** is used to refer to a nonspecific direct object or a direct object that is expressed as an idea or a phrase (instead of a person or object).

| | |
|---|---|
| *¿Sabes dónde está el gato?* | Do you know where the cat is? |
| *No, no **lo** sé.* | No, I don't know (**it**). |

---

### 29  ¡Sí, los veo! 👥 🎧

With a classmate, take turns asking and answering whether or not you can see the following from where you are sitting.

**MODELO**  A: ¿Ves la puerta?
B: Sí, (No, no) la veo.
A: ¿Ves los marcadores?
B: Sí, (No, no) los veo.

1. ¿Ves la pizarra?
2. ¿Ves el pupitre?
3. ¿Ves las revistas?
4. ¿Ves la computadora?

5. ¿Ves los libros de español?
6. ¿Ves el reloj?
7. ¿Ves el mapa?
8. ¿Me ves?

## 30  Mi fin de semana

Completa el párrafo, eligiendo de las siguientes palabras.

| me | nos | la |
|----|-----|-----|
| las | lo | los |

Este fin de semana voy a ir a Puntarenas para estar con mis abuelos. No **(1)** veo mucho porque mi familia y yo vivimos en San José. Pero ellos **(2)** ven en el verano porque les gusta ir a la capital. A mí me gusta pasar tiempo en Puntarenas porque mi abuelo Raúl **(3)** comprende. A él le gusta mucho la música y **(4)** toca también en el piano. Las canciones de amor son sus canciones favoritas. Siempre **(5)** canta. También compra muchos CDs y **(6)** escucha todos los días. Mi abuelo Raúl es muy cariñoso. ¡**(7)** quiero mucho!

### Estrategia

**Avoiding interference with English**

Try to avoid letting English interfere with new structures and vocabulary that you are learning in Spanish. For example, the pronouns *lo* and *la* are the Spanish equivalents of the English pronoun **it** only when it functions as a direct object of the verb. When it is the subject of a sentence, the Spanish subject pronoun is omitted.

¿**Lo** ves?  Do you see **it**?

No, no **lo** veo.  No, I do not see **it**.

but:

No está aquí.  **It** is not here.

Es bonito.  **It** is pretty.

## 31  Unas preguntas

Alterna con un(a) compañero/a de clase en hacer y contestar las siguientes preguntas.

1. ¿A quién ves ahora?
2. ¿Buscas a tus amigos los fines de semana para escuchar CDs?
3. ¿A quién llamas hoy por teléfono?
4. ¿A quién escribes un correo electrónico hoy?
5. ¿Comprendes a tu profesor(a) de español?
6. ¿Ves a tus amigos todos los días?

*Veo a mis padres todos los días.*

## 32  ¿Qué haces todos los días?

Trabajando con un compañero o una compañera, contesta las siguientes preguntas. Usa **lo**, **los**, **la** o **las** para las respuestas.

MODELO  A: ¿Practicas tenis todos los días?
B: Sí, (No, no) lo practico.

1. ¿Llevas a tu perro a caminar todos los días?
2. ¿Montas en bicicleta todos los días?
3. ¿Lees revistas en español todos los días?
4. ¿Escuchas discos compactos de tu cantante favorito/a todos los días?
5. ¿Llamas a tus parientes todos los días?
6. ¿Cantas canciones de amor todos los días?
7. ¿Ves películas en DVD todos los días?

# Todo en contexto

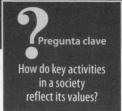
## ¡Comunicación!

### 33 Divertido y educativo 👥 Presentational Communication

Imagine that you and a friend are making plans to visit Costa Rica. Discuss with your classmate what you are going to do to prepare for the trip, things you will need to take, places you will visit, and activities to do there. Then make a presentation to the class. Include visuals, such as an itinerary (include pre-planning and the actual trip) and photos (from magazines or the Internet) with captions to identify items needed for the trip, places you will visit, and activities you will do there. Use words from the word bank and/or consult the Internet to help you with your presentation.

reproductor de MP3    llamar    nadar    visitar un parque natural

dinero    maleta    fin de semana    hacer ecoturismo

ver animales    buscar    teléfono celular    ir a la playa

## ¡Comunicación!

### 34 ¡Yo soy tico! 👥 Interpersonal Communication

Working in pairs, imagine you are a *tico* or *tica* and your classmate is from the United States. Investigate a museum and a typical festival in Costa Rica. In a conversation, tell your friend that you want to visit this museum. Explain where it is and when you will go. Tell one thing you would like (*me gustaría*) to see or do there that is important to you as a *tico*. Then, tell what the typical festival is, when and where you are going to go, and something you would like to do or see there. Switch roles. A table like the one below may help you put your ideas in order.

| | |
|---|---|
| Nombre del museo | |
| Dónde está | |
| Cuándo voy a ir | |
| Qué voy a ver o hacer | |
| Nombre del festival | |
| Dónde y cuándo es | |
| Qué voy a ver o hacer | |

*Museo de Arte Costarricense en San José*

# Lectura informativa

## Antes de leer

1. Have you ever done any kind of extreme sport? What did you think of the experience?

2. Have you ever visited a natural park or wildlife reserve? Where? What did you see there?

## Unas vacaciones de aventura

*El ocelote es un felino de las Américas.*

*Volando sobre el bosque nuboso*

### Estrategia

**Illustrations**

When reading about an unfamiliar topic, be sure to study any photos, illustrations, and captions first. These will give you important clues about the subject and may explain some vocabulary terms.

*Un puente sobre el bosque*

¿Te gustan las actividades extremas? ¡Visita el Parque Natural Monteverde en Costa Rica! Este bosque nuboso[1] es una aventura, pero también es una reserva biológica y un santuario de la flora y la fauna.

**Qué hacer:** Si te gusta sentir[2] la adrenalina en tus venas, ¿qué tal volar[3] sobre la selva suspendido en un cable? ¿O en un columpio[4] gigante? Si prefieres ir a pie, puedes[5] pasar por una serie de puentes increíbles. Los puentes se extienden a altitudes de 12 a 60 metros sobre cañones, bosques y ríos. ¡Y su longitud es hasta 170 metros! Abajo[6] viven grandes felinos como jaguares y ocelotes, aves exóticas como el quetzal y el tucán, y anfibios como la rana "blue jeans". Si te gusta salir

*Un tucán en el bosque nuboso de Monteverde*

*Una rana "blue jeans"*

de noche, puedes caminar por la selva y admirar la fauna nocturna, como insectos, tarántulas, serpientes y armadillos.

Y lo más importante: Lleva tu cámara. Te prometemos que tus fotos van a ser ¡espectaculares!

[1] cloud forest   [2] feel   [3] flying   [4] swing   [5] you can   [6] below

**Búsqueda:** parque natural monteverde, flora y fauna costarricense

---

### 35 Comprensión | Interpretive Communication

1. What is *el Parque Natural Monteverde?* What can you do there?

2. What are three ways to see the forest from above?

3. Name four kinds of wildlife you can see in the park.

### 36 Analiza

How do the activities at Monteverde reflect Costa Ricans' values?

*Un colibrí* (hummingbird) *de Costa Rica*

## Extensión

Because of its location and climate, Costa Rica is home to an astounding variety of species. Some have names almost as intriguing as the animals themselves, like glass frog, howler monkey, bellbird, white-faced capuchin, and olingo. Research these animals and explain the origin of their names.

**Búsqueda:** wildlife costa rica

# ✎Escritura

**37  Mi excursión de ecoturismo**    **Presentational Communication**

Plan your own three-day nature trip to Costa Rica. Research online a place that offers ecotourism with activities that are interesting and educational. Write a day-by-day itinerary describing what you are going to see and do each morning, afternoon, and evening of the visit. Photos or illustrations with captions may help clarify your location and activities for your classmates. Use a chart like the one below to organize your ideas. Then present your report to the class.

### Para escribir más

| | |
|---|---|
| conocer | *to see for the first time* |
| disfrutar | *to enjoy* |
| explorar | *to explore* |
| visitar | *to visit* |
| las aves | *birds* |
| la naturaleza | *nature* |
| las plantas | *plants* |

## Mi visita a _____

| Día | Horas | Actividades |
|---|---|---|
| viernes | mañana | |
| | tarde | |
| | noche | |

# Repaso de la Lección A

## A Escuchar: ¿Quién busca qué? 🎧 (pp. 202–203)

Write the names Marcos and Sofía. Next, listen and list under their names what they are looking for at an electronics store. Then circle any items on the lists that are the same.

| Marcos | Sofía |
|--------|-------|
|        |       |

## B Gramática: Un DVD para Gloria (p. 206)

Completa el diálogo con las formas apropiadas de **tener**.

**Maripili:** Voy a ver si la tienda de artículos electrónicos **(1)** un DVD para Gloria.

**Inés:** ¿**(2)** dinero?

**Maripili:** No, no **(3)** mucho, pero sé que a ella le gusta Chris Pine y no **(4)** su nueva película.

**Inés:** Muy bien, vamos a preguntar.

**Maripili:** Buenos días, señor. ¿**(5)** Uds. la nueva película de Chris Pine en DVD?

**Señor:** Nosotros **(6)** muchos DVDs, pero no el de la nueva película de Chris Pine.

**Maripili:** ¡Qué lástima! Muchas gracias.

## C Gramática: Respuesta apropiada (p. 208)

Contesta las preguntas de la izquierda con la respuesta más apropiada de la derecha.

1. ¿Vamos a jugar al tenis?                         A. ¡Qué computadora!
2. Mis audífonos están en el agua.                  B. ¡Qué amable!
3. Sé cómo usar mi nuevo quemador de CDs.           C. No, amigo. ¡Qué cansado estoy!
4. Aquí tienes el libro que necesitas.              D. ¡Qué horrible!
5. Tengo una computadora rápida.                    E. ¡Qué fantástico!

## D Gramática: ¿Qué buscan? (p. 216)

Completa los diálogos con el pronombre de complemento directo (*direct object pronoun*) apropiado.

1. A: ¿Buscas tus audífonos?
   B: Sí, ___ busco.

2. A: ¿Buscas a tu gato?
   B: No, no ___ busco. Aquí está.

3. A: ¿Buscas tu tableta?
   B: Sí, ___ busco.

4. A: ¿___ buscas? Estoy aquí.
   B: No, yo no ___ busco.

5. A: ¿Buscas tu dinero?
   B: Sí, ___ busco. ¿Sabes donde está?

6. A: ¿___ buscan Uds.? Estamos aquí.
   B: Sí, ___ buscamos.

7. A: ¿Buscas tus CDs?
   B: No, no ___ busco.

8. A: ¿Buscas a tus compañeras?
   B: Sí ___ busco. ¿Dónde están?

The *cultura* readings about Costa Rica make several assertions about this Central American country. Reread the pages carefully and pick out at least two sentences that make specific claims. Use a graphic organizer like the one shown to write the topic, the claims, and also the arguments offered in support of each one. Do you find that each claim is adequately supported by one or more convincing arguments?

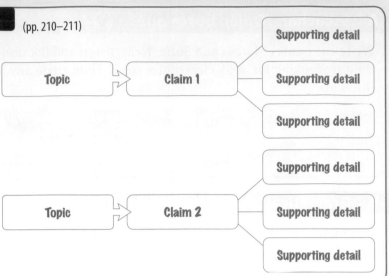

## Vocabulario

| Actividades | Artículos electrónicos | Otras expresiones | | Pronombres |
|---|---|---|---|---|
| la actividad | | el amor | un poco | la |
| (hacer) el deporte | el artículo electrónico | cada | primero | las |
| (hacer) la maleta | los audífonos | la canción | que | lo |
| (hacer) el viaje | la consola de juegos | ¡caramba! | ¡qué (+ *noun/adjective*)! | los |
| (ir a) la librería | el DVD | el compañero, la | que viene | me |
| (ir a) la práctica | el estéreo | compañera | la semana | nos |
| | el quemador de CDs | el dinero | si | te |
| | la película | el fin de semana | la sorpresa | |
| | el reproductor de CDs/ | el gato, la gata | tan | |
| | DVDs/MP3 | la lástima | tener (+ *number*) años | **Verbos** |
| | la tableta | la maleta | todos los días | abrir |
| | | el perro, la perra | | buscar |
| | | | | entrar |
| | | | | llamar |
| | | | | llevar |
| | | | | montar |
| | | | | pasar |
| | | | | tener |

## Gramática

| tener | |
|---|---|
| tengo | tenemos |
| tienes | tenéis |
| tiene | tienen |

Remember to use *tener* + number to indicate someone's age.

> *Marta tiene 15 años.*   Marta is 15 years old.

### Expressing strong feelings with *¡Qué* + (adjective/noun)*!*

In Spanish, to express strong feelings about something or someone, use the construction *¡Qué* + (adjective/noun)*!*

> *¡Qué bueno!*   How great!
> *¡Qué camisa!*   What a shirt!

### Direct object pronouns

Direct objects answer the questions **What?** or **Whom?** in a sentence. Direct object pronouns can be used to substitute the direct object in a sentence if the direct object has already been stated or is implied. *Lo, la, los,* and *las* may replace people or things, and they must agree in number and gender with the direct object they are replacing.

| singular | plural |
|---|---|
| me | nos |
| te | os |
| lo | los |
| la | las |

## Lección B

# Vocabulario 1

Nicaragua

emcpassport.com

WB 1–2
LA 1
GV 1–2

## ¿Qué fecha celebramos? 🎧

Me llamo Paula. Soy de Managua. El martes, 2 de **diciembre**, **fue** mi **cumpleaños**.

| DICIEMBRE | | | | | | |
|---|---|---|---|---|---|---|
| LUNES | MARTES | MIÉRCOLES | JUEVES | VIERNES | SÁBADO | DOMINGO |
| 1 | 2 | 3 HOY | 4 | 5 | 6 | 7 |
| 8 | 9 | 10 | 11 | 12 | 13 | 14 |
| 15 | 16 | 17 | 18 | 19 | 20 | 21 |
| 22 | 23 | 24 | 🎄25 | 26 | 27 | 28 |
| 29 | 30 | 🎉31 | | | | |

Mis primos y mis amigos siempre **vienen** a mi fiesta de cumpleaños.

El lunes **primero** de diciembre fue el cumpleaños de mi hermanito **menor**.

El cumpleaños de mi tía es el primero de enero, el día de **Año Nuevo**.

Mi hermana **mayor** y yo vamos a hacer las compras de **Navidad** por la computadora. ¡El 25 de diciembre viene pronto!

**Temprano** en la mañana del 25, toda mi familia **celebra** la Navidad en casa de mis abuelos.

Mis amigos y yo celebramos la noche de fin de **año** en la plaza.

## Para conversar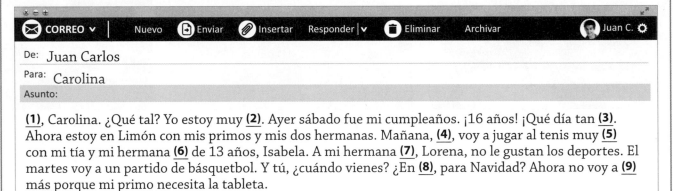

**T**o ask what day it was:

¿Qué día fue **ayer**?
*What day was yesterday?*

¿Qué día fue **anteayer**?
*What day was the day
before yesterday?*

**T**o ask about a future date:

¿Qué día es tu
cumpleaños?
*What day is your birthday?*

Es **pasado mañana**.
*It's the day after tomorrow.*

## 1 ¿Qué día es?

Escoge una respuesta correcta a cada pregunta que escuchas.

1. **A.** Navidad
   **B.** Año Nuevo
   **C.** mi cumpleaños

2. **A.** sábado
   **B.** lunes
   **C.** viernes

3. **A.** sábado
   **B.** martes
   **C.** jueves

4. **A.** miércoles
   **B.** sábado
   **C.** domingo

5. **A.** 24 de diciembre
   **B.** 25 de diciembre
   **C.** 31 de diciembre

## 2 Un correo electrónico

Juan Carlos escribe a su amiga Carolina. Completa el correo electrónico de una manera lógica.

| ✉ CORREO ﹀ | Nuevo | ▣ Enviar | ✏ Insertar | Responder ﹀ | 🗑 Eliminar | Archivar | Juan C. ⚙ |
|---|---|---|---|---|---|---|---|

De: Juan Carlos
Para: Carolina
Asunto:

**(1)**, Carolina. ¿Qué tal? Yo estoy muy **(2)**. Ayer sábado fue mi cumpleaños. ¡16 años! ¡Qué día tan **(3)**. Ahora estoy en Limón con mis primos y mis dos hermanas. Mañana, **(4)**, voy a jugar al tenis muy **(5)** con mi tía y mi hermana **(6)** de 13 años, Isabela. A mi hermana **(7)**, Lorena, no le gustan los deportes. El martes voy a un partido de básquetbol. Y tú, ¿cuándo vienes? ¿En **(8)**, para Navidad? Ahora no voy a **(9)** más porque mi primo necesita la tableta.
Adiós,
Juan Carlos

## 3 Las fechas

Contesta las siguientes preguntas.

1. Si hoy es jueves, ¿qué día es mañana?
2. Si hoy es jueves, ¿qué día es pasado mañana?
3. Si hoy es jueves, ¿qué día fue ayer?
4. Si hoy es jueves, ¿qué día fue anteayer?
5. Si ayer fue domingo, ¿qué día es hoy?
6. Si mañana es martes, ¿qué día fue ayer?
7. Si hoy es miércoles, ¿qué día es mañana?
8. ¿Qué día es hoy?

# Diálogo

## ¿Cuándo es tu cumpleaños?

**Isabel:**   Oye, Sergio, ¿cuándo es tu cumpleaños?

**Sergio:**   ¡Chica! ¡Mi cumpleaños es pasado mañana!

**Isabel:**   ¡Ay, sí!

**Darío:**   Y, ¿cómo lo vas a celebrar?

**Sergio:**   Voy a tener una fiesta. Mi hermano mayor viene de Arizona. Mis primos van a estar aquí también.

**Isabel:**   ¡Fantástico!

**Darío:**   ¿Y cuándo viene tu hermano Jaime?

**Sergio:**   Viene mañana temprano.

**Isabel:**   ¿Y tu hermana menor?

**Sergio:**   Ella está en la Florida, pero viene para la Navidad.

## 4   ¿Qué recuerdas?

1. ¿Cuándo es el cumpleaños de Sergio?
2. ¿Cómo va a celebrar su cumpleaños?
3. ¿Quién viene de Arizona?
4. ¿Cuándo viene Jaime?
5. ¿Dónde está la hermana menor de Sergio?

## 5   Algo personal

1. ¿Cómo vas a celebrar tu cumpleaños este año?
2. ¿Celebras los cumpleaños con tu familia?
3. ¿Tienes un(a) hermano/a mayor? ¿Menor? ¿Cómo se llama?

## 6   ¿Cuál es la respuesta?

Escoge una respuesta correcta a lo que escuchas.

1. **A.** mi hermano mayor          **B.** mi hermano menor
2. **A.** el jueves                 **B.** el domingo
3. **A.** el 25 de diciembre        **B.** el 31 de diciembre
4. **A.** su hermano mayor          **B.** su hermano menor
5. **A.** el viernes                **B.** el sábado
6. **A.** el día de Navidad         **B.** el día de Año Nuevo

*¡Feliz cumpleaños!*

# Gramática

## Telling Where Someone Is Coming From: *venir*

- The present tense of **venir** (to come) is very similar to that of the irregular verb *tener*.

| venir | | | |
|---|---|---|---|
| yo | **vengo** | nosotros<br>nosotras | **venimos** |
| tú | **vienes** | vosotros<br>vosotras | **venís** |
| Ud.<br>él<br>ella | **viene** | Uds.<br>ellos<br>ellas | **vienen** |

- Use **venir** to tell that someone is coming to a place or an event.

| | |
|---|---|
| *Ellos **vienen** a mi casa para la Navidad.* | **They are coming** to my house for Christmas. |
| *¿**Vienes** tú para el Año Nuevo?* | **Are you coming** for New Year's Day? |

- Use **venir de** to tell where someone comes from or is coming from.

| | |
|---|---|
| *¿**De** dónde **vienen** Uds?* | Where **do you come from**? |
| ***Venimos de** Managua.* | **We come from** Managua. |
| *¿**De** dónde **vienes**, Alex?* | Where **are you coming from**, Alex? |
| ***Vengo de** la fiesta de fin de año.* | **I'm coming from** the New Year's Eve party. |

### Un poco más

**¿Ir o venir?**

In English, the verbs to go and to come are used interchangeably. You can say "I'm going to your house" or "I'm coming to your house." Unlike English, **ir** and **venir** are not interchangeable in Spanish. How do you know when to use each? The rule of thumb is to use **ir** to indicate movement toward a location away from the speaker: *Voy a la casa de mi amigo.* Use **venir** to indicate movement toward the place where the speaker is (meaning "here"): *Mis amigos vienen a mi casa.*

*¿Vienes al cumpleaños de la abuela?*

### 7 Vamos a celebrar el cumpleaños de la abuela

Completa el párrafo que sigue con las formas apropiadas de **venir**.

Pasado mañana es el cumpleaños de la abuela. Va a cumplir ochenta años y hay una fiesta grande en mi casa. Pero, ¿cómo **(1)** todos a la fiesta? Pues, mis tíos y mis primos **(2)** en carro de León. ¡Mi tío siempre **(3)** a celebrar el cumpleaños de la abuela! Francisca, la nieta favorita de la abuela, **(4)** en avión de Costa Rica. Doris y Leonardo **(5)** de Granada el día de la fiesta. El tío Ricardo **(6)** en bicicleta porque también vive muy, muy cerca. Y tú, ¿cómo **(7)**? Yo no **(8)** porque vivo aquí.

## 8 La fiesta de Año Nuevo

Sergio's parents are having a New Year's party. Working in pairs, take turns asking and answering how each of the guests will arrive. Include an appropriate means of transportation (*a pie, en autobús, bicicleta, carro, metro, taxi*) in your answers.

*Tú vienes en metro.*

**MODELO**   A: **¿Cómo vienen tus abuelos a la fiesta?**

   B: **Mis abuelos vienen en taxi.**

1. los tíos
2. Isabel y tu hermana
3. Darío
4. el primo de Sergio

5. los padres de Sergio
6. mis abuelos
7. yo
8. tú

## 9 ¿A qué hora y de dónde?

Several people are arriving at Augusto C. Sandino International Airport in Managua, Nicaragua. Tell where they are coming from and at what time, according to the information.

**MODELO**   yo / Santa María / 8:30 AM

**Yo vengo de Santa María a las ocho y media de la mañana.**

1. la familia Torres / Matagalpa / 2:45 PM
2. el señor Peralta y su esposa / Somoto / 7:15 AM
3. tú / Rivas / 10:50 AM
4. mis abuelos / Palo Blanco / 12:00 PM
5. la señorita Ochoa / Estelí / 5:25 AM
6. mi amigo Óscar / Somotillo / 9:15 PM

## 10 ¿Ir o venir?

Completa las siguientes oraciones con la forma correcta de **ir** o **venir** según el contexto.

1. Mis abuelos__ a mi casa el fin de semana.
2. ¿ __ tú a la fiesta de Carmen el sábado?
3. Tú y yo __ al museo esta tarde.
4. ¿ __ Uds. a mi fiesta de cumpleaños el domingo?
5. Mañana, yo __ a un restaurante con mis padres.
6. Marisa no__ a nuestra fiesta de fin de año.

## Present Tense to Indicate the Future

- You have learned to use the present tense of a verb to say what people are doing now or what they do frequently.

- The present tense of a verb can also be used to refer to the not-too-distant future as long as a future time expression is used.

| | |
|---|---|
| Ella **viene** a mi casa el fin de semana. | She **is coming** to my house on the weekend. |
| Mañana **celebro** mi cumpleaños. | Tomorrow **I am celebrating** my birthday. |
| ¿**Estás** en casa el domingo? | **Will you be** home on Sunday? |
| Laura **va** a la fiesta el sábado. | Laura **is going** to the party on Saturday. |

## 11 El concierto navideño 👥

Pretend that you and your partner are in charge of the invitations for the Christmas holiday concert at your school. Using this incomplete invitation list, take turns asking and answering questions about who is attending on Saturday night and who is attending on Sunday night.

**MODELO**
A: ¿Cuándo viene el Sr. Robles?
B: El Sr. Robles viene el domingo.

### Lista de invitaciones

| sábado | domingo |
|---|---|
| Gabriel y su prima | Srta. Rodríguez y su hermano |
| Sara | Sr. Robles |
| yo | mis padres |
| tú | yo |
| la madre de Enrique Rivera | tú |

1. ¿Mis padres?
2. ¿Sara?
3. ¿La Srta. Rodríguez y su hermano?
4. ¿Gabriel y su prima?
5. ¿Tú?
6. ¿La madre de Enrique Rivera?
7. ¿Yo?
8. ¿Tú y yo?

El Colegio
**La Merced**
*los invita al:*

Gran Concierto de
**Navidad**

## ¡Comunicación!

### 12 Mis planes del mes | Interpersonal Communication

Pretend today is **el miércoles 8**. In pairs, take turns talking about activities that happened (*¿Cuándo fue?*) or will happen (*¿Cuándo es?*) this month. Among the activities that will happen, include a birthday celebration that you are having for someone you know and say who is coming to the celebration. Use the calendar as a guide.

MODELO

A: ¿Cuándo fue la fiesta para celebrar el cumpleaños de Sara?

B: Fue anteayer, el lunes seis.

A: ¿Y cuándo es el cumpleaños de tu hermano mayor?

B: Es pasado mañana, el viernes diez. Vienen muchos amigos y parientes.

| CALENDARIO | | | | | | |
|---|---|---|---|---|---|---|
| L | M | M | J | V | S | D |
| | | 1 | 2 | 3 | 4 | 5 |
| 6 | 7 | 8 | 9 | 10 | 11 | 12 |
| 13 | 14 | 15 | 16 | 17 | 18 | 19 |

## ¡Comunicación!

### 13 El año nuevo | Presentational Communication

Imagine today is December 26th and you are writing an e-mail to your best friend to tell him/her about the New Year's party your family is having for your relatives and special friends. Include the following information in your e-mail:

- where is the party
- who is coming
- where are they coming from
- when are they coming
- how are they coming (*en carro, en metro, a pie, en avión*, etc.)

Include as many details as you can. Remember to include a greeting and a closing. Then read your e-mail to the class.

¡Feliz Año Nuevo!

¡Vamos a hacer una fiesta!

# Cultura

## Días de fiesta en Nicaragua 🎧

¿Cuál es el origen de los días de fiesta de un país? En Estados Unidos son una combinación de fiestas declaradas por el gobierno y otras fiestas religiosas. En Nicaragua las principales fiestas tienen una conexión con la religión católica. Casi todas las ciudades y pueblos de Nicaragua celebran una fiesta patronal para honrar a sus santos. Las fiestas patronales revelan el carácter y la personalidad de los nicaragüenses: hospitalarios, festivos, serviciales y orgullosos[1] de sus tradiciones.

*Miles de personas participan en la procesión.*

Una de las fiestas patronales más importantes se celebra cada año en la capital, Managua, el primero y el diez de agosto. En esos dos días, las personas salen a las calles para celebrar las fiestas de Santo Domingo, o "Minguito". Para muchos nicaragüenses, este es un momento de gran devoción religiosa. Miles[2] de personas participan en la procesión del santo. Por el camino[3], los espectadores comparten[4] bebidas y comidas tradicionales. Es una procesión de mucho color y ambiente festivo. Los ciudadanos de Managua saludan al santo y participan en danzas, música y explosiones de pólvora[5]. También, se celebra un desfile de caballos y de carrozas[6], al que va una enorme cantidad de personas para disfrutar y participar del ambiente de fiesta en las calles.

[1]proud  [2]thousands  [3]along the way  [4]share  [5]gunpowder  [6]horse and carriage parade

🔍 **Búsqueda:** procesión de santo domingo managua

### Prácticas  Conéctate: la historia

*La estatuilla de Santo Domingo*

Every year on August 1st and 10th, the residents of Managua celebrate the "descending of the saint" and the "ascending of the saint," respectively. In this ceremony, the small statuette of Santo Domingo (affectionately known as "Minguito") is taken from its shrine in a residential area of the city and brought into the city center for the patron saint processions. The statuette was discovered in 1885 by a peasant named Vincente Aburto in the hollow of a burnt tree in *Las Sierritas*, an area just outside Managua. The local priest identified it as the image of *Santo Domingo de Guzmán*. When the priest tried to give the saint a permanent home in his parish church, the statue disappeared and reappeared back in the hollow of the tree. The priest interpreted this as the desire of the saint to stay in *Las Sierritas*, where it has remained since that time.

### 14 Comprensión  Interpretive Communication

1. What do the main holidays in Nicaragua have in common?
2. What is one of the most important holidays in Managua?
3. How do people in Managua show their hospitality and pride during the *fiestas patronales*?
4. What is the origin of the *Fiesta de Santo Domingo*?

### 15 Analiza

1. Why do you think Nicaragua has a strong connection to the Catholic religion?
2. What holidays in the United States have a religious background? Why do you think that is?

**Pregunta clave** How do key activities in a society reflect its values?

# La procesión de los perros

*Participando del día de San Lázaro*

Los nicaragüenses son devotos a sus santos y también a sus perros. ¿Una combinación curiosa? ¡No te creas![1] Una vez al año en la ciudad de Masaya, un poco antes de la Semana Santa (*Holy Week*), los nicaragüenses celebran la fiesta de San Lázaro, una celebración que refleja la relación entre la cultura nicaragüense y la religión.

Según la Biblia, Lázaro era un hombre tan pobre y enfermo[2], que sus únicos[3] amigos eran los perros. (Quizás de esa relación viene la expresión "El perro es el mejor amigo del hombre".) Los nicaragüenses honran al santo cuando llevan a sus perros a visitarlo en la iglesia de Santa María Magdalena. La gente le da las gracias a Lázaro por su ayuda durante el año y le pide milagros[4] para sus parientes y para sus mascotas[5]. Los perros llevan trajes[6] atractivos y originales creados especialmente para esa ocasión. Al final de la fiesta hay premios[7] para los perros con los trajes más originales.

Hoy esta fiesta curiosa es una de las tradiciones religiosas más coloridas e interesantes de Nicaragua, en la que los nicaragüenses combinan su devoción religiosa con su amor hacia los animales y su buen sentido del humor.

[1] Don't you believe it!   [2] poor and sick   [3] only   [4] miracles   [5] pets   [6] outfits   [7] prizes

*Una visita a San Lázaro*

🔍 **Búsqueda:** masaya, historia de san lázaro

## Prácticas

Every year on December 8th, thousands of Nicaraguans get together to celebrate *la Purísima* (Purest one), the feast of the Immaculate Conception of the Virgin Mary. During this celebration families display altars in honor of the Virgin to pray and thank her for granting their wishes throughout the year. Families hosting the feast invite friends and neighbors to gather around the altar to pray and sing traditional songs. It is a joyous celebration where the host distributes fruits, candies, traditional drinks, and gifts to the guests. The celebration often extends to entire neighborhoods, where colorful firework displays add to the cheerful atmosphere of the *Purísima*.

*Celebración de la Purísima*

## 16 Comprensión   Interpretive Communication

1. Explain why people in Nicaragua take their dogs to church to visit *San Lázaro*.
2. What happens at the end of this *fiesta*?
3. What happens during the feast of *la Purísima*?

## Perspectivas

There's a saying in Spanish: *El trabajo sin reposo convierte al hombre en un soso.* (Work without rest makes for a dull man.) How does Nicaraguan culture reflect this attitude?

## 17 Analiza

Why are holidays and traditional celebrations important to a culture?

# Vocabulario 2

## ¿En qué mes estamos? 🎧

Me llamo Mónica. Soy una chica muy **joven**. **Cumplo** 13 años el 15 de marzo pero quiero tener 18 años muy **rápidamente**. Mi hermanito menor, mi mamá y yo hacemos muchas actividades todos los meses.

Mi hermanito Luis es menor que yo. Él cumple 11 años en el mes de octubre.

**Los meses del año**

marzo, abril, mayo

En los meses de marzo, abril y mayo, montamos en bicicleta por las tardes. Mi mamá viene con nosotros.

junio, julio, agosto

En junio, julio y agosto, practicamos deportes y vamos a la playa, **a veces** por la mañana y a veces por la tarde.

septiembre, octubre, noviembre

En septiembre, octubre y noviembre, nos gusta leer en el parque.

diciembre, enero, febrero

En diciembre, enero y febrero, nos gusta pasar un momento **feliz**.

## Los números del 101 al 999.999

| | | | |
|---|---|---|---|
| 101 | ciento uno | 700 | setecientos/as |
| 122 | ciento veintidós | 800 | ochocientos/as |
| 200 | doscientos/as | 900 | novecientos/as |
| 201 | doscientos uno | 1.000 | mil |
| 300 | trescientos/as | 1.001 | mil uno |
| 400 | cuatrocientos/as | 1.999 | mil novecientos noventa y nueve |
| 500 | quinientos/as | 2.000 | dos mil |
| 600 | seiscientos/as | 100.000 | cien mil |

## Para conversar

*T*o talk about dates and birthdays:

¿En qué mes es tu cumpleaños?
*In what month is your birthday?*

Mi cumpleaños es en febrero.
*My birthday is in February.*

¿**De veras**? ¿En qué **fecha**?
*Really? On what date?*

El 29 de febrero.
*February 29th.*

¡Fantástico! Solo cumples años cada cuatro años.
*Fantastic! You only have a birthday every four years.*

### Para decir más

| | |
|---|---|
| las estaciones | *seasons* |
| el invierno | *winter* |
| el otoño | *fall* |
| la primavera | *spring* |
| el verano | *summer* |
| el año bisiesto | *leap year* |
| las hojas | *leaves* |
| la nieve | *snow* |

## 18 ¿Cuándo cumplen años? 🎧

Selecciona la letra de la fecha que corresponde con lo que escuchas.

**A.** 16.06          **C.** 20.05          **E.** 12.11

**B.** 02.03          **D.** 30.08          **F.** 23.01

## 19 ¡Me gusta! 🎧

Say how much you like or dislike the following situations, using *gustar* and any expressions you have learned.

**MODELO**    El mes que viene es diciembre. ¡Es Navidad!

**¡Qué bueno! Me gusta mucho./No me gusta ni un poquito.**

1. Las horas de clase no pasan rápidamente.

2. Mi cumpleaños es en enero.

3. Un día vamos a ser viejos.

4. Soy muy joven.

5. Hoy es el día de mi cumpleaños.

6. Tengo una fiesta y vienen todos mis amigos.

7. A veces celebro mi cumpleaños con mis abuelos.

8. No tengo CDs ni reproductor de CDs.

## 20 Las series de números 👥    Conéctate: las matemáticas

With a partner, alternate counting up to the number shown in parentheses. Follow the established pattern.

1. ciento cincuenta, trescientos, cuatrocientos cincuenta... (1.050)

2. cuatrocientos, seiscientos, ochocientos... (2.000)

3. nueve mil, ocho mil, siete mil... (1.000)

4. treinta y cinco mil seiscientos, treinta mil quinientos, veinticinco mil cuatrocientos... (5.000)

5. cien mil, noventa mil, ochenta mil... (10.000)

## 21 ¿Cuál es la respuesta?

Empareja cada oración de la columna I con una respuesta apropiada de la columna II.

**I**

1. ¿Qué fecha es hoy?

2. Mi cumpleaños es el 25 de diciembre.

3. Pasado mañana es el cumpleaños de mi hermana.

4. ¿Celebras tu cumpleaños con tus abuelos?

5. Mi gato tiene 20 años.

6. ¿Celebras tu cumpleaños en un restaurante?

**II**

**A.** ¿Ah sí? ¿Cuántos años cumple?

**B.** A veces, sí.

**C.** Es el cinco de abril.

**D.** No, la idea no me gusta ni un poquito.

**E.** ¡Es muy viejo!

**F.** ¿De veras?

# Diálogo

## ¡Feliz cumpleaños!

**Isabel:** ¿Cuál es la fecha de hoy?

**Darío:** Hoy es el veinticinco de octubre.

**Isabel:** ¡Hoy es el cumpleaños de Sergio!

**Darío:** ¡Pues vamos a su casa!

*(Más tarde)*

**Isabel:** ¡Feliz cumpleaños, Sergio!

**Darío:** ¿Cuántos años cumples? ¿Veinticinco? ¿Treinta?

**Sergio:** ¡Oye, no! Yo soy joven. Cumplo diecisiete años.

**Darío:** Ja, ja. Pero los años pasan rápidamente.

**Sergio:** ¡Los años y el tiempo pasan rápidamente!

**Isabel:** Sí, en dos meses estamos en Navidad.

**Sergio:** ¡Qué bueno!

**Darío:** ¿Bueno? No me gusta la idea ni un poquito.

## 22 ¿Qué recuerdas?

1. ¿Cuándo es el cumpleaños de Sergio?
2. ¿Cuántos años cumple Sergio?
3. ¿Qué pasan rápidamente?
4. ¿Le gusta la idea de la Navidad a Darío?

*¿Te gusta la Navidad?*

## 23 Algo personal

1. ¿Cuándo es la fecha de tu cumpleaños?
2. ¿Cuántos años vas a cumplir?
3. En tu opinión, ¿pasan los años rápidamente?

## 24 ¡Feliz cumpleaños, Sergio!

Di si lo que oyes es **cierto** o **falso**, según el Diálogo. Si es falso, corrige la información.

## ¡Comunicación!

### 25 Preguntas de cumpleaños — Interpersonal Communication

With a partner, take turns talking about your birthdays. Include dates, how old you are going to be, where you are going to celebrate it and with whom, and any other relevant information.

MODELO
> A: ¿Cuál es la fecha de tu cumpleaños?
>
> B: El primero de julio.
>
> A: ¿Cuántos años cumples?
>
> B: Catorce años. Y tú, ¿cuándo es tu cumpleaños?

# Gramática

## Using the Numbers 101–999,999

- You have already learned to use *cien* (100) before a noun. Use **ciento** in place of *cien* for the numbers 101 to 199: *Tengo* **cien** *DVDs y* **ciento** *veinte CDs.*

- The numbers from 200 to 999 have masculine and feminine forms that agree with the noun they describe: *Hay quinientos ochenta chicos y seiscientas cincuenta chicas en el colegio.*

- *Mil* (1,000) has only one form. Numbers beginning with *mil* are written with a period in Spanish instead of a comma: 1.000. (**Note**: Sometimes four-digit numbers are written without any punctuation, just like in English.)

  | | | |
  |---|---|---|
  | 3.000 | = | tres mil |
  | 106.500 | = | ciento seis mil quinientos |
  | 999.999 | = | novecientos noventa y nueve mil, novecientos noventa y nueve |

- The year may be written in Spanish with or without a period. When it is spoken, it is read like any other four-digit number, **not** grouped two numbers at a time, as is done in English.

  | | | |
  |---|---|---|
  | 1492 | = | mil cuatrocientos noventa y dos |

---

## 26  Regalos para todos

Imagine you are shopping for a birthday gift while visiting friends in Managua and you see the following items. Make a list of each article along with the price written out. The prices are given in *córdobas nicaragüenses (NIO)*.

**MODELO**  **el reproductor de DVDs**
**cinco mil cuatrocientos cincuenta y seis**

NIO 5.456

**1.** NIO 582

**2.** NIO 6.499

**3.** NIO 11.640

**4.** NIO 7.275

**5.** NIO 2.910

**6.** NIO 873

## 27 ¿Cuántos vienen? 🎧 Conéctate: las matemáticas

Imagine that Nicaragua is hosting a world youth meeting (*reunión juvenil mundial*) and you are in charge of recording how many boys and girls are attending the event and where they are from. Write out how many people are coming from each of the following countries.

*¿Cuántos muchachos vienen de Ecuador?*

MODELO 2.800 / Ecuador
**Vienen dos mil ochocientos muchachos de Ecuador.**

1. 153 / El Salvador
2. 721 / Bolivia
3. 2.199 / Argentina
4. 362 / Venezuela

5. 586 / Colombia
6. 93.537 / México
7. 3.738 / Chile
8. ¿Cuántos muchachos vienen en total?

## 28 ¿Cuánto dinero? 👥

Trabajando en parejas, alternen en preguntar y contestar cuánto dinero tienen las personas indicadas y qué van a comprar.

MODELO él / NIO 200

A: **¿Cuánto dinero tiene él?**
B: **Tiene doscientos córdobas.**
A: **¿Qué va a comprar?**
B: **Va a comprar unos calcetines.**

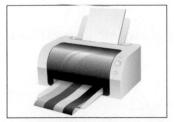
1. tus padres / NIO 4.500

2. Tita / NIO 950

3. Félix / NIO 5.700

4. los hermanos Méndez / NIO 18.000

5. la estudiante / NIO 820

6. yo / NIO 250

# Gramática

## ¡Comunicación!

**29 ¡Feliz fin de año escolar!** 👥 **Interpersonal Communication**

Imagine you and a friend are in charge of organizing a party for 200 people to celebrate the end of the year at your school. The school has allocated a budget of $5,000 (*dólares*) for the party. Working in pairs, prepare a list of the things you would need for the party and discuss how much money you would need to allocate for each item. Be creative!

*Una fiesta en el colegio*

| refrescos | comida |
| música | decoraciones |

**MODELO**

**A:** Bueno, necesitamos mil cuatrocientos dólares para comida.

**B:** Mil cuatrocientos es mucho. Para comida necesitamos ochocientos.

**A** Está bien. ¿Y para refrescos?

**B:** Para los refrescos necesitamos doscientos cincuenta dólares.

## Asking For and Giving the Date

- Use *¿Cuál es la fecha de hoy?* to ask for the date in Spanish. The answer follows this pattern:

> *Es el* + **number for day of month (or *primero*)** + *de* + **month** (+ *de* + **year**)

    *Es el ocho de marzo.*          It is March eighth.

**Note:** The word ***primero*** (abbreviated *1º*) is used for the first day of a month instead of *uno*.

    *Es el **primero** de enero.*      It is January **first**.

- In written form the date may appear as follows:

    *8 de marzo de 2015*    or    *8.3.15* (or *8/3/15*) (or *8-3-15*)

**Note:** The order of the month and the day is opposite to how it is written in English.

- The following expressions may be helpful when talking about days and dates:

    *¿Qué día es hoy?*         *Hoy es viernes.*

    *¿En qué mes estamos?*    *Estamos en mayo.*

    *¿En qué año?*          *En 2016.*

- When you want to express "on" in Spanish, use the definite article *el* or *los*.

    *No voy **el** sábado. Trabajo **los** lunes.*    I am not going **on** Saturday. I work **on** Mondays.

## 30 Fechas para recordar

Give the following dates, first in numbers and then in words. Remember to put the day first and then the month, following the Spanish pattern.

1. (day, month, and year you were born)
2. (date you obtained or plan to obtain your driver's license)
3. (year you plan to buy a car)
4. (year you will be able to vote)
5. (year of your high school graduation)
6. (date of some other important future event in your life)

¿Cuál es la fecha de tu graduación?

## 31 Fechas importantes 👥 Conéctate: la historia

In pairs, take turns asking and answering questions about several important dates in Nicaragua's history. Follow the model.

**MODELO** Nicaragua / declarar / la independencia de España: 1821

   **A:** ¿En qué año declara Nicaragua su independencia de España?

   **B:** Nicaragua declara su independencia de España en 1821.

1. los nicaragüenses / celebrar / 200 años de independencia: 2021
2. los nicaragüenses / celebrar / el Día de la Liberación: 19 de julio
3. en Nicaragua / el Día del Trabajo / ser: 1° de mayo
4. Nicaragua / tener / su fiesta nacional de independencia: septiembre

# 💬 ¡Comunicación!

## 32 Días memorables 👥 Interpersonal/Presentational Communication

With another student, talk about events or special occasions you celebrate during the year. Discuss when these special days occur (name the day of the week, if appropriate); say what you do to make the day(s) special, and mention what you do or do not like about each occasion. If possible, bring a photo that depicts how you celebrate or observe the special event. Show the class your photo and make a small presentation.

**MODELO** A: ¿Qué celebras en julio?

   **B:** Celebro el Día de la Independencia. Es el cuatro de julio.

   **A:** ¿Qué haces para celebrar?

   **B:** Voy a ver los desfiles. Me gustan las carrozas.

### Para decir más

| | |
|---|---|
| la banda | band |
| la bandera | flag |
| la carroza | parade float |
| el desfile | parade |
| el discurso | speech |
| los fuegos artificiales | fireworks |
| desfilar | to parade |
| marchar | to march |

# Todo en contexto

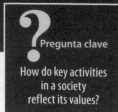
## ¡Comunicación!

### 33  ¿Cuál es tu fiesta favorita?  **Presentational Communication**

You are an exchange student living in Nicaragua, and you are amazed by the abundance of festivals and holidays that take place throughout the year. You start to reflect on holidays and festivals in your own culture, and you want to share one with your Nicaraguan classmates. Write the name of your favorite holiday in the middle circle in Spanish. Fill in the outside circles on the graphic organizer by answering the questions. Then present your holiday to the class, and include visuals.

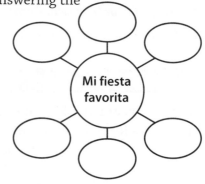

- ¿Cuándo celebras esta fiesta?

- ¿Dónde la celebras?

- ¿Con quién(es) la celebras?

- ¿Hay alguna comida especial que te gusta comer en la fiesta?

- ¿Qué actividades especiales asocias con esta celebración?

- ¿Por qué es un día importante?

## ¡Comunicación!

### 34  Un calendario muy festivo  **Interpersonal Communication**

Here are some important holidays that are celebrated (*se celebra*) throughout the Spanish-speaking world. With a partner, ask each other when these holidays are celebrated. Include at least one follow-up question.

**MODELO**

A:  ¿Cuándo se celebra el Día del Trabajo?

B:  En el mundo hispanohablante se celebra el primero de mayo. En Estados Unidos se celebra el primer lunes de septiembre.

A:  ¿Qué haces para celebrar?

B:  Voy a un desfile con mi familia.

1. el Día de Año Nuevo (*New Year's Day*)
   el primero de enero

2. el Día de los Reyes Magos (*Three Kings Day*)
   el 6 de enero

3. el Día de San Valentín (*Valentine's Day*)
   el 14 de febrero

4. la Semana Santa (*Holy Week*)
   una semana en marzo o abril

5. el Día del Trabajo (*Labor Day*)
   el primero de mayo

6. el Día de la Raza/de la Hispanidad
   (*Columbus Day*) el 12 de octubre

7. el Día de Todos los Santos (*All Saints' Day*)
   el primero de noviembre

8. la Nochebuena (*Christmas Eve*)
   el 24 de diciembre

9. la Navidad (*Christmas*) el 25 de diciembre

10. el Día de los Santos Inocentes (*Fools' Day*)
    el 28 de diciembre

11. la Nochevieja (*New Year's Eve*)
    el 31 de diciembre

# Lectura

## Antes de leer

### 35 Preparación

1. Have you ever seen people playing music and dancing in the street? What was the occasion?

2. If you could choose to honor someone with a public holiday, whom would you choose? Why?

3. Can you recite any poems by heart? Which ones?

### Estrategia

**Predicting**

Try to predict what a reading will be about before you begin. Look at the headings, captions, and illustrations, and try to imagine what the subject will be. As you read, decide whether your prediction was correct, and modify it as needed.

### 36 ¿Cuál es el tema?

With a partner, compare the different images on this page. Do they seem to refer to the same thing? What do they have in common? What makes them different? What do you think might be a common thread that links them all together?

## Las fiestas Darianas

### Una fiesta para un poeta: Rubén Darío (1867–1916)

Todos los años en el mes de enero, la Ciudad Darío en Nicaragua celebra una semana completa de fiesta para honrar al poeta famoso Rubén Darío. Durante esa semana, la gente hace cosas divertidas: canta, baila, escucha música, juega… y también recita poesía.

*Una carreta antigua adornada de flores*

Rubén Darío nació[1] en esta ciudad que lleva su nombre. Es considerado el padre de la poesía modernista y sus poemas son famosos en todo el mundo hispanohablante. En la celebración de la semana Dariana, los nicaragüenses quieren dar homenaje[2] a Darío y también a toda la cultura y las tradiciones de su país. Por eso, el programa incluye actividades culturales, tradicionales y recreativas. Hay juegos populares, conferencias y conciertos, recitales de poesía, espectáculos[3] de baile y música, y desfiles[4].

[1] was born  [2] honor  [3] shows  [4] parades

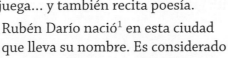

*Monumento al poeta Rubén Darío en Nicaragua. En el centro, la musa de la poesía.*

Una actividad popular durante la celebración es el juego del palo lucio[1]. Grupos de muchachos buscan un premio[2] (por ejemplo, dinero) que está en un palo muy alto y engrasado. Otra actividad es la elección de la Musa Dariana. Las candidatas son bonitas pero también deben demostrar que conocen[3] y admiran la vida y la poesía de Rubén Darío. Siempre hay también un desfile de carretas[4] antiguas decoradas con flores, que van por todas las calles de la ciudad.

*Una escuela de marimba se presenta en las fiestas darianas.*

Toda la comunidad dariana participa en esta semana de festividades. Al final, las actividades terminan con una fiesta popular en la plaza central de Ciudad Darío. ¡Nicaragua quiere mucho a su poeta nacional!

[1] greased pole    [2] prize
[3] are familiar with    [4] carts

🔍 **Búsqueda:** ciudad darío, fiestas darianas

*Muchachos jugando al palo lucio*

## 37 Comprensión    Interpretive Communication

Say if the following statements are *cierto* or *falso*. Correct the false ones.

1. The holiday in honor of Rubén Darío is all about poetry.
2. Rubén Darío is known as the father of traditional Nicaraguan poetry.
3. Rubén Darío is well known throughout the Spanish-speaking world.
4. The *palo lucio* is a tall pole covered with grease that entices climbers with a prize at the top.
5. The "Darian Muse" is elected only for her beauty and charm.

## 38 Analiza

1. What do you think of mixing cultural activities and games the way Nicaraguans do at *las fiestas Darianas*?
2. Do you think it makes sense for a town to celebrate a poet for an entire week? Why or why not?
3. What cultural values are reflected in the activities of this festival?

# Repaso de la Lección B

## A  Escuchar: ¿Qué día es hoy?  (pp. 223–224)

Escribe la respuesta correcta a las seis preguntas que escuchas.

## B  Vocabulario: La palabra apropiada  (pp. 223–224, 232–233)

Completa las oraciones con la palabra apropiada según el contexto.

1. Hoy mi padre (*cumple / es*) cuarenta años.
2. Yo tengo catorce años. Mi hermana (*mayor / menor*) tiene dieciocho años.
3. Hoy es martes; (*ayer / anteayer*) fue domingo.
4. El primero de enero celebramos (*el Año Nuevo / el fin de año*).
5. **A:** ¿Sabes que cumplo años el día de Navidad?
   **B:** (*¡Qué lástima! / ¿De veras?*)
6. Mi hermanita tiene cinco años. Ella es muy (*vieja / joven*).
7. **A:** A veces los años pasan (*rápidamente / temprano*).
   **B:** (*No me gusta ni un poquito. / ¡Feliz cumpleaños!*)

## C  Gramática: ¿Cómo vienen al colegio?  (p. 226)

Completa las siguientes oraciones con la forma apropiada de **venir**.

1. Andrea y Mercedes siempre __ en el autobús del colegio.
2. **A:** Francisco, tú __ en carro con tu hermana, ¿verdad?
   **B:** No, nosotros __ en bicicleta.
3. Yo __ en carro unos días. Otros días tomo el autobús.
4. **A:** Sr. Díaz, ¿ __ Ud. en metro al colegio?
   **B:** No, yo casi siempre __ en taxi.
5. Ella y yo __ a pie porque vivimos cerca del colegio.
6. Mi hermano mayor siempre __ en moto.

## D  Vocabulario/Gramática: ¿En qué mes celebramos...?  (pp. 232–233)

Di en qué mes celebramos las fiestas siguientes.

1. la Navidad
2. el Día de la Independencia
3. el Día de la Madre
4. el Día de Acción de Gracias
5. el cumpleaños de George Washington
6. el Día de la Raza/Hispanidad
7. el Año Nuevo
8. el Día del Padre

A. mayo
B. junio
C. febrero
D. enero
E. julio
F. octubre
G. diciembre
H. noviembre

Escribe los siguientes números. Escribe el punto (*decimal point*) si es necesario.

1. cuatro mil quinientos cincuenta
2. cinco mil setecientos
3. dieciocho mil trescientos ochenta y nueve
4. siete mil trescientos ochenta y nueve
5. novecientos cuarenta y cinco
6. dos mil novecientos treinta y tres
7. doscientos cuarenta
8. mil trecientos noventa
9. quinientos ochenta y nueve
10. setecientos veintiuno

## F Cultura: Fiestas en Nicaragua (pp. 230–231)

Sort the following into the correct category. Then choose five to write a one-sentence description or explanation.

| Managua | la semana Dariana | Rubén Darío | la procesión del santo |
| Minguito | Vicente Aburto | las Sierritas | las fiestas patronales |
| la Purísima | la procesión de los perros | San Lázaro | la Virgen María |

| PERSONAJES | LUGARES | FIESTAS |
| --- | --- | --- |
| _____ | _____ | _____ |
| _____ | _____ | _____ |

## Vocabulario

| Para describir | Números | Fechas | | Verbos | Otras expresiones |
| --- | --- | --- | --- | --- | --- |
| feliz | ciento | abril | julio | celebrar | |
| joven | doscientos/as | agosto | junio | cumplir (años) | a veces |
| mayor | trescientos/as | el año | marzo | fue | ¿de veras? |
| menor | cuatrocientos/as | el Año Nuevo | mayo | venir | ¡Feliz cumpleaños! |
| pasado/a | quinientos/as | anteayer | el mes | | la idea |
| poquito | seiscientos/as | ayer | la Navidad | | ni |
| primero/a | setecientos/as | el cumpleaños | noviembre | | temprano |
| rápidamente | ochocientos/as | diciembre | octubre | | la vez (pl. veces) |
| viejo/a | novecientos/as | enero | pasado mañana | | |
| | mil | febrero | septiembre | | |
| | | la fecha | | | |

## Gramática

| venir | |
| --- | --- |
| vengo | venimos |
| vienes | venís |
| viene | vienen |

**Asking for and giving the date**

Question: **¿Cuál es la fecha de hoy?** What is the date today?

Answer: **Es** + **el** + the date + **de** + month + **de** + year

*Es el cinco de mayo de dos mil quince.* It is May 5, 2015.

# Para concluir

## ? Pregunta clave

How do key activities in a society reflect its values?

## Proyectos

### A  ¡Manos a la obra!  👥

Imagine it is December, time to organize your activities for the coming year. You plan to enter special occasions in your new calendar app. But first, you need to get your information together. Make a list of ten occasions, including special birthdays, holidays, the beginning and end of school vacations and school year, weekend trips, etc. For each item, indicate the occasion and the exact date(s), including the day of the week. Also include one activity you will do to mark the occasion. Put this information in a computer calendar or a calendar app. When you have finished, compare your calendar with a classmate's in Spanish.

**JULIO 2016**

| DOM | LUN | MAR | MIE | JUE | VIE | SAB |
|-----|-----|-----|-----|-----|-----|-----|
|  |  |  |  | 1 | 2 | 3 |
| hacer una fiesta en mi casa 4 | 5 | 6 | 7 | 8 | 9 | 10 |
| 11 | 12 | ir de compras con mis amigos 13 | 14 | 15 | 16 | 17 |
| 18 | 19 | 20 | cumpleaños de mi mamá 21 | 22 | 23 | 24 |
| 25 | 26 | 27 | 28 | 29 | 30 | 31 |

### B  En resumen

In this unit you have been asked to reflect on how key activities in a society reflect its values. This same question could also be applied to the other parts of the Spanish-speaking world that you have studied so far. Starting with Costa Rica and Nicaragua, fill in the chart below as you reflect on this essential question. Then, from the list, choose two other regions of the Spanish-speaking world and fill in the same information. Try to write as much in Spanish as possible. You may insert more rows for the countries where you are able to highlight the connections between values and activities.

**Países**

Estados Unidos (los hispanohablantes)

México

Puerto Rico

la República Dominicana

| País | Valor | Actividad(es) |
|------|-------|---------------|
| **Costa Rica** | la naturaleza | |
| **Nicaragua** | | |
| | | |
| | | |

### C  ¡A escribir!

Go online and find a web site for an electronics store in a Spanish-speaking country. Make a list of ten items you find on the site and how much they cost. Write five to seven sentences in Spanish describing what you see. Include your reaction to the price, the language you see (cognates or terms in English), or anything unusual you find. Use the words in the *Para escribir más* box as well as vocabulary and expressions from the unit to help you compose your sentences.

#### Para escribir más

| | |
|---|---|
| **comprender** | *understand* |
| **la página web** | *web page* |
| **el sitio web** | *web site* |
| **más caro/ barato que** | *more expensive/ cheaper than* |
| **¡Qué sorpresa!** | *What a surprise!* |

## D  Una celebración especial 👥

Working with a partner, choose a Spanish-speaking country and find
out how the people there celebrate a special holiday of your choosing.
You can do your research at the library, online, or, if the resources are
there, in your community. Find out about traditions that make the
holiday unique, and special foods or clothing involved in the celebration.
Then, share your findings in a small group. An idea map like the one
below may be useful for organizing your ideas.

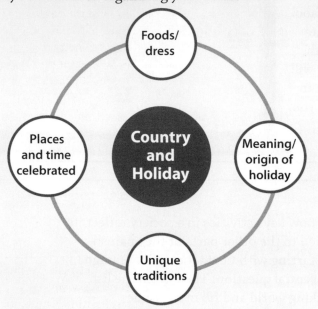

*Fiesta Nacional del Inmigrante,
en Argentina*

*Fiesta de la Vendimia* (grape harvest),
en España

## E  ¡Nos gusta la música!

Conduct a survey (*encuesta*) identifying what kind of music your
peers enjoy. Ask if they are familiar with Hispanic music (cumbia,
Latin rock, reggaeton, etc.). Then find out where they listen to
musical performances in Spanish (such as MP3 or television) and
if so, when. Share your findings with the class.

| Nombre | Tipo de música | Música hispana que conocen | Dónde escuchan cantantes en español |
|--------|----------------|----------------------------|-------------------------------------|
| yo | popular | Latin Rock | por la noche en mi MP3 |
| Carlos | hip hop | reggaeton | en las fiestas |

MODELO    A mí me gusta la música popular. La música hispana que conozco es el Latin Rock
y lo escucho por la noche en mi reproductor de MP3. A Carlos le gusta el hip hop.
La música hispana que conoce es el reggaeton. Le gusta escucharlo en las fiestas.

# Vocabulario de la Unidad 5

**a veces** sometimes, at times *5B*
**abril** April *5B*
**abrir** to open *5A*
la **actividad** activity *5A*
**agosto** August *5B*
el **amor** love *5A*
**anteayer** the day before yesterday *5B*
el **año** year *5B*
el **Año Nuevo** New Year's Day *5B*
el **artículo** article, item *5A*
los **audífonos** earphones, headphones *5A*
**ayer** yesterday *5B*
**buscar** to look for *5A*
**cada** each, every *5A*
la **canción** song *5A*
**¡caramba!** wow! *5A*
**celebrar** to celebrate *5B*
**ciento** one hundred *5B*
el **compañero, la compañera** classmate, partner *5A*
la **consola de juegos** game console/gaming system *5A*
**cuatrocientos/as** four hundred *5B*
el **cumpleaños** birthday *5B*
**cumplir (+ años)** to become (+ number of years), to reach *5B*

**¿de veras?** really? *5B*
el **deporte** sport *5A*
**diciembre** December *5B*
el **dinero** money *5A*
**doscientos/as** two hundred *5B*
el **DVD** DVD *5A*
**electrónico/a** electronic *5A*
**enero** January *5B*

**entrar** to go in, to come in, to enter *5A*
el **estéreo** sound system *5A*
**febrero** February *5B*
la **fecha** date *5B*
**feliz** happy *5B*
**¡Feliz cumpleaños!** Happy Birthday! *5B*
el **fin de semana** weekend *5A*
**fue** was *5B*
el **gato, la gata** cat *5A*
**hacer un viaje** to take a trip *5A*
la **idea** idea *5B*
**joven** young *5B*
**julio** July *5B*
**junio** June *5B*
la **her, it, you (dop)** *5A*
**las** them, you (dop) *5A*
la **lástima** shame *5A*
la **librería** bookstore *5A*
**llamar** to call, to telephone *5A*
**llevar** to take, to carry *5A*
**lo** him, it, you (dop) *5A*
**los** them, you (dop) *5A*
la **maleta** suitcase *5A*
**marzo** March *5B*
**mayo** May *5B*
**mayor** older, oldest *5B*
**me** me (dop) *5A*
**menor** younger *5B*
el **mes** month *5B*
**mil** thousand *5B*
**montar** to ride *5A*
la **Navidad** Christmas *5B*
**ni** not even *5B*
**nos** us (dop) *5A*
**novecientos/as** nine hundred *5B*
**noviembre** November *5B*
**ochocientos/as** eight hundred *5B*
**octubre** October *5B*
**pasado/a** past *5B*
**pasado mañana** the day after tomorrow *5B*
**pasar** to pass, to spend (time) *5A*
la **película** movie, film *5A*
el **perro, la perra** dog *5A*

**poquito** a very little (bit) *5B*
la **práctica** practice *5A*
**primero** first (adverb) *5A*
**primero** first (of the month) *5B*
**que** that, which *5A*
**¡qué (+ adjective)!** how (+ adjective)! *5A*
**¡qué (+ noun)!** what a (+ noun)! *5A*
**que viene** upcoming, next *5A*
el **quemador de CDs** CD burner *5A*
**quinientos/as** five hundred *5B*
**rápidamente** rapidly *5B*
el **reproductor de CDs/DVDs/MP3** CD/DVD/MP3 player *5A*

**seiscientos/as** six hundred *5B*
la **semana** week *5A*
**septiembre** September *5B*
**setecientos/as** seven hundred *5B*
**si** if *5A*
la **sorpresa** surprise *5A*
la **tableta** tablet *5A*
**tan** so *5A*
**te** you (dop) *5A*
**temprano** early *5B*
**tener** to have *5A*
**tener (+ number) años** to be (+ number) years old *5A*
**todos los días** every day *5A*
**trescientos/as** three hundred *5B*
**un poco** a little (bit) *5A*
**venir** to come *5B*
la **vez (pl. veces)** time *5B*
el **viaje** trip *5A*
**viejo/a** old *5B*

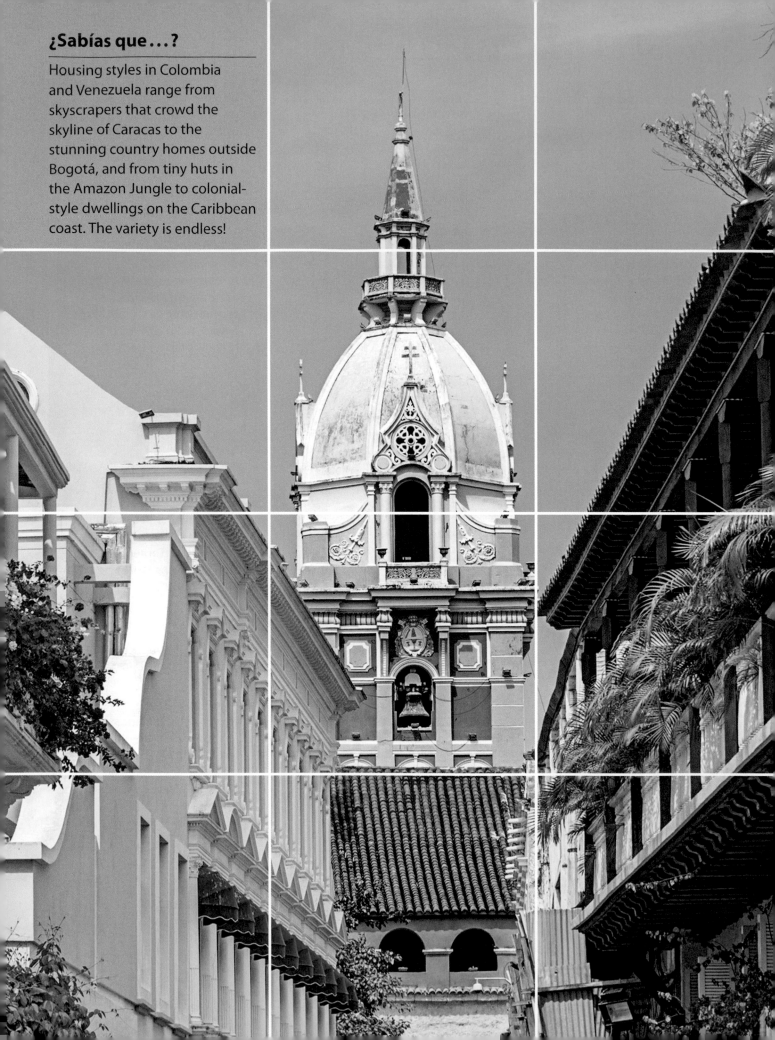

**¿Sabías que...?**

Housing styles in Colombia and Venezuela range from skyscrapers that crowd the skyline of Caracas to the stunning country homes outside Bogotá, and from tiny huts in the Amazon Jungle to colonial-style dwellings on the Caribbean coast. The variety is endless!

# Mi casa es su casa

Scan the QR code to watch this episode of *El cuarto misterioso*.

**Where did José find the key to *el cuarto misterioso*?**

A. en un escritorio
B. en uno de los libros de su tío
C. en la puerta

*Pregunta clave*

## ?

**What does a house and its contents tell us about the people who live there?**

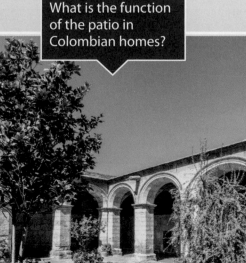

What is the function of the patio in Colombian homes?

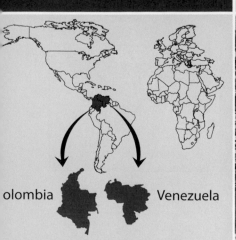

Colombia        Venezuela

## Mis metas

**Lección A  I will be able to:**

▶ identify items in the kitchen and dining room
▶ express obligation using **tener que** and **deber**
▶ talk about plans and preferences using stem-changing verbs (**e → ie**)
▶ describe different types of housing in Venezuela
▶ talk about typical Venezuelan foods
▶ describe table settings
▶ use demonstrative adjectives to point things out
▶ describe various geographic regions of Venezuela

**Lección B  I will be able to:**

▶ identify rooms and floors of a house
▶ report what other people say using the verb **decir**
▶ express wishes using **querer** and **gustaría**
▶ describe housing styles in Colombia
▶ tell how I and others feel using expressions with **tener**
▶ make requests using stem-changing verbs (**e → i**)
▶ recognize when to use **pedir** and **preguntar**
▶ read and discuss a poem by Rafael Pombo

## ¿Qué hay en la cocina? 🎧

el refrigerador

¿Qué cosas tenemos que hacer en la cocina?

Después, tienen que **ayudar** a **poner la mesa**.

Para **empezar**, Juliana **debe cerrar** la puerta del refrigerador.

los cubiertos

la estufa

el fregadero

el horno microondas

el lavaplatos

Estos son los platos de todos los días.

los platos especiales

las servilletas

los vasos

la lámpara

la luz (las luces)

la mesa

el comedor

encender

## Para conversar

*T*o talk about plans you and others have:

¿Van a **viajar** los abuelos **otra vez**?
*Are grandma and grandpa going to travel again?*

Sí, **piensan** que **ya** es hora de regresar a casa.
*Yes, they think it is now time to return home.*

**Entonces**, ¿**quieres** hacer una comida especial?
*Then, do you want to make a special meal?*

No, **prefiero** ir con ellos a su restaurante favorito.
*No, I prefer to go with them to their favorite restaurant.*

### Para decir más

| | |
|---|---|
| el abrelatas | *can opener* |
| el agarraollas | *potholder* |
| la bandeja | *tray* |
| la cafetera | *coffee pot* |
| la cena | *dinner* |
| el congelador | *freezer* |
| los individuales | *placemats* |
| la jarra | *pitcher* |
| la licuadora | *blender* |
| la olla | *pot* |
| la sartén | *skillet* |
| la tostadora | *toaster* |
| la vajilla | *silverware, place setting* |

### En otros países

| | |
|---|---|
| la estufa | *la cocina (Costa Rica)* |
| el fregadero | *la pileta (Uruguay, Argentina)* |
| el lavaplatos | *el lavavajillas (España, Argentina)* |
| el refrigerador | *la nevera (Colombia, España)* |
| | *la heladera (Argentina)* |
| | *el frigo(rífico) (España)* |

*Preferimos comer en este restaurante.*

## 1 ¿Qué tenemos que hacer en la cocina? 🎧

Selecciona la foto que corresponde con lo que oyes.

A

B

C

D

E

F

## 2 ¿A quién llamar?

Imagine you live in Caracas, Venezuela, and several appliances in your home are broken. Decide whom you would call to come and have them fixed.

**A**

**Taller Palma** ¡Los mejores técnicos en reparación de electrodomésticos en Caracas!

Todas las marcas: estufas, lavaplatos, fregaderos y trituradores de desperdicios, lavadoras, secadoras, aspiradoras, planchas. Garantía total, domicilios, Av. Junín.

☎ Llámenos hoy: 614-22-64

**B**

**Refrigas** Servicio las **24 horas** del día. Línea directa: 215-58-78

Somos especialistas en la reparación de microondas, refrigeradores, lavaplatos, licuadoras, tostadoras, procesadores de comida. Servicio a domicilio. Venta de repuestos.

**40** AÑOS SIRVIENDO A CARACAS.

1

2

3

4

5

## Diálogo

### ¿Me vas a ayudar?

**Julio:** ¿Qué haces, mamá?

**Mamá:** Hago la comida. ¿Me vas a ayudar?

**Julio:** ¿Qué debo hacer?

**Mamá:** ¿Por qué no enciendes el lavaplatos?

**Julio:** ¿Qué más?

**Mamá:** ¿Por qué no limpias el refrigerador?

**Julio:** No, ¡el refrigerador no! Prefiero otra cosa, mamá.

**Mamá:** Bueno, ¿por qué no pones la mesa?

**Julio:** ¡Sí, cómo no!

---

### 3  ¿Qué recuerdas?

1. ¿Qué hace la mamá de Julio?
2. ¿Va a ayudar Julio a su mamá?
3. ¿Qué hace Julio primero?
4. ¿Julio va a limpiar el refrigerador o prefiere hacer otra cosa?

### 4  Algo personal

1. ¿Ayudas en la cocina en tu casa?
2. ¿Qué cosas haces para ayudar en la cocina?
3. ¿Qué cosas hay en la cocina de tu casa?

---

### 5  ¿Qué hacen para ayudar?

Mira las palabras de la lista. Di la que corresponde con lo que oyes.

**el vaso**   *la lámpara*   *el refrigerador*

**la estufa**   *el fregadero*   *la mesa*

# Gramática

## Expressing Obligations with *tener que* and *deber*

Use the expressions **tener que** (+ infinitive) and *deber* (+ infinitive) when you wish to express what someone has to do or is obligated to do. Whereas **tener que** (+ infinitive) indicates what someone **has** to do, **deber** (+ infinitive) implies more of a moral obligation or what someone **should** do.

| | |
|---|---|
| **Tengo que** *poner la mesa.* | **I have** to set the table. |
| **Debo** *ayudar a mi madre.* | **I should (ought)** to help my mother. |

### 6 Muchas obligaciones

Complete the following sentences with the correct form of *tener que* or *deber* as appropriate.

1. Mi abuela tiene mucho que hacer en la cocina. Yo __ ayudarla.
2. Mañana hay un examen de matemáticas. Nosotros __ estudiar mucho hoy.
3. Mañana viajo a Colombia. __ salir temprano.
4. Si quieres comida caliente en cinco minutos, __ usar el horno microondas y no la estufa.
5. Uds. __ tomar ocho vasos de agua todos los días. Es muy importante.
6. Estas servilletas están sucias. Tú no __ ponerlas en la mesa.

### 7 ¿Deben hacerlo o tienen que hacerlo? 🎧

Create sentences using the following cues and adding the appropriate form of either *deber* or *tener que*, according to what fits logically.

> **MODELO**  lavar los platos mañana (*Pedro*)
> **Pedro tiene que lavar los platos mañana.**
>
> estudiar primero y hacer deportes después (*los estudiantes*)
> **Los estudiantes deben estudiar primero y hacer deportes después.**

1. ayudar a su madre (*ellos*)
2. llamar a nuestra abuela (*mi hermana*)
3. poner los platos sucios en el lavaplatos (*yo*)
4. cerrar siempre la puerta del refrigerador (*tú*)

## ¡Comunicación!

### 8 ¿Qué tienes que hacer? 👥 Interpersonal Communication

First, create a list of at least two things you have to do and two things you should do this week. Use a variety of time expressions. Then, in small groups, ask and answer about your schedules and obligations.

> **MODELO**  A: El jueves tengo que comprar la comida y debo llamar a mis abuelos. ¿Y tú? ¿Qué debes (tienes que) hacer esta semana?
> B: Mañana tengo que limpiar la estufa y pasado mañana debo ayudar a mi mamá a hacer la comida.

*El jueves tengo que ayudar a hacer la comida.*

# Gramática

## Stem-Changing Verbs: *e → ie*

The verb *pensar* (to think, to plan) belongs to a special group called stem-changing verbs. In these verbs the *e* of the stem changes to **ie** in all its forms except *nosotros* and *vosotros*.

These verbs are sometimes called "shoe verbs" or "boot verbs" because the forms that take a stem change display the shape of a shoe or boot in the chart.

| pensar (ie) | | | |
|---|---|---|---|
| yo | p**ie**nso | nosotros nosotras | pensamos |
| tú | p**ie**nsas | vosotros vosotras | pensáis |
| Ud. él ella | p**ie**nsa | Uds. ellos ellas | p**ie**nsan |

The verb *pensar* can have several different meanings depending on its use.

- When followed immediately by an infinitive, *pensar* indicates what someone plans or intends to do.

  **Pienso ir** *a Venezuela.*          **I plan to go** to Venezuela.

- When combined with **de**, *pensar* is used to ask for an opinion. Use *pensar* followed by **que** to express your opinion or thoughts.

  *¿Qué **piensas de** las servilletas rojas?*          What **do you think of** the red napkins?

  **Pienso que** *son bonitas.*          **I think (that)** they are pretty.

- *Pensar* may be combined with **en** to indicate whom or what someone is thinking about.

  *¿**En qué piensas**?*          What **are you thinking about**?

  **Pienso en** *el verano.*          **I'm thinking about** summer.

*Pensar* (**ie**) is just one of many *e → ie* stem-changing verbs. Others include the following: *cerrar* (to close), *empezar* (to start, to begin), *encender* (to light, to turn on), *preferir* (to prefer), *querer* (to want, to love a person), and *sentir* (to feel sorry, to regret).

**Note:** The verb *empezar* is used with **a** when an infinitive follows.

  **Empiezo a** *estudiar.*          **I am beginning** to study.

*¿En qué piensas?*

## 9   ¿Qué piensan...?

Tell what these people are planning to do, using words from each column and the
appropriate form of *pensar*. Verb forms may be repeated.

| I | II | III |
|---|---|---|
| Roberto y Raúl | pienso | hacer un almuerzo especial |
| mis primos y yo | piensas | encender la luz |
| yo | piensa | comer en el comedor |
| una amiga | pensamos | buscar  las servilletas |
| Julia y Esther | piensan | poner la mesa |
| tú | | ayudar en la cocina |

## 10   Una ocasión especial

Completa el siguiente párrafo con la forma correcta de los
verbos indicados entre paréntesis.

### ¡Ojo!   👁

As well as paying careful attention to
whether the verb form needs a stem change
or not, pay attention to what kind of verb
you are conjugating (-*ar*, -*er*, -*ir*) so you
choose the appropriate endings.

Martín y Andrea (**1.** *pensar*) hacer un almuerzo especial
para su prima Elvira porque ella va a Colombia a estudiar por un año. Andrea (**2.** *pensar*) hacer unas
arepas y Martín (**3.** *querer*) hacer un postre especial. Ellos (**4.** *empezar*) a hacer la comida muy temprano.
Otros amigos (**5.** *pensar*) venir al almuerzo. Rafael (**6.** *venir*) y Leandra y Sara (**7.** *pensar*) venir también.
Graciela lo (**8.** *sentir*) mucho, pero no (**9.** *venir*) al almuerzo porque tiene que estudiar. David (**10.** *deber*)
ayudar a sus padres en la casa y (**11.** *preferir*) venir después del almuerzo. Él (**12.** *querer*) decirle "adiós" a
Elvira. Y tú, ¿qué (**13.** *pensar*)? ¿(**14.** *venir*) al almuerzo?

## 11   Somos diferentes   🎧

Use the cues that follow to create sentences that compare and contrast how different
Sara and Julio are from their parents.

> **MODELO**   empezar a escuchar música / empezar a leer
> **Si nosotros empezamos a escuchar música, ellos empiezan a leer.**

1. querer nadar en la playa / querer caminar en
   la playa
2. pensar ir al parque / pensar ir a un museo
3. encender el reproductor de CDs / encender el
   televisor
4. tener que hacer la tarea / tener que lavar
   los platos
5. querer comer en un restaurante / querer hacer
   arepas y comer en casa otra vez
6. cerrar la puerta / abrir las ventanas
7. preferir ir al cine / preferir ver un DVD
   en casa
8. empezar a ver la televisión / empezar a
   escuchar la radio

## ¡Comunicación!

### 12 ¿En qué piensan? 👥 Interpersonal Communication

In pairs, take turns asking and answering questions about what your family and friends are thinking about, according to the illustrations, as you all prepare for a holiday dinner. Then, take turns discussing how and with whom you celebrate your favorite holiday.

MODELO   tu padre
A: ¿En qué piensa tu padre?
B: Mi padre piensa en la mesa y las sillas.

1. yo

2. Elena

3. tus hermanos

4. Juana y Alberto

5. mis primos y yo

6. tú

## ¡Comunicación!

### 13 ¿Qué piensan hacer? 👥 Interpersonal/Presentational Communication

In small groups, talk about some things you are planning to do this year or at some other future time. Be creative. You might also discuss what you think of each person's plans. Then decide what your remarks have in common. One student should take notes and report the results of your discussion to the class.

MODELO   A: Este año yo pienso ayudar a mis padres en casa y leer cien libros.
B: ¡Qué bueno! Pues yo pienso viajar a otro país. Quiero ir a Venezuela en octubre.
C: Vas a necesitar mucho dinero. Yo pienso cantar con Shakira en un concierto. ¿Qué piensan de mi plan?

# Cultura

**?** Pregunta clave

What does a house and its contents tell us about the people who live there?

*Casas indígenas en el agua*

## Los venezolanos y sus casas

Do you know where the name Venezuela originated? The Spanish explorers saw houses built on stilts in the waters of Lake Maracaibo and decided to call the area "Little Venice." Venezuelans trace their origins to those early Europeans, but also to various indigenous tribes, and to the blacks brought from Africa to work on the sugar and cotton plantations.

*Los ranchos cerca de Caracas*

Venezuelan homes are as diverse as the people themselves. The varied living spaces and lifestyles are evidence of Venezuela's rapid social and economic change since the oil boom of the 1970s. In large cosmopolitan cities like Caracas and Maracaibo, you find high-rise apartment buildings with all the modern conveniences. The owners usually work in the city to take advantage of job opportunities and the proximity to museums, shopping, and restaurants. The housing shortage in Caracas has caused many rural newcomers seeking employment to build small homes and shacks (*ranchos*) crowded together in slums on the hillsides surrounding the city. Wealthier families prefer houses with more living space in quiet residential districts.

Indigenous groups have their own styles of housing. The Yanomami, a tribe that lives in the Amazon rainforest, choose communal living. Entire villages live under a common roof called the *shabono*. And on the shores of Lake Maracaibo, you can still find settlements built on stilts over the water, similar to the housing units viewed by the Spanish back in the 16th century.

**Búsqueda:** venezuela housing, 1970s venezuelan oil boom

## Productos

Los indígenas del Estado Amazonas en Venezuela producen los mejores productos artesanales (*handicrafts*) del país. Un producto que está presente en todos los hogares (*homes*) indígenas de Venezuela es el *chinchorro*. Esta hamaca de muchos colores se usa para dormir o descansar (*rest*) y también como decoración. Hoy, las comunidades indígenas producen *chinchorros* artesanales para todo el país. Son tan populares que en muchos hogares de las grandes ciudades venezolanas hay un *chinchorro* en el patio o en el balcón.

*Un chinchorro*

## 14 Comprensión

1. What is the origin of the name Venezuela?
2. Name three types of housing in Venezuela and a positive aspect of each.
3. Why are the *chinchorros* so popular in Venezuelan homes?

## 15 Analiza

What effects, positive and negative, do you think the Venezuelan oil boom of the 1970s had on people's living situation?

### Comparaciones

What types of homes exist where you live? How are they similar to, and different from, the types of homes in Venezuela?

# Los venezolanos y su comida 🎧

Imagina esta escena en una casa en Venezuela. Sandra sale del colegio tarde y, ¡quiere comer! En la cocina, abre el refrigerador. Nada. Entonces abre un gabinete y, ¿qué ve? Allí hay harina de maíz[1], sal y aceite[2]. Sandra tiene todo lo que necesita para hacer unas deliciosas *arepas*.

Siempre hay una arepa en la mesa venezolana. La arepa es un pan[3] de maíz delgado. Para prepararlas combinas harina de maíz con agua y un poquito de aceite. Formas la arepa y la pones sobre la estufa caliente. Comes la arepa como pan. O si prefieres, la abres y pones adentro carne[4], pollo o vegetales.

*Una arepa rellena*

*Una comida típica: el pabellón criollo*

Otro plato delicioso es el *pabellón criollo*. Tiene arroz[5], frijoles negros (*caraotas* en Venezuela) y carne. El pabellón criollo es el plato venezolano más típico porque la carne simboliza la raza indígena, las caraotas la raza negra y el arroz la raza europea.

Con la harina de maíz se hace otro plato típico: *la hallaca*. Se prepara la harina de maíz pero no se pone en la estufa. Se rellena[6] con carnes, vegetales y especias y se pone al vapor, en hojas[7] de plátano (una variedad de banano grande). Es difícil hacer hallacas. Por eso, los venezolanos no las preparan con mucha frecuencia. Pero sí comen hallacas todos los años en la Navidad, con una taza de chocolate caliente. ¡A los venezolanos les gusta mucho la comida!

*Comida navideña: una hallaca*

[1] corn meal  [2] oil  [3] bread  [4] meat  [5] rice  [6] stuffed  [7] leaves

🔍 **Búsqueda:** comida típica venezolana

## Perspectivas

"When a Venezuelan cooks, she does it in grand style, to share that bit of family tradition and bring out smiles with that first bite." Comment on the value of home-cooked meals in Venezuela, based on this translated quote from an online recipe site.

## 16 Comprensión | Interpretive Communication

1. What are some foods you might find in a Venezuelan kitchen?

2. What ingredients do you need to make *arepas*?

3. Name the three main ingredients in *pabellón criollo*.

4. How is plantain used to make *hallacas*?

5. Why are *hallacas* eaten only on special occasions?

## 17 Analiza

1. Do you think the *pabellón criollo* is a good choice for Venezuela's most typical or characteristic food? Why?

2. Why do you think so many Latin American foods have corn as their base?

# Vocabulario 2

## ¿Qué hay en la mesa? 🎧

el mantel

la cucharita / la cuchara

el cuchillo / el tenedor

la taza

el aceite

la sal / la pimienta

el azúcar

el pan / la mantequilla

**Este postre** ya está. Lo vamos a llevar a la mesa.

Por favor, **pásame esos** panes.

Quiero poner **un poco de** pimienta a **la sopa**.

Por favor, pásame **aquel** plato.

## Para conversar 🎧

*T*o ask someone to pass you something at the table:

Pásame **esa** servilleta, por favor.
*Pass me that napkin, please.*

¡Claro! ¿Algo más?
*Of course! Anything else?*

Sí, una cucharita y **aquel** postre que está **allá**.
¡Gracias!
*Yes, a teaspoon and that dessert that's over there.*
*Thanks!*

### Para decir más

| | |
|---|---|
| la mayonesa | *mayonnaise* |
| la mostaza | *mustard* |
| la salsa de tomate | *ketchup* |
| el sabor | *flavor* |
| agrio/a | *sour* |
| delicioso/a | *delicious* |
| dulce | *sweet* |
| picante | *spicy* |
| sabroso/a | *delicious* |
| salado/a | *salty* |

## 18 A la mesa

Completa las siguientes oraciones, según las fotos.

**1.** El __ es de nuestra abuela.

**2.** Pásame la __, por favor.

**3.** Necesito la __.

**4.** Prefiero un poco de __, por favor.

**5.** Me gusta la __ bien caliente.

**6.** Quiero más __ para la ensalada.

**7.** Necesitan esas __ para el postre.

**8.** Son las __ de todos los días.

**9.** Prefiero estos __ para la cena de hoy.

## 19 ¿Qué necesitas? ¿Qué quieres? 👥

Bring in a photo or an illustration of a table that is set for dinner. Working with a partner, ask what he or she needs or wants. Your partner must respond by asking you to pass an item that is shown in the photo. Check the items off as they are used.

**MODELO**
A: ¿Qué necesitas? (¿Qué quieres?)
B: Pásame la mantequilla, por favor.

*Pásame la sal, por favor.*

# Diálogo

## ¿Te gusta la sopa?

**Julio:** Mamá, pásame esa cucharita, por favor.

**Mamá:** ¿Cuál? ¿Esta cucharita?

**Julio:** Sí, esa cucharita, mamá.

**Papá:** Sara, ¿cómo está la sopa?

**Sara:** Me gusta, pero necesita un poco más de sal.

**Julio:** Mira, aquí está la sal.

**Mamá:** ¿Y tú, amor? ¿Te gusta la sopa?

**Papá:** No sé. No tengo cuchara.

**Mamá:** Lo siento. Aquí está.

**Papá:** Esta arepa está buena.

## 20 ¿Qué recuerdas?

1. ¿Qué quiere Julio?
2. ¿Le gusta a Sara la sopa?
3. ¿Qué necesita un poco más de sal?
4. ¿Qué no tiene el papá?
5. ¿Qué le gusta al papá?

## 21 Algo personal

1. ¿Tiene comedor tu casa?
2. ¿Cómo es la mesa del comedor de tu casa?
3. ¿Qué sopa te gusta? Explica.

*Esta casa tiene un comedor elegante.*

## 22 Yo necesito...

Selecciona la letra de la frase que completa lógicamente cada oración que oyes. *(Select the letter of the phrase that logically completes each sentence you hear.)*

**A.** de agua mineral

**B.** sal

**C.** tenedor

**D.** el lavaplatos

**E.** arepas

**F.** sobre el pan caliente

**G.** una cuchara y un plato

**H.** mantel

# Gramática

emcpassport.com

WB 13–16
LA 6
GV 13

## Pointing Out Someone or Something: Demonstrative Adjectives

Use a demonstrative adjective (*adjetivo demostrativo*) before a noun to point out or draw attention to where someone or something is located in relation to yourself ("this house," "that car," etc.).

| Los adjetivos demostrativos | | | |
|---|---|---|---|
| **singular** | | **plural** | |
| masculino | femenino | masculino | femenino |
| **este** vaso *(this glass)* | **esta** taza *(this cup)* | **estos** vasos *(these glasses)* | **estas** tazas *(these cups)* |
| **ese** vaso *(that glass)* | **esa** taza *(that cup)* | **esos** vasos *(those glasses)* | **esas** tazas *(those cups)* |
| **aquel** vaso *(that glass over there)* | **aquella** taza *(that cup over there)* | **aquellos** vasos *(those glasses over there)* | **aquellas** tazas *(those cups over there)* |

When pointing out people or objects that are nearby, use **este**, **esta**, **estos**, or **estas** (this/ these). Use **ese**, **esa**, **esos**, or **esas** (that/those) to draw attention to people or objects that are farther away. Call attention to people or objects that are even farther away ("over there") by using **aquel**, **aquella**, **aquellos**, or **aquellas** (that/those over there).

| | | |
|---|---|---|
| near speaker (**aquí**) | Me gusta **esta** taza. | I like **this** cup. |
| away from speaker (**allí**) | ¿Te gustan **esas** tazas? | Do you like **those** cups? |
| far away from speaker (**allá**) | Prefiero **aquella** taza. | I prefer **that** cup (over there). |

*Aquella taza*

*Esa taza*

*Esta taza*

## 23 ¡Una nueva cocina!

Completa las oraciones con la forma apropiada de **este**.

Quiero una nueva cocina para mi casa porque **(1)** cocina es muy fea. **(2)** paredes tienen un color muy triste. La puerta de **(3)** horno microondas no cierra. **(4)** fregadero es muy pequeño, necesito un fregadero doble. **(5)** refrigerador está muy viejo y **(6)** lavaplatos es muy malo. **(7)** luces no encienden y **(8)** lámpara es muy fea. No me gusta **(9)** mesa y **(10)** sillas son horribles.

## 24 ¿Qué vamos a poner en la mesa?

With a classmate, pretend you are discussing whether or not you need the following items as you are preparing the table for dinner. Answer each question negatively as shown in the model.

**MODELO** las servilletas verdes

A: ¿Quieres estas servilletas verdes?

B: No, no quiero esas servilletas verdes.

1. los cubiertos
2. el mantel
3. la mantequilla

4. el aceite
5. los platos de sopa
6. las tazas

7. el cuchillo
8. los vasos nuevos
9. la silla

## 25 ¿Este, ese o aquel?

Imagine you are in a department store buying kitchenware. Use the appropriate form of *este, ese,* or *aquel* to say what items you prefer, based upon the cues shown in the illustration.

**MODELO** ¿Qué platos prefieres?
**Prefiero aquellos platos.**

**1.** ¿Qué vasos prefieres?

**2.** ¿Qué lámpara prefieres?

**3.** ¿Qué servilletas prefieres?

**4.** ¿Qué cubiertos prefieres?

**5.** ¿Qué taza prefieres?

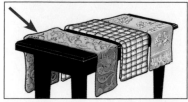

**6.** ¿Qué mantel prefieres?

## 26 ¿Qué te gusta?

Imagine that you and a friend are at a housewares store. Talk about the things you like and prefer using a form of *ese* and *aquel*. Follow the model.

**MODELO**   servilletas blancas / servilletas rojas

A: ¿Te gustan esas servilletas blancas?

B: Sí, pero prefiero aquellas servilletas rojas que están allá.

1. mantel amarillo / mantel azul
2. lámparas verdes / lámparas blancas
3. platos de todos los días / platos especiales
4. mesa negra / mesa gris
5. tazas verdes / tazas blancas
6. cucharitas pequeñas / cucharas grandes

# ¡Comunicación!

## 27 Compras para poner la mesa    Interpersonal Communication

With a classmate, play the roles of customer and sales clerk to talk about some dinnerware items you would like to buy. Use the list below to get you started or create one of your own. Make sure to include the appropriate forms of *este, ese,* or *aquel* in your conversation.

**MODELO**   A: Buenas tardes. Quiero ver esas cucharitas de postre.

B: ¿Estas cucharitas que están aquí?

A: No, aquellas cucharitas que están allá. Son más bonitas.

B: ¿Necesita otra cosa?

A: Sí, busco un mantel grande.

B: ¿Le gusta este mantel azul?

A: No, ya tengo un mantel azul. Prefiero aquel mantel blanco que está allá.

> unas cucharitas de postre
> una cuchara para la sopa
> una cuchara grande
> unos tenedores pequeños
> un cuchillo grande
> unos platos de todos los días
> unos vasos grandes
> unas tazas especiales
> un mantel grande
> unas servilletas blancas

*Prefiero estos platos de todos los días.*

# ¡Comunicación!

## 28 Un almuerzo en Caracas · Interpersonal Communication

During lunch with a friend in Caracas, you discuss your plans for the week. Talk about some things you want to do, ought to do, have to do, or prefer to do each day this week. Make the conversation realistic by politely interrupting one another, asking for things to be passed to you and commenting on things and people you see. Use the word bank to help you get started.

**tengo**    *debo*    ese    *cuchara*    **tenedor**

*lavaplatos*    *cucharita*    **aquel**    estufa    *mantel*    servilletas

**platos**    *cuchillo*    *vasos*    este    *lámpara*    *quiero*

MODELO    A: El martes tengo que ir con mi mamá a la tienda a mirar unas estufas nuevas.

B: ¿Unas estufas?... ¡Ay, qué aburrido! Por favor, pásame esa cucharita.

A: Sí, cómo no. ¡Mira! Aquella muchacha es Ana, ¿no?

# ¡Comunicación!

## 29 En el restaurante · Presentational Communication

Working in small groups, prepare a short skit by pretending you are having dinner together in a restaurant in Venezuela. Each member of the group should create at least four statements or questions, including some of the following: requests for items at the table, questions about what your friends think and want, comments about the food, questions about what your friends have to do during the week, and so on. Be polite (use *por favor* and *gracias*). After you have established your dialogue, present it in front of the class.

*Las arepas están buenas.*

MODELO    A: Pásame ese pan y el aceite, por favor.

B: Aquí tienes. ¿Qué piensan de aquellas arepas?

C: Están muy buenas, pero esta sopa necesita un poco de sal.

*El aceite*

# Todo en contexto

**?** Pregunta clave

What does a house and its contents tell us about the people who live there?

## ¡Comunicación!

### 30  Dos viviendas venezolanas  👥  Presentational Communication

Imagine two very different styles of housing in Venezuela: an apartment in the city or a house in the suburbs; a house on stilts on the shores of Lake Maracaibo or a *rancho* in the shantytowns above Caracas; a *shabono* or an *hacienda* on the open plains. What might be the similarities and differences? Drawing on the knowledge you gained in the reading *"Los venezolanos y sus casas"* on p. 258, and any additional research you would like to do online, work with a partner to compare and contrast two types of Venezuelan housing and possible lifestyles of the people who live there. Be sure to take into account architectural style, kitchen and dining room furnishings, family life, food, daily activities, and other factors as you imagine life in the two types of dwellings. Use a Venn diagram or another type of graphic to organize your ideas. As you present your ideas to the class, include illustrations and also ideas on what these types of dwellings might tell you about the people who live there.

*Un shabono en los llanos de Venezuela.*

## ¡Comunicación!

### 31  Una receta venezolana  👥  Presentational Communication

In small groups, research a typical Venezuelan dish. Learn about its origin and ingredients. What region is it from? What can you learn about the people from that region by what they eat? Would this dish seem exotic to someone from the United States? Why? What makes it a typical dish, from that region of Venezuela? Use pictures to tell the class about your dish including a map of Venezuela indicating the region where it originated. Show pictures of your ingredients to help identify them. Using a combination of visuals and words, tell the class how to make the dish. Use expressions from the *Para decir más* and *Estrategia* boxes, and be sure to include a lot of visuals to communicate your ideas. Use a table like the one below to help you organize your ideas.

| Para decir más | |
|---|---|
| agregar | *to add* |
| asar | *to grill, roast* |
| cocinar | *to cook* |
| hervir | *to boil* |
| hornear | *to bake* |
| mezclar | *to mix* |
| rellenar | *to stuff* |

| Una receta venezolana | |
|---|---|
| Plato | |
| Región donde lo comen | |
| Origen | |
| Cuándo lo comen | |
| Ingredientes | |
| Cómo lo hacen | |

### Estrategia

**Review and recycle**

Use these words for connecting sentences:

| | |
|---|---|
| primero | *first* |
| para empezar | *to begin, to start* |
| después | *after* |
| entonces | *then* |
| luego | *then* |

# Lectura informativa

## Antes de leer

1. Have you read books or seen movies about the jungle? How far away does it seem from your own life?

2. What do you know about cattle raising? Have you ever been to a cattle ranch?

## Estrategia

### Summarize

When you read a text with a lot of information, a good way to remember it is to summarize as you read. Make a chart and write down important data as you go. Be sure to organize your data by categories or headings to keep everything clear in your mind.

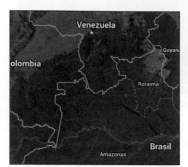

*La Amazonía o selva del Amazonas*

*El Salto Ángel, cataratas más altas del mundo*

## La gente y las viviendas en otras regiones de Venezuela 🎧

No todos los venezolanos habitan en Caracas o Maracaibo. Muchos viven en la selva[1] del Amazonas o en los grandes llanos[2].

### El Amazonas

Suramérica tiene la zona tropical más grande del mundo. Es la selva del Amazonas, que incluye partes de ocho países: Brasil, Perú, Colombia, Bolivia, Ecuador, Guayana, Venezuela y Surinam. ¿Quiénes viven en la Amazonía venezolana? Hay diferentes tribus

*Una guacamaya en la selva venezolana*

*El llano es una zona de ganadería.*

indígenas pequeñas. Los yanomamis, por ejemplo viven en casas grandes comunales de forma circular llamadas *shabonos*. Varias familias viven en una casa. Por la noche se reúnen[3] para comer, hablar y explicar sus historias, mitos y leyendas a los niños y luego todos los niños y adultos duermen[4] en hamacas.

En el Amazonas donde viven estas tribus es posible admirar animales como las guacamayas de color azul y rojo y ver el espectacular Salto Ángel, las cataratas más altas del mundo.

### Los llanos

Esta es una zona grande y caliente con ríos enormes como el Orinoco. Pero a veces también hay lluvias torrenciales. La actividad principal en los llanos es la ganadería[5], pero también hay agricultura y explotación de petróleo.

En esta zona viven los llaneros, similares a los *cowboys* de Estados Unidos. Los llaneros viven en haciendas grandes y altas con mucho espacio interior y exterior. La actividad principal del llanero es cuidar ganado[6] pero también le gusta cantar con su arpa o con una guitarra pequeña llamada *cuatro*.

Muchas haciendas se dedican al agroturismo, un tipo de turismo que ofrece a los visitantes la oportunidad de observar la fauna y la flora de la región y comer comidas típicas del llano como la carne asada[7].

Los shabonos del Amazonas y las haciendas de los llanos reflejan aspectos fascinantes de la vida de los habitantes de estas regiones venezolanas.

[1] (tropical) forest   [2] plains   [3] get together   [4] sleep   [5] cattle raising   [6] take care of the cattle   [7] roast meat

# Casa agroturística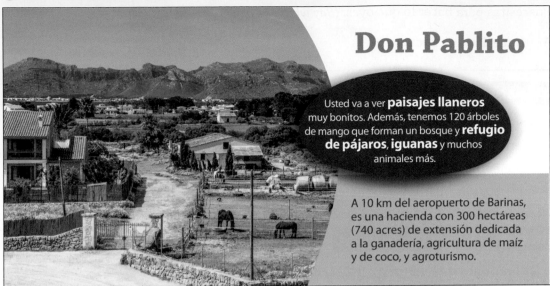

## Don Pablito

Usted va a ver **paisajes llaneros** muy bonitos. Además, tenemos 120 árboles de mango que forman un bosque y **refugio de pájaros**, **iguanas** y muchos animales más.

A 10 km del aeropuerto de Barinas, es una hacienda con 300 hectáreas (740 acres) de extensión dedicada a la ganadería, agricultura de maíz y de coco, y agroturismo.

**Búsqueda:** regiones venezuela

## 32 Comprensión  Interpretive Communication

1. ¿Quiénes son los yanomamis? ¿Dónde viven?
2. ¿Dónde viven los llaneros? ¿Cuál es su actividad principal?
3. Compara y contrasta la geografía y el clima del Amazonas y los llanos.

## 33 Analiza

1. What can you infer about the people who live in *un shabono* and in *una hacienda*?
2. Describe what you think *agroturismo* is. What makes it special in *los llanos*?

## Escritura

### 34 Mi estilo de vida  Presentational Communication

Choose one area of Venezuela and pretend you live there. Write a paragraph describing your life. The table will help you outline your ideas.

| Mi vida en _____ | |
| --- | --- |
| Quién soy | un vaquero |
| Dónde vivo | en los llanos |
| El clima donde vivo | |
| Mi casa | |
| Mis actividades | |
| La comida | |

#### Para escribir más

| | |
| --- | --- |
| lluvia/lluvioso | *rain/rainy* |
| seco | *dry* |
| trabajar | *to work* |
| el agricultor, la agricultora | *farmer* |
| el clima | *climate, weather* |
| el petrolero, la petrolera | *oil worker* |

# Repaso de la Lección A

## A  Escuchar: ¿Qué necesitas? 🎧 (pp. 260–261)

Di lo que necesitas para hacer lo que oyes. *(Say what you need in order to do what you hear.)*

**MODELO**  Necesito una cuchara.

## B  Vocabulario: La palabra lógica (pp. 250–251, 260–261)

Completa las oraciones con una palabra lógica del vocabulario de la lección.

1. Voy a encender la __ porque no veo bien.
2. Vamos a poner un __ nuevo en la mesa.
3. Tienes que poner los platos sucios en el __.
4. El tenedor y el cuchillo son __.
5. Me gusta el pan con __.
6. Necesito una __ para comer la sopa.

## C  Gramática: ¿*Debo* o *tengo que*? (p. 254)

Completa las oraciones con la forma correcta de **deber** o **tener que**.

1. Tú no __ comer el postre antes de la sopa.
2. Los platos están sucios. Uds. __ ponerlos en el lavaplatos.
3. Si no te gusta el agua fría, no __ ponerla en el refrigerador.
4. Los niños no __ encender la estufa.
5. ¿No hay mucha luz? Entonces tú __ abrir las ventanas.
6. Oye, hijo, __ ayudar a abuelita a poner la mesa.

## D  Gramática: En la casa (p. 255)

Completa las oraciones con la forma correcta del verbo entre paréntesis.

1. Yo (*pensar*) en viajar a Venezuela.
2. La película (*empezar*) a las diez de la noche.
3. Pablo, ¿(*querer*) ayudar en la cocina?
4. Yo (*preferir*) poner la mesa.
5. Mamá (*encender*) las luces del comedor.
6. Sara, ¿(*querer*) un poco de sal?
7. Lo (*sentir*), pero no me gusta la sal.
8. Eduardo y Carlos no (*querer*) comer postre hoy.

## E  Gramática: ¿*Este, ese* o *aquel*? (p. 263)

Crea conversaciones con el adjetivo demostrativo que corresponda, según el contexto. Sigue el modelo.

**MODELO**  este libro

> A:  ¿Quieres este libro?
> B:  No, no quiero ese libro. Prefiero aquel libro allá.

1. estas servilletas
2. estos cubiertos
3. estas tazas rojas
4. esta cuchara y este plato
5. este vaso de agua mineral
6. estas lámparas

**Cultura: Cómo viven los venezolanos** (pp. 258–259, 268)

Think about the different types of homes, foods, and regions of Venezuela. Then complete the chart below while also adding additional items and descriptions. What general conclusions can you draw about the country and its people?

| Home/Food/Regions | Description or Statement |
|---|---|
| **high-rise buildings** | **People live in big cities for access to jobs and services.** |
| **pabellón criollo** | |
| **los llanos** | |
| | |

## Vocabulario

### En la cocina/En el comedor

| | |
|---|---|
| el aceite | el mantel |
| el azúcar | la mantequilla |
| la cocina | la mesa |
| el comedor | el pan |
| los cubiertos | la pimienta |
| la cuchara | el plato |
| la cucharita | el postre |
| el cuchillo | el refrigerador |
| la estufa | la sal |
| el fregadero | la servilleta |
| el horno microondas | la sopa |
| la lámpara | la taza |
| el lavaplatos | el tenedor |
| la luz (las luces) | el vaso |

### Otras expresiones

allá
aquel, aquella (aquellos, aquellas)
la cosa
de todos los días
después
entonces
ese, esa (esos, esas)
especial
este, esta (estos, estas)
otra vez
un poco de
ya

### Verbos

ayudar
cerrar (ie)
deber
empezar (ie)
encender (ie)
pásame
pensar (ie) de/en/que
poner (la mesa)
preferir (ie)
querer (ie)
sentir (ie)
tener que
viajar

## Gramática

### Expressing obligations: *tener que* and *deber*

#### *tener que* + infinitive

| | |
|---|---|
| **Tengo que** estudiar para el examen. | *I have* to study for the test. |

#### *deber* + infinitive

| | |
|---|---|
| **Debo** ayudar a mi hermano. | *I should* help my brother. |

### Stem-changing verbs: e →ie

When conjugating stem-changing verbs, the endings change as well as the stem. Remember to change the stem in the forms that fall within the shape of the shoe/boot.

#### pensar (ie)

| | |
|---|---|
| **pie**nso | pensamos |
| **pie**nsas | pensáis |
| **pie**nsa | **pie**nsan |

### Demonstrative adjectives

Demonstrative adjectives are used before a noun to point out where someone or something is located in relation to the speaker.

| | | this/these | that/those | that/those (over there) |
|---|---|---|---|---|
| masculine | singular | **este** | **ese** | **aquel** |
| | plural | **estos** | **esos** | **aquellos** |
| feminine | singular | **esta** | **esa** | **aquella** |
| | plural | **estas** | **esas** | **aquellas** |

## La casa de Julián

¡Hola! Soy Francisco. Vivo en Caracas. Ahora estoy en Cartagena en la casa de mi primo Julián. La casa de Julián es muy bonita y grande.

Primero, voy a llamar **por teléfono** a mis padres para **decirles** que estoy bien. Más tarde, me **gustaría escribirles** sobre la casa **donde** vive Julián y mis vacaciones.

el primer piso
la planta baja
una casa de dos pisos

el garaje

la sala

la piscina

Para ir al primer piso está **la escalera**.

En el primer piso está **el cuarto** de Julián.

También está **el baño**.

El cuarto de Ana es grande y **cómodo**.

**Por la noche** comemos en **el patio**. Allí hay muchas **plantas**.

Esta semana vamos a **aprender** a montar a caballo.

**Tengo ganas de** caminar con amigos.

Más tarde, vamos a hacer **un dibujo** de nuestra casa ideal.

## Para conversar 🎧

**T**o start a letter to a friend:

**Querido/a** amigo/a:
*Dear friend,*

Escribo esta **carta desde** Cartagena.
*I am writing this letter from Cartagena.*

**T**o close a letter:

**Un abrazo** grande, Inés
*A big hug, Inés*

### Para decir más

| | |
|---|---|
| Recordado/a | *Dear...* |
| Con cariño, | *With affection,* |
| ¡Cuídate! | *Take care!* |
| Te quiere, | *Love you,* |

### En otro país (México)

| | |
|---|---|
| el cuarto | la recámara |
| el garaje | la cochera |
| el patio | la yarda |
| la piscina | la alberca |

**T**o describe your room:

¿Cómo es tu cuarto?
*What's your bedroom like?*

Es **pequeño** pero muy cómodo. Me gusta **cuando** la luz entra **por** la ventana.
*It's small but very comfortable. I like it when the light comes in through the window.*

¿Dónde está?
*Where is it?*

En el primer piso, **al lado del** baño.
*On the first floor, next to the bathroom.*

### Un poco más

**La planta baja *vs* el primer piso**

In most Spanish-speaking countries, the term *la planta baja* refers to the ground floor, or what we would call the first floor. The term *el primer piso* refers to what we would call the second floor. ¡Ojo! When you get on an elevator, remember to press the button that says *PB* to get to the ground floor, not the button that says 1!

### 1 ¿Qué hacen en tu casa?

Completa las oraciones con las palabras del recuadro, según el contexto.

| una escalera | cuarto | un baño | la piscina | el patio |
|---|---|---|---|---|
| teléfono | la planta baja | el garaje | la sala | dibujos |

1. Mi hermano nada en __.
2. Papá pone el carro en __.
3. Mi familia ve la televisión en __.
4. Cuando estoy cansado voy a mi __ y cierro la puerta.
5. Los domingos siempre hacemos una comida en __.
6. Mi casa tiene __ porque es una casa de dos pisos.
7. El comedor está en __.
8. Hay __ en cada piso.
9. A mi hermano menor le gusta hacer __ de nuestro gato.
10. Voy a llamar a mis abuelos por __.

*Mi hermana nada.*

## 2 Dictado 🎧

Escucha la información y escribe lo que oyes.

## 3 ¿Dónde en la casa?

Look at these photographs and tell what Francisco's relatives are doing somewhere in their house in Cartagena.

**1.** su prima menor

**2.** su abuelo

**3.** su prima Ana

**4.** su tío

**5.** su tía

**6.** su madre

## 4 ¿Adónde deben ir? 🎧

Read the statements and say where the people should go.

MODELO    Quiero un vaso de agua.

**Debes ir a la cocina.**

**1.** Mi hermana quiere buscar una naranja y un refresco.

**2.** Mis padres necesitan usar el carro.

**3.** Yo tengo ganas de ver televisión.

**4.** Mis abuelos están aquí para comer con la familia.

**5.** Mi hermana viene de jugar al fútbol.

**6.** Voy a leer y escuchar CDs.

## ¡Comunicación!

## 5 ¿Cómo es tu casa? Presentational Communication

Create a floor plan of your home (real or imaginary) and label the rooms in Spanish. Write five sentences in Spanish that describe your floor plan. State if it is a house (*casa*) or an apartment (*apartamento*), how many floors it has, how large it is, the number of rooms, outdoor features, etc. Present your floor plan and describe it to the class.

# Diálogo 🎧

## La casa de Elisa

**Javier:** Juan dice que la casa de Elisa es muy grande.

**Rosa:** Sí, yo tengo ganas de ir a su casa.

**Javier:** A mí también me gustaría mucho verla.

**Rosa:** ¡Vamos mañana!

**Javier:** Mira, allí está Juan.

**Rosa:** Oye, Juan, ¿cómo es la casa de Elisa?

**Juan:** Es una casa grande e interesante. Tiene tres pisos.

**Rosa:** ¡Qué grande!

**Juan:** Sí, tiene siete u ocho cuartos, dos salas y una piscina.

**Javier:** ¡Es la casa ideal!

**Rosa:** ¿Ideal? No pienso eso, prefiero casas pequeñas.

### 6 ¿Qué recuerdas? 🎧

1. ¿Quién dice que la casa de Elisa es grande?
2. ¿Quién tiene ganas de ir a la casa de Elisa?
3. ¿A quién le gustaría mucho ver la casa de Elisa?
4. ¿Cómo es la casa de Elisa?
5. ¿Cuántos pisos tiene la casa de Elisa?
6. ¿Y cuántos cuartos tiene?

### 7 Algo personal 🎧

1. ¿Cómo es tu casa ideal?
2. ¿Te gustan las casas grandes o pequeñas? Explica.

### Un poco más

**Las palabras *e* y *u***

Before words that begin with *i* or *hi*, the word *y* becomes *e*. Similarly, the word *o* changes to *u* before words that begin with *o* or *ho*.

*Marcos **e** Inés viven en Cartagena. Dicen que van a montar a caballo mañana **u** otro día.*

## 💬 ¡Comunicación!

### 8 A describir 👥 Interpersonal Communication

Trabajando en parejas, menciona un cuarto de la casa. Tu compañero/a tiene que describirlo.

**MODELO**  A: tu cuarto
B: Es pequeño y bonito. Está en el primer piso al lado del baño.

# Gramática

## Telling What Someone Says: *decir*

- The present tense of **decir** (to say, to tell) has an irregular *yo* form. In addition, it is a "shoe verb," so it requires a stem change (*e* → *i*) for all forms except *nosotros/as* and *vosotros/as*. Use **decir** to tell what someone says.

  *Mi hermanito **dice** muchas cosas tontas.*        My little brother **says** a lot of silly things.

| decir (i) | | | |
|---|---|---|---|
| yo | **digo** | nosotros nosotras | decimos |
| tú | dices | vosotros vosotras | decís |
| Ud. él ella | dice | Uds. ellos ellas | dicen |

- When you are summarizing or reporting what someone says, use **que** between **decir** and the expression or phrase that follows:

  *¿Qué **dice** Luisa?*        What does Luisa **say**?

  ***Dice** que el cuarto de Elvira es muy pequeño.*   **She says (that)** Elvira's room is very small.

---

### 9   Todos dicen algo

Completa las siguientes oraciones con la forma apropiada del verbo **decir**.

1. Rafael __ que su cuarto favorito es la sala.
2. A veces tú __ cosas tontas.
3. Los niños __ que están cansados.
4. Mi hermana y yo nunca __ secretos.
5. Ud. __ que tenemos tarea.
6. Yo siempre __ gracias por ayudarme.
7. Mi padre __ que está apurado.

---

### 10   ¿Qué dicen?  🎧

What might the response be to what the following people say?

MODELO     ¿Cómo te llamas? (Ramiro)
           **Ramiro dice "Me llamo Ramiro".**

*Ana dice que está contenta.*

1. Estoy enfermo. (yo)
2. Hoy es mi cumpleaños. (nosotros)
3. No hay luz en mi casa. (Uds.)
4. ¿Te gustan mis plantas? (tú)
5. Voy a comprar una casa con una piscina muy grande. (ellas)
6. ¡Aló! ¿Puedo hablar con Daniela? (Daniela)

## 11 Encuesta de viaje de intercambio

Results of a poll show who would like to spend the summer in Colombia as part of an exchange program with a high school in Cartagena. Summarize whether the indicated people say they would like to participate or not. Report a final tally of how many people say yes and how many people say no.

**MODELO**  Silvia
**Silvia dice que sí.**

1. Julia
2. Miguel y la señorita Oquendo
3. el señor Martín y Carlos
4. Ud.
5. la señora Abreu y Eva
6. Ernesto y yo
7. Enrique

### Viaje de intercambio

| | sí | no |
|---|---|---|
| Silvia | ● | ○ |
| yo | ● | ○ |
| Ernesto | ● | ○ |
| la señorita Oquendo | ● | ○ |
| Miguel | ● | ○ |
| Julia | ○ | ● |
| Enrique | ● | ○ |
| Eva | ○ | ● |
| Ud. | ○ | ● |
| el señor Martín | ○ | ● |
| la señora Abreu | ○ | ● |
| Carlos | ○ | ● |

## ¡Comunicación!

## 12 ¿Cómo hacen en tu casa?   Interpersonal/Presentational Communication

In small groups, dicuss what is similar or different about your homes (*casa* or *apartamento*) and what activities you do there. Assign one classmate to take notes. You may include some of the following activities or add others of your choice:

- ver televisión
- hacer la comida
- comer
- escuchar música
- estudiar
- leer
- hablar por teléfono
- usar la computadora

*Toda la familia come en el comedor.*

Report to the class what you've discussed.

**MODELO**
A: **¿Dónde come tu familia?**
B: **Comemos en la cocina. ¿Y Uds.?**
A: **Nosotros comemos en la sala y vemos televisión.**
C: **En mi casa comemos en la sala, pero no los domingos. Los domingos comemos en el comedor.**
A: **B dice que en su casa...**

# Gramática

## Expressing Wishes with *querer* or *gustaría*

You have learned to express someone's wishes by using a form of **querer** (to want) and an infinitive. You can also express wishes by combining *me*, *te*, *le*, *nos*, *os*, or *les* with the more polite but less emphatic *gustaría* (would like) and an infinitive.

| | |
|---|---|
| **Quiero viajar** a Bogotá. | **I want to travel** to Bogotá. |
| *Me gustaría viajar* a Bogotá. | **I would like to travel** to Bogotá. |
| **Quieren comprar** un lavaplatos nuevo. | **They want to buy** a new dishwasher. |
| *Les gustaría comprar* un lavaplatos nuevo. | **They would like to buy** a new dishwasher. |

### 13 ¿Qué les gustaría?

Choose a word or expression from each column and create complete sentences telling what members of the Rodríguez family would like when they buy a new house.

**MODELO**   **A mí me gustaría tener plantas en el patio.**

*Nos gustaría tener plantas en el patio.*

| I | II |
|---|---|
| yo | quieren tener cuartos en el primer piso |
| a ti | les gustaría tener un garaje para dos carros |
| mi hermano | queremos comprar una casa grande |
| a mis padres | te gustaría tener un cuarto en la planta baja |
| a nosotros | me gustaría tener plantas en el patio |
| a mí | quiero tener una piscina |
| mis hermanas | nos gustaría tener una sala cómoda |
| nosotros | quiere una cocina con un horno microondas |

### 14 Me gustaría...

Completa las oraciones de una manera original.

**MODELO**   Me gustaría tener...
**Me gustaría tener una casa con piscina.**

1. Me gustaría vivir...
2. Me gustaría aprender a...
3. Me gustaría viajar...
4. No me gustaría vivir...
5. Me gustaría comprar...
6. No me gustaría ir...

# ¡Comunicación!

## 15  ¿Cómo es tu casa ideal?  Interpersonal/Presentational Communication

What are some of the rooms and outdoor features that an ideal house should have?
Start a small group discussion and then share the results with the rest of the class.

MODELO  A:  ¿Cómo es tu casa ideal?

B:  Me gustaría tener una casa grande de dos pisos.

C:  Yo prefiero una casa pequeña con una piscina.

A:  B dice que le gustaría tener una casa grande
de dos pisos y C dice que prefiere una casa
pequeña con una piscina.

# ¡Comunicación!

## 16  Me gustaría alquilar una casa  Interpersonal Communication

You are looking for a place to rent near a beach in Cartagena, Colombia. With a
classmate, discuss the type of house or apartment you would like to rent, based on the
information on this online rental site. Include as many details as possible.

MODELO  A:  Me gustaría alquilar una casa para la semana del 5 de julio.

B:  ¿Para cuántas personas?

A:  Para cuatro. Yo, mis dos hermanas y mi prima. Necesitamos 3 o 4
cuartos con 2 o más baños.

B:  ¿Quieres televisión con cable?

A:  Sí y también me gustaría tener WiFi.

cartagenavacaciones.com

**¿Cuándo piensan comenzar sus vacaciones?**
**(Deben elegir de una a cuatro semanas)**

● 21 junio   ● 28 junio   ● 5 julio   ● 12 julio   ● 19 julio
● 26 julio   ● 2 agosto   ● 9 agosto   ● 16 agosto   ● 23 agosto

**Precio (en dólares)**
● por día (1 a 4 días) $308 a $800 por día
● por semana (1 a 4 semanas) $1,780 a $6,800 por semana

**Tipo**   ● apartamento   ● casa

**Número de personas**   ● 1   ● 2   ● 3 o más

**Distancia a la playa**  ● caminar a la playa   ● en la playa

**Exterior de la casa**   ● patio   ● piscina   ● jardín

**Interior de la casa**   ● lavaplatos   ● lavadora/secadora
● horno microondas   ● televisión con cable
● WiFi   ● se permiten perros o gatos

## Cultura

En Cartagena puedes observar el estilo colonial.

# Las diferentes casas colombianas 🎧

**? Pregunta clave**

What does a home and its contents tell us about the people who live there?

Al observar las casas de un pueblo o ciudad, es posible aprender sobre las personas que viven allí y su estilo de vida.

En Colombia, los diferentes estilos de las casas están determinados por los distintos climas y por la diversidad cultural del país. La mayoría[1] de los colombianos son descendientes de españoles, y muchas casas de los pueblos y ciudades de Colombia son del estilo colonial español. La ciudad de Cartagena, en la costa del Caribe, preserva un estilo de arquitectura colonial que atrae a muchos artistas y escritores. Estas casas son grandes (de dos pisos) y de colores alegres. ¡Son perfectas para familias numerosas! Los balcones ofrecen la oportunidad de tomar aire fresco[2], plantar flores y relajarse.

En las ciudades grandes como Bogotá, la vida es dinámica y moderna. Allí residen muchos profesionales que prefieren vivir cerca del trabajo en edificios de apartamentos de estilo contemporáneo donde los espacios son más pequeños y fáciles de limpiar. Pero los jardines, plantas y flores que adornan estos edificios son evidencia de que los colombianos admiran la naturaleza.

Rascacielos en Bocagrande, Cartagena

Las casas de San Andrés, en el Caribe, nos hablan del origen de sus habitantes: ingleses y sus esclavos[3] africano-americanos. El estilo de construcción es inglés, pero los colores vivos y alegres son típicos de la cultura caribeña. Las casas tienen un porche delante o en la parte de atrás. Aquí los sanadresanos, que son personas sociables y tranquilas, disfrutan de un espacio fresco[4] para relajarse y conversar con sus vecinos[5].

[1] majority   [2] get fresh air   [3] slaves   [4] cool   [5] neighbors

Casa en la zona del Caribe

🔍 **Búsqueda:** casas coloniales en colombia, arquitectura moderna en bogotá

## Productos

El museo Quinta de Bolívar

*La Quinta de Bolívar* was given to Simón Bolívar, famed liberator of much of South America, as a token of Colombia's appreciation for his service to the nation. This *quinta*, or farm, is a fine example of a colonial-style home. Here, Bolívar could relax, write, and walk in the beautiful gardens. In 1922 it became a museum dedicated to Bolívar's life and times. You can visit the different rooms, including the library, and see his furniture and personal belongings, as well as reminders of the War of Independence.

## 17 Comprensión — Interpretive Communication

1. What type of housing is most common in Colombia's big cities? Why?
2. Describe the homes and the residents of San Andrés.
3. What does the Quinta de Bolívar tell you about the personality of Simón Bolívar?

## 18 Analiza

1. What factors do you think influence Colombians' housing choices?
2. Which style of Colombian home is most similar to homes where you live?

## Antes de leer

Is there a special place in your home where you like to spend time? Where? Why?

# El patio

What comes to mind when you hear the word "patio"? One of the most outstanding characteristics of colonial-style homes built in Colombia, and in many other Latin American countries, is the *patio*, or courtyard. This unique element of the traditional colonial house plays a key role in the lives of the people who live there. There's a certain prestige attached to these colonial homes which makes them very attractive to members of the upper middle class who can afford them. These homes do not favor landscapes or grand views of the outside world; on the contrary, they focus their attention inwards. The need for privacy and tranquility is essential to the lifestyle of the people who live in these houses. The patio functions as a refuge from the hot or cold weather. It also serves as a source of light and air circulation to the rooms that only open onto the patio. Residents grow local plants and flowers there to add color and beauty, and these are complemented sometimes with fountains and small trees. As the heart of the home, it represents an open space where family members can meet, talk, eat meals, and spend time together.

Un patio colonial

🔍 **Búsqueda:** patios coloniales en colombia

## Comparaciones

Are there any features unique to the houses in your region? What do those features reflect about the people who live there?

## 19 Comprensión

1. Where is the main focus in traditional Colombian colonial homes?
2. Explain two functions that patios serve in traditional colonial homes.
3. What are some possible features of a patio?

## 20 Analiza

1. Do you think that having an indoor patio in your house would be a good idea or a bad idea? Explain.
2. What type of person or family can you envision living in a typical colonial home in Colombia? Explain and give details from the readings on these two pages to support your answer.

## Perspectivas

Colombians have a *dicho* (saying) about houses: *"Tener casa no es riqueza, pero no tenerla sí es pobreza."* (Owning a house does not make you rich, but not owning one makes you poor.) From this saying, explain what you see as the value of a home for Colombians. Find statistics online to discover how many Colombians own their own homes.

# Vocabulario 2

## Un día con Verónica

Me llamo Verónica. Vivo en Santa Marta, Colombia. Me gusta hacer muchas actividades con mi familia y mis amigos. **Lo que** más me gusta es ir a la playa.

En la playa

En la casa

**Tenemos** mucho **calor**. Nos gustaría nadar.

Mis amigas toman bebidas calientes porque **tienen frío**.

**Tengo** mucha **sed**. Debo tomar más agua.

¡Hay mucha comida! Mi familia **tiene hambre**.

Nos gusta **correr**. Después, tenemos calor y sed.

**Tenemos miedo** cuando vemos películas de terror.

Tenemos ganas de tocar música y cantar.

Estamos muy cansados y **tenemos** mucho **sueño**.

> Sabes que debes **pedir permiso** para usar el carro y no debes decirle **mentiras** a tu madre.

> Sí, lo siento. Voy a pedirle **perdón** a mamá.

**Tenemos prisa** para ir a casa.

## Para conversar

*T*o talk about things you should and should not do:

No debes pedir **prestado** dinero.
*You should not borrow money.*

No debes **repetir** las mentiras que dicen otros.
*You should not repeat the lies others say.*

Siempre debes decir **la verdad**.
*You should always tell the truth.*

*T*o ask others what they feel like doing:

¿Tienes ganas de comer algo?
*Do you feel like eating something?*

No, gracias. Tengo **poca** hambre.
*No, thanks. I'm not very hungry.*

### Para decir más

| | |
|---|---|
| devolver | *to give back* |
| engañar | *to deceive* |
| pedir disculpas | *to apologize* |
| ser honesto | *to be honest* |
| tener cuidado | *to be careful* |
| tener razón | *to be right* |

*Tenemos ganas de ir a la playa.*

### 21 ¿Cuál es la palabra?

Completa las oraciones con la palabra apropiada.

1. Es la hora del almuerzo. Tengo mucha __. *(hambre / prisa)*
2. Debes decir la verdad. No debes decir __. *(gracias / mentiras)*
3. No queremos ir a la playa. No tenemos __. *(ganas / miedo)*
4. Estoy cansada y tengo mucho __. *(prisa / sueño)*
5. Lo siento. Voy a pedirle __ a papá. *(prestado / perdón)*
6. Necesito tomar más agua. Tengo mucha __. *(sed / frío)*

## 22 ¿Lógico o no? 🎧

Di si lo que oyes es lógico o no. Si no es lógico explica por qué.

*Paco tiene hambre. Va a comer.*

## 23 ¿Qué tiene?

With a classmate, take turns asking and answering the following questions, according to the photos.

MODELO    Cristina

       **A:** **¿Qué tiene Cristina?**

       **B:** **Cristina tiene sed.**

**1.** Nicolás

**2.** Verónica

**3.** Erica

**4.** abuelo

**5.** Mateo

**6.** ellos

**7.** Julio

**8.** tú

## 24 Situaciones con tener

Use an appropriate expression with *tener* to make a statement about the following situations.

**1.** El señor Álvarez está en Alaska en febrero.

**2.** Son las 12:30 de la noche y Belinda está muy cansada.

**3.** Martita tiene ocho años. Está sola en casa y son las 10:00 de la noche.

**4.** Rita busca algo de comer pero no hay nada en el refrigerador.

**5.** Jorge corre para tomar el autobús.

**6.** La señora Díaz necesita tomar agua después de correr en un maratón.

**7.** Estás en Florida en agosto.

**8.** Tú y tus amigos no quieren estudiar.

# Diálogo

## Tengo mucho calor

**Javier:** Tengo mucho calor.

**Rosa:** Ya estamos cerca de la casa de Elisa.

**Javier:** También tengo mucha sed.

**Rosa:** ¡Allí está la casa de Elisa! ¡Qué grande y bonita es tu casa!

**Elisa:** Muchas gracias. Es tu casa también.

**Javier:** A Rosa no le gusta tu casa.

**Rosa:** Mentira, Elisa. No es verdad.

**Javier:** Pero dices que te gustan las casas pequeñas.

**Rosa:** Lo que digo es que prefiero una casa pequeña.

**Elisa:** Está bien. Yo comprendo. ¡Vamos a la playa!

**Javier:** Buena idea. Tengo mucho calor.

## 25 ¿Qué recuerdas?

1. ¿Quién tiene mucho calor?
2. ¿Quién tiene mucha sed?
3. ¿De quién es la casa grande y bonita?
4. ¿Es verdad que a Rosa no le gusta la casa de Elisa?
5. ¿Adónde quiere ir Elisa?

## 26 Algo personal

1. ¿Tienes calor? ¿Y sed?
2. ¿Dices mentiras? Explica.
3. ¿Adónde vas cuando hace mucho calor?

Cuando tenemos mucho calor vamos a la playa.

## 27 ¿Qué tienen?

Selecciona la ilustración apropiada que corresponda con lo que oyes.

| A | B | C | D | E | F |

# Gramática

## Regular -ar, -er, and -ir Verbs

You are already familiar with the forms of regular verbs:

|  | hablar | comer | vivir |
|---|---|---|---|
| yo | hablo | como | vivo |
| tú | hablas | comes | vives |
| Ud. él ella | habla | come | vive |
| nosotros nosotras | hablamos | comemos | vivimos |
| vosotros vosotras | habláis | coméis | vivís |
| Uds. ellos ellas | hablan | comen | viven |

## 28  Elena y su familia

Completa el siguiente párrafo con las formas apropiadas de los verbos entre paréntesis.

Me llamo Elena y (**1.** *vivir*) con mi familia en Cartagena, Colombia. Nosotros (**2.** *tener*) una casa muy grande con cinco cuartos y cuatro baños. En casa todos (**3.** *hablar*) inglés porque mi padre (**4.** *ser*) de San Antonio, Texas. Mi hermana Raquel y yo (**5.** *estudiar*) en el colegio Jorge Washington. Nosotras (**6.** *caminar*) al colegio todos los días porque está muy cerca. Por las tardes, Raquel (**7.** *practicar*) deportes y yo (**8.** *ir*) a la biblioteca y (**9.** *leer*) libros de historia y de biología. Raquel (**10.** *pensar*) que es aburrido, pero a mí me (**11.** *gustar*) mucho. A veces mis amigas y yo (**12.** *salir*) a tomar un refresco o (**13.** *caminar*) por la playa. Después en casa, Raquel y yo (**14.** *hacer*) la tarea en nuestro cuarto, (**15.** *escribir*) correos electrónicos a nuestros amigos y (**16.** *jugar*) con el perro. Por las noches, toda la familia (**17.** *comer*) en el patio y después (**18.** *ver*) televisión en la sala.

¿Te gustaría ir a Cartagena, Colombia?

# Gramática

## Stem-Changing Verbs: e → i

You have already learned to use stem-changing verbs ("shoe verbs") like *pensar* (*ie*) that have the spelling change **e → ie**: *yo pienso, nosotros pensamos*. The verb *pedir* is also a stem-changing verb. In this verb the **e** of the stem changes to **i** in all its forms except for *nosotros* and *vosotros*.

| pedir | | | |
|---|---|---|---|
| yo | pido | nosotros nosotras | pedimos |
| tú | pides | vosotros vosotras | pedís |
| Ud. él ella | pide | Uds. ellos ellas | piden |

*Pedir* is the English equivalent of "to ask for, to request, to order (in a restaurant)." Don't confuse *pedir* with *preguntar* or *hacer una pregunta*, which are both used for "to ask a question."

Other expressions with *pedir*:

- **Pedir ayuda** is "to ask for help."
- **Pedir perdón** can be used to excuse yourself and to apologize.
- **Pedir permiso** (*para*) is "to ask for permission (to do something)."
- **Pedir prestado/a** is "to ask for a loan" or "to borrow something."

The verbs *repetir* (to repeat) and *decir* (to say, to tell) follow the same pattern as *pedir*, with the exception of the irregular *yo* form of *decir: digo*.

### Un poco más

**Con permiso y Perdón**

Although *permiso* and *perdón* may be used with the verb *pedir*, *Con permiso* and *Perdón* can also be used alone for "Excuse me" or "Pardon me."

---

## 29  Mi amigo Pablo

Completa este párrafo con la forma apropiada de los verbos **pedir** o **repetir**.

Hola, soy Eduardo. Pablo y yo somos amigos. Pablo siempre **(1)** prestadas muchas cosas. Un día **(2)** prestado un cuchillo; otro día **(3)** un tenedor. A veces tiene que **(4)** prestado dinero para comer más porque siempre tiene hambre. Cuando él y su hermano van a un restaurante **(5)** muchos refrescos porque siempre tienen sed, y cuando están en el colegio siempre **(6)** ropa prestada a sus amigos porque siempre tienen frío. Yo nunca **(7)** prestado nada, y lo **(8)**, nada. A mí no me gusta cuando las personas **(9)** cosas prestadas. ¡Es muy malo! Yo siempre le debo **(10)** a Pablo una y otra vez: "No debes pedir más cosas prestadas" pero él dice que yo soy egoísta. Mmm, ¿qué opinas si nosotros le **(11)** cosas prestadas a Pablo todos los días? ¿Qué va a pensar?

*Siempre me pide cosas prestadas.*

## 30 ¿Preguntar o pedir?

Completa las siguientes oraciones con la forma apropiada de **preguntar** o **pedir**.

1. Mis padres siempre me __ adónde voy.

2. Mi hermano y yo __ ¿cuándo vamos a viajar a Bogotá?

3. ¿ __ siempre tú permiso para usar el carro de tu papá?

4. Mi hermana menor siempre __ ayuda para encender la estufa.

5. Jorge siempre __ mucho en la clase de matemáticas.

6. A veces Susana tiene que __ faldas prestadas a su mamá.

7. ¿ __ ayuda con tu tarea a tus hermanos?

8. Mi primo siempre __ perdón cuando no comprende lo que dice el profesor.

## 31 Respuesta apropiada

Choose an appropriate response from the column on the right to go with the situations on the left.

1. Buscas algo para escribir.

2. Dices una mentira a tu amiga y ella lo sabe.

3. Dices lo que no debes decir a tu madre.

4. Tienes que poner una mesa para doce parientes invitados.

5. Quieres salir del comedor.

6. Caminas en la calle y tienes prisa.

7. No comprendes nada en la clase de matemáticas.

*Pedimos ayuda a nuestro profesor.*

A. Pido prestado un lápiz.

B. Digo "con permiso".

C. Hago preguntas al profesor.

D. Pido perdón.

E. Pido ayuda.

## 32 En familia

¿Qué dices o pides en estas situaciones? Sigue el modelo.

MODELO     Situación: Tu madre te pide hacer muchos quehaceres antes de poder ver la televisión.
                **Pido ayuda a mis hermanos menores.**

1. Situación: Estás en el comedor y tu madre dice que debes hablar poco y comer más.

2. Situación: Eres el primero/la primera en terminar de comer y quieres ir a tu cuarto porque tienes mucho sueño.

3. Situación: Quieres ir con tus amigos a una fiesta por la noche.

4. Situación: Tú dices que tienes mucha sed y tu madre te pasa un refresco.

5. Situación: Vas a salir para el colegio y ves que no tienes una camisa limpia.

## ¡Comunicación!

### 33 ¿Cuándo pides...? 👥 Interpersonal Communication

En grupos, hablen de situaciones donde tienen que
**pedir perdón**, **pedir prestado/a**, **pedir ayuda** o **pedir permiso**.

MODELO
A: Pedro, ¿cuándo pides perdón?

B: Pido perdón cuando salgo de noche sin pedir permiso.
Amalia, ¿qué pides prestado?

C: A veces pido prestado dinero.

## ¡Comunicación!

### 34 ¿Qué pide? 👥 Interpersonal Communication

En grupos pequeños hablen de un pariente y luego digan lo que él o
ella pide para su cumpleaños pero nunca lo recibe (*but never receives it*).

MODELO
A: Tienes una hermana mayor, ¿verdad?

B: Sí. Se llama Elena. Tiene diecisiete años.

C: ¿Qué pide siempre tu hermana para su
cumpleaños?

B: Mi hermana siempre pide un carro nuevo
pero nunca lo recibe.

*Mi hermana pide un carro nuevo para su cumpleaños.*

## ¡Comunicación!

### 35 ¿Qué piden? 👥 Interpersonal Communication

You and a classmate must each create a two-column list with the headings *¿Quién?*
and *¿Qué?*. Name six family members or friends in the first column. Leave the second
column blank. Exchange lists and use them to ask what the people listed ask to
borrow. Write down the borrowed item next to the person's name.

MODELO
A: ¿Qué pide siempre prestado tu hermano?

B: Siempre pide prestada ropa.

| ¿Quién? | ¿Qué? |
| --- | --- |
| tu hermano | ropa |
| Ana y Diego | |
| mi amigo Juan | |
| mi hermana | |
| yo | |
| mi hermano | |

# Todo en contexto

? Pregunta clave

What does a house and its contents tell us about the people who live there?

## ¡Comunicación!

### 36 Como en tu casa    Interpretive Communication

Answer the questions according to the advertisement below.

No se aceptan mascotas

**¡Alquila nuestra casa en Cartagena!**

Ven a pasar unos días en Cartagena de Indias y disfruta de una casa cómoda con:

- 2 habitaciones con balcón
- 1 baño completo
- 1 salón-comedor
- Cocina grande y moderna
- Patio con flores, plantas y fuente
- Magníficas vistas
- Garaje para estacionar el auto

La casa está situada en el centro de Cartagena con acceso fácil a la playa y a muchos restaurantes, cines, y el centro comercial. Visita nuestro sitio web para consultar precios, calendario y ver más fotografías.

1. Where is this rental house located?
2. How can you find out about the prices?
3. Can you take your dog with you?
4. State three other facts you learned about this house from this ad.

5. What can you infer about the people who would rent this house? Be creative, but use information from the ad to support your answer.

## ¡Comunicación!

### 37 Mi casa ideal    Interpretive/Presentational Communication

You are going to describe your ideal home in Colombia, and your partner is going to sketch it along with a floor plan according to your description. First, review the vocabulary and the cultural readings in this lesson to decide which style of Colombian home you would choose. Then make a list of desired features your home would have, and include those in your description. Make sure to include:

- style of Colombian home
- location (city, suburbs, country)
- number of floors

- number of rooms and where they are
- outdoor features such as a patio, garden, or swimming pool

With your partner, review the sketch and floor plan that he or she created to ensure that it includes all the features you described. Then be prepared to make a presentation to the class.

MODELO    Mi casa ideal es una casa de estilo colonial. Tiene dos pisos y es grande. En la planta baja hay una sala. Al lado de la sala hay un comedor y una cocina. En el primer piso...

# Lectura

## La pobre viejecita (*The Poor Old Lady*)
### de *Rafael Pombo*
#### Sobre el autor

Rafael Pombo (1833–1912) once famously said, "*De que soy poeta apenas tengo estos datos: Que no sirvo para nada, sino para hacer versos*". ("As for my being a poet, I have only this information: That I am no good at anything except writing verses.") Some years later, in 1905, this diplomat, writer, mathematician, and engineer was named Colombia's National Poet.

Pombo was also a respected translator. In fact, one of his most famous works came about when he was commissioned by a publisher in New York to translate some of the traditional English nursery rhymes and songs into Spanish. The result was two children's books, which took original stories like "Simple Simon" and "Froggy Went A-Courtin'" and transformed them into modernist Spanish poems that made him famous all over the world.

The poem on the next page is from one of those books, titled *Cuentos morales para niños formales*. In it, the poet uses gentle humor and irony to examine some wrong attitudes that are common everywhere. You just might know someone like the little old lady in this poem.

### Antes de leer

#### 38 Preparación

1. Have you ever complained about something that was not really worth complaining about? What was it?

2. Look at the illustration. What kind of life does the woman in the illustration seem to have? Does she seem happy?

#### 39 ¿Hay una exageración?

As you look at the illustration, is there anything that seems excessive in the house or its contents? At first glance, how do you imagine the lady feels? Keep your findings in mind as you read.

### Estrategia

#### Irony

Sometimes authors say one thing in words, but the real message they transmit is different. They intentionally lead us to believe something, but, as we continue reading, we realize that the truth is not what it appears to be. In fact, it may be the exact opposite. Pay attention when a description or statement seems overly positive or overly negative. This might be a clue to look for a different meaning than the obvious.

## La pobre viejecita (*The Poor Old Lady*) 🎧
### de *Rafael Pombo*

| | |
|---|---|
| Érase una viejecita | *There was a poor old lady* |
| sin nadita que comer, | *Who had nothing much to eat,* |
| sino carnes, frutas, dulces, | *Except fruits and sweets, and cakes, and eggs,* |
| tortas, huevos, pan y pez. | *and bread, and fish, and meat.* |
| | |
| Bebía caldo, chocolate, | *She drank broth and cups of chocolate,* |
| leche, vino, té y café, | *Milk and coffee, wine and tea,* |
| y la pobre no encontraba | *But not a single beverage,* |
| qué comer ni qué beber. | *Not a thing to eat had she.* |
| | |
| Y esta vieja no tenía | *This poor old lady did not own* |
| ni un ranchito en que vivir | *A house in which to stay,* |
| fuera de una casa grande | *Just a large one with an orchard* |
| con su huerta y su jardín. | *and a garden down the way.* |
| | |
| Se murió del mal de arrugas, | *She died from all her wrinkles,* |
| ya encorvada como un tres, | *Old and curved like a number three* |
| y jamás volvió a quejarse | *And never more did she complain* |
| ni de hambre ni de sed. | *Of hunger, thirst, or heat.* |
| | |
| Duerma en paz, y Dios permita | *Rest in peace, oh poor old lady,* |
| que logremos disfrutar | *And perhaps, if God so wills,* |
| las pobrezas de esa pobre | *We can live in that same poverty,* |
| y morir del mismo mal. | *And die of those same ills.* |

## 40 Comprensión · Interpretive Communication

Indica la respuesta correcta.
1. ¿Qué come la viejecita?
   A. Comida típica
   B. Muchas cosas
   C. Solo pollo y pan
2. ¿Qué bebe la viejecita?
   A. Refrescos
   B. Jugo de naranja
   C. Muchas cosas
3. ¿Dónde vive la viejecita?
   A. En una casa pequeña
   B. En un apartamento
   C. En una casa grande
4. ¿Por qué dice el poema que murió de arrugas (*wrinkles*)?
   A. Porque es muy vieja.
   B. Porque come mucho.
   C. Porque es muy canosa.

## 41 Analiza

1. Why do you think the lady in the poem complains so much?
2. What is the author really saying in the last three lines of the poem? Explain the irony.

# Repaso de la Lección B

## A  Escuchar: ¿Está en la casa, en el colegio o en el parque?  (pp. 272–273)

Di dónde están las siguientes personas según lo que oyes.

*Está en la casa.*   **Está en el parque.**   *Está en el colegio.*

## B  Vocabulario: La palabra apropiada (pp. 272–273, 282–283)

Completa las oraciones con una palabra apropiada del vocabulario de la lección.

1. Por favor, pásame ese vaso de agua. Tengo __.
2. Para ir a la planta baja está la __.
3. Cuando no llevo mucha ropa tengo __.
4. El carro de mi hermano está en el __.
5. Necesito un lápiz para hacer un __ de mi casa.
6. Voy a llamar a mis abuelos por __.
7. Estoy cansada. No tengo __ de jugar.
8. Me gustaría nadar en la __.

## C  Gramática: Planes de la semana (p. 278)

Jorge escribe en su agenda sus planes, y los de su familia y sus amigos, para la semana. ¿Qué les gustaría hacer, qué tienen ganas de hacer o qué quieren hacer ellos? Escribe tres oraciones para cada día de la semana con la forma correcta de **gustaría**, **tener ganas de** y **querer**.

**MODELO**  yo / patinar sobre ruedas

**El lunes me gustaría patinar sobre ruedas.**

**El lunes tengo ganas de patinar sobre ruedas.**

**El lunes quiero patinar sobre ruedas.**

| lunes | martes | miércoles | jueves | viernes | sábado | domingo |
|---|---|---|---|---|---|---|
| yo / patinar sobre ruedas | mamá y mi hermana / hacer un postre | Ricardo / correr en la playa | yo / escribirles una carta a mis abuelos | papá / comer en el patio | Julieta y Sandra / ir de compras | mi hermano y yo / jugar al tenis |

## D  Gramática: El verbo correcto (pp. 276, 287)

Completa las frases con la forma del verbo apropiado según el contexto.

1. Mi hermano siempre (*preguntar / pedir*) prestada mi ropa.
2. Yo nunca (*decir / preguntar*) mentiras.
3. Tú y yo siempre (*decir / repetir*) "con permiso" cuando queremos salir de la clase.
4. Nosotros (*preguntar / pedir*) comida cuando tenemos hambre.
5. Los estudiantes (*preguntar / repetir*) las palabras en la clase de español.
6. ¿A veces (*decir / pedir*) tú mentiras a tus amigos?
7. Cuando salgo por las noches, mis padres me (*preguntar / pedir*) a qué hora voy a estar en casa.
8. Los niños (*pedir / repetir*) todo lo que escuchan.
9. ¿(*preguntar / pedir*) Uds. perdón cuando hacen algo que no deben hacer?

Place the information from the box about the different types of homes in Colombia in the appropriate column in the table.

| influencia española | espacios pequeños | patio central | dos pisos | porche delante o detrás |
| grandes ciudades | balcones | colores vivos y alegres | vida urbana | influencia inglesa |

**Estilos de casas en Colombia**

| Coloniales | Apartamentos | Costa Caribe |
| --- | --- | --- |
| | | |
| | | |
| | | |
| | | |

## Vocabulario

| La casa | Para describir | Qué tienes | Otras expresiones | Verbos |
| --- | --- | --- | --- | --- |
| el baño | al lado de | el calor | el abrazo | aprender (a) |
| el cuarto | cómodo/a | el frío | la carta | correr |
| la escalera | cuando | las ganas | el dibujo | decir |
| el garaje | desde | el hambre (f.) | entonces | escribir |
| el patio | donde | el miedo | lo que | gustaría |
| la piscina | pequeño/a | la prisa | me/te/le/nos/les | pedir (i) |
| el piso | poco/a | la sed | gustaría | repetir (i) |
| la planta | por | el sueño | la mentira | |
| la planta baja | por la noche | tener (calor, frío, | pedir (ayuda, perdón, | |
| el primer piso | | ganas de, hambre, | permiso, | |
| la sala | | miedo de, prisa, | prestado/a) | |
| | | sed, sueño) | por la noche | |
| | | | por teléfono | |
| | | | la planta | |
| | | | querido/a | |
| | | | la verdad | |

## Gramática

### Stem-changing verbs: e → i

The verb *pedir* is a stem changing verb except in the *nosotros* and *vosotros* forms.

**pedir (i)**

| | |
| --- | --- |
| pido | pedimos |
| pides | pedís |
| pide | piden |

The verb *repetir* follows the same e → i pattern.
The verb *decir* follows the same e → i pattern except for the *yo* form: *digo*.

### Expressing wishes: *querer* and *gustaría*

| | | | |
| --- | --- | --- | --- |
| | *querer* | + infinitive | *Quiero bailar en la fiesta* |
| me | | | |
| te | | | |
| le | | | |
| nos | *gustaría* | + infinitive | *Me gustaría bailar en la fiesta* |
| os | | | |
| les | | | |

# *Para concluir*

**?** Pregunta clave

What does a home and its contents tell us about the people who live there?

## Proyectos

### A ¡Manos a la obra! 👥

Choose a Spanish-speaking country and use online resources to find out about the types of homes that exist there. You may want to include such topics as the influence of geography, climate, and history on architectural styles, the types of construction materials used in housing, the advantages and disadvantages of living in urban, suburban, or rural areas, and so on. Work in a small group to prepare a class presentation combining your knowledge of *Unidad 6* and what you've discovered in your research. Use maps and visuals to accompany your presentation.

### B En resumen

How does each culture reading in *Unidad 6* answer the *Pregunta clave*: "What does a home and its contents tell us about the people who live there?" Use the chart to organize your ideas. Present your findings to the class.

Los venezolanos y sus casas ⇨

Los venezolanos y su comida ⇨

La gente y las viviendas en otras regiones de Venezuela ⇨

Las diferentes casas colombianas ⇨

El patio ⇨

## Extensión

Working in groups of three, talk about what you know about housing and home life in the United States and in Spanish-speaking parts of the world such as Venezuela, Colombia, Puerto Rico, and the Dominican Republic. Then, use a graphic organizer such as a Venn diagram to make a side-by-side comparison between the United States and another Spanish-speaking country, listing at least five similarities or differences.

## C  ¡A escribir!

You are visiting the home of a friend in Venezuela or Colombia. Write a paragraph that describes the home where you are staying. Include information such as what the house looks like, where it is located, what kind of rooms it has, how many windows and doors it has, where the rooms are located, and any other details you wish to include. Use transition words to connect your ideas.

### Estrategia

**Connecting phrases**

Your writing style may seem choppy in Spanish unless you connect your thoughts using transition words like *y* (and), *también* (also), *primero* (first), *después* (later), *entonces* (then), and *pero* (but). These words can act like adhesive to bind together the ideas in a paragraph as a connected unit.

## D  Casa moderna para alquilar

In small groups, search online for real estate rental ads in Colombia or Venezuela that are similar to the illustrated ad shown below. Take note of the main features advertised. Then create an ad in Spanish using the vocabulary in *Unidad 6*. Make sure to include a photo and a floor plan with labels for each room. Present your ad to the class.

VENTA DE CASAS

• 2 baños  • 4 cuartos  • cocina
• patio  • comedor  • sala
• garaje para dos carros

**Casa moderna**
de dos pisos para alquilar

**José Martí 2048**
📞 **57 1 3210338**

# Vocabulario de la Unidad 6

el **abrazo** hug *6B*
el **aceite** oil *6A*
**al lado de** next to, beside *6B*
**allá** over there *6A*
**aprender (a)** to learn *6B*
**aquel, aquella (aquellos, aquellas)** that, (those) far away *6A*
**ayudar** to help *6A*
el **azúcar** sugar *6A*
el **baño** bathroom *6B*
el **calor** heat *6B*
la **carta** letter *6B*
**cerrar (ie)** to close *6A*
la **cocina** kitchen *6A*
el **comedor** dining room *6A*
**cómodo/a** comfortable *6B*
**correr** to run *6B*
la **cosa** thing *6A*
**cuando** when *6B*
el **cuarto** room, bedroom *6B*
los **cubiertos** silverware *6A*

la **cuchara** spoon *6A*
la **cucharita** teaspoon *6A*
el **cuchillo** knife *6A*
**de todos los días** everyday *6A*
**deber** should, to have to, must, ought *6A*
**decir (i)** to tell, to say *6B*
**desde** since, from *6B*
**después** afterwards, later, then *6A*
el **dibujo** drawing, sketch *6B*
**donde** where *6B*
**e** and (used before a word beginning with *i* or *hi*) *6B*
**empezar (ie)** to begin, to start *6A*
**encender (ie)** to light, to turn on (a light) *6A*

**entonces** then *6A*
la **escalera** stairway, stairs *6B*
**escribir** to write *6B*
**ese, esa (esos, esas)** that (those) *6A*
**especial** special *6A*
**este, esta (estos, estas)** this (these) *6A*
la **estufa** stove *6A*
el **fregadero** sink *6A*
el **frío** cold *6B*
las **ganas** desire *6B*
el **garaje** garage *6B*
**gustaría** would like *6B*
el **hambre (f.)** hunger *6B*
el **horno microondas** microwave oven *6A*
el **lado** side *6B*
la **lámpara** lamp *6A*
el **lavaplatos** dishwasher *6A*
**lo que** what, that which *6B*
la **luz (pl.) luces** light *6A*
el **mantel** tablecloth *6A*
la **mantequilla** butter *6A*
**me/te/le/nos/les gustaría** I/you/he/she/it/we/they would like *6B*
la **mentira** lie *6B*
la **mesa** table *6A*
el **miedo** fear *6B*
**otra vez** again, another time *6A*
el **pan** bread *6A*
**pásame** pass me *6A*
el **patio** courtyard, patio, yard *6B*
**pedir (i)** to ask for, to order, to request; **pedir ayuda** to ask for help; **pedir perdón** to say you are sorry; **pedir permiso (para)** to ask for permission (to do something); **pedir prestado/a** to borrow *6B*
**pensar (ie)** to think, to intend, to plan *6A*
**pensar de/en/que** to think about *6A*
**pequeño/a** small *6B*
el **permiso** permission *6B*
la **pimienta** pepper (seasoning) *6A*
la **piscina** swimming pool *6B*
el **piso** floor *6B*
la **planta** plant *6B*
la **planta baja** ground floor *6B*

el **plato** dish, plate *6A*
**poco/a** not very, little *6B*
**poner** to put, to place *6A*
**poner la mesa** to set the table *6A*
**por** through, by *6B*
**por la noche** at night *6B*
**por teléfono** by phone *6B*
el **postre** dessert *6A*
**preferir (ie)** to prefer *6A*
el **primer piso** first floor *6B*
la **prisa** rush, hurry, haste *6B*
**querer (ie)** to love, to want *6A*
**querido/a** dear *6B*
el **refrigerador** refrigerator *6A*
**repetir (i)** to repeat *6B*
la **sal** salt *6A*
la **sala** living room *6B*
la **sed** thirst *6R*
**sentir (ie)** to be sorry, to feel sorry, to regret *6A*
la **servilleta** napkin *6A*
la **sopa** soup *6A*
el **sueño** sleep *6B*
la **taza** cup *6A*

el **tenedor** fork *6A*
**tener (calor, frío, hambre, miedo de, prisa, sed, sueño)** to be (hot, cold, hungry, afraid, in a hurry, thirsty, sleepy) *6B*
**tener ganas de** to feel like *6B*
**tener que** to have (to) *6A*
**u** or (used before a word that starts with *o* or *ho*) *6B*
el **vaso** glass *6A*
la **verdad** truth *6B*
**viajar** to travel *6A*
**ya** now *6A*

### ¿Sabías que...?

Latin America, like Australia, has its own "land down under." The southern cone is shared by Argentina and Chile. Geography makes these two countries different from the rest of the Spanish-speaking world, but there is one thing they all have in common— *el fútbol.*

# 7

# Las diversiones de todo el año

**Where does Francisco invite Ana?**

**A. a mirar su práctica de fútbol**
**B. a tomar un refresco**
**C. a estudiar en la biblioteca**

*Pregunta clave*

**?**

**How does geography affect the sports and leisure of a nation?**

## Mis metas

**Lección A  I will be able to:**

▸ talk about leisure activities
▸ use **o → ue** and **u → ue** stem-changing verbs
▸ discuss Argentina, its geography, and pastimes
▸ talk about pastimes
▸ say how long something has been happening using **hace** + time expression + **que**
▸ describe what is happening right now using the present progressive
▸ discuss popular sports in Argentina

**Lección B  I will be able to:**

▸ talk about seasons and weather
▸ use verbs with special accentuation like **esquiar**, **enviar**, and **continuar**
▸ use the present tense of **dar** and **poner**
▸ discuss how Chile's geography affects its sports and leisure activities
▸ identify people who participate in sports using **-dor(a)** and **-ista**
▸ use ordinal numbers to indicate order
▸ discuss the island of **Rapa Nui** and its inhabitants

Chile    Argentina

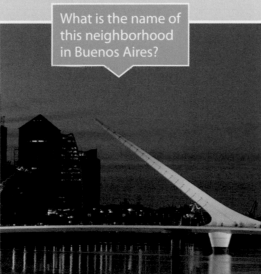

What is the name of this neighborhood in Buenos Aires?

## Las diversiones

Me llamo Miguel. Soy de Buenos Aires, Argentina. Mis amigos y yo tenemos muchos **pasatiempos** los fines de semana. Lo que más nos gusta es jugar al **básquetbol**.

Estas son nuestras actividades favoritas.

hacer aeróbicos

jugar al básquetbol

jugar al fútbol americano

jugar al voleibol

jugar a los videojuegos

jugar al ajedrez

jugar a las damas

jugar a las cartas

el televisor

Antes de comer, me gusta ver las telenovelas.

Necesito **un minuto** más. Quiero ver mi **programa** favorito.

Sabes que no **puedes** ver la televisión **después de** las 9 de la noche.

Nos gustan los programas sobre **la vida** de personas famosas.

Nos gusta ver a nuestro **equipo** favorito de fútbol en televisión.

## Para conversar 🎧

**T**o talk about things you are going to do:

¿Quieres ver el partido en la televisión?
*Do you want to watch the game on TV?*

**Todavía** no puedo. Tengo que terminar mi tarea.
*I can't yet. I have to finish my homework.*

Bueno, entonces **vuelvo esta noche**.
*OK, then I will come back tonight.*

**T**o talk about things you would like to do:

Me gustaría comprar un televisor, pero **cuestan** mucho.
*I'd like to buy a TV, but they cost a lot.*

Me gustaría aprender a **dibujar**, pero es difícil.
*I'd like to learn how to draw, but it is difficult.*

**T**o talk about shows you would like to watch:

¿Qué hay esta noche en la televisión?
*What's on TV tonight?*

No sé. No **recuerdo**.
*I don't know. I don't remember.*

### Para decir más

| | |
|---|---|
| el aficionado/la aficionada | *fan* |
| el jugador/la jugadora | *player* |
| el tiempo libre | *free time* |
| estar en forma | *to be in shape* |
| ganar | *to win* |
| perder | *to lose* |

### 1 ¿Qué contestas?

Empareja cada oración de la columna I con la respuesta apropiada de la columna II.

**I**

1. ¿Sabes cómo se llama ese programa de tele?
2. ¿Te gusta tu clase de arte?
3. ¿Cuáles son tus pasatiempos favoritos?
4. Mamá, ¿puedo ver este programa?
5. ¿Cómo se llama tu equipo de fútbol americano favorito?

**II**

A. Sí, pero no dibujo muy bien.
B. No, ya sabes que no puedes ver la televisión después de comer.
C. Los Delfines de Miami.
D. Lo siento, pero no recuerdo.
E. Jugar a las cartas y ver telenovelas.

## 2 ¿Qué actividad es? 🎧

Identifica la actividad que oyes.

A

B

C

D

E

F

## 3 ¡Ya sé el pasatiempo! 👥

Create a list of at least ten leisure activities.
Include new expressions from this unit, and
also previously learned vocabulary. Then,
working in small groups, take turns playing
charades to act out activities on your list.
The winner is the person who first says *¡Ya
sé el pasatiempo!* and guesses correctly.

### *Un poco más*

**¿Damas en los baños?**

The games *ajedrez* (chess) and *damas* (checkers)
are two of the world's oldest pastimes. However,
if you see the word *Damas* (Ladies) on the door of
a public restroom not very far from another door
labeled *Caballeros* (Gentlemen), do not assume you
are going in to play checkers. Remember what you
have learned: The meaning of any word may vary
according to the context in which the word is used.

## ¡Comunicación!

## 4 En la casa y en el parque 👥  Interpersonal Communication

En grupos de tres, túrnense (*take turns*) para hablar de sus pasatiempos favoritos en la
casa y en el parque.

MODELO    A: ¿ Cuál es tu pasatiempo favorito en la casa?

B: Me gusta jugar a las damas. ¿Y a ti?

C: A mí me gusta más ver telenovelas.

A: ¿Y cuál es tu pasatiempo favorito en el parque?

B: Me gusta jugar al voleibol.

C: Yo prefiero jugar al tenis.

# Diálogo 🎧

## ¿No quieres jugar al ajedrez?

**Luz:** ¿No quieres jugar al ajedrez?

**Hugo:** Sí, pero después de este programa.

**Luz:** ¿Qué programa es?

**Hugo:** Es mi telenovela favorita.

*(Más tarde)*

**Luz:** ¿Ahora sí?

**Hugo:** ¿Por qué no vienes en dos horas?

**Luz:** ¿Cómo? ¿No vamos a jugar al ajedrez?

**Hugo:** Es que el equipo de Argentina va a jugar ahora.

*(Más tarde)*

**Luz:** ¡Veo que ya no sabes jugar al ajedrez!

**Hugo:** Sí, ya no recuerdo cómo jugar.

**Luz:** ¡Claro! Tu vida ahora es ver televisión.

**Hugo:** No. ¡Mi vida ahora es ver televisión y jugar al fútbol!

---

### 5  ¿Qué recuerdas? 🎧

1. ¿A qué quiere jugar Luz?
2. ¿Qué programa ve Hugo?
3. ¿Qué equipo va a jugar?
4. ¿Qué va a ver Hugo?
5. ¿Cómo es ahora la vida de Hugo?

---

### 6  Algo personal 🎧

1. ¿Sabes jugar al fútbol?
2. ¿Te gusta jugar al ajedrez?
3. ¿Qué vas a hacer esta noche?
4. ¿Te gusta ver televisión?

---

### 7  ¿Qué comprendiste? 🎧

Di si lo que oyes es **cierto** o **falso**, según el Diálogo.

*¿Sabes jugar al ajedrez?*

---

### Un poco más

#### La fiebre del gol

It is easy to understand why Hugo is distracted as he talks with Luz. For many people in Argentina and throughout the Spanish-speaking world, soccer (*el fútbol*) is more than just a simple pastime. During the World Cup (*la Copa Mundial*) fans of all ages follow the action, and nearly everyone has *la fiebre del gol* (goal fever).

# Gramática

## Stem-Changing Verbs: o → ue and u → ue

- Some verbs have the stem change **o → ue** (*poder*) or **u → ue** (*jugar*) in all their present-tense forms except for *nosotros* and *vosotros*. These stem changes do not affect regular verb endings. Remember to keep in mind the "shoe" or "boot" shape to visualize which forms require the stem change.

| poder (ue) | | | |
|---|---|---|---|
| yo | puedo | nosotros nosotras | podemos |
| tú | puedes | vosotros vosotras | podéis |
| Ud. él ella | puede | Uds. ellos ellas | pueden |

| jugar (ue) | | | |
|---|---|---|---|
| yo | juego | nosotros nosotras | jugamos |
| tú | juegas | vosotros vosotras | jugáis |
| Ud. él ella | juega | Uds. ellos ellas | juegan |

- Other **o → ue** stem-changing verbs include *costar* (to cost), *recordar* (to remember), and *volver* (to return, to go back).

## 8  Todos quieren ayudar 🎧

If everyone works together they will be free to do what they want later in the day.
Say what these people can do to help with lunch, according to the cues.

**MODELO**   Marta (buscar los platos)
**Marta puede buscar los platos.**

1. papá (comprar leche y pan)
2. yo (buscar los cubiertos)
3. mi mamá (hacer el almuerzo)

4. tú (poner la mesa)
5. nosotros (preparar un postre)
6. mis hermanos (poner los platos sucios en el lavaplatos)

## 9  La televisión en casa

Completa el siguiente párrafo con la forma apropiada de uno de los siguientes verbos:
**poder, costar, volver, jugar, recordar**.

Yo siempre **(1)** cuando **(2)** el equipo de Chile. Mi papá y yo vemos el partido en la televisión. A mi hermana también le gustaría ver el partido pero ella no **(3)** porque tiene que estudiar para un examen. Nosotros no **(4)** tener otro televisor en casa porque **(5)** mucho. Cuando mi mamá **(6)** a casa a las cuatro, ella **(7)** ver su telenovela favorita y entonces yo **(8)** al fútbol con mis amigos en el parque.

## 10  Una invitación

In pairs, take turns inviting one another to do the indicated activities. Answer by either refusing or accepting the invitation, giving an excuse if you refuse or changing the suggested time if you accept.

**MODELO**   jugar al básquetbol

A: **¿Puedes jugar al básquetbol hoy?**

B: **Lo siento, pero no puedo. Es muy tarde. / No puedo hoy, pero puedo jugar el sábado.**

1. jugar a los videojuegos esta tarde
2. ver mis fotos de Chile ahora
3. ir al cine pasado mañana
4. jugar al fútbol americano el sábado
5. jugar al voleibol a las 6:30
6. hacer aeróbicos mañana

## 11  ¿Recuerdas a qué hora vuelven?

In pairs, talk about when these people will be returning from the places mentioned.

**MODELO**   Inés / el colegio

A: **¿Recuerdas a qué hora vuelve Inés del colegio?**

B: **Ella vuelve del colegio a la tres menos cuarto de la tarde.**  2:45 PM

1. José y Gisela / la piscina  8:40 AM
2. tú y yo / la tienda  1:25 PM
3. tú / el cine  1:50 PM
4. Juanito / el partido 9:30 PM

## 12  ¿Qué hacen?

With a classmate, ask and answer questions about what these people are doing.

**MODELO**   Enrique

A: **¿Qué hace Enrique?**

B: **Él juega al béisbol.**

1. Olivia
2. Ana y Melisa
3. Fernando y Juan
4. Alex y Esteban

**?** Pregunta clave

How does geography affect the sports and leisure of a nation?

# Argentina: Un país de mucha variedad

When you think of Argentina, do you imagine wide-open plains? Mountainous regions? Subtropical forests? Glaciers? Argentina has all of these. Its land mass stretches from the subtropical forests in the north to the frigid climate conditions near Antarctica in the south, and from the Atlantic Ocean in the east to the Andes Mountains in the west. This diverse geography influences how Argentinians as well as visitors spend their free time and get to know the country, and it creates opportunities for amazing sports and leisure activities all year long.

The subtropical region of the north is home to the spectacular Iguazú Falls which, in addition to being a World Heritage Site, are also a perfect location for hiking, rowing, and dancing the *chacarera*, a folkloric dance which consists of men stomping

*Parque Nacional Los Glaciares*

their boots and women swirling their colorful skirts. *Las pampas*, or the plains, are home to the famed gaucho. This beef-eating, *mate*-drinking cowboy, with his wide-brimmed hat and flared pants, is a symbol of Argentina's struggle to preserve its traditions against European influences. Known for his great horsemanship, the gaucho's tradition lives on at the many *estancias* (ranches) on the *pampas,* where people enjoy horseback riding, playing polo, and other outdoor activities suited to the open plains.

The province of Mendoza in the Andean foothills is dotted with vineyards and olive trees. Its music, art, and festivals celebrate hope, hard work, and the products of the land. Mendoza also attracts hikers, rafters, and skiers, as well as climbers headed for Aconcagua Peak, the highest in the Americas. Patagonia, the southern cone of Argentina, is home to the Andean town of Bariloche with its winter sports, and also the *Parque Nacional Los Glaciares*.

*Un gaucho a caballo*

**Búsqueda:** geography of argentina, world heritage sites, el mate

### Prácticas 🎧

El mate es una infusión herbal caliente similar al té verde. Pero es mucho más. Tomar mate es una experiencia entre amigos. El mate se prepara en una calabaza (*gourd*) y se toma con una bombilla de plata (*silver straw*). Es muy común ver a grupos de amigos compartiendo (*sharing*) un mate en los parques mientras escuchan música, juegan o conversan. ¿Quieres un mate?

*Mate en una calabaza con una bombilla de plata*

### 13 Comprensión

1. What are three leisure activities that you can enjoy around Iguazú Falls?

2. Why is the *gaucho* an important symbol of Argentina?

3. What sports and leisure activities are popular in the province of Mendoza?

### 14 Analiza

1. What values do you think are promoted by drinking *mate*?

2. Despite the diverse geography of their country, what values do you think all Argentinians share? Explain with information from the readings.

# El río[1] de Buenos Aires 🎧

Las aguas del Río de la Plata bañan la costa[2] de la ciudad de Buenos Aires. Miles y miles de personas y toneladas de mercaderías[3] pasan por el puerto de la ciudad. Desde la época colonial, gracias a la proximidad del río, Buenos Aires es un centro importante de comercio y de turismo y recreación.

*Puerto Madero y el río*

Al lado del río, cerca de los rascacielos[4] del moderno barrio de Puerto Madero, está la Reserva Ecológica donde puedes disfrutar de la naturaleza y practicar actividades como dar paseos, montar en bicicleta y sacar fotos de la vegetación y los animales.

Hacia el norte, bordeando la costa del río, se extiende la avenida Costanera, rodeada de parques y centros deportivos y de recreación. Pero la pesca[5] es la actividad por excelencia del lugar. Si pasas por la Costanera un domingo, puedes ver a las familias *porteñas* (así es cómo llaman a los residentes de Buenos Aires) practicando la pesca y disfrutando de la vista interminable[6] del río.

[1] river  [2] wash the coast  [3] tons of goods  [4] skyscrapers  [5] fishing  [6] unending view

*Tardes de pesca en la Costanera*

🔍 **Búsqueda:** puerto de buenos aires, puerto madero, avenida costanera rafael obligado

## Productos

Tango is synonymous with Argentina and especially with Buenos Aires. The songs that accompany this popular dance are characterized by a marked rhythm and lyrics that reveal the values of ordinary men and women of the city. From its origin in the modest waterfront neighborhood of *La Boca*, in Buenos Aires, it spread to the rest of the world. A street sign in *La Boca* with the name *Caminito* indicates a short dead-end street that gave its name to one of Argentina's most famous tangos. *Che, bailá conmigo.*

*Bailando tango en una calle de La Boca*

## Perspectivas

This fragment of the tango "Buenos Aires, colina chata" by Homero Manzi describes the city of Buenos Aires:

"On a flat hill / Garay traced four winds; / on one side the Pampa, / on the other side a stream / with the river at its back / and the desert against its chest / with a horizon made of straw / and the sky as its roof." What do you think Manzi is trying to show the world about Buenos Aires through his lyrics?

## 15 Comprensión — Interpretive Communication

1. ¿Qué importancia tiene el Río de la Plata para la ciudad de Buenos Aires?

2. ¿Qué actividades recreativas pueden hacer los porteños cerca del río?

3. ¿Qué barrio de Buenos Aires es famoso por el tango?

## 16 Analiza

What is the main idea of the reading *"El río de Buenos Aires"*?

# Vocabulario 2

## En mi tiempo libre

Me llamo Catalina. Soy de Mendoza, Argentina. Me gusta mucho **alquilar** películas.

**Por la noche**...

Me gusta hacer **una lista** de las películas que voy a alquilar. No quiero ver las **mismas** películas del mes pasado.

Yo uso **el control remoto** para buscar mis programas favoritos. También lo necesito para encender y **apagar** el televisor.

¿Cuánto tiempo hace que estás hablando con Anita?

Hace como una hora.

Bueno, debes decirle adiós y empezar a hacer tus tareas **ahora mismo**.

Sí, sí, en **un segundo**...

Mis padres me **permiten dormir** con mi perro. ¡Qué bueno!

## Para conversar

*T*o suggest going out:

Hace **casi** una semana que no nos vemos.
*We haven't seen each other for almost a week.*

Es verdad, hace como **un siglo**. ¿Por qué no salimos esta noche?
*It's true, it's been like a century. Why don't we go out tonight?*

**¡Estupendo**!
*Wonderful!*

### *Para decir más*

| | |
|---|---|
| ¿Por qué no nos encontramos en...? | *Why don't we meet at...?* |
| ¡No me dejan! | *They won't let me!* |
| ¡Ya voy! | *Coming!* |

### *En otros países*

| | |
|---|---|
| **el control remoto** | *el mando a distancia (España)* |
| **ahora mismo** | *ahorita (muchos países)* |
| **¡Estupendo!** | *¡Chévere! (muchos países)* |
| | *¡Guay! (España)* |
| | *¡ Padrísimo! (México)* |

### 17  El tiempo libre 🎧

Selecciona la ilustración que corresponde con lo que oyes.

A

B

¡Alquilar DVDs!
**Nuevas películas**
- *Historia de amor*
- *El hombre araña V*
- *El cuarto misterioso*

C

**11:50** PM

D

### 18  ¿Cuánto tiempo hay en...? 🎧  Conéctate: las matemáticas

Contesta las siguientes preguntas.

1. ¿Cuántas semanas hay en un año?
2. ¿Cuántos años hay en un siglo?
3. ¿Cuántas horas hay en un día?
4. ¿Cuántos cuartos de hora hay en una hora?
5. ¿Cuántos segundos hay en un minuto?
6. ¿Cuántos minutos hay en una hora?
7. ¿Cuántos segundos hay en una hora?
8. ¿Cuántas horas hay en una semana?

*¿Cuántos segundos hay en un minuto?*

# Diálogo

## Quiero alquilar una película

**Hugo:** ¿Estás durmiendo?

**Luz:** No. Estoy viendo televisión. ¿Por qué?

**Hugo:** Porque quiero ir a alquilar una película.

**Luz:** ¿Ahora mismo?

**Hugo:** Sí, quiero ir antes de comer. ¿Quieres ir?

**Luz:** Un segundo.... Ya voy.

*(Más tarde)*

No quiero ver las mismas películas otra vez.

**Hugo:** ¿Cuánto tiempo hace que no ves una película?

**Luz:** ¡Uy! Hace mucho tiempo. Casi dos meses.

**Hugo:** ¡Entonces no vas a ver las mismas películas!

---

### 19  ¿Qué recuerdas?

1. ¿Está Luz durmiendo?
2. ¿Qué quiere hacer Hugo?
3. ¿Cuándo quiere ir Hugo?
4. ¿Cuánto tiempo hace que Luz no ve una película?

### 20  Algo personal

1. ¿Cuánto tiempo hace que no alquilas una película?
2. ¿Haces una lista de películas antes de ir a alquilar una?
3. ¿Cuánto tiempo hace que no ves una película?
4. ¿Por cuánto tiempo ves televisión en una semana?
5. ¿Cuánto tiempo libre tienes en una semana? ¿Qué haces?

### 21  ¿Adentro o afuera?

Di **sí**, si las actividades que se mencionan se hacen adentro (*inside*). Di **no**, si se hacen afuera (*outside*).

---

## ¡Comunicación!

### 22  ¿Qué haces en tu tiempo libre?   Interpersonal/Presentational Communication

Haz una encuesta a cinco compañeros/as usando la pregunta: **¿Qué haces en tu tiempo libre?** Anota los resultados y luego preséntalos a la clase.

**MODELO**

A: ¿Qué haces en tu tiempo libre?

B: Hago una lista de las películas que voy a alquilar.

C: Yo prefiero jugar a las damas con mi hermano.

Resultados: Jorge hace una lista de las películas que va a alquilar.
Sara prefiere jugar a las damas con su hermano.

# Gramática

emcpassport.com

WB 11–12
LA 5
GV 9–10

## Expressions with *hace*

- You can describe an action that began in the past and has continued into the present using this formula:

> **hace + *time expression* + que + *present-tense verb***

**Hace diez minutos que veo** *televisión.*

**I have been watching** television **for ten minutes**.

- Reverse the order of **hace** and the time expression if a form of **¿cuánto?** introduces the question.

**¿Cuánto tiempo hace que ves** *televisión?*

**How long have you been watching** television?

### 23 ¿Cuánto tiempo hace?

Say how long the following activities have been taking place.

**MODELO**    haces aeróbicos / una hora
> **Hace una hora que haces aeróbicos.**

1. juegan al béisbol en los Estados Unidos / más de un siglo
2. jugamos al voleibol / un año
3. vivo aquí / quince años
4. Uds. juegan a los videojuegos / veinte minutos
5. mi sobrina dibuja una casa / un cuarto de hora
6. jugamos al ajedrez / treinta segundos

*Hace una hora que hacen aeróbicos.*

### 24 Preguntas con *hace*

Lee las respuestas para hacer preguntas con **hace**. Sigue el modelo.

**MODELO**    Hace tres años que vivo aquí.
> **¿Cuántos años hace que vives aquí?**

1. Hace dos años que voy a este colegio.
2. Hace cuatro semanas que no veo telenovelas.
3. Hace diez días que no alquilo películas.
4. Hace cinco minutos que estoy aquí.
5. Hace dos meses que no juego al ajedrez.
6. Hace cinco años que toco el piano.

**¡Ojo!**

The form of *cuánto* changes to agree with the time expression immediately following it: *¿Cuántas semanas hace que lees ese libro?*

## 25 ¿Qué haces?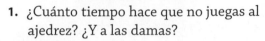

In pairs, take turns asking and answering the following questions.
Then summarize your partner's answers for each question.

MODELO
A: ¿Juegas a los videojuegos?
B: Sí, juego a los videojuegos.
A: *Write:* B juega a los videojuegos.

Jugamos a los videojuegos.

1. ¿Cuánto tiempo hace que no juegas al ajedrez? ¿Y a las damas?
2. ¿Sabes jugar al ajedrez o a las damas?
3. ¿Cuánto tiempo hace que no lees una revista?
4. ¿Qué revistas lees?
5. ¿Cuánto tiempo hace que dibujas?
6. ¿Sabes dibujar?

7. ¿Cuánto tiempo hace que no ves una telenovela?
8. ¿Te gusta ver televisión? ¿Te gustan las telenovelas?
9. ¿Cuánto tiempo hace que estudias español?
10. ¿Cuánto tiempo hace que no escribes una carta?

# ¡Comunicación!

## 26 En mi tiempo libre    Interpersonal Communication

Prepare a list of your pastimes. Include at least eight or nine activities. Then, with a partner, take turns asking and answering questions about your favorite activities and how long you've been participating in them.

MODELO
A: ¿Qué te gusta hacer en tu tiempo libre?
B: Me gusta dibujar.
A: ¿Cuánto tiempo hace que dibujas?
B: Hace dos años que dibujo. Y tú, ¿qué haces en tu tiempo libre?

Hace diez minutos que vemos televisión.

¿Cuánto tiempo hace que dibujas?

# Gramática

## Saying What Is Happening: Present Progressive

- To express what is happening right now, use the *presente progresivo*, which consists of the present tense of **estar** plus a present participle (*gerundio*).

> **estar + present participle**

| | |
|---|---|
| *¿Qué* **estás haciendo**? | What **are you doing**? |
| *Mónica* **está escuchando** *música.* | Mónica **is listening to** music. |
| **Estoy escribiendo** *una carta.* | **I am writing** a letter. |

- To form the present participle (*gerundio*) of most verbs, drop the infinitive endings (-*ar*, -*er*, -*ir*) and add -**ando** to the stem of -**ar** verbs and -**iendo** to the stem of -**er** and -**ir** verbs.

| -ar | -er | -ir |
|---|---|---|
| alqui**lar** → alqui**lando** | hac**er** → hac**iendo** | permit**ir** → permit**iendo** |

- Some -*ir* verbs with a stem change in the present tense require a different stem change in the present participle. This second change is shown in parentheses after infinitives in this book. Three verbs that follow this pattern are *dormir (ue, **u**)*, *preferir (ie, **i**)*, and *sentir (ie, **i**)*.

| verbo | presente | gerundio |
|---|---|---|
| dormir (ue, **u**) | duermo | durmiendo |
| preferir (ie, **i**) | prefieren | prefiriendo |
| sentir (ie, **i**) | siento | sintiendo |

- Some verbs have minor irregularities in their present participles. For example, the *i* in -*iendo* changes to **y** after most verb stems that end in a vowel: *leer* (stem: *le*) → *leyendo*. The present participle for the irregular verb *venir* requires a change in the stem from **e** to **i**: *venir* → *viniendo*. The present participle for *poder* involves a stem change from **o** to **u**: *pudiendo*.

### 27 Todos están haciendo algo

Using the *presente progresivo* and the provided cues, say what these people are doing right now.

**MODELO** nosotros / leer el periódico
**Nosotros estamos leyendo el periódico.**

1. mi padre y mi madre / salir de casa
2. mi hermano / buscar el control remoto
3. Esteban / alquilar una película estupenda
4. tú / pensar en tus pasatiempos
5. Uds. / apagar la luz de la cocina
6. María / poner la mesa

*Nosotros estamos leyendo el periódico.*

In pairs, take turns asking and answering what you are doing right now, according to the photos.

MODELO    A: ¿Qué estás haciendo?
          B: Estoy escuchando música.

1

2

3

4

5

Pretend you are sitting in an outdoor café in Buenos Aires. Using the present progressive, describe at least seven things that you see from your table.

MODELO    Una chica está usando la tableta.

# ¡Comunicación!

30 **¿Qué está pasando?** 👥 Interpersonal Communication

Working in pairs, imagine you are in the following places: *una cafetería, una librería, una tienda de artículos electrónicos, una tienda de ropa, el centro de Buenos Aires, la sala de la casa, el museo, la calle, el parque.* Pretend you are talking on the phone with a friend and discussing what you are doing right now. Add to the conversation by asking such things as who is with you, where each place is located, etc.

MODELO
A: ¿Dónde estás?
B: Estoy en una tienda de artículos electrónicos.
A: ¿Dónde está la tienda?
B: Está en La Boca.
A: ¿Qué estás haciendo?
B: Estoy comprando CDs de tango.

# ¡Comunicación!

**31 ¿Puedo hablar con...?** 👥 Interpersonal Communication

With a classmate, pretend you go to visit a friend, but the person is out. The person opening the door must apologize and say the friend you are trying to see is not home and then say what the person is doing. Try again with more friends. Be creative!

MODELO
A: Hola, ¿está Roberto?
B: Lo siento. Roberto no está. Está jugando al fútbol ahora mismo.

## Comparaciones

### Comparando inglés y español

You have learned to combine the present tense of *estar* with a present participle (*gerundio*) of a verb in Spanish to describe what is going on right now. This verb form is comparable to the *-ing* form of a verb in English. Notice, however, that words ending in *-ing* in English may require an infinitive in Spanish if the English word functions as a noun instead of a verb. Compare the following:

| | |
|---|---|
| *Me gusta jugar al voleibol.* | I like playing volleyball. (*noun*) |
| *Nadar es divertido.* | Swimming is fun. (*noun*) |

but:

| | |
|---|---|
| *Estoy jugando al voleibol.* | I am playing volleyball. (*verb*) |
| *¿Estás nadando?* | Are you swimming? (*verb*) |

# Gramática

## Direct Object Pronouns

- You have already learned to distinguish the direct object in a sentence, the person or thing that receives the action of the verb. Do you remember the direct object pronouns that can replace them?

| Los pronombres de complemento directo | | | |
|---|---|---|---|
| **me** | me | **nos** | us |
| **te** | you | **os** | you |
| **lo** | him, it, you | **los** | them, you |
| **la** | her, it, you | **las** | them, you |

- Recall that direct object pronouns are placed directly before the conjugated verb.

| | |
|---|---|
| *No **la** veo.* | I do not see **her**.<br>I do not see **it**. (*la sal*) |
| *Nunca **lo** buscas.* | You never look for **him**.<br>You never look for **it**. (*el programa*) |

## Using the Present Progressive with Direct Object Pronouns

- You know that direct object pronouns usually precede conjugated verbs. However, direct object pronouns may also be attached to an infinitive.

| | |
|---|---|
| ***La** voy a alquilar.*<br>*Voy a alquilar**la**.* | I am going to rent **it**. (*la película*) |

- Similarly, you can attach a direct object pronoun to the end of a present participle (*gerundio*). When doing so, remember to add an accent mark to the present participle in order to maintain the original pronunciation of the *gerundio* without the pronoun.

| | |
|---|---|
| ***Lo** estamos leyendo.*<br>*Estamos leyéndo**lo**.* | We are reading **it**. (*el libro*) |

### 32 Lo estamos haciendo 🎧

Tell what the following people are doing right now, using direct object pronouns.

1. la señora Herrera / empezar / un viaje a Venezuela
2. Uds. / escribir / la lista de películas nuevas
3. nosotros / leer / un libro sobre Buenos Aires ahora
4. yo / escuchar / la radio ahora
5. Pilar / buscar / el control remoto

*Estoy viendo una película.*

## 33 De nuevo

Redo *Actividad 32* by attaching the direct object pronouns to the end of the present participle. Make any other appropriate changes.

## 34 ¿Qué están haciendo en clase?

Mira a cuatro o cinco personas que están en tu clase ahora. ¿Qué están haciendo? Si quieres, puedes agregar más detalles (*you may include more details*).

**MODELO**   Mi compañero está dibujando un mapa. Lo está dibujando con un lápiz.

## 35 Haciéndolo

Imagine you and your friend are watching television and commenting on various characters and programs. Working in pairs, take turns asking and answering questions using the provided cues. Follow the model, attaching direct object pronouns to the vebs in each sentence.

**MODELO**   los hermanos / leer el diario de la hermana

A: ¿Están leyendo los hermanos el diario de la hermana?

B: Sí, están leyéndolo.

1. tú / buscar el programa
2. el cantante / cantar una canción de amor
3. Julia / escuchar la radio
4. nosotros / ver esta telenovela
5. Mónica / dibujar un mapa en la servilleta
6. mi equipo favorito / jugar un partido importante

# ¡Comunicación!

## 36 Tu pasatiempo favorito    Interpersonal Communication

Write at least five or six of your favorite pastimes. Then, working with a partner, take turns asking and answering questions about each other's pastimes, where and with whom you practice the activity, and how long you have been doing it.

**MODELO**   A: ¿Cuál es tu pasatiempo favorito?

B: Mi pasatiempo favorito es jugar al voleibol.

A: ¿Dónde y con quién lo juegas?

B: Lo juego en la playa con mis amigos.

A: ¿Cuánto tiempo hace que juegas al voleibol?

B: Hace dos años que lo juego.

# Todo en contexto

**Pregunta clave**

How does geography affect the sports and leisure of a nation?

## ¡Comunicación!

### 37 ¿Cuáles son tus pasatiempos? — Interpersonal Communication

Pretend that you and a classmate are two Argentinians talking about typical pastimes in your country. Discuss what you do, what you like to do, what you would like to do, or what you want to do in your free time. Say where and when you do these activities, and how long you have been doing them. Add other topics, such as places in Argentina where you want to go, where you would like to go, and things you can and can't do there. Refer to the culture readings on pp. 306–307 for ideas as well as the information in the *Productos* and *Prácticas* sections. You may do additional research online as well.

MODELO
A: ¿Qué te gusta hacer en tu tiempo libre?
B: Los sábados voy a la Reserva Ecológica en Buenos Aires, pero me gustaría jugar al polo en las pampas. ¿Y tú?
A: Yo prefiero jugar al fútbol en el parque.
B: ¿Cuánto tiempo hace que juegas al fútbol?
A: Hace casi ocho años.

*Un juego de polo*

*¿Cuánto tiempo hace que juegas al fútbol?*

## ¡Comunicación!

### 38 ¿Qué es Argentina para mí? — Presentational Communication

Research a place, a pastime, a tradition, or an activity online that is unique due to Argentina's geography. Use the information to make a poster including basic information and plenty of visual details. Then, present the poster to a group of classmates and explain why you made this choice.

MODELO
Título: La Boca
Qué es: Una parte de Buenos Aires
Datos interesantes: El tango viene de allá.
Por qué es interesante: Me gustaría ir allí un día porque me gusta la música y el baile.

# Lectura informativa

## Antes de leer

1. Do you play any sports? Which ones? What do you like about these sports?

2. What sports do you like to watch, either live or on television/online? What makes them fun to watch?

3. What sports are popular in Spanish-speaking countries?

### Estrategia

**Main points**

Before starting to read, skim the material and pick out the main points. As you read, keep in mind the general topic as well as the main points.

## Los deportes en Argentina

Un jugador pasa la pelota entre el aro en el juego del pato.

¿Cuál es el deporte más popular en Argentina? El fútbol, ¡claro! Este país ha producido[1] jugadores de fama mundial, como Diego Maradona y Lionel Messi. Además, la Selección Argentina (equipo nacional) siempre es uno de los equipos favoritos para ganar la Copa Mundial. El fútbol es un deporte de adultos, jóvenes y niños. Para empezar a jugar, ¡solamente se requiere una pelota!

Pero la geografía argentina favorece una gran variedad de deportes. ¿Te gustaría esquiar en agosto? Puedes ir a Bariloche, en el sur[2] de Argentina. Allí el frío y las montañas te invitan a hacer este deporte todos los años de junio a septiembre. Si estás en las pampas[3], puedes hacer el deporte nacional: el juego del pato[4]. En esta competencia, dos equipos de jugadores, montados a caballo, deben pasar una pelota entre un aro[5] alto, como en el básquetbol. El juego del pato se llama así porque originalmente lo jugaban con un pato real, no con una pelota.

De las pampas viene también el polo. Introducido por los ingleses en el siglo XIX, este deporte tiene mucha popularidad en las grandes estancias, o haciendas, donde el caballo es un protagonista importante. Argentina ha sido[6] cuatro veces campeón mundial de polo.

Otros deportes populares que se practican en Buenos Aires y el resto del país son el boxeo, el tenis y el básquetbol. Los argentinos son fans de casi todos los deportes.

Argentina y México buscan un "cabezazo" en la Copa Mundial.

Esquiadores en Cerro Bayo, entre Argentina y Chile

[1] has produced  [2] south  [3] plains, grasslands  [4] duck game  [5] ring  [6] has been

**Búsqueda:** deporte en argentina

## 39 Comprensión — Interpretive Communication

1. ¿Cuál es el deporte nacional de Argentina? ¿Cuál es el más popular?

2. ¿Cuál es un buen mes para esquiar en Argentina?

3. ¿Cuáles son dos deportes con caballos que se practican en Argentina?

4. Nombra otros tres deportes populares en Argentina.

## 40 Analiza

1. Why do you think polo and *pato* became popular in *las pampas*?

2. What sports or leisure activities are popular where you live due to climate and/or geography?

## Extensión

Para las personas a quienes no les gustan los deportes, hay muchos otros pasatiempos en Argentina. Los jóvenes, como en todas partes, leen, escuchan música, navegan por la internet, o ven unos DVDs. Un pasatiempo favorito es tomar mate y conversar con los amigos en un café o restaurante. ¿Y a quién no le gusta un buen asado argentino? Esta tradición del fin de semana incluye carnes, pescados, pollo y salchichas.

**Búsqueda:** asado argentino

*Un asado típico argentino*

# ✏ Escritura

## 41 El mejor pasatiempo   Presentational Communication

Is there something you have always wanted to try? Or some place you would love to go after school or on a weekend? Now you can plan a week of leisure activities and describe them in a paragraph or two. These are things that you actually do or would like to do. A brainstorming session should turn up some favorites and also some new ideas, and the Internet may reveal others. Start by jotting down your ideas on a chart like the one shown.

| Mis pasatiempos de la semana | | |
| --- | --- | --- |
| Cuándo | Dónde | Me gustaría... |
| los lunes por la tarde | en mi casa | hacer un postre de chocolate y comerlo |
| | | |
| | | |

**Búsqueda:** pasatiempos favoritos

### Para escribir más

| | |
| --- | --- |
| descansar | *to relax* |
| ir de excursión | *to hike* |
| pasar el día/la tarde | *to spend the day/afternoon* |
| pintar | *to paint, draw* |
| subir | *to climb* |
| tomar una clase de... | *to take a class on...* |

*Me gustaría hacer un postre de chocolate.*

# Repaso de la Lección A

## A  Escuchar: ¿Cierto o falso?  (pp. 300–301)

Di si lo que oyes es **cierto** o **falso** según las fotos.

1

2

3

4

## B  Gramática: Tu pasatiempo favorito (p. 304)

Completa las oraciones con la forma correcta de los verbos **poder** o **jugar** según
el contexto.

1. **A:** ¿ __ tú al voleibol?
   **B:** Sí, yo lo __ jugar muy bien. Pero no __ bien al básquetbol.
2. **A:** Lorena __ al ajedrez, ¿verdad?
   **B:** Sí, pero no lo __ jugar muy bien. Ella __ a los videojuegos.
3. **A:** ¿ __ tú y tus amigos al fútbol?
   **B:** Sí, lo __. Y también __ jugar al fútbol americano.
4. **A:** Mi hermano __ a las cartas. ¿Y tú?
   **B:** Yo no __ a las cartas. Pero __ jugar muy bien a las damas.

## C  Gramática: ¿Cuánto tiempo hace que...? (p. 311)

Di cuánto tiempo hace que estas personas (no) hacen estas actividades.

**MODELO**  ellos/ alquilar películas / dos años
**Hace dos años que ellos alquilan películas.**

1. yo / no ver una telenovela / un siglo
2. Uds. / leer revistas en español / seis meses
3. tú y yo / ver las mismas películas / tres meses
4. tú / dibujar a tu gato / quince minutos

## D  Gramática: ¿Qué están haciendo? (pp. 313, 316)

¿Qué están haciendo estas personas y dónde? Usa el presente progresivo (*present
progressive*) y el pronombre de complemento directo (*direct object pronoun*) apropiado.

**MODELO**  Ana / ver una telenovela / en la sala
**Ana está viendo una telenovela. La está viendo en la sala. (Está viéndola...)**

1. mi abuelo / tomar un mate / el comedor
2. tú / ver tu equipo favorito / la televisión
3. yo / buscar las revistas / la sala
4. mis amigos y yo / oír tangos / la radio

La geografía de Argentina tiene una gran influencia en los deportes y pasatiempos que se practican en el país. Vuelve a leer las lecturas culturales y la lectura informativa y completa la gráfica con los deportes o pasatiempos que se practican en cada región.

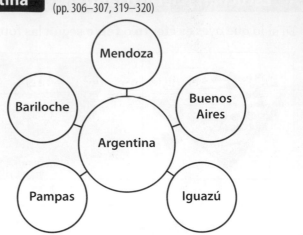

## Vocabulario

| Pasatiempos | Expresiones de tiempo | Verbos | Expresiones y otras palabras |
|---|---|---|---|
| los aeróbicos | ahora mismo | alquilar | americano/a |
| el ajedrez | antes de | apagar | casi |
| el básquetbol | ¿Cuánto (+ *time expression*) hace que (+ *present tense of verb*)... ? | costar (ue) | el control remoto |
| las cartas | después de | dibujar | estupendo/a |
| las damas | esta noche | dormir (ue, u) | la lista |
| el equipo | hace (+ *time expression*) que | jugar (ue) | mismo/a |
| el fútbol americano | el minuto | permitir | el televisor |
| hacer aeróbicos | por la (mañana, tarde, noche) | poder (ue, u) | la vida |
| el pasatiempo | el segundo | recordar (ue) | |
| el programa | el siglo | volver (ue) | |
| la telenovela | todavía | | |
| el videojuego | | | |
| el voleibol | | | |

## Gramática

### Stem-changing verbs: o → ue and u → ue

The verbs *poder* (ue) and *jugar* (ue) are stem-changing verbs except in the *nosotros* and *vosotros* forms.

| poder (ue) | | jugar (ue) | |
|---|---|---|---|
| p**ue**do | podemos | j**ue**go | jugamos |
| p**ue**des | podéis | j**ue**gas | jugáis |
| p**ue**de | p**ue**den | j**ue**ga | j**ue**gan |

### Saying what is happening: present progressive

Use the present tense of **estar** + present participle (*gerundio*)

| -*ar* verbs | -*er* verbs | -*ir* verbs |
|---|---|---|
| habl**ar** → **ando** habl**ando** | com**er** → **iendo** com**iendo** | escrib**ir** → **iendo** escrib**iendo** |

*¡Ojo! Some verbs require a spelling change or stem change in the present participle.

### Expressions with *hace*

Question: ¿**Cuánto tiempo hace que** ves televisión?
Answer: **Hace dos horas que** veo televisión.

### Using the present progressive with direct object pronouns

Direct object pronouns can precede a conjugated verb or can be attached to the end of an in infinitive or gerund.

| | |
|---|---|
| **Lo** leo en el parque. | *I read **it** in the park.* |
| Voy a leer**lo** en el parque. | *I am going to read **it** in the park.* |
| **La** estamos alquilando. | *We are renting **it**.* |
| Estamos alquilándo**la**. | *We are renting **it**.* |

## Lección B

# Vocabulario 1

emcpassport.com

WB 1–3
LA 1
GV 1–2

Chile

## ¿Cuándo son las estaciones en Chile?

El verano es en diciembre, enero y febrero.

el sol
Hace mucho sol.

dar un paseo por la playa

**El otoño** es en marzo, abril y mayo.

No hace mucho calor.

la patineta
montar en patineta

**El invierno** es en junio, julio y agosto.

Hace frío.

esquiar

el hielo
patinar sobre hielo

**La primavera** es en septiembre, octubre y noviembre.

Este **lugar** es **excelente** en la primavera.

Hay **flores por todos lados**.

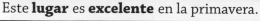

No me gusta esquiar, pero **en cambio** me gusta escribir correos electrónicos a mis amigos.

¿Todavía **continúas** en la tableta?

Sí, pero ya estoy **lista**.

## Para conversar

*T*o talk about sharing information:

Te voy a **enviar** las fotos de Chile por correo electrónico.
*I am going to send you the photos of Chile by e-mail.*

¡Excelente! ¿Puedes **copiar** a Carlos? Sé que le van a gustar.
*Excellent! Can you copy Carlos? I know he is going to like them.*

## 1 Las estaciones

Escoge la estación correcta, según lo que oyes.

el verano   el invierno   el otoño   la primavera

## 2 Las estaciones en Chile

Contesta las siguientes preguntas.

1. ¿En qué estación pueden patinar sobre hielo en Chile?
2. ¿En qué meses hay flores en Chile?
3. ¿En qué meses están esquiando en Chile?
4. ¿Qué estación es en abril y mayo en Chile?
5. ¿Qué estación es en enero y febrero en Chile?
6. ¿Qué estación es en junio y julio en Chile?

### Un poco más

**¿Cuándo es verano?**

In the Southern Hemisphere, the seasons are the reverse of the seasons in the Northern Hemisphere. People ski in Chile from June to August because it is winter there. Similarly, the summer months in Chile are December, January, and February.

## ¡Comunicación!

### 3 Mi estación favorita    Interpersonal Communication

Con tu compañero/a hablen de su estación favorita y de las actividades que les gusta hacer en esa estación.

**MODELO**
A: ¿Cuál es tu estación favorita?

B: Mi estación favorita es el invierno porque hace frío y puedo patinar sobre hielo. Y tú, ¿cuál es tu estación favorita?

A: Yo prefiero la primavera porque no hace mucho calor y me gusta dar paseos con mi perro.

*En la primavera me gusta dar paseos con mi perro.*

# Diálogo 🎧

## ¡Vamos a esquiar!

**Diego:** ¿Vamos a dar un paseo por la playa?

**Pablo:** No, gracias. Hace mucho calor.

**Elena:** Yo prefiero montar en patineta.

**Pablo:** ¡Vamos a esquiar!

**Elena:** ¡En enero no podemos esquiar en Chile!

**Pablo:** No, aquí, no. ¡Vamos a Colorado!

**Elena:** ¡Qué tonto eres!

**Pablo:** Me gusta el invierno.

**Elena:** ¡Ya está bien! Vamos a tomar un refresco.

## 4 ¿Qué recuerdas? 🎧

1. ¿Quién quiere dar un paseo por la playa?
2. ¿Por qué no quiere Pablo ir a la playa?
3. ¿Qué prefiere hacer Elena?
4. ¿Qué quiere hacer Pablo?
5. ¿A quién le gusta el invierno?

## 5 Algo personal 🎧

1. ¿Cuál es tu estación favorita? Explica.
2. ¿Qué te gusta hacer en tu estación favorita?
3. ¿Qué deportes practicas donde tú vives en la primavera? ¿Y en el verano? ¿Y en el otoño? ¿Y en el invierno?

## 6 ¿Qué actividades puedes hacer? 🎧

Escucha la información y di qué actividad o actividades puedes hacer.

**MODELO**  **Puedo montar en patineta en el parque.**

*Me gusta montar en patineta.*

# Gramática

## Verbs that Require Special Accentuation

Sometimes verbs that end in **-uar** or **-iar** (*esquiar, enviar,* and *continuar,* for example) require a written accent mark to indicate that a vowel should be stressed for all present-tense forms except for *nosotros.* You will have to learn which verbs follow this pattern since some verbs that end in **-uar** or **-iar** may not follow this pattern (such as the verbs *estudiar* and *copiar*).

**esquiar**: esquío, esquías, esquía, esquiamos, esquiáis, esquían

**enviar**: envío, envías, envía, enviamos, enviáis, envían

**continuar**: continúo, continúas, continúa, continuamos, continuáis, continúan

**but:**

**copiar**: copio, copias, copia, copiamos, copiáis, copian

**estudiar**: estudio, estudias, estudia, estudiamos, estudiáis, estudian

---

### 7    ¿Qué hacen?

Indica qué hacen estas personas en su tiempo libre. Usa la forma correcta del verbo entre paréntesis.

**MODELO**   Yo (*esquiar*) todos los inviernos.

Yo **esquío** todos los inviernos.

1. Tú (*continuar*) dando paseos por las calles de la ciudad.
2. Mi tía siempre me (*enviar*) un libro nuevo para mi cumpleaños.
3. Claudia y Alberto (*esquiar*) en Portillo.
4. Victoria y Patricia (*enviar*) correos electrónicos a sus amigos.
5. Nosotros (*esquiar*) en Colorado.
6. Mamá (*enviar*) cartas a nuestros abuelos.
7. Luis (*alquilar*) DVDs.
8. Sara (*patinar*) sobre hielo.
9. Elena (*continuar*) montando en patineta, su actividad favorita.
10. Yo (*esquiar*) con mis padres.
11. Mis amigas y yo (*estudiar*) por la tarde.
12. Eva (*copiar*) canciones de la internet.
13. Tere (*continuar*) hablando español después de la clase.
14. Mis primos y yo (*esquiar*) los fines de semana en los Andes.

*Yo patino sobre hielo con mi hermana.*

## 8 Todos hacemos algo

Read the following statements and indicate where there are missing accent marks.
Then identify the letter of the illustration that best matches each statement.

1. Él envia una carta.
2. Hace frío.
3. Ellos esquian ahora mismo.
4. Hace calor y están en la playa.

5. Es invierno.
6. Ellos continuan esquiando.
7. Continua haciendo sol.
8. Ella copia el número de teléfono.

A

B

# ¡Comunicación!

## 9 Amigos por correo electrónico 👥 Interpersonal Communication

Imagine you have a key pal in Portillo, Chile. Write an e-mail telling him or her about
your home and school life. You may want to say:

- you like to ski during the winter
- how often you and your family ski
- you would like to go to Portillo
- you continue studying Spanish at school
- you are sending pictures of you and your family
  with the e-mail

Remember to add a greeting and a closing. Add
additional details, including three questions for your
key pal. Then exchange messages with another student
in class so you can respond to each other's e-mail.

*Le envío un correo electrónico a mi amigo que vive en Chile.*

# Gramática

## Present Tense of *dar* and *poner*

The verbs ***dar*** (*to give*) and ***poner*** (*to put, place, set*) have irregular present-tense *yo* forms. In addition, the verb ***dar*** has an irregular *vosotros/as* form. Other verbs that are regular in the present tense except for the *yo* form include: ***hacer*** (*yo hago*), ***saber*** (*yo sé*), ***ver*** (*yo veo*), ***salir*** (*yo salgo*).

| dar | | | |
|---|---|---|---|
| yo | **doy** | nosotros/as | damos |
| tú | das | vosotros/as | **dais** |
| Ud., él, ella | da | Uds., ellos, ellas | dan |

| poner | | | |
|---|---|---|---|
| yo | **pongo** | nosotros/as | ponemos |
| tú | pones | vosotros/as | ponéis |
| Ud., él, ella | pone | Uds., ellos, ellas | ponen |

### 10 ¿Dan un paseo a pie o en carro?

Create logical sentences using the expression *dar un paseo* and either *a pie* or *en carro*, according to what makes the most sense.

**MODELO** Enrique / por el parque

**Enrique da un paseo por el parque a pie.**

1. yo / por la playa
2. tú / por la ciudad
3. nosotros / por el centro
4. Marta y Esperanza / por la calle
5. mi amigo / por la Avenida de la Independencia
6. mis padres / por la plaza

*Ellos dan un paseo por el parque.*

### 11 ¡A ponerlo en su lugar!

Completa las oraciones con la forma apropiada del verbo **poner**.

**MODELO** Esteban **pone** la bicicleta en el garaje.

1. Lola __ las servilletas en la mesa del comedor.
2. Yo __ las flores en el escritorio.
3. Pedro y Laura __ sus patinetas en el patio.
4. Todos nosotros __ los platos sucios en el fregadero.
5. Tú __ los refrescos en el refrigerador.
6. Mi padre __ el televisor en la sala.

## 12 ¡Qué bonita es la primavera!

Completa el siguiente párrafo con la forma apropiada de **comer**, **poner**, **dar**, **salir** y **ver** para saber por qué Ingrid dice que le gusta la primavera.

En la primavera yo siempre **(1)** con mi madre los sábados por la mañana a buscar flores. Yo **(2)** flores por toda la casa. Casi todas las mañanas yo **(3)** un paseo por el parque con mi hermana y por la tarde vamos de compras a las tiendas que están cerca de la casa. Mi padre siempre me **(4)** dinero para ir de compras. Claro, a veces, nos quedamos en casa y **(5)** televisión o **(6)** a dar un paseo por la noche. Antes de comer, mis hermanos y yo **(7)** la mesa. Hoy vamos a **(8)** en el patio porque no hace calor y hay flores allí. ¡Me gusta la primavera!

# ¡Comunicación!

## 13 Preguntas personales 👥 🎧 Interpersonal Communication

En parejas, alternen en hacer y contestar las siguientes preguntas en español.

1. ¿Qué haces cuando tienes tiempo libre?
2. ¿Te gusta dar paseos? ¿Dónde?
3. ¿Dan tu familia y tú paseos en carro los fines de semana? ¿Adónde van?
4. ¿Cómo das paseos en el verano? ¿En carro? ¿A pie? ¿En bicicleta?
5. ¿Dan tus amigos y tú paseos en el verano? ¿Adónde?
6. ¿En qué estación del año te gusta más dar paseos? ¿Por qué?
7. ¿Adónde vas de viaje con tu familia en el verano? ¿En la primavera? ¿En el otoño? ¿En el invierno?
8. ¿Quién pone las maletas en el carro cuando vas de viaje con tu familia?
9. ¿Pones flores en tu casa en la primavera? ¿Quién las pone?
10. ¿Dónde pones tu mochila en las vacaciones, cuando no hay clases?
11. ¿...?

En mi tiempo libre les envío fotos a mis amigos

# ¡Comunicación!

## 14 Actividades para cada estación 👥 Interpersonal/Presentational Communication

Working in small groups, ask and answer about the activities you and your classmates enjoy doing according to different seasons. Include any favorite pastimes from this unit or previously learned vocabulary. Include details such as when and with whom you do an activity, what the weather is like at that time of year and why you like the activity. Prepare a summary presentation for the class including visuals.

MODELO  A: ¿Qué actividades haces en el invierno?

B: En el invierno esquío con mis padres todos los fines de semana. A mi padre y a mí nos gusta mucho el frío.

**? Pregunta clave**

How does geography affect the sports and leisure of a nation?

# La geografía y la identidad chilena 🎧

*El desierto de Atacama*

Hoy en día hay más de 17 millones de personas viviendo en Chile. Su capital, Santiago, es el centro del país y donde se concentra la mitad[1] de la población. La identidad de los chilenos —su personalidad, sus pasatiempos favoritos— está fuertemente determinada por las características geográficas del país.

Chile está rodeado por barreras naturales que lo separan del resto de los países latinoamericanos: el océano, la cordillera[2] y el desierto. Estas barreras impiden el contacto fluido con los países de al lado. Es como vivir en una isla. La particular geografía y el clima severo influyen en el carácter de los chilenos, que se distinguen por su tenacidad y capacidad de superar obstáculos.

*Santiago de Chile y los Andes detrás*

La cordillera de los Andes, con montañas de más de 6.000 metros de altura, es un lugar fantástico para esquiar o escalar[3]. El desierto de Atacama (el más árido del mundo) ofrece oportunidades para hacer caminatas y tomar fotos. Allí también se realizan[4] campeonatos de rally (competición de coches) porque las dunas del desierto son ideales para este deporte. Y con 4.300 km de extenso océano, Chile es un lugar excelente para practicar deportes acuáticos, especialmente el surf. El balneario[5] de Pichilemu es el paraíso de los surfistas por las excelentes condiciones del viento y las olas.[6] Más al sur,[7] existen cientos de lagos que también son ideales para la práctica de deportes como kayak, regatas y rafting.

[1] half   [2] mountain range   [3] climb   [4] take place   [5] seaside resort   [6] wind and waves   [7] further south

🔍 **Búsqueda:** geografía de chile, deporte en chile

## Prácticas

*Un huaso chileno*

The national sport of Chile is rodeo, not soccer. The practice dates back to the 16th century when lost cattle were rounded up and herded into the *Plaza de Armas* (town square) to be branded. In time, this roundup became a traditional sport with established rules, and it now takes place in an established half-moon arena called a *medialuna*.

Unlike rodeos in the United States, there is no bull riding or calf roping. The Chilean rodeo consists mainly of two riders, or *huasos,* pinning a cow up against a padded wall. This practice replicates the traditional work on the range, where the *huaso* identifies a cow and then maneuvers his horse to push it into an area where it can be controlled. The national rodeo championships, held each spring in the city of Rancagua, draw huge crowds who come to see the impressive skills of both horse and rider.

## 15 Comprensión   Interpretive Communication

1. ¿Qué determina las actividades de los chilenos?
2. ¿Qué barreras naturales separan a Chile? ¿Qué actividades puedes hacer allí?
3. ¿Qué actividades acuáticas se practican en Chile?

## 16 Analiza

1. What challenges might Chile's geography pose in daily life?
2. Why do you think Chilean rodeos attract huge crowds?

# Naturaleza, tradiciones y deportes chilenos

Did you know that in Chile, because of its narrow geography, you can climb a snow-covered volcano in the morning, take a refreshing lakeside swim after lunch, and be soaking in thermal baths by sunset? Chileans enjoy skiing in Portillo (on the border with Argentina); surfing and rafting in the Pacific and the southern lakes region; glacier and cave exploring in Patagonia in the south; and thermal bathing in the northern, central, and southern regions. Chile's unique topography and climate allow *los chilenos* to enjoy many different outdoor pastimes and sports.

*Las cavernas de mármol en la Patagonia*

Besides enjoying outdoor activities in beautiful natural settings, there are two games that Chileans appreciate and enjoy: *el palín* and *el fútbol*.

A traditional activity in the farming communities of the south is *el palín*, a game inherited from the

*Un juego de palín*

indigenous group the Mapuche that is still played today. The participants are often from two community groups or tribes. Play begins by placing a hard ball made of wood, leather, or metal in a hole in the center of a long, rectangular field or court. Players use a curved wooden stick (*palín*) to advance the ball in an effort to score on the opposing team at the extreme end of the field. The game is always part of a larger celebration in which a religious ceremony, dancing, and food are included. Regardless of who wins or loses, the home team provides the refreshments. And of course Chile, like many other countries, enjoys its *fútbol*. Along with the rodeo, it is enjoyed by Chileans across the entire country regardless of geography.

**Búsqueda:** cavernas de mármol, el palín (juego)

## 17 Comprensión

1. Why is it possible for Chileans to go from climbing volcanoes to soaking in thermal baths in a short time?
2. Name seven pastimes available to *los chilenos*, and explain the connection to the geography of the region.
3. What is *el palín*?

## Perspectivas

"Chileans love the rodeo because it is imprinted in their DNA. We are proud of this unique sport, which comprises expressions of our culture, tradition, craftsmanship, and folklore."
According to this translated quote by the president of the Chilean Rodeo Federation, how is the rodeo a reflection of what Chile values?

## 18 Analiza

1. How does the geography of your region affect your leisure activities?
2. How does the geography of a region impact the personality of the people who live there?

## Comparaciones

Which sports do you know that share characteristics with *el palín*? How are they alike? How are they different?

# Vocabulario 2

## ¿Qué tiempo hace para los deportistas? 🎧

Está soleado.

la corredora

el futbolista / el jugador de fútbol

Está nublado.

Hace quince grados.

la esquiadora

Hay neblina.

Hace fresco.

el patinador

Hace viento.

la tenista

el basquetbolista

la nieve

la lluvia

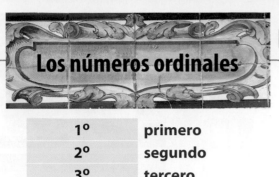

## Los números ordinales

| 1º | primero |
| 2º | segundo |
| 3º | tercero |
| 4º | cuarto |
| 5º | quinto |
| 6º | sexto |
| 7º | séptimo |
| 8º | octavo |
| 9º | noveno |
| 10º | décimo |

## Para conversar

**T**o talk about the weather:

**Hace buen tiempo**.
*The weather is good.*

**Hace mal tiempo**.
*The weather is bad.*

¿Cuál es **la temperatura máxima**?
*What is the maximum temperature?*

¿Cuál es **la temperatura mínima**?
*What is the minimum temperature?*

¿Cuándo **nieva** en Chile?
*When does it snow in Chile?*

¿Cuándo **llueve** más en tu país?
*When does it rain the most in your country?*

## 19 ¿Quién es?

Selecciona la foto de la persona apropiada.

A

B

C

D

E

F

## 20 El tiempo

Contesta las siguientes preguntas en español.

1. ¿En qué estación hace mucho frío?
2. ¿En qué estación llueve mucho?
3. ¿Cuándo hace mucho calor?

4. Cuando va a llover, ¿cómo está el día?
5. ¿Qué tiempo hace en primavera? ¿Y en verano? ¿Y en otoño? ¿Y en invierno?

# Diálogo

## ¿Qué temperatura hace?

**Diego:**   ¡Qué buen refresco!

**Pablo:**   ¿Qué temperatura hace?

**Elena:**   Hace calor. Hace treinta y cinco grados.

**Diego:**   ¡Vamos a jugar al básquetbol!

**Pablo:**   Soy mal jugador de básquetbol.

**Elena:**   Eres un buen basquetbolista.

**Pablo:**   No, soy un buen esquiador.

**Elena:**   En julio podemos ir a esquiar a Portillo.

**Diego:**   ¿Quién va a ser el primero en terminar el refresco?

**Pablo:**   ¡Yo! Y el segundo vas a ser tú.

## 21  ¿Qué recuerdas?

1. ¿Dice Elena que hace calor o hace frío?

2. ¿A qué quiere jugar Diego?

3. ¿Quién es un buen esquiador?

4. ¿Adónde pueden ir a esquiar en julio?

5. ¿Quién va a ser el primero en terminar el refresco?

## 22  Algo personal

1. ¿Qué temperatura hace ahora?

2. ¿Qué tiempo hace?

3. ¿Te gusta cuando hace mucho calor? ¿Y cuando hace frío?

## 23  ¿Qué tiempo hace?

Selecciona la ilustración que corresponde con lo que oyes.

**A**

**B**

**C**

**D**

**E**

**F**

# Gramática

## Describing People Using -dor and -ista

You can identify someone who participates in a particular sport or activity by changing the ending on the verb to **-dor** (**-dora**) and the ending on the noun to **-ista** (which remains the same for males or females).

| | | | | |
|---|---|---|---|---|
| patinar | – el patina**dor**/la patina**dora** | el tenis | – | el/la ten**ista** |
| esquiar | – el esquia**dor**/la esquia**dora** | el básquetbol | – | el/la basquetbol**ista** |
| correr | – el corre**dor**/la corre**dora** | el fútbol | – | el/la futbol**ista** |
| jugar | – el juga**dor**/la juga**dora** | los deportes | – | el/la deport**ista** |

**Note:** The accent mark is not used on the newly formed word when these endings are added.

### 24 ¿Qué son? 🎧

Describe a estas personas usando las siguientes palabras:
**basquetbolista, beisbolista, corredor(a), deportista, esquiador(a), futbolista, nadador(a), patinador(a), tenista.**

> **MODELO** Mis primas nadan en la piscina.
> **Son nadadoras.**

1. Juan está jugando al fútbol.
2. Beatriz está patinando sobre hielo.
3. Nosotros tenemos práctica de deportes.
4. Marta está jugando al tenis.
5. Jorge e Iván esquían muy bien.
6. Estoy jugando al básquetbol.
7. Tú estás listo para jugar al béisbol.
8. Estoy corriendo en el parque.

*Marta está jugando al tenis.*

## ¡Comunicación!

### 25 ¿Qué clase de deportista eres? 👥 Interpersonal Communication

Con tu compañero/a, túrnense para preguntar qué deportes practican y para contestar qué clase de deportista son y por qué.

> **MODELO** jugar al tenis
> **A:** ¿Juegas al tenis?
> **B:** Sí, soy un tenista excelente / No, soy un tenista muy malo.

1. jugar al béisbol
2. nadar
3. patinar
4. jugar al fútbol
5. correr
6. esquiar

## 26 ¿Qué tipo de deportistas son?

Di qué tipo de deportistas son las personas de las fotografías.

MODELO     Es beisbolista.

1

2

3

4

5

6

## ¡Comunicación!

## 27 Mi deportista favorito     Interpersonal Communication

Either from previous knowledge or Internet research, make a list of ten famous athletes from Spanish-speaking countries. In small groups, talk about these athletes. Say the person's name, sport, and where the person is from. If the person plays with a team, name the team. Be as specific and detailed as you can about the athletes on your list, and add any information you can to your classmates' descriptions.

MODELO
    A: Mi deportista favorito es Leo Messi. Es futbolista y es de Argentina.

    B: Juega con el Fútbol Club de Barcelona en España, ¿verdad?

    A: Sí y también juega para el equipo nacional de Argentina. Es un futbolista fantástico.

    C: Pues mi deportista favorito es un beisbolista. Se llama Miguel Cabrera. Juega con los Tigres de Detroit.

# Gramática

## Using Ordinal Numbers

- Use ordinal numbers to place things in order (first, second, third, etc.). In Spanish, only the first ten ordinal numbers are used often. They generally follow definite articles and precede nouns. Like other adjectives in Spanish, the ordinal numbers agree in gender (masculine/feminine) and number (singular/plural) with the noun they modify.

  | | |
  |---|---|
  | *¿Cuáles son los **primeros** esquiadores en terminar?* | Who are the **first** skiers to finish? (Which skiers came in first place?) |

- When *primero* and *tercero* appear before a masculine singular noun, they are shortened to *primer* and *tercer*.

  | | |
  |---|---|
  | *Luis es el **primer** esquiador en terminar.* | Luis is the **first** skier to finish. |
  | *Gustavo es el **tercer** esquiador en terminar.* | Gustavo is the **third** skier to finish. |

- You can abbreviate ordinal numbers ending in **-o**, **-a**, **-os**, **-as**, or **-er** by placing those letters at the upper right-hand side of the number:

  *primero* → $1^o$,  *primera* → $1^a$,  *primeros* → $1^{os}$,  *primeras* → $1^{as}$,  *primer* → $1^{er}$,  *tercer* → $3^{er}$.

---

### 28 La competencia anual del colegio

El Colegio San Ignacio de Santiago tiene una competencia de esquí en Portillo todos los años. Completa los resultados de la competencia de este año con el número ordinal apropiado.

**MODELO**   Ingrid fue la <u>décima</u> esquiadora en terminar.

| Competencia Anual | |
|---|---|
| 1ª Olga | 6º Javier |
| 2º Edgar | 7ª Paula |
| 3º Hugo | 8ª Paz |
| 4ª Natalia | 9º Alfonso |
| 5º Enrique | 10ª Ingrid |

*Ingrid fue la décima esquiadora en terminar.*

1. Javier fue el __ esquiador en terminar.
2. Paula fue la __ esquiadora en terminar.
3. Alfonso fue el __ esquiador en terminar.
4. Paz fue la __ esquiadora en terminar.
5. Hugo fue el __ esquiador en terminar.
6. Olga fue la __ esquiadora en terminar.
7. Edgar fue el __ esquiador en terminar.
8. Natalia fue la __ esquiadora en terminar.
9. Enrique fue el __ esquiador en terminar.
10. Ingrid fue la __ esquiadora en terminar.

## 29 Nuestro pasatiempo nacional

Isabel loves soccer and would like to find out the standings for her favorite Chilean teams. Use the information provided in the chart to update her.

| Tabla de posiciones | | | | | |
|---|---|---|---|---|---|
| Equipos | PJ | PG | PE | PP | Pts. |
| 1. Colo Colo | 38 | 32 | 2 | 4 | 66 |
| 2. Antofagasta | 38 | 30 | 4 | 4 | 64 |
| 3. O'Higgins | 38 | 27 | 5 | 3 | 59 |
| 4. Everton | 38 | 24 | 3 | 11 | 51 |
| 5. Palestino | 38 | 23 | 2 | 13 | 48 |
| 6. Huachipato | 38 | 20 | 5 | 13 | 45 |
| 7. Iquique | 38 | 18 | 6 | 14 | 42 |
| 8. Cobreloa | 38 | 15 | 10 | 13 | 40 |
| 9. La Calera | 38 | 12 | 5 | 21 | 29 |
| 10. Cobresal | 38 | 9 | 7 | 22 | 25 |
| PJ: Partidos jugados; PG: Partidos ganados; PE: Partidos empatados; PP: Partidos perdidos; Pts.: Puntos | | | | | |

1. El Everton es el __ equipo.
2. El Iquique es el __ equipo.
3. El O'Higgins todavía es el __ equipo.
4. El Palestino es el __ equipo.
5. El Cobresal es el __ equipo.

6. El Cobreloa es el __ equipo.
7. Antofagasta es el __ equipo.
8. El Colo Colo es el __ equipo.
9. La Calera es el __ equipo.
10. El Huachipato es el __ equipo.

## 30 ¿Quién fue el primero?

Working in pairs, talk about the final results of the girls' and boys' race.

**MODELO**
A: ¿Quién fue la séptima en terminar?
B: Marta fue la séptima en terminar.

| muchachos | muchachas |
|---|---|
| 1° Enrique | 1ª Adina |
| 2° Edgar | 2ª Olga |
| 3° Hugo | 3ª Natalia |
| 4° Javier | 4ª Paula |
| 5° Alfonso | 5ª Paz |
| 6° Víctor | 6ª Ingrid |
| 7° Alejandro | 7ª Marta |
| 8° Jorge | 8ª Raquel |
| 9° Ramiro | 9ª Juliana |
| 10° Roberto | 10ª Susana |

*¿Quién va a ser el primero en terminar?*

# ¡Comunicación!

## 31 ¿Qué deporte practicas? 👥 Interpersonal Communication

Athletes participate in different sports throughout the year. Working in pairs, using the pictures, vocabulary, and information provided, talk about what each person is doing, what the season is, what the weather is like or anything else you can say in Spanish. Correct any information your partner says that you think is wrong.

MODELO
A: **En la primera foto es invierno.**

B: **No, no es invierno, es primavera. La temperatura es perfecta para jugar en el parque. Ana está jugando al tenis.**

A: **Sí, y en la segunda foto Pedro está jugando al básquetbol.**

**1.** Ana

**2.** Pedro  **3.** Carmen

**4.** Rosa

**5.** Alejandro

**6.** Esteban

# ¡Comunicación!

## 32 ¿Qué quieres hacer en el verano? 👥 Interpersonal Communication

Working in groups of three, each of you must create a list of eight summer activities in order from most to least favorite, using ordinal numbers. Then discuss the order of your preferences and why.

MODELO
A: **Primero, quiero ir a la piscina a nadar porque en verano hace calor y buen tiempo. Segundo, me gustaría jugar al tenis porque es un deporte muy divertido.**

B: **Bueno, primero me gustaría dar paseos por la playa. Me encanta cuando hace sol.**

C: **Pues a mí, primero me gustaría leer libros en el patio porque allí no hace mucho calor.**

*1° nadar en la piscina*

*2° jugar al tenis*

*3° ver partidos de fútbol en la televisión*

# Todo en contexto

? Pregunta clave

How does geography affect the sports and leisure of a nation?

## ¡Comunicación!

### 33 ¿Qué tiempo hace hoy en Chile? 👥 Interpretive Communication

Lee este mapa del pronóstico del tiempo en Chile. Luego usa el vocabulario, las lecturas culturales de las páginas 330–331 de esta lección y *Un poco más* para ayudarte a contestar las preguntas.

1. ¿Qué tiempo hace en Pichilemu? ¿Qué deportes puedes practicar allí?
2. ¿Qué tiempo hace en Atacama? ¿Qué actividades puedes hacer allí?
3. ¿Dónde está nublado? ¿Qué deporte puedes practicar allí?
4. ¿Cuál es la temperatura máxima en Santiago de Chile? ¿Y la temperatura mínima?
5. Si quieres disfrutar el calor, ¿adónde vas?
6. ¿Cuál es la temperatura máxima en grados Fahrenheit en Atacama?
7. ¿Cuál es la temperatura mínima en grados Fahrenheit en Portillo?

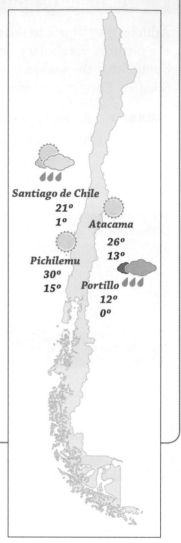

Santiago de Chile
21°
1°

Atacama
26°
13°

Pichilemu
30°
15°

Portillo
12°
0°

#### Un poco más

**Celsius vs Fahrenheit**

In the Spanish-speaking world, temperatures are always given in degrees Celcius (°C). To convert Celsius (°C) to Fahrenheit (°F) use the following formula:

Multiply by 1.8, then add 32. Thus, °C 30 = °F 86

## ¡Comunicación!

### 34 ¡Bienvenidos a Chile! 👥 Presentational Communication

In pairs or small groups, you're going to write a tourist pamphlet for visitors to Chile. Your pamphlet should focus on information about one of the main climatic regions of Chile: the Atacama Desert, the Central Valley, the lakes and volcanoes region, Patagonia in the south, or the Pacific Islands. It should include a description of the region, information about the average climate and temperatures (both in Celsius and Fahrenheit), and recommended activities for each season. Remember that in Chile the seasons are reversed! Use the Internet as well as the information provided in the culture readings about Chile, and add visuals to illustrate your guide. Be prepared to make a presentation to the class.

# Lectura AP

## Antes de leer

### 35 Preparación

1. Do you know about Stonehenge or other mysterious civilizations that erected huge stones?
2. Have you ever heard of Easter Island?
3. Have you ever visited a UNESCO (United Nations Educational, Scientific and Cultural Organization) World Heritage Site, such as Yellowstone National Park or the Statue of Liberty? Can you name any others?

> **Estrategia**
>
> **Read on and go back**
>
> If a word is unfamiliar, you can skip it and read the rest of the sentence. Then go back and see if you can figure out the meaning in context. The most important thing is to understand the idea of the whole sentence.

### 36 ¿Qué verbo es?

Look at each of the following unfamiliar forms of verbs from the reading. Try to name a verb infinitive you already know that would go with each one to help you better understand what you read.

1. viajaron
2. descubierta

3. describió
4. hacían

## Rapa Nui

Rapa Nui es la isla habitada más remota del planeta. No hay otra porción de tierra en el mundo tan aislada en el mar y esa misma condición le da un aura de fascinante misterio.

Es un Parque Nacional, declarado Patrimonio Mundial por la UNESCO, y que tiene de todo y para todos: playas de color rosa (como la playa de Ovahe), volcanes, flora y fauna marinas para descubrir cuando estás nadando, cavernas para recorrer[1] en silencio, y moáis (estatuas gigantescas) que fueron testigos[2] del auge y la caída[3] de una sociedad estratificada y compleja.

[1] to go through    [2] witnesses    [3] witnessed the rise and fall

**Búsqueda:** rapa nui

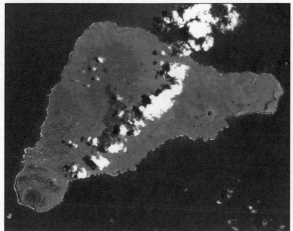

*La isla polinesia de Rapa Nui (Easter Island)*

*Una fila de misteriosos "moáis" (esculturas)*

# Los habitantes de Rapa Nui 🎧

Se estima que los primeros habitantes de Rapa Nui viajaron desde las Islas Marquesas en el siglo VI y que durante más de mil años no tuvieron contacto con el exterior. Eso, hasta que el domingo de Pascua[1] de 1722 la isla fue descubierta para el mundo occidental por el marinero holandés Jakob Roggevcen, quien describió a los rapa nui como *"un sutil pueblo de mujeres bonitas y hombres amables"*.

El espíritu de esta cultura sigue vivo en sus habitantes, su lengua, su ropa, su música, sus bailes, su artesanía y sus comidas. Cada mes de febrero, los habitantes celebran la fiesta de Tapati, una fiesta de dos semanas... donde los rapa nui se pintan el cuerpo[2] como lo hacían sus ancestros, hacen competencias fantásticas, cantan, bailan y eligen a su reina[3].

[1] Easter    [2] paint their bodies    [3] queen

*Enormes moáis hechos de roca volcánica*

*Baile tradicional de los rapa nui*

🔍 **Búsqueda:** los habitantes de rapa nui

*Los moáis dominan la costa de Rapa Nui.*

## 37 Comprensión 🎧 Interpretive Communication

1. ¿Cómo se conoce en inglés a Rapa Nui?
2. Menciona cuatro cosas que puedes ver en Rapa Nui.
3. ¿Qué es un *moái*?
4. ¿Cómo celebran los habitantes de Rapa Nui su fiesta anual?

## 38 Analiza

1. What do you think is the significance of the *moái*? Justify your answer.
2. How do you think the ancient Rapa Nui were able to transport and lift the huge rocks to build the *moái*?

# Repaso de la Lección B

## A  Escuchar: ¿Es lógico o no? 🎧 (pp. 323–324)

Di si lo que oyes sobre las cuatro estaciones es **lógico** o **ilógico**. Si es ilógico, di por qué.

## B  Vocabulario: Di qué estación es (p. 323)

Indica cuál es la estación según el contexto.

1. Hace mucho sol. Me encanta tomar el sol y nadar. Es __.
2. Hay flores por todos lados. Ahora puedo jugar al fútbol. Es __.
3. Hace frío y puedo esquiar en la nieve. Es __.
4. Empieza a hacer frío y ahora puedo ver los partidos de fútbol americano. Es __.

## C  Gramática: Tiempo libre (pp. 326, 328)

Indica qué hacen estas personas cuando tienen tiempo libre. Usa la forma apropiada del verbo entre paréntesis.

1. Tú (*esquiar*) todos los fines de semana.
2. Luis (*continuar*) montando en patineta.
3. Yo (*saber*) patinar sobre hielo.
4. Marina (*copiar*) la lista de películas.
5. Uds. (*poder*) esquiar muy bien.
6. Yo (*poner*) la patineta en mi cuarto.
7. Tú y yo (*dar*) un paseo en la playa.
8. Paz y Esther (*enviar*) correos electrónicos.
9. Mi hermano menor (*copiar*) dibujos de las revistas.
10. Yo (*dar*) un paseo con mi perro.
11. Álvaro (*alquilar*) DVDs.

## D  Gramática: ¿Qué son? (p. 335)

Describe a estas personas usando la palabra apropiada.

**MODELO**  Me gusta correr en el parque.
**Soy corredora.**

1. Enrique y Daniel nadan todas las mañanas.
2. Mi mamá corre en el parque.
3. A Maite le gusta jugar al tenis.
4. Nosotros estamos listos para jugar al béisbol.
5. Mis primos siempre practican deportes.
6. Mi papá va a esquiar todos los inviernos.
7. Me gusta patinar sobre hielo.
8. Mis hermanos juegan al voleibol todos los fines de semana.

## E  Vocabulario/Gramática: ¿Cuál es el orden? (pp. 333, 337)

Escribe los números ordinales que faltan en la serie.

décimo, __, octavo, __, __, quinto, __, tercero, __, __.

How are your pastimes similar to and different from the Chileans'? Include information from the culture readings *"La geografía y la identidad chilena"* and *"Naturaleza, tradiciones y deportes chilenos"* and take into account the seasons, climate, and geography to compare and contrast. Use a Venn diagram to organize your ideas.

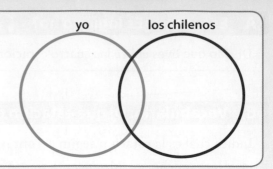
yo          los chilenos

## Vocabulario

| El tiempo |
|---|
| está nublado/a / soleado/a |
| la estación |
| fresco |
| el grado |
| hace (+ *weather expression*) |
| hay neblina / sol |
| el hielo |
| el invierno |
| la lluvia |
| máximo/a |
| mínimo/a |
| la neblina |
| la nieve |
| nublado/a |
| el otoño |
| la primavera |
| ¿Qué tiempo / temperatura hace? |
| el sol |
| soleado/a |
| la temperatura |
| el tiempo |
| el viento |

| Para describir |
|---|
| buen |
| cuarto/a |
| décimo/a |
| excelente |
| listo/a |
| mal |
| noveno/a |
| octavo/a |
| quinto/a |
| segundo/a |
| séptimo/a |
| sexto/a |
| tercero/a (tercer) |
| todavía |

| Deportistas |
|---|
| el/la basquetbolista |
| el corredor, la corredora |
| el deportista, la deportista |
| el esquiador, la esquiadora |
| el/la futbolista |
| el jugador, la jugadora |
| el patinador, la patinadora |
| el/la tenista |

| Verbos |
|---|
| continuar |
| copiar |
| dar (un paseo) |
| enviar |
| esquiar |
| llover (ue) |
| montar en patineta |
| nevar (ie) |
| patinar sobre hielo |

| Expresiones y otras palabras |
|---|
| en cambio |
| la flor |
| el lugar |
| el paseo |
| la patineta |
| por |
| por todos lados |

## Gramática

### Present tense of *dar* and *poner*

The verbs *dar* and *poner* are irregular in the present tense *yo* form. *Dar* has an irregular *vosotros* form, also.

| dar | | poner | |
|---|---|---|---|
| **doy** | damos | **pongo** | ponemos |
| das | **dais** | pones | ponéis |
| da | dan | pone | ponen |

### Verbs that require special accentuation

Some verbs that end in *-uar* or *-iar* require a written accent, **except** for the *nosotros* form.

| continuar | | esquiar | |
|---|---|---|---|
| contin**ú**o | continuamos | esqu**í**o | esquiamos |
| contin**ú**as | continuáis | esqu**í**as | esquiáis |
| contin**ú**a | contin**ú**an | esqu**í**a | esqu**í**an |

### Using ordinal numbers

Ordinal numbers match the noun in gender and number.

| | |
|---|---|
| Hoy es el **primer** día de clase. | Today is the **first** day of class. |
| Las **segundas** páginas son más interesantes. | The **second** pages are more interesting. |

### Describing people using *-dor* and *-ista*

To identify someone who participates in a particular sport or activity, change the ending of the verb to *-dor* and the noun to *-ista*.

| patinar | → | el patina**dor**/la patina**dora** |
|---|---|---|
| el fútbol | → | el/la futbol**ista** |

# *Para concluir*

## Proyectos

**?** Pregunta clave

How does geography affect the sports and leisure of a nation?

### A ¡Manos a la obra!

Find a website that gives weather information for different Spanish-speaking cities around the world. Then write a brief weather report in Spanish for ten cities. Be sure to include the following: a symbol to represent the weather conditions, a description of today's weather, and the current temperature. Also, tell what season it is. Predict what people are doing now in each city due to the weather. Present your weather report to a small group.

**MODELO** En Córdoba, Argentina, la temperatura hoy es de 20ºC (68ºF). Es la primavera y hay flores, pero también mucha lluvia. Las personas están en sus casas viendo películas o jugando a las damas.

### B En resumen

Chile and Argentina have many characteristics in common, yet each has its own individual personality as a nation. List the traits that contribute to make each of these countries what it is. Then, on a large Venn diagram, show which characteristics they share and which are unique to each country. Be sure to include climate, geography, language, culture, sports, and other features.

Argentina    Chile

Spanish-speaking

## C  ¡A escribir!

Write a short paragraph to compare sports that are popular where you live with what you know about sports in Spanish-speaking countries. Are the same sports popular? Does the weather have an effect on the sports being practiced? Are the sports played at the same time of the year? During the same season? Incorporate vocabulary and information from *Unidad 7* as well as previously learned material.

## D  ¿El *Silicon Valley* de América Latina?

In groups of three, research the Chilean government program called "Start-Up Chile," created to promote young entrepreneurs. Find as much information as you can. Then, brainstorm some ideas that you would submit for admission to the program. Be creative! You won't actually have to carry them out, but think of projects that would be meaningful to Chile in the 21$^{st}$ century. Choose the one you like best, and present it to the class. Be sure to include visuals and diagrams to educate your classmates on your idea.

*Estos jóvenes participan en el programa* Start-Up Chile.

## E  Tango  Conéctate: la música y el baile

Prepare a project on the *tango*, choosing from one of the following options or making up your own:

- Search the word *tango* on the Internet or find a book at the library and write a summary of your findings.

- Play a tango for the class, comparing it to another musical style.

- With a partner, find an instructional video on how to dance the tango. Learn a few steps, and show the class.

## F  Dos hemisferios  Conéctate: la geografía

Study a map of the Western Hemisphere. Compare some Spanish-speaking cities to cities in the United States and Canada in terms of their distance from the Equator and from the North or South Poles. Which cities are in the Temperate Zones? Which are in the Tropical Zone? Now, compare their altitudes. How would you expect the climate to compare between any two pairs of cities? Use the Internet to check your answers. Create a visual representation with as much as possible in Spanish, and present your findings to the class.

# Vocabulario de la Unidad 7

los **aeróbicos** aerobics 7A

**ahora mismo** right now 7A

el **ajedrez** chess 7A

**alquilar** to rent 7A

**americano/a** American 7A

**antes de** before 7A

**apagar** to turn off 7A

el **básquetbol** basketball 7A

el **basquetbolista**, la **basquetbolista** basketball player 7B

**buen** good 7B

las **cartas** playing cards 7A

**casi** almost 7A

**continuar** to continue 7B

el **control remoto** remote control 7A

**copiar** to copy 7B

el **corredor**, la **corredora** runner 7B

**costar (ue)** to cost 7A

**¿Cuánto** (+ *time expression*) **hace que** (+ *present tense of verb*) ... ? How long ... ? 7A

**cuarto/a** fourth 7D

las **damas** checkers 7A

**dar** to give 7B

**dar un paseo** to go for a walk, to go for a ride 7B

**décimo/a** tenth 7B

el **deportista**, la **deportista** athlete 7B

**después de** after 7A

**dibujar** to draw, to sketch 7A

**dormir (ue, u)** to sleep 7A

**en cambio** on the other hand 7B

**enviar** to send 7B

el **equipo** team 7A

el **esquiador**, la **esquiadora** skier 7B

**esquiar** to ski 7B

**esta noche** tonight 7A

**está nublado/a / soleado/a** it's cloudy / sunny 7B

la **estación** season 7B

**estupendo/a** wonderful, marvelous 7A

**excelente** excellent 7B

la **flor** flower 7B

el **fresco** cool 7B

el **fútbol americano** football 7A

el **futbolista**, la **futbolista** soccer player 7B

el **grado** degree 7B

**hace** (+ *weather expression*) it is (+ weather expression) 7B

**hace** (+ *time expression*) **que** (time expression +) ago 7A

**hacer aeróbicos** to do aerobics 7A

**hay neblina / sol** it is misting / sunny 7B

el **hielo** ice 7B

el **invierno** winter 7B

el **jugador**, la **jugadora** player 7B

**jugar (ue)** to play 7A

la **lista** list 7A

**listo/a** ready 7B

**llover (ue)** to rain 7B

la **lluvia** rain 7B

el **lugar** place 7B

**mal** bad 7B

**máximo/a** maximum 7B

**mínimo/a** minimum 7B

el **minuto** minute 7A

**mismo/a** same 7A

**montar en patineta** to skateboard 7B

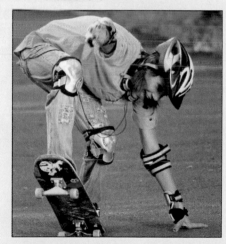

la **neblina** mist 7B

**nevar (ie)** to snow 7B

la **nieve** snow 7B

**noveno/a** ninth 7B

**nublado/a** cloudy 7B

**octavo/a** eighth 7B

el **otoño** autumn 7B

el **pasatiempo** pastime, leisure activity 7A

el **paseo** walk, ride, trip 7B

el **patinador**, la **patinadora** skater 7B

**patinar sobre hielo** to ice-skate 7B

la **patineta** skateboard 7B

**permitir** to permit 7A

**poder (ue, u)** to be able to 7A

**por** along 7B

**por la mañana** in the morning 7A

**por la noche** at night 7A

**por la tarde** in the afternoon 7A

**por todos lados** everywhere 7B

la **primavera** spring 7B

**primero/a (primer)** first 7B

el **programa** program 7A

**¿Qué temperatura hace?** What is the temperature? 7B

**¿Qué tiempo hace?** How is the weather? 7B

**quinto/a** fifth 7B

**recordar (ue)** to remember 7A

el **segundo** second (time increment) 7A

**segundo/a** second 7B

**séptimo/a** seventh 7B

**sexto/a** sixth 7B

el **siglo** century 7A

el **sol** sun 7B

**soleado/a** sunny 7B

la **telenovela** soap opera 7A

el **televisor** television set 7A

la **temperatura** temperature 7B

el **tenista**, la **tenista** tennis player 7B

**tercero/a (tercer)** third 7B

el **tiempo** weather 7B

**todavía** yet 7A

**todavía** still 7B

la **vida** life 7A

el **verano** 7B

el **videojuego** 7A

el **viento** wind 7B

el **voleibol** volleyball 7A

**volver (ue)** to return, to go back, to come back 7A

# La rutina diaria

Scan the QR code to watch this episode of *El cuarto misterioso*.

**Who is coming to lunch?**
A. **Rafael y Conchita**
B. **Conchita y Ana**
C. **Conchita, Ana y Rafael**

Pregunta clave

**?**

**How do routines inside and outside the home reflect cultural values?**

## Mis metas

**Lección A  I will be able to:**
▶ talk about household chores
▶ use indirect object pronouns to say to whom or for whom something is done
▶ say what just happened using **acabar de**
▶ discuss daily life in Spain for adults and teenagers
▶ talk about party preparations
▶ use the present tense of **oír** and **traer**
▶ talk about the past using the preterite tense of **-ar** verbs
▶ talk about how people spend their time in Spain

**Lección B  I will be able to:**
▶ identify and describe foods
▶ talk about preparing a meal
▶ make comparisons
▶ talk about a typical Sunday in Spain
▶ describe where Spaniards shop for food
▶ purchase food at a market
▶ use the preterite tense of **dar** and **estar**
▶ read and discuss a popular Spanish short story

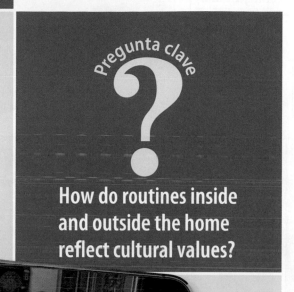

España

What is the name of this plaza in Madrid, and how does it fit into the daily life of Spaniards?

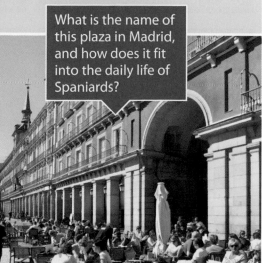

# *Vocabulario 1*

## Haciendo quehaceres 🎧

Vamos a **cocinar** para **las personas** de la familia. Nos gusta estar **juntos**.

Hay mucho **trabajo** para hacer en casa, pero todos ayudamos con **los quehaceres**.

preparar la comida

limpiar la cocina

adornar las paredes

hacer la cama

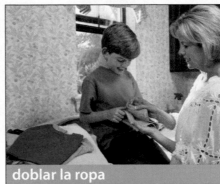

doblar la ropa

colgar la ropa

trabajar en el jardín

el abrigo

llegar a casa y colgar el abrigo

subir algo al cuarto

## Para conversar

*T*o talk about household chores:

Es un día bonito. Toda **la gente** está de paseo. ¿Quieres ir al parque?
*It's a beautiful day. All the people are out for a walk. Do you want to go to the park?*

**Quizás** esta tarde. **Acabo de** limpiar mi cuarto y estoy un poco cansada.
*Maybe this afternoon. I have just cleaned my room and I'm a little tired.*

¿Te puedo ayudar en **algo** más?
*Can I help you with anything else?*

No. **Solo** tengo que doblar mi ropa.
*No. I only have to fold my clothes.*

¿Sabes dónde está tu abrigo?
*Do you know where your coat is?*

Sí. Siempre lo **dejo** en la sala.
*Yes, I always leave it in the living room.*

### Estrategia

**Increasing your vocabulary**

When reading or learning new vocabulary in Spanish, you can figure out the meaning of a new word by relating it to your knowledge of other words that are spelled similarly. Such groups of similar words are called "word families." All the "members" of a word family share a common, easily recognizable root. Can you see how the verb *cocinar* (to cook) and the noun *cocina* (kitchen) are related in this way since people cook in a kitchen? Recognizing word families can help you expand your Spanish vocabulary and can make learning new words easier.

### En otros países

| | |
|---|---|
| **adornar** | *decorar (Latinoamérica)* |
| **hacer la cama** | *tender la cama (Latinoamérica)* |
| **el abrigo** | *el sobretodo (varios países)* |
| | *el tapado (Argentina)* |

### 1  ¿Qué tienen que hacer?

Write the names Julia and Enrique. Next, listen and list under each of their names what chores (*quehaceres*) each of them has to do. Then circle any items on the lists that they both have to do. The first one has been done for you.

MODELO

| Julia | Enrique |
|---|---|
| **adornar la sala** | |

### Para decir más

| | |
|---|---|
| **compartir** | *to share* |
| **cortar el césped** | *to mow the lawn* |
| **desempolvar** | *to dust* |
| **fregar** | *to wash, to scrub* |
| **guardar** | *to put away* |
| **pasarlo bien** | *to have fun* |
| **planchar** | *to iron* |
| **regar las plantas** | *to water the plants* |
| **secar los platos** | *to dry the dishes* |
| **solo/a** | *alone* |

### 2  En tu casa

Haz una lista de los quehaceres que hacen en tu casa según las expresiones en el Vocabulario 1. Luego, di quién hace cada uno de esos quehaceres en tu familia.

MODELO

| | |
|---|---|
| **limpiar la cocina** | **mi hermana mayor** |
| **colgar la ropa** | **yo** |
| **preparar la comida** | **mi mamá** |

### Un poco más

**El verbo *colgar***

The present tense of *colgar* (to hang) follows the pattern of other *o → ue* stem-changing verbs: *cuelgo, cuelgas, cuelga, colgamos, colgáis, cuelgan.*

## 3 ¿Cuál es el intruso?

Busca al intruso y explica por qué.

**MODELO** personas / gente / abrigo

**abrigo: Es una cosa.**

1. llegar / doblar / ropa
2. comida / cocinar / subir
3. gente / trabajo / quehaceres

4. colgar / abrigo / cama
5. cocina / comedor / jardín
6. juntos / personas / paredes

## 4 ¿Cuál es la palabra?

Completa los diálogos con las palabras del recuadro.

| quehaceres | gente | subir | camas |
|---|---|---|---|
| personas | limpiar | trabajo | algo |

1. **A:** ¿Hay mucha __ en tu familia?

   **B:** Sí, somos diez __.

2. **A:** ¿Ayudan Uds. con los __?

   **B:** Sí, siempre hay mucho __ en casa.

3. **A:** ¿Quién hace las __?

   **B:** Yo, y también ayudo a __ la cocina.

4. **A:** ¿Te puedo ayudar en __?

   **B:** Sí. ¿Puedes __ la ropa al primer piso?

*Hay muchas personas en nuestra familia.*

## ¡Comunicación!

## 5 ¿Lo hacemos juntos?  **Interpersonal Communication**

Conversa con un(a) compañero/a sobre los quehaceres de la casa. Invítalo/la a hacerlos juntos como se ve en el modelo. Él/ella va a decir que no y te va a invitar a hacer otra cosa juntos.

**MODELO** A: **¿Colgamos la ropa juntos?**

B: **No, prefiero hacerlo solo/a. Pero podemos cocinar juntos.**

*Tengo que colgar la ropa.*

## Diálogo

### ¿Me ayudas?

**Inés:** Víctor, ¿qué haces?

**Víctor:** Hago unos quehaceres.

**Inés:** ¡Qué aburrido! ¿Por qué no vamos al cine?

**Víctor:** Tengo que terminar de limpiar la casa. ¿Me ayudas?

**Inés:** Sí, dejo mi abrigo aquí y te voy a limpiar la cocina.
*(Más tarde)*
Bueno, la cocina ya está limpia. Hola, señora Zea.

**Sra. Zea:** Hola, Inés. Hola, Víctor. ¡Qué casa tan limpia!

**Víctor:** Gracias, mamá. Ahora voy al cine con Inés.

---

### 6 ¿Qué recuerdas?

1. ¿Qué hace Víctor?
2. ¿Adónde quiere ir Inés?
3. ¿Qué tiene que terminar Víctor primero?
4. ¿Qué limpia Inés?
5. ¿Qué dice la Sra. Zea?

---

### 7 Algo personal

1. ¿Cómo ayudas con los quehaceres en casa?
2. ¿Piensas que hacer los quehaceres es aburrido? Explica.
3. ¿Te gusta ir al cine?

---

### 8 ¿Me ayudas?

Mira las tres fotos que van con el diálogo y di si lo que oyes va con la primera, la segunda o la tercera foto.

**MODELO** Va con la tercera foto.

---

## ¡Comunicación!

### 9 ¿Ayudas en tu casa? 👥 Interpersonal Communication

Con un(a) compañero/a, túrnense para hablar de los quehaceres que hacen en casa y de los quehaceres que no les gusta hacer.

**MODELO**
**A:** ¿Qué quehaceres haces en tu casa?
**B:** Limpio mi cuarto, hago mi cama y a veces doblo la ropa.
**A:** ¿Qué quehaceres no te gusta hacer?
**B:** No me gusta preparar la comida o limpiar la cocina. ¿Y a ti?

# Direct Object Pronouns

- You have already learned that the direct object in a sentence is the person or thing that receives the action of the verb directly, and it answers the question **what?** or **whom?** Direct object pronouns replace the direct object in the sentence.

| Los pronombres de complemento directo | | | |
|---|---|---|---|
| **me** | me | **nos** | us |
| **te** | you | **os** | you |
| **lo** | him, it, you | **los** | them, you |
| **la** | her, it, you | **las** | them, you |

- Direct object pronouns can precede conjugated verbs, be attached to the end of an infinitive, or be attached to the end of a present participle. If attaching the pronoun to the end of a present participle, remember to add an accent mark on the participle to maintain the original pronunciation.

Susana está poniendo la mesa.

Susana **la** está poniendo.
Susana está poniéndo**la**.

## 10  Todos están haciendo quehaceres

Sigue el modelo para decir la misma oración de forma diferente, usando un pronombre de complemento directo.

MODELO    Yo estoy doblando *la ropa*.

**Yo la estoy doblando. / Yo estoy doblándola.**

1. Alfredo está buscando *las tazas*.
2. María y Fernando están preparando *la comida*.
3. Estamos adornando *el cuarto*.
4. Carlos está limpiando *la cocina*.
5. Mis hermanos están haciendo *las camas*.
6. Yo estoy colgando *los abrigos*.
7. Estamos haciendo juntos *los trabajos de la casa*.

Están preparando la comida.

# Gramática

## Indirect Object Pronouns

An indirect object indicates **to whom** or **for whom** something is said or done. An indirect object pronoun (*pronombre de complemento indirecto*) may replace an indirect object. Indirect object pronouns look the same as direct object pronouns except for *le* and *les*. You have already learned to use indirect object pronouns with the verb *gustar*.

| Los pronombres de complemento indirecto | | | |
|---|---|---|---|
| me | *to me, for me* | nos | *to us, for us* |
| te | *to you, for you* | os | *to you, for you* |
| le | *to you, for you*<br>*to him, for him*<br>*to her, for her* | les | *to you, for you*<br>*to them, for them* |

Indirect object pronouns follow the same rules for placement in a sentence that you learned for the direct object pronouns.

- They usually precede the conjugated form of the verb, but they also may follow and attach to an infinitive or a present participle. (Add an accent mark to the present participle in order to maintain the original pronunciation.)

  *Pamela **me** va a preparar un café.*
  *Pamela va a preparar**me** un café.*

  Pamela is going to prepare a coffee **for me**.

  ***Te** estoy hablando.*
  *Estoy hablándo**te**.*

  I am talking **to you**.

- Place negative expressions (e.g. *no, nunca*) before the indirect object pronouns.

  *Nunca **nos** preparan la comida.*

  They **never** make the food **for us**.

- Add the word *a* plus a pronoun or noun to a sentence in order to clarify the meaning of *le* and *les*, or in order to add emphasis.

  *Le escribo*    *a ella.*
            *a Jorge.*
            *a mi primo.*

  *Les escribo*    *a ellas.*
             *a Jorge y a Andrea.*
             *a mis primos.*

*Le escribo a Daniela.*

Raúl y su familia van de vacaciones y sus vecinos (*neighbors*) van a ayudar a la familia a prepararse para el viaje. Completa las oraciones con **me**, **te**, **le**, **nos** o **les**, para decir qué van a hacer.

**MODELO**   Ana **nos** va a limpiar la cocina. (*a nosotros*)

1. Esteban __ va a buscar las maletas. (*a mí*)
2. Ana __ va a doblar la ropa. (*a mi madre*)
3. La Sra. Tovar __ va a preparar la comida. (*a mis padres*)
4. El Sr. Tovar __ va a colgar los abrigos. (*a mi padre*)
5. Esteban y Ana __ van a hacer las camas. (*a nosotros*)

### Un poco más

**El uso de vosotros**

It is common to use the direct and indirect object pronoun *os* in Spain in the same circumstances in which you have learned to use *vosotros*: when talking informally to two or more people.

Estás hablando de los quehaceres de la casa con unos amigos. ¿Cómo puedes decir la misma oración de otra manera (*another way*)?

**MODELO**   *¿Me* estás colgando la ropa?

**¿Estás colgándome la ropa?**

1. Él nunca *le* puede limpiar la casa.
2. Quizás Carlos *te* puede poner la mesa.
3. ¿No *me* quieres preparar la comida?
4. Quizás *te* debo escribir una lista de quehaceres.

*Estoy colgándote los abrigos.*

5. *Les* estamos colgando la ropa.
6. ¿No *nos* está Ud. adornando el cuarto?

In pairs, take turns asking one another for help with the indicated tasks. The person responding may agree or refuse to help.

**MODELO**   colgar los abrigos

A:  **¿Me cuelgas los abrigos?**
B:  **Sí, (No, no) te cuelgo los abrigos.**

1. limpiar el patio
2. doblar las servilletas
3. limpiar la mesa del comedor
4. buscar la sal
5. encender las luces del comedor
6. hacer las camas
7. poner la mesa
8. subir la ropa a mi cuarto

## 14 Los quehaceres en casa

Las personas en las fotos están ayudándote en los quehaceres de la casa. Describe lo que hace cada una de las personas.

**MODELO** Juana

**Juana me está limpiando la cocina. /
Juana está limpiándome la cocina.**

**1.** Doris y Julia

**2.** María y sus hijos

**3.** Andrés

**4.** Carlota

# ¡Comunicación!

## 15 Para ayudar 👥 Interpersonal Communication

Make a list of your household chores and another list of what you do to help specific members of your family. Then talk with a classmate about what you do to help around the house and whom you help with the household duties.

**MODELO**
A: **¿Qué haces para ayudar en tu casa?**
B: **Pongo la mesa y limpio el comedor después de comer. ¿Y tú? ¿Ayudas a tus padres?**
A: **Sí, les limpio la ropa, la doblo y la pongo en su lugar.**

# ¡Comunicación!

## 16 ¿Cuándo me puedes ayudar? 👥 Interpersonal Communication

A group of exchange students from Spain will be staying with families in your community. With a classmate, take turns asking one another when each of you will be able to help with various chores to prepare for their visit. Indicate if and when you will be able to help with the indicated tasks.

**MODELO**
A: **¿Cuándo me puedes hacer las camas?**
B: **Quizás te puedo hacer las camas por la tarde. /
Quizás puedo hacerte las camas por la tarde.**

# Gramática

## ¡Comunicación!

### 17 ¿Qué nos gusta hacer? · Interpersonal Communication

In small groups, discuss your favorite and least favorite household chores. Assign one person to make a list of at least three chores you all like to do and a second list of three chores that you all do not like to do. Then talk with members of other groups to find out how your lists compare.

MODELO    A: ¿Les gusta poner la mesa?

B: Sí, nos gusta ponerla.

A: A nosotros también nos gusta.

| Nos gusta | No nos gusta |
|---|---|
| - poner la mesa | - cocinar |

## Saying What Just Happened with *acabar de*

You can say what has just happened using a form of the verb **acabar** (to finish, to complete) followed by **de** and an infinitive.

$$\boxed{\textbf{acabar de} \quad + \quad \textbf{infinitive}}$$

| | |
|---|---|
| *Acabo de limpiar* el baño. | **I have just cleaned** the bathroom. |
| *Mi padre acaba de llegar* a casa. | My father **has just arrived** home. |

### 18 Gracias por la ayuda 🎧

Francisco tiene muchos quehaceres y muchos buenos amigos. A sus amigos les gusta ayudar con sus quehaceres. Contesta las preguntas para decir quién acaba de hacer cada quehacer, usando las pistas entre paréntesis.

MODELO    ¿Los platos? (Alicia / limpiar)

**Alicia acaba de limpiarlos.**

1. ¿Las camisas? (Ana / doblar)
2. ¿Las camas? (Pedro y Pablo / hacer / ahora mismo)
3. ¿El cuarto? (Alejandro y yo / limpiar / juntos)
4. ¿La sala? (Elena / adornar)
5. ¿Los abrigos? (yo / colgar)
6. ¿Las ventanas? (Ángel / limpiar / hace media hora)

*Alicia acaba de limpiar los platos.*

## 19 La fiesta de despedida

You and a friend are organizing the farewell party for the Spanish exchange students who spent the last week with families in your community. Take turns asking and answering questions to find out what everyone has just done to help out.

**MODELO** Uds. / limpiar la cocina

**A:** ¿Qué acaban de hacer Uds.?

**B:** Acabamos de limpiar la cocina.

1. Ana / poner la mesa
2. Andrés y Rosa / adornar las paredes
3. tú / limpiar las ventanas
4. Jaime y Cristina / preparar la comida
5. Mercedes / llegar con la comida
6. yo / leer la lista de quehaceres

## Comunidades

### Estudiante de intercambio

It is becoming more and more popular for language students to spend time overseas as exchange students. After you have studied Spanish for a couple of years, it would be a great opportunity for you to become an exchange student in Spain or in another Spanish-speaking country. Living within the culture in a different country, practicing the language you have learned with native speakers, developing lifelong friendships, and gathering firsthand experience will be very rewarding and exciting. Participating in a study abroad program is a great way to connect with people in Spanish-speaking communities.

## ¡Comunicación!

### 20 ¿Qué haces? — Interpersonal Communication

Imagine it is Saturday and you are texting a friend to discuss some things each of you did just recently and what you are going to do later in the day. You may want to include something interesting that someone in your family or a friend did recently, too.

*Acabo de doblar la ropa.*

¿Qué haces?

Bueno, yo acabo de doblar la ropa. ¿Y tú?

Pues, yo acabo de limpiar la cocina. Mis padres dicen que puedo salir. ¿Quieres hacer algo?

# *Cultura*

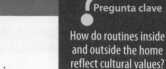
**?** Pregunta clave

How do routines inside and outside the home reflect cultural values?

Cafés en la Plaza Mayor de Madrid

## La vida diaria en España 🎧

En España los horarios de la gente que trabaja reflejan una vida tranquila y social. Después del desayuno a las 7:00, hay una pausa a media mañana para comer algo ligero[1]. "La comida" (o almuerzo) es entre las 14:00 y las 16:00 horas. De primer plato hay ensalada, sopa o verduras. Después viene un plato principal con carne o pescado y, para terminar, postre y café… y mucha conversación. Muchas personas llevan su "comida" al trabajo o van a un restaurante. ¡La vida moderna no deja tiempo para siestas! Muchos españoles trabajan hasta las 19:00 o 20:00 horas, con otra pausa para la merienda[2] sobre las 17:00 o 18:00 horas. Después del trabajo, muchas personas salen a comer una tapa[3] con sus compañeros y vuelven a su casa a estar con la familia. La cena es ligera y se sirve a las 21:00 o 22:00 horas.

La vida española refleja la solidaridad familiar. No es raro encontrar tres generaciones viviendo juntas. Los viejos son atendidos[4] por sus parientes, y muchos hijos viven con sus padres hasta terminar la universidad o hasta casarse[5]. La familia extensa siempre está cerca para acompañar y ayudar. Un cambio moderno es que las mujeres trabajan fuera de la casa y el esposo y los hijos ayudan más con los quehaceres.

A los españoles les encanta la vida social al aire libre[6]. Por la tarde y los fines de semana, las calles (como Las Ramblas en Barcelona) y las plazas (como la Plaza Mayor en Madrid) se llenan[7] de familias que dan un paseo o amigos que disfrutan en la terraza de un café. Los cafés y los restaurantes cierran tarde.

Dando un paseo por Las Ramblas, Barcelona

[1] light  [2] afternoon snack  [3] small snack  [4] cared for  [5] they marry  [6] outdoors  [7] fill up

🔍 **Búsqueda:** spanish lifestyle, la siesta en españa

### *Perspectivas*

According to a survey on how Spaniards spend their time, household chores in Spain are currently more equally shared between men and women. However, women still spend up to two more hours each day on chores than men. What do these statistics reveal about cultural attitudes in Spain?

¿Quién trabaja más en la casa?

### 21 Comprensión — Interpretive Communication

1. ¿Cuáles son las horas para las diferentes comidas en España?

2. ¿Por qué ahora hay más padres e hijos españoles ayudando con los quehaceres?

3. ¿Adónde van muchos españoles con sus amigos por la tarde?

4. ¿Qué miembro de la familia española generalmente hace más quehaceres?

### 22 Analiza

1. The text says, "Modern life doesn't allow for siestas." What do you think this means?

2. Why do you think Spanish children live with their parents for so long?

# ¿Cómo viven los chicos españoles?

En España los jóvenes dividen su tiempo entre la casa, el colegio y la vida social, probablemente igual que tú. En casa, colaboran con los quehaceres como hacer recados[1], comprar pan, recoger la mesa o sacar la basura. En el colegio generalmente hay clases por la mañana y por la tarde, con dos horas para almorzar en casa o en el colegio. Las clases terminan más o menos a las cinco de la tarde.

*Vida social en una calle de Salamanca*

Para los chicos, es importante aprender, pero también divertirse. Por la tarde hacen actividades extraescolares, quizás en el colegio o en un centro privado o municipal. Estudian inglés o música, o practican deportes. Muchas ciudades tienen piscinas o campos de fútbol para el público. Otras tienen un

centro polideportivo con deportes como balonmano[2], básquetbol y tenis. ¡Y cómo no!, los chicos también pasan tiempo en las redes sociales[3]. Por la noche entre semana los jóvenes están en casa, cenando con la familia y haciendo la tarea.

El fin de semana, ¡es para la vida social! A los chicos les gusta salir con sus amigos en un ambiente[4] informal. A diferencia de los jóvenes estadounidenses, los chicos españoles no se reúnen en las casas de sus amigos. Pasan tiempo en los parques, practican deportes o dan un paseo por la ciudad. Más tarde, salen a tomar algo en la terraza de un café. Luego, la diversión continúa con baile, una película o un concierto.

*Una competencia en el polideportivo de Oviedo*

[1]do errands  [2]handball  [3]social media  [4]atmosphere

**Búsqueda:** actividades para jóvenes en madrid

## Prácticas

Los sábados por la noche, los chicos españoles se divierten bailando en clubes para gente joven (discotecas light).  Estos clubes admiten solo a jóvenes de 14 a 18 años de edad. No sirven alcohol, pero sí ofrecen música, baile y fiestas. Abren de 6:00 de la tarde a 11:00 de la noche y son muy populares porque ofrecen la oportunidad de bailar y divertirse en un ambiente sano (*healthy environment*) y seguro.

### 23 Comprensión — Interpretive Communication

1. ¿Cuáles son algunos quehaceres de los jóvenes españoles?
2. ¿Qué es un **polideportivo**?
3. ¿En qué son similares la vida social de un joven español y la de un adulto español?

### 24 Analiza

1. Compare and contrast your daily life with that of a Spanish teen.
2. Why do you think Spanish teens don't gather in each other's homes?
3. What can you infer about Spanish values from the readings on these two pages?

# Vocabulario 2

## Mucho por hacer 🎧

Esta noche es la fiesta de cumpleaños de la abuela y todos tenemos que ayudar.

barrer el piso

la aspiradora

pasar la aspiradora

recoger la mesa

la olla

lavar las ollas

dar de comer al perro

sacar la basura

la leche

traer la leche a casa

## Para conversar 🎧

*T*o talk about party preparations:

Elisa… ¡Elisa! ¿No me **oyes**? ¿**Arreglaste** la sala para la fiesta de tu abuela?
*Elisa… Elisa! Can't you hear me? Did you straighten up the living room for Grandma's party?*

Sí, mamá. Y también adorné las paredes.
*Yes, Mom. And I also decorated the walls.*

¡Qué **lista** eres!
*How smart you are!*

### Para decir más

| | |
|---|---|
| hacer las tapas | *to make snacks* |
| hacer los preparativos | *to do the preparations* |
| sacudir | *to dust* |
| trapear | *to mop* |

### 25  Los quehaceres 🎧

Selecciona la foto de la persona que corresponda con lo que oyes.

**A**

**B**

**C**

**D**

### 26  ¿Qué debes hacer?

Di qué quehaceres debes hacer, según las fotos.

**MODELO**  Debo barrer la sala.

**A**

**B**

**C**

**D**

**E**

**F**

# Diálogo

## Hay mucho por hacer

**Sra. Zea:** Ayer trabajasteis mucho, pero hoy hay quehaceres también.

**Víctor:** Pues, yo voy a recoger la mesa y lavar las ollas.

**Sra. Zea:** Entonces, David puede pasar la aspiradora. ¿Quién va a la tienda a buscar leche?

**David:** ¿Qué?

**Sra. Zea:** ¿No me oyes? ¡Qué listo! ¿Puedes ir a buscar leche a la tienda?

**David:** ¿Y por qué yo? ¿Por qué no va Víctor?

**Sra. Zea:** Porque él va a lavar las ollas. ¿Quieres hacer eso?

## 27  ¿Qué recuerdas?

1. ¿Quiénes trabajaron mucho ayer?
2. ¿Qué va a hacer Víctor?
3. ¿Quién pasa la aspiradora?
4. ¿Quién es listo?
5. ¿Qué no quiere hacer David?

## 28  Algo personal

1. ¿Qué quehaceres haces en casa?
2. ¿Eres listo/a?
3. ¿Te gusta ir a la tienda a buscar leche o pan? Explica.
4. ¿Quién saca la basura en tu casa? ¿Quién pasa la aspiradora?

### Un poco más

#### El cambio de *g* → *j*

You have learned to use several verbs that are regular in the present tense except for a minor stem change (*poder, jugar*) or a spelling change. These changes do not affect the verb's present-tense endings. For verbs that end in *-ger* (such as *recoger*) the letter *g* changes to *j* before the letters *o* and *a* to maintain pronunciation:

*Yo recojo la mesa muchas veces.*

## 29  ¿Vais a hacer un quehacer o un deporte?

Las siguientes personas van a hablar de sus actividades de hoy. Di si lo que oyes es **un quehacer** o **un deporte**.

# Gramática

## Present Tense of *oír* and *traer*

The verbs **oír** (to hear, to listen) and **traer** (to bring) have irregularities in the present tense.

| oír | | | |
|---|---|---|---|
| yo | **oigo** | nosotros<br>nosotras | **oímos** |
| tú | **oyes** | vosotros<br>vosotras | **oís** |
| Ud.<br>él<br>ella | **oye** | Uds.<br>ellos<br>ellas | **oyen** |
| | | gerundio: **oyendo** | |

| traer | | | |
|---|---|---|---|
| yo | **traigo** | nosotros<br>nosotras | **traemos** |
| tú | **traes** | vosotros<br>vosotras | **traéis** |
| Ud.<br>él<br>ella | **trae** | Uds.<br>ellos<br>ellas | **traen** |
| | | gerundio: **trayendo** | |

## 30  Oyendo la radio

Completa el siguiente párrafo con las formas correctas del verbo **oír**.

A toda mi familia le gusta oír la radio. Mis hermanas **(1)** un programa de ciencias todas las noches. Son muy listas. Mi mamá **(2)** un programa de música clásica por la tarde. Mi papá **(3)** partidos de fútbol, cuando no puede verlos en la televisión. Si mi hermano y mi padre están trabajando en el garaje, **(4)** música popular y cantan. Mamá y yo siempre **(5)** el pronóstico del tiempo para saber si va a llover. Yo **(6)** la radio cuando escribo correos electrónicos y también siempre estoy **(7)** música cuando hago la tarea. Y tú, ¿cuándo **(8)** la radio?

*A mis hermanos les gusta oír música.*

Todos los años la familia de Martín y los vecinos (*neighbors*) hacen una fiesta juntos. Para la fiesta, cada persona tiene que traer algo diferente. Trabajando en parejas, alterna con tu compañero/a para preguntar y responder qué trae cada persona.

MODELO    A:  ¿Qué traen tus padres?

                B:  Mis padres traen la ensalada.

**1.** Tomás

**2.** Manolo

**3.** Blanca y Paloma

**4.** Pedro

**5.** mi hermano y yo

**6.** Graciela y Patricia

# ¡Comunicación!

## 32 Quehaceres en tu casa 👥  Interpersonal Communication

Working in pairs, talk about how your families or friends balance fun and work on the weekends. Include favorite pastimes and the types of chores that people like and don't like to do. Each of you can prepare in advance a list of chores and pastimes to help you get started.

| Pasatiempos | Quehaceres |
|---|---|
| hacer una fiesta | arreglar el cuarto |
| ver la televisión | lavar las ollas |
| oír la radio | |

MODELO    A:  En mi familia nos gusta limpiar la casa los sábados y, luego, a veces hacemos una fiesta. Vienen amigos y familia. Mis amigos siempre traen mucha comida y música para bailar.

                B:  Yo siempre oigo la radio cuando arreglo mi cuarto. A veces tengo que lavar las ollas pero no me gusta. Por la tarde, veo fútbol en la televisión.

# Gramática

## Talking About the Past: Preterite Tense of -ar Verbs

To talk about activities that were completed in the past, use the preterite tense (*el pretérito*). To conjugate verbs in the preterite tense, follow a similar pattern to conjugating verbs in the present tense: remove the ending from the infinitive and add new endings according to the subject. Here are the endings for regular **-ar** verbs in the preterite.

| lavar | | | | | |
|---|---|---|---|---|---|
| yo | lav**é** | *I washed* | nosotros nosotras | lav**amos** | *we washed* |
| tú | lav**aste** | *you washed* | vosotros vosotras | lav**asteis** | *you washed* |
| Ud. él ella | lav**ó** | *you washed* *he washed* *she washed* | Uds. ellos ellas | lav**aron** | *you washed* *they washed* *they washed* |

**Note:** Regular verbs that end in -**car** (*buscar, explicar, sacar, tocar*), -**gar** (*apagar, arreglar, colgar, jugar, llegar*), and -**zar** (*empezar*) require a spelling change in the *yo* form of the preterite in order to maintain the original sound of the infinitive.

| bus**car** | c → **qu** | yo bus**qué** |
|---|---|---|
| apa**gar** | g → **gu** | yo apa**gué** |
| empe**zar** | z → **c** | yo empe**cé** |

*Le **expliqué** a María cómo lavar los platos.*    **I explained** to Mary how to wash the dishes.

**Llegué** *tarde al colegio ayer.*    **I arrived** late to school yesterday.

**Empecé** *a cocinar a las diez de la mañana.*    **I started** cooking at ten in the morning.

### 33 ¿Qué pasó ayer?

Completa las siguientes oraciones con la forma correcta del pretérito de los verbos entre paréntesis para decir lo que pasó ayer en la casa de Elena.

1. Todos sus amigos (*llegar*) temprano para ayudar.
2. Su máma (*cocinar*) desde las diez.
3. Uds. (*trabajar*) todo el día ayudándola.
4. Yo la (*ayudar*) mucho también.
5. Elena (*pasar*) la aspiradora por la sala.
6. Paco (*limpiar*) el piso del comedor.
7. Tú (*sacar*) la basura antes de comer.
8. Todos (*hablar*) bien de la comida.
9. Después de comer, Daniel (*lavar*) los platos.
10. Luego, nosotros (*bailar*) en la sala.

*Empecé a cocinar a las diez.*

## 34 A comer

Completa el siguiente párrafo con la forma apropiada del pretérito de los verbos entre paréntesis.

Yo (**1.** *cocinar*) una paella ayer en mi casa para toda la familia. Mi hermana me (**2.** *ayudar*). Yo (**3.** *empezar*) a preparar todo por la mañana. Primero yo (**4.** *buscar*) los ingredientes y le (**5.** *explicar*) a mi hermana cómo preparar la paella. Luego (**6.** *lavar*) la olla y (**7.** *sacar*) los cubiertos y los platos. Después (**8.** *preparar*) unos postres. Al terminar de cocinar, (**9.** *apagar*) la estufa y (**10.** *arreglar*) los platos en la mesa. Entonces, (**11.** *llamar*) a todos a comer.

> **¡Ojo!**
>
> Remember to look for spelling changes in the *yo* form of *-car, -gar,* and *-zar* verbs.

## 35 ¿Qué hiciste?

In pairs, take turns asking whether your classmate has completed the indicated chores. Your partner should say that he or she did not do each task because someone else already did it.

*No compré el pan.*

**MODELO** comprar el pan / Roberto

A: **¿Compraste el pan?**

B: **No, yo no compré el pan porque Roberto ya lo compró.**

1. buscar los platos / Ernesto
2. apagar la estufa / Miguel
3. sacar la basura / Pedro
4. colgar los abrigos / Alfonso y Ana
5. preparar la comida / Jorge y Luisa
6. lavar la olla grande / Isabel

## ¡Comunicación!

## 36 Los quehaceres    Interpersonal Communication

Working in pairs, talk about some of the chores that needed to be done around the house recently and whether or not either of you did any of them. Use ideas from the word bank and add other activities you know how to say.

| | | |
|---|---|---|
| preparar la comida | sacar la basura | lavar las ollas |
| pasar la aspiradora | comprar la leche | comprar el pan |
| colgar la ropa en tu cuarto | arreglar el cuarto | doblar la ropa |

**MODELO**

A: **¿Doblaste la ropa?**

B: **Sí, (No, no) la doblé. Tengo que doblarla ahora. ¿Y tú? ¿Sacaste la basura?**

A: **Sí, acabo de sacarla.**

# Todo en contexto

? Pregunta clave

How do routines inside and outside the home reflect cultural values?

## ¡Comunicación!

### 37 Jóvenes y adultos españoles | Presentational Communication

Create a Venn diagram comparing the daily routines of a typical adult and a typical teenager in Spain. Show the adult's daily activities and times on the left and those for the teenager on the right. Remember to include any activities they have in common in the area where the circles intersect.

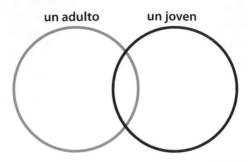

un adulto    un joven

## ¡Comunicación!

### 38 ¿Qué haces todo el día? | Interpersonal Communication

With a classmate, pretend that one of you lives in the United States and the other in Spain. Compare your weekday routines, including what you do in the home and outside the home, with whom, and when you do it.

**MODELO**
A: Yo almuerzo al mediodía en la cafetería del colegio.
B: Yo no. Yo almuerzo en casa a las dos de la tarde.

## ¡Comunicación!

### 39 ¿Quién va a hacer los quehaceres? | Interpersonal/Presentational Communication

In groups of three, pretend that you are a family in Spain. One of you is the parent and the other two are the children. Prepare a conversation about household chores. The parent assigns the chores, and the children decide which ones they can't or shouldn't do and why. To prepare, review the lesson vocabulary, grammar, and culture, as well as other words that will help you come up with some creative reasons. The parent has the final decision on who does what and when.

**MODELO**
A: Natalia, hoy debes doblar la ropa.
B: ¿Yo? ¡Pero acabo de llegar y tengo muchas tareas por hacer! ¿Por qué no la dobla Riqui?
C: ¿Yo? Yo la doblé ayer y también arreglé toda la sala. Y ahora no puedo porque voy a tomar algo en la plaza con mis amigos.

# Lectura informativa

## Antes de leer 🎧

1. ¿Qué actividades haces en un día? ¿Cuánto tiempo dedicas a cada actividad?

2. ¿Qué quehaceres haces?

3. ¿Cuánto tiempo estudias en un día de semana?

### Estrategia

**Compare and contrast related readings**

Often, you will read two texts that touch on similar subjects. There may be differences in their approach or in the aspects they choose to stress, but there are also similarities. Exploring similarities between two texts on the same or similar topics helps you to understand them both.

The following text, for example, continues the theme of daily activities in Spain. As you read, look for ideas or facts that you recognize from the *Cultura* readings. Notice also what new information is provided to increase your understanding.

## ¿Quién hace qué? 🎧

En España, el Instituto Nacional de Estadística (INE) hace una encuesta[1] sobre las actividades de la gente. Mira los resultados en la página 371 y analiza cuánto tiempo dedican las personas a hacer diferentes cosas en un día. La encuesta de 2009–2010 muestra unas tendencias interesantes, especialmente entre la gente joven.

*Mucha gente usa tabletas.*

Un dato interesante es que mientras la participación de las mujeres[2] en el mercado laboral sube cada día, la desigualdad entre los sexos todavía existe en las tareas domésticas. Las mujeres dedican en promedio[3] 1 hora y 57 minutos diarios más a las actividades de hogar[4] y familia que los hombres. Sin embargo, esta diferencia ha disminuido 41 minutos en los últimos siete años. La distribución de las responsabilidades familiares del hogar incluye la cocina, mantenimiento del hogar, cuidado de la ropa, jardinería, cuidado de animales, construcción y reparaciones, compras y servicios, cuidado de niños y ayuda a adultos miembros del hogar.

Los menores de 25 años se caracterizan por el tiempo dedicado al estudio (tres horas y 13 minutos) y el poco tiempo que destinan a las tareas domésticas (poco más de una hora). En cambio, el tiempo que dedican a la informática[5] (juegos de computadora, motores de búsqueda, aplicaciones de redes sociales) aumenta: casi una hora y media, o el doble que hace siete años. Si incluimos a los adultos, la cantidad de personas que en España dedican tiempo a los pasatiempos y la informática ha aumentado más de 10 % con respecto a 2003 (30 % versus 17,9 %).

[1] survey   [2] women   [3] on average   [4] household chores   [5] computers

*Hay que limpiar la casa.*

🔍 **Búsqueda:** INE spain, la vida diaria en españa

## • Tiempo diario dedicado a cada actividad, 2009–2010 (horas y minutos)

|  | Hombres | Mujeres |
|---|---|---|
| **Hogar y familia** | 2:32 | 4:29 |
| - Cocinar y recoger | 0:55 | 1:44 |
| - Mantenimiento del hogar | 0:53 | 1:17 |
| - Cuidado de la ropa | 0:35 | 1:08 |
| - Jardinería y cuidado de animales | 1:54 | 1:08 |
| - Cuidado de niños | 1:46 | 2:22 |
| - Ayuda a adultos miembros del hogar | 1:41 | 1:40 |
| **Trabajo voluntario** | 2:10 | 1:51 |
| - Trabajo voluntario al servicio de una organización | 2:34 | 2:40 |
| - Ayudas informales a otros hogares | 2:13 | 2:03 |
| **Vida social y diversión** | 1:54 | 1.43 |
| - Deportes y actividades al aire libre | 2:03 | 1:40 |
| - Pasatiempos e informática | 2:05 | 1:38 |
| - Medios de comunicación (TV, etc.) | 3:06 | 2:49 |

**Fuente:** Encuesta de Empleo del Tiempo 2009–2010. INE

## 40 Comprensión 🎧 Interpretive Communication

1. ¿Qué analiza la encuesta del INE?
2. ¿Cuáles son algunas actividades incluidas en la encuesta?
3. ¿A qué actividades dedican más tiempo los jóvenes que los adultos?

## 41 Analiza

1. Why do you think women work outside the home more than before but also do more housework than men?
2. What trends might the next survey show for teen use of time on computers and on housework? Explain.

# ✎ Escritura

## 42 Los quehaceres en mi casa — Presentational Communication

Write a paragraph about the types of chores you and your family (real or fictional) commonly do at home. Explain when you do each chore and what you think of it. Describe who else does chores at home, what each person does, and his/her opinion of it. Before you start to write, review the lesson vocabulary and grammar, and take notes using a table like the one below.

| Los quehaceres | Quién los hace y cuándo | Opinión |
|---|---|---|
|  |  |  |
|  |  |  |

# Repaso de la Lección A

## A  Escuchar: ¿Lógico o ilógico? 🎧 (pp. 350–351, 362–363)

Di si lo que oyes es **lógico** o **ilógico**. Si es ilógico, explica por qué.

## B  Vocabulario: La palabra lógica (pp. 350–351, 362–363)

Completa las oraciones con una palabra lógica del vocabulario.

1. Hay diez __ en la cocina. ¡Es mucha gente!
2. Todos los días tengo que __ mi cama.
3. Cuando tengo frío llevo un __.
4. Pablo, ¿puedes __ los platos de la mesa?
5. Ana y yo __ el piso todos los días.
6. No puedo salir ahora. __ esta tarde.

## C  Gramática: ¿Qué van a hacer? (p. 355)

Completa las oraciones con **me**, **te**, **le**, **nos** o **les** para decir qué van a hacer.

MODELO   Yo __ voy a preparar la comida. (*a Uds.*)
Yo **les** voy a preparar la comida.

1. Ellos __ van a lavar la ropa. (*a nosotros*)
2. Teresa __ va a doblar la ropa. (*a su mamá*)
3. Elisa __ va a colgar la ropa. (*a ellos*)
4. Teresa y Elisa __ van a hacer la cama. (*a ti*)
5. Gustavo __ va a limpiar la sala. (*a mí*)
6. Jorge __ va a barrer el cuarto. (*a Teresa*)

## D  Gramática: Una fiesta en casa (p. 365)

Completa el siguiente párrafo con las formas correctas de los verbos **oír** y **traer**.

A mi familia le gustan las fiestas familiares. Mis tías (**1.** *traer*) la paella, yo (**2.** *traer*) la ensalada y mi mamá (**3.** *traer*) el postre. Mis primos y yo también (**4.** *traer*) la música. A toda mi familia le gusta bailar. Mis primos (**5.** *oír*) música rock, pero también (**6.** *traer*) música popular para poder bailar. Yo (**7.** *oír*) mucho la radio. Si la gente no (**8.** *traer*) buena música, nosotros (**9.** *oír*) la radio durante la fiesta.

## E  Gramática: Lo acabo de hacer (pp. 354, 358, 367 )

Crea diálogos con la forma correcta del pretérito de los verbos y **acabar de** más el complemento directo apropiado. Sigue el modelo.

MODELO   tú / cocinar el pollo
A:  ¿Cocinaste el pollo?
B:  Sí, acabo de cocinarlo.

1. Ud. / doblar la ropa
2. Sara y tú / lavar las ollas
3. yo / apagar las luces
4. José / colgar su abrigo
5. Elisa y Mariela / empezar la comida
6. tú / sacar la basura

What is daily life in Spain like? Include information from the culture readings "*La vida diaria en España*" and "*¿Cómo viven los chicos españoles?*" to complete a chart like the one below.

| horarios de trabajo / horas de colegio | ⟹ | |
| vida en familia | ⟹ | |
| vida social | ⟹ | |

## Vocabulario

### En casa

el abrigo
la aspiradora
la basura
la cama
dar de comer (al perro)
la gente
hacer la cama
el jardín
la leche
la olla
pasar la aspiradora
la persona
el quehacer
recoger la mesa
sacar la basura
el trabajo

### Verbos

| | |
|---|---|
| acabar | limpiar |
| adornar | llegar |
| arreglar | oír |
| barrer | preparar |
| cocinar | recoger |
| colgar (ue) | sacar |
| dejar | subir |
| doblar | trabajar |
| lavar | traer |

### Expresiones y otras palabras

acabar de (+ *infinitive*)
algo
juntos/as
listo/a
quizás
solo

## Gramática

### Indirect object pronouns

Indirect object pronouns indicate **to whom** or **for whom**.

| singular | | plural | |
|---|---|---|---|
| **me** | *to me, for me* | **nos** | *to us, for us* |
| **te** | *to you, for you* | **os** | *to you, for you* |
| **le** | *to you, for you to him, for him to her, for her* | **les** | *to you, for you to them, for them* |

### Saying what just happened with *acabar de*

| *acabar de* + infinitive | |
|---|---|
| *Acabo de llegar.* | I have just arrived. |

### Irregular verbs: Present tense of *oír* and *traer*

| oír | | traer | |
|---|---|---|---|
| oigo | oímos | traigo | traemos |
| oyes | oís | traes | traéis |
| oye | oyen | trae | traen |
| gerundio: **oyendo** | | gerundio: **trayendo** | |

### Preterite tense of regular *-ar* verbs

| cocinar | |
|---|---|
| cocin**é** | cocin**amos** |
| cocin**aste** | cocin**asteis** |
| cocin**ó** | cocin**aron** |

# Gramática

## Making Comparisons

- You can use the following patterns when making comparisons in Spanish:

> **más/menos + noun/adjective/adverb + que**

Hay **más/menos sal que** ajo.      There is **more/less salt than** garlic.

> **tanto/a/os/as + noun + como**

Hay **tanto pollo como** arroz en esa paella.      There is **as much chicken as** rice in that paella.

> **tan + adjective/adverb + como**

Estos tomates no están **tan maduros como** esos tomates.      These tomatoes are not **as ripe as** those tomatoes.

> **tanto como**

Sebastián cocina **tanto como** Esteban.      Sebastián cooks **as much as** Esteban.

> **más que/menos que**

Luis cocina **más que** Sara.      Luis cooks **more than** Sara.

- You can also make comparisons by singling out a person, group, object or attribute as the best, most, or least by using the following patterns:

> **definite article (+ noun) + más/menos + adjective**

El pescado es **el ingrediente más importante**.      Fish is **the most important ingredient**.

> **lo + más/menos + adverb + posible**

Debes prepararlo **lo más pronto posible**.      You should prepare it **as early as possible**.

- Use **más de** or **menos de** and a number for stating there are "more than" or "fewer than" the number of items or people indicated.

Necesito **más de/menos de** cuatro pimientos.      I need **more than/fewer than** four peppers.

The following adjectives and adverbs have irregular comparative forms:

| mejor | *better* |
|-------|----------|
| peor | *worse* |
| mayor | *older* |
| menor | *younger* |

*Esos pimientos son **buenos**, pero aquellos pimientos son **mejores** y estos pimientos son **los mejores de todos**.*

Those peppers are **good**, but those peppers over there are **better** and these peppers are **the best of all**.

**Note:** When referring to quantity, the comparative forms of *pequeño* and *grande* are **menor** (lesser, smaller, fewer) and **mayor** (greater, larger).

*Hay un **menor** (**mayor**) número de tomates en lata que de tomates frescos.*

There is a **smaller** (**greater**) number of canned tomatoes than fresh tomatoes.

## 7 Haciendo compras

Estás haciendo compras en el mercado. Completa estas comparaciones **con más/menos... que**.

**MODELO**   Estos pimientos son **más grandes** que esos pimientos. (+ grande)
Estos pimientos son **menos grandes** que esos pimientos. (– grande)
Estas lechugas son **menos frescas** que esas lechugas. (– fresco)
Estas lechugas son **más frescas** que esas lechugas. (+ fresco)

1. Este pescado está __ que ese pescado. (– fresco)
2. Este pollo es __ que el otro. (+ pequeño)
3. Ese aguacate está __ que este aguacate. (– maduro)
4. Estos ajos son __ que esos ajos. (+ pequeño)
5. Aquellos tomates están __ que esos tomates. (+ maduro)
6. Esta receta es __ que esa receta. (– difícil)
7. Aquellas cebollas son __ que estas cebollas. (+ grande)
8. Este mercado está __ que ese supermercado. (+ cerca)
9. Esa ensalada tiene __ que la otra. (– sal)
10. Los guisantes de esta paella son __ que los de la otra. (– fresco)

*¡Estos tomates son los mejores de todos!*

Use the information provided to make as many comparisons as you can.

> **MODELO**
> Ana puede ir de compras al supermercado en una hora pero yo necesito dos horas para ir de compras al supermercado.
>
> **Comparación 1:** No puedo ir de compras al supermercado tan rápidamente como Ana.
>
> **Comparación 2:** Ana puede ir de compras al supermercado más rápidamente que yo.
>
> **Comparación 3:** Yo puedo ir de compras al supermercado menos rápidamente que Ana.

1. Javier tiene dos kilos de arroz y Clara tiene dos kilos de arroz.
2. Las lechugas del supermercado Día son pequeñas pero las lechugas del supermercado Hypercor son grandes.
3. Alberto va al supermercado tres veces al mes y Ana va al supermercado tres veces al mes.
4. Hay mucho pescado en una paella valenciana pero no hay muchos guisantes.
5. Teresa y Armando compran dos latas de tomates y dos latas de guisantes.
6. Belén tiene cincuenta recetas y Alfonso tiene solo cinco recetas.

## 9 ¿Qué necesitas?

You are preparing a *paella valenciana* using the ingredients below. Complete these sentences saying what you will need, and compare whether you will need more, less, or the same amount of each of the listed ingredients.

| **Para decir más** | |
|---|---|
| la almeja | *clam* |
| el azafrán | *saffron* |
| la gamba | *prawn* |
| el langostino | *shrimp* |
| el mejillón | *mussel* |

> **MODELO**
> Necesito **tantos** tomates **como** zanahorias.

1. Necesito __ mejillones __ gambas.
2. Necesito __ latas de almejas __ latas de pimientos rojos.
3. Necesito __ tazas de guisantes __ tazas de arroz.
4. Necesito __ pimiento verde __ cebolla.
5. Necesito __ gambas __ langostinos.
6. Necesito __ agua __ aceite de oliva.

**La Paella**

*(ingredientes para seis personas)*

1 pollo en pedazos
1/2 kg de gambas
1/2 kg de langostinos
1/4 kg de mejillones
1 lata de almejas (200 gramos)
2 tazas de arroz
1 cebolla, troceada
2 dientes de ajo, troceados
2 zanahorias, limpias y cortadas
2 tomates grandes
1 pimiento verde, troceado
1 lata de pimientos rojos, troceados
1 taza de guisantes

5 hilos de azafrán
4 tazas de agua
5 cucharadas de aceite de oliva
sal y pimienta

## 10  ¡Deben hacer lo siguiente!

If you were the owner of a restaurant, what instructions might you give your employees during the week?

**MODELO**  abrir el restaurante / temprano
**Debes abrir el restaurante lo más temprano posible.**

1. preparar las recetas / bien
2. hacer las comidas / pronto
3. recoger las mesas / rápidamente
4. barrer el suelo / bien

5. limpiar la cocina / bien
6. sacar la basura / pronto
7. cerrar el restaurante / tarde

## 11  El mejor supermercado

Compara lo que ves en las ilustraciones de estos dos supermercados, según las pistas.

**MODELO**  cebollas / ser grandes
**Las cebollas del supermercado Supermax son más grandes que las cebollas del supermercado Ciudad.**

1. los guisantes / costar más
2. los tomates / costar más
3. el señor / ser menor
4. la señora / ser mayor
5. las lechugas / ser pequeñas
6. los aguacates / ser grandes
7. los ajos / costar menos
8. los pimientos / ser peores
9. las lechugas / costar más
10. los tomates / ser mejores
11. las cebollas / costar menos
12. una comparación original

## ¡Al mercado!

Me gusta mucho ir al **mercado** en Las Ramblas. Los productos son muy frescos y **las frutas** son las mejores de la ciudad.

los plátanos

las fresas

las uvas

las manzanas

el maíz

las papas

las habichuelas

las zanahorias

el vinagre

el café

el chocolate

los huevos

el helado

el queso

el jamón

la carne

el chorizo

el kilo

¿Cuánto cuesta el kilo de jamón?

Está a solo 14 euros el kilo.

## Para conversar

*T*o buy products at a market:

¿A qué **precio** está el kilo de uvas?
*How much is (What's the price for) a kilo of grapes?*

Está a solo cuatro euros el kilo.
*It's only four euros a kilo.*

### En otros países

| | |
|---|---|
| las fresas | las frutillas (*América del Sur*) |
| las habichuelas | las judías verdes (*España*) |
| | las chauchas (*Argentina*) |
| | los ejotes (*México*) |
| el maíz | el choclo (*Latinoamérica*) |
| las papas | las patatas (*España*) |
| los plátanos | las bananas (*Argentina, Ecuador*) |
| | los guineos (*Puerto Rico, República Dominicana*) |

## ¡Comunicación!

### 22 ¡Vamos de compras!   Interpersonal/Presentational Communication

Imagine you and your friend want to prepare a meal together, but one of you knows nothing about recipes and ingredients. Before going to the market, you have to make a list of the things you need to buy. Choose the meal you want to prepare and act out a dialogue in which you discuss the shopping list. Use the vocabulary from this and the previous lesson, and follow the model.

MODELO
A: Vamos a preparar una paella. ¿Necesitamos comprar carne?

B: No. Necesitamos comprar pollo y pescado.

A: ¿Y qué verduras necesitamos? ¿Maíz?

B: No. Necesitamos pimientos, tomates, ajo, cebollas y zanahorias.

## 23 En el mercado

Selecciona la foto que corresponde con lo que oyes.

**A**

**B**

**C**

**D**

**E**

**F**

## 24 Fuera de lugar

Say which food item does not belong in each of the following groups.

1. maíz / habichuela / zanahoria / chocolate
2. queso / mantequilla / jamón / leche
3. huevo / manzana / fresa / naranja
4. café / cebolla / pimiento / zanahoria
5. carne / pescado / pollo / papa
6. fresa / maíz / uva / plátano

## ¡Comunicación!

## 25 La mejor dieta 👥 Presentational Communication

Trabajando en parejas, escriban una dieta equilibrada (*balanced*) con todas las comidas básicas para los siete días de la semana. La dieta debe incluir el desayuno (*breakfast*), el almuerzo y la cena (*dinner*).

# Diálogo

## Comprando chorizo

**Inés:** Ayer estuve con Víctor en el supermercado.

**Eva:** ¿Y qué compraste?

**Inés:** Compramos los ingredientes para hacer paella.

**Eva:** Entonces, ¿qué venimos a hacer al mercado?

**Inés:** Quiero comprar chorizo. El chorizo del supermercado no me gusta.

**Eva:** Bueno, este mercado es el mejor mercado de la ciudad.

**Inés:** Señora, ¿a qué precio tiene el kilo de chorizo?

**Señora:** El chorizo está a 4,00 € el kilo.

**Inés:** De acuerdo, llevo un kilo por favor.

## 26 ¿Qué recuerdas?

1. ¿Qué compró Inés ayer en el supermercado?
2. ¿Qué quiere comprar Inés en el mercado?
3. ¿Es bueno el mercado donde están las chicas?
4. ¿A qué precio está el kilo de chorizo?
5. ¿Compra Inés el chorizo?

## 27 Algo personal

1. ¿Hay un mercado en tu ciudad? ¿Dónde está?
2. ¿Prefieres ir al mercado o al supermercado? Explica.
3. ¿Cuál es el mercado o supermercado más grande de tu ciudad?

## Un poco más

### El euro

The symbol for the euro is €, which became the common currency of most European Union (EU) countries in 2002. Spain became a member of the EU in 1986, and it uses the euro as its currency.

## 28 ¿Qué comprendiste?

Escucha lo que dicen las personas del diálogo *"Comprando chorizo"* y di si lo que oyes es **cierto** o **falso**. Corrige lo que no es cierto.

# Gramática

*Repaso rápido*

## Preterite Tense of Regular -*ar* Verbs

Do you remember how to form the preterite tense of a regular -*ar* verb? Remove the last two letters from the infinitive and add the indicated endings.

| hablar | | | |
|---|---|---|---|
| yo | hablé | nosotros nosotras | hablamos |
| tú | hablaste | vosotros vosotras | hablasteis |
| Ud. él ella | habló | Uds. ellos ellas | hablaron |

**Note:** Remember that regular verbs that end in -*car* (*buscar, explicar, sacar, tocar*), -*gar* (*apagar, colgar, jugar, llegar*) and -*zar* (*empezar*) require a spelling change in the *yo* form of the preterite.

c → qu

g → gu

z → c

---

### 29 El diario de Marta

Marta siempre escribe en su diario por la noche. Haz oraciones completas con las pistas que se dan para saber lo que escribe esta noche.

1. nosotros / comprar zanahorias
2. mi madre / buscar el pollo
3. yo / buscar mi receta favorita
4. mi padre / trabajar todo el día

---

## Preterite Tense of *dar* and *estar*

The verbs *dar* (to give) and *estar* (to be) are irregular in the preterite tense.

| dar | | | |
|---|---|---|---|
| yo | di | nosotros nosotras | dimos |
| tú | diste | vosotros vosotras | disteis |
| Ud. él ella | dio | Uds. ellos ellas | dieron |

| estar | | | |
|---|---|---|---|
| yo | estuve | nosotros nosotras | estuvimos |
| tú | estuviste | vosotros vosotras | estuvisteis |
| Ud. él ella | estuvo | Uds. ellos ellas | estuvieron |

---

### 30 Estuvieron en el mercado

Di cuándo las siguientes personas estuvieron en el mercado.

MODELO Enrique / el martes pasado
**Enrique estuvo el martes pasado.**

1. Daniel y Gloria / esta mañana
2. mi tía / el mes pasado
3. los chicos / el fin de semana pasado
4. mis primas / anteayer
5. Ud. / el viernes
6. yo / el sábado pasado
7. Uds. / ayer
8. tú / el jueves

## 31 Ayudamos con la comida

Last week your neighborhood held a food drive. In pairs, take turns reporting what food items people donated. Follow the model.

MODELO  Elena

A: ¿Qué dio Elena?

B: Elena dio unas naranjas.

**1.** yo

**2.** Paco

**3.** tú y yo

**4.** el Sr. y la Sra. Pérez

**5.** mi padre

**6.** los hermanos García

## 32 Mi cumpleaños

Completa el siguiente párrafo con la forma apropiada del pretérito de los verbos entre paréntesis.

El viernes pasado mi hermana mayor (**1.** *dar*) una fiesta para mi cumpleaños. Muchos de mis amigos (**2.** *estar*) allí. Mi amiga Ana no (**3.** *estar*) y mis mejores amigas, Catalina y Fabiana, tampoco (**4.** *estar*), pero me (**5.** *enviar*) correos electrónicos para desearme feliz cumpleaños. Nosotros (**6.** *estar*) muy contentos. Mi hermana me (**7.** *dar*) un libro que me (**8.** *gustar*) mucho y mis padres me (**9.** *dar*) un reproductor de MP3 fabuloso. Luego, mis amigos Juan y Esteban (**10.** *dar*) un concierto muy bueno. Juan (**11.** *cantar*) cuatro canciones y Esteban las (**12.** *tocar*) en el piano. Yo (**13.** *estar*) muy contento porque mis amigos (**14.** *estar*) muy contentos. Todos le (**15.** *dar*) las gracias a mi hermana. ¡Fue una fiesta fantástica!

## ¡Comunicación!

## 33 ¿Dónde estuviste?    Interpersonal Communication

Working in pairs, talk about where you and the people you know were last weekend, adding any details you wish.

MODELO  A: ¿Dónde estuviste el fin de semana pasado?

B: Estuve en la playa con mis amigos. Nadamos mucho. ¿Y tú?

# Todo en contexto

**? Pregunta clave**

How do routines inside and outside the home reflect cultural values?

## ¡Comunicación!

### 34 La comida del domingo   Presentational Communication

Imagina que eres español y vives en Galicia. Le escribes un correo electrónico a un amigo para describir la gran comida que tu abuela preparó el domingo pasado. Elige un aperitivo, un primer plato y un segundo plato. Luego di si tomaron postre y café o no, y si les gustó la comida. Usa los siguientes verbos en pretérito: **dar**, **preparar**, **empezar**, **estar**, **tomar**, **gustar**.

## ¡Comunicación!

### 35 Vamos de compras   Interpersonal Communication

Tú y tu compañero/a están en España en un programa de intercambio estudiantil (*student exchange program*). Su familia anfitriona (*host family*) les da una lista de las comidas que tienen que comprar. Usen la información de la lectura "*¿Dónde compran los alimentos los españoles?*" y la tabla de alimentos y precios del supermercado y el mercado para decidir dónde van a comprar cada cosa.

### Para decir más

| | |
|---|---|
| la carnicería | *butcher shop* |
| la frutería/la verdulería | *greengrocer's* |
| la panadería | *bakery* |
| la pescadería | *fish market* |
| la pollería | *poultry market* |

MODELO

**A:** Yo voy a comprar las hamburguesas.

**B:** ¿Las vas a comprar en el mercado?

**A:** No, voy a ir al supermercado porque cuestan menos.

- zanahorias
- cebollas
- tomates
- pan
- hamburguesas
- pescado

### Supermercado

| cebollas<br>5 €/kilo | hamburguesas<br>pollo<br>1,5 €/unidad | tomates<br>en lata<br>1,5 €/kilo | pan<br>1,30 €/ kilo | pescado<br>en lata<br>5,50 €/kilo | zanahorias<br>en lata<br>0,75 €/kilo |
|---|---|---|---|---|---|

### Mercado

| cebollas<br>5 €/kilo | hamburguesas<br>pollo<br>2,5 €/unidad | tomates<br>frescos<br>2,50 €/kilo | pan<br>1,25 €/ kilo | pescado<br>fresco<br>14 €/kilo | zanahorias<br>frescas<br>1,30 €/kilo |
|---|---|---|---|---|---|

# Lectura AP

## Una moneda de ¡Ay!
### de Juan de Timoneda

#### Sobre el autor

Juan de Timoneda (hacia 1520–1583) fue un escritor español que compiló muchos cuentos populares. El cuento "Una moneda de ¡Ay!" es parte de la colección de cuentos *Sobremesa y alivio de caminantes* (*After Dinner and Relief for Walkers*). Estos cuentos eran muy cómicos y servían para entretener a los caminantes (*walkers, hikers*) después de una buena comida.

## Antes de leer

### 36 Vocabulario

La lectura que vas a leer incluye las siguientes palabras en negrita (*bold*). Usa el contexto de la oración para determinar qué quieren decir. Conecta cada palabra de la columna I con su equivalente en inglés de la columna II.

| I | II |
|---|---|
| 1. Dicen que Pedro es un muchacho **tonto** porque no es muy inteligente. | **A.** makes fun of |
| 2. **Los criados** del señor hacen los quehaceres de la casa. | **B.** nettles |
| | **C.** silly |
| 3. El señor le da a Pedro dos **monedas** para comprar uvas. | **D.** bag |
| | **E.** servants |
| 4. El señor es malo y **se burla** de Pedro. | **F.** coins |
| 5. Cuando Pedro va al mercado pone las uvas en **una bolsa**. | |
| 6. Cuando el señor toca **las ortigas** dice ¡Ay! | |

### Estrategia

**Context clues**

Context refers to the other words and sentences that are around a new word. These act as hints or clues to help you understand the meaning of unknown words. Before reading this selection, skim the story and identify the words that have been glossed. Read them in context (without looking at the footnotes), and guess their meaning. Then verify their definition in the footnotes.

### 37 Los guiones de diálogo

Spanish uses *guiones* (dashes, —) instead of quotation marks to set off a dialogue. If there is no text after a spoken dialogue, no closing dash is needed. Find the lines of dialogue in the story and identify whether they are spoken by *Pedro* or by the *Señor*.

# Una moneda¹ de ¡Ay!
## de *Juan de Timoneda*

Tenía un caballero un criado nuevo, un mozo² llamado Pedro que parecía³ un poco tonto. Para burlarse⁴ de él, le dio dos monedas y le dijo:

—Pedro, vete al mercado y cómprame una moneda de uvas y otra de ¡ay!

El pobre mozo compró las uvas, pero cada vez que pedía una moneda de ¡ay! todos se reían y mofaban⁵ de él.

Al darse cuenta⁶ de la burla de su amo, puso las uvas en el fondo de una bolsa y sobre las uvas un manojo de ortigas⁷.

Cuando regresó a su casa, le dijo su amo:

—¿Lo traes todo?

Contestó el mozo:

—Sí, señor, está todo en la bolsa.

El caballero extrañado⁸ metió rápidamente la mano⁹ y al tocar las ortigas, exclamó:

—¡Ay!

A lo que dijo el mozo:

—Debajo están las uvas, señor.

¹coin   ²lad   ³seemed   ⁴make fun of   ⁵laughed and mocked   ⁶when he realized
⁷handful of nettles   ⁸surprised   ⁹quickly put his hand

---

## 38 Comprensión  🎧  Interpretive Communication

1. ¿Qué tipo de muchacho piensa el señor que es Pedro?
2. ¿Qué debe comprar Pedro en el mercado?
3. ¿Qué hay en la bolsa que Pedro le da al señor?
4. ¿Cómo reacciona el señor cuando mete la mano en la bolsa?

---

## 39 Analiza

1. How does Pedro feel when he realizes that his master is making fun of him? What is his reaction?
2. Irony is when a speaker says one thing but actually means the opposite. Based on what Pedro says at the end, would you say that this story has an ironic ending? Why or why not?
3. Have you read any other stories that employ irony? If so, give an example.

# Repaso de la Lección B

## A  Escuchar: ¿Es lógico o ilógico? 🎧 (pp. 374–375, 386–387)

Escucha las siete oraciones y di si lo que oyes es **lógico** o **ilógico**.

## B  Vocabulario: Preparo una comida (pp. 374–375, 386–387)

Completa las oraciones con las palabras del recuadro según el contexto.

| frescos | ingredientes | paella | mercado | receta | olvidar |
|---------|--------------|--------|---------|--------|---------|

1. No sé cómo preparar una __. Necesito leer la __.
2. Llevo la lista de la compra para no __ nada.
3. Compro los __ en el __ porque son más __.

## C  Gramática: Comparaciones (pp. 378–379)

Haz comparaciones usando **más/menos que**, **más/menos de**, **tan/tanto/a/os/as como**, **mejor** y **mayor**, según el contexto.

1. Yo tengo quince años. Mi hermana tiene diez años. Yo soy __ que mi hermana.
2. Julián compró cuatro manzanas. Eva compró dos manzanas. Eva compró __ manzanas __ Julián.
3. Juan estudia ocho horas. Esteban estudia ocho horas. Juan estudia __ horas __ Esteban.
4. Esta ensalada de aguacates es muy buena. Es la __ ensalada de todas.
5. Para esta receta necesitas __ cuatro pimientos. Necesitas añadir uno más.
6. Las papas cuestan 4 € el kilo y los ajos cuestan 3 € el kilo. Las papas cuestan __ los ajos.

## D  Gramática: El pretérito (p. 390)

Completa las oraciones con la forma correcta del pretérito de los verbos entre paréntesis.

1. Ayer mi hermano y yo (dar) una fiesta fabulosa para nuestros padres.
2. Yo (olvidar) añadir vinagre a la ensalada.
3. A: ¿Dónde (estar) tú ayer? Yo te (buscar) por todos lados.
   B: Yo (estar) en el mercado con mi mamá.
4. Nosotros (estar) tres horas en la cocina preparando pollo con arroz.
5. A: Mamá, tu no me (dar) el dinero para comprar el pescado.
   B: Sí, te lo (dar) ayer. ¿No recuerdas?
6. Ellas me (dar) una receta para hacer paella. Yo la (colgar) en el refrigerador.
7. A: ¿(estar) Uds. en el restaurante anoche?
   B: Sí, nosotros (estar) pero mi hermana no (estar). Ella nunca (llegar).
8. Susi (olvidar) traer la receta al mercado. No (comprar) todos los ingredientes.
9. A: Papi, ¿a qué hora (empezar) a trabajar hoy?
   B: (empezar) muy temprano, a las siete.
10. A: ¿Te (gustar) la paella que (preparar) mi madre?
    B: Sí, pero la (cocinar) con mucha sal.

## E Cultura: Lo que escogen los españoles (pp. 384–385)

Look at the following options and decide which one would be the preferred choice by many Spaniards according to what you read in the *cultura* selections in this lesson. Why do you think many Spanish people make those choices? And what would you choose? How are your choices similar to or different from Spaniards' preferences?

- comer en casa o comer afuera los fines de semana
- comer con amigos o comer con la familia el domingo
- hacer una comida que dura (*lasts*) mucho o poco tiempo
- comprar alimentos en tiendas tradicionales o en el supermercado
- comprar alimentos frescos o procesados
- comprar en una tienda o comprar por internet

## Vocabulario

### En el mercado/el supermercado

| | | |
|---|---|---|
| el aguacate | el helado | el pimiento |
| el ajo | el huevo | el plátano |
| el arroz | el ingrediente | el precio |
| el café | el jamón | el queso |
| la carne | el kilo | la receta |
| la cebolla | la lata | el supermercado |
| el chocolate | la lechuga | el tomate |
| el chorizo | el maíz | la uva |
| la fresa | la manzana | la verdura |
| la fruta | el mercado | el vinagre |
| el guisante | la paella | la zanahoria |
| la habichuela | la papa | |

### Para describir

fresco/a
maduro/a
mayor
mejor
menor
peor

### Verbos

añadir
escoger
hacer falta
importar
olvidar
parecer
prestar

### Para describir

el/la/los/las (+ *noun*)
   más/menos (+ *adjective*)
el/la/los/las mejor/mejores/
   peor/peores (+ *noun*)
lo más/menos
   (+ *adverb*) posible
más/menos
   (+ *noun/adjective/adverb*) que
sin
tan (+ *adjective/adverb*) como
tanto como
tanto/a (+ *noun*) como

## Gramática

### Making comparisons

**más/menos** + *noun/adjective/adverb* + **que**
**tanto/a/os/as** + *noun* + **como**
**tan** + *adjective/adverb* + **como**
**tanto como**
**más que/menos que**
*definite article with noun* + **más/menos** + *adjective*
**lo** + **más/menos** + *adverb* + **posible**

### Irregular verbs: Preterite tense of *dar* and *estar*

| dar | | estar | |
|---|---|---|---|
| di | dimos | estuve | estuvimos |
| diste | disteis | estuviste | estuvisteis |
| dio | dieron | estuvo | estuvieron |

# *Para concluir*

**? Pregunta clave**

How do routines inside and outside the home reflect cultural values?

## Proyectos

### A  ¡Manos a la obra!

Working with two classmates, draw up a KWL chart to find out more about Spain. Write down what you know and what you want to know. Then, use the Internet to research some topics you want to know more about, and write the results in the final column. When you have finished, choose the two topics you found most interesting and make a brief presentation about them to the class. Use visuals to make your presentation more interesting.

| Lo que sé | Lo que quiero saber | Lo que aprendí |
|---|---|---|
|  |  |  |
|  |  |  |
|  |  |  |
|  |  |  |

### B  En resumen

You have just completed your second week as an exchange student living with a Spanish family. Now that you are getting used to the lifestyle, fill out a weekly planner, which you can design yourself or download from the Internet. Write your routine activities for next week, both inside and outside the home, keeping in mind what you know about Spanish culture and lifestyle. Include the times when you will do each activity, with whom (friends and/or host family), and also your plans for the weekend.

**PLANEADOR**

| LUNES | MARTES | MIÉRCOLES | JUEVES |
|---|---|---|---|
| **VIERNES** | **SÁBADO** | **DOMINGO** | **LUNES** |

## C ¡A escribir!

Imagine that you're an exchange student in Spain. Based on the weekly planner from *Actividad B*, write an email back home. Tell about things you do in your daily routine, as well as some new or special things you did last week. Be sure to include vocabulary from *Unidad 3* as well as previously learned vocabulary. Mention other host family members and what some of them do every day.

*Amigas tomando una foto en España*

## D ¿Cuánto pesa? ¿Cuánto cuesta?  Conéctate: las matemáticas

Imagina que vas a un mercado en España a comprar los siguientes ingredientes para preparar una paella. Cambia los pesos (*weights*) a libras u onzas, según la pista (*clue*) entre paréntesis. También observa los precios de los ingredientes. Luego, cambia los euros a dólares, para saber cuánto te cuesta en total comprar todo lo que necesitas.

**Receta de Paella**

1 kg de cebollas (libras)

1/2 kg de pimientos rojos (onzas)

2 kg de mejillones (libras)

1/2 kg de gambas (onzas)

1 pollo

2 kilos de arroz blanco (libras)

2 chorizos

1 kg de tomates (libras)

1/2 kg de limones (onzas)

1 cabeza de ajo

| |
|---|
| pimientos rojos 1,60 €/kg |
| gambas 15 €/kg |
| tomates rojos 0,70 €/kg |
| pollo 12 € |
| arroz blanco 3 €/kg |
| cebollas 0,75 €/kg |
| mejillones 6,50 €/kg |
| ajo 0,20 €/cabeza |
| chorizo 3,50 €/unidad |
| limón 1 €/kg |

### Un poco más

**¿Cuánto pesa?**

| | | |
|---|---|---|
| 1 kilogram, kg. (*kilo, kg*) | = | 2.2 pounds, lbs. (*libras, lb*) |
| 1 kilogram | = | 1000 grams, gr. (*gramos, gr*) |
| 28.35 grams | = | 1 ounce, oz. (*onza, oz*) |

## E La comida en casa

If you know someone, or if there is a resource in your community from another country (preferably Spanish-speaking), interview him or her about meals at home. (If you don't know anyone, then do the activity with someone from another state.) Ask about dishes the family likes and who prepares the meals. Ask also who buys the ingredients, sets the table, and cleans up. Finally, learn about one or more dishes from the person's place of origin. Find out the ingredients, where you can buy them, and then ask for the recipe. Report your findings to the class. If you are able, make the recipe and report on your experience.

# Vocabulario de la Unidad 8

el **abrigo** coat *8A*

**acabar** to finish *8A*

**acabar de** (+ *infinitive*) to have just (done something) *8A*

**adornar** to decorate *8A*

el **aguacate** avocado *8B*

el **ajo** garlic *8B*

**algo** something, anything *8A*

**añadir** to add *8B*

**arreglar** to arrange, to straighten, to fix *8A*

el **arroz** rice *8B*

la **aspiradora** vacuum cleaner *8A*

**barrer** to sweep *8A*

la **basura** garbage *8A*

el **café** coffee *8B*

la **cama** bed *8A*

la **carne** meat *8B*

la **cebolla** onion *8B*

el **chocolate** chocolate *8B*

el **chorizo** sausage (seasoned with red peppers) *8B*

**cocinar** to cook *8A*

**colgar (ue)** to hang *8A*

**dar de comer** to feed *8A*

**dejar** to leave (something behind) *8A*

**doblar** to fold *8A*

**escoger** to choose *8B*

la **fresa** strawberry *8B*

**fresco/a** fresh *8B*

la **fruta** fruit *8B*

la **gente** people *8A*

el **guisante** pea *8B*

la **habichuela** green bean *8B*

**hacer falta** to be necessary, to be lacking *8B*

el **helado** ice cream *8B*

el **huevo** egg *8B*

**importar** to be important, to matter *8B*

el **ingrediente** ingredient *8B*

el **jamón** ham *8B*

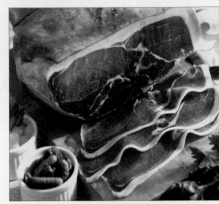

el **jardín** garden *8A*

**juntos/as** together *8A*

el **kilo (kg)** kilogram *8B*

la **lata** can *8B*

**lavar** to wash *8A*

la **leche** milk *8A*

la **lechuga** lettuce *8B*

**limpiar** to clean *8A*

**listo/a** smart *8A*

**llegar** to arrive *8A*

**maduro/a** ripe *8B*

el **maíz** corn *8B*

la **manzana** apple *8B*

**más** (+ *noun/adjective/adverb*) **que** more (+ noun/adjective/ adverb) than *8B*

**mejor** better *8B*

**menor** lesser, least *8B*

**menos** (+ *noun/adjective/adverb*) **que** less (+ noun/adjective/ adverb) than *8B*

el **mercado** market *8B*

**oír** to hear, to listen *8A*

la **olla** pot, saucepan *8A*

**olvidar** to forget *8B*

la **paella** traditional Spanish rice dish *8B*

la **papa** potato *8B*

**parecer** to seem *8B*

**pasar la aspiradora** to vacuum *8A*

**peor/peores** worse *8B*

la **persona** person *8A*

el **pimiento** bell pepper *8B*

el **plátano** banana *8B*

el **precio** price *8B*

**preparar** to prepare *8A*

**prestar** to lend *8B*

el **quehacer** chore *8A*

el **queso** cheese *8B*

**quizás** maybe, perhaps *8A*

la **receta** recipe *8B*

**recoger** to pick up *8A*

**recoger la mesa** to clear the table *8A*

**sacar** to take out *8A*

**sin** without *8B*

**solo** only, just *8A*

**subir** to climb, to go up, to go upstairs, to take up, to bring up, to carry up *8A*

el **supermercado** supermarket *8B*

**tan** (+ *adjective/adverb*) **como** as (+ adjective/adverb) as *8B*

**tanto como** as much as *8B*

**tanto/a** (+ *noun*) **como** as many/ much (+ noun) as *8B*

el **tomate** tomato *8B*

**trabajar** to work *8A*

el **trabajo** work, job *8A*

**traer** to bring *8A*

la **uva** grape *8B*

la **verdura** greens, vegetables *8B*

el **vinagre** vinegar *8B*

la **zanahoria** carrot *8B*

## ¿Sabías que...?

Panama has one of the fastest growing economies in Latin America. Most of its revenue comes from fees from the Panama Canal, banking, its duty-free zone, and tourism.

# ¡Vamos de compras!

Scan the QR code to watch this episode of *El cuarto misterioso*.

**What did José find in the briefcase?**

A. una llave y un viejo abrigo
B. una máscara de oro Azteca y un viejo mapa
C. un viejo abrigo y un mapa

*Pregunta clave*

**?**

**What can you learn about a country from the products and services it provides?**

## Mis metas

**Lección A  I will be able to:**

▸ describe clothing in terms of color and fabric
▸ identify parts of the body
▸ use adjectives as nouns
▸ talk about the past using the preterite tense of **-er** and **-ir** verbs
▸ talk about the Panama Canal, and the products and services that Panama provides
▸ talk about shopping for clothing
▸ use the preterite of **ir** and **ser**
▸ use affirmative and negative expressions in conversations
▸ read about and discuss a shopping mall in Panama

**Lección B  I will be able to:**

▸ talk about gifts and accessories
▸ use diminutives to express affection or size
▸ use the preterite of **leer**, **oír**, **ver**, **decir**, **hacer**, and **tener**
▸ discuss the connection between Ecuador's geography and the products and services it provides
▸ talk about prices and payment practices in a store
▸ use prepositions with their corresponding pronouns
▸ read about and discuss **el Mercado de Otavalo**

Why is this representative product from Ecuador called *el sombrero panameño?*

Panamá

Ecuador

## 2 Comprando ropa 🎧

Selecciona la ilustración que corresponde con lo que oyes.

A

B

C

D

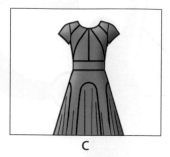

E

F

## 3 ¿De qué color es?

Describe la ropa de la actividad anterior, usando los colores.

1. la corbata
2. la blusa
3. el traje de baño
4. el vestido
5. las botas
6. el pijama

### Estrategia

**Review and recycle** ♻

| amarillo | | negro |
| rojo | | blanco |
| azul | | gris |
| verde | | |

## 4 Partes del cuerpo

Di las partes del cuerpo indicadas.

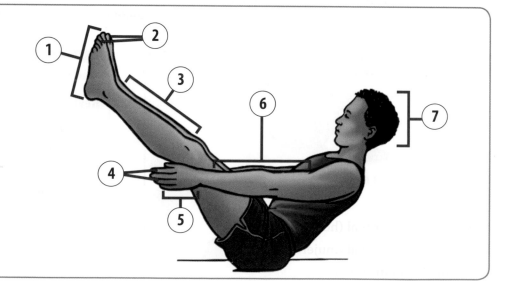

# Diálogo

## ¿Cuál prefieres?

**Rocío:** ¿Dónde está el departamento de ropa para mujeres?

**Pedro:** ¿Qué buscas?

**Rocío:** Busco un vestido de seda para la fiesta del sábado.

(*Más tarde*)

Aquí hay unos vestidos. ¿Cuál prefieres?

**Pedro:** Prefiero el vestido rosado. Y no cuesta mucho.

**Rocío:** ¿El rosado? No me gusta ni un poquito. Prefiero el morado.

**Pedro:** Con el rosado puedes llevar unas medias verdes.

**Rocío:** ¿Unas medias verdes? ¡Estás loco!

**Pedro:** Sí, te vas a ver muy bonita, como una flor.

## 5 ¿Qué recuerdas?

1. ¿Qué busca Rocío?
2. ¿Qué vestido prefiere Pedro?
3. ¿Cuesta mucho el vestido rosado?
4. ¿Le gusta el vestido rosado a Rocío?
5. ¿Qué vestido prefiere Rocío?
6. Según Pedro, ¿qué puede llevar Rocío con el vestido rosado?

## 6 Algo personal

1. ¿Cuál es tu color favorito?
2. ¿Tienes un color favorito para la ropa?
3. ¿Qué ropa te gustaría comprar?
4. ¿Qué colores te gusta llevar juntos?
5. ¿Te gusta ayudar a tus amigos/as a comprar ropa? Explica.

## 7 ¿Cuál prefieres?

Selecciona la letra de la ilustración que corresponde con lo que las siguientes personas prefieren.

A

B

# Gramática

## Adjectives as Nouns

- Frequently colors are used as adjectives in Spanish, that is, to describe something. In those cases, a definite article is not required. When a color is used as a noun, the definite article is required, just as with other nouns in Spanish.

  *Compré unas botas rojas para mi hermana.*   I bought a pair of red boots for my sister.

**but:**

  *Me gusta **el** (color) **rosado**.*   I like (the color) **pink**.

- Sometimes an item being described may be omitted in order to avoid repetition. In such cases the definite article remains, and the adjective (in this case the color) must agree with the noun that was omitted.

  *¿Te gusta la blusa azul o **la** (blusa) **morada**?*   Do you like the blue blouse or **the purple one**?
  *Compré el traje gris, no **el marrón**.*   I bought the gray suit, not **the brown one**.

### 8  Mi ropa es de color...

Completa cada oración con el adjetivo apropiado para describir los artículos de ropa en tu cuarto.

**MODELO**   **Tengo un vestido gris.**

1. Tengo unas botas __.
2. Tengo un traje de baño __.
3. Tengo unos zapatos __.
4. Tengo un pijama __.
5. Tengo una camisa __.
6. Tengo mucha ropa __.

### 9  ¿Qué les gusta?

Completa las siguientes oraciones con un artículo definido si es necesario.

1. A mi prima le gustaría comprar un vestido __ amarillo.
2. A Miriam le gusta __ color verde.
3. Mi hermana tiene una blusa de seda __ rosada porque es su color favorito.
4. __ anaranjado es mi color favorito.
5. El color favorito de Juan es __ morado.
6. A Julio le gustan sus botas __ negras.

*El gris es mi color favorito.*

7. Esperanza compró la ropa interior azul ayer, no __ blanca.
8. ¿Prefiere Selena los calcetines marrones o __ rojos?

## ¡Comunicación!

**10 ¡De compras!** **Presentational Communication**

Imagina que tienes $500. Haz una lista de la ropa que te gustaría comprar. Incluye los colores y los materiales que te gustan. Comparte tu lista con la clase.

### Estrategia

**Developing language survival skills: *regatear***

Most shops and stores in Spanish-speaking parts of the world have a fixed price (*precio fijo*), and trying to negotiate a lower price would be inappropriate. However, in some instances, negotiating (*regatear*) the price for an item is a common and accepted practice. For example, street vendors selling clothing, baskets, jewelry, etc., in Panama City would expect you to negotiate with them on prices. How might knowing Spanish help you negotiate a price while visiting a Spanish-speaking country? Do you feel confident enough with your Spanish skills to be able to negotiate a price?

## ¡Comunicación!

**11 En la tienda** **Interpersonal Communication**

Trabajando en parejas, un estudiante hace de cliente (*customer*) y el otro de vendedor(a) (*salesperson*). Alternen en regatear los precios de los artículos en las fotos.

MODELO A: ¿Cuánto cuestan los pantalones?
B: Los pantalones cuestan $70.
A: Le doy $60.
B: No puedo venderlos a menos de $65.

1

2

3

### Un poco más

**Regatear**

Is there a flea market where you live? Go there and practice bargaining for items. Learning how to bargain will be beneficial if you travel to a Spanish-speaking country where you can combine this skill with your ability to speak Spanish.

4

5

6

## ¡Comunicación!

**12** **¿Qué vas a comprar?** 👥 **Interpersonal Communication**

Trabajando en parejas, habla con tu compañero/a sobre los artículos de ropa del Vocabulario 1. Miren las fotos y digan qué les gustaría comprar.

**MODELO**   A: ¿Qué te gustaría comprar en la tienda?

B: Me gustaría comprar un traje gris. Los negros no me gustan.

## ¡Comunicación!

**13** **¿Qué llevan hoy?** 👥 **Interpersonal Communication**

In pairs, discuss your classmates' clothing. You say who is wearing the article of clothing and your partner describes it. Name and describe at least five articles each.

**MODELO**   A: Estoy mirando las botas de Teresa.

B: Sus botas son negras de tacón.

*Me gusta llevar botas de tacón.*

## Preterite of -ar Verbs

*Repaso rápido*

You are already familiar with how to conjugate the preterite of **-ar** verbs:

| comprar | | | |
|---|---|---|---|
| yo | comp**ré** | nosotros | comp**ramos** |
| tú | comp**raste** | vosotros | comp**rasteis** |
| él | comp**ró** | Uds. | comp**raron** |

**Note:** Stem changes in **-ar** verbs for the present tense do not occur in the preterite tense:

**Infinitive:** *recordar*   **Present:** *yo recuerdo*   **Preterite:** *yo recordé*

**14** **En la tienda por departamentos**

Usa elementos de cada columna para crear oraciones con la forma correcta del pretérito.

| I | II | III |
|---|---|---|
| mis hermanas | | unas medias de colores |
| tú | | una blusa rosada |
| mi hermano | buscar | un traje marrón |
| yo | mirar | un vestido morado de seda |
| mis amigas y yo | comprar | una camisa de algodón y una |
| tú y tu padre | | corbata anaranjada |

**¡Ojo!**

Verbs ending in -car change their spelling in the *yo* form in the preterite:
*bus**car*** → *bus**qué***.

# Gramática

## Talking About the Past: Preterite Tense of *-er* and *-ir* Verbs

- Form the preterite tense of regular **-er** and **-ir** verbs by removing the last two letters from the infinitive and adding the same set of endings for either type of verb.

| correr | | | |
|---|---|---|---|
| yo | corr**í** | nosotros/as | corr**imos** |
| tú | corr**iste** | vosotros/as | corr**isteis** |
| Ud. él ella | corr**ió** | Uds. ellos ellas | corr**ieron** |

| escribir | | | |
|---|---|---|---|
| yo | escrib**í** | nosotros/as | escrib**imos** |
| tú | escrib**iste** | vosotros/as | escrib**isteis** |
| Ud. él ella | escrib**ió** | Uds. ellos ellas | escrib**ieron** |

| ¿Quién **corrió** a la tienda por departamentos? | Who **ran** to the department store? |
|---|---|
| ¿Le **escribió** Mirta un e-mail a su primo? | **Did** Mirta **write** an e-mail to her cousin? |

**Note:** Stem changes that occur in the present tense for *-ar* and *-er* verbs do not occur in the preterite tense. However, **-ir** verbs that have a stem change in the present tense require a different stem change in the preterite tense for *Ud., él, ella, Uds., ellos,* and *ellas*. This second change is shown in parentheses after infinitives in this book. Some verbs that follow this pattern include *dormir* (ue, **u**), *pedir* (i, **i**), *preferir* (ie, **i**), *repetir* (i, **i**), and *sentir* (ie, **i**). The stem changes do not interfere with the verb endings.

| dormir | | | |
|---|---|---|---|
| yo | dormí | nosotros/as | dormimos |
| tú | dormiste | vosotros/as | dormisteis |
| Ud. él ella | d**u**rmió | Uds. ellos ellas | d**u**rmieron |

| pedir | | | |
|---|---|---|---|
| yo | pedí | nosotros/as | pedimos |
| tú | pediste | vosotros/as | pedisteis |
| Ud. él ella | p**i**dió | Uds. ellos ellas | p**i**dieron |

| preferir | | | |
|---|---|---|---|
| yo | preferí | nosotros/as | preferimos |
| tú | preferiste | vosotros/as | preferisteis |
| Ud. él ella | pref**i**rió | Uds. ellos ellas | pref**i**rieron |

## 15 En la tienda de ropa

Working in pairs, one person plays the part of the owner of a clothing store who has returned from vacation and one person plays the part of an employee who has been managing the store during the owner's absence. What might the conversation sound like, based upon the provided cues?

**MODELO**  recoger las corbatas nuevas

A: ¿Recogiste las corbatas nuevas?

B: Sí, (No, no) las recogí.

1. aprender a arreglar los pantalones
2. barrer siempre el suelo de la tienda por la mañana
3. pedir las camisas
4. escoger las corbatas para los clientes
5. subir la ropa nueva a la oficina

## 16 ¿Qué pasó ayer?

Usa elementos de cada columna para hacer siete oraciones completas y decir lo que pasó ayer.

**MODELO**  **Yo pedí cuatro medias.**

> **¡Ojo!**
>
> Remember that the verb *estar* is irregular in the preterite: *estuve, estuviste, estuvo, estuvimos, estuvisteis, estuvieron*.

| I | II | III |
|---|---|---|
| tú y yo | pedir | al departamento de ropa para hombres |
| tú y Nacho | estar | comprarte unas botas marrones |
| el profesor | dormir | toda la noche |
| Ud. | correr | ropa interior blanca |
| las chicas | preferir | en la tienda por departamentos |
| tú | repetir | dos corbatas nuevas |
| yo | | los trajes de baño |
| | | el precio dos veces |

*Estuvimos en la tienda por departamentos.*

## 17 ¡Vamos de compras!

En parejas, hablen de lo que pasó en la tienda por departamentos ayer, según las pistas y las fotos.

**MODELO**   Carmen / pedir ver

     **A:** ¿Qué pidió ver Carmen?

     **B:** Carmen pidió ver ropa interior.

**1.** Joaquín y Esteban / pedir ver

**2.** Elena y su mamá / escoger

**3.** Andrés y su primo / volver para comprar

**4.** Pepe / preferir comprar

**5.** Miguel / escoger

**6.** la amiga de Enrique / correr a comprar

## ¡Comunicación!

## 18 ¿Qué hicieron la semana pasada?    Interpersonal Communication

Tú y un(a) compañero/a deben hacer una lista de las actividades que hicieron la semana pasada. Alternen para hablar de las actividades de la lista. Digan lo que hicieron, cuándo lo hicieron, con quién(es) lo hicieron, y cualquier (*any*) otra información importante. Pueden incluir actividades como las siguientes u otras: escribir un correo electrónico, salir con amigos, dormir tarde, comer en un restaurante y comprar (un artículo de ropa).

**MODELO**   **A:** Compré ropa nueva. Fui de compras con Mayra el viernes.

     **B:** ¿Qué compraste?

     **A:** Compré unos zapatos de tacón bonitos.

     **B:** ¿Cuánto costaron?

     **A:** Solo cincuenta dólares.

 # Cultura

*Las playas de Panamá*

## Panamá, país comercial 🎧

Casi podemos decir que Panamá nació[1] para ser un país comercial. Uno de sus servicios principales es el turismo, que ofrece a los visitantes hermosas playas de agua cálida y arena blanca. Cuenta también con el famoso Canal de Panamá que conecta dos océanos, el Atlántico y el Pacífico, por el cual pasan cada año casi 14.000 barcos enormes con productos de todo el mundo. El servicio que presta[2] el Canal de Panamá es muy importante para el mundo porque les ahorra mucho tiempo y dinero a las industrias que llevan productos de un lado del mundo al otro.

Otros servicios importantes en Panamá son los bancos para el comercio internacional y las oficinas de importación y exportación. Las bajas tarifas de importación[3] en Panamá atraen a inversionistas[4] de Europa, las Américas, Israel, India y los países árabes que vienen a comprar y vender. Otra atracción para los inversionistas es la Zona Libre[5] de la ciudad de Colón. Allí venden artículos de todas clases al por mayor[6] sin tarifas de importación y exportación. Las transacciones se hacen en dólares y en balboas, la moneda nacional del país. Panamá también exporta productos como antibióticos, plátanos, camarones[7], azúcar, café y ropa.

> **Pregunta clave**
> What can you learn about a country from the products and services it provides?

*La Zona Libre de Colón*

[1] was born　[2] offers　[3] low import tariffs　[4] investors　[5] duty-free zone　[6] wholesale　[7] shrimp

🔍 **Búsqueda:** canal de panamá, economía de panamá, molas, polleras

## Productos

Las molas son diseños (*designs*) textiles en forma de panel con aplicaciones de diversos colores. Antes, los indios kunas pintaban (*painted*) su cuerpo con figuras geométricas. Después, empezaron a poner esos diseños en molas. Hoy también crean diseños de flores y animales. Las mujeres kunas usan las molas como parte de su blusa tradicional. Las molas resultan muy atractivas para los turistas, quienes las llevan de recuerdo de su paso por Panamá.

*Una mola de los indios kunas*

## Prácticas

Cada año, el festival "Mil Polleras" celebra la ropa tradicional panameña. La pollera es una falda típica con encajes (*lace*), perlas y bordados (*embroidery*). Las mujeres y niñas participan en un desfile (*parade*) llevando polleras bonitas hechas a mano.

*El festival "Mil Polleras"*

### 19 Comprensión　Interpretive Communication

1. ¿Qué océanos conecta el Canal de Panamá?
2. ¿Qué servicios ofrece Panamá? ¿Qué productos exporta?
3. ¿Qué son las molas y las polleras?

### 20 Analiza

1. What makes Panama's services so attractive to investors?
2. Explain the importance of *molas* and *polleras* in Panama's culture today.

# El Canal de Panamá 🎧

Gracias al Canal de Panamá, un barco tarda solo entre 8 y 10 horas en ir desde el océano Atlántico (y el Caribe) hasta el océano Pacífico. El Canal de Panamá es un sistema de vías fluviales[1] que une los dos océanos. ¿Por qué es Panamá un buen lugar para un canal? Primero, por su localización estratégica entre dos océanos. Segundo, por su geografía. Es un país pequeño, pero tiene lagos[2] y valles grandes. Gracias a esto, los ingenieros pudieron[3] hacer una "calle" de agua desde un océano hasta el otro.

Un barco contenedor en las esclusas del canal

¿Cómo hicieron la "calle"? Primero, llenaron un valle enorme con agua para hacer un lago artificial (el Gatún). Lo conectaron con otro lago natural llamado Miraflores. Después, excavaron canales para conectar cada lago con un océano.

Pero estos lagos están 85 pies más arriba del nivel del mar[4]. ¿Cómo pueden subir y bajar los barcos? El canal incluye un sistema de esclusas[5], o "elevadores de agua", que suben el barco desde el nivel del océano hasta los lagos. Luego, el barco continúa por los lagos y baja por otras esclusas al océano del otro lado.

Los Estados Unidos empezaron a construir el canal en 1904 y lo terminaron en diez años. Estuvo bajo su control hasta 1999, cuando se transfirió a Panamá. Hoy, Panamá administra el canal, y cada barco que va a cruzar debe pagar. Hoy en día Panamá está trabajando en un proyecto para ampliar[6] el canal, ¡para que puedan cruzar más barcos!

[1]waterways  [2]lakes  [3]were able  [4]above sea level
[5]locks  [6]enlarge

🔍 **Búsqueda:** canal de panamá

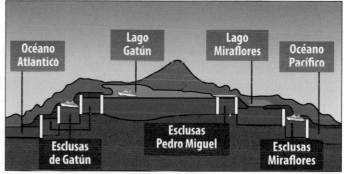
Diagrama del Canal de Panamá

## Perspectivas

"Panamanians from the interoceanic era are cosmopolitan, they give more value to negotiation than to confrontation. They are tolerant of diversity. That is why you see Jewish and Arab partners in Colon's duty-free zone. That is the culture of the interoceanic era." According to this translated quote from a cultural anthropologist, what is the attitude of *los panameños* toward the international services it provides?

## 21 Comprensión — Interpretive Communication

1. How did Panama's geography favor the construction of a canal?
2. What are the two large bodies of water in the canal system?
3. What role do the locks (*esclusas*) play?
4. Who controls the passage of ships through the canal?

## 22 Analiza

1. Why is the Panama Canal strategic for world trade?
2. Do you think the Panama Canal will be as important in the next 50 years as it is now? Why or why not?

# Vocabulario 2

## Artículos para todos 🎧

| INICIO | ARTÍCULOS | MUJER | HOMBRE | CASA |

**CENTRO COMERCIAL PLAZA PAITILLA**
INICIO > TIENDAS

HORARIO lunes a sábado
11:00 AM a 9:00 PM

### La tienda de
### LOS GUANTES

Tenemos guantes de muchos colores para **combinar** con toda tu ropa.
¡Visítanos en el local 83!

### La tienda de
### LOS SOMBREROS

Tenemos lo mejor en sombreros. **Nadie** nos gana, **ni** en precio **ni** en cantidad.
¡Visítanos en el local 240!

### La tienda de
### LOS SUÉTERES

Suéteres para tus **vacaciones** de invierno. No hay mejores suéteres en **ninguna** parte.
¡Visítanos en el local 101!

### La tienda de
### LAS CHAQUETAS

DESCUENTOS
del **20%**

**Vendemos** chaquetas para todos los gustos y para todos los meses del año.
¡Visítanos en el local 145!

### La tienda de
### LOS IMPERMEABLES

Excelente servicio. Siempre hay **alguien** listo para ayudarte.
¡Visítanos en el local 225!

Le **prometí** a mi hija una chaqueta como esta, pero a ella no le gusta el marrón.

Parece que no la tienen en **ningún** otro color. ¡Qué lástima!

¿Qué piensas de esta chaqueta?

¡Me encanta! Ese color **te queda** muy bien.

## Para conversar

***T***o talk about shopping:

¿Puedo ayudarla en algo?
*Can I help you with something?*

Sí, me **contaron** que aquí venden guantes **de lana**, pero no los veo.
*Yes, I was told you sell wool gloves here, but I don't see them.*

Lo siento. No nos **queda ninguno**, pero tenemos **algunos** de algodón.
*I'm sorry. We don't have any left, but we have some cotton ones.*

Estos me gustan. ¿Los tiene en **algún** otro color?
*I like these. Do you have them in any other color?*

Vienen **o** en negro **o** en marrón. **Nada** más.
*They come either in black or brown. Nothing else.*

### Para decir más

| | |
|---|---|
| la bufanda | *scarf* |
| las gafas de sol | *sunglasses* |
| el gorro | *hat* |
| la sudadera | *sweatshirt* |
| la sudadera con capucha | *hoodie* |
| abrigado/a | *warm (clothing)* |
| ajustado/a | *tight-fitting* |
| de cuero | *(made) of leather* |
| elegante | *elegant* |
| informal | *casual* |
| ligero/a | *lightweight (clothing)* |

### 23  ¿Qué es?

Escribe el artículo de ropa que oyes.

MODELO   el <u>sombrero</u>

1. los __
2. un __
3. una __
4. un __
5. tu __
6. el __

### 24  ¿Cuándo?

Listen carefully to statements made by several people. Indicate whether each sentence you hear is in the **pretérito** or in the **presente**.

## Diálogo 🎧

### Un vestido de seda

**Rocío:** ¿Hay alguien a quien preguntar por otros vestidos?

**Pedro:** Sí, allí. Señora, ¿nos puede ayudar?

**Señora:** Sí, cómo no.

**Rocío:** Busco un vestido de seda.

**Señora:** ¿No le gusta ninguno de aquí?

**Rocío:** No, ninguno. Bueno, este azul, pero no me queda bien.

**Señora:** Bueno, aquí hay otros, pero son de lana.

**Rocío:** No, los vestidos de lana no me gustan nada.

**Señora:** ¿Le gustaría ver algo más, guantes, abrigos, faldas?

¿Te gusta este vestido de seda?

### 25 ¿Qué recuerdas? 🎧

1. ¿Hay alguien a quien preguntar por otros vestidos?

2. ¿Le gustan los vestidos de seda a Rocío?

3. ¿Qué vestidos no le gustan a Rocío?

4. ¿Qué más puede ver Rocío?

### 26 Algo personal 🎧

1. ¿Prefieres los vestidos de lana o los de seda?

2. ¿Qué color de ropa te queda bien?

3. ¿Qué ropa compras cuando vas de vacaciones?

## ¡Comunicación!

### 27 ¿Qué llevan? 👥 Interpersonal Communication

Busca fotos o ilustraciones en la internet de personas en la playa y en la nieve. Trabajando con un(a) compañero/a, alternen para hablar de la ropa que lleva cada persona y expliquen por qué la lleva. Usen las palabras en Para decir más en las páginas 403 y 415 para ampliar (*extend*) la conversación.

**MODELO**
    **A:** ¿Qué ropa lleva la muchacha en la foto?
    **B:** Lleva un gorro morado, una bufanda verde y roja y un suéter morado.
    **A:** ¿Qué tiempo hace en la foto?

¿Qué llevas cuando hay nieve?

# Gramática

## Preterite Tense of *ir* and *ser*

You have already seen one form of the preterite tense of **ser**: **fue** (was). The irregular preterite-tense forms of **ir** (to go: went) and **ser** (to be: was, were) are identical. The meaning will be clear from context.

| ir/ser | | | |
|---|---|---|---|
| yo | **fui** | nosotros/as | **fuimos** |
| tú | **fuiste** | vosotros/as | **fuisteis** |
| Ud.<br>él<br>ella | **fue** | Uds.<br>ellos<br>ellas | **fueron** |

| | |
|---|---|
| Inés **fue** de compras ayer. | Inés **went** shopping yesterday. |
| ¿**Fuiste** al centro comercial? | **Did you go** to the mall? |

**but:**

| | |
|---|---|
| ¿Qué día **fue** tu cumpleaños? | What day **was** your birthday? |
| Esos inviernos **fueron** muy fríos. | Those winters **were** very cold. |

### 28  ¿Pretérito de *ser* o *ir*?

Decide si el verbo de las siguientes oraciones es una forma del pretérito de **ir** o de **ser** y explica por qué según el contexto.

MODELO    Ayer fui al centro comercial. **Pretérito de *ir* porque habla de ir a un lugar.**
Ese programa fue muy aburrido. **Pretérito de *ser* porque describe un programa.**

1. Ayer mi hermana y yo fuimos al centro.
2. Mi hermana fue a una tienda de ropa interior.
3. La señora de la tienda fue muy amable con ella.
4. Yo fui en metro a una tienda de zapatos.
5. Al mediodía mi mamá fue con nosotras a un restaurante.
6. La comida fue muy buena.
7. Los meseros fueron muy simpáticos.
8. Por la noche todos nosotros fuimos al cine.
9. La película fue muy cómica.
10. Fue un día muy divertido.
11. Y Uds., ¿adónde fueron ayer?

*¿Fueron ellas al centro comercial?*

## 29 ¿Adónde fueron ayer? 🎧

Indica adónde fueron ayer estas personas, según las fotos.

**MODELO** Ana y Pablo

**Ana y Pablo fueron al cine ayer.**

**1.** yo

**2.** tú

**3.** Julia

**4.** mis padres

**5.** mi amigo y yo

**6.** Raúl e Inés

## 30 De vacaciones en la isla Contadora

Completa el siguiente párrafo con el pretérito de los verbos entre paréntesis para decir qué ropa compraron Sara y sus dos hermanas en la isla Contadora en Panamá.

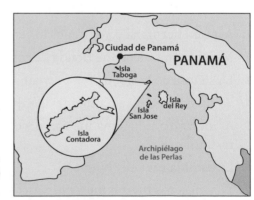

Primero yo (**1.** *escoger*) un traje de baño porque el que tengo no me queda bien. Lo (**2.** *comprar*) por poco dinero. Mis hermanas también (**3.** *ir*) a la misma tienda y (**4.** *comprar*) unas blusas de algodón muy bonitas. Cuando nosotras (**5.** *volver*) al centro comercial, yo (**6.** *ir*) a buscar otro traje de baño para mí. Ese día, en la tienda, los dependientes (**7.** *ser*) muy amables y (**8.** *vender*) todos los trajes de baño rápidamente. Nosotras (**9.** *comprar*) el último. Me gustaría tener dos. Luego, mi tía Iris (**10.** *ir*) con nosotras de compras. Ella (**11.** *prometer*) comprarme ropa para mi cumpleaños y yo le (**12.** *pedir*) unos zapatos de tacón, de color anaranjado. ¡Qué bonitos son! Nosotras (**13.** *estar*) comprando todo el día y (**14.** *llegar*) tarde al hotel, ¡cansadas pero contentas! (**15.** *ser*) un día fantástico.

## 31 Lo que compramos

Di lo que las siguientes personas fueron a comprar. Sigue el modelo.

MODELO    Melinda
          **Melinda fue a comprar una blusa amarilla.**

**1.** Juan        **2.** Lisa y Rebeca        **3.** tú        **4.** nosotros        **5.** yo

## ¡Comunicación!

## 32 Fuimos y nos gustó    Interpersonal/Presentational Communication

En parejas, alternen para hablar de lo que sus familias y amigos hicieron ayer, la semana pasada, el mes pasado o el año pasado. Incluyan en su conversación adónde fueron estas personas, con quién fueron y qué hicieron. Luego, uno de Uds. debe presentar un resumen (*summary*) de la conversación a la clase.

MODELO    A:  ¿Adónde fueron tú y tu familia la semana pasada?
          B:  Fuimos a ver una película al nuevo centro comercial.
          A:  ¿Les gustó?
          B:  Sí, nos gustó mucho. ¡Fue fantástica!
          Resumen:  Andy y su familia fueron a ver una película fantástica en el nuevo centro comercial la semana pasada. Les gustó a todos.

## ¡Comunicación!

## 33 La semana pasada    Presentational Communication

Usa una tabla como la de abajo para entrevistar a cinco compañeros/as sobre sus actividades de la semana pasada. Luego presenta los resultados de la entrevista a la clase.

| Nombre | ¿Qué hiciste la semana pasada? | ¿Cuándo? | ¿Con quién? |
|--------|-------------------------------|----------|-------------|
| Liz | ir de compras | el sábado | amigas |

MODELO    Resumen: Liz fue de compras el sábado pasado con sus amigas.

# Gramática

## Affirmative and Negative Words

- In Spanish it is sometimes possible (and necessary) to use two negative expressions in the same sentence. The following chart contains a list of common affirmative expressions along with their negative counterparts.

| Expresiones afirmativas | Expresiones negativas |
|---|---|
| • **sí** (*yes*)<br>**Sí**, vendemos chaquetas. | • **no** (*no*)<br>**No**, **no** vendemos chaquetas. |
| • **algo** (*something, anything*)<br>¿Quieres tomar **algo**? | • **nada** (*nothing, anything*)<br>**No** quiero tomar **nada**. |
| • **alguien** (*somebody, anybody*)<br>¿Lo sabe **alguien**? | • **nadie** (*nobody, anybody*)<br>**No**, **nadie** lo sabe |
| • **algún**, **alguna**, **-os**, **-as** (*some, any*)<br>¿Le gusta **algún** impermeable?<br>¿Le gusta **alguna** bufanda?<br>¿Compras **algunos** zapatos?<br>¿Buscas **algunas** medias? | • **ningún**, **ninguna**, **-os**, **-as** (*none, not any*)<br>No, **ningún** impermeable me gusta.<br>No, **ninguna** me gusta.<br>No, **no** compro **ningunos** zapatos.<br>No, **no** busco **ningunas** medias. |
| • **o... o** (*either... or*)<br>Puedes comprar **o** un abrigo **o** un sombrero. | • **ni... ni** (*neither... nor*)<br>**No** voy a comprar **ni** un abrigo **ni** un sombrero. |
| • **siempre** (*always*)<br>Él **siempre** lleva corbata. | • **nunca** (*never*)<br>Él **nunca** lleva corbata. |
| • **también** (*also, too*)<br>Ella **también** viene hoy. | • **tampoco** (*neither, either*)<br>Él **tampoco** viene hoy. |

**Note:** The words *alguno/a* (some, any) and *ninguno/a* (none, not any) are sometimes used as pronouns.

¿Va **alguno** *de Uds. al centro esta semana?*    No, **ninguno** *de nosotros va al centro esta semana.*

- When combining negative expressions in one sentence in Spanish, it is often possible to use one of the negative expressions before the verb and another negative expression (and sometimes even more than one) after the verb. However, *no*, *nada*, *nadie*, *nunca*, *tampoco*, and forms of *ninguno* may be used alone, before the verb, without the word *no*.

*No voy **nunca** a las tiendas.*
***Nunca** voy a las tiendas.*

I **never** go to the stores.

*No estoy haciendo **nada tampoco**.*
***Tampoco** estoy haciendo **nada**.*

I am **not** doing **anything either**.

• When *nadie* or a form of *ninguno* are direct objects referring to people, they require the personal *a*.

| | |
|---|---|
| *No veo **a** **nadie** aquí.* | I don't see **anyone** here. |
| *No veo **a** **ningún** amigo aquí.* | I don't see **any** friends here. |

## 34 Mini-diálogos

Completa estos mini-diálogos lógicamente, usando una de las siguientes palabras:
**algo**, **alguien**, **nada** o **nadie**.

1. **A:** __ tiene que ir con Uds.

   **B:** No, no queremos ir con __.

2. **A:** ¿Sabe __ dónde está la tienda?

   **B:** No, __ lo sabe.

3. **A:** ¿Va __ con Uds.?

   **B:** Sí, Iris va con nosotras porque quiere comprar __.

4. **A:** ¿Ves a __ en el departamento de ropa de hombres?

   **B:** No, no veo a __.

5. **A:** ¿ __ me puede ayudar?

   **B:** Ahora no te puede ayudar __.

6. **A:** ¿Quieres comprar __?

   **B:** No, no me gusta __.

## 35 ¡No! 🎧

Contesta las preguntas en forma negativa.

**MODELO**   ¿Qué quieres mirar?

**No quiero mirar nada.**

1. Yo no voy a la tienda de ropa. ¿Y tú?
2. ¿Con quién fueron Uds. de compras ayer?
3. ¿Prefieres las botas anaranjadas o las verdes?
4. ¿Viste alguna falda de algodón?
5. ¿Ves a algún amigo del colegio?
6. ¿Compraron Uds. el suéter rojo o el suéter azul?
7. ¿Sus padres siempre les dan dinero para ir de compras?
8. ¿Te gustaría vender ropa interior o carros?
9. ¿Siempre van Uds. de compras al centro?
10. ¿Quiénes de Uds. son de Panamá?

*¿Prefieres la blusa anaranjada o la de muchos colores?*

## 36 ¡Estoy enfermo/a y no quiero hacer nada! 👥 🎧

Estás de mal humor porque estás enfermo/a y tus padres te hacen muchas preguntas. Trabajando en parejas, alternen en hacer las siguientes preguntas y en dar respuestas negativas a cada una.

**MODELO**  A: ¿Piensas ir de compras o vas a estudiar?

B: No, no pienso ni ir de compras ni estudiar.

1. ¿Qué vas a hacer hoy?
2. ¿Quién te va a visitar en casa?
3. ¿Siempre juegas con el perro cuando estás enfermo/a?
4. ¿Quieres comer algo?
5. ¿Vas a hablar con alguien por teléfono?
6. ¿Quieres ver alguna película en DVD?
7. ¿Te puedo comprar algo?

## ¡Comunicación!

### 37 Las cosas que no se hacen 👥  Presentational Communication

Con un(a) compañero/a hagan una lista de diez cosas que nadie hace nunca. Luego, deben leer las mejores oraciones de la lista a la clase.

**MODELO**  Nadie va nunca a un restaurante sin camisa.

## ¡Comunicación!

### 38 Tu ropa favorita 👥  Interpersonal Communication

Hablen en parejas sobre su artículo de ropa favorito. Incluyan la siguiente información:

- cuándo lo llevan
- qué colores prefieren
- con qué otros artículos de ropa combina
- cuando y dónde lo compraron o quién les dio ese artículo de ropa

*Me gusta llevar mi pantalón rosado.*

**MODELO**  A: ¿Qué ropa te gusta llevar mucho?

B: Me gusta llevar un pantalón rosado porque combina muy bien con mi camiseta negra. Lo llevo casi todos los días.

A: ¿Dónde lo compraste?

B: Lo compré el mes pasado en el centro comercial. Y a ti, ¿qué ropa te gusta llevar?

A: Mi ropa favorita es mi chaqueta azul de lana. Me gusta mucho porque combina con todos mis pantalones. Siempre la llevo en invierno cuando hace frío.

B: ¿Dónde la compraste?

A: No la compré. Mi mamá me dio la chaqueta para mi cumpleaños.

# Todo en contexto

**?** Pregunta clave

What can you learn about a country from the products and services it provides?

## ¡Comunicación!

### 39 En la Zona Libre de Colón 👥 Interpersonal Communication

Imagine that you own a store in the United States where you sell clothes from different parts of the world, and that you went to Panama to buy typical Panamanian items in the Zona Libre de Colón. On the flight home, you get into a conversation with the person next to you about the items you purchased. With a partner, discuss the items you bought and what they tell about the country. You can search the Internet and refer to the *Para decir más* box below, the culture readings, and the vocabulary sections from this lesson for help.

**MODELO**
  A: ¿Compró algo en la Zona Libre de Colón?
  B: Sí, compré muchas blusas adornadas con molas. Son tradicionales de las mujeres kuna y son muy populares.

### Para decir más

| | |
|---|---|
| el descuento | *discount* |
| la docena | *dozen* |
| el impuesto | *tax* |
| barato/a | *cheap* |
| caro/a | *expensive* |
| extranjero/a | *foreign* |

## ¡Comunicación!

### 40 ¡Cruzamos el Canal de Panamá! 👥 Presentational Communication

En parejas o en grupos pequeños, van a describir un viaje que hicieron en barco por el Canal de Panamá. Usen las lecturas en las páginas 412 413 e investiguen en la internet para informar a otros miembros de la clase. Incluyan el itinerario del barco desde el océano Atlántico hasta el océano Pacífico: en qué ciudad empezaron y en qué fecha; en qué ciudad terminaron y en qué fecha; y los nombres de los lagos (*lakes*), de las esclusas (*locks*) y de los puentes (*bridges*) por los que pasaron. Expliquen por qué la operación del Canal de Panamá es un servicio tan importante para todo el mundo. Por último, comenten cómo creen que el canal ha influido en la cultura y la vida de los panameños. Incluyan un mapa, fotos o ilustraciones para acompañar su presentación a la clase.

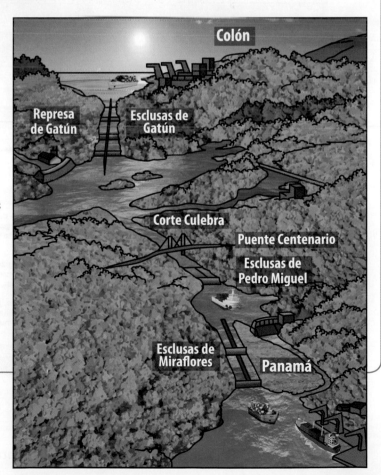

# Lectura informativa

## Antes de leer 🎧

1. ¿Te gusta ir de compras al centro comercial? ¿Qué te gusta comprar cuando vas allá?

2. ¿Qué más haces cuando vas al centro comercial?

### Estrategia

**Using visual format to predict meaning**

Visual details of printed information such as the style and format of printed media can tell you a lot about its probable content. Before starting to read, look at the layout, the artwork, the pictures, the titles, and the format of the writing for hints about its content and meaning.

## Una visita al centro comercial 🎧

## 41 Comprensión 🎧 Interpretive Communication

1. ¿Qué es Multicentro?
2. ¿Qué cosas puedes hacer en Multicentro?
3. ¿Qué servicios encuentras en un centro comercial grande?

## 42 Analiza

1. Do you think this ad would attract more locals or tourists to the mall? Why?
2. Why might a store in Panama attract foreign visitors?

# ✏️ Escritura

## 43 Mi visita reciente a un centro comercial — Presentational Communication

When was the last time you went to a mall or other shopping area? Write a real or imaginary account of a trip to the mall. Tell where you went and with whom, what you did, and what you bought. Be sure to describe your purchases in detail, giving colors and why you bought them. If you saw items you did not like, explain why. Tell where you stopped to rest or eat, and what else you did at the shopping center. Be sure to use connecting words for making smooth transitions and for telling the sequence of events. Use a diagram like the one below to organize your ideas before you start writing.

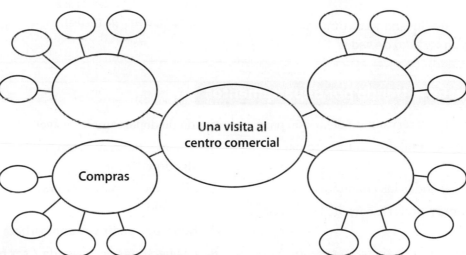

## Estrategia

### Indicating sequence

You have already learned to use transition words to make your writing flow smoothly. When writing about past activities or events, transition words indicate the sequence in which actions occurred. Some sequence words you may want to use in your writing include the following: *primero* (first), *luego* (later, then), *antes de* (before), *después de* (after), *finalmente* (finally).

### Para escribir más

| | |
|---|---|
| el puesto (de comida) | (food) stand |
| barato/a | inexpensive, cheap |
| caro/a | expensive |
| ahorrar | to save money |
| descansar | to rest |
| gastar | to spend (money) |
| pagar | to pay |

# Repaso de la Lección A

## A Escuchar: ¿Qué fueron a comprar?  (pp. 402–403, 414–415)

Selecciona la foto del artículo de ropa que corresponde con lo que oyes.

A

B

C

D

E

## B Vocabulario: ¿Qué llevan? (pp. 402–403, 414–415)

Completa las oraciones con la palabra apropiada entre paréntesis.

1. Ana lleva un sombrero rojo en (*la cabeza / el brazo*).

2. En el invierno llevo un abrigo de (*seda / lana*).

3. Julián lleva unos zapatos negros en (*los dedos / los pies*).

4. Para ir a la fiesta Susana va a comprar (*un guante / un vestido*) de seda.

5. Cuando tengo frío en las manos llevo (*los guantes / los calcetines*).

6. Va a llover. Debes llevar (*el traje de baño / el impermeable*).

7. No me gustan las blusas de seda, prefiero las (*de algodón / de tacón*).

## C Gramática: En la tienda por departamentos (pp. 409, 417)

Haz oraciones en el pretérito para decir qué pasó en la tienda de departamentos ayer.

1. Jorge y Enrique / ir al departamento para hombres

2. Teresa / vender todas las chaquetas

3. Sara y su mamá / preferir comprar unas botas moradas

4. Elisa / escoger un traje de baño rosado

5. Gustavo / correr a comprar un pijama de algodón

6. Miranda / ir para comprar un vestido de seda amarillo

7. Roberto / pedir ver una corbata roja

8. Las personas de la tienda / ser muy amables

## D Gramática: Expresiones negativas (pp. 420–421)

Contesta las preguntas en forma negativa.

**MODELO** ¿Ves a algún amigo del colegio?

**No, no veo a ningún amigo del colegio.**

1. ¿Venden aquí algunos zapatos de tacón?

2. ¿Compraste el vestido anaranjado o el rosado?

3. ¿Te da tu tía dinero para ir de compras?

4. ¿Viste alguna camisa de algodón?

5. ¿Siempre vas de compras al centro?

6. Yo no voy al centro comercial. ¿Y tú?

7. ¿Vas de compras con alguien mañana?

8. ¿Tienes que comprar algo en esta tienda?

## E   Cultura: Productos y servicios de Panamá (pp. 412–413)

Repasa lo que leíste sobre los servicios y productos que encuentran los visitantes en Panamá y resume la información en una tabla como la que sigue. Escribe una frase para describir cada producto o servicio, como se ve en el modelo.

**Productos y servicios de Panamá**

| Producto | Servicio | Descripción |
|----------|----------|-------------|
| las molas |  | unos textiles para decorar las blusas |
|  |  |  |
|  |  |  |

## Vocabulario

### Para describir

algún, alguna
anaranjado/a
marrón
morado/a
ningún,
  ninguna
rosado/a

### Pronombres

alguien
alguno/a
nada
nadie
ninguno/a

### La ropa

la bota
la chaqueta
la corbata
el guante
el impermeable
las medias
el pijama
la ropa interior
el sombrero
el suéter
el traje (de baño)
el vestido
el zapato (bajo/de tacón)

### Partes del cuerpo

el brazo
la cabeza
el cuerpo
el dedo
la mano
el pie
la pierna

### Verbos

combinar
contar (ue)
prometer
vender

### Otras expresiones

el algodón
el centro comercial
el departamento
el hombre
la lana
la mujer
ni... ni
o... o
quedarle algo a alguien
quedarle bien a uno
la seda
las vacaciones

## Gramática

### Adjectives as nouns

The definite article is necessary with the adjective when it becomes a noun.

*¿Te gusta la camisa roja?*   Do you like the red shirt?

*Sí, me gusta **la roja**.*   Yes, I like **the red one**.

### Preterite tense of regular -er and -ir verbs

| correr | |
|--------|--------|
| corr**í** | corr**imos** |
| corr**iste** | corr**isteis** |
| corr**ió** | corr**ieron** |

**Note:** -ir verbs that have stem changes in the present tense will also have a stem change in the preterite tense indicated by the second vowel in parentheses after the infinitive. For example: ***dormir (ue, u)*** or ***pedir (i, i)***.

### Preterite tense of *ir* and *ser*

| ir/ser | |
|--------|--------|
| fui | fuimos |
| fuiste | fuisteis |
| fue | fueron |

### Affirmative and negative expressions

| Expresiones afirmativas | Expresiones negativas |
|-------------------------|-----------------------|
| sí | no |
| algo | nada |
| alguien | nadie |
| algún, alguno/a/os/as | ningún, ninguno/a/os/as |
| o…o | ni…ni |
| siempre | nunca |
| también | tampoco |

## Regalos para todos 🎧

| INICIO | REGALOS | HOMBRE | MUJER |

**CENTRO COMERCIAL CUENCA**
**Boutique** LOS ANDES

HORARIO lunes a sábado
11:00 AM a 9:00 PM

¡**Regalos** para todos los gustos!

los anillos

los aretes de oro

las joyas

los bolsos de material sintético

las pulseras de plata

el collar de perlas

las billeteras

el cinturón de cuero

el perfume

las bufandas

los pañuelos

el paraguas

¡Este mes
**descuentos**
del **20%**
en todas
las joyas!

¡Visítenos en el local 207!

Esta bufanda está **demasiado larga**.

¿Prefiere una más **corta**?

Preferimos **usar la escalera mecánica**.

Yo prefiero usar **el ascensor**.

## Para conversar

*T*o talk about buying presents:

Mi hermana me dijo que quiere **recibir** un bolso para su cumpleaños.
*My sister told me that she wants to get a purse for her birthday.*

¿Te gusta esta bufanda para ella? Es **perfecta** y está muy **barata**.
*Do you like this scarf for her? It's perfect and it's very cheap.*

Sí, y es **bastante linda**.
*Yes, and it is quite pretty.*

### Para decir más

| | |
|---|---|
| la caja de bombones | *box of chocolates* |
| el moño | *bow (for a gift)* |
| el obsequio | *present* |
| la pluma | *fountain pen* |
| el ramo de flores | *bouquet of flowers* |

### En otros países

| | |
|---|---|
| el anillo | *la argolla (Chile)* |
| | *la sortija (México)* |
| los aretes | *los zarcillos (Venezuela)* |
| | *los aros (Argentina)* |
| | *los pendientes (Costa Rica, España)* |
| el bolso | *la cartera (Chile, Puerto Rico)* |
| | *la bolsa (México, Guatemala)* |
| el paraguas | *la sombrilla (Puerto Rico, México)* |
| la pulsera | *el brazalete (Argentina)* |

### 1   ¿Cuál es la palabra?

Adivina las palabras según las pistas. *(Guess the words according to the clues.)*

1. Es una joya que llevas en el dedo.

2. Es un artículo de cuero donde pones tu dinero.

3. Es algo que necesitas cuando llueve.

4. Lo usas para ir de un piso a otro.

5. Es un artículo de cuero que usas con el pantalón o la falda.

6. Es una joya que te pones en el brazo.

7. Es un sinónimo de bonito.

## 2 ¿Qué les gustaría recibir de regalo? 🎧

Selecciona la letra de la foto que corresponde con lo que oyes.

A

B

C

D

E

F

## 3 Los artículos de la tienda

Contesta las siguientes preguntas.

1. ¿Cuándo llevas bufanda?
2. ¿Qué joyas te gusta llevar?
3. ¿Qué puede ser de oro?
4. ¿De qué materiales puede ser una billetera?
5. ¿Cuándo llevas pañuelo?

6. ¿Qué puede ser de cuero?
7. ¿Te gusta usar perfume? Explica.
8. ¿Qué puede ser de plata?
9. ¿Qué puede ser de perlas?
10. ¿Prefieres usar bufandas largas o cortas?

## 4 Regalos para toda tu familia

Prepara una lista de sugerencias de regalos para toda tu familia como la de abajo.
Da por lo menos cuatro sugerencias para cada miembro de tu familia.

| Lista de regalos para mi familia | | |
|---|---|---|
| para mamá | para papá | para mi hermano/a |
| unos aretes de perlas | | |
| | | |
| | | |
| | | |

# Diálogo

## Busco un regalo

**Daniel:** Busco un regalo, bueno, bonito y barato.

**Señora:** ¿Para hombre o para mujer?

**Daniel:** Para mujer.

**Señora:** ¿Qué le parece una pulsera de oro?

**Daniel:** No. Ella dijo que joyas no.

**Señora:** Entonces, ¿qué le parece este perfume?

**Daniel:** El perfume es perfecto.

### 5 ¿Qué recuerdas?

1. ¿Qué busca Daniel?
2. ¿Qué tipo de regalo busca?
3. ¿Para quién busca algo Daniel?
4. ¿Va a comprar Daniel una pulsera de oro?
5. ¿Qué le parece perfecto?

### 6 Algo personal

1. Cuando buscas un regalo, ¿lo buscas bueno, bonito y barato? Explica.

2. ¿Piensas que es más fácil comprar un regalo para un hombre o una mujer?

3. En tu opinión, ¿qué regalos piensas que son para hombres? ¿Y para mujeres?

### 7 Bueno, bonito y barato

Selecciona la letra de la ilustración que corresponde con lo que las siguientes personas buscan.

A

B

# Gramática

## Diminutives

- Diminutives can be used to show affection or convey the idea that something is small.
- To form the diminutive of a noun, replace the final vowel with the endings *-ito*, *-ita*, *-itos*, and *-itas*.

    *Ana* → *An**ita***

**Note:** Some words may require a spelling change: *poco* → *po**quito***.

- For nouns that end in a consonant, add the endings *-cito*, *-cita*, *-citos*, or *-citas* to the complete word.

    *collar* → *collar**cito***

- Additional diminutive endings you may encounter include: *-illo*, *-illa*, *-uelo*, *-uela*, *-ico*, and *-ica*.
- Although many exceptions exist for the diminutive forms, most are easily recognized: *hotelito (hotel)*, *Danielito (Daniel)*. It is best to learn the variations as you encounter them since they can vary from country to country and even from one person to another within countries.

### 8  Todo es pequeñito 🎧

Cambia las siguientes palabras al diminutivo.

1. el bolso
2. la billetera
3. el cinturón
4. el pañuelo
5. la bufanda
6. el collar
7. las botas
8. los guantes
9. el suéter

### 9  ¿De dónde vienen? 🎧

Indica la palabra original.

**MODELO**  el regalillo → el regalo

1. la chaquetilla
2. el zapatico
3. las joyitas
4. el trajecillo
5. la portezuela
6. el sombrerito
7. la corbatica
8. el jardincito
9. el hijuelo

## ¡Comunicación!

### 10  Comprar un regalo 👥  Interpersonal Communication

With a partner, imagine you and a close friend are in a department store shopping for a graduation gift for someone you both like a lot. Role-play using the diminutive to refer to the objects you are considering buying and to convey your affection for the person for whom you are shopping.

**MODELO**  A: Mira estas pulseritas tan lindas para Sarita. Me gustan mucho.

B: No me gustan mucho. Me gusta más este bolsito.

A: El bolsito no está mal, pero prefiero algo un poquito mejor para Sarita.

B: ¿Qué te parece este collar de perlitas?

# Gramática

## Preterite Tense of *leer*, *oír*, *ver*, *decir*, *hacer*, and *tener*

- The verbs **leer**, **oír**, **ver**, **decir**, **hacer**, and **tener** all have irregularities in the preterite tense.
- In the verbs *leer* and *oír*, the *i* between the two vowels changes to *y* in the *él*, *ella*, *Ud.*, and *ellos*, *ellas*, *Uds.* forms. In the other forms, *leer* and *oír* require an accent mark on the *i* to separate vowel sounds and to indicate how these words are pronounced.

| leer | | | |
|---|---|---|---|
| yo | leí | nosotros/as | leímos |
| tú | leíste | vosotros/as | leísteis |
| Ud. él ella | leyó | Uds. ellos ellas | leyeron |

| oír | | | |
|---|---|---|---|
| yo | oí | nosotros/as | oímos |
| tú | oíste | vosotros/as | oísteis |
| Ud. él ella | oyó | Uds. ellos ellas | oyeron |

- The preterite tense of the verb *ver* uses the regular *-er* verb endings, but without any accent marks.

| ver | | | |
|---|---|---|---|
| yo | vi | nosotros/as | vimos |
| tú | viste | vosotros/as | visteis |
| Ud. él ella | vio | Uds. ellos ellas | vieron |

- Learning the irregular preterite-tense stem of *decir (dij)*, *hacer (hic)*, and *tener (tuv)* and the endings *-e*, *-iste*, *-o*, *-imos*, *-isteis*, and *-ieron* will help you to use the preterite tense of these three irregular verbs. You will notice that *tener* is conjugated exactly like *estar* minus the *es-* prefix.

**Note:** The *c* in the preterite tense stem for *hacer* changes to *z* in *hizo*; *dijeron* is also an exception to the above because no *i* is required for the preterite ending.

| decir | | | |
|---|---|---|---|
| yo | dije | nosotros/as | dijimos |
| tú | dijiste | vosotros/as | dijisteis |
| Ud. él ella | dijo | Uds. ellos ellas | dijeron |

| hacer | | | |
|---|---|---|---|
| yo | hice | nosotros/as | hicimos |
| tú | hiciste | vosotros/as | hicisteis |
| Ud. él ella | hizo | Uds. ellos ellas | hicieron |

| tener | | | |
|---|---|---|---|
| yo | tuve | nosotros/as | tuvimos |
| tú | tuviste | vosotros/as | tuvisteis |
| Ud. él ella | tuvo | Uds. ellos ellas | tuvieron |

## 11  No te oí

Imagina que estás en un restaurante con tu familia donde todos te dicen algo al mismo tiempo y no oyes algunos de los comentarios. ¿Qué dices?

**MODELO**  mi papá

**¿Qué dijo mi papá? No lo oí.**

1. mi mamá
2. el mesero
3. mi primo y mi tía
4. tú
5. mis hermanas
6. mi hermano

*¿Qué dijo mi padre?*

## 12  ¿Qué le(s) gustaría recibir?

Di qué dijeron las siguientes personas que les gustaría recibir de regalo para su cumpleaños, según las indicaciones.

**MODELO**  mi padre

**Mi padre dijo que le gustaría recibir unos pañuelos.**

1. yo
2. mis primos
3. mi tía
4. mi mamá

5. mi hermano
6. nosotros
7. tú
8. Uds.

## 13  ¿Qué hice?

Di cuáles de las siguientes cosas hiciste o no hiciste ayer.

**MODELO**  leer un libro

**Sí, leí un libro ayer. / No, no leí un libro ayer.**

1. tener que ir a la tienda para comprar pan y leche
2. oír un CD de mi cantante favorito
3. ver televisión
4. hacer la tarea de español
5. decir una mentira
6. comprar un regalo para alguien
7. tener un examen
8. leer una revista

## 14 ¿Qué pasó en la tienda por departamentos?

Di lo que hicieron algunas personas el viernes pasado en la tienda, según las ilustraciones y los verbos indicados.

**MODELO** comprar

**Algunas personas compraron joyas.**

**1.** arreglar

**2.** tener

**3.** oír

**4.** leer

**5.** hacer

**6.** ver

## ¡Comunicación!

## 15 El fin de semana pasado     Interpersonal/Presentational Communication

Con un(a) compañero/a de clase, escriban un mini-diálogo de las actividades que hicieron el fin de semana pasado. Luego presenten el mini-diálogo a la clase.

**MODELO**

A: ¿Qué hiciste el sábado?

B: Vi una película estupenda con mi familia.

A: ¿Y qué más hiciste?

B: Tuve que ir al centro comercial para comprar un regalo. ¿Y tú? ¿Qué hiciste?

## ¡Comunicación!

## 16 En la tienda de joyas     Interpersonal Communication

Imagina que trabajas en una tienda de joyas los sábados y tu compañero/a trabaja en la misma tienda los domingos. Hablen de las actividades que hicieron y decidan quién tuvo que hacer más trabajo.

**MODELO**

A: El sábado tuve muchas cosas que hacer en el trabajo.

B: ¿Qué tuviste que hacer?

A: Primero, tuve que llegar muy temprano...

**Pregunta clave**

What can you learn about a country from the products and services it provides?

*Orquídea de Ecuador*

# Los productos de Ecuador

Si conoces[1] los productos y servicios de un país, puedes comprender mejor su clima, su industria, sus platos típicos y el tipo de trabajo que realizan sus habitantes. Ecuador se llama "el país de las orquídeas", y hoy en día es uno de los principales exportadores de flores en todo el mundo.

Las temperaturas estables, la alta humedad y su rico suelo[2] hacen de Ecuador el lugar ideal para cultivar flores. Estas mismas características climáticas ayudan a Ecuador a ser uno de los mayores productores mundiales de bananas. ¡Produce alrededor de 8 millones de toneladas de bananas al año!

Ecuador también produce camarones[3]. Hoy en día, hay muchas granjas[4] de camarones que exportan al mundo entero. Al estar localizado en la costa del Pacífico, Ecuador tiene las condiciones naturales ideales para el cultivo[5] de este crustáceo. Tanto las bananas como los camarones forman parte de muchos de los platos típicos de Ecuador. Ecuador es también un exportador importante de petróleo y de cacao. Su especial geografía y su clima tropical le permiten producir productos únicos.

*Bananas ecuatorianas*

[1] you know, are familiar with [2] rich soil [3] shrimp [4] farms [5] farming

**Búsqueda:** productos de ecuador, servicios que ofrece ecuador

## Productos

Uno de los productos más representativos de Ecuador es el sombrero de paja toquilla (*toquilla straw*) o sombrero panamá. Sí, leíste bien, sombrero panamá. El nombre nació porque muchas personas que trabajaron en la construcción del Canal de Panamá lo usaron para protegerse del sol. Luego, cuando terminó la construcción del canal, el presidente Theodore Roosevelt visitó el sitio llevando un sombrero de estos y desde ese momento el sombrero se hizo popular en todo el mundo.

*Un sombrero panamá*

El sombrero panamá se caracteriza por su ligereza (*lightness*), frescura, elegancia y calidad (*quality*).

## 17 Comprensión | Interpretive Communication

1. ¿Qué aspectos de la geografía ecuatoriana favorecen la producción de flores?
2. ¿Qué productos típicos puedes encontrar a menudo en la cocina ecuatoriana?
3. ¿Por qué se le llama sombrero panamá al sombrero tradicional de Ecuador?

## 18 Analiza

1. In what ways does a country benefit from exporting its products?
2. What are some of the factors that determine the products and services a country has to offer?

# Unas islas únicas en el mundo 🎧

*Una iguana toma el sol*

Uno de los servicios más importantes que Ecuador ofrece es el turismo, y las islas Galápagos es uno de los destinos más famosos en Ecuador. Las Galápagos son un archipiélago de islas volcánicas que se extienden a lo largo de[1] la línea ecuatorial.

Cinco corrientes marinas se unen[2] en las Galápagos creando una ecología marina única en el mundo. Debido a la singularidad de estas islas y a sus aguas hay un gran número de especies que solo viven en estas islas, como tortugas gigantes, iguanas, delfines, albatros y más de cincuenta especies de peces. Charles Darwin, el naturalista inglés, escribió un estudio sobre estas especies durante su viaje por las islas. El estudio sirvió de base para su famosa teoría de la evolución de las especies. Las Galápagos fueron declaradas Patrimonio de la Humanidad[3] por la UNESCO en 1978 y sus aguas se convirtieron en 1990 en un santuario para ballenas[4]. Estas islas atraen aproximadamente a unas 70.000 personas al año. Pero los ecuatorianos son conscientes de la fragilidad de este ecosistema y hacen todo lo posible para protegerlo.

*Las islas Galápagos*

Las Galápagos son vigiladas cuidadosamente[5] por científicos y organizaciones ecológicas. Las islas Galápagos contribuyen a incrementar[6] la riqueza natural de Ecuador al mismo tiempo que proporcionan unos ingresos[7] importantes para la economía del país.

[1] along　[2] converge　[3] a World Heritage Site　[4] whales　[5] carefully monitored
[6] increase　[7] provide revenues

🔍 **Búsqueda:** galápagos, patrimonio de la humanidad

## 19 Comprensión — Interpretive Communication

1. ¿Qué tipo de islas son las Galápagos?
2. ¿Por qué son las Galápagos unas islas tan especiales?
3. ¿Cómo fue reconocida la importancia de estas islas a nivel mundial?

## 20 Analiza

1. How do the Galapagos contribute to increase Ecuador's wealth?
2. How is it possible for Ecuador to promote tourism at the Galapagos and at the same time protect the islands' ecosystem?

### Comparaciones

Are there natural reserves in the United States that are similar to the Galapagos? What animals and plants would you find there?

### Perspectivas

"Because of their nature and biodiversity, as well as their unique ecosystems, these islands are considered an important place for humanity. As administrators, we have the responsibility of preserving them and guaranteeing their sustainable development."

What does this translated quote by Edwin Naula, Director of *Parque Nacional Galápagos*, reveal about the attitude of Ecuadorians toward the islands as a service to the rest of the world?

# Vocabulario 2

## ¡Vamos a pagar! 🎧

el dependiente

la caja

las ofertas
-10% -20% -35% -50%

pagar en efectivo

el cambio

la tarjeta de crédito
pagar a crédito

el recibo

Me gusta mucho **la calidad** de este suéter.

Me gusta **el tamaño** del bolso. No es ni grande ni pequeño.

Quiero **cambiar** estos zapatos.

## Para conversar 🎧

***T****o talk about shopping:*

Gracias por venir **conmigo** a la tienda.
*Thanks for coming with me to the store.*

¿Te gusta el tamaño de esta billetera?
*Do you like the size of this wallet?*

Sí, y no es muy **cara** porque está en oferta.
Entonces vamos a **ahorrar** dinero.
*Yes, and it's not very expensive because it's on sale.*
*So we're going to save money.*

¡Por eso me gusta ir **contigo** de compras!
*This is why I like to go shopping with you!*

### Para decir más

| el escaparate | shop window |
| la etiqueta | label, tag |
| el mostrador | counter |
| el probador | fitting room |

### En otros países

| el/la dependiente | el vendedor, la vendedora (Argentina, Uruguay) el empleado, la empleada (varios países) |
| la oferta | la rebaja (España) la venta (Argentina) la barata (México) |

## 21  ¿Cuál es la palabra?

Completa las oraciones con una palabra apropiada según el contexto.

1. Voy a pagar con la tarjeta de crédito porque no tengo __.
2. Gracias por venir __. No me gusta ir al centro comercial solo.
3. Aquí tiene su __. Lo va a necesitar si quiere cambiar algo.
4. Esta chaqueta me queda grande. Necesito una chaqueta de __ más pequeño.
5. Voy a preguntarle al __ cuánto cuesta esta pulserita.
6. Estos aretes son muy baratos porque están en __.
7. No debes comprar demasiado. Tienes que __ tu dinero.
8. En esta tienda solo vendemos artículos de buena __.

*tamaño*
*conmigo*
*recibo*
*efectivo*
*dependiente*
*ahorrar*
*efectivo*
*calidad*
*oferta*

## 💬 ¡Comunicación!

## 22  ¿Qué compraste?  👥  Interpersonal Communication

Imagina que te encuentras con un(a) compañero/a en el centro comercial. Túrnense para hablar de las cosas que compraron. Digan cuánto les costó cada cosa y cómo la pagaron.

MODELO  A: Mira, compré este anillo de oro. ¿Te gusta?

B: ¡Qué lindo! ¿Te costó mucho?

A: Sí, bastante, pero pagué con tarjeta de crédito. Y tú, ¿qué compraste?

*Este vestido me queda perfecto.*

Escoge la letra de la respuesta correcta a lo que oyes.

**A.** Sí, es una seda muy buena.

**B.** Necesitas el recibo.

**C.** Pago con tarjeta de crédito.

**D.** No, está en oferta.

**E.** Son tres dólares con cincuenta.

**F.** Sí, voy contigo.

## 24 Decir lo opuesto

Completa las siguientes oraciones para decir lo opuesto de las palabras indicadas.

**MODELO** No compré el collar *caro,* preferí el collar **barato**.

*Compré un perfume muy caro.*

1. No vi cinturones *en oferta*, solo vi cinturones demasiado __.
2. No le pagué a *la dependienta*, le pagué __.
3. No me gustó el bolso *de tamaño grande*, me gustó el bolso __.
4. No me gusta ir de compras *contigo*, porque a ti no te gusta ir de compras __.
5. No compré ningún perfume *de mala calidad*, compré un perfume __.
6. No pagué *a crédito*, pagué __ en una de las cajas.
7. No vi los aretes *caros*, vi los aretes __.
8. No me gustan las bufandas *cortas*, prefiero las __.
9. No vi aretes *feos*; solo vi aretes __.

# Diálogo

## ¿Cómo va a pagar?

**Daniel:** ¿Cuánto cuesta el perfume?

**Señora:** Está en oferta. Cuesta treinta dólares.

**Daniel:** Sí, no está caro. Lo llevo.

**Señora:** ¿Cómo va a pagar? ¿En efectivo o a crédito?

**Daniel:** Voy a pagar en efectivo.

**Señora:** Aquí tiene diez dólares de cambio y su recibo.

**Daniel:** Muchas gracias.

## 25 ¿Qué recuerdas?

1. ¿Qué está en oferta?
2. ¿Cuánto cuesta el perfume?
3. ¿Cómo va a pagar Daniel?
4. ¿Cuánto es el cambio?
5. ¿Qué más le da la señora a Daniel?

*¿Cuánto cuestan los perfumes?*

## 26 Algo personal

1. ¿Qué compras en oferta?
2. ¿Prefieres pagar a crédito o en efectivo? Explica.
3. ¿Te gusta dar regalos caros o baratos? Explica.
4. ¿Qué haces con el dinero que recibes de cambio?

*En esta tienda todo está en oferta.*

## 27 ¿Sí o no?

¿Son lógicos los diálogos? Corrige lo que no es lógico.

# Gramática

## Prepositions

How many of the following prepositions (*preposiciones*) in Spanish do you remember?

a  de  para  con  desde

por  en  sin  hasta  sobre

---

### 28 | Unos aretes para mi hermana

Completa las siguientes oraciones, escogiendo una palabra apropiada del recuadro.

| con | de | desde | en |
|-----|-----|-------|-----|
| para | por | sin | sobre |

1. ¿Cuánto cuestan los aretes que están __ aquella mesa?

2. Los aretes son __ oro y cuestan cien dólares.

3. ¿Va a pagarlos __ efectivo?

4. No, voy a pagarlos __ tarjeta de crédito.

5. Los aretes son __ mi hermana.

6. Mi hermana usa aretes __ pequeña.

7. Ella nunca sale a la calle __ aretes.

8. Muchas gracias __ su compra.

---

## Using Prepositions

- You have already learned to use prepositions with prepositional pronouns, for example, with the preposition *a* to add emphasis or clarity: ***A ella*** *le gusta ir de compras con sus amigas.* The following prepositional pronouns may also be used with the other prepositions you have learned.

| Los pronombres después de la preposiciones | | | |
|---|---|---|---|
| (para) **mí** | *(for) me* | (para) **nosotros/as** | *(for) us* |
| (para) **ti** | *(for) you* | (para) **vosotros/as** | *(for) you* |
| (para) **Ud.** | *(for) you* | (para) **Uds.** | *(for) you* |
| (para) **él** | *(for) him* | (para) **ellos** | *(for) them* |
| (para) **ella** | *(for) her* | (para) **ellas** | *(for) them* |

- Two exceptions are the words ***conmigo*** (with me), which is used instead of *con* followed by *mí*, and ***contigo*** (with you), which is used instead of *con* followed by *ti*.

| | |
|---|---|
| *¿Quieres ir al cine* ***conmigo****?* | Do you want to go to the movies **with me**? |
| *Sí, me gustaría ir al cine* ***contigo****.* | Yes, I would like to go to the movies **with you**. |

## 29  Un regalo para Miguel

Completa este correo electrónico con palabras del recuadro. Puedes usar las palabras más de una vez.

| conmigo | contigo | ella | él | mí | nosotros | ti |
|---|---|---|---|---|---|---|

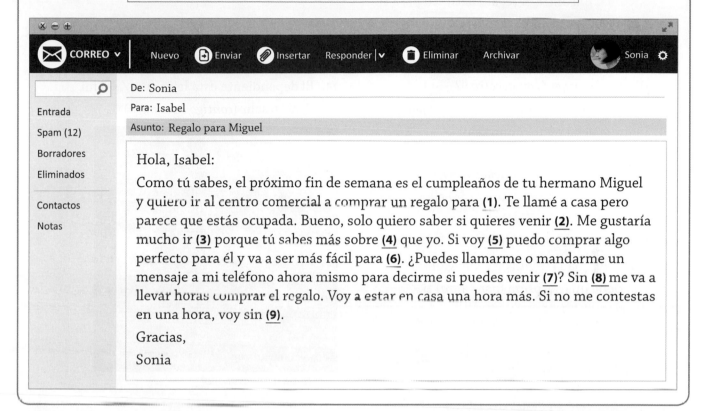

**De:** Sonia

**Para:** Isabel

**Asunto:** Regalo para Miguel

Hola, Isabel:

Como tú sabes, el próximo fin de semana es el cumpleaños de tu hermano Miguel y quiero ir al centro comercial a comprar un regalo para **(1)**. Te llamé a casa pero parece que estás ocupada. Bueno, solo quiero saber si quieres venir **(2)**. Me gustaría mucho ir **(3)** porque tú sabes más sobre **(4)** que yo. Si voy **(5)** puedo comprar algo perfecto para él y va a ser más fácil para **(6)**. ¿Puedes llamarme o mandarme un mensaje a mi teléfono ahora mismo para decirme si puedes venir **(7)**? Sin **(8)** me va a llevar horas comprar el regalo. Voy a estar en casa una hora más. Si no me contestas en una hora, voy sin **(9)**.

Gracias,

Sonia

## 30  ¿Puedes venir conmigo?

Trabajando con un(a) compañero/a de clase, alternen en hacer las invitaciones indicadas y en dar excusas para cada invitación.

**MODELO**    al cine

A:  ¿Puedes venir conmigo al cine?

B:  No, no puedo ir contigo porque no tengo dinero.

1. el banco
2. a comprar unos zapatos que están en oferta
3. la tienda de artículos electrónicos
4. la tienda por departamentos
5. el centro comercial
6. a cambiar un cinturón que compré y ahora no me gusta

*¿Puedes venir conmigo al cine?*

## 31 La preposición correcta

Escoge la preposición correcta según el contexto.

**MODELO**  Encontré el regalo perfecto (*por / para*) ti.
Encontré el regalo perfecto **para** ti.

1. Nos fuimos de compras (*de / sin*) ella.
2. Fuimos al cine (*sin / menos*) ti.
3. ¿Vienes (*contigo / con nosotros*)?
4. Su hija es lo más importante (*para / por*) él.
5. Siempre llevo mi teléfono celular (*conmigo / contigo*).
6. Estuvimos todos en la fiesta (*sin / menos*) tú.
7. Él tiene mucho amor (*para / con*) ellos.
8. No puedo vivir (*de / sin*) ti.
9. Trabajo (*conmigo / contigo*) todos los sábados.
10. Por favor, ¡baila (*contigo / conmigo*)!
11. Ella tiene una sorpresa (*por / para*) ti.

12. Tienes algo (*para mí / para ti*), ¿verdad?
13. ¿Vienes a la fiesta (*contigo / conmigo*)?
14. El dependiente está lejos (*por / de*) mí.
15. Quiero salir (*contigo / conmigo*).

*¿Vienes con nosotros al cine?*

## 32 Situaciones y conclusiones

Da conclusiones apropiadas para las siguientes situaciones, usando las preposiciones y pronombres apropiados. Sigue las indicaciones entre paréntesis.

**MODELO**  **Situación:** Él llegó a la casa a las cuatro de la tarde, su hermana llegó a las cuatro menos diez y tú llegaste a la casa a las tres y media. (*Él / después de*)
**Conclusión: Él llegó después de Uds.**

1. **Situación:** Tú llegaste después porque vives más lejos de la tienda que yo. (*yo / más cerca de*)
2. **Situación:** Mi amiga y yo nos compramos regalos la una para la otra. Yo compré un regalo para mi amiga. (*ella / para*)
3. **Situación:** Son las cinco de la tarde y mi amiga y yo estamos mirando zapatos en el departamento de mujeres y tú y tu amiga están mirando bolsas en el mismo departamento. (*Uds. / al lado de*)
4. **Situación:** Tu profesor me dijo que vive en la Calle 128, N° 151, y mi familia y yo vivimos en la Calle 128, N° 153. (*él / cerca de*)
5. **Situación:** Yo voy a recibir un bolso de mi amigo y tú también vas a recibir un bolso de tu amigo. (*nosotras / de*)

# ¡Comunicación!

Compramos muchos regalos.

## 33 Necesito comprar un regalo 👥 Interpersonal Communication

Imagina que estás en una tienda por departamentos con un amigo y que necesitas comprar unos regalos. Con un(a) compañero/a habla de los artículos que te gustaría comprar, para quién son y cuánto puedes pagar. Tu compañero/a te puede ayudar con la selección de los regalos.

**MODELO**
A: Me gustaría comprar unos aretes para mi hermana.
B: En esa mesa hay algunos de plata y están en oferta.
A: Sí, pero a ella no le gustan las joyas de plata.
B: Entonces, ¿por qué no le compras estos aretes de oro con perlas?
A: Sí, son muy lindos pero también muy caros y, ¡yo necesito ahorrar!

# ¡Comunicación!

## 34 En la tienda por departamentos 👥 Interpersonal Communication

Con un(a) compañero/a de clase, preparen un diálogo de cinco o seis oraciones sobre el proceso de comprar un artículo. Uno de Uds. es el dependiente y la otra persona es el cliente. Pueden hablar de lo que el cliente quiere comprar, el precio, la calidad, el tamaño y cómo va a pagar. Recuerden usar la forma apropiada de las preposiciones.

**MODELO**
A: Quiero comprar un perfume para mi prima.
B: Si viene conmigo le puedo enseñar algunos perfumes.
A: Quiero un perfume no muy caro pero de buena calidad.
B: Este es muy bueno y lo tenemos en oferta. Cuesta treinta dólares.
A: Me gusta mucho y pienso que a mi hermana le va a gustar también. Lo llevo.
B: ¿Cómo va a pagar, en efectivo o con tarjeta de crédito?

# ¡Comunicación!

## 35 Nos fuimos de compras 👥 Presentational Communication

Interview five students and ask them what item they bought the last time they went shopping and for whom. Record their answers in a table and then report your findings to the class.

**MODELO**
A: ¿Qué compraste la última vez que fuiste de compras?
B: Compré un suéter rojo de lana para mí.
En resumen: La última vez que Marta fue de compras compró un
suéter rojo de lana para ella.

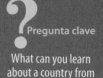

## ¡Comunicación!

**36 Un regalo especial** · **Interpretive Communication**

Estás en Ecuador visitando Quito y quieres comprarle un sombrero de paja toquilla a tu papá. Lee el anuncio de esta tienda y contesta las preguntas.

SOMBRERÍA **PÓLIT**

**VENTA DE SOMBREROS MUY ELEGANTES HECHOS A MANO EN ECUADOR**

Ofrecemos diferentes tamaños y colores.

Nuestros sombreros de paja toquilla son elaborados en Ecuador con paja extraída del bosque húmedo tropical de Santa Elena y el sur de Manabí. La fabricación de nuestros sombreros requiere un proceso que lleva entre un día y ocho meses de trabajo, según su calidad y finura.

Sombrero Fino: $145
Sombrero Súper Fino: $195
Sombrero Extra Fino: $295

**Abierto de lunes a sábado de 9:00 hs. a 20:00 hs.**

1. ¿Dónde hacen estos sombreros?
2. ¿Cuánto tiempo lleva fabricar un sombrero de paja toquilla?
3. Según el anuncio, ¿de dónde viene la paja para hacer los sombreros?
4. ¿A qué hora cierran la tienda el martes?
5. ¿Qué tipos de sombreros venden?
6. ¿Cuánto cuesta cada tipo de sombrero?
7. ¿Piensas que los sombreros son caros o baratos?
8. ¿Cuántos días a la semana está abierta la sombrería Pólit?
9. ¿A qué hora abren la tienda? ¿A qué hora cierran?

## ¡Comunicación!

**37 ¡Vamos a Galápagos!** · **Presentational Communication**

Con un(a) compañero/a preparen un folleto (*brochure*) sobre las atracciones turísticas de las islas Galápagos. Usen la lectura "*Unas islas únicas en el mundo*" y la internet para buscar información sobre los servicios que estas islas ofrecen a los turistas. Incluyan información sobre las excursiones de turismo ecológico, la geografía de las islas, el clima, los animales y las plantas que pueden ver allí. Usen fotos o ilustraciones para hacer su folleto más interesante. Luego presenten el folleto a la clase.

# Lectura ⓐ

## Antes de leer

### 38 Preparación

1. Is there anything handmade in your home? What is it? Where was it made?

2. Have you ever shopped at a street market? What did you learn or gain from the experience?

### 39 ¿Qué va a decir?

Look at the title of the text and the photo captions. Then, write at least three ideas that you think may come up in the reading.

### Estrategia

**Predict ideas**

When preparing to read a text, first look for all the clues that can help you predict the topic or topics to be presented. The title, of course, will give you the general topic, but photos and illustrations can fill in many details. Try to put all the clues together and form some ideas of what the text will probably include.

# El mercado de Otavalo 🎧

El mundialmente reconocido mercado de artesanías de los sábados, en Otavalo, es uno de los más famosos en toda la región andina. Los tejedores[1] indígenas que habitan en los pueblos[2] cerca de Otavalo se encuentran entre los más talentosos de Ecuador. Los otavaleños, ingeniosos para adaptar sus productos a las demandas del mercado, han ganado[3] no solo reconocimiento internacional sino también prosperidad.

El mercado de los sábados es el más grande y famoso de Ecuador, pero cualquier[4] día de la semana es posible comprar en el laberíntico mercado de artesanías de la Plaza de Los Ponchos. Entre los artículos más importantes se cuentan telas exquisitamente tejidas[5], ponchos de lana, sombreros, suéteres tejidos a mano, mantas[6], bufandas, joyas y hasta instrumentos musicales andinos.

[1] weavers  [2] towns  [3] have gained  [4] any  [5] woven fabrics  [6] blankets

El mercado de Otavalo

Un hombre indígena tejiendo

También los sábados, muchos visitantes llegan temprano en la mañana al mercado de animales, donde hay desde llamas hasta caballos y perros. Este mercado se localiza a la salida de Otavalo y puede ser visitado antes del mercado artesanal… También es posible visitar el mercado de alimentos y enseres del hogar[1] que se encuentra muy cerca del artesanal.

Otavalo está a dos horas al norte de Quito, en la región andina, a una altitud de 2.500 metros sobre el nivel del mar. Su población es de alrededor de 40.000 habitantes.

[1] home goods

*Una otavaleña vendiendo sombreros de lana*

*Cuyes para la venta en el mercado de animales pequeños*

## 40 Comprensión 🎧 Interpretive Communication

1. ¿De dónde son los mejores tejedores de Ecuador?
2. Nombra cuatro cosas que se venden en el mercado de Otavalo.
3. ¿Dónde está ubicado (*located*) Otavalo?

## 41 Analiza

1. What marketing strategy do the *otavaleños* have in common with sellers of modern products?
2. Would a modern shopping center make more sense in Otavalo than a traditional open-air market? What might be some advantages and disadvantages of each?

# Repaso de la Lección B

Selecciona la foto que corresponde con lo que oyes.

| A | B | C | D | E |

**B   Vocabulario: En el centro comercial** (pp. 428–429, 438–439)

Completa las oraciones con la palabra correcta entre paréntesis, según el contexto.

1. Este sombrerito es muy (*caro / barato*) porque está en oferta.

2. Voy a comprar un collar de (*perlas / algodón*) para mi mamá.

3. Señor, los sombreros están en el primer piso. Puede usar (*la escalera mecánica / la caja*).

4. Esta bufanda está demasiado larga. ¿Tiene una más (*barata / corta*)?

5. No tengo dinero. Voy a pagar (*en efectivo / con tarjeta de crédito*).

**C   Gramática: ¿Qué hicieron?** (p. 433)

Di qué hicieron las siguientes personas, usando las pistas que se dan.

**MODELO**   mi amigo: leer una revista / y / ver una película

**Mi amigo leyó una revista y vio una película.**

1. tu madre: tener que ir a trabajar a la tienda / y / arreglar los perfumes y los collares de perlas

2. tu hermana: comprar unos aretes de plata / y / tener que hacer unos quehaceres

3. mis tías: hacer un viaje a las islas Galápagos / pero / olvidar llevar sus trajes de baño

4. él: leer un libro muy interesante / y / ver una película divertida en el cine

5. Uds.: tener que comprar un regalo para ella / y / hacerlo por la internet

6. mis hermanos: hacer la tarea / y / oír música con sus amigos

**D   Gramática: Preposiciones con pronombres** (p. 442)

Completa las oraciones, usando el pronombre correcto según las pistas en paréntesis.

**MODELO**   Marta invita a **nosotras** al centro comercial porque somos buenas amigas. (*us*)

1. Estoy aquí por __. (*you, inf.*)

2. Janet compró un regalo para __. (*him*)

3. Ella va de compras __ todos los sábados. (*with me*)

4. Lola, ¿está mi hermana __ en las tiendas? (*with you*)

5. Yo puedo ir a comprarle un regalo a mi mamá sin __. (*you, inf.*)

6. El suéter azul es de __. (*his*)

Completa la siguiente gráfica con la información sobre la geografía, el clima, los productos y los servicios que ofrece Ecuador.

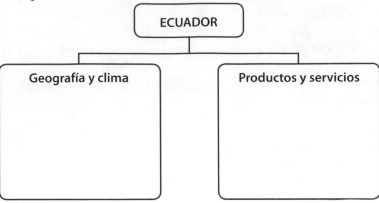

## Vocabulario

| Para describir |
| --- |
| barato/a |
| bastante |
| caro/a |
| corto/a |
| demasiado |
| largo/a |
| lindo/a |
| perfecto/a |
| sintético/a |

| En la tienda | |
| --- | --- |
| el anillo | la escalera mecánica |
| el arete | la joya |
| el ascensor | el material |
| la billetera | la oferta |
| el bolso | el oro |
| la bufanda | el pañuelo |
| la caja | el paraguas |
| la calidad | el perfume |
| el cambio | la perla |
| el cinturón | la plata |
| el collar | la pulsera |
| el crédito | el recibo |
| el cuero | el regalo |
| el dependiente, | el tamaño |
| la dependienta | la tarjeta (de crédito) |
| el efectivo | |

| Verbos |
| --- |
| ahorrar |
| cambiar |
| pagar |
| recibir |
| usar |

| Expresiones y otras palabras |
| --- |
| a crédito |
| conmigo |
| contigo |
| en efectivo |
| estar en oferta |

## Gramática

| Preterite tense of irregular verbs: *leer, oír, ver, decir, hacer,* and *tener* | | | |
| --- | --- | --- | --- |
| **leer** | | **oír** | |
| leí | leímos | oí | oímos |
| leíste | leísteis | oíste | oísteis |
| leyó | leyeron | oyó | oyeron |
| **ver** | | **decir** | |
| vi | vimos | dije | dijimos |
| viste | visteis | dijiste | dijisteis |
| vio | vieron | dijo | dijeron |
| **hacer** | | **tener** | |
| hice | hicimos | tuve | tuvimos |
| hiciste | hicisteis | tuviste | tuvisteis |
| hizo | hicieron | tuvo | tuvieron |

# *Para concluir*

## Proyectos

?  Pregunta clave

What can you learn about a country from the products and services it provides?

### A  ¡Manos a la obra!  👥

In a small group, research three famous markets in the Spanish-speaking world, such as Otavalo (Ecuador), Chichicastenango (Guatemala), and Pisac (Peru). Compare and contrast the three, using diagrams or charts to make the comparisons clear. Include characteristics such as who buys there, products sold, location, days and hours of operation, and any additional services or attractions offered by the markets that make them similar to, or different from, the others.

*Mercado de Chichicastenango*

### B  En resumen

Review what you have learned in this unit about Panama and Ecuador. On the chart below, list the products and services offered by each country. Explain how each of those products or services reveals an aspect of that country.

| País | Producto o servicio | Lo que aprendí |
|------|--------------------|----------------|
| Panamá | | |
| | | |
| | | |
| | | |
| | | |
| | | |
| Ecuador | | |
| | | |
| | | |
| | | |
| | | |
| | | |

## C   ¡A escribir!

What kind of clothes do you like to wear? What accesories do you use? Write a paragraph in Spanish comparing and contrasting how you generally dress during summer and winter. What colors, fabrics, and accessories do you prefer? Incorporate vocabulary from *Unidad 9* as well as previously learned vocabulary. Use a Venn diagram to organize your ideas before you start writing.

**verano**   **invierno**

un traje de baño

un bolso de cuero

un suéter de lana

## D   La agencia de publicidad   | Conéctate: el arte y el diseño

Imagine you work for an advertising agency. Find advertisements and pictures of different clothing items from fashion magazines and the Internet, and design a poster-sized advertisement for clothing and accessories. Include in your collage various types of clothing in different colors and sizes. Then, present your poster to the class and explain each item in the advertisement, including what the people are wearing, the colors and materials of each article, the price, and why others should buy them. After all the presentations are made, students will vote on the most convincing one.

*Nos gusta la ropa de buena calidad.*

## E   Ahora, ¡hay que pagar!

In small groups, prepare a skit. Two friends are shopping and the third is a *dependiente*. The two shoppers discuss the items, the prices, and what they think of them. The *dependiente* should try to convince the shoppers to buy, making comments about how the items fit and look. When they are ready to pay, there is a discussion with the *dependiente* about the total price, whether or not anything is on sale, how the shoppers will pay, and the receipt. Make the dialogue as lively and detailed as you can. You may use props to make the skit more realistic.

*¿Cuánto cuesta este bolso?*

# Vocabulario de la Unidad 9

ahorrar to save 9B
el algodón cotton 9A
alguien someone, anyone, somebody, anybody 9A
algún, alguna some, any 9A
alguno/a some, any 9A
anaranjado/a orange (color) 9A
el anillo ring 9B
el arete earring 9B
el ascensor elevator 9B
barato/a cheap 9B
bastante quite, rather, fairly, sufficiently, enough, sufficient 9B
la billetera wallet, billfold 9B
el bolso purse, handbag 9B
la bota boot 9A
el brazo arm 9A
la bufanda scarf 9B

la cabeza head 9A
la caja cash register 9B
la calidad quality 9B
cambiar to change, to exchange 9B
el cambio change 9B
caro/a expensive 9B
el centro comercial shopping center, mall 9A
la chaqueta jacket 9A
el cinturón belt 9B
el collar necklace 9B
combinar to combine 9A
conmigo with me 9B
contar (ue) to tell (a story) 9A

contigo with you 9B
la corbata necktie 9A
corto/a short (not long) 9B
el crédito credit 9B
a crédito on credit 9B
el cuero leather 9B
el cuerpo body 9A
el dedo finger 9A
demasiado too (much) 9B
el departamento department 9A
el dependiente, la dependienta clerk 9B
el efectivo cash 9B
en efectivo in cash 9B
la escalera mecánica escalator 9B
estar en oferta to be on sale 9B
el guante glove 9A
la joya jewel 9B
el hombre man 9A
el impermeable raincoat 9A
la lana wool 9A
largo/a long 9B
lindo/a pretty 9B
la mano hand 9A
marrón brown 9A
el material material 9B
las medias pantyhose, nylons 9A
morado/a purple 9A
la mujer woman 9A
nada nothing 9A
nadie nobody 9A
ni... ni neither... nor 9A
ningún, ninguna none, not any 9A
ninguno/a none, not any 9A
o... o either... or 9A
la oferta sale 9B

*Fuimos de compras.*

el oro gold 9B
pagar to pay 9B
el pañuelo handkerchief, hanky 9B

el paraguas umbrella 9B
perfecto/a perfect 9B
el perfume perfume 9B
la perla pearl 9B
el pie foot 9A
la plerna leg 9A
el pijama pajamas 9A
la plata silver 9B
prometer to promise 9A
la pulsera bracelet 9B
quedarle (algo a alguien) to have (something) left 9A
quedarle bien a uno to fit, to be becoming 9A
recibir to receive 9B
el recibo receipt 9B
el regalo gift 9B
la ropa interior underwear 9A
rosado/a pink 9A
la seda silk 9A
sintético/a synthetic 9B
el sombrero hat 9A
el suéter sweater 9A
el tamaño size 9B
la tarjeta (de crédito) (credit) card 9B
el traje (de baño) (swim) suit 9A
usar to use 9B
las vacaciones vacation 9A
vender to sell 9A
el vestido dress 9A
el zapato bajo flat shoe 9A
el zapato de tacón high-heeled shoe 9A

## ¿Sabías que...?

Central and South America were home to great civilizations. You can get a glimpse of them in the remains of ancient cities, tall pyramids, agricultural practices, and in their descendants who populate those areas to this day.

# 10

# El fin de curso

Scan the QR code to watch this episode of *El cuarto misterioso*.

**Whom do Conchita, Ana, José, and Francisco see when they approach the house?**

A. a una mujer con una llave
B. a un hombre salir de la casa con una maleta pequeña
C. al papá de José con un mapa

*Pregunta clave*

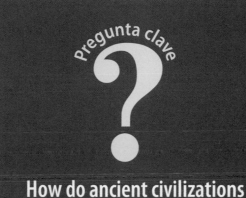

**?**

**How do ancient civilizations live on in the present?**

## Mis metas

**Lección A  I will be able to:**

▶ talk about the past school year
▶ talk about what I liked, using the preterite of **gustar**
▶ interview classmates about the school year
▶ describe my favorite Spanish-speaking country
▶ compare and contrast ancient and modern-day Peru
▶ discuss a trip to Machu Picchu

**Lección B  I will be able to:**

▶ talk about summer plans
▶ review compound verb structures: **ir a**, **tener que**, **tener ganas de**, and **acabar de**
▶ plan a trip to a Spanish-speaking country
▶ describe the ancient Mayan civilizations and their presence in Guatemala today
▶ discuss the mythology and the importance of the ***Popol Vuh***

Guatemala

Perú

Who built and lived in this ancient lost city?

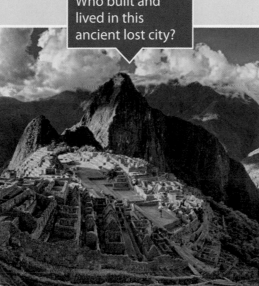

# Lección A

## Diálogo 🎧

### Fue un año divertido

**Mario:** ¡Un año más! No hay más tareas por unos meses.

**Silvia:** ¡Qué bueno! Fue un año divertido.

**Mario:** Estudié mucho.

**Silvia:** ¿Qué fue lo que más te gustó?

**Mario:** ¡Jugar al fútbol y las clases de historia!

**Silvia:** A mí me gustó más la clase de biología.

**Mario:** A mí la biología no me gusta.

**Silvia:** Sí, yo sé. Bueno, también hice nuevos amigos.

**Mario:** ¿Tus amigos del equipo de voleibol?

**Silvia:** Sí, y voy a verlos ahora. Adiós.

### 1  ¿Qué recuerdas? 🎧

1. ¿Qué no hay por unos meses?
2. ¿Quién estudió mucho?
3. ¿Qué fue lo que más le gustó a Mario?
4. ¿Qué le gustó más a Silvia?
5. ¿Qué no le gusta a Mario?
6. ¿Quién tiene amigos en el equipo de voleibol?

### 2  Algo personal 🎧

1. ¿Fue tu año divertido? Explica.
2. ¿Te gusta hacer tareas? ¿Por qué?
3. ¿Qué fue lo que más te gustó del colegio este año?
4. ¿Qué deporte jugaste más este año?

*¿Qué fue lo que más te gustó del colegio este año?*

### 3  Fue un año divertido 🎧

Di si lo que oyes es **cierto** o **falso**, según el Diálogo. Si es falso, corrige la información.

## The Preterite Tense of *gustar*

- You have already seen forms of the preterite tense of **gustar**. Remember that the verb *gustar* requires an indirect object pronoun.

| me | te | le | nos | os | les |
|----|----|----|-----|----|-----|
| **+ gustó** | | | **+ gustaron** | | |

*Me **gustó** la película de anoche.*      **I liked** last night's movie.

*¿Te **gustaron** las clases este año?*      **Did you like** your classes this year?

- Other verbs that behave in a similar way are: **hacer falta**, **importar**, and **parecer**.

### 4 ¿Qué les gustó?

¿Qué les gustó de este año escolar? Reemplaza el sujeto de la columna I con el pronombre de complemento indirecto apropiado y elige la forma correcta de **gustar**, para hablar de lo que le gustó a cada persona.

MODELO    **A mis primos y a mí nos gustaron los deportes de invierno.**

| I | II | III |
|---|----|-----|
| una amiga | | todas las clases |
| tú | | hacer nuevos amigos |
| yo | gustó | la comida de la cafetería |
| mis primos y yo | gustaron | practicar deportes |
| Ivette y María | | tocar en la banda escolar |
| tú y tus amigos | | los deportes de invierno |

## ¡Comunicación!

### 5 Una entrevista para el blog del colegio    Interpersonal/Presentational Communication

Prepara una entrevista de entre siete y diez preguntas para un(a) compañero/a sobre sus experiencias y actividades durante este año. Pregúntale sobre las cosas más importantes que hizo, las más divertidas, las más aburridas, lo que más le gustó del año, lo que menos le gustó, algo interesante que le pasó y cualquier otra información de su vida en el colegio. Luego, escribe un artículo para el blog del colegio sobre la entrevista que hiciste. Preséntalo a la clase.

### Estrategia

**The importance of reviewing**

It is important to review what you have learned during the year. No one will expect you to remember everything you learned, but reviewing will help make the transition to next year easier.

MODELO    A: **¿Qué fue lo que más te gustó del colegio este año?**

           B: **Me gustó mucho tocar en la banda, hacer nuevos amigos y la clase de español. Fue un año divertido.**

## ¡Comunicación!

### 6 Encuesta de estudiantes · Presentational Communication

Haz la siguiente encuesta a diez compañeros(as) de tu clase de español para averiguar (*to find out*) cuáles fueron sus clases favoritas este año. Primero, hazte la encuesta a ti mismo, y luego a tus compañeros(as). Finalmente, organiza los resultados del grupo en una tabla o una gráfica y preséntalos a la clase.

**ENCUESTA SOBRE LAS CLASES FAVORITAS DEL AÑO**

*Por cada una de las siguientes clases, di el número que representa mejor tu opinión.*

| | | 0 | 1 | 2 | 3 | 4 |
|---|---|---|---|---|---|---|
| 1. | el arte | ⓪ | ① | ② | ③ | ④ |
| 2. | las ciencias (biología, química, etc.) | ⓪ | ① | ② | ③ | ④ |
| 3. | la computación | ⓪ | ① | ② | ③ | ④ |
| 4. | la educación física | ⓪ | ① | ② | ③ | ④ |
| 5. | el español | ⓪ | ① | ② | ③ | ④ |
| 6. | los estudios sociales | ⓪ | ① | ② | ③ | ④ |
| 7. | la historia | ⓪ | ① | ② | ③ | ④ |
| 8. | el inglés | ⓪ | ① | ② | ③ | ④ |
| 9. | las matemáticas (álgebra, geometría, etc.) | ⓪ | ① | ② | ③ | ④ |
| 10. | la música (banda, orquesta, coro, etc.) | ⓪ | ① | ② | ③ | ④ |
| 11. | (¿otras?) _____ | ⓪ | ① | ② | ③ | ④ |

0 = No sé. No tengo una opinión.
1 = Fue horrible. Me disgustó (*disliked*) mucho.
2 = Fue aburrida. No me gustó mucho.
3 = Fue buena. Me gustó.
4 = Fue excelente. Me gustó mucho.

## ¡Comunicación!

### 7 Encuesta por internet · Presentational Communication

Usa la encuesta que hiciste a tus compañeros de la clase de español en la actividad anterior y crea una encuesta electrónica que puedan llenar fácilmente por internet estudiantes de cualquier otra clase de español de tu colegio o de otro colegio. Escribe un correo electrónico donde expliques cómo llenar la encuesta y pidas a los estudiantes que la contesten también por la internet. Comparte los resultados con la clase, comparando y contrastando los resultados de la encuesta.

## ¡Comunicación!

### 8 Tu país favorito · Presentational Communication

¿Cuál fue tu país hispanohablante favorito del año? Crea una presentación visual para la clase que represente al país hispanohablante que encontraste (*found*) más interesante durante tu año de clases de español. ¡Sé creativo/a! Puedes buscar más información en la internet sobre tu país favorito, usar fotos, crear un collage, usar mapas, etc. Luego, muestra tu presentación a la clase de manera digital o en papel y da una corta explicación de por qué es tu favorito.

*Estoy buscando información sobre mi país favorito.*

emcpassport.com
WB 8–10
LA 4

**? Pregunta clave**
How do ancient civilizations live on in the present?

## Perú: Una civilización antigua 🎧

Durante el Renacimiento europeo en los siglos XV al XVI, una gran civilización apareció en los Andes. El Imperio inca, con seis millones de habitantes y territorios en el sur de Ecuador, partes de Perú, Bolivia y Chile, llegó a ser el imperio más grande del mundo.

Los incas son famosos por sus avances en agronomía y arquitectura. Tallaron[1] montañas, secaron pantanos[2] y construyeron un acueducto. Hicieron ciudades de piedra[3] arriba de una montaña como la magnífica ciudad de Machu Picchu, que aún[4] hoy sorprende a los visitantes.

Machu Picchu, ciudad antigua de los incas

Los incas hicieron estas terrazas para agricultura.

Cusco era[5] la capital del imperio, pero la mayoría de las personas vivían en pueblos pequeños y viajaban a Cusco para los festivales o para comprar y vender. La base de la economía inca era la agricultura. Los incas construyeron terrazas en las montañas como escaleras verdes gigantes. Allí hicieron sistemas de irrigación para cultivar papas, maíz, algodón y otros productos. También tenían llamas y alpacas para llevar cosas y para obtener lana. Aún hoy en Perú, la lana de estos animales juega un papel muy importante en la industria textil. Los incas también inventaron un sistema de finanzas con cuerdas y nudos[6] llamado *quipu*. Lo usaron para registrar el número de personas y productos que pasaban por los Andes.

Otro avance de los incas fue un sistema de calles para unir todo el imperio. El sistema de calles iba por lo alto[7] de los Andes, pasando por valles, montañas con nieve, túneles y puentes de cuerdas[8] sobre los precipicios. Este sistema de calles aún existe hoy y es otra evidencia de que el legado inca continúa hoy en día en la vida de todos los peruanos.

[1] carved  [2] drained swamps  [3] stone  [4] even  [5] was  [6] strings and knots
[7] stretched along the top  [8] suspension bridges

Los quipus son cuerdas de colores con nudos.

🔍 **Búsqueda:** imperio inca

### Productos 🎧

Una estampilla moderna honra el pasado de Perú en el Señor de Sipán, una momia (*mummy*) pre-incaica. Los arqueólogos descubrieron una tumba magnífica, con cetros (*scepters*) y joyas de oro, plata y piedras semipreciosas. Al lado del monarca estaban sus guardias y varias mujeres jóvenes.

Estampilla con una joya del Señor de Sipán

---

### 9 Comprensión | Interpretive Communication

1. ¿Qué territorios formaron parte del Imperio inca?
2. ¿Cuáles son algunos avances tecnológicos de los incas?
3. ¿Qué son los *quipus*? ¿Para qué los usaron los incas?

### 10 Analiza

Why do you think the Incas invented such sophisticated agricultural and road systems?

# Perú hoy

El español Francisco Pizarro conquistó a los incas en 1532. Entonces empezó el período colonial, con Lima como capital. Sin embargo[1], la cultura inca continúa viva dentro del Perú moderno. Se ve en las ruinas maravillosas, como el Templo del Sol en Machu Picchu. Se ve en la vida diaria de los pueblos de los Andes, donde los viejos hablan *quechua* (el idioma inca) y tocan música con trompetas de caracol[2] y quenas[3]. Su religión dice que toda la vida viene de la Madre Tierra, y en el solsticio de verano todavía celebran un antiguo festival en honor del sol, llamado *Inti Raymi* por los incas. Mucha gente viene a ver las ceremonias y a admirar la música y los bailes.

La influencia española continúa en Perú. Los españoles trajeron fiestas religiosas cristianas como la Navidad y la Semana Santa que hoy en día se celebran. La influencia española se vive todos los días en el idioma y en la arquitectura de los edificios, iglesias[4] y casas. En la cocina se combinan lo indígena y lo colonial. Un plato popular es papas a la huancaína, que combina la papa nativa con las aceitunas (olivas) y el queso, dos productos introducidos por los españoles.

*Un administrador lleva un quipu durante el Festival del Sol.*

La combinación de las razas indígena y europea se llama *mestizaje*. Un modelo de la cultura mestiza fue el Inca Garcilaso de la Vega. Hijo de un conquistador español y una princesa inca, fue educado en casa de su padre. De adulto, escribió un libro sobre la vida, cultura y conquista del Imperio inca. Algunos consideran al Inca Garcilaso como el "primer mestizo biológico y espiritual de América".

[1]However   [2]conch shell   [3]reed flute   [4]churches

*El patio de un convento en Lima*

**Búsqueda:**

## Perspectivas

"Aquí no hay una raza ni varias, sino todas y ninguna. Aquí los blancos no son blancos, ni los negros son negros, aquí hay blancos negros y negros blancos, blancos indios e indios chinos, chinos blancos y negros indios". What can you infer from this quote by the Peruvian blogger Pepe Farfán about how Peruvians view their identity?

*Jóvenes limeñas*

---

## 11 Comprensión | Interpretive Communication

1. ¿Qué es el *quechua*?
2. ¿En qué zona de Perú se preservan muchas costumbres incas?
3. ¿Qué es *Inti Raymi*?
4. Nombra tres influencias españolas en Perú.

## 12 Analiza

1. Why do you think the Inca culture is still so prevalent in Peru?
2. With respect to el Inca Garcilaso de la Vega, what do you think is meant by a "spiritual mestizo?"

# Todo en contexto

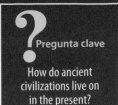
## ¡Comunicación!

**13 ¿Quién sabe más?**  **Interpersonal Communication**

In groups of three, review the information on Peru in the *Cultura* and *Lectura informativa* sections. On individual cards, write questions in Spanish (one per card) about Peru's past and present. At the bottom of the card be sure to include the answer in Spanish and in English so whoever reads the question can verify that it is answered correctly. Place the cards in a box. Take turns drawing out questions to ask your group members, alternating who has the first opportunity to answer each question. Continue until all the questions have been asked and answered, keeping track of who answers the most questions correctly. Score one point for each correct answer and two points if the question was answered in Spanish.

### Estrategia

**Review and recycle** ♻

| | | | |
|---|---|---|---|
| **¿Cómo?** | *How?* | **¿Dónde?** | *Where?* |
| **¿Cuál?** | *Which (one)?* | **¿Por qué?** | *Why?* |
| **¿Cuáles?** | *Which (ones)?* | **¿Qué?** | *What?* |
| **¿Cuándo?** | *When?* | **¿Quién?** | *Who?* |
| **¿Cuánto?** | *How much?* | **¿Quiénes?** | *Who? (pl.)* |
| **¿Cuántos/as?** | *How many?* | | |

• To form questions using question words, the verb precedes the subject:

   **¿Cuándo** llegaron los españoles? ***When** did the Spaniards arrive?*

• Some question words are used in combination with prepositions:

   **¿De dónde** eres tú?    ***Where** are you **from**?*

## ¡Comunicación!

**14 Perú antiguo y moderno**   **Presentational Communication**

You are planning a one-week trip to Peru. You may use the information from the readings in *Lección A* or do online research about other areas of the country. Make a chart like the one below to list all the things you want to see or do while you are there, in order of importance to you. Include different experiences such as food, music, ancient sites, and language. Use your notes to present to the class a brief overview of your upcoming trip. When presenting, try to work from notes rather than reading complete sentences. Talk about each item of interest and its connection to the past and the present. You may also use visuals to illustrate your presentation.

**MODELO**   **El primer día, voy a visitar la ciudad de Cusco. Quiero ver...**

### Para decir más

| | |
|---|---|
| **el puente** | *bridge* |
| **antiguo/a** | *ancient* |
| **típico/a** | *typical* |
| **conocer** | *to see (for the first time)* |
| **cruzar** | *to cross* |
| **había** | *there was* |
| **participar** | *to participate* |
| **tenían** | *(they) had* |
| **usaban** | *(they) used* |

| Mi viaje a Perú | | | |
|---|---|---|---|
| Ciudad/Lugar | Quiero visitar/ver | Pasado | Presente |
| | | | |
| | | | |
| | | | |

# Lectura informativa

## Antes de leer

1. Are you intrigued by mysterious, far-off places?
2. What ancient civilizations do you know about?
3. Would you like to travel for adventure?

*El tren que va a Machu Picchu*

### Estrategia

**Use background knowledge**

Before starting to read, think about the topic and recall what you already know about it. As you read, connect new information to your prior knowledge.

## Viajar a Machu Picchu: Siete consejos útiles para el viajero (*fragmento*)

### 1. Cuándo ir

De noviembre a marzo es la época de lluvia y es preferida por los latinos. De julio a septiembre es la época de los europeos.

### 2. Cómo llegar al parque arqueológico

La forma más rápida y cómoda de llegar a la Ciudadela es por tren. Existen tres compañías con servicios hacia Aguas Calientes. Todas tienen frecuencias diarias desde la estación de Ollantaytambo. Los precios son similares y los servicios también. La principal diferencia son sus horarios.

### 3. Sobre el Camino del Inca

Si su plan es subir por el Camino del Inca, debe reservar su lugar con, por lo menos[1], cinco meses de anticipación. Solo se permiten 500 personas por día.

### 4. Cómo ingresar[2] a Machu Picchu

Las personas que prefieren pagar el ticket con tarjeta de crédito pueden hacerlo en el sitio web del Santuario. La manera más simple de comprar la entrada en efectivo es directamente en la Casa de la Cultura de Aguas Calientes. Cuesta 126 soles (no aceptan dólares) y cierra a las 20.30. No olvide llevar su pasaporte para ingresar a la Ciudadela.

*La ciudad perdida*

### 5. Trepar[3] el Huayna Picchu

La "montaña joven" tiene 2.667 metros de alto; hacer cumbre[4] en él es llegar a una perspectiva distinta, amplificada, de Machu Picchu, y encontrar importantes vestigios arqueológicos. Para subir, hay que tener buen estado físico y presentarse en el parque a las cuatro y media de la mañana. Es la única manera de asegurarse[5] un lugar en uno de los dos únicos turnos por día, para un máximo de 400 personas en total. El ascenso es de dificultad media, y demanda entre 45 y 60 minutos. Importante: llevar agua y calzado[6] para trekking.

[1] at least   [2] enter   [3] Climbing   [4] reaching the summit
[5] ensure   [6] footwear

*Parque Arqueológico Nacional de Machu Picchu*

**Búsqueda:** machu picchu

## 15 Comprensión 🎧 Interpretive Communication

Responde **cierto** o **falso**. Corrige las oraciones falsas.

1. Más de mil personas suben por el Camino del Inca cada día.
2. Los trenes a Machu Picchu viajan todos los días.
3. Puedes comprar boletos para entrar en Machu Picchu en efectivo o con tarjeta de crédito.
4. Subir a pie al Huayna Picchu es muy fácil.
5. La mejor hora para salir a Huayna Picchu es al mediodía.

## 16 Analiza

1. What sort of travelers might be attracted to Machu Picchu? Who might shy away from visiting it?
2. What adjectives would you anticipate a visitor to Machu Picchu might use to describe the site and his or her reactions?

# ✏️ Escritura

## 17 Un viaje de aventura — Presentational Communication

Imagine you are on an adventure trip anywhere in the Spanish-speaking world. Write a blog about two places you went and what happened there. Provide details, and make sure the blog is about an adventure. You can tell about something you discovered or something you found amazing or unexpected. You can also compare and contrast the two places. The trip can be fictional, but it must be realistic and take place in a real location. For additional vocabulary, see *Para escribir más*. Before you write, you may want to organize your thoughts in a table like the one shown below.

| Fecha | |
|---|---|
| Título | |
| Lugar | |
| Qué pasó | |
| Qué hice | |
| Conclusión | |

### Para escribir más

| | |
|---|---|
| aterrador(a) | *frightening* |
| extraordinario/a | *extraordinary* |
| increíble | *incredible* |
| inolvidable | *unforgettable* |
| maravilloso/a | *wonderful* |
| sorprendente | *surprising* |
| único/a | *unique* |

# Repaso de la Lección A

## A  Escuchar: Números 🎧 (pp. 11, 31, 233)

Escribe los quince números que escuchas.

## B  Vocabulario: Palabras interrogativas (p. 461)

Usa la palabra interrogativa apropiada del recuadro según el contexto.

| ¿Quién? | ¿Qué? | ¿Cómo? | ¿Cuándo? | ¿Por qué? | ¿Cuál? |
|---|---|---|---|---|---|

1. ¿ __ es el presidente de los Estados Unidos?
2. ¿ __ vas a volver a la casa? ¿En carro o a pie?
3. ¿ __ vas a comer hoy?
4. ¿ __ vienes a visitarme?
5. ¿ __ quieres ir al parque hoy?
6. ¿ __ es la capital de Perú?

## C  Gramática: Los verbos en el presente (pp. 78, 136, 157)

Di lo que hacen estas personas, usando el presente de los verbos entre paréntesis.

1. Sara (*estudiar*) en la biblioteca.
2. Tina y yo (*tomar*) el autobús.
3. Martín y José (*correr*) en el parque.
4. Yo (*comer*) cuando estoy nervioso.
5. Lisa (*hablar*) mucho.
6. Mis hermanos y yo (*vivir*) en Lima.
7. ¿(*ver*) tú muchas películas?
8. Mirna (*leer*) muchos libros en la playa.

## D  Gramática: Los verbos en el pretérito (pp. 367, 390, 409, 417, 433)

Di lo que hicieron los estudiantes durante el año escolar, usando el pretérito de los verbos.

Este año mi amigo Pedro y yo (**1.** *hacer*) muchos deportes. Pedro (**2.** *jugar*) con el equipo de fútbol y yo (**3.** *nadar*) en la piscina. Pedro (**4.** *estar*) muy contento porque su equipo (**5.** *ganar*) todos los partidos. Mi clase de matemáticas (**6.** *ser*) bastante difícil y el profesor nos (**7.** *dar*) muchos exámenes. En la clase de historia, mis compañeros (**8.** *leer*) sobre muchos países y (**9.** *escribir*) muchos informes. Al fin del año escolar, el colegio nos (**10.** *permitir*) tener una fiesta. Mis compañeros y yo (**11.** *bailar*) y (**12.** *cantar*) toda la noche. (**13.** *ser*) una fiesta fabulosa. Y tú, ¿que (**14.** *hacer*) este año?

## E  Cultura: Herencia de los incas (pp. 459–460)

Repasa las lecturas culturales de esta lección y busca ejemplos de la influencia inca y la influencia española en Perú hoy en día. Luego, compara los ejemplos en un diagrama de Venn, como se ve a continuación.

influencia inca       influencia española

papas a la huancaína

# Lección B

## Diálogo

### ¿Adónde van de vacaciones?

**Luis:** Hola, Inés.

**Inés:** Hola, Luis. ¿Qué hiciste el sábado?

**Luis:** Tuve que ayudar a mis padres.

**Inés:** ¿Van a ir de vacaciones?

**Luis:** Vamos a ir a las ruinas de Tikal.

**Inés:** Fui a Tikal el año pasado. Me gustó mucho.

**Luis:** Y tú, ¿qué vas a hacer en las vacaciones?

**Inés:** No sé. Me gustaría ir a California a la casa de mi tía, o trabajar en la tienda de mi padre.

**Luis:** Pienso que debes ir a California. Va a ser más divertido.

---

### 1 ¿Qué recuerdas?

1. ¿Qué hizo Luis el sábado pasado?
2. ¿Adónde va Luis de vacaciones?
3. ¿Adónde fue Inés el año pasado?
4. ¿Adónde le gustaría a Inés ir de vacaciones?

### 2 Algo personal

1. ¿Qué hiciste el sábado pasado?
2. ¿Qué vas a hacer en las vacaciones?
3. ¿Adónde te gustaría ir de vacaciones?
4. ¿Piensas que trabajar durante las vacaciones es una buena idea?

### 3 ¿Quién dijo qué?

¿Quién dijo lo siguiente, Inés o Luis?

---

## Estrategia

### Review and recycle

Remember to use *gustaría* combined with *me, te, le, nos,* and *les* in order to make a request, to politely express a wish, or to ask about another person's wishes.

**Me gustaría** ir a California.

**¿Te gustaría** ir de vacaciones?

# Verb Phrases

- Remember that, in Spanish, many useful expressions are formed by combining two verbs. When this happens, the first verb is conjugated, while the second verb remains in the infinitive form.

- **Ir a** + infinitive is used to say that someone is going to do something in the future. It is often used as an alternative to the future tense.

| ir a + infinitive |
|---|

**Voy a** *nadar en la piscina.*          **I am going** to swim in the pool.
Mañana **vamos a** *viajar a Guatemala.*          Tomorrow **we are going** to travel to Guatemala.

- **Tener que** + infinitive is one way to express obligation or necessity.

| tener que + infinitive |
|---|

**Tengo que** *hacer la maleta.*          **I have** to pack the suitcase.
**Tienes que** *comprar un regalo.*          **You have** to buy a gift.

- **Tener ganas de** + infinitive is used to say that someone feels like doing something.

| tener ganas de + infinitive |
|---|

**Tengo ganas de** *caminar en el parque.*          **I feel like** walking in the park.
¿**Tienes ganas de** *salir?*          **Do you feel like** going out?

- **Acabar de** + infinitive is used to say that someone has done something in the recent past. It is often used as an alternative to the past tense.

| acabar de + infinitive |
|---|

**Acabamos de** *estudiar el pretérito.*          **We have just** studied the preterite.

## 4  Actividades de verano

Usa palabras de cada columna para hacer oraciones sobre las actividades de verano de estas personas.

| I | II | III |
|---|---|---|
| Marcos | | trabajar en una tienda de ropa |
| tú y tus hermanos | ir a | practicar el piano |
| tú y yo | tener que | estudiar en otro país |
| Julia y Estela | tener ganas de | ir a la playa |
| tú | acabar de | jugar al béisbol |
| Uds. | | montar a caballo |
| mis padres | | viajar a Guatemala |
| yo | | hacer muchos quehaceres en casa |

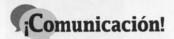

## ¡Comunicación!

### 5  Otra entrevista para el blog de tu colegio  ·  Interpersonal Communication

Hazle las cinco preguntas de abajo a un(a) compañero/a de clase para conocer sus planes para el verano. Luego, hazle otras cinco preguntas creadas por ti.

| Trabajos de verano para adolescentes | |
|---|---|
| cuidar niños, mascotas o casas | vender helados |
| cortar el césped | trabajar en un restaurante |
| ayudar en un campamento de verano | reparar o lavar carros |
| trabajar en una tienda | pintar casas |
| trabajar en una oficina | limpiar casas |

1. ¿Tienes ganas de trabajar este verano? ¿Por qué (no)?

2. ¿Cuál(es) de los trabajos de la lista te gustaría hacer este verano? ¿En cuál(es) no te gustaría trabajar? ¿Por qué?

3. ¿Tienes experiencia en alguno de estos trabajos? ¿En cuál? ¿Cuánta experiencia tienes?

4. ¿Tienes que ayudar en casa este verano? ¿Qué tienes que hacer?

5. ¿Vas a viajar durante tus vacaciones de verano? ¿Adónde?

6.–10. ¿...?

## ¡Comunicación!

### 6  Un folleto turístico  ·  Presentational Communication

Trabajando en grupos de tres a cinco estudiantes, busquen información en la internet sobre algún lugar en un país hispanohablante adónde les gustaría ir de vacaciones. Luego, preparen un folleto turístico sobre el lugar, indicando las principales actividades que se pueden hacer allí y creando un eslogan para decir por qué creen Uds. que este lugar es el mejor para ir de vacaciones. Finalmente, presenten el folleto a la clase.

**¡Bienvenidos!**

- Finca familiar tradicional. Tres generaciones produciendo café y banano.
- Cultivos diversificados y agroindustria de fruta seca.
- Reserva natural privada con vegetación tropical exuberante.
- Lindas vistas del volcán más activo de Centroamérica.

**¡Les esperamos!**

**Actividades**

- Introducción a la caficultura y diversificación de cultivos con recorrido y presentación en español, inglés, alemán, francés.
- Caminatas de aventura o moderadas adecuadas a cada edad y grupo.
- Hospedaje y gastronomía local e internacional.
- Programas educativos, retiros y campamentos de trabajo voluntario.

**Ubicación**

Fácil acceso por carretera asfaltada.

km. 186, carretera a Quetzaltenango. Entrada a Palmarcito, 400 metros del asfalto. Apartado Postal 9-11005, San Felipe, Reu

Reservaciones:
Tel: (502) 7772-5294  agrl@softhome.net
www.portal.anacafe.org/fincasantaelena

**Finca Santa Elena y Anexos**

Descubra el mundo del Caficultor

Disfrute de la naturaleza y la paz

**GUATEMALA**

# *Cultura*  PRE AP

**? Pregunta clave**
How do ancient civilizations live on in the present?

## Una antigua civilización en el presente

*El futuro de la cultura maya está en manos de los jóvenes.*

La antigua civilización maya fue una de las culturas más fascinantes e influyentes de la historia de nuestro mundo. Situadas en el bosque tropical de América Central (en lo que hoy en día es México, Guatemala, Honduras, Belice y El Salvador), las ciudades mayas, como Tikal o Chichén Itzá, eran[1] grandes centros de desarrollo[2] científico y artístico. Cuando los españoles llegaron a Guatemala hace 500 años, muchos mayas vivían alejados en las montañas. Este aislamiento les permitió mantener gran parte de su propia cultura y tradiciones. Hoy en día, los descendientes de los mayas todavía viven en los límites de su antiguo imperio.

Guatemala, considerada como la cuna[3] de la civilización maya, conserva una población maya muy activa. De los casi seis millones de mayas que hay, la mayoría viven en Guatemala. Una parte muy importante de la cultura maya es el idioma. Hoy en día, más del 40% de los guatemaltecos hablan un idioma indígena. Muchos de ellos se sienten más cómodos conversando en su idioma nativo que en español.

Como antes, la mayoría de los mayas siguen viviendo de la agricultura. Cultivan maíz y frijoles de la misma manera que sus ancestros. La religión maya actual combina sus antiguos rituales con la religión católica. Todavía sacrifican animales vivos a imágenes cristianas, y en algunas ceremonias se adoran imágenes católicas con dioses[4] mayas. Otro aspecto importante de la cultura maya que todavía está presente son sus avances científicos. Los mayas inventaron un calendario civil de 365 días, similar al que usamos ahora. Sin computadoras ni telescopios, los mayas podían predecir los movimientos de los planetas y eclipses solares y lunares al segundo más cercano. Su sistema numérico era similar al sistema binario que usamos en las computadoras e incluía el concepto de cero.

El antiguo imperio maya desapareció repentinamente[5], pero sus descendientes todavía habitan América Central y tienen un patrimonio de gran riqueza.

[1]were   [2]development   [3]birth place, cradle   [4]gods   [5]suddenly

**Búsqueda:** los mayas

### Productos

Un área en la que la cultura maya se ve hoy en día es en su tradición textil. Las mujeres mayas crean blusas y vestidos llamados *huipil* con complicados bordados (*embroideries*). La ropa que los mayas llevan cada día ofrece gran cantidad de información sobre la persona que la lleva, como su estatus social en la comunidad, su grupo étnico y el área donde vive.

*Cada comunidad maya tiene su propio huipil.*

### 7 Comprensión — Interpretive Communication

1. ¿Cuántos mayas viven hoy en día en América Central y dónde viven?
2. ¿Qué aspectos de la cultura maya existen hoy?
3. ¿Qué información ofrece *el huipil* de una persona?

### 8 Analiza

What do you think caused the sudden disappearance of the Mayan civilization? Explain.

# Descubriendo Tikal 🎧

*Todavía queda por explorar una gran parte de Tikal.*

Tikal, la antigua ciudad de los mayas, es uno de los sitios arqueológicos más fascinantes del mundo. Esta ciudad-estado maya se sitúa en una remota selva[1] entre México y Guatemala. Su atractivo principal es que gran parte de esta ciudad está por explorar. Hoy en día todavía puedes ver a arqueólogos trabajando en estas ruinas. Tikal sigue dándonos aun más información que nos permite conocer[2] cómo vivían los mayas.

Tikal fue habitada desde el siglo VI a.C. hasta el siglo X d.C. El arte maya y la escritura que los arqueólogos descubren en Tikal contienen historias de batallas, ceremonias religiosas, sacrificios y torturas. También sabemos que las ciudades-estado mayas como Tikal prosperaron como centros de agricultura y comercio. La principal moneda de intercambio[3] era el grano de cacao. Hoy en día el chocolate sigue formando parte de muchos platos de los descendientes mayas.

El arte y la arquitectura de los mayas todavía tienen mucha importancia en las civilizaciones modernas. Su arte se puede observar en la belleza de los objetos de arcilla[4], piedra y jade encontrados en Tikal. La arquitectura de las pirámides en terrazas y la planificación detallada de Tikal son señales de la ingeniería sofisticada de los mayas. El Templo del Gran Jaguar en Tikal es el edificio maya más conocido. Se llama Gran Jaguar porque hay un jaguar tallado en el dintel[5] de la puerta principal del templo. El templo tiene una forma de pirámide, con nueve terrazas y una escalera que va desde la base hasta la cima[6] de la pirámide. Hoy en día, los descendientes de los mayas todavía viven en casas similares a las de sus ancestros, con paredes construidas de caña[7] y adobe, y techos de paja[8].

*Templo del Gran Jaguar*

[1]jungle   [2]know   [3]exchange currency   [4]clay   [5]carved in the top of the frame   [6]top   [7]reeds   [8]straw roofs

🔍 **Búsqueda:** tikal

## 9 Comprensión   Interpretive Communication

1. ¿Por qué sabemos tanto sobre la civilización maya?
2. ¿Cuál era la moneda de intercambio en el antiguo Imperio maya?
3. ¿Qué es el Templo del Gran Jaguar?

## 10 Analiza

Which Mayan achievements do you think have made the greatest impact in today's modern world? Why?

## Comparaciones

Now that you know about the Mayan civilization, how does it compare with indigenous cultures in your region or in your country of origin?

## Perspectivas

In 1979, Tikal National Park was the first archeological site accepted as a World Heritage site by UNESCO. Why is Tikal important and relevant to Guatemalans today?

# *Todo en contexto*

**?** Pregunta clave

How do ancient civilizations live on in the present?

## ¡Comunicación!

### 11  Visitar el Parque Nacional de Tikal | Interpretive Communication

Estás planeando un viaje a Guatemala y quieres visitar Tikal. Lee este anuncio y contesta las preguntas.

**Tikal** PARQUE NACIONAL

**2 días / 1 noche** comenzando en
**Ciudad de Guatemala**
Ruinas mayas, selva sub tropical húmeda, vida salvaje
**Hotel Selva Lodge**

**DÍA 1**  Muy temprano en la mañana tendrá un traslado desde su hotel hacia el Aeropuerto Internacional de la Aurora para su vuelo hacia Flores. Necesita estar en el aeropuerto a las 5:15 AM. Su vuelo sale a las 6:30 AM. A su llegada, tomará el bus hacia el Parque Nacional de Tikal. Tendrá un tour de Tikal con un guía profesional. Almuerzo incluido en su tour. Después del almuerzo, puede visitar el Museo Sylvannus Morley para ver una magnífica colección de arte maya.

**DÍA 2**  Después del desayuno, día libre para explorar por su cuenta este magnífico lugar. A las 2 PM, traslado desde el Parque Nacional de Tikal hacia el Aeropuerto Internacional Mundo Maya para su vuelo hacia Guatemala.

**PRECIO POR PERSONA EN HABITACIÓN SENCILLA**
US$ 360 por medio de transferencia bancaria o cheque.

Qué incluye: Vuelo doméstico Guatemala—Flores—Guatemala, traslados terrestres en bus, entradas al parque, tour de Tikal con un guía profesional, almuerzo (solo el día 1), alojamiento en Hotel Selva Lodge, desayuno (día 2).

No está incluido: Vuelo internacional, gastos personales, propinas, impuesto de aeropuertos.

1. ¿Dónde empieza y termina el viaje?
2. ¿Qué tipo de ropa vas a necesitar? ¿Por qué?
3. ¿Cuántos días dura la visita?
4. ¿En qué hotel vas a dormir?
5. ¿Cómo vas a ir del aeropuerto al Parque Nacional de Tikal?
6. ¿Están las comidas incluidas en el precio total? ¿Están las propinas incluidas en el precio total?
7. ¿Cómo se llama el museo que puedes visitar? ¿Qué puedes ver en ese museo?
8. ¿Qué quieres aprender en este viaje?

## ¡Comunicación!

### 12  Una cultura viva 👥 | Presentational Communication

Con un(a) compañero/a escriban un blog en internet sobre cómo la cultura maya sigue presente en la vida de los guatemaltecos. Añadan características e historia de los mayas antiguos usando los verbos del recuadro *Para decir más*. Escriban cómo se mantiene viva la cultura maya en los siguientes tres aspectos de la vida en Guatemala:

| idioma | religión | comida |

**Para decir más**

| cazaban | used to hunt |
| comían | used to eat |
| compraban | used to buy |
| cosechaban | used to plant |
| hablaban | used to speak |
| vendían | used to sell |
| vivían | used to live |

# Lectura  🅰🅿

## Antes de leer

### 13 Preparación

1. Do you know of any texts written by ancient civilizations?
2. Do you enjoy reading legends about how something originated?
3. What would you use for writing if you had no paper?

### Estrategia

#### Activate prior knowledge

Review what you know about the ancient Maya. When and where did they live? How advanced were they? Did they leave behind works of art and architecture? What writing tools did they use? This knowledge will help you place yourself inside the Mayan culture and gain a better appreciation of its literary and artistic output.

## El libro sagrado de los mayas  🎧

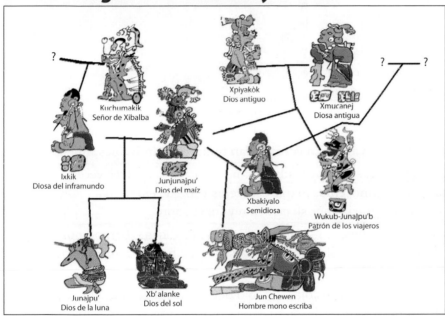

Página ilustrada de un antiguo libro maya

Una versión del Popol Vuh

El *Popol Vuh* es el libro sagrado de los mayas. Fue escrito en Guatemala en el siglo XVI. Sus mitos e historias hablan del origen del mundo, los humanos y el Imperio maya. La expresión *Popol Vuh* en el idioma quiché significa literalmente "libro de la estera"[1]. Para los mesoamericanos, las esteras eran símbolo de la autoridad de los reyes[2]. El *Popol Vuh* habla primero de la creación del mundo. Luego, dice que los dioses[3] quieren crear personas que hablen y los adoren. Crean animales, pero los animales no hablan. Crean hombres de lodo[4], pero no pueden moverse. Entonces crean hombres de madera[5], pero no tienen inteligencia. Finalmente, crean hombres ¡de maíz!

El *Popol Vuh* original, escrito en el idioma de los antiguos mayas, se perdió[6], pero existe una traducción al español hecha por un religioso en tiempos de la Conquista española. El libro se divide en tres partes. La primera es una descripción de la creación, la segunda describe las aventuras de los semidioses Hunahpú e Ixbalanqué, y la tercera es una historia detallada sobre el origen de los pueblos indígenas de Guatemala. En la página siguiente, vas a leer un extracto de la Tercera Parte, Capítulo I.

[1] reed mat  [2] kings  [3] gods  [4] mud  [5] wood  [6] was lost

# Popol Vuh, Tercera Parte (*fragmento*) 🎧

## Capítulo I

Y dijeron los Progenitores, los Creadores y Formadores, que se llaman Tepeu y Gucumatz: "[Llegó] el tiempo... que aparezca[1] el hombre, la humanidad, sobre la superficie de la tierra". Así dijeron...

Había [comida] de todas clases... plantas pequeñas y plantas grandes... Y moliendo[2] entonces las mazorcas[3] amarillas y las mazorcas blancas, hizo Ixmucané nueve bebidas, y de [esta comida] provinieron la fuerza[4] y la gordura y con él crearon los músculos y el vigor del hombre. Esto hicieron los Progenitores, Tepeu y Gucumatz... De maíz amarillo y de maíz blanco se hizo su carne; de masa de maíz se hicieron los brazos y las piernas del hombre. Únicamente masa de maíz entró en la carne de nuestros padres, los cuatro hombres que fueron creados...

Los mayas también ponían su escritura, llamada "glifos", en piedra.

Grande era su sabiduría[5]; su vista[6] llegaba hasta los bosques[7], las rocas, los lagos... las montañas y los valles. En verdad eran hombres admirables...

Luego dieron las gracias al Creador y al Formador: —¡En verdad os damos gracias dos y tres veces! Hemos sido creados... hablamos, oímos, pensamos... y conocemos lo que está lejos y lo que está cerca...¡Oh abuela nuestra! ¡Oh nuestro abuelo!, dijeron dando las gracias por su creación y formación...

Pero el Creador y el Formador no oyeron esto con gusto... —No está bien lo que dicen. ¿No son por su naturaleza simples criaturas [nuestras]? ¿Han de[8] ser ellos también dioses?... Se han de igualar ellos a nosotros, sus autores... que lo sabemos y vemos todo?...

Entonces el Corazón del Cielo les envió un vaho[9] sobre los ojos... y solo pudieron ver lo que estaba cerca... Así fue destruida su sabiduría y todos los conocimientos de los cuatro hombres, origen y principio [de la raza quiché].

Así fueron creados y formados nuestros abuelos, nuestros padres, por el Corazón del Cielo, el Corazón de la Tierra.

[1]appear    [2]grinding    [3]ears of corn    [4]strength    [5]wisdom    [6]sight    [7]forests    [8]Should they    [9]vapor

## 14 Comprensión 🎧 Interpretive Communication

1. ¿Por qué no estaban contentos los dioses con los hombres admirables que hicieron?

2. ¿Qué hicieron los dioses para hacer más aceptables a los hombres?

## 15 Analiza

1. Do you think the original readers of the *Popol Vuh* were expected to believe the stories it contains? Why or why not?

2. Why do you think the Mayan authors chose corn to create man?

# Repaso de la Lección B

## A  Escuchar: ¿En las vacaciones o en el colegio? 🎧

Di si lo que oyes en las ocho oraciones pasó en **las vacaciones** o en **el colegio**.

## B  Gramática: Frases verbales  (p. 466)

Carlos les escribe un e-mail a sus abuelos en Guatemala. Usa la frase verbal apropiada del recuadro, según el contexto.

| tener que | tener ganas de | ir a |

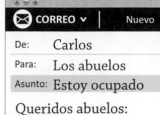

✉ CORREO ∨  |  Nuevo  📄 Enviar  📎 Insertar  Responder|∨  🗑 Eliminar  Archivar  👤 Carlos ⚙

De:  Carlos
Para:  Los abuelos
Asunto:  Estoy ocupado

Queridos abuelos:

¿Cómo están? Yo estoy muy bien pero siempre estoy muy ocupado. Mamá dice que ahora yo **(1)** terminar la tarea y más tarde **(2)** ayudar a papá a limpiar el carro. Esta noche mis amigos **(3)** ir al cine, pero yo no **(4)** ir con ellos porque sé que **(5)** estar muy cansado. Mis padres dicen que **(6)** viajar a Guatemala porque hace mucho tiempo que no los ven a Uds. A mí también me gustaría ir pero no voy a poder porque **(7)** ir al colegio. ¡Qué lástima!

Un abrazo de su nieto,

Carlos, el ocupado

## C  Gramática: Verbos irregulares en el pretérito  (pp. 367, 390, 409, 433)

Completa las oraciones con la forma pretérita correcta del verbo entre paréntesis.

1. ¿Sabes dónde están mis maletas? Las (*buscar*) por todos lados.

2. Después del viaje, mis hermanos (*dormir*) hasta las diez de la mañana.

3. Carlos (*leer*) en una revista que Chichén Itzá es un lugar fantástico.

4. Mis padres (*decir*) que tenemos que dar un paseo por Lima.

5. Ayer, mamá (*hacer*) papas a la huancaína. (*ser*) un plato delicioso.

6. Pilar y yo no (*tener*) tiempo para ir al Templo del Sol.

7. ¿(*ver*) tú las ruinas de Machu Picchu?

8. ¿Cuántos días (*estar*) Uds. en Cusco?

9. Mamá me (*dar*) un *huipil* auténtico de Guatemala para mi cumpleaños.

## D  Cultura: Guatemala ayer y hoy  (pp. 468–469)

Completa una tabla como la siguiente sobre cómo vivían los mayas antiguamente y cómo viven sus descendientes hoy en día en Guatemala. Usa las lecturas culturales de esta lección como referencia. Incluye información sobre los idiomas, la forma de vida, las costumbres religiosas, etc.

| Antigua civilización maya | Descendientes mayas hoy en día |
| --- | --- |
|  |  |

# *Para concluir*

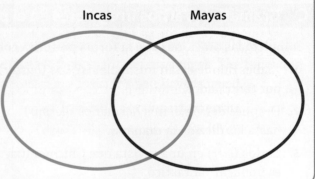
**? Pregunta clave**

How do ancient civilizations live on in the present?

## Proyectos

### A   ¡Manos a la obra!

With a friend, talk about joining an exchange program in one of the Spanish-speaking countries you have studied. Choose one of these countries and do research online as if you were going to be an exchange student there. Think about why you want to go to that particular country and what you hope to gain from the exchange. Also, think about what you have to offer your host family. Research available programs for that country and their requirements, and share what you find with the class. If you get really interested, put your research into practice. An exchange program is something you really can do!

Intercambios estudiantiles

Estudia en un país de habla hispana
España, Colombia, México, Bolivia...

### B   En resumen

Compare the Inca and the Mayan civilizations. Use a Venn diagram to note their similarities and differences. Then, write two or three paragraphs comparing and contrasting these two ancient cultures and their presence today.

Incas        Mayas

### C   Una cultura de mi región

In groups of three, research an indigenous culture from the state or area where you live, or from your heritage culture. Find out all you can about this culture, including the name, where and how they lived, how many members there were, what their society was like, and what forms of communication they had. Are there any descendants of that community? If possible, get in touch by Internet or phone with a descendant of the group and conduct a brief interview. Ask about the differences in the life and makeup of the community then and now. Report your findings to the class.

## D  ¡A escribir!

The purpose of this writing assignment is to describe yourself, using the format of an acrostic poem. In an acrostic poem, certain letters of each line spell out the letters of a specific word the author has in mind. Use the letters of your name or nickname, in their correct order, as your acrostic word. Design the pattern for placing a letter of your name in each line. For instance, you might choose to highlight the first letter of each line, the first letter of the last word in each line, etc.

Then, within the content of the poem, include some information to describe yourself and your preferences. Also, incorporate some information about things you do or have done. Be sure to make the letters of your acrostic word stand out in the poem (as was done in the example on this page). Finally, you may wish to accompany your poem with artwork or graphics to make it more visually appealing.

### Estrategia

**Defining your purpose for writing**

Before you begin a writing assignment, it is a good idea to identify your purpose. Then keep your purpose in mind throughout the writing process as you brainstorm your topic, formulate your rough draft, and edit your finished product.

> **J**uego al fútbol, al básquetbol, y mucho más. Soy **u**n jugador
> fuerte y rápido. Quiero jugar **a**l fútbol profesional algún día.
> Las matemáticas **n**o me gustan ni un poquito.

## E  Una canción en español  👥  Conéctate: la música

Working in small groups, find a song you like in any language (or make up your own). Using the music for the song, create lyrics in Spanish about some of the things you have learned in this class: the Spanish language, culture, people, a grammar point, or a mix of these. The song may be as serious, as funny, or as silly as you want. Sing it to the class.

## F  Culturas antiguas de América  👥  Conéctate: la historia

In groups of three to five students, research an ancient group or culture from what is now the Spanish-speaking world. Research where they lived, their economic structure and lifestyle, number of inhabitants, and what ruins or remains may be found. Share the results with another group of students, comparing the degree of development attained by the two civilizations.

# Appendices

## Appendix A

# Grammar Review

## Definite articles

|  | Singular | Plural |
|---|---|---|
| **Masculine** | el | los |
| **Feminine** | la | las |

## Indefinite articles

|  | Singular | Plural |
|---|---|---|
| **Masculine** | un | unos |
| **Feminine** | una | unas |

## Adjective/noun agreement

|  | Singular | Plural |
|---|---|---|
| **Masculine** | El chico es alto. | Los chicos son altos. |
| **Feminine** | La chica es alta. | Las chicas son altas. |

## Pronouns

| Singular | Subject | Direct object | Indirect object | Object of preposition |
|---|---|---|---|---|
| **1st person** | yo | me | me | mí |
| **2nd person** | tú<br>Ud. | te<br>lo/la | te<br>le | ti<br>Ud. |
| **3rd person** | él<br>ella | lo<br>la | le<br>le | él<br>ella |

| Plural |  |  |  |  |
|---|---|---|---|---|
| **1st person** | nosotros<br>nosotras | nos<br>nos | nos<br>nos | nosotros<br>nosotras |
| **2nd person** | vosotros<br>vosotras<br>Uds. | os<br>os<br>los/las | os<br>os<br>les | vosotros<br>vosotras<br>Uds. |
| **3rd person** | ellos<br>ellas | los<br>las | les<br>les | ellos<br>ellas |

# Interrogatives

| | |
|---|---|
| qué | *what* |
| cómo | *how* |
| dónde | *where* |
| cuándo | *when* |
| cuánto/a/os/as | *how much, how many* |
| cuál/cuáles | *which (one)* |
| quién/quiénes | *who, whom* |
| por qué | *why* |
| para qué | *why, what for* |

# Demonstrative adjectives

| Singular | | Plural | |
|---|---|---|---|
| **Masculine** | **Feminine** | **Masculine** | **Feminine** |
| este | esta | estos | estas |
| ese | esa | esos | esas |
| aquel | aquella | aquellos | aquellas |

# Possessive adjectives

| Singular | Singular nouns | Plural nouns |
|---|---|---|
| **1st person** | mi hermano<br>mi hermana | mis hermanos<br>mis hermanas |
| **2nd person** | tu hermano<br>tu hermana<br>su hermano<br>su hermana | tus hermanos<br>tus hermanas<br>sus hermanos<br>sus hermanas |
| **3rd person** | su hermano<br>su hermana | sus hermanos<br>sus hermanas |

| Singular | Singular nouns | Plural nouns |
|---|---|---|
| **1st person** | nuestro hermano<br>nuestra hermana | nuestros hermanos<br>nuestras hermanas |
| **2nd person** | vuestro hermano<br>vuestra hermana<br>su hermano<br>su hermana | vuestros hermanos<br>vuestras hermanas<br>sus hermanos<br>sus hermanas |
| **3rd person** | su hermano<br>su hermana | sus hermanos<br>sus hermanas |

# Appendix B — Verbs

## Present tense (indicative)

| Regular present tense | | |
|---|---|---|
| **hablar**<br>(*to speak*) | hablo<br>hablas<br>habla | hablamos<br>habláis<br>hablan |
| **comer**<br>(*to eat*) | como<br>comes<br>come | comemos<br>coméis<br>comen |
| **escribir**<br>(*to write*) | escribo<br>escribes<br>escribe | escribimos<br>escribís<br>escriben |

## Preterite tense (indicative)

| | | |
|---|---|---|
| **hablar**<br>(*to speak*) | hablé<br>hablaste<br>habló | hablamos<br>hablasteis<br>hablaron |
| **comer**<br>(*to eat*) | comí<br>comiste<br>comió | comimos<br>comisteis<br>comieron |
| **escribir**<br>(*to write*) | escribí<br>escribiste<br>escribió | escribimos<br>escribisteis<br>escribieron |

## Present participle

The present participle is formed by replacing the *-ar* of the infinitive with *-ando* and the *-er* or *-ir* with *-iendo*.

| | |
|---|---|
| hablar | hablando |
| comer | comiendo |
| vivir | viviendo |

## Progressive tenses

The present participle is used with the verbs *estar, continuar, seguir, andar* and some other motion verbs to produce the progressive tenses. They are reserved for recounting actions that are or were in progress at the time in question.

# Present tense of stem-changing verbs

Stem-changing verbs are identified in this book by the presence of vowels in parentheses after the infinitive. If these verbs end in -*ar* or -*er*, they have only one change. If they end in -*ir*, they have two changes. The stem change of -*ar* and -*er* verbs and the first stem change of -*ir* verbs occur in all forms of the present tense, except *nosotros* and *vosotros*.

| cerrar (ie) (*to close*) | e → ie | cierro cierras cierra | cerramos cerráis cierran |
|---|---|---|---|

Verbs like **cerrar:** calentar (*to heat*), comenzar (*to begin*), despertar (*to wake up*), despertarse (*to awaken*), empezar (*to begin*), encerrar (*to lock up*), nevar (*to snow*), pensar (*to think*), recomendar (*to recommend*), sentarse (*to sit down*)

| contar (ue) (*to tell*) | o → ue | cuento cuentas cuenta | contamos contáis cuentan |
|---|---|---|---|

Verbs like **contar:** acordar (*to agree*), acordarse (*to remember*), almorzar (*to have lunch*), colgar (*to hang*), costar (*to cost*), demostrar (*to demonstrate*), encontrar (*to find, to meet someone*), probar (*to taste, to try*), recordar (*to remember*)

| jugar (ue) (*to play*) | u → ue | juego juegas juega | jugamos jugáis juegan |
|---|---|---|---|

| perder (ie) (*to lose*) | e → ie | pierdo pierdes pierde | perdemos perdéis pierden |
|---|---|---|---|

Verbs like **perder:** defender (*to defend*), descender (*to descend, to go down*), encender (*to light, to turn on*), entender (*to understand*), extender (*to extend*), tender (*to spread out*)

| volver (ue) (*to return*) | o → ue | vuelvo vuelves vuelve | volvemos volvéis vuelven |
|---|---|---|---|

Verbs like **volver:** devolver (*to return something*), doler (*to hurt*), llover (*to rain*), morder (*to bite*), mover (*to move*), resolver (*to resolve*), soler (*to be in the habit of*), torcer (*to twist*)

| pedir (i, i) (*to ask for*) | e → i | pido pides pide | pedimos pedís piden |
|---|---|---|---|

Verbs like **pedir:** conseguir (*to obtain, to attain, to get*), despedirse (*to say good-bye*), elegir (*to choose, to elect*), medir (*to measure*), perseguir (*to pursue*), repetir (*to repeat*)

| sentir (ie, i) (to feel) | e → ie | siento sientes siente | sentimos sentís sienten |
|---|---|---|---|

Verbs like **sentir:** advertir (*to warn*), arrepentirse (*to regret*), convertir (*to convert*), convertirse (*to become*), divertirse (*to have fun*), herir (*to wound*), invertir (*to invest*), mentir (*to lie*), preferir (*to prefer*), requerir (*to require*), sugerir (*to suggest*)

| dormir (ue, u) (to sleep) | o → ue | duermo duermes duerme | dormimos dormís duermen |
|---|---|---|---|

Another verb like **dormir:** morir (*to die*)

## Present participle of stem-changing verbs

Stem-changing verbs that end in -*ir* use the second stem change in the present participle.

| | |
|---|---|
| dormir (ue, u) | durmiendo |
| seguir (i, i) | siguiendo |
| sentir (ie, i) | sintiendo |

## Preterite tense of stem-changing verbs

Stem-changing verbs that end in -*ar* and -*er* are regular in the preterite tense. That is, they do not require a spelling change, and they use the regular preterite endings.

| pensar (ie) | | volver (ue) | |
|---|---|---|---|
| pensé | pensamos | volví | volvimos |
| pensaste | pensasteis | volviste | volvisteis |
| pensó | pensaron | volvió | volvieron |

Stem-changing verbs ending in -*ir* change their third-person forms in the preterite tense, but they still require the regular preterite endings.

| sentir (ie, i) | | dormir (ue, u) | |
|---|---|---|---|
| sentí | sentimos | dormí | dormimos |
| sentiste | sentisteis | dormiste | dormisteis |
| sintió | sintieron | durmió | durmieron |

## Verbs with irregularities

The following charts provide some frequently used Spanish verbs with irregularities.

| buscar (*to look for*) | |
|---|---|
| preterite | busqué, buscaste, buscó, buscamos, buscasteis, buscaron |
| Similar to: | explicar (*to explain*), sacar (*to take out*), tocar (*to touch, to play an instrument*) |

| dar (*to give*) | |
|---|---|
| present | doy, das, da, damos, dais, dan |
| preterite | di, diste, dio, dimos, disteis, dieron |

## decir (*to say, to tell*)

| | |
|---|---|
| **present** | digo, dices, dice, decimos, decís, dicen |
| **preterite** | dije, dijiste, dijo, dijimos, dijisteis, dijeron |
| **present participle** | diciendo |

## enviar (*to send*)

| | |
|---|---|
| **present** | envío, envías, envía, enviamos, enviáis, envían |
| **Similar to:** | esquiar (*to ski*) |

## estar (*to be*)

| | |
|---|---|
| **present** | estoy, estás, está, estamos, estáis, están |
| **preterite** | estuve, estuviste, estuvo, estuvimos, estuvisteis, estuvieron |

## hacer (*to do, to make*)

| | |
|---|---|
| **present** | hago, haces, hace, hacemos, hacéis, hacen |
| **preterite** | hice, hiciste, hizo, hicimos, hicisteis, hicieron |

## ir (*to go*)

| | |
|---|---|
| **present** | voy, vas, va, vamos, vais, van |
| **preterite** | fui, fuiste, fue, fuimos, fuisteis, fueron |
| **present participle** | yendo |

## leer (*to read*)

| | |
|---|---|
| **preterite** | leí, leíste, leyó, leímos, leísteis, leyeron |
| **present participle** | leyendo |

## llegar (*to arrive*)

| | |
|---|---|
| **preterite** | llegué, llegaste, llegó, llegamos, llegasteis, llegaron |
| **Similar to:** | colgar (*to hang*), pagar (*to pay*) |

## oír (*to hear, to listen*)

| | |
|---|---|
| **present** | oigo, oyes, oye, oímos, oís, oyen |
| **preterite** | oí, oíste, oyó, oímos, oísteis, oyeron |
| **present participle** | oyendo |

## poder (*to be able*)

| | |
|---|---|
| **present** | puedo, puedes, puede, podemos, podéis, pueden |
| **preterite** | pude, pudiste, pudo, pudimos, pudisteis, pudieron |
| **present participle** | pudiendo |

## poner (*to put, to place, to set*)

| | |
|---|---|
| **present** | pongo, pones, pone, ponemos, ponéis, ponen |
| **preterite** | puse, pusiste, puso, pusimos, pusisteis, pusieron |

## querer (*to love, to want*)

| | |
|---|---|
| **present** | quiero, quieres, quiere, queremos, queréis, quieren |
| **preterite** | quise, quisiste, quiso, quisimos, quisisteis, quisieron |

## saber (*to know*)

| | |
|---|---|
| **present** | sé, sabes, sabe, sabemos, sabéis, saben |
| **preterite** | supe, supiste, supo, supimos, supisteis, supieron |

## salir (*to go out, to leave*)

| | |
|---|---|
| **present** | salgo, sales, sale, salimos, salís, salen |

## ser (*to be*)

| | |
|---|---|
| **present** | soy, eres, es, somos, sois, son |
| **preterite** | fui, fuiste, fue, fuimos, fuisteis, fueron |

## tener (*to have*)

| | |
|---|---|
| **present** | tengo, tienes, tiene, tenemos, tenéis, tienen |
| **preterite** | tuve, tuviste, tuvo, tuvimos, tuvisteis, tuvieron |

## traer (*to bring*)

| | |
|---|---|
| **present** | traigo, traes, trae, traemos, traéis, traen |
| **preterite** | traje, trajiste, trajo, trajimos, trajisteis, trajeron |
| **present participle** | trayendo |

## venir (*to come*)

| | |
|---|---|
| **present** | vengo, vienes, viene, venimos, venís, vienen |
| **preterite** | vine, viniste, vino, vinimos, vinisteis, vinieron |
| **present participle** | viniendo |

## ver (*to see, to watch*)

| | |
|---|---|
| **present** | veo, ves, ve, vemos, veis, ven |
| **preterite** | vi, viste, vio, vimos, visteis, vieron |

# Appendix C Numbers

## Cardinal numbers 0–1.000

| | | | |
|---|---|---|---|
| 0—cero | 13—trece | 26—veintiséis | 90—noventa |
| 1—uno | 14—catorce | 27—veintisiete | 100—cien/ciento |
| 2—dos | 15—quince | 28—veintiocho | 200—doscientos/as |
| 3—tres | 16—dieciséis | 29—veintinueve | 300—trescientos/as |
| 4—cuatro | 17—diecisiete | 30—treinta | 400—cuatrocientos/as |
| 5—cinco | 18—dieciocho | 31—treinta y uno | 500—quinientos/as |
| 6—seis | 19—diecinueve | 32—treinta y dos | 600—seiscientos/as |
| 7—siete | 20—veinte | 33—treinta y tres, etc. | 700—setecientos/as |
| 8—ocho | 21—veintiuno | 40—cuarenta | 800—ochocientos/as |
| 9—nueve | 22—veintidós | 50—cincuenta | 900—novecientos/as |
| 10—diez | 23—veintitrés | 60—sesenta | 1.000—mil |
| 11—once | 24—veinticuatro | 70—setenta | |
| 12—doce | 25—veinticinco | 80—ochenta | |

## Ordinal numbers

| | |
|---|---|
| 1—primero/a (primer) | 6—sexto/a |
| 2—segundo/a | 7—séptimo/a |
| 3—tercero/a (tercer) | 8—octavo/a |
| 4—cuarto/a | 9—noveno/a |
| 5—quinto/a | 10—décimo/a |

# Vocabulary

## Spanish / English

All active words introduced in *¡Qué chévere! 1* appear in this end vocabulary. The number and letter following an entry indicate the lesson in which an item is first actively used. Additional words and expressions are included for reference and have no number. Obvious cognates and expressions that occur as passive vocabulary for recognition only have been excluded from this end vocabulary.

**Abbreviations:**

| | |
|---|---|
| d.o.p. | direct object pronoun |
| f. | feminine |
| i.o.p. | indirect object pronoun |
| m. | masculine |
| pl. | plural |
| s. | singular |

## A

**a** to, at, in *2B; a caballo* on horseback *3A; a crédito* on credit *9B; a pie* on foot *3A; ¿a qué hora?* at what time? *2B; a veces* sometimes, at times *5B; a ver* let's see

**abierto/a** open *4A*

**abran:** see *abrir*

el **abrazo** hug *6B*

**abre:** see *abrir*

la **abreviatura** abbreviation

el **abrigo** coat *8A*

**abril** April *5B*

**abrir** to open *5A; abran (Uds.* command) open; *abre (tú* command) open

la **abuela** grandmother *4A*

el **abuelo** grandfather *4A*

**aburrido/a** bored, boring *4B*

**acabar** to finish, to complete, to terminate *8A; acabar de* (+ infinitive) to have just *8A*

el **aceite** oil *6A*

la **aceituna** olive

el **acento** accent *1A*

la **acentuación** accentuation

**aclarar** to make clear, to explain

la **actividad** activity *5A*, exercise

el **acuerdo** accord; *de acuerdo* agreed, okay *3B*

**adiós** good-bye *1A*

el **adjetivo** adjective; *adjetivo posesivo* possessive adjective

**¿adónde?** (to) where? *3A*

**adoptar** to adopt

**adornar** to decorate *8A*

el **adverbio** adverb

los **aeróbicos** aerobics *7A*

el **aeropuerto** airport

la **agencia** agency; *agencia de viajes* travel agency

**agosto** August *5B*

el **agricultor** farmer

el **agua** *f.* water *3B; agua mineral* mineral water *3B*

el **aguacate** avocado *8B*

**ahora** now *3B; ahora mismo* right now *7A*

**ahorrar** to save *9B*

el **ajedrez** chess *7A*

el **ajo** garlic *8B*

**al** to the *3A; al lado de* next to, beside *6B*

**alegre** happy, merry, lively

el **alfabeto** alphabet

el **álgebra** algebra

**algo** something, anything *8A*

el **algodón** cotton *9A*

**alguien** someone, anyone, somebody, anybody *9A*

**algún, alguna** some, any *9A*

**alguno/a** some, any *9A*

**allá** over there *6A*

**allí** there *2B*

la **almeja** clam

el **almuerzo** lunch *2B*

**aló** hello (telephone greeting) *2B*

**alquilar** to rent *7A*

**alterna** alternate (*tú* command)

**alternen** alternate (*Uds.* command)

**alto/a** tall, high *4B*

**amable** kind, nice *4A*

**amarillo/a** yellow *2B*

**ambiguo/a** ambiguous

la **América** America; *América Central* Central America; *América del Sur* South America

**americano/a** American *7A; el fútbol americano* football *7A*

el **amigo, la amiga** friend *2A; amigo/a por correspondencia* pen pal

el **amor** love *5A*

**anaranjado/a** orange (color) *9A*

**andino/a** Andean, of the Andes Mountains

el **anillo** ring *9B*

**anteayer** the day before yesterday *5B*

**anterior** preceding

**antes de** before *7A*

**añade:** see *añadir*

**añadir** to add *8B; añade (tú* command) add

el **año** year *5B; Año Nuevo* New Year's Day *5B; ¿Cuántos años tienes?* How old are you? *1A; tener* (+ number) *años* to be (+ number) years old *5A*

**apagar** to turn off *7A*

el **apartamento** apartment

el **apellido** last name, surname

el **apodo** nickname

**aprender** to learn

**apropiado/a** appropriate

**apunta:** see *apuntar*

**apuntar** to point; *apunta (tú* command) point (at); *apunten (Uds.* command) point (at)

**apunten:** see *apuntar*

**apurado/a** in a hurry *4A*

**aquel, aquella** that (far away) *6A*

**aquellos, aquellas** those (far away) *6A*

**aquí** here *1A; Aquí se habla español.* Spanish is spoken here.

el **árbol** tree; *árbol genealógico*

family tree

el **arete** earring *9B*

la **Argentina** Argentina *1A*

**arreglar** to arrange, to straighten, to fix *8A*

**arroba (@)** at *(the symbol (@) used for e-mail addresses) 2B*

el **arroz** rice *8B*

el **arte** art *2B*

la **artesanía** handicrafts

el **artículo** article *5A*

el **artista** artist

el **ascensor** elevator *9B*

la **asignatura** subject

la **aspiradora** vacuum *7A; pasar la aspiradora* to vacuum *8A*

el **Atlántico** Atlantic *(Ocean)*

la **atracción** attraction

los **audífonos** earphones, headphones *5A*

**aunque** although

el **autobús** bus *3A*

la **avenida** avenue *3B*

**aventurero/a** adventurous

el **avión** airplane *3A*

**¡ay!** oh! *2A*

**ayer** yesterday *5B*

la **ayuda** help; *pedir ayuda* to ask for help *6B*

**ayudar** to help *6A*

el **azafrán** saffron

los **aztecas** Aztecs

el **azúcar** sugar *6A*

**azul** blue *2B*

# B

**bailar** to dance *4B*

**bajo/a** short (not tall), low *4B; planta baja* ground level *6B*

**balanceado/a** balanced

el **baloncesto** basketball

el **banco** bank *3A*

el **baño** bathroom *6B; traje de baño* swimsuit *9A*

**barato/a** cheap *9B*

el **barco** boat, ship *3A*

**barrer** to sweep *8A*

el **barril** barrel

**basado/a** based

el **básquetbol** basketball *7A*

el **basquetbolista, la basquetbolista** basketball player *7B*

**bastante** quite, rather, fairly, sufficiently; enough, sufficient *9B*

la **basura** garbage *8A*

la **bebida** drink *3B*

el **béisbol** baseball *4B*

la **biblioteca** library *3A*

la **bicicleta** bicycle, bike *3A*

**bien** well *1B*

**bienvenido/a** welcome

la **billetera** wallet *9B*

la **biología** biology *2B*

**blanco/a** white *2B*

la **blusa** blouse *2B*

la **boda** wedding

el **bolígrafo** pen *2A*

**Bolivia** Bolivia *1A*

el **bolo** bowling pin; *jugar a los bolos* to bowl

el **bolso** handbag, purse *9B*

**bonito/a** pretty, good-looking, attractive *4A*

**borra:** see *borrar*

el **borrador** eraser *2A*

**borrar** to erase; *borra (tú* command) erase; *borren (Uds.* command) erase

**borren:** see *borrar*

la **bota** boot *9A*

el **brazo** arm *9A*

**buen** good (form of *bueno* before a *m., s.* noun) *7B*

**bueno** well, okay (pause in speech) *3B;* hello (telephone greeting)

**bueno/a** good *4B; buena suerte* good luck; *buenas noches* good night *1B; buenas tardes* good afternoon *1B; buenos días* good morning *1B*

la **bufanda** scarf *9B*

**buscar** to look for *5A*

# C

el **caballero** gentleman

el **caballo** horse *3A; a caballo* on horseback *3A*

la **cabeza** head *9A*

**cada** each, every *5A*

el **café** coffee *8B*

la **cafetería** cafeteria

la **caja** cash register *9B*

el **calcetín** sock *2B*

el **calendario** calendar

la **calidad** quality *9B*

**caliente** hot *4A*

la **calle** street *3B*

el **calor** heat *6B; hace calor* it is hot *7B; tener calor* to be hot *6B*

**calvo/a** bald *4B*

la **cama** bed *8A*

el **camarón** shrimp

**cambiar** to change, to exchange *9B*

el **cambio** change *9B; en cambio* on the other hand *7B*

**caminar** to walk *3A*

el **camión** truck *3A;* bus (Mexico); *en camión* by truck *3A*

la **camisa** shirt *2B*

la **camiseta** jersey, polo, t-shirt *2B*

la **canción** song *5A*

**canoso/a** white-haired, gray-haired *4B*

**cansado/a** tired *4A*

el **cantante, la cantante** singer *3B*

**cantar** to sing *4B*

la **cantidad** quantity

la **capital** capital *1A*

el **capitán** captain

el **capítulo** chapter

la **cara** face

la **característica** characteristic, trait; *características de personalidad* personality traits; *características físicas* physical traits

**¡caramba!** wow! *5A*

**cariñoso/a** affectionate *4A*

el **carnaval** carnival

la **carne** meat *8B*

**caro/a** expensive *9B*

la **carrera** career, race

el **carro** car *3A; en carro* by car *3A*

la **carta** letter *6B,* playing card *7A*

la **casa** home, house *4A; en casa* at home

**casi** almost *7A*

**catorce** fourteen *1A*

el **CD** CD (compact disc) *2B*

la **cebolla** onion *8B*

**celebrar** to celebrate *5B*

el **censo** census

el **centavo** cent

el **centro** downtown, center *3B; centro comercial* shopping center, mall *9A*

**cerca (de)** near *3A*

**cero** zero *1A*

**cerrado/a** closed *4A*

**cerrar (ie)** to close *6A; cierra (tú* command) close; *cierren (Uds.* command) close

el **cesto de papeles** wastebasket *2A*

**chao** bye

la **chaqueta** jacket *9A*

**charlando** talking, chatting

la **chica** girl *2A*

el **chico** boy *2A*, man, buddy

**Chile** Chile *1A*

el **chocolate** chocolate *8B*

el **chorizo** sausage (seasoned with red peppers) *8B*

el **ciclismo** cycling

**cien** one hundred *1B*

la **ciencia** science

**ciento** one hundred (when followed by another number) *5B*

**cierra:** see *cerrar*

**cierren:** see *cerrar*

**cinco** five *1A*

**cincuenta** fifty *1B*

el **cine** movie theater *3A*

el **cinturón** belt *9B*

la **ciudad** city *3A*

la **civilización** civilization

el **clarinete** clarinet

**¡claro!** of course! *3A*

la **clase** class *2A*

el **clima** climate

el **coche** car; *en coche* by car

la **cocina** kitchen *6A*

**cocinar** to cook *8A*

el **cognado** cognate

el **colegio** school *2B*

**colgar (ue)** to hang *8A*

el **collar** necklace *9B*

**Colombia** Colombia *1A*

la **colonia** colony

el **color** color *2B*

**combinar** to combine *9A*

el **comedor** dining room *6A*

**comer** to eat *3B; dar de comer* to feed *8A*

**cómico/a** comical, funny *4B*

la **comida** food *3B*, lunch (Spain)

**como** like, since, as

**¿cómo?** how?, what? *1A; ¿Cómo?* What (did you say)? *2B; ¿Cómo está (Ud.)?* How are you (formal)? *1B; ¿Cómo están (Uds.)?* How are you (pl.)? *1B; ¿Cómo estás (tú)?* How are you (informal)? *1B; ¡Cómo no!* Of course! *3B; ¿Cómo se dice...?* How do you say...? *2A; ¿Cómo se escribe...?* How do you write (spell)...? *1A; ¿Cómo se llama (Ud./él/ella)?* What is (your/ his/ her) name? *2A; ¿Cómo te llamas?* What is your name? *1A*

**comodidad** comfort

**cómodo/a** comfortable *6B*

el **compañero, la compañera** classmate, partner *5A*

**comparando** comparing

la **competencia** competition

**completa:** see *completar*

**completar** to complete; *completa (tú command)* complete

la **compra** purchase *4B; ir de compras* to go shopping *4B*

**comprar** to buy *4B*

**comprender** to understand *2A; comprendo* I understand *2A*

**comprendo:** see *comprender*

la **computadora** computer (machine) *2B*

la **computación** computer science *2B*

**común** common

**con** with *1A; con (mucho) gusto* I would be (very) glad to *1B; con permiso* excuse me (with your permission), may I *1B*

el **concierto** concert *3B*

la **conjunción** conjunction

**conmigo** with me *9B*

**conquistar** to conquer

**conseguir (i, i)** to obtain, to attain, to get

la **consola de juegos** game console/system *5A*

la **contaminación** contamination, pollution; *contaminación ambiental* environmental pollution

**contar (ue)** to tell (a story) *9A; cuenta (tú command)* tell; *cuenten (Uds. command)* tell; to count

**contento/a** happy, glad *4A; estar contento/a (con)* to be satisfied (with) *4A*

**contesta:** see *contestar*

**contestar** to answer *4B; contesta (tú command)* answer; *contesten (Uds. command)* answer

**contesten:** see *contestar*

el **contexto** context

**contigo** with you (*tú*) *9B*

**continúa:** see *continuar*

**continuar** to continue *7B; continúa (tú command)* continue; *continúen (Uds. command)* continue

**continúen:** see *continuar*

la **contracción** contraction

el **control remoto** remote control *7A*

**copiar** to copy *7B*

la **corbata** tie *9A*

**correcto/a** right, correct

el **corredor, la corredora** runner *7B*

el **correo** mail; *correo electrónico* e-mail *2B*

**correr** to run *6B*

la **cortesía** courtesy

**corto/a** short (not long) *9B*

la **cosa** thing *6A*

la **costa** coast

**Costa Rica** Costa Rica *1A*

**costar (ue)** to cost *7A*

**crear** to create

el **crédito** credit *9B; a crédito* on credit *9B; la tarjeta de crédito* credit card *9B*

**creer** to believe

el **crucero** cruise ship

**cruzar** to cross

el **cuaderno** notebook *2A*

**¿cuál?** which?, what?, which one? (*pl. ¿cuáles?*) which ones? *2B*

la **cualidad** quality

**cualquier** any

**cuando** when *6B*

**¿cuándo?** when? *3A*

**¿cuánto/a?** how much? *2B* (*pl. ¿cuántos/as?*) how many? *2B; ¿Cuántos años tienes?* How old are you? *1A; ¿Cuánto* (+ time expression) *hace que* (+ present tense of verb)...? How long...? *7A*

**cuarenta** forty *1B*

el **cuarto** quarter *1B*, room, bedroom *6B; cuarto de baño* bathroom; *menos cuarto* a quarter to, a quarter before *1B; y cuarto* a quarter after, a quarter past *1B*

**cuarto/a** fourth *7B*

**cuatro** four *1A*

**cuatrocientos/as** four hundred *5B*

**Cuba** Cuba *1A*

los **cubiertos** silverware *6A*

la **cuchara** tablespoon *6A*

la **cucharita** teaspoon *6A*

el **cuchillo** knife *6A*

**cuenta:** see *contar*

**cuenten:** see *contar*

el **cuero** leather *9B*

el **cuerpo** body *9A*

**cuidar** to take care of

el **cumpleaños** birthday *5B; ¡Feliz cumpleaños!* Happy birthday! *5B*

**cumplir** to become, to become (+ number) years old, to reach *5B; cumplir años* to have a birthday *5B*

# D

la **dama** lady

las **damas** checkers *7A*

**dar** to give *7B; dar un paseo* to go for a walk, to go for a ride *7B; dar de comer* to feed *8A; dé (Ud.* command) give

**de** from, of *1A; de acuerdo* agreed, okay *3B; ¿de dónde?* from where? *1A; ¿De dónde eres?* Where are you from? *1A; de la mañana* in the morning, a.m. *1B; de la noche* at night, p.m. *1B; de la tarde* in the afternoon, p.m. *1B; de nada* you are welcome, not at all *1B; de todos los días* everyday *6A; ¿de veras?* really? *5B; ¿Eres (tú) de...?* Are you from...? *1A*

**dé:** see *dar*

**deber** should, must, ought (expressing a moral duty) *6A*

**décimo/a** tenth *7B*

**decir (i)** to tell, to say *6B; ¿Cómo se dice...?* How do you say...? *2A; di (tú* command) say, tell; *díganme (Uds.* command) tell me; *dime (tú* command) tell me; *¿Qué quiere decir...?* What is the meaning (of)...? *2A; querer decir* to mean *6B; quiere decir* it means *2A; se dice* one says *2A*

el **dedo** finger, toe *9A*

**dejar** to leave (something behind) *8A*

**del** of the, from the *3A*

**delgado/a** thin *4B*

**demasiado** too (much) *9B*

la **democracia** democracy

el **dentista, la dentista** dentist *3A*

el **departamento** department *9A*

el **dependiente, la dependienta** clerk *9B*

el **deporte** sport *5A*

el **deportista, la deportista** athlete *7B*

**desaparecido/a** missing

el **desastre** disaster

el **desayuno** breakfast

**describe** *(tú* command) describe

**descubrir** to discover

**desde** since, from *6B*

**desear** to wish

el **deseo** wish

la **despedida** farewell

**después** afterwards, later, then *6A; después de* after *7A*

**di:** see *decir*

el **día** day *2B; buenos días* good morning *1B; de todos los días* everyday *5A; todos los días* every day *5A*

el **diálogo** dialog

**diario/a** daily

**dibuja:** see *dibujar*

**dibujar** to draw, to sketch *7A; dibuja (tú* command) draw; *dibujen (Uds.* command) draw

**dibujen:** see *dibujar*

el **dibujo** drawing, sketch *6B*

**diciembre** December *5B*

el **dictado** dictation

**diccinueve** nineteen *1A*

**dieciocho** eighteen *1A*

**dieciséis** sixteen *1A*

**diecisiete** seventeen *1A*

**diez** ten *1A*

la **diferencia** difference

**diferente** different

**difícil** difficult, hard *4B*

**diga** hello (telephone greeting)

**dígame** tell me, hello (telephone greeting)

**díganme:** see *decir*

**dime:** see *decir*

el **dinero** money *5A*

la **dirección** address *2B; dirección de correo electrónico* e-mail address *2B*

el **director, la directora** director, principal

**dirigir** to direct

el **disco compacto** compact disc *2B*

**disfrutar** to enjoy

**divertido/a** fun *4A*

**doblar** to fold *8A*

**doce** twelve *1A*

el **doctor, la doctora** doctor

el **dólar** dollar

**domingo** Sunday *2B; el domingo* on Sunday

**don** title of respect used before a man's first name

**donde** where *6B*

**¿dónde?** where? *1A*

**doña** title of respect used before a woman's first name

**dormir (ue, u)** to sleep *7A*

**dos** two *1A*

**doscientos/as** two hundred *5B*

**Dr.** abbreviation for *doctor*

**Dra.** abbreviation for *doctora*

**durante** during

el **DVD** DVD *5A; el reproductor de DVDs* DVD player *5A*

# E

**e** and (used before a word beginning with *i* or *hi*) *6B*

la **ecología** ecology

el **Ecuador** Ecuador *1A*

la **edad** age

el **edificio** building *3B*

la **educación física** physical education

el **efectivo** cash *9B; en efectivo* in cash *9B*

**egoísta** selfish *4B*

el **ejemplo** example; *por ejemplo* for example

**el** the *(m., s.) 2A*

**él** he *1B;* him (after a preposition) *4B; Él se llama....* His name is.... *2A*

**eléctrico/a** electric

**electrónico/a** electronic *5A*

**El Salvador** El Salvador *1A*

**ella** she *1B;* her (after a preposition) *4B; Ella se llama....* Her name is.... *2A*

**ellos/as** they *2A;* them (after a preposition) *4B*

**empatados:** see *empate*

el **empate** tie; *los partidos empatados* tie games

**empezar (ie)** to begin, to start *6A*

**en** in, on, at *2A; en* (+ vehicle) by (+ vehicle) *3A; en cambio* on the other hand *7B; en casa* at home; *en efectivo* in cash *9B; en resumen* in short

**encantado/a** delighted, the pleasure is mine *3A*

**encender (ie)** to light, to turn on (a light) *6A*

**encontrar (ue)** to find

la **encuesta** survey, poll

**enero** January *5B*

el **énfasis** emphasis

el **enfermero, la enfermera** nurse

**enfermo/a** sick *4A*

la **ensalada** salad *3B*
**enseñar** to teach, to show
**entero/a** whole
**entonces** then *6A*
**entrar** to go in, to come in *5A*
**entre** between, among
la **entrevista** interview
**enviar** to send *7B*
el **equipo** team *7A*
**equivocado** mistaken; *número equivocado* wrong number *2B*
**eres:** see *ser*
**es:** see *ser*
**escalar** to climb
la **escalera** stairway, stairs *6B*; *escalera mecánica* escalator *9B*
la **escena** scene
**escoger** to choose *8B*; *escogiendo* choosing
**escogiendo:** see *escoger*
**escriban:** see *escribir*
**escribe:** see *escribir*
**escribir** to write *6B*; *¿Cómo se escribe...?* How do you write (spell)...? *1A*; *escriban (Uds. command)* write; *escribe (tú command)* write; *se escribe* it is written *1A*
el **escritorio** desk *2A*
**escucha:** see *escuchar*
**escuchar** to listen (to) *4B*; *escucha (tú command)* listen; *escuchen (Uds. command)* listen
**escuchen:** see *escuchar*
la **escuela** school *3A*
**ese, esa** that *6A*
**eso** that (neuter form)
**esos, esas** those *6A*
el **espacio** space
**España** Spain *1A*
el **español** Spanish (language) *2B*
**español, española** Spanish
**especial** special *6A*
**especializado/a** specialized
el **espectáculo** showcase
la **esposa** wife, spouse *4A*
el **esposo** husband, spouse *4A*
el **esquiador, la esquiadora** skier *7B*
**esquiar** to ski *7B*
**está:** see *estar*
**establecieron** settled, established
la **estación** season *7B*
el **estadio** stadium
el **Estado Libre Asociado** Commonwealth
los **Estados Unidos (EE.UU.)** United States (of America) *1A*
**están:** see *estar*
**estar** to be *2B;¿Cómo está (Ud.)?* How are you (formal)? *1B*; *¿Cómo están (Uds.)?* How are you (pl.)? *1B; ¿Cómo estás (tú)?* How are are you (informal)? *1B; está nublado/a* it's cloudy *7B; está soleado/a* it's sunny *7B; están* they are *1B; estar contento/a (con)* to be satisfied (with) *4A; estar en oferta* to be on sale *9B; estar listo/a* to be ready *7B; estás* you (informal) are *1B; estoy* I am *1B*
**estás:** see *estar*
**este** well, so (pause in speech)
**este, esta** this *6A; esta noche* tonight *7A*
el **estéreo** sound system *5A*
**estos, estas** these *6A*
**estoy:** see *estar*
la **estructura** structure
**estudia:** see *estudiar*
el **estudiante, la estudiante** student *2A*
**estudiar** to study *2B; estudia (tú command)* study; *estudien (Uds. command)* study
**estudien:** see *estudiar*
el **estudio** study
la **estufa** stove *6A*
**estupendo/a** wonderful, marvellous *7A*
el **examen** exam, test *2B*
**excelente** excellent *7B*
el **éxito** success
**explica:** see *explicar*
la **explicación** explanation
**explicar** to explain; *explica (tú command)* explain
el **explorador, la exploradora** explorer
la **exportación** exportation
el **exportador, la exportadora** exporter
**expresar** to express
la **expresión** expression
la **extensión** extension

# F

**fácil** easy *4B*
la **falda** skirt *2B*
**falso/a** false
la **familia** family *4A*

**famoso/a** famous
**fantástico/a** fantastic, great *3A*
el **favor** favor; *por favor* please *1B*
**favorito/a** favorite *3B*
**febrero** February *5B*
la **fecha** date *5B*
**felicitaciones** congratulations
**feliz** happy (pl. *felices*) *5B*; *¡Feliz cumpleaños!* Happy birthday! *5B*
**femenino/a** feminine
**feo/a** ugly *4B*
el **ferrocarril** railway, railroad
la **fiesta** party *3A*
la **filosofía** philosophy
el **fin** end *5A; fin de semana* weekend *5A*
la **física** physics *6A*
la **flauta** flute
la **flor** flower *7B*
la **florcita** small flower
la **forma** form
la **foto(grafía)** photo *4A*
la **frase** phrase, sentence
el **fregadero** sink *6A*
la **fresa** strawberry *8B*
**fresco** cool *7B; hace fresco* it is cool chilly *7B*
**fresco/a** fresh *8B*
los **frijoles** beans *3B*
el **frío** cold *4A; hace frío* it is cold *7B; tener frío* to be cold *6B*
**frío/a** cold *4A*
la **fruta** fruit *8B*
**fue** was *5B*
**fuerte** strong
el **fútbol** soccer *4B; fútbol americano* football *7A*
el **futbolista, la futbolista** soccer player *7B*
el **futuro** future

# G

las **ganas** desire *6B; tener ganas de* to feel like *6B*
**ganados:** see *ganar*
**ganar** to win; *los partidos ganados* games won
el **garaje** garage *6B*
el **gato, la gata** cat *5A*
el **género** gender
**generoso/a** generous *4B*
la **gente** people *8A*
la **geografía** geography
la **geometría** geometry

el **gerundio** present participle

el **gesto** gesture

el **gimnasio** gym

la **gira** tour

el **gobernador, la gobernadora** governor

**gordo/a** fat *4B*

**gracias** thanks *1B; muchas gracias* thank you very much *1B*

el **grado** degree *7B*

**gran** big (form of *grande* before a *m., s.* noun)

**grande** big *3B*

**gris** gray *2B*

el **grupo** group; *grupo musical* musical group

el **guante** glove *9A*

**guapo/a** good-looking, attractive, handsome, pretty *4A*

**Guatemala** Guatemala *1A*

el **guía, la guía** guide

**Guinea Ecuatorial** Equatorial Guinea *1A*

el **guisante** pea *8B*

la **guitarra** guitar

**gusta:** see *gustar*

**gustar** to like, to be pleasing *4B; me/te/le/nos/vos/les gustaría...* I/you/he/she/it/we/they would like... *6B*

**gustaría:** see *gustar*

el **gusto** pleasure, delight, taste *3A; con (mucho) gusto* I would be (very) glad to *1B; el gusto es mío* the pleasure is mine *3A; ¡Mucho gusto!* Glad to meet you! *1A; Tanto gusto.* So glad to meet you. *3A*

## H

la **habichuela** green bean *8B*

la **habitación** room, bedroom

el **habitante, la habitante** inhabitant

**habla:** see *hablar*

**hablar** to speak *2B; habla (tú command)* speak; *hablen (Uds. command)* speak; *Se habla español.* Spanish is spoken.

**hablen:** see *hablar*

**hace:** see *hacer*

**hacer** to do, to make *3B; ¿Cuánto (+ time expression)*

*hace que (+ present tense of verb)...?* How long...? *7A; hace buen (mal) tiempo* the weather is nice (bad) *7B; hace fresco* it is cool *7B; hace frío (calor)* it is cold (hot) *7B; hace (+ time expression) que* ago *7A; hace sol* it is sunny *7B; hace viento* it is windy *7B; hacer aeróbicos* to do aerobics *7A; hacer falta* to be necessary, to be lacking *8B; hacer un viaje* to take a trip *5A; hacer una pregunta* to ask a question *3B; hagan (Uds. command)* do, make; *haz (tú command)* do, make; *haz el papel* play the part; *hecha* made

**hagan:** see *hacer*

el **hambre** *f.* hunger *6B; tener hambre* to be hungry *6B*

**hasta** until, up to, down to *1A; hasta la vista* so long, see you later; *hasta luego* so long, see you later *1A; hasta mañana* see you tomorrow *1B; hasta pronto* see you soon *1B*

**hay** there is, there are *2A; hay neblina* it is misting *7B; hay sol* it is sunny *7B*

**haz:** see *hacer*

**hecha:** see *hacer*

el **helado** ice cream *8B*

la **hermana** sister *4A*

el **hermano** brother *4A*

el **hielo** ice *7B; patinar sobre hielo* to ice skate *7B*

la **hija** daughter *4A*

el **hijo** son *4A*

**hispano/a** Hispanic

**hispanohablante** Spanish-speaking *1A*

la **historia** history *2B*

la **hoja** sheet; *hoja de papel* sheet of paper; leaf

**hola** hi, hello *1A*

el **hombre** man *9A*

**Honduras** Honduras *1A*

la **hora** hour *1B; ¿a qué hora?* at what time? *2B; ¿Qué hora es?* What time is it? *1B*

el **horario** schedule *2B*

el **horno microondas** microwave oven *6A*

**horrible** horrible *4B*

el **hotel** hotel *3A*

**hoy** today *3B*

el **huevo** egg *8B*

## I

la **idea** idea *5B*

**ideal** ideal *4B*

**imagina:** see *imaginar*

la **imaginación** imagination

**imaginar** to imagine; *imagina (tú command)* imagine

el **impermeable** raincoat *9A*

**importante** important *4B*

**importar** to be important, to matter *8B*

la **impresora láser** laser printer *2B*

los **incas** Incas

**incluir** to include

**indefinido/a** indefinite

la **independencia** independence

**indica:** see *indicar*

la **indicación** cue

**indicado/a** indicated

**indicar** to indicate; *indica (tú command)* indicate

**indígena** native

el **informe** report

el **inglés** English (language) *2B*

el **ingrediente** ingredient *8B*

**inicial** initial

**inmenso/a** immense

la **inspiración** inspiration

**inteligente** intelligent *4B*

**interesante** interesting *4B*

**interrogativo/a** interrogative

el **invierno** winter *7B*

la **invitación** invitation

**invitar** to invite

**ir** to go *3A; ir a (+ infinitive)* to be going (to do something) *3B; ir de compras* to go shopping *4B; ¡vamos!* let's go! *3A; ¡vamos a (+ infinitive)!* let's (+ infinitive)! *3B; vayan (Uds. command)* go to; *ve (tú command)* go to

la **isla** island

## J

el **jamón** ham *8B*

el **jardín** garden *8A*

la **jirafa** giraffe

los **jeans** jeans, blue jeans *2B*

**joven** young *5B*

la **joya** jewel *9B*

el **juego** game

**jueves** Thursday *2B; el jueves* on
Thursday

el **jugador, la jugadora**
player *7B*

**jugar (ue)** to play *4B, jugar a* (+
sport/game) *4B*

el **jugo** juice *3B*

**julio** July *5B*

**junio** June *5B*

**juntos/as** together *8A*

# K

el **kilo (kg)** kilogram *8B*

# L

**la** the *(f., s.)* *2A;* her, it, you
*(d.o.p)* *5A; a la...* at...o'clock *2B*

el **lado** side *6B; al lado (de)* next
to, beside *6B; por todos lados*
everywhere *7B*

la **lámpara** lamp *6A*

la **lana** wool *9A*

la **langosta** lobster

**lanzar** to throw

el **lápiz** pencil *(pl. lápices)* *2A*

**largo/a** long *9B*

**las** the *(f., pl.)* *2A;* them, you
*(d.o.p)* *5A; a las...* at...o'clock *2B*

la **lástima** shame; *¡Qué lástima!*
What a shame! *5A*

la **lata** can *8B*

el **lavaplatos** dishwasher *6A*

**lavar** to wash *8A*

**le** to, for him, to, for her, to, for
you (formal)*(i.o.p)* *3A*

**lean:** see *leer*

la **lección** lesson

la **leche** milk *8A*

la **lechuga** lettuce *8B*

la **lectura** reading

**lee:** see *leer*

**leer** to read *3B; lean (Uds.*
command) read; *lee (tú*
command) read

**lejos (de)** far (from) *3A*

la **lengua** language

**lento/a** slow *4B*

**les** (to, for) them, (to, for) you
*(pl.)(i.o.p)* *3A*

la **letra** letter

**levantarse** to get up, to rise;
*levántate (tú* command) get up;

*levántense (Uds.* command) get
up

**levántate:** see *levantarse*

**levántense:** see *levantarse*

la **libertad** liberty, freedom

la **libra** pound

**libre** free *4A*

la **librería** bookstore *5A*

el **libro** book *2A*

el **líder** leader

**limitar** to limit

**limpiar** to clean *8A*

**limpio/a** clean *4A*

**lindo/a** pretty *9B*

la **lista** list *7A*

**listo/a** ready *7B;* smart *8A; estar*
*listo/a* to be ready *7B; ser listo/a*
to be smart *8A*

la **literatura** literature

**llama:** see *llamar*

**llamar** to call, to telephone *5A;*
*¿Cómo se llama (Ud./él/*
*ella)?* What is (your/his/her)
name? *2A; ¿Cómo te llamas?*
What is your name? *1A;*
*llamaron* they called (preterite
of *llamar*); *me llamo* my name
is *1A; se llaman* their names are;
*te llamas* your name is *1A; (Ud./*
*Él/Ella) se llama....* (Your [formal]/
His/Her)
name is.... *2A*

**llamaron:** see *llamar*

**llamas:** see *llamar*

**llamo:** see *llamar*

**llegar** to arrive *8A; llegó* arrived
(preterite of *llegar*)

**llegó:** see *llegar*

**llevar** to wear *2B;* to take, to
carry *5A*

**llover (ue)** to rain *7B*

la **lluvia** rain *7B*

**lo** him, it, you *(d.o.p)* *5A; lo que,*
that which *6B; lo siento* I am
sorry *1B*

**loco/a** crazy *4A*

**lógicamente** logically

**lógico/a** logical

**los** the *(m., pl.)* *2A;* them, you
*(d.o.p)* *5A*

**luego** then, later, soon *1A; hasta*
*luego* so long, see you later *1A*

el **lugar** place *7B*

**lunes** Monday *2B; el lunes* on
Monday

la **luz** light *(pl. luces)* *6A*

# M

la **madrastra** stepmother

la **madre** mother *4A*

**maduro/a** ripe *8B*

el **maestro** teacher, master;
*La práctica hace al maestro.*
Practice makes perfect.

el **maíz** corn *8B*

**mal** badly *1B;* bad *7B*

la **maleta** suitcase *5A*

**malo/a** bad *4B*

la **mamá** mother, mom

la **manera** manner, way

la **mano** hand *9A*

el **mantel** tablecloth *6A*

la **mantequilla** butter *6A*

la **manzana** apple *8B*

**mañana** tomorrow *1B; hasta*
*mañana* see you tomorrow *1B;*
*pasado mañana* the day after
tomorrow *5B*

la **mañana** morning *1B; de*
*la mañana* a.m., in the
morning *1B; por la mañana* in
the morning *7A*

el **mapa** map *2A*

la **maravilla** wonder, marvel

el **marcador** marker *2A*

**mariachi** popular Mexican
music and orchestra

el **marisco** seafood, shellfish

**marrón** brown *9A*

**martes** Tuesday *2B; el martes* on
Tuesday

**marzo** March *5B*

**más** more, else *4A; el/la/los/*
*las* (+ noun) *más* (+ adjective)
the most (+ adjective) *8B; lo*
*más* (+ adverb) *posible* as
(+ adverb + noun) as
possible *8B; más* (+ noun/
adjective/ adverb) *que* more
(+ noun/ adjective/adverb)
than *8B*

**masculino/a** masculine

las **matemáticas** mathematics *2B*

el **material** material *9B*

**máximo/a** maximum *7B*

**maya** Mayan

los **mayas** Mayans

**mayo** May *5B*

**mayor** older, oldest *5B;* greater,
greatest *8B*

la **mayúscula** capital letter *1A*

**me** to, for me *(i.o.p)* *4B;* me
*(d.o.p)* *5A; me llaman* they call
me; *me llamo* my name is *1A*

**mecánico/a** mechanic *9B*; *la escalera mecánica* escalator *9B*

la **medianoche** midnight *1B; Es medianoche.* It is midnight. *1B*

**mediante** by means of

las **medias** pantyhose, nylons *9A*

el **médico, la médica** doctor *3A*

**medio/a** half; *y media* half past *1B*

**medio tiempo (trabajo)** part-time (work)

el **mediodía** noon; *Es mediodía.* It is noon. *1B*

**mejor** better *8B; el/la/los/las mejor/mejores* (+ noun) the best (+ noun) *8B*

**menor** younger, youngest *5B*; lesser, least *8B*

**menos** minus, until, before, to (to express time) *1B*; less *8B; el/la/los/las* (+ noun) *menos* (+ adjective) the least (+ adjective + noun) *8B; lo menos* (+ adverb) *posible* as (+ adverb) as possible *8B; menos* (+ noun/ adjective/ adverb) *que* less (+ noun/ adjective/adverb) than *8B; por lo menos* at least

**mentir (ie, i)** to lie

la **mentira** lie *6B*

el **menú** menu *3B*

el **mercado** market *8B*

el **merengue** merengue (dance music)

el **mes** month *5B*

la **mesa** table *6A; poner la mesa* to set the table *6A; recoger la mesa* to clear the table *8A*

el **mesero, la mesera** food server *3B*

el **metro** subway *3A*

**mexicano/a** Mexican

**México** Mexico *1A*

**mi** my *2A; (pl. mis)* my *4A*

**mí** me *4B;* me (after a preposition) *4B*

el **miedo** fear *6B; tener miedo de* to be afraid of *6B*

el **miembro** member, part

**mientras que** while

**miércoles** Wednesday *2B; el miércoles* on Wednesday

**mil** thousand *5B*

**mínimo/a** minimum *7B*

la **minúscula** lowercase letter *1A*

el **minuto** minute *7A*

**mío/a** my, mine; *el gusto es mío*

the pleasure is mine *3A*

**mira:** see *mirar*

**mirar** to look (at) *4B; mira (tú* command) look *2B;* hey, look (pause in speech); *miren (Uds.* command) look; hey, look (pause in speech)

**miren:** see *mirar*

**mismo** right (in the very moment, place, etc.) *7A; ahora mismo* right now *7A*

**mismo/a** same *7A*

el **misterio** mystery

la **mochila** backpack *2A*

el **modelo** model

**moderno/a** modern

el **momento** moment *3B*

el **mono** monkey

**montar** to ride *5A; montar en patineta* to skateboard *7B*

**morado/a** purple *9A*

**moreno/a** brunet, brunette, dark-haired, dark-skinned *4B*

la **moto(cicleta)** motorcycle *3A*

la **muchacha** girl, young woman *1A*

el **muchacho** boy, guy, young man *1A*

**muchísimo** very much, a lot

**mucho** much, a lot of, very much *4A*

**mucho/a** much, a lot of, very *3B; (pl. muchos/as)* many *3B; con (mucho) gusto* I would be (very) glad to *1B; muchas gracias* thank you very much *1B; ¡Mucho gusto!* Glad to meet you! *1A*

la **mujer** woman *9A*

el **mundo** world; *todo el mundo* everyone, everybody

la **muralla** wall

el **museo** museum *3B*

la **música** music *2B*

**muy** very *1B*

## N

la **nación** nation

**nacional** national

**nada** nothing *9A; de nada* you are welcome, not at all *1B*

**nadar** to swim *4B*

**nadie** nobody *9A*

la **naranja** orange *3B*

**natal** birth

la **Navidad** Christmas *5B*

la **neblina** mist *7B; hay neblina* it is misting *7B*

**necesitar** to need *2B*

**negativo/a** negative

el **negocio** business; *el hombre de negocios* businessman; *la mujer de negocios* businesswoman

**negro/a** black *2B*

**nervioso/a** nervous *4A*

**nevar (ie)** to snow *7B*

**ni** not even *5B; ni...ni* neither... nor *9A*

**Nicaragua** Nicaragua *1A*

la **nieta** granddaughter *4A*

el **nieto** grandson *4A*

la **nieve** snow *7B*

**ningún, ninguna** none, not any *9A*

**ninguno/a** none, not any *9A*

el **niño** boy (child)

la **niña** girl (child)

**no** no *1A*

la **noche** night *1B; buenas noches* good night *1B; de la noche* p.m., at night *1B; esta noche* tonight *7A; por la noche* at night *6B*

el **nombre** name

el **norte** north

**nos** to, for us *(i.o.p)* *4B;* us *(d.o.p)* *5A*

**nosotros/as** we *2A;* us (after a preposition) *4B*

la **nota** grade

la **noticia** news

**novecientos/as** nine hundred *5B*

**noveno/a** ninth *7B*

**noventa** ninety *1B*

la **novia** girlfriend

**noviembre** November *5B*

el **novio** boyfriend

**nublado/a** cloudy *7B; está nublado* it is cloudy *7B*

**nuestro(s)/a(s)** our *4A*

**nueve** nine *1A*

**nuevo/a** new *2A; el Año Nuevo* New Year's Day *5B*

el **número** number *2B; número de teléfono/de fax/de teléfono celular* telephone/fax/ cellular telephone number *2B, número equivocado* wrong number *2B*

**nunca** never *4A*

# O

o or *2B; o...o* either...or *9A*

la **obra** work, play

**ochenta** eighty *1B*

**ocho** eight *1A*

**ochocientos/as** eight hundred *5B*

**octavo/a** eighth *7B*

**octubre** October *5B*

**ocupado/a** busy, occupied *4A*

**ocupar** to occupy

la **odisea** odyssey

la **oferta** sale *9B; estar en oferta* to be on sale *9B*

**oficial** official

la **oficina** office *3A*

**oigan** see *oír*

**oigo** see *oír*

**oír** to hear, to listen *8A; oigan* hey, listen (pause in speech); *oigo* hello (telephone greeting); *oye* hey, listen (pause in speech) *3B*

la **olla** pot, saucepan *8A*

**olvidar** to forget *8B*

la **omisión** omission

**once** eleven *1A*

el **opuesto** opposite

la **oración** sentence

el **orden** order

la **organización** organization

el **órgano** organ

el **oro** gold *9B*

**os** to, for you (Spain, informal, *pl., i.o.p),* you (Spain, informal, *pl., d.o.p)*

el **otoño** autumn *7B*

**otro/a** other, another *(pl. otros/ as) 4A; otra vez* again, another time *6A*

**oye** hey, listen (pause in speech) *3B*

# P

el **Pacífico** Pacific (Ocean)

el **padrastro** stepfather

el **padre** father *4A; (pl. padres)* parents

la **paella** paella (traditional Spanish dish with rice, meat, seafood and vegetables) *8B*

**pagar** to pay *9B*

la **página** page *2A*

el **país** country *1A*

la **palabra** word *2A; palabra interrogativa* question word; *palabras antónimas* antonyms, opposite words

el **pan** bread *6A*

**Panamá** Panama *1A*

la **pantalla** screen *2B*

el **pantalón** pants *2B*

el **pañuelo** handkerchief, hanky *9B*

la **papa** potato *8B*

el **papá** father, dad

los **papás** parents

el **papel** paper *2A; haz el papel* play the role; *la hoja de papel* sheet of paper

**para** for, to, in order to *3A*

el **paraguas** umbrella *9B*

el **Paraguay** Paraguay *1A*

**parecer** to seem *8B*

la **pared** wall *2A*

la **pareja** pair, couple

el **pariente, la pariente** relative *4A*

**parientes políticos** in-laws

el **parque** park *3A*

el **párrafo** paragraph

la **parte** part

el **partido** game, match *4B; partidos empatados* tied games; *partidos ganados* games won; *partidos perdidos* games lost

**pasado/a** past, last *5B; pasado mañana* the day after tomorrow *5B*

**pásame:** see *pasar*

**pasar** to pass, to spend (time) *5A;* to happen, to occur; *pásame* pass me *6A; pasar la aspiradora* to vacuum *8A; ¿Qué te pasa?* What is wrong with you?

el **pasatiempo** pastime, leisure activity *7A*

la **Pascua** Easter

el **paseo** walk, ride *7B; dar un paseo* to go for a walk, to go for a ride *7B*

el **patinador, la patinadora** skater *7B*

**patinar** to skate *4B; patinar sobre ruedas* to in-line skate *4B; patinar sobre hielo* to ice skate *7B*

la **patineta** skateboard *7B*

el **patio** courtyard, patio, yard *6B*

**pedir (i, i)** to ask for, to order, to request *6B; pedir ayuda* to ask for help *6B; pedir perdón* to say you are sorry *6B; pedir permiso (para)* to ask for permission (to do something) *6B; pedir prestado/a* to borrow *6B*

la **película** movie, film *5A*

**pelirrojo/a** red-haired *4B*

la **pelota** ball

**pensar (ie)** to think, to intend, to plan *6A; pensar de* to think about (i.e., to have an opinion) *6A; pensar en* to think about (i.e., to focus one's thoughts on) *6A; pensar en* (+ infinitive) to think about (doing something)

**peor** worse *8B; el/la/los/las peor/peores* (+ noun) the worst (+ noun) *8B*

**pequeño/a** small *6B*

**perder (ie)** to lose; *los partidos perdidos* games lost

**perdidos:** see *perder*

**perdón** excuse me, pardon me *1B; pedir perdón* to say you are sorry *6B*

**perezoso/a** lazy

**perfecto/a** perfect *9B*

el **perfume** perfume *9B*

el **periódico** newspaper *2A*

el **periodista, la periodista** journalist, reporter

el **período** period

la **perla** pearl *9B*

el **permiso** permission *7A; con permiso* excuse me (with your permission), may I *1B; pedir permiso (para)* to ask for permission (to do something) *6B*

**permitir** to permit *7A*

**pero** but *3B*

el **perro, la perra** dog *5A*

la **persona** person *8A*

**personal** personal; *el pronombre personal* subject pronoun

el **Perú** Peru *1A*

el **pescado** fish *3B*

el **petróleo** oil

el **piano** piano *4B*

el **pie** foot *9A; a pie* on foot *3A*

la **pierna** leg *9A*

el **pijama** pajamas *9A*

la **pimienta** pepper (seasoning) *6A*

el **pimiento** bell pepper *8B*
**pintar** to paint
la **pirámide** pyramid
la **piscina** swimming pool *6B*
el **piso** floor *6B; el primer piso* first floor *6B*
la **pista** clue
la **pizarra** blackboard *2A*
la **planta** plant *6B; planta baja* ground floor *6B*
la **plata** silver *9B*
el **plátano** banana *8B*
el **plato** dish, plate *6A*
la **playa** beach *4A*
la **plaza** plaza, public square *3B*
**poco/a** not very, little, few *6B; un poco* a little (bit) *5A*
**poder (ue)** to be able *7A*
**políticamente** politically
el **pollo** chicken *3B*
**poner** to put, to place *6A;* to turn on (an appliance); *poner la mesa* to set the table *6A*
**popular** popular *4A*
un **poquito** a very little (bit)
**por** through, by *6B;* in *7A;* along *7B; por ejemplo* for example; *por favor* please *1B; por la mañana* in the morning *7A; por la noche* at night *6B; por la tarde* in the afternoon *7A; por teléfono* by telephone, on the telephone *6B; por todos lados* everywhere *7B; por lo general* generally
**¿por qué?** why? *3A*
**porque** because *3A*
la **posibilidad** possibility
la **posición** position, place
el **póster** poster
el **postre** dessert *6A*
la **práctica** practice *5A; La práctica hace al maestro.* Practice makes perfect.
el **precio** price *8B*
**preferir (ie, i)** to prefer *6A*
la **pregunta** question *3B; hacer una pregunta* to ask a question *3B*
**preguntar** to ask *3B*
el **premio** award, prize
la **preparación** preparation
**preparar** to prepare *8A*
el **preparativo** preparation
la **preposición** preposition
**presenciar** to witness
la **presentación** introduction

**presentar** to introduce, to present; *le presento a* let me introduce you (formal, *s.*) to *3A; les presento a* let me introduce you (pl.) to *3A; te presento a* let me introduce you (informal, *s.*) to *3A*
**presente** present
**presento:** see *presentar*
**prestado/a** on loan *6B; pedir prestado/a* to borrow *6B*
**prestar** to lend *8B*
la **primavera** spring *7B*
**primer** first (form of *primero* before a *m., s.* noun) *6B; el primer piso* first floor *6B*
**primero/a** first *5B*
**primero** first (adverb) *5A*
el **primo, la prima** cousin *4A*
**principal** main
la **prisa** rush, hurry, haste *6B; tener prisa* to be in a hurry *6B*
el **problema** problem *3A*
**produce** produces
el **producto** product
el **profesor, la profesora** teacher *2A; el profe* teacher
el **programa** program, show *7A*
**prometer** to promise *9A*
el **pronombre** pronoun; *pronombre personal* subject pronoun
el **pronóstico** forecast
**pronto** soon, quickly *1B; hasta pronto* see you soon *1B*
la **pronunciación** pronunciation
el **propósito** aim, purpose
**próximo/a** next
la **publicidad** publicity
**público/a** public
la **puerta** door *2A*
**Puerto Rico** Puerto Rico *1A*
**pues** thus, well, so, then (pause in speech) *3B*
la **pulsera** bracelet *9B*
el **punto** point, dot *(term used in Internet addresses) 2B*
la **puntuación** punctuation
el **pupitre** desk *2A*

# Q

**que** that, which *5A; lo que* what, that which *6B; más (+ noun/adjective/adverb) que* more (+ noun/adjective/

adverb) than *8B; que viene* upcoming, next *5A*
**¡qué (+ adjective)!** how (+ adjective)! *4A*
**¡qué (+ noun)!** what a (+ noun)! *5A*
**¿qué?** what? *2A; ¿a qué hora?* at what time? *2B; ¿Qué comprendiste?* What did you understand?; *¿Qué hora es?* What time is it? *1B; ¿Qué quiere decir...?* What is the meaning (of)...? *2A; ¿Qué tal?* How are you? *1B; ¿Qué te pasa?* What is wrong with you?; *¿Qué temperatura hace?* What is the temperature? *7B; ¿Qué (+ tener)?* What is wrong with (someone)? *6B; ¿Qué tiempo hace?* How is the weather? *7B*
**quedarle (algo a alguien)** to have (something) left *9A; quedarle bien a uno* to fit, to be becoming *9A*
el **quehacer** chore *8A*
el **quemador de discos compactos (CDs)** compact disc (CD) burner *5A*
**querer (ie)** to love, to want, *6A; ¿Qué quiere decir...?* What is the meaning (of)...? *2A; quiere decir* it means *2A; quieres* (do) you want *3A; quiero* I love *4A;* I want *3A*
**querido/a** dear *6B*
el **queso** cheese *8B*
**¿quién?** who? *2A;* **¿quiénes?** who? pl *2A*
**quiere:** see *querer*
**quiero:** see *querer*
la **química** chemistry
**quince** fifteen *1A*
**quinientos/as** five hundred *5B*
**quinto/a** fifth *7B*
**quisiera** would like
**quizás** perhaps *8A*

# R

la **radio** radio (broadcast) *4B; el radio* radio (apparatus)
**rápidamente** rapidly *5B*
**rápido/a** rapid, fast *4B*
el **rascacielos** skyscraper
el **ratón** mouse *(pl. ratones) 2B*
la **razón** reason
**real** royal

la **realidad** reality
la **receta** recipe *8B*
**recibir** to receive *9B*
el **recibo** receipt *9B*
**recoger** to pick up *8A; recoger la mesa* to clear the table *8A*
**recordar (ue)** to remember *7A*
**redondo/a** round
el **refresco** soft drink, refreshment *3B*
el **refrigerador** refrigerator *6A*
el **regalo** gift *9B*
**regañar** to scold
**regatear** to bargain, to haggle
la **regla** ruler *2A*
**regresar** to return, to go back
**regular** average, okay, so-so, regular *1B*
**relacionado/a** related
el **reloj** clock, watch *2A*
**remoto/a** remote *7A*
**repasar** to reexamine, to review
el **repaso** review
**repetir (i, i)** to repeat *6B; repitan (Uds.* command) repeat; *repite (tú* command) repeat
**repitan:** see *repetir*
**repite:** see *repetir*
**reportando** reporting
el **reproductor** player *5A; reproductor de CDs* CD player *5A; reproductor de DVDs* DVD player *5A; reproductor de MP3* MP3 player *5A*
la **República Dominicana** Dominican Republic *1A*
**resolver (ue)** to resolve, to solve
**responder** to answer
la **respuesta** answer
el **restaurante** restaurant *3A*
el **resultado** result
el **resumen** summary; *en resumen* in short
la **reunión** meeting
la **revista** magazine *2A*
**rico/a** rich
el **riel** rail
el **río** river
el **ritmo** rhythm
**rojo/a** red *2B*
la **ropa** clothing *2B; ropa interior* underwear *9A*
**rosado/a** pink *9A*
**rubio/a** blond, blonde *4B*
la **rutina** routine

# S

**sábado** Saturday *2B; el sábado* on Saturday
**saber** to know *3B; sabes* you know *3B; (no) sé* I (don't) know *2A*
**sabes:** see *saber*
el **sacapuntas** pencil sharpener *2A*
**sacar** to take out *8A; sacar fotos* to take photographs
la **sal** salt *6A*
la **sala** living room *6B*
**salir** to go out *4A*
la **salsa** salsa (dance music)
la **salud** health
el **saludo** greeting
el **salvavidas** lifeguard
la **sangre** blood
el **santo** saint's day; *Todos los Santos* All Saints' Day
el **saxofón** saxophone
**se** *¿Cómo se dice...?* How do you say...? *2A; ¿Cómo se escribe...?* How do you write (spell)...? *1A; ¿Cómo se llama (Ud./él/ ella)?* What is (your/his/ her) name? *2A; se considera* it is considered; *se dice* one says *2A; se escribe* it is written *1A; Se habla español.* Spanish is spoken.; *se llaman* their names are; *(Ud./Él/Ella) se llama....* (Your [formal]/His/ Her) name is.... *2A*
**sé:** see *saber*
**sea:** see *ser*
la **sed** thirst *6B; tener sed* to be thirsty *6B*
la **seda** silk *9A*
**seguir (i, i)** to follow, to continue, to keep on; *sigan (Uds.* command) follow; *sigue (tú* command) follow
**según** according to
el **segundo** second *7B*
**segundo/a** second *7A*
**seguro/a** safe
**seis** six *1A*
**seiscientos/as** six hundred *5B*
**selecciona** select *(tú* command)
la **selva** jungle; *selva tropical* tropical rain forest
la **semana** week *5A; el fin de semana* weekend *5A; Semana Santa* Holy Week
**sentarse (ie)** to sit (down);

*siéntate (tú* command) sit (down); *siéntense (Uds.* command) sit (down)
**sentir (ie, i)** to be sorry, to feel sorry, to regret *6A; lo siento* I am sorry *1B*
**señalar** to point to, to point at, to point out; *señalen (Uds.* command) point to
**señalen:** see *señalar*
el **señor** gentleman, sir, Mr. *1B*
la **señora** lady, madame, Mrs. *1B*
la **señorita** young lady, Miss *1B*
**septiembre** September *5B*
**séptimo/a** seventh *7B*
**ser** to be *2A; eres* you are *1A; ¿Eres (tú) de...?* Are you from...? *1A; es* you (formal) are, he/she/it is *1B; es la una* it is one o'clock *1B; Es medianoche.* It is midnight. *1B; Es mediodía.* It is noon. *1B; fue* you (formal) were, he/she/it was (preterite of *ser*) *5B; ¿Qué hora es?* What time is it? *1B; sea* it is; *son* they are *2A; son las* (+ number) it is (+ number) o'clock *1B; soy* I am *1A*
**serio/a** serious
la **servilleta** napkin *6A*
**sesenta** sixty *1B*
**setecientos/as** seven hundred *5B*
**setenta** seventy *1B*
**sexto/a** sixth *7B*
**si** if *5A*
**sí** yes *1A*
**siempre** always *3B*
**siéntate:** see *sentarse*
**siéntense:** see *sentarse*
**siento:** see *sentir*
**siete** seven *1A*
**sigan:** see *seguir*
el **siglo** century *7A*
los **signos de puntuación** punctuation marks
**sigue:** see *seguir*
**siguiente** following; *lo siguiente* the following
la **silabificación** syllabification
el **silencio** silence
la **silla** chair *2A*
el **símbolo** symbol
**similar** alike, similar
**simpático/a** nice, pleasant *3A*
**sin** without *8B*
**sintético/a** synthetic *9B*

la **situación** situation

**sobre** on, over, on top of  *2B,* about; *patinar sobre hielo* to ice skate  *4B; patinar sobre ruedas* in-line skate  *4B*

la **sobrina** niece  *4A*

el **sobrino** nephew  *4A*

el **sol** sun  *7B; hace sol, hay sol* it is sunny  *7B*

**solamente** only

**soleado/a** sunny  *7B; está soleado* it is sunny  *7B*

**solo/a** alone

**solo** only, just  *8A*

el **sombrero** hat  *9A*

**son:** see *ser*

el **sondeo** poll

el **sonido** sound  *5A*

la **sopa** soup  *6A*

la **sorpresa** surprise  *5A*

**soy:** see *ser*

**Sr.** abbreviation for *señor*  *1B*

**Sra.** abbreviation for *señora*  *1B*

**Srta.** abbreviation for *señorita*  *1B*

**su, sus** his, her, its, your *(Ud./ Uds.)*, their  *4A*

**suave** smooth, soft

el **subdesarrollo** under-development

**subir** to climb, to go up, to go upstairs, to take up, to bring up, to carry up  *8A*

el **suceso** happening

**sucio/a** dirty  *4A*

el **sueño** sleep  *6B; tener sueño* to be sleepy  *6B*

el **suéter** sweater  *9A*

el **supermercado** supermarket  *8B*

el **sur** south

el **sustantivo** noun

# T

la **tableta** tablet  *5A*

**tal** such, as, so; *¿Qué tal?* How are you?  *1B*

el **tamal** tamale

el **tamaño** size  *9B*

**también** also, too  *3A*

el **tambor** drum

**tampoco** either, neither  *2B*

**tan** so  *5A; tan* (+ adjective/adverb) *como* (+ person/item) as (+ adjective/adverb) as

(+ person/item)  *8B*

**tanto/a** so much  *3A; tanto/a* (+ noun) *como* (+ person/ item) as much/many (+ noun) as (+ person/item)  *8B; tanto como* as much as  *8B; Tanto gusto.* So glad to meet you.  *3A*

la **tapa** tidbit, appetizer

la **tarde** afternoon  *1B; buenas tardes* good afternoon  *1A; de la tarde* p.m., in the afternoon  *1B; por la tarde* in the afternoon  *7A;* late

la **tarea** homework  *4B*

la **tarjeta** card  *9B; tarjeta de crédito* credit card  *9B*

el **taxi** taxi  *3A*

la **taza** cup  *6A*

**te** to, for you *(i.o.p)*  *3A;* you *(d.o.p)*  *5A; ¿Cómo te llamas?* What is your name?  *1A; te llamas* your name is  *1A*

el **teatro** theater  *3B*

el **teclado** keyboard  *2B*

el **teléfono** telephone  *2B; el número de teléfono* telephone number  *2B; por teléfono* by phone, on the telephone  *6B*

la **telenovela** soap opera  *7A*

la **televisión** television  *4B; ver la televisión* to watch television  *4B*

el **televisor** television set  *7A*

el **tema** theme, topic

la **temperatura** temperature  *7B; ¿Qué temperatura hace?* What is the temperature?  *7B*

**temprano** early  *5B*

el **tenedor** fork  *6A*

**tener** to have  *5A; ¿Cuántos años tienes?* How old are you?  *1A; ¿Qué* (+ *tener)?* What is wrong with (person)?  *6B; tener calor* to be hot  *6B; tener frío* to be cold  *6B; tener ganas de* to feel like  *6B; tener hambre* to be hungry  *6B; tener miedo de* to be afraid  *6B; tener* (+ number) *años* to be (+ number) years old  *5A; tener prisa* to be in a hurry  *6B; tener que* to have (to do something)  *6A; tener sed* to be thirsty  *6B; tener sueño* to be sleepy  *6B; tengo* I have  *1A; tengo* (+ number) *años* I am (+ number) years old  *1A; tiene* it has; *tienes* you have  *1A*

**tengo:** see *tener*

el **tenis** tennis  *4B*

el **tenista, la tenista** tennis player  *7B*

**tercer** third (form of *tercero* before a *m., s.* noun)  *7B*

**tercero/a** third  *7B*

**terminar** to end, to finish  *2B*

**ti** you (after a preposition)  *4B*

la **tía** aunt  *4A*

el **tiempo** time  *4A;* weather  *7B;* verb tense; *Hace buen (mal) tiempo.* The weather is nice (bad).  *7B; ¿Qué tiempo hace?* How is the weather?  *7B*

la **tienda** store  *3B*

**tiene:** see *tener*

**tienes:** see *tener*

el **tío** uncle  *4A*

**típico/a** typical

el **tipo** type, kind

la **tiza** chalk  *2A*

**toca:** see *tocar*

**tocar** to play (something musical)  *4B;* to touch; *toca* (*tú* command) touch; *toquen* (*Uds.* command) touch

**todavía** yet  *7A;* still  *7B*

**todo/a** all, every, whole, entire  *4A; de todos los días* everyday  *6A; por todos lados* everywhere  *7B; todo el mundo* everyone, everybody; *todos los días* every day  *5A*

**todos/as** everyone, everybody

**tolerante** tolerant

**tomar** to take  *3A;* to drink, to have  *3B*

el **tomate** tomato  *8B*

**tonto/a** silly  *4B*

el **tópico** theme

**toquen:** see *tocar*

**trabajar** to work  *8A; trabajando en parejas* working in pairs

el **trabajo** work  *8A*

**traer** to bring  *8A*

el **traje** suit  *9A; traje de baño* swimsuit  *9A*

el **transporte** transportation  *3A*

**tratar (de)** to try (to do something)

**trece** thirteen  *1A*

**treinta** thirty  *1B*

el **tren** train  *3A*

**tres** three  *1A*

**trescientos/as** three hundred  *5B*

triste sad *4A*
el trombón trombone
la trompeta trumpet
tu your (informal) *2B; (pl. tus)*
your (informal) *4A*
tú you (informal) *1A*
la tumba tomb
el turista, la turista tourist

# U

u or (used before a word that
starts with *o* or *ho*) *6B*
Ud. you (abbreviation of
*usted*) *1B;* you (after a
preposition) *4B; Ud. se llama....*
Your name is.... *2A*
Uds. you (abbreviation of
*ustedes*) *1B;* you (after a
preposition) *4B*
último/a last
un, una a, an, one *2A*
único/a only, unique *4A*
unido/a united
la universidad university
uno one *1A*
unos, unas some, any,
a few *2A*
el Uruguay Uruguay *1A*
usar to use *9B*
usted you (formal, *s.*) *1B;* you
(after a preposition) *4B*
ustedes you *(pl.)* *1B;* you (after a
preposition) *4B*
la uva grape *8B*

# V

las vacaciones vacation *9A*
Vallenato a combination
of African, European and
Colombian folkloric sounds
¡vamos! let's go! *3A; ¡vamos a* (+
infinitive)*!* let's
(+ infinitive)*!* *3B*
varios/as several
el vaso glass *6A*
vayan: see *ir*
ve: see *ir*
veinte twenty *1A*

veinticinco twenty-five *1B*
veinticuatro twenty-four *1B*
veintidós twenty-two *1B*
veintinueve twenty-nine *1B*
veintiocho twenty-eight *1B*
veintiséis twenty-six *1B*
veintisiete twenty-seven *1B*
veintitrés twenty-three *1B*
veintiuno twenty-one *1B*
vender to sell *9A*
Venezuela Venezuela *1A*
vengan: see *venir*
venir to come *5B; vengan (Uds.*
command) come
la ventana window *2A*
ver to see *3B; a ver* let's see;
*ver la televisión* to watch
television *4B*
el verano summer *4A*
el verbo verb
verdad true
la verdad truth *6B*
¿verdad? right? *3A*
verde green *2B*
la verdura greens,
vegetables *8B*
ves: see *ver*
el vestido dress *9A*
la vez time *(pl. veces)* *5B; a veces* at
times, sometimes *5B;* (number
+) *vez/veces al/a la* (+ time
expression) (number +) time(s)
per (+ time expression)*; otra vez*
again, another time *6A*
viajar to travel *6A*
el viaje trip *5A; hacer un viaje* to
take a trip *5A; la agencia de
viajes* travel agency
la vida life *7A*
el videojuego video game *7A*
viejo/a old *5B*
el viento wind *7B; hace viento* it is
windy *7B*
viernes Friday *2B; el viernes* on
Friday
el vinagre vinegar *8B*
la vista view; *hasta la vista* so long,
see you later
vivir to live *4A*
el vocabulario vocabulary
la vocal vowel; *vocales abiertas*
open vowels; *vocales cerradas*
closed vowels

el voleibol volleyball *7A*
volver (ue) to return, to go back,
to come back *7A*
vosotros/as you (Spain,
informal, *pl.*) *1B*
vuestros/as your (Spain,
informal, *pl.*)

# Y

y and *1A; y cuarto* a quarter
past, a quarter after *1B;
y media* half past *1B*
ya now *6A; ¡ya lo veo!*
I see it!
yo I *1A*

# Z

la zanahoria carrot *8B*
el zapato shoe *2B; zapato bajo* flat
(shoe) *9A; zapato de tacón*
high-heel shoe *9A*

# Vocabulary

## English / Spanish

## A

**a** un, una *1B; a few* unos, unas *1B; a lot (of)* mucho *4B,* muchísimo
**about** sobre
**accent** el acento *1A*
**activity** la actividad *5A*
to **add** añadir *8B*
**address** la dirección *2B*
to **adopt** adoptar
**aerobics** los aeróbicos *7A; to do aerobics* hacer aeróbicos *7A*
**affectionate** cariñoso/a *4A*
**afraid** asustado/a; *to be afraid of* tener miedo de *6B*
**after** después de *7A*
**afternoon** la tarde *1B; good afternoon* buenas tardes *1A; in the afternoon* de la tarde *1B; por la tarde 7A*
**afterwards** después *7A*
**again** otra vez *6A*
**age** la edad
**agency** la agencia; *travel agency* agencia de viajes
**ago** hace *(+ time expression)* que *7A*
**agreed** de acuerdo *3B*
**airplane** el avión *3A; by airplane* en avión *3A*
**airport** el aeropuerto
**algebra** el álgebra
**all** todo/a *4A*
**almost** casi *7A*
**alone** solo/a
**along** por *7B*
**already** ya *6A*
**also** también *3A*
**alternate** alterna (tú *command*); alternen (Uds. *command*)
**although** aunque
**always** siempre *3B*
**American** americano/a *7A*
**an** un, una *2A*
**and** y *1A;* e *(used before a word beginning with i or hi) 6B*
**another** otro/a *2A; another time* otra vez *4B*
**answer** la respuesta
to **answer** contestar *4B*
**any** unos, unas *2A;* alguno/a, algún, alguna *8A;* cualquier

**anybody** alguien *9A*
**anyone** alguien *9A*
**anything** algo *9A*
**apartment** el apartamento
**apple** la manzana *8B*
**April** abril *5B*
**Argentina** la Argentina *1A*
**arm** el brazo *9A*
to **arrange** arreglar *8A*
to **arrive** llegar *8A*
**art** el arte *2B*
**article** el artículo *5A*
**artist** el artista, la artista
**as** tal *1B;* como; *as (+ adverb) as possible* lo más/menos *(+ adverb)* posible *8B; as (+ adjective/adverb) as (+ person/item)* tan *(+ adjective/adverb)* como *(+ person/item) 8B; as much/many (+ noun) as (+ person/item)* tanto/a *(+ noun)* como *(+ person/item) 8B; as much as* tanto como *8B*
to **ask** preguntar *3B; to ask a question* hacer una pregunta *3B; to ask for* pedir (i, i) *6B; to ask for help* pedir ayuda *6B; to ask for permission (to do something)* pedir permiso (para) *6B*
**at** en; *(@) symbol for e-mail address* arroba *2B; at home* en casa *9B; at night* de la noche *1B,* por la noche *6B; at... o'clock* a la(s)... *2B; at times* a veces *5B; at what time?* ¿a qué hora? *2B*
**athlete** el deportista, la deportista *7B*
to **attain** conseguir (i, i)
**attractive** bonito/a, guapo/a *4A*
**August** agosto *5B*
**aunt** la tía *4A*
**autumn** el otoño *7B*
**avenue** la avenida *3B*
**average** regular *1B*
**avocado** el aguacate *8B*
**award** el premio

## B

**backpack** la mochila *2A*
**bad** malo/a *4B*

**bald** calvo/a *4B*
**ball** pelota, bola
**banana** el plátano *8B*
**bank** el banco *3A*
to **bargain** regatear
**baseball** el béisbol *4B*
**basketball** el básquetbol *7A;* el baloncesto; *basketball player* el basquetbolista, la basquetbolista *7B*
**bathroom** el baño *6B;* el cuarto de baño
to **be** ser *2A; to be able* poder (ue) *7A; to be afraid of* tener miedo de *6B; to be hot* tener calor *6B; to be hungry* tener hambre *6B; to be important* importar *8B; to be in a hurry* tener prisa *6B; to be lacking* hacer falta *8B; to be necessary* hacer falta *8B; to be (+ number) years old* tener (+ ) años *5A; to be pleasing to* gustar *4B; to be ready* estar listo/a *7B; to be satisfied (with)* estar contento/a (con) *4A; to be sleepy* tener sueño *6B; to be smart* ser listo/a *8A; to be sorry* sentir *6A; to be thirsty* tener sed *6B*
**beach** la playa *4A*
**beans** los frijoles *3B*
**because** porque *3A*
to **become** cumplir *5B; to become (+ number) years old* cumplir *(+ number)* años *5B*
**bed** la cama *8A*
**bedroom** el cuarto *6B,* la habitación
**before** antes de *7A*
to **begin** empezar (ie) *6A*
to **believe** creer
**belt** el cinturón *9B*
**beside** al lado (de) *6B*
**best** mejor *8B; the best (+ noun)* el/la/los/las mejor/mejores *(+ noun) 8B*
**better** mejor *8B*
**between** entre
**bicycle** la bicicleta *3A*
**big** grande *3B;* gran *(form of* grande *before a m., s. noun)*
**bike** la bicicleta *3A*
**biology** la biología *2B*
**birthday** el cumpleaños *5B; Happy birthday!* ¡Feliz

cumpleaños! *5B; to have a birthday* cumplir años *5B*
**black** negro/a *2B*
**blackboard** la pizarra *2A*
**blond, blonde** rubio/a *4B*
**blouse** la blusa *2B*
**blue** azul *2B; blue jeans* los jeans *2B*
**boat** el barco *3A*
**body** el cuerpo *9A*
**Bolivia** Bolivia *1A*
**book** el libro *2A*
**bookstore** la librería *5A*
**boot** la bota *9A*
**bored** aburrido/a *4B*
**boring** aburrido/a *4B*
to **borrow** pedir prestado/a *6B*
**boy** el chico *2A;* el muchacho *1A;* el niño
**boyfriend** el novio
**bracelet** la pulsera *9B*
**bread** el pan *6A*
**breakfast** el desayuno
to **bring** traer *8A*
to **bring up** subir *8A*
**brother** el hermano *4A*
**brown** marrón *9A*
**brunet, brunette** moreno/a *4B*
**building** el edificio *3B*
**bus** el autobús *3A*
**busy** ocupado/a *4A*
**but** pero *3B*
**butter** la mantequilla *6A*
to **buy** comprar *4B*
**by** by *(+ vehicle)* en *(+ vehicle) 3A; by telephone* por teléfono *6B; by means of* mediante

# C

**cafeteria** la cafetería
**calendar** el calendario
to **call** llamar *5A*
**can** la lata *8B*
**capital** la capital *1A*
**car** el carro *3A;* el coche; *by car* en carro *3A;* en coche
**card** la tarjeta *9B; credit card* tarjeta de crédito *9B; playing card* la carta *7A*
**carrot** la zanahoria *8B*
to **carry** llevar *5A; to carry up* subir *8A*
**cash** el efectivo *9B; in cash* en efectivo *9B*
**cash register** la caja *9B*

**cat** el gato, la gata *5A*
**CD** el CD, el disco compacto *2B; CD player* el reproductor de CDs *5A; CD burner* el quemador de CDs *5A*
to **celebrate** celebrar *5B*
**census** el censo
**center** el centro *3B; shopping center* el centro comercial *9A*
**century** el siglo *7A*
**chair** la silla *2A*
**chalk** la tiza *2A*
**change** el cambio *9B*
to **change** cambiar *9B*
**cheap** barato/a *9B*
**checkers** las damas *7A*
**cheese** el queso *8B*
**chemistry** la química
**chess** el ajedrez *7A*
**chicken** el pollo *3B*
**child** el niño, la niña
**Chile** Chile *1A*
**chilly** fresco/a *7B*
**chocolate** el chocolate *8B*
to **choose** escoger *8B*
**chore** el quehacer *8A*
**Christmas** la Navidad *5B*
**city** la ciudad *3A*
**clam** la almeja
**clarinet** el clarinete
**class** la clase *2A*
**classmate** el compañero, la compañera *5A*
**clean** limpio/a *4A*
to **clean** limpiar *8A*
**clerk** el dependiente, la dependienta *9B*
to **climb** subir *8A;* escalar
**clock** el reloj *2A*
to **close** cerrar (ie) *6A*
**closed** cerrado/a *4A*
**clothing** la ropa *2B*
**cloudy** nublado/a *7B; it is cloudy* está nublado *7B*
**coat** el abrigo *8A*
**coffee** el café *8B*
**cold** frío/a *4A;* el frío *4A; it is cold* hace frío *7B; to be cold* tener frío *6B*
**Colombia** Colombia *1A*
**color** el color *7B*
to **combine** combinar *9A*
to **come** venir *5B; to come back* volver (ue) *7A; to come in* entrar *5A*
**comfort** comodidad
**comfortable** cómodo/a *6B*
**comical** cómico/a *4B*
**common** común

**compact disc** el disco compacto (CD) *2B; CD player* el reproductor de discos compactos (CDs) *5A; CD burner* el quemador de discos compactos (CDs) *5A*
**competition** la competencia
to **complete** completar, acabar *8A*
**computer** la computadora *2B*
**computer science** la computación *2B*
**concert** el concierto *3B*
**congratulations** felicitaciones
to **conquer** conquistar
to **continue** continuar *7B,* seguir (i, i)
to **cook** cocinar *8A*
**cool** el fresco *7B; it is cool* hace fresco *7B*
to **copy** copiar *7B*
**corn** el maíz *8B*
to **cost** costar (ue) *7A*
**Costa Rica** Costa Rica *1A*
**cotton** el algodón *9A*
to **count** contar
**country** el país *1A*
**couple** la pareja
**courtyard** el patio *6B*
**cousin** el primo, la prima *4A*
**crazy** loco/a *4A*
to **create** crear
**credit** el crédito *9B; credit card* la tarjeta de crédito *9B; on credit* a crédito *9B*
to **cross** cruzar
**Cuba** Cuba *1A*
**cup** la taza *6A*
**cycling** ciclismo

# D

**dad** el padre *4A;* el papá
to **dance** bailar *4B*
**dark** oscuro/a; *dark-haired, dark-skinned* moreno/a *4B*
**date** la fecha *5B*
**daughter** la hija *4A*
**day** el día *2B; every day* todos los días *6A; the day after tomorrow* pasado mañana *5B; the day before yesterday* anteayer *5B*
**dear** querido/a *5B*
**December** diciembre *5B*
to **decorate** adornar *8A*
**degree** el grado *7B*
**delighted** encantado/a *3A*

**dentist** el dentista, la dentista  *3A*
**department** el departamento  *9A*
**desire** la gana  *6B*
**desk** el escritorio, el pupitre  *2A*
**dessert** el postre  *6A*
**difficult** difícil  *4B*
**dinner** la comida, la cena
to **direct** dirigir
**director** el director, la directora
**dirty** sucio/a  *4A*
**disaster** el desastre
**disc** el disco  *2B; compact disc (CD)* el disco compacto  *2B; CD player* el reproductor de discos compactos (CDs)  *5A; CD burner* el quemador de discos compactos (CDs)  *5A*
to **discover** descubrir
**dish** el plato  *6A*
**dishwasher** el lavaplatos  *6A*
to **do** hacer  *3B; to do aerobics* hacer aeróbicos  *7A*
**doctor** el médico, la médica  *3A,* el doctor, la doctora
**dog** el perro, la perra  *5A*
**dollar** el dólar
**Dominican Republic** la República Dominicana  *1A*
**door** la puerta  *2A*
**dot** punto  *2B*
**downtown** el centro  *3B*
to **draw** dibujar  *7A*
**drawing** el dibujo  *6B*
**dress** el vestido  *9A*
**drink** el refresco  *3B;* la bebida
to **drink** tomar  *3B*
**drum** el tambor
**during** durante
**DVD** el DVD  *5A; DVD player* el reproductor de DVDs  *5A*

# E

**e-mail** el correo electrónico  *2B*
**each** cada  *5A*
**early** temprano  *5B*
**earring** el arete  *2B*
**Easter** la Pascua
**easy** fácil  *4B*
to **eat** comer  *3B*
**Ecuador** el Ecuador  *1A*
**egg** el huevo  *8B*
**eight** ocho  *1A*
**eight hundred** ochocientos/as

*5B*
**eighteen** dieciocho  *1A*
**eighth** octavo/a  *7B*
**eighty** ochenta  *1B*
**either** tampoco  *2B; either...or* o...o  *9A*
**electronic** electrónico/a  *2B*
**elevator** el ascensor  *9B*
**eleven** once  *1A*
**El Salvador** El Salvador  *1A*
**else** más  *4A*
**end** el fin  *5A*
to **end** terminar  *2B*
**English** el inglés  *(language)*  *2B*
to **enjoy** disfrutar
**earphones** los audífonos  *5A*
**enough** bastante  *9B*
to **erase** borrar
**eraser** el borrador  *2A*
**escalator** la escalera mecánica  *9B*
**every** todo/a  *1A;* cada  *5A; every day* todos los días  *5A*
**everybody** todo el mundo, todos/as
**everyday** de todos los días  *5A*
**everyone** todo el mundo, todos/as
**everywhere** por todos lados  *7B*
**exam** el examen  *5A*
**example** el ejemplo; *for example* por ejemplo
**excellent** excelente  *7B*
to **exchange** cambiar  *9B*
**excuse me** perdón, con permiso  *1B*
**expensive** caro/a  *9B*
to **explain** explicar, aclarar
**explanation** la explicación
**exporter** el exportador, la exportadora

# F

**face** la cara
**fairly** bastante
**family** la familia  *4A; family tree* el árbol genealógico
**famous** famoso/a
**fantastic** fantástico/a  *3A*
**far (from)** lejos (de)  *3A*
**fast** rápido/a  *4B*
**fat** gordo/a  *4B*
**father** el padre  *4A*
**favorite** favorito/a  *3B*
**fear** el miedo  *6B; to be afraid of*

tener miedo de  *6B*
**February** febrero  *5B*
to **feed** dar de comer  *8A*
to **feel like** tener ganas de  *6B*
to **feel sorry** sentir (ie)  *6A*
**few** poco/a  *6A*
**fifteen** quince  *1A*
**fifth** quinto/a  *7B*
**fifty** cincuenta  *1B*
**film** la película  *5A*
to **find** encontrar (ue)
**finger** el dedo  *9A*
to **finish** terminar  *2B,* acabar  *8A*
**first** primero/a  *5B;* primer *(form of primero before a m., s. noun)*  *6B;* primero *(adverb)*  *5B; first floor* el primer piso  *6B*
**fish** el pescado  *3B*
to **fit** quedarle bien a uno  *9A*
**five** cinco  *1A*
**five hundred** quinientos/as  *5B*
to **fix** arreglar  *8A*
**floor** el piso  *6B; first floor* el primer piso  *6B; ground floor* la planta baja  *6B*
**flower** la flor  *7B*
**flute** la flauta
to **fold** doblar  *8A*
to **follow** seguir (i, i); *the following* lo siguiente
**food** la comida  *3B; food server* el mesero, la mesera  *3B*
**foot** el pie  *9A; on foot* a pie  *3A*
**football** el fútbol americano  *7A*
**for** por, para  *3A; for example* por ejemplo  *1B*
to **forget** olvidar  *8B*
**fork** el tenedor  *6A*
**forty** cuarenta  *1B*
**four** cuatro  *1A*
**four hundred** cuatrocientos/as  *5B*
**fourteen** catorce  *1A*
**fourth** cuarto/a  *7B*
**free** libre  *4A*
**fresh** fresco/a  *8B*
**Friday** viernes  *2B; on Friday* el viernes
**friend** el amigo, la amiga  *2A*
**from** de  *1A;* desde  *6B; from the* de la/del (de + el)  *3A; from where?* ¿de dónde?  *1A*
**fruit** la fruta  *8B*
**fun** divertido/a  *4A*
**funny** cómico/a  *4B*

# G

**game** el partido *4B*, el juego
**game console/system** la consola de juegos *5A*
**garage** el garaje *6B*
**garbage** la basura *8A*
**garden** el jardín *8A*
**garlic** el ajo *8B*
**generally** generalmente
**generous** generoso/a *4B*
**geography** la geografía
**geometry** la geometría
**to get** conseguir (i, i)
**to get together** reunir
**gift** el regalo *9B*
**girl** la chica *2A*, la muchacha *1A;* la niña
**girlfriend** la novia
**to give** dar *7A*
**glad** contento/a *2A; Glad to meet you!* ¡Mucho gusto! *1A; I would be glad to* con (mucho) gusto *1A; So glad to meet you.* Tanto gusto. *1A*
**glass** el vaso *4B*
**glove** el guante *9A*
**to go** ir *3A; let's go!* ¡vamos! *3A; to be going (to do something)* ir a (+ infinitive) *3B; to go back* regresar, volver (ue) *7A; to go in* entrar *5A; to go out* salir *4A; to go shopping* ir de compras *4B; to go up* subir *8A; to go upstairs* subir *8A*
**gold** el oro *9B*
**good** bueno/a *4B*, buen (*form of* bueno *before a m., s. noun*) *7B; good afternoon* buenas tardes *1B; good luck* buena suerte; *good morning* buenos días *1B; good night* buenas noches *1B*
**good-bye** adiós *1A*
**good-looking** guapo/a *4A*, bonito/a *4A*
**grade** la nota, la calificación
**granddaughter** la nieta *4A*
**grandfather** el abuelo *4A*
**grandmother** la abuela *4A*
**grandson** el nieto *4A*
**grape** la uva *8B*
**gray** gris *2B*
**gray-haired** canoso/a *4B*
**great** fantástico/a *3A*
**greater** mayor *8B*
**greatest** mayor *8B*

**green** verde *2B*
**green bean** la habichuela *8B*
**greens** la verdura *8B*
**group** el grupo; *musical group* grupo musical
**Guatemala** Guatemala *1A*
**guitar** la guitarra
**guy** el muchacho *1A*
**gym** el gimnasio

# H

**half** medio/a; *half past* y media *1B*
**ham** el jamón *8B*
**hand** la mano *9A; on the other hand* en cambio *7B*
**handbag** el bolso *9B*
**handkerchief** el pañuelo *9B*
**handsome** guapo/a *4A*
**to hang** colgar (ue) *8A*
**to happen** pasar
**happy** contento/a *4A;* feliz (*pl.* felices) *5B;* alegre; *Happy birthday!* ¡Feliz cumpleaños! *5B*
**hard** difícil *4B*
**hat** el sombrero *9A*
**to have** tomar *3B;* tener *5A;* to *have a birthday* cumplir años *5B; to have just* acabar de (+ infinitive) *8A; to have (something) left* quedarle (algo a alguien) *9A; to have (to)* deber, tener que *6A*
**he** él *1B*
**head** la cabeza *9A*
**headphones** los audífonos *5A*
**to have** *(something) left* quedarle (algo a alguien) *9A;*
**health** la salud
**to hear** oír *8A*
**heat** el calor *6B*
**hello** hola *1A; hello (telephone greeting)* aló *2B;* diga
**help** la ayuda; *pedir ayuda to ask for help 6B*
**to help** ayudar *6A*
**her** su, sus *4A;* la (*d.o.p.*) *5A;* le (*i.o.p.*) *1A; (after a preposition)* ella *4B*
**here** aquí *1A*
**hey** mira, miren, oye, oigan
**hi** hola *1A*
**him** lo (*d.o.p.*) *5A;* le (*i.o.p.*) *3A; (after a preposition)* él *4B*
**his** su, sus *4A*

**Hispanic** hispano/a
**history** la historia *2B*
**hockey** el hockey
**home** la casa *4A; at home* en casa
**homework** la tarea *4B*
**Honduras** Honduras *1A*
**horrible** horrible *4B*
**horse** el caballo *3A; on horseback* a caballo *3A*
**hot** caliente *4A; it is hot* hace calor *7B; to be hot* tener calor *6B*
**hotel** el hotel *3A*
**hour** la hora *1B*
**house** la casa *4A*
**how?** ¿cómo? *1A; How are you?* ¿Qué tal? *1B; How are you (formal)?* ¿Cómo está (Ud.)? *1B; How are you (informal)?* ¿Cómo estás (tú)? *1B; How are you (pl.)?* ¿Cómo están (Uds.)? *1B; How do you say...?* ¿Cómo se dice...? *2A; How do you write (spell)...?* ¿Cómo se escribe...? *1A; How is the weather?* ¿Qué tiempo hace? *7B; How long...?* ¿Cuánto (+ time expression) hace que (+ present tense of verb)...? *7A; how many?* ¿cuántos/as? *2B; how much?* ¿cuánto/a? *2B; How old are you?* ¿Cuántos años tienes? *1A*
**how (+ adjective)!** ¡qué (+ adjective)! *4A*
**hug** el abrazo *6B*
**hunger** el hambre *f. 6B*
**hungry: to be hungry** tener hambre *6B*
**hurry** la prisa *6B; in a hurry* apurado/a *4A; to be in a hurry* tener prisa *6B*
**husband** el esposo *4A*

# I

**I** yo *1A*
**ice** el hielo *7B; to ice skate* patinar sobre hielo *7B*
**ice cream** el helado *8B*
**idea** la idea *5B*
**ideal** ideal *4B*
**if** si *5A*
**to imagine** imaginar
**important** importante *4B*
**in** en *2A;* por *4A*

**in-laws** los parientes políticos
**ingredient** el ingrediente *8B*
**in order** para *3A*
**intelligent** inteligente *4B*
to **intend** pensar (ie) *6A*
**interesting** interesante *4B*
to **introduce** presentar *3A; let me introduce you (formal, s.) to* le presento a *3A; let me introduce you (informal, s.) to* te presento a *3A; let me introduce you (pl.) to* les presento a *3A*
**invitation** la invitación
to **invite** invitar
**island** la isla
**it** la *(d.o.p.)*, lo *(d.o.p.) 5A; it was* fue *5B*
**its** su, sus *4A*

# J

**jacket** la chaqueta *9A*
**January** enero *5B*
**jeans** los jeans *2B*
**jersey** la camiseta *2B*
**jewel** la joya *9B*
**juice** el jugo *3B*
**July** julio *5B*
**June** junio *5B*
**just** solo

# K

to **keep on** seguir (i, i)
**keyboard** el teclado *2B*
**kilogram** el kilo (kg)
**kind** amable *4A;* el tipo
**kitchen** la cocina *6A*
**knife** el cuchillo *6A*
to **know** saber *3B; I don't know* no sé *2A*

# L

**lady** la señora, Sra. *1B;* la dama; *young lady* la señorita *1B*
**lamp** la lámpara *6A*
**language** la lengua, el idioma
**last** pasado/a *5B;* último/a
**late** tarde
**later** luego *1A;* después *6A; see you later* hasta luego *1A;* hasta la vista

**lazy** perezoso/a
to **learn** aprender
**leather** el cuero *9B*
to **leave** *(something behind)* dejar *8A*
**leg** la pierna *9A*
to **lend** prestar *8B*
**less** menos *8B; less (+ noun/ adjective/adverb) than* menos (+ noun/adjective/adverb) que *8B; the least (+ adjective + noun)* el/la/los/las (+ noun) menos (+ adjective) *8B*
**let's (+ infinitive)!** ¡vamos a (+ infinitive)! *3B*
**let's go!** ¡vamos! *3A*
**letter** la carta *6B;* la letra; *capital letter* la mayúscula *1A; lowercase letter* la minúscula *1A*
**lettuce** la lechuga *8B*
**library** la biblioteca *3A*
**lie** la mentira *6B*
to **lie** mentir (ie, i)
**life** la vida *7A*
**light** la luz *(pl. luces) 6A*
to **light** encender (ie) *6A*
**like** como
to **like** gustar *4B; I/you/he/she/it/ we/they would like...* me/te/le/ nos/os/les gustaría... *6B*
**list** la lista *7A*
to **listen (to)** escuchar *4B*
**little** poco/a *6B; a little (bit)* un poco *5A; a very little (bit)* un poquito
to **live** vivir *4A*
**living room** la sala *6B*
**lobster** la langosta
**long** largo/a *9B*
to **look (at)** mirar *4B; to look for* buscar *3A*
to **lose** perder (ie)
**love** el amor *5A*
to **love** querer *6A*
**lunch** el almuerzo *2B*

# M

**magazine** la revista *2A*
to **make** hacer *3B*
**mall** el centro comercial *9A*
**man** el hombre *9A*
**many** muchos/as *3B*
**map** el mapa *2A*
**March** marzo *5B*
**marker** el marcador *2A*

**market** el mercado *8B*
**match** el partido *4B*
**material** el material *9B*
**mathematics** las matemáticas *2B*
to **matter** importar *8B*
**maximum** máximo/a *7B*
**May** mayo *5B*
**me** me *(i.o.p.) 4B;* me *(d.o.p.) 5A; they call me* me llaman; *(after a preposition)* mí
to **mean** querer decir *6B; it means* quiere decir *2A; What is the meaning (of)...?* ¿Qué quiere decir...? *2A*
**meat** la carne *8B*
**mechanic** mecánico/a *9B;* la escalera mecánica *9B*
**menu** el menú *3B*
**Mexico** México *1A*
**microwave oven** horno microondas *6A*
**midnight** la medianoche *1B; It is midnight.* Es medianoche. *1B*
**milk** la leche *8A*
**mine** mío/a; *the pleasure is mine* el gusto es mío *3A*
**minimum** mínimo/a *7B*
**minus** menos *1B*
**minute** el minuto *7A*
**Miss** la señorita, Srta. *1B*
**mist** la neblina *7B*
**mistaken** equivocado *2B*
**modern** moderno/a
**mom** la madre *4A;* la mamá
**moment** el momento *3B*
**Monday** lunes *2B; on Monday* el lunes
**money** el dinero *5A*
**month** el mes *5B*
**more** más *4A; more (+ noun/ adjective/adverb) than* más (+ noun/adjective/adverb) que *8B*
**morning** la mañana *1B; good morning* buenos días *1B; in the morning* de la mañana *1B;* por la mañana *7A*
**most: the most (+ adjective + noun)** el/la/los/ las (+ noun) más (+ adjective) *8B*
**mother** la madre *4A*
**motorcycle** la moto(cicleta) *3A*
**mouse** ratón *(pl. ratones) 2B*
**movie** la película *5A; movie theater* el cine *3A*
**Mr.** el señor, Sr. *1B*

**Mrs.** la señora, Sra.  *1B*
**much** mucho/a, mucho  *4B; very much* muchísimo
**museum** el museo  *3B*
**music** la música  *2B*
**must** deber  *6A*
**my** mi  *2A; (pl. my)* mis  *4A; my name is* me llamo  *1A*

## N

**name** el nombre; *last name* el apellido; *my name is* me llamo  *1A; their names are* se llaman; *What is your name?* ¿Cómo te llamas?  *2A; What is (your/his/ her) name?* ¿Cómo se llama (Ud./él/ella)?  *1A; (Your [formal]/His/Her) name is....* (Ud./ Él/Ella) se llama....  *2A; your name is* te llamas  *1A*
**napkin** la servilleta  *6A*
**near** cerca (de)  *3A*
**necklace** el collar  *9B*
to **need** necesitar  *2B*
**neither** tampoco  *2B; neither... nor* ni...ni  *9A*
**nephew** el sobrino  *4A*
**nervous** nervioso/a  *4A*
**never** nunca  *4A*
**new** nuevo/a  *2A; New Year's Day* el Año Nuevo  *5B*
**news** la noticia
**newspaper** el periódico  *2A*
**next** próximo/a; que viene  *5A; next to* al lado (de)  *6B*
**Nicaragua** Nicaragua  *1A*
**nice** simpático/a  *3A; amable* *4A; the weather is nice* hace buen tiempo  *7B*
**nickname** el apodo
**niece** la sobrina  *4A*
**night** la noche  *1B; at night* de la noche  *1B; por la noche  *6B; good night* buenas noches  *1B*
**nine** nueve  *1A*
**nine hundred** novecientos/as  *5B*
**nineteen** diecinueve  *1A*
**ninety** noventa  *1B*
**ninth** noveno/a  *7B*
**no** no  *1A*
**nobody** nadie  *9A*
**none** ninguno/a, ningún, ninguna  *9A*

**noon** el mediodía; *It is noon.* Es mediodía.  *1B*
**north** el norte
**not: not any** ninguno/a, ningún, ninguna  *9A; not even* ni  *5B; not very* poco/a  *6B*
**notebook** el cuaderno  *2A*
**nothing** nada  *9A*
**November** noviembre  *5B*
**now** ahora  *2B; right now* ahora mismo  *7A*
**number** el número  *2B; telephone/fax/cellular telephone number* número de teléfono/ de fax/de teléfono celular  *2B; wrong number* número equivocado  *2B*
**nylons** las medias  *9A*

## O

to **obtain** conseguir (i, i)
**occupied** ocupado/a  *4A*
to **occur** pasar
**October** octubre  *5B*
**of** de  *1A; of the* de la/del (de + el)  *1A*
**of course!** ¡claro!  *3A; ¡Cómo no!*  *3B*
**office** la oficina  *3A*
**official** oficial
**oh!** ¡ay!  *2A*
**oil** el aceite  *6A; el petróleo*
**okay** de acuerdo  *3B; regular  1B; (pause in speech)* bueno  *3B*
**old** viejo/a  *5B; How old are you?* ¿Cuántos años tienes?  *1A; to be (+ number) years old* tener (+ number) años  *5A*
**older** mayor  *5B*
**oldest** el/la mayor  *5B*
**on** en  *2A; sobre  2B; on credit* a crédito  *9B; on foot* a pie  *3A; on loan* prestado/a  *6B; on the other hand* en cambio  *7B; on the telephone* por teléfono  *6B*
**one** un, una, uno  *2A*
**one hundred** cien  *1B; (when followed by another number)* ciento  *5B*
**onion** la cebolla  *8B*
**only** único/a  *4A; solo  8A; solamente*
**open** abierto/a  *4A*
to **open** abrir  *5A*
**or** o  *2B; u (used before a word*

*that starts with o or ho)  6B; either...or* o...o  *9A*
**orange** la naranja  *3B; anaranjado/a (color)*  *9A*
to **order** pedir (i, i)  *6B*
**organ** el órgano
**other** otro/a  *4A*
**ought** deber  *6A*
**our** nuestro(s)/a(s)  *4A*
**over** sobre  *2B; over there* allá  *6A*

## P

**paella** la paella  *8B*
**page** la página  *2A*
**pair** la pareja
**pajamas** el pijama  *9A*
**Panama** Panamá  *1A*
**pants** el pantalón  *2B*
**pantyhose** las medias  *9A*
**paper** el papel  *2A; sheet of paper* la hoja de papel
**Paraguay** el Paraguay  *1A*
**pardon me** perdón  *1B*
**parents** los padres  *2A; los papás*
**park** el parque  *3A*
**part-time (work)** medio tiempo (trabajo)
**partner** el compañero, la compañera  *5A*
**party** la fiesta  *3A*
to **pass** pasar  *5A; pass me* pásame  *6A*
**past** pasado/a  *5B; half past* y media  *1B*
**pastime** el pasatiempo  *7A*
**patio** el patio  *6B*
to **pay** pagar  *9B*
**pea** el guisante  *8B*
**pearl** la perla  *9B*
**pen** el bolígrafo  *2A*
**pencil** el lápiz (pl. lápices)  *2A; pencil sharpener* el sacapuntas  *2A*
**people** la gente  *8A*
**pepper** la pimienta (seasoning)  *6A; bell pepper* el pimiento  *8B*
**perfect** perfecto/a  *9B*
**perfume** el perfume  *9B*
**perhaps** quizás  *8A*
**permission** el permiso  *7A; to ask for permission (to do something)* pedir permiso (para)  *6B*

to **permit** permitir *7A*
**person** la persona *7A*
**personal** personal
**Peru** el Perú *1A*
**philosophy** la filosofía
**photo** la foto(grafía) *4A*
**physics** la física *6A*
**piano** el piano *4B*
to **pick up** recoger *8A*
**pink** rosado/a *9A*
**place** el lugar *7B*; la posición
to **place** poner *6A*
to **plan** pensar (ie) *6A*
**plant** la planta *6B*
**plate** el plato *6A*
to **play** jugar (ue) *4B*; *(something musical)* tocar *4B*; *(+ a sport/game)* jugar a *4B*
**player** el jugador, la jugadora *7B*; *CD player* el reproductor de CDs *5A*; *DVD player* el reproductor de DVDs *5A*; *MP3 player* el reproductor de MP3 *5A*
**playing card** la carta *7A*
**plaza** la plaza *3B*
**pleasant** simpático/a *3A*
**please** por favor *1B*
**pleasure** el gusto *3A*; *the pleasure is mine* encantado/a, el gusto es mío *3A*
**plural** el plural
**point** el punto
to **point** apuntar; *to point to (at, out)* señalar
**politically** políticamente
**pollution** la contaminación ambiental
**polo** la camiseta *2B*
**popular** popular *4A*
**pot** la olla *8A*
**potato** la papa *8B*
**pound** la libra
**practice** la práctica *5A*
to **prefer** preferir (ie, i) *6A*
to **prepare** preparar *8A*
**pretty** bonito/a *2A*; guapo/a *2A*; lindo/a *8B*
**price** el precio *8B*
**printer (laser)** la impresora (láser) *2B*
**problem** el problema *3A*
**program** el programa *7A*
to **promise** prometer *9A*
**public** público/a; *public square* la plaza *3B*
**Puerto Rico** Puerto Rico *1A*

**purple** morado/a *9A*
**purpose** el propósito
**purse** el bolso *9B*
to **put** poner *6A*

# Q

**quality** la calidad *9B*
**quarter** el cuarto *1B*; *a quarter after, a quarter past* y cuarto *1B*; *a quarter to, a quarter before* menos cuarto *1B*
**question** la pregunta *3B*; *to ask a question* hacer una pregunta *3B*
**quickly** pronto *1B*
**quite** bastante *9B*

# R

**radio (broadcast)** la radio *4B*; el radio
**rain** la lluvia *7B*
to **rain** llover (ue) *7B*
**raincoat** el impermeable *9A*
**rapid** rápido *4B*
**rapidly** rápidamente *5B*
**rather** bastante *9B*
to **reach** cumplir *5B*
to **read** leer *3B*
**reading** la lectura
**ready** listo/a *7B*; *to be ready* estar listo/a *7B*
**really?** ¿de veras? *5B*
**receipt** el recibo *9B*
to **receive** recibir *9B*
**recipe** la receta *8B*
**red** rojo/a *2B*
**red-haired** pelirrojo/a *4B*
**refreshment** el refresco *3B*
**refrigerator** el refrigerador *6A*
to **regret** sentir (ie, i) *6A*
**regular** regular *1B*
**relative** el pariente, la pariente *4A*
to **remain** quedar *9A*
**remains** restos
to **remember** recordar (ue) *7A*
**remote** remoto/a *7A*; *remote control* el control remoto *7A*
to **rent** alquilar *7A*
to **repeat** repetir (i, i) *6B*
**report** el informe
**reporter** el periodista, la periodista

to **request** pedir (i, i) *6B*
to **resolve** resolver (ue)
**restaurant** el restaurante *3A*
to **return** volver (ue) *4A*; regresar
to **review** repasar
**rice** el arroz *8B*
**ride** el paseo *7B*; *to go for a ride* dar un paseo *7B*
to **ride** montar *5A*
**right** correcto/a; *right now* ahora mismo *7A*
**right?** ¿verdad? *3A*
**ring** el anillo *9B*
**ripe** maduro/a *8B*
**river** el río
**room** el cuarto *6B*; *dining room* el comedor *6A*; *living room* la sala *6B*
**ruler** la regla *2A*
to **run** correr *6B*
**runner** el corredor, la corredora *7B*
**rush** la prisa *6B*

# S

**sad** triste *4A*
**safe** seguro/a
**saint's day** el santo; *All Saints' Day* Todos los Santos
**salad** la ensalada *3B*
**sale** la oferta *9B*; *to be on sale* estar en oferta *9B*
**salt** la sal *6A*
**same** mismo/a *7A*
**satisfied:** *to be satisfied (with)* estar contento/a (con) *4A*
**Saturday** sábado *2B*; *on Saturday* el sábado
**saucepan** la olla *8A*
**sausage** el chorizo *(seasoned with red peppers)* *8B*
to **save** ahorrar *9B*
**saxophone** el saxofón
to **say** decir *6B*; *How do you say...?* ¿Cómo se dice...? *2A*; *one says* se dice *2A*; *to say you are sorry* pedir perdón *6B*
**scarf** la bufanda *9B*
**schedule** el horario *2B*
**school** el colegio *2B*; la escuela *3A*
**science** la ciencia
to **scold** regañar
**screen** la pantalla *2B*

**season** la estación  *7B*
**second** el segundo  *7B;* segundo/a  *7A*
to **see** ver  *3B; I see it!* ¡ya lo veo!; *let's see* a ver; *see you later* hasta la vista, hasta luego  *1A; see you soon* hasta pronto  *1B; see you tomorrow* hasta mañana  *1B; you see* ves
to **seem** parecer  *8B*
**selfish** egoísta  *4B*
to **sell** vender  *9A*
to **send** enviar  *7B*
**sentence** la oración, la frase
**September** septiembre  *5B*
**settled** establecieron
**seven** siete  *1A*
**seven hundred** setecientos/ as  *5B*
**seventeen** diecisiete  *1A*
**seventh** séptimo/a  *7B*
**seventy** setenta  *1B*
**several** varios/as
**shame** la lástima; *What a shame!* ¡Qué lástima!  *5A*
**she** ella  *1B*
**sheet** la hoja; *sheet of paper* la hoja de papel
**ship** el barco  *3A*
**shirt** la camisa  *2B*
**shoe** el zapato  *2B; high-heel shoe* zapato de tacón  *9A; low-heel shoe* zapato bajo  *8A*
**short** bajo/a *(not tall)  4B;* corto/a *(not long)  9B; in short* en resumen
**should** deber  *6A*
**show** el programa  *7A*
to **show** enseñar
**shrimp** el camarón
**sick** enfermo/a  *4A*
**side** el lado  *6B*
**silk** la seda  *9A*
**silly** tonto/a  *4B*
**silver** la plata  *9B*
**silverware** los cubiertos  *6A*
**since** desde  *6B;* como
to **sing** cantar  *4B*
**singer** el cantante, la cantante  *3B*
**sink** el fregadero  *6A*
**sir** el señor, Sr.  *1B*
**sister** la hermana  *4A*
**six** seis  *1A*
**six hundred** seiscientos/a  *5B*
**sixteen** dieciséis  *1A*
**sixth** sexto/a  *7B*
**sixty** sesenta  *1B*

**size** el tamaño  *9B*
to **show** enseñar
to **skate** patinar  *4B; to ice skate* patinar sobre hielo  *7B; to in-line skate* patinar sobre ruedas  *4B*
**skateboard** la patineta  *7B*
to **skateboard** montar en patineta  *7B*
**skater** el patinador, la patinadora  *7B*
**sketch** el dibujo  *6B*
to **sketch** dibujar  *7A*
to **ski** esquiar  *7B*
**skier** el esquiador, la esquiadora  *7B*
**skirt** la falda  *2B*
**skyscraper** el rascacielos
to **sleep** el sueño  *6B*
to **sleep** dormir (ue, u)  *7A*
**slow** lento/a  *4B*
**small** pequeño/a  *6B*
**smart** listo/a  *8A; to be smart* ser listo/a  *8A*
**smooth** suave
**snow** la nieve  *7B*
to **snow** nevar (ie)  *7B*
**so** tal, tan  *5A*
**soap opera** la telenovela  *7A*
**soccer** el fútbol  *4B; soccer player* el futbolista, la futbolista  *7B*
**sock** el calcetín  *2B*
**soft** suave; *soft drink* el refresco  *3B*
**so long** hasta luego  *1A*
to **solve** resolver (ue)
**some** unos, unas  *2A;* alguno/a, algún, alguna  *9A*
**somebody** alguien  *9A*
**someone** alguien  *9A*
**something** algo  *9A*
**sometimes** a veces  *5B*
**son** el hijo  *4A*
**song** la canción  *5A*
**soon** luego  *1A;* pronto  *1B; see you soon* hasta pronto  *1B*
**sorry:** *I am sorry* lo siento  *1B; to feel sorry* sentir (ie, i)  *6A; to say you are sorry* pedir perdón  *6B*
**so-so** regular  *1B*
**sound system** el estéreo  *5A*
**soup** la sopa  *6A; soup bowl* el plato de sopa  *6A*
**south** el sur
**Spain** España  *1A*
**Spanish** el español *(language)  2B;* español, española; *Spanish-speaking*

hispanohablante  *1A*
to **speak** hablar  *2B*
**special** especial  *6A*
to **spend (time)** pasar  *5A*
**sport** el deporte  *5A*
**spouse** el esposo, la esposa  *4A*
**spring** la primavera  *7B*
**stadium** el estadio
**stairway** la escalera  *6B*
to **start** empezar (ie)  *6A*
to **stay** quedar  *9A*
**stepfather** el padrastro
**stepmother** la madrastra
**still** todavía  *7B*
**store** la tienda  *3B*
**stove** la estufa  *6A*
to **straighten** arreglar  *8A*
**strawberry** la fresa  *8B*
**street** la calle  *3B*
**strong** fuerte
**student** el estudiante, la estudiante  *2A*
**study** el estudio
to **study** estudiar  *2B*
**subject** la asignatura
**subway** el metro  *3A*
**such** tal
**sufficient** bastante  *9B*
**sufficiently** bastante  *9B*
**sugar** el azúcar  *6A*
**suit** el traje  *9A*
**suitcase** la maleta  *5A*
**summer** el verano  *4A*
**sun** el sol  *7B*
**Sunday** domingo  *2B; on Sunday* el domingo
**sunny** soleado/a  *7B; it is sunny* está soleado  *7B;* hay sol  *7B;* hace sol  *7B*
**supermarket** el supermercado  *8B*
**surprise** la sorpresa  *5A*
**sweater** el suéter  *9A*
to **sweep** barrer  *8A*
to **swim** nadar  *4B*
**swimming pool** la piscina  *6B*
**swimsuit** el traje de baño  *9A*
**synthetic** sintético/a  *9B*

# T

**table** la mesa  *6A; to clear the table* recoger la mesa  *8A; to set the table* poner la mesa  *6A*
**tablecloth** el mantel  *6A*
**tablespoon** la cuchara  *6A*

**tablet** la tableta  *5A*

to **take** tomar  *3A;* llevar  *5A; take turns* alterna (tú *command);* alternen (Uds. *command); to take a trip* hacer un viaje  *5A; to take out* sacar  *8A; to take up* subir  *8A*

**tall** alto/a  *4B*

**taste** gusto

to **taste** probar

to **teach** enseñar

**teacher** el profesor, la profesora  *2A*

**team** el equipo  *7A*

**teaspoon** la cucharita  *6A*

**telephone** el teléfono  *2B; by telephone, on the telephone* por teléfono  *6B; telephone number* el número de teléfono  *2B; cellular telephone number* número de teléfono celular

to **telephone** llamar  *5A*

**television** la televisión  *4B; to watch television* ver la televisión  *4B*

**television set** el televisor  *7A*

to **tell** decir  *6B; (a story)* contar (ue)  *9A; tell me* dígame (Ud command)*

**temperature** la temperatura  *7B; What is the temperature?* ¿Qué temperatura hace?  *7B*

**ten** diez  *1A*

**tennis** el tenis  *4B*

**tennis player** el tenista, la tenista  *7B*

**tenth** décimo/a  *7B*

to **terminate** acabar  *8A*

**test** el examen  *2B*

**than: more/less (+ noun/ adjective/adverb) than** más/ menos (+ *noun/adjective/ adverb*) que  *8B*

**thanks** gracias  *1B; thank you very much* muchas gracias  *1B*

**that** que  *5A;* ese, esa  *6A; (far away)* aquel, aquella  *6A; (neuter form)* eso; *that which* lo que  *6B*

**the** el *(m., s.)*  *2A;* la *(f., s.)*  *2A;* las *(f., pl.)*  *2A;* los *(m., pl.)*  *2A; to the* al  *3A*

**theater** el teatro  *3B*

**their** su, sus  *4A*

**them** les *(i.o.p)*  *3A;* los/las *(d.o.p.)*  *5A; (after a preposition)* ellos/as  *4B*

**theme** el tema, el tópico

**then** luego  *1A;* después  *6A;* entonces  *6A; (pause in speech)* pues  *3B*

**there** allí  *2A; there is, there are* hay  *2A; over there* allá  *6A*

**these** estos, estas  *6A*

**they** ellos/as  *2A; they are* son  *2A; they were* fueron

**thin** delgado/a  *4B*

**thing** la cosa  *6A*

to **think** pensar (ie)  *6A; to think about (i.e., to have an opinion)* pensar de  *6A; to think about (i.e., to focus one's thoughts)* pensar en  *6A; to think about (doing something)* pensar en (+ *infinitive*)

**third** tercero/a, tercer *(form of tercero before a m., s. noun)*  *7B*

**thirst** la sed  *6B; to be thirsty* tener sed  *6B*

**thirteen** trece  *1A*

**thirty** treinta  *1B*

**this** este *(m., s.),* esta *(f., s.)*  *6A*

**those** esos, esas  *6A; (far away)* aquellos, aquellas  *6A*

**thousand** mil  *5B*

**three** tres  *1A*

**three hundred** trescientos/ as  *5B*

**through** por  *6B*

to **throw** lanzar

**Thursday** jueves  *2B; on Thursday* el jueves

**thus** pues  *3B*

**tie** la corbata  *9A*

**time** el tiempo  *4A;* la vez *(pl. veces)*  *5B; at times, sometimes* a veces  *5B; at what time?* ¿a qué hora?  *2B; (number +) time(s) per (+ time expression) (number +)* vez/veces al/a la (+ *time expression); What time is it?* ¿Qué hora es?  *1B*

**tired** cansado/a  *4A*

to **a**  *2B*

**today** hoy  *3B*

**toe** el dedo  *9A*

**together** juntos/as

**tomato** el tomate  *8B*

**tomorrow** mañana  *1B; see you tomorrow* hasta mañana  *1B; the day after tomorrow* pasado mañana  *5B*

**tonight** esta noche  *7A*

**too** también  *3A; too (much)* demasiado  *9B*

to **touch** tocar

**train** el tren  *3A*

**transportation** el transporte  *3A*

to **travel** viajar  *6A*

**tree** el árbol; *family tree* el árbol genealógico

**trip** el paseo  *7B;* el viaje  *5A; to take a trip* hacer un viaje  *5A*

**trombone** el trombón

**truck** el camión

**trumpet** la trompeta

**truth** la verdad  *6B*

to **try (to do something)** tratar (de)

**t-shirt** la camiseta  *2B*

**Tuesday** martes  *2B; on Tuesday* el martes

to **turn off** apagar  *7A*

to **turn on** encender (ie)  *6A;* poner

**twelve** doce  *1A*

**twenty** veinte  *1A*

**twenty-eight** veintiocho  *1B*

**twenty-five** veinticinco  *1B*

**twenty-four** veinticuatro  *1B*

**twenty-nine** veintinueve  *1B*

**twenty-one** veintiuno  *1B*

**twenty-seven** veintisiete  *1B*

**twenty-six** veintiséis  *1B*

**twenty-three** veintitrés  *1B*

**twenty-two** veintidós  *1B*

**two** dos  *1A*

**two hundred** doscientos/as  *5B*

**typical** típico/a

# U

**ugly** feo/a  *4B*

**umbrella** el paraguas  *9B*

**uncle** el tío  *4A*

to **understand** comprender  *2A; I understand* comprendo  *2A*

**underwear** la ropa interior  *9A*

**unique** único/a  *4A*

**united** unido/a

**United States (of America)** los Estados Unidos (EE.UU.)  *1A*

**university** la universidad

**until** hasta  *1A; (to express time)* menos  *1B*

**upcoming** que viene  *5A*

**Uruguay** el Uruguay  *1A*

**us** nos *(i.o.p.)*  *4B;* nos *(d.o.p.)*  *5A; (after a preposition)* nosotros  *4B*

to **use** usar  *9B*

# V

**vacation** las vacaciones *9A*
**vacuum** la aspiradora *8A; to vacuum* pasar la aspiradora *8A*
**vegetable** la verdura *8B*
**Venezuela** Venezuela *1A*
**verb** el verbo
**very** muy, mucho/a *3B; very much* mucho, muchísimo *4A; not very* poco/a *6B*
**video game** el videojuego *7A*
**vinegar** el vinagre *8B*
**volleyball** el voleibol *7A*

# W

**walk** el paseo *7B; to go for a walk* dar un paseo *7B; to walk* caminar *3A*
**wall** la pared *2A;* la muralla
**wallet** la billetera *9B*
**to want** querer *6A; I want* quiero *3A; (do) you want* quieres *3A*
**was** fue *5B*
**to wash** lavar *8A*
**wastebasket** el cesto de papeles *2A*
**watch** el reloj *2A*
**to watch** ver *3B; to watch television* ver la televisión
**water** el agua *f. 4B; mineral water* el agua mineral *3B*
**way** la manera
**we** nosotros/as *2A*
**to wear** llevar *2B*
**weather** el tiempo *7B; How is the weather?* ¿Qué tiempo hace? *7B; the weather is nice (bad)* hace buen (mal) tiempo *7B*
**Wednesday** miércoles *2B; on Wednesday* el miércoles
**week** la semana *5A*
**weekend** el fin de semana *5A*
**welcome** bienvenido/a; *you are welcome* de nada *1B*
**well** bien *1B; (pause in speech)* bueno, este, pues *3B*
**what a (+ noun)!** ¡qué (+ *noun)!* *5A*
**what?** ¿qué? *2A;* ¿cuál? *2B; at what time?* ¿a qué hora? *2B;*

*What is the meaning (of)...?* ¿Qué quiere decir...? *2A; What is the temperature?* ¿Qué temperatura hace? *7B; What is wrong with (someone)?* ¿Qué (+ tener)? *6B; What is wrong with you?* ¿Qué te pasa?; *What is your name?* ¿Cómo te llamas? *2A; What is (your/his/her) name?* ¿Cómo se llama (Ud./él/ella)? *1A; What time is it?* ¿Qué hora es? *1B*
**when** cuando *6B*
**when?** ¿cuándo? *3A*
**where** donde *6B*
**where?** ¿dónde? *1A; from where?* ¿de dónde? *1A; (to) where?* ¿adónde? *3A*
**which** que *5A; that which* lo que *6B*
**which?** ¿cuál? *2B; which one?* ¿cuál? *2B; which ones?* ¿cuáles? *2B*
**white** blanco/a *2B*
**white-haired** canoso/a *4B*
**who?** ¿quién? *2A; (pl.)* ¿quiénes? *2A*
**whole** entero/a
**why?** ¿por qué? *3A*
**wife** la esposa *4A*
**to win** ganar; *games won* los partidos ganados
**wind** el viento *7B; it is windy* hace viento *7B*
**window** la ventana *2A*
**winter** el invierno *7B*
**to wish** desear
**with** con *1A; with me* conmigo *9B; with you* (tú) contigo *9B*
**without** sin *8B*
**to witness** presenciar
**woman** la mujer *9A*
**wonderful** estupendo/a *7A*
**wool** la lana *9A*
**word** la palabra *2A*
**work** el trabajo *8A;* la obra
**to work** trabajar *8A*
**world** el mundo
**worse** peor *8B*
**worst: the worst (+ noun)** el/la/los/las peor/peores *8B*
**wow!** ¡caramba! *5A*
**to write** escribir *6B; How do you write...?* ¿Cómo se escribe...? *1A; it is written* se escribe *1A*

# Y

**yard** el patio *6B*
**year** el año *5B; New Year's Day* el Año Nuevo *5B; to be (+ number) years old* tener (+ *number)* años *5A*
**yellow** amarillo/a *8A*
**yes** sí *1A*
**yesterday** ayer *5B; the day before yesterday* anteayer *5B*
**yet** todavía *7A*
**you** tú *(informal) 1A;* usted (Ud.) *(formal, s.) 1B;* ustedes (Uds.) *(pl.) 1B;* vosotros/as *(Spain, informal, pl.) 1B; (after a preposition)* ti *4B;* usted (Ud.), ustedes (Uds.), vosotros/as *1B;* la, lo, *(d.o.p.) 5A;* las, los, *(d.o.p.) 5A;* te *(d.o.p.) 6A;* os *(Spain, informal, pl., d.o.p.),* le *(formal, i.o.p.),* les *(pl., i.o.p.) 1A;* os *(Spain, informal, pl., i.o.p.),* te *(i.o.p.) 3A; Are you from...?* ¿Eres (tú) de...? *1A; you are* eres *1A; you (formal) are* es *1B; you (pl.) were* fueron
**young** joven *5B; young lady* la señorita *1B; young man* el muchacho *1A; young woman* la muchacha *1A*
**younger** menor *5B*
**youngest** el/la menor *5B*
**your** tu *(informal) 2B;* tus *(informal, pl.) 4A;* su, sus (Ud./Uds.) *4A;* vuestro/a/os/as *(Spain, informal, pl.)*

# Z

**zero** cero *1A*

# Index

# Credits

## Acknowledgments

The authors wish to thank the many people of the Caribbean Islands, Central America, South America, Spain, and the United States who assisted in the photography used in the textbook and videos. Also helpful in providing photos and materials were the National Tourist Offices of Argentina, Chile, Costa Rica, Colombia, Ecuador, Guatemala, the Dominican Republic, Honduras, Mexico, Nicaragua, Panamá, Perú, Puerto Rico, Spain, and Venezuela. We would like to thank the Bilingual Press/Editorial Bilingüe, Arizona State University, Tempe, AZ, for permission to reprint *Coplas 1* and *9* from *Puentes y Fronteras/Bridges and Borders* (1996) by Gina Valdés, appearing on page 94 of this textbook. We would also like to thank the following institutions for permission to reproduce the paintings by Frida Kahlo on pp. 141-142 (*Autorretrato con mono,* 1938, and *Raíces,* 1943): Banco de México Diego Rivera and Frida Kahlo Museums Trust, Av. 5 de Mayo No. 2, Col. a Centro, Del. Cuauhtémoc 06059, México, D.F. Instituto Nacional de Bellas Artes y Literatura, Dirección de Asuntos Jurídicos, Edificio "La Nacional" 8° Piso, Av. Juárez No. 4 esq. Eje Central Lázaro Cárdenas, Col. Centro, 06050, México, D.F. Photographs of these paintings are © Albright-Knox Art Gallery / CORBIS and © SuperStock, Inc., respectively.

### Abbreviations:

| | |
|---|---|
| (t) | top |
| (b) | bottom |
| (r) | right |
| (l) | left |
| (c) | center |
| (mod.) | modelo |
| act. | actividad |

## Literary Credits

The Publisher would like to thank the following people and/or institutions for the right to reproduce their content:

**94** Bilingual Press/Editorial Bilingüe and Gina Valdés: "Coplas 1 and 9" from *Puentes y Fronteras/Bridges and Borders*. Bilingual Press/Editorial Bilingüe, Arizona State University (Tempe, AZ); **292** Rafael Pombo: "La pobre viejecita" from http://es.wikisource.org/wiki/La_pobre_viejecita; **341** Servicio Nacional de Turismo: "Rapa Nui, el ombligo del mundo" from http://chile.travel/donde-ir/tres-islas-tres-culturas-un-solo-pais/isla-de-pascua/. Servicio Nacional de Turismo (Chile); **394** El huevo de chocolate and Francisco José Briz Hidalgo: "Una moneda de ¡ay!" from http://www.elhuevodechocolate.com/cuentos/cuento27.htm; **447** Casa Mojanda: "El Mercado de Otavalo" from http://www.casamojanda.com/actividades-locales/el-mercado-de-otavalo/?lang=es. Casa Mojanda, Apartado 160 (Otavalo, Ecuador); **462** Lugares de Viaje: "Viajar al Machu Picchu: 7 consejos útiles para el viajero" from http://www.lugaresdeviaje.com/nota/viajar-al-machu-picchu-7-consejos-utiles-para-el-viajero. Revista Lugares, La Pampa 2455 Belgrano (Buenos Aires, Argentina)

## Photo Credits

**Cover photo** Nikada/iStock; **0** andresrimaging/iStock; **1** (b) Image Source Plus/Alamy; (c) maxbabakovi/Stock; **2** (tl) shootingankauf/Fotolia; (cl) fotostorm/iStock; (tr) asiseeit/iStock; **3** (c) Rtimages/Fotolia; (tl) Odua Images/Fotolia; (tr) Valua Vitaly/shutterstock; **4** fstop123/iStock; **5** Francisco, Timothy; **6** Stockrocket/iStock; **7** Juanmonino/iStock; **8** (t) Image Source Plus/Alamy; (b) CarolinaSmith/iStock; **9** (t) IS_ImageSource/iStock; (b) webphotographeer/iStock; **10** chokkicx/iStock; ("Soy de México") billnoll/iStock; ("Soy de España") Cultura Creative (RF)/Alamy; ("Soy de Perú") SensorSpot/iStock; ("Soy de Argentina") manuart/Fotolia; ("Soy de Estados Unidos") catnap72/iStock; ("Soy de Chile") spfoto/iStock; ("Soy de Colombia") JenniferPhotographyImaging/iStock; ("Yo soy de Guinea Ecuatorial") valeriebarry/iStock; ("Yo soy de Puerto Rico") alejandrophotography/iStock; **11** dulsita/Fotolia; (b) Blend Images/iStock; **12** VikaValter/iStock; **13** (tl) Francisco, Timothy; act. 27:

(mod.)(#1, #2) Creatas Images; (#3) Sanger, David; (#4) Peterson, Chip and Rosa María de la Cueva; **15** (tl) castillodominici/iStock; (tr) tifonimages/iStock; (bl) DC_Colombia/iStock; (br) rchphoto/iStock; **16** (t) alex_black/iStock; act. 33: (A) dnberty/iStock; (B) Preston, Neal/CORBIS; (C) Stockbyte Images/iStock; (D) lisafx/iStock; **17** act. 35: Joelle Maslaton/Wikimedia; act. 36: Ashwin82/iStock; **18** IPGGutenbergUKLtd/iStock; **19** (c) Aurelie1/iStock; (r) janza/iStock; **20** Picksel/iStock; **23** (tl) Edward J Bock 111/Dreamstime; (cr) Goodluz/Dreamstime; (tr) Pavel Losevsky/Fotolia; (cl) asiseeit/iStock; (br) Lighthaunter/iStock; **25** Francisco, Timothy; **26** act. 8: (#1) Simson, David; (#2) Creatas Images; (#3) Corbis Royalty-Free; (#4) Jung, Michael/Shutterstock; (#5) Pawlowska, Edyta/Shutterstock; **27** act. 9: (mod.) Kraft, Wolfgang; (#1) Stockbyte Images; (#2) Corbis Royalty-Free; (#3) Creatas Images; (#4) Andresr/iStockphoto; (#5) drbimages/iStock; (#6) marcelmooij (MaMoPictures)/iStock; **28** (t) izusek/iStock; (c) monkeybusinessimages/iStock; **29** (c) Monkey Business Images/iStock; (t) Almeida, Helder/iStock; **30** (tl) Monkey Business Images/Dreamstime; (tr) Queerstock, Inc./Alamy; (bl) IS_ImageSource/iStock; (br) skynesher/iStock; **31** (t) dulsita/Fotolia; (c) lisafx/iStock; **33** (t) Francisco, Timothy; act. 24: FingerMedium/iStock; **36** aldomurillo/iStock; **37** ("Shakira") Georges Biard/Wikimedia; ("Gabriel García Márquez") Festival Internacional de Cine en Guadalajara/Wikimedia; ("Salto Ángel") Paulo Caplotti/Wikimedia; ("Carolina Herrera") Christopher Peterson/Wikimedia; ("Coté de Pablo") TixGirl.com/Wikimedia; ("Isabel Allende") Mutari/Wikimedia; ("Jorge Luis Borges") Pepe Fernández/Wikimedia; ("Viggo Mortensen") Alan Langford Uploaded/Wikimedia; **38** ("Frida Kahlo") Carl Van Vechten/Wikimedia; ("Alicia Alonso") Moré/Cubarte; ("El rey y la reina de España") joan llado/Alamy; ("Harry Shum, Jr.") Gage Skidmore/Wikimedia; ("J.D. Pardo") Genevieve/Wikimedia; ("Sonia Sotomayor") Steve Petteway source/Wikimedia; **39** act. B: (mod.) free/Dreamstime; (#1) monkeybusinessimages/iStock; (#2) furtaev/iStock; (#3) JackF/iStock; (#4) Stockphoto4u/iStock; (#5) JackF/iStock; **41** (t) Jose Lara/Wikimedia; (b) aldomurillo/iStock; **42** Andresr/shutterstock; **44** monkeybusinessimages/iStock; **45** (c) maxkabakov/istock; (b) Leonard J. DeFrancisci/Wikimedia; **46** (tl) kali9/iStock; (tr) fstop123/iStock; (bl) CEFutcher/iStock; (br) Monkey Business/Fotolia; **47** act. 1: (A) Strauss,

edificio") Abalcazar/iStock; ("la tienda") contrastaddict/iStock; ("el teatro") shemara/iStock; ("el concierto") drxy/iStock; ("el/la cantante") robbiesaurus/Wikipedia; ("la plaza") MoreISO/iStock; ("la avenida/la calle") ntzolov/iStock; **127** act. 1: (A) Brown, Katrina/iStock; (B) MoreISO/iStock; (C ) iStock; (D) Varvaki, Vasiliki/iStock; (E) abalcazar/iStock; (F) Lau, Karin/iStock; (G) Edwards, Jeremy/iStock; (H) Ramirez Lee, Rafae/iStock; **128** (t) Béjar Latonda, Mónica; **112** (B) Linke, Heinz/iStock; (C) Chen, Chun Wu/iStock; (D) Pallardo del Rio, Miguel Ángel/iStock; **131** (tr) stockcam/iStock; (br) Torresigner/iStock; **132** (tr) Shakzu/iStock; (br) Nsaum75/Wikipedia; **133** (tl) Asiseeit/iStock; ("el mesero") IS_ImageSource/iStock; ("el menu") Nilswey/iStock; ("la ensalada") Robynmac/iStock; ("los frijoles") ncognet0/iStock; ("el pescado") tomonikon /iStock; ("el pollo") barol16/iStock; ("el agua") maxicam/iStock; ("el jugo") Okea/iStock; ("el refresco") RTimages/iStock; ("comer") Juanmonino/iStock; ("tomar") Studio-Annika/iStock; ("leer") keeweeboy/iStock; ("ver") eyecrave/iStock; **134** Coast-to-Coast/iStock; **135** (t, c) Béjar Latonda, Mónica; **137** Frontpage/Shutterstock; **138** act. 26: (mod.) Image More Co. Ltd./Getty Images; (#1) Dapino, Carlo/Shutterstock; (#2) Facotria Singular/iStockphoto; (#3) Lena S/Shutterstock; (#4) Jupiterimages/Getty Images; (#5) Image Source/iStock; (#6) DeGrie Photo Illustration/iStock; **140** kornemuz/Wikipedia; **141** (l) Bettmann/CORBIS; **147** (t) simcoemedia/iStock; (b) Torresigner/iStock; **148** kevinruss/iStock; **149** (c) maxkabakov/iStock; (b) Garylves/iStock; **150** ("Alejandro") Monkey Business/Fotolia; ("Pedro") Rob/Fotolia; ("Enrique") Felix MiZioznikov/Fotolia; ("Sarita") Blend Images/Fotolia; ("Mónica") Fotoluminate LLC/Fotolia; ("Álvaro") Gino Santa Maria/Fotolia; ("Patricia") carmebalcells/iStock; ("José") Juanmonino/iStock; ("Guillermo") Alina555/iStock; ("Ana María") DianaLundin/iStock; ("Cristina") bowdenimages/iStock; ("Isabel") digitalskillet/iStock; ("Rodrigo") Rauluminate/iStock; ("Clara") WhitneyLewisPhotography/iStock; ("Natalia") Juanmonino/iStock; (bl) MartaKimball; **151** (tc, cr) Monkey Business Images/Shutterstock; (cc) spotmatik/Shutterstock; (tr) Max Topchii/Shutterstock; (tl) Aspen Photo/Shutterstock; (b) CEFutcher/iStock; **152** act. 1: (tr)Felix Miozioznikov/Fotolia; (tl)Juanmonino/iStock; act. 4: Monkey Business/Fotolia; **153** (t) Francisco, Timothy; act. 8: (A) Alina555/iStock; (B) bowdenimages/iStock; (C) Juanmonino/iStock; (D) Rauluminate/iStock; **154** Hollingsworth, Jack; **155** AlexRaths/iStock; **156** monkeybusinessimages/iStock; **157** monkeybusinessimages/iStock; **159** monkeybusinessimages/iStock; **160** (t) aldomurillo/iStock; (b) kilan 14/iStock; **161** (cl) Lisa F. Young/Shutterstock; (tr) Garylves/iStock; (bl) arenacreative/iStock; **162** (tl) Studio D/Fotolia; (tc) Studio D/Fotolia; (tr) Sabphoto/Fotolia; (cl) CareyHope/iStock; (cr) Juanmonino/iStock; (cc) aldomurillo/iStock; (br) BartekSzewczyk/iStock; (bl) Nitr/Shutterstock; (bc) Marzia Giacobbe/Shutterstock; **163** act. 24: quintanilla/iStock; **164** (t, c, b) Francisco, Timothy; act. 27: Francisco, Timothy; **165** act. 28: (#1) Peterson, Chip and Rosa María de la Cueva; (#2) Woraput/iStock; (#3) mythja/iStock; (#4) neiromobile/iStock; (#5) Monkey Business Images/Shutterstock, iStock; (#6) Zurijeta/iStock; **166** omgimages/iStock; **168** act. 33: (tl) James Atoa/Alamy; (tr) Eva Rinaldi/Wikimedia; act. 34: (bl) jhorrocks/iStock; (br) Murillo, Aldo/iStock; **170** (r) monkeybusinessimages/iStock; **171** (r) Julie Hewitt/iStock; (l) Yobro10/iStock; **173** act. E: travelpixpro/iStock; **174** ("ver la televisión") monkeybusinessimages/iStock;

("cantar") joel-t/iStock; ("comprar ropa") wildworx/Fotolia; ("hacer las tareas") diego cervo/Fotolia; ("mirar fotos") apops/Fotolia; ("nadar") aabejon/iStock; ("patinar") druvo/iStock; ("jugar al tenis") gchutka/iStock; ("ir de compras") fstop123/iStock; ("tocar el piano") OJO_Images/iStock; ("bailar") franckreporter/iStock; (tl) ipag/iStock; ("ir a un partido de fútbol") Pavel L Photo and Video/Shutterstock; **175** act. 2: (A) Givaga/iStock; (B)(C)(F) CORBIS Royalty-Free; (D) Simson, David; (E) Pakhnyushchyy/iStock; **176** (t) Francisco, Timothy; act. 6: monkeybusinessimages/iStock; **177** LuminaStock/iStock; **178** act. 8: (mod.) IPGGutenbergUKLtd/iStock; (#1) zoliki/iStock; (#3) Maridav/iStock; (#4) saiko3p/iStock; (#6) Werner, Tom/iStock; act. 9: (bl) maxkabakov/istock; **179** shironosov/iStock; **180** Frei, Franz-Marc/CORBIS; **181** act.13: Chagin/iStock; act. 15: val_th/iStock; **182** act. 17: (tr) RuslanDashinsky/iStock; (br) maxkabakov/istock; **183** (t) Rafalkrakou/iStock; (b) Wavebreak Media Ltd/bigstock; **184** (br) Julio Etchart/Alamy; (tl) ZUMA/Alamy; **185** ("pelirroja") druvo/iStock; ("canosa") Andres Rodriguez/Fotolia; ("calvo") EMPPhotography/iStock; ("calvo") ValuaVitaly/iStock; ("moreno") eurobanks/iStock; ("alto y bajo") Serg Salivon/Shutterstock; ("cómica") gekaskr/Fotolia; ("inteligente") ManoAfrica/iStock; ("tonto") Elena Rostunova/Shutterstock; ("gorda") Petra Kohlstädt/Fotolia; ("delgado") ginastancel/iStock; ("importante") Junial Enterprises/Fotolia; ("buena") Nataliiap/iStock; ("malo") bbevren/iStock; ("rápido") PeopleImages/iStock; ("lento") Evgeny Bakharev/Shutterstock; ("egoísta") dimj/iStock; ("generosas") monkeybusinessimages/iStock; ("horrible") Benjamin Simeneta/Fotolia; ("feo") nevenm/Fotolia; ("ideal") Natalia Pushchina/Fotolia; **186** act. 22: (#1) Peterson, Chip and Rosa María de la Cueva; (#2)(#8) Corbis Royalty-Free; (#3) (#4) Stockbyte Image; (#5) Jung, Michael/Shutterstock; (#6) CORBIS; (#7) fstop123/iStock; **187** (t, c) Francisco, Timothy; act. 26: Stockbyte Images; **188** shadrin_andrey/iStock; **189** act. 29: mandygodbehear/iStock; act. 30: (#1) Murillo, Aldo/iStock; (#2) Glumack, Ben; (#3) Creatas Images; (#4) monkeybusinessimages/iStock; **190** Eneas De Troya/Wikimedia; **191** (l) Feverpitched/iStock; (c) RaghuVickramvanshi/iStock; (r) Stocknroll/iStock; **192** Monkey Business Images/Shutterstock; **193** (b) Keith Allison/Wikimedia; (c) Keith Dannemiller/Alamy; **194** (tr) AP/WideWorldPhotos; (l) Keith Dannemiller/Alamy; (cr) SecondPrint/Wikimedia; act. 40: (br) Keith Allison/Wikimedia; **195** act. A: (A) Lichtmeister/Shutterstock; (B) Arruza, Tony/CORBIS; (C) Goran Bogicevic/Shutterstock; (D) Latif, Andrees/CORBIS; (E) Francisco, Timothy: **197** kevinruss/iStock; **198** Sean De Burca/Shutterstock; **199** (l) mythja/iStock; (c) eurobanks/iStock; (r) Yobro10/iStock; **200** daveamsler/iStock; **201** (c) maxkabakov/istock; (b) Esteban Felix/AP; **202** (t) Juanmonino/iStock; ("la tableta") karandaev/iStock; ("el estéreo") IvanWuPI/iStock; ("los audífonos") maxuser/iStock; ("la consola de juegos") pagadesign/iStock; ("el quemador de CDs") ashumskiy/Fotolia; ("el reproductor de MP3") pokomeda/Fotolia; ("el reproductor de CDs") studo58/iStock; ("el reproductor de DVDs") HSNPhotography/iStock;" **203** CREATISTA/iStock; **204** act. 3: (A) cveltri/iStock; (B) Alex Kotlov/iStock; (C) Jonas/iStock; (D) Lateci/iStock; (E) IvanWuPI/iStock; (F) Paha_L/iStock; act. 4: dnberty/iStock; **205** (t, c) Francisco, Timothy, act. 5: Pablosebastian/iStock; **206** mangostock/iStock; **207** act. 9: (mod.) Jonas/iStock; (#1) karandaev/iStock; (#2) tentan/iStock; (#3) papa1266/

Shutterstock; **301** (tl) Minerva Studio/iStock; (tr) 4774344sean/iStock; ANDRE DURAO/Shutterstock; **302** Act. 2: (A) Corbis Royalty-Free; (B, D) Peterson, Chip and Rosa María de la Cueva; (C) Rangel, Francisco; (E) Dra Schwartz/iStock; **303** act. 6: Digital Vision; **305** act. 12: (mod.) IPGGutenbergUKLtd/iStock; (#1) ScrappinStacy/iStock; (#2) Ljupco/iStock; (#3) ActionPics/iStock; (#4) selimaksan/iStock; **306** (tr) Marianocecowski/Wikimedia; (br) Magdalena Zurawska/Shutterstock; (cr) Bernardo Galmarin/Alamy; **307** (tr) elnavegante/iStock; (br) David R. Frazier Photolibrary, Inc./Alamy; (cl) Magaiza/iStock; **308** (t) mangostock/Shutterstock; (cl) damircudic/iStock; (br) igorr1/iStock; (bl) MachineHeadz/iStock; (cr) mady70/Shutterstock; **309** act. 18: popovaphoto/iStock; **310** (t, b) Béjar Latonda, Mónica **311** Get4Net/iStock; **312** act. 25: Ridofranz/iStock; act. 26: (bl) monkeybusinessimages/iStock; (br) bo1982/iStock; **313** Yuri/iStock; **314** act. 28: (mod.) skynesher/iStock; (#1) LittleBee80/iStock; (#2) 4774344sean/iStock; (#3) Elenathewise/iStock; (#4) Elegor/iStock; (#5) Corbis Royalty-Free; **316** monkeybusinessimages/iStock; **317** omgimages/iStock; **318** act. 37: (l) JOSE ALBERTO TEJO/Shutterstock; (r) vphowe001/iStock; **319** (tl) Jonathan Larsen/Diadem Images/Alamy; (tr) Beatrice Murch/Wikimedia; (cl) Gareth Roberts/Alamy; **320** (br) martinturzak/iStock; (tr) South American Images/Alamy; **321** act. A: (#1) muzon/iStock; (#2) monkeybusinessimages/iStock; (#3) SerrNovik/iStock; (#4) amriphoto/iStock; **323** ("montar en patineta") DenisNata/Fotolia; (bl) grafikplusfoto/Fotolia; ("esquiar") Sportstock/iStock; ("Hace mucho sol") R9_RoNaLdO/iStock; ("No hace mucho calor") YinYang/iStock; ("patinar sobre hielo") VLIET/iStock; ("Hace frío") skynesher/iStock; (cl) jakobradlgruber/iStock; (br) funstock/iStock; ("dar un paseo por la playa") oliveromg/Shutterstock; (cr) Mayovskyy Andrew/Shutterstock; **324** Etchison, Sonya/Shutterstock; **325** (t, c) Béjar Latonda, Mónica; act. 6: gilltrejos/iStock; **326** Lana K/Shutterstock; **327** (b) TarpMagnus/iStock; **328** targovcom/iStock; **329** kamil/iStock; **330** (cr) kastianz/Shutterstock; (tl) BMJ/Shutterstock; (br) BMJ/Alamy; **331** (tr) Serjio74/Shutterstock; (cl) Ovalle, Alonso/Wikimedia; **332** ("Hace quince grados") Delices/Shutterstock; ("la tenista") nickp37/iStock; ("Hay neblina") CoolR/Shutterstock; ("el basquetbolista") Alexander Raths/Shutterstock; ("el patinador") Valeriy Lebedev/Shutterstock; ("Está nublado") Efired/Shutterstock; ("la corredora") Ariwasabi/Shutterstock; ("Hace viento") Robert Hoetink/Shutterstock; ("la esquiadora") Kamil Macniak/Shutterstock; ("el futbolista") grafvision/Shutterstock; ("Está soleado") Vibrant Image Studio/Shutterstock; ("la nieve") Valentyn Volkov/Shutterstock; ("la lluvia") gpointstudio/Shutterstock; ("Hace fresco") luanateuzzi/iStock; **333** act. 19: (A, B, E) Corbis Royalty-Free; (C, F) Stockbyte Images; (D) Duomo/CORBIS **334** (tr, cr) Béjar Latonda, Mónica; **335** Blulz60/iStock; **336** act. 26: (mod.) Corbis Royalty-Free; (#1) Yin Yang/iStock; (#2) Jupiterimages/Getty Images; (#3) Corbis Royalty-Free; (#4) asiseeit/iStock; (#5) Thinkstock Royalty-Free; (#6) technotr/iStock; **337** extremal/iStock; **338** Songbird839/iStock; **339** act. 31: (#1) McIninch/iStock; (#2) MSPhotographic/iStock; (#3) bendzhik/iStock; (#4) YanLev/iStock; (#5) blende64/iStock; (#6) goldenangel/iStock; **341** (bl) Jesse Allen/Wikimedia; (br) Tero Hakala/Shutterstock; **342** (cr) AlbertoLoyo/iStock; (tr) Andrzej Gibasiewicz/Shutterstock; (cl) sebikus/Shutterstock; **346** act. D: startupchile.org; act. F: jgroup/iStock; **347** DenisNata/Fotolia; **348** alle12/iStock;

**349** (c) maxkabakov/istock; (b) Pavel L Photo and Video/Shutterstock; **350** (tr) monkeybusinessimages/iStock; ("preparar la comida") TAGSTOCK1/iStock; ("limpiar la cocina") JackF/iStock; ("adornar las paredes") Iakov Filimonov/Shutterstock; ("hacer la cama") evok20/iStock; ("doblar la ropa") ("trabajar en el jardín") spwidoff/iStock; ("colgar la ropa") Africa Studio/Fotolia; ("llegar a casa") JackF/iStock; ("subir algo al cuarto") PeopleImages/iStock; **352** act. 4: Hollingsworth, Jack; act. 5: NicolasMcComber/iStock; **353** (t, c, b) Béjar Latonda, Mónica; **354** act. 10: 4774344sean/iStock; **355** SnowWhiteimages/iStock; **356** hundreddays/iStock; **357** act. 14: (mod.) Elenathewise/iStock; (#1) bmcent1/iStock; (#2) bikeriderlondon/Shutterstock; (#3) JackF/iStock; (#4) kzenon/iStock; **358** act. 17: daboost/iStock; act. 18: Juanmonino/iStock; **359** act. 20: (br) maxkabakov/iStock; (chat women, men) omgimages/iStock; (bl) Ashrafov/iStock; **360** (tl) Pavel L Photo and Video/Shutterstock; (br) Radius Images/Alamy; (cr) Tupungato/Shutterstock; **361** (tl) Yulia Grigoryeva/Shutterstock; (cr) José Antonio Alonso/Wikimedia; (b) clownbusiness/iStock; **362** (t) SolStock/iStock; ("barrer el piso") JackF/Fotolia; ("pasar la aspiradora") CEFutcher/iStock; ("lavar las ollas") s-cphoto/iStock; ("traer la leche a casa") Danilin/iStock; ("recoger la mesa") AVAVA/Shutterstock; ("dar de comer al perro") Chalabala/iStock; ("sacar la basura") Monkey Business Images/Shutterstock; **363** act. 25: (A) Figure8Photos/iStock; (B) Jim West / Alamy (C) lucubaghs/iStock; (D) guenterguni/iStock; act. 26: (mod.) fstop123/iStock; (A) AVAVA/iStock; (B) ShutterBee/iStock; (C) Ljupco/iStock; (D) JackF/iStock; (E) JackF/iStock; (F) astrocady/iStock; **364** (t, b) Béjar Latonda, Mónica **365** Erdosain/iStock; **366** act. 31: (mod.) robynmac/iStock; (#1) ajafoto/iStock; (#2) Smirnoff, Debbi/iStock; (#3) Julia Ivantsova/Shutterstock; (#4) Aleksangel/Shutterstock; (#5) scanrail/iStock; (#6) Bombaert/iStock; **367** Fotosmurf03/iStock; **368** Julia Ivantsova/Shutterstock; **370** (br) extender_01/Shutterstock; (tl) bikeriderlondon/Shutterstock; **374** (tc) JackF/Fotolia; ("biografiasyvidas") marco mayer/Shutterstock; ("los aguacates") Tupungato/Fotolia; ("las cebollas") Africa Studio/Fotolia; ("guisantes") Supertrooper/Shutterstock; ("la lechuga") hardyuno/Fotolia; ("el ajo") Mariusz Prusaczyk/Fotolia; ("los pimientos rojos") Kondor83/Fotolia; ("los tomates maduros") jeancliclac/iStock; ("el arroz") olya_dn/Fotolia; ("las verduras") Steve Vidler/Alamy; (bc) XiXinXing/iStock; **375** act. 1: (A) Givaga/iStock; (B) PicturePartners/iStock; (C) lepas2004/iStock; (D) grublee/iStock; (E) eyewave/iStock; (F) dcbog/iStock; **376** act. 3: (mod.) evgenyb/iStock; (#1) fotofermer/iStock; (#2) bworld/iStock; (#3) gzorgz/iStock; (#4) Yasonya/iStock; (#5) Lilun_Li/iStock; (#6) aluxum/iStock; (#7) AlexMax/iStock; (#8) brookebecker/iStock; (#9) Natikka/iStock; **377** (t, c) Béjar Latonda, Mónica; act. 6: (A) bedo/iStock; (B) vincomfoto/iStock; (C) JoeGough/iStock; (D) piotr_malczyk/iStock; (E) westlaker/iStock; (F) dollyllama/iStock; **379** AmbientIdeas/iStock; **380** glesik/iStock; **382** Fertnig/iStock; **383** holgs/iStock; **384** (tr) Radius Images/Alamy; (br) Paul_Brighton/iStock; **385** (tl) Per Andersen/Alamy; (br) Ken Welsh/Alamy; **386** ("los plátanos") Steve Vidler/Alamy; ("las papas") great_photos-/Fotolia; ("las manzanas") miff32/Fotolia; ("las uvas") Mariusz Prusaczyk/Fotolia; ("el helado") Viktor/Fotolia; ("el queso") Ferrante Pietro/Fotolia; ("el maíz") sneska/iStock; ("las habichuelas") dirkr/iStock; ("el café") chang/iStock; ("el chocolate") fcafotodigital/iStock; ("los huevos") Andrey Burmakin/Shutterstock; ("el vinagre")